Teaching with
The Norton Anthology of English Literature

EIGHTH EDITION

A Guide for Instructors

Sondra Archimedes
UNIVERSITY OF CALIFORNIA, SANTA CRUZ

Elizabeth Fowler
UNIVERSITY OF VIRGINIA

Laura Runge
UNIVERSITY OF SOUTH FLORIDA

Philip Schwyzer
EXETER UNIVERSITY

W. W. NORTON & COMPANY
New York • London

ISBN 10: 0-393-92708-3
ISBN 13: 978-0-393-92708-5

W. W. Norton & Company, Inc., 500 Fifth Avenue, New York, NY 10110-0017
www.wwnorton.com

W. W. Norton & Company Ltd., Castle House,
75/76 Wells Street, London W1T 3QT

Contents

Authors and Selections

General Editor's Preface

Instructors reading this guide face a challenging and exciting task: that of shaping successful undergraduate survey courses out of the vast resources of *The Norton Anthology of English Literature* (*NAEL*). Chances are good that the scope of the course extends beyond any one instructor's expertise; that preparation time—time to read through the mass of materials, to plan the course, to prepare individual classes and assignments—is short and that students will arrive with little or no background in literature, and skeptical about its potential for pleasure and interest. The purpose of this guide is to help instructors succeed at the task. To that end, it offers practical, focused help, from syllabi for courses using *NAEL*, to teaching strategies for individual authors and texts, to assistance with exam preparation, essay topics, and study questions.

Reconceived, reformatted, and substantially rewritten to make it easy to find help quickly, the guide includes the following features:

Help with Planning and Managing Your Course From pacing, to designing assigments, to using technology in the classroom, the first four chapters cover the pedagogic challenges—some perennial, some new to our electronic age—that teachers face in planning and managing a course. Collaboratively written by the guide authors, this material reflects decades of experience teaching undergraduates in different institutional settings.

Sample Syllabi To help instructors envision different kinds of courses, from seminars to lectures, from a one-semester Middle Ages–Twenty-first Century survey to less rapidly paced period courses, Chapter 2 of the Guide provides ten sample syllabi.

Teaching Clusters For each period, the guide offers several Teaching Clusters that give instructors thematic maps to navigate groups of texts. Each Teaching Cluster is described in general terms in the "Introducing the Period" section and then treated more specifically in relevant Author/Work entries. The clusters are general enough to let teachers explore their own and their students' interests, but connected enough to convey a sense of development among the texts within them. Whether exploring recurrent themes and ideas, studying the development of particular genres, examining successive cultural moments (and the disruptions that lead from one to another), or investigating literary, cultural, or social history, the Teaching Clusters will help instructors present both the importance of a theme and the unique way each text addresses it.

Author/Work Entries are designed for reference and usually include a teaching "hook"—an idea about how to begin a class, which passages might be good to focus on, and what questions are likely to elicit interesting responses. "Quick Read" sections offer a refresher list on the basics of a literary work—brief summary, form, key passages, and the like. "Teaching Suggestions" call out interesting textual or contextual aspects of a writer's works and offer pedagogic strategies. Discussion questions include both questions that teachers can pose in class and questions that might accompany a reading assignment. Where appropriate, the questions connect *NAEL's* print and media selections.

Media Guide and Syllabus In addition to cross-references to the *NAEL* media in the period chapters, the guide includes a separate chapter (Chapter 4) and syllabus suggesting ways to integrate the *NAEL* online topics and archive selections with the print selections and how to use these materials in traditional or distance-learning courses.

Sample Essay Topics and Exam Questions focus on individual authors and on links and larger themes.

The guide has been a collaborative effort from start to finish. The guide authors and *NAEL* editors are indebted to previous guide authors, notably Alfred David, whose work is woven throughout this edition. Elizabeth Fowler, with contributions from James Simpson and Alfred David, wrote the chapter on the Middle Ages. Philip Schwyzer wrote the Sixteenth and Early Seventeenth Century sections and Chapter 4, "Teaching with Norton's Online Media Resources." Laura Runge wrote the chapters on the Restoration and the Eighteenth Century, the Romantic Period, and Chapter 1, "Getting Started." Sondra Archimedes wrote the chapters on the Victorian Age, the Twentieth Century and Beyond, and Chapter 3, "Using Technology in the Classroom." All authors contributed syllabi and exam topics and questions. The *NAEL* editors advised and commented on the chapters for their respective periods.

Stephen Greenblatt
General Editor

CHAPTER 1

Getting Started

CONSTRUCTING YOUR SYLLABUS

Congratulations! The first step in designing a course is selecting the text, and if you are reading this you probably have already identified *NAEL* as your starting place. Because there is no way you could possibly teach everything in *NAEL* in one course, the next step is to select the literary works you want to teach and to organize them into an effective pedagogical schedule. There are, of course, many methods of selection, and the wealth of literature contained in the anthology's pages may at first seem overwhelming. What follows are some practical suggestions to help you make choices that feel right and that take advantage of all that the anthology has to offer.

Primary Considerations

Good teaching is a product of many variables, and what works for one teacher may not always work for another. The art of teaching capitalizes on the individual strengths of the instructor. Become cognizant of your teaching style and learn to develop courses that correspond to it. For example, if you are a phenomenal orator and vastly entertaining, you probably will be an effective lecturer, and so your syllabus might contain as many works as you can adequately discuss in a class period. If you excel at leading discussions, your classes might spend an entire hour discussing the implications of a few lines of poetry. Your syllabus should be devoted to deeper coverage of fewer works.

Remember that good teaching also considers the many different learning styles of students. Some students prefer the organized, outlined lecture from which they can derive reliable notes and further their understanding of the literature on their own outside of class. Other students will be bored by this one-way flow of information; they might benefit from thought-provoking discussion questions, oral processing of information, and collaborative activities in the classroom. Some students demonstrate their mastery of the course material best by independent writing assignments outside of class, taking advantage of technologies such as discussion boards; others prefer to answer questions in class and raise points about which they are curious or uncertain. Effective teaching tries to reach as many different learners as possible, and so we recommend that you incorporate a variety of teaching strategies in your courses. Most of the Author/Work entries contain a "hook" and interesting textual issues around which to organize lectures; they also contain discussion questions and some creative assignments.

After accounting for teaching and learning styles, you will want to consider what your course should achieve or the learning objectives the students should reach when they complete your course. At this point it is appropriate to consider how you will be testing your students. The wording of your objectives depends closely on what your evaluative measures will be. Unfortunately, a full discussion of evaluation is beyond the scope of this guide. In general, you should consider how you will test or measure a student's competency in achieving the course objectives. For example, if you want students to demonstrate knowledge of the literature of the twentieth century, you might use a series of essay exams to test their general familiarity with a wide range of texts from the period. See Chapter 12 for some sample test questions. On the other hand, if your objective is "to introduce students to the literature of the Middle Ages," you can be satisfied that the students have met the objective if they have read the works on the syllabus. This can be evaluated through informal writing or discussion.

It is also important to consider the relationship between how you teach and what you expect the students to learn. For example, if yours is a collaborative or discussion-oriented classroom, it's unfair to test the students on a set of received ideas that they may not have learned. Rather, you might design writing assignments that allow for independent analysis or exam questions that pick up on some of the issues that were central to class discussion. Again, you will find suggestions for assignments in Chapter 12. Most of the sample syllabi in Chapter 2 include course objectives related to the reading. Your course objectives should include expectations about skills beyond reading and comprehending, such as writing about literature, analyzing literature, and so on. These will relate specifically to the assignments you make, such as journals, bibliographies, research papers, exams, and close-reading exercises.

Most instructors who use *NAEL* will be teaching a survey course, but chronological scope and focus can differ widely. The first objective, therefore, will probably include some aspect of coverage, whether it is to introduce the literature to the students or to have students demonstrate particular knowledge of it. Now the process of selection begins. It is sometimes helpful to identify objectives keyed to your interests in the range of literature for which you are responsible. Objectives that contain words that inspire your love of literature or your particular angle on literature are useful guides for selecting which texts to teach. For example, if you are interested in gender, popular culture, and class, the following might be one of your objectives: To learn about issues of gender, popular culture, and class in Victorian literature. Or, if you are particularly interested in book history: To understand the history of books and publishing as it relates to the literature of the Romantic period. Then you can choose works with themes or subjects related to your interest or that provide good examples for your teaching angle.

In other cases, however, you may have to design a course to fulfill a department's requirements, but you can certainly make this imposed structure work with your objectives. For example, if the course must cover "major works and major authors," you can include the objective "To become familiar with major works and major authors of the Restoration and Eighteenth Century." Your selection of works will then conform to your understanding of what is "major." On the one hand, this might eliminate more marginal voices from your syllabus; on the other, contrasting different types of texts might create the opportunity to explore what "major" means. Similarly, you might be expected to teach genres, in which case you might include the objective "To become familiar with the genres of epic, lyric, and romance in the literature of the Sixteenth Century." Or epistolary novel and travel narratives; or tragedy and comedy; or autobiographical writings and religious tracts—the possibilities are many. These objectives will help clarify which works to include, and they will make the syllabus seem far less arbitrary to your students.

Pacing the Course

Before you struggle in vain for complete coverage of any era, you should know that coverage is a mythic ideal. Though the *NAEL* editors have put together a balanced, up-to-date, and coherent anthology of English literature, they would be the first to admit that much literature lies beyond the book's scope and purpose. The process of selection has already begun, therefore, before you start making your syllabus. As you plan your course, remember that you cannot include everything and that often the most difficult choices have to do with what *not* to cover. The Author/Work entries in this guide can help by giving you insights into the teaching strengths and challenges of particular texts.

The most common problem that new instructors have is trying to do too much. In general, you will be more effective in getting your students to achieve your objectives if you limit the materials you include. Keeping in mind that different courses and teaching styles call for different reading assignments and evaluative measures, the following points may provide some practical advice for pacing your course.

You alone know how much you can teach in one class period, and this knowledge comes with experience. When you are starting out as an instructor, keep a few things in mind. Some people believe a lecture for a fifty-minute class should include no more than three major points. That is all that students are likely to take away from it. (It can be sobering to read the notes a student takes during your lectures.) Most students cannot absorb new material after fifteen minutes of lecture—if they can stay focused that long. This suggests that you might want to introduce important concepts and ideas at the beginning of class. It also suggests that you may want to break up the one-way flow of information with discussion questions and other forms of active learning. Don't let the students remain passive in their seats for too long; you may lose them.

It is ludicrous to believe that you can teach the full significance of a major work, with the possible exception of a lyric poem, in one class sitting. Consequently, you must decide what points, passages, and themes you want to highlight. The "Quick Read" sections can give you a sense of how to break down a work for teaching. You might introduce the form—mock-epic, for example—with definitions and examples from the work on the syllabus. Then you might introduce key themes and offer a lecture/discussion around the passages that develop the theme. Finally, you might conclude with discussion based on the questions you provided in advance. Keep your students engaged by presenting them with opportunities to analyze the passages or perform close readings of the lines. Be attentive to how the students are responding and learn to read their capacities so that you can push them just a little farther.

Be prepared at the start of a course to spend time on general concepts of reading and responding to literature, such as summary, paraphrase, close-reading, analysis, and evaluation. As the students become more practiced in these skills, you can move more quickly through the demonstration of them in class. Make sure the students know when you're paraphrasing a text or breaking down a metaphor into its parts and drawing out the implications and connotations. Provide opportunities for them to model the skill in class. As the course progresses, the students should become more adept at reading the literature, and you will find that they can cover more in one class. You may want to schedule your readings accordingly, with shorter, more accessible works at the start and increasingly long or complex works later on. You can always assign more reading than you will discuss in class, but it might be productive to highlight on your syllabus which works you will be addressing at length. In part, the objective of teaching literature is to give students the skills and the desire to read more literature on their own. So, point out additional works for their pleasure, but keep the assigned readings to the maximum you can adequately discuss. You can also get students to begin active reading before the class by assigning reading questions with each work. Requiring informal responses to the reading to be submitted to a discussion board before class can facilitate active reading, prompt discussion in class, and increase the likelihood that the students are doing the reading.

Finally, you should maintain realistic expectations about how much information you can relate or solicit for any given work. If you are teaching a longer survey course covering several hundred years, attention to detail will necessarily be somewhat cursory. If you are teaching a period course, you can likely afford to spend more time on a given work. Keep in mind the objectives for the class and plan to allot a reasonable amount of time to each text. Assign sufficient material to meet the objectives without overburdening the syllabus. It is better to teach one work well than three works poorly. Also keep in mind the difficulty and length of the works you are assigning, being careful not to assign three epics or novels in succession. If you expect students to read the texts, you need to pace the class so that they have the time. You might consider bracketing complete works of substantial length with shorter poems or excerpts from NAEL. Be sure to alert the students to upcoming long works well in advance of covering them in class so that they can devote time to reading them.

Organizing the Readings

Traditionally, survey courses are organized chronologically either by author or by work. NAEL is organized chronologically by date of author's birth and date of publication, so it lends itself easily to this type of course. The guide follows suit in featuring the work of each author in the same order as the Anthology. There are obvious benefits to structuring your course this way. The students approach the literature in the same historical direction that it was produced in, so they are more likely to appreciate allusions and parodies that draw on the work of previous years. You can also feature the role of literary influence by tracing the impact of a work on following generations of writers. There are drawbacks to this structure, however. If you focus on one author per class or week, you may end up teaching a range of works written throughout the author's lifetime. The next author may have been born later but have written earlier or at the same time as the previous author. In this case, strict chronology is violated, which might be confusing. Also, publication dates do not always correspond to dates of composition, and this can affect the way you teach the poems.

Following a chronological order may also affect which authors you include. If you focus on authors and make your decision based on the overall achievement of his or her oeuvre, you may neglect some excellent pieces of literature produced by otherwise minor writers. You can include a wider variety of authors in a chronological survey if you organize the syllabus by the date of the work. However, this structure will affect the amount of biographical information you bring to each work. In this case you may be teaching several poems by different authors in one class, and so time will be spent on the works rather than on the achievements of the individual authors. Also in this structure, a major author may appear on a syllabus at several different points in the course. Allowances need to be made for the weaknesses of each method of organization.

In general, *NAEL* is ideally arranged for a chronological survey. The detailed introductions to each historical period, including a helpful timeline, provide broad overviews that touch on each author and illuminate the cultural and frequently political context in which to situate the works. The headnotes to each author and before each major work provide additional biographical and historical information to round out a student's understanding of the author's or work's significance in the chronology.

As practical as they may be, however, the pedagogical benefits of chronological surveys may be limited by the fact that many students fail to take their courses in chronological order. Moreover, recent literary studies place greater emphasis on cultural trends and thematic issues than on traditional studies of allusion and influence. In light of this, the organization of a survey course by theme or topic can be another productive way to teach. With this structure you can target exactly the works that address a given subject regardless of chronology or author, and so you can teach a wider range of works, including excerpts, without creating a sense of disorder. This is a particularly useful strategy for incorporating some of the newly recovered voices in literature, such as early women, Anglo-African, working-class, and colonial and postcolonial authors. Not only does this shift the focus of study from a dominant tradition of influence, where such writers presumably have little impact, but also it provides opportunities for illustrative groupings that cross chronological barriers. For example, you might cover representations of slavery in early modern Britain and include Behn's *Oroonoko*, Equiano's *Interesting Narrative*, and Wordsworth's sonnet "To Toussaint l'Ouverture." Thematic organization allows for a variety of methods of teaching. Or you might thread a thematic contrast through the course by pairing writers who represent different cultural positions, such as a male and a female, or an aristocratic and a working-class writer, or English and Celtic. Such pairings highlight the distinctive choices of individual authors and provide clear entries for class discussion. Over the course of a term, the class accumulates a fairly solid understanding of the writings from diverse cultural perspectives. For suggestions on period topics, see the Teaching Cluster suggestions in Chapters 5–11. These describe a topical focus that emerges from the period's writings and identify different ways an instructor might expand on the theme or subject. The Teaching Clusters also list works suitable for the topic. You will find additional ideas for creative groupings in the author entries.

One may find with thematic organization, however, a lack of awareness of the actual order of literary production. You think it is obvious that Shakespeare wrote before Milton, but your students probably don't know it. The effect is greater for writers of less fame—Jonson or Johnson, Behn, Barbauld, Bowen . . . One way to counter such confusion is to require students to keep their own timeline of the works and authors.

Given the strengths and weaknesses we've just been discussing, you may find it useful to combine approaches. You can divide the syllabus into short chronological periods within which you can address a variety of authors and works in thematic groupings. Such an organization moves away from the "major authors" approach but retains the sense of chronological order. To challenge traditional literary categories, you might pair works that in author surveys would not be taught together, such as John Webster's *Duchess of Malfi* and Elizabeth Cary's *Tragedy of Mariam*, or Pope's *Epistle to a Lady* and Mary Leapor's *Essay on Woman*. This organization benefits from the historical context provided by *NAEL*'s introductions as well as the illustrative contrasts produced by the creative pairing.

TEACHING CLUSTERS, NORTON TOPICS ONLINE, AND IN-TEXT TOPICS

While the organization of *NAEL* facilitates the chronological approach to literature, the guide, *Norton Topics Online*, and the anthology all have features that can aid a thematic approach. As mentioned above, this guide identifies a variety of Teaching Clusters to help you select texts for thematic treatment. In fact, you could design an entire period course around two or three clusters; for an example, see the syllabus in Chapter 2 on Romantic literature: "Innocence and the Child; Sin and the Outcast." When planning a longer survey, you might connect Teaching Clusters from period to period, particularly when they continue a subject. For instance, one can link the clusters on religion from the Middle Ages through the Victorian era or create a series of clusters around questions of exploration and science from the sixteenth century through the nineteenth.

Often the *Norton Topics Online* complement the Teaching Clusters identified in the guide, and an instructor can incorporate additional information on context, texts, and relevant illustrations by assigning readings from the Web site or introducing them in the classroom. If this is the first survey you've taught, you might explore the topics suggested either in the Teaching Clusters or on *Norton Topics Online* and organize your readings around these themes.

The anthology also includes sections of "in-text topics," which, like the Teaching Clusters, focus on issues from the literary discourse of the era. These are designed to re-create a dialogue about a pressing cultural issue, such as war and conflict ("Crisis of Authority" in the Early Seventeenth Century, "Voices from World War I" and "Voices from World War II" in the Twentieth Century) or gender issues ("Women in Power" in the Sixteenth Century, "The Gender Wars" in the Early Seventeenth Century, "Debating Women" in the Restoration and Eighteenth Century, "The Woman Question" in the Victorian period). Each in-text topic begins with a brief historical overview of the subject that offers ways to understand the significance of the works included. Many times the in-text topics include excerpts from longer works of cultural—if not always literary—

importance. In this way, the anthology is able to present significant works that would otherwise be too long for inclusion in the book. The editors have selected excerpts and works that complement one another and teach well as a group. Generally, you could devote a class to the readings in the in-text topic and bring in additional information on the subject through lecture or outside readings. The guide provides suggestions for readings and illustrations from *Norton Topics Online* that can supplement the in-text topics. Alternatively, you might use the in-text topic to introduce a subject before assigning a full-length text. For example, following the in-text topic "Literary Gothic and the Development of a Mass Readership" in the Romantic section, you could assign any one of a number of gothic novels to round out the picture suggested by the anthologized works. Each of the in-text topics has an entry in this guide, with discussion questions and suggestions for how to teach the section.

CHAPTER 2

Syllabi for Courses Using *The Norton Anthology of English Literature*

This chapter offers sample syllabi for ten courses using *The Norton Anthology of English Literature*, Eighth Edition, and for one course using *The Norton Anthology of English Literature*, The Major Authors, Eighth Edition. Chapter 4 of the guide includes a syllabus that shows how one might integrate *NAEL*'s media resources into a two-semester course covering English literature from the Middle Ages to the present.

Please note that we have not forced the sample syllabi into any particular format. Some are fairly detailed, while others are quite simple; some spell out course objectives, and others offer exercises and assignments. These differences, among many others, demonstrate the wide variety of ways in which instructors approach courses in English literature. We hope that the syllabi will help you in working with *NAEL* and in figuring out which authors and texts you want to explore with your students each semester.

Survey Courses

THE MIDDLE AGES THROUGH THE EARLY MODERN PERIOD: A SURVEY COURSE WITH EXERCISES

This course will introduce you to the first ten centuries of literature in English (Old, Middle, Early Modern) and will help you develop the skills to master a lot of material quickly. Both lectures and sections meet twice weekly and are required.

Tools: My advice for reading a lot of material well involves your head, your heart, and a .5 mm mechanical pencil and a good soft eraser. Write in the margins. Don't write over the text with a highlighter; you want to "see" the poem again. Use your pencil to (1) list (perhaps near the head-note) genre, verseform, cast of characters, settings; (2) divide the text into its primary sections; (3) give a running plot synopsis at the top of the page; (4) bracket, attribute, and give a synopsis of speeches; (5) mark, in the margins, important theses, keywords, structuring images, and central tropes. Using a pencil allows you to find your way around the text quickly and to articulate its larger shapes.

Week 1
Introduction
Beowulf
Skill of the week: Reading for STYLE. Exercise 1 due.

Week 2
Sir Gawain and the Green Knight
Skill of the week: Reading for THEME. Exercise 2 due.

Week 3
Geoffrey Chaucer, *The Canterbury Tales,*
   The Pardoner's Prologue and Tale
Julian of Norwich, *Showings* (all selections)
Skill of the week: Reading for IMAGERY. Exercise 3 due.
Memorize the first eighteen lines of the General Prologue to recite to
   your instructor during office hours.

Week 4
Chaucer, *The Canterbury Tales*, The Wife of Bath's Tale (but not the
    Prologue), the Nun's Priest's Tale, and the Miller's Tale
Skill of the week: Reading with and against GENRE. Exercise 4 due.

Week 5
Chaucer, *The Canterbury Tales*, The General Prologue
The Chester Play of Noah's Flood
The Wakefield Second Shepherds' Play
Skill of the week: Reading for LEXIS. Exercise 5 due.

Week 6
Reading day
Thomas Malory, *Morte Darthur* (all selections)
Midterm Examination

Week 7
Edmund Spenser, *The Faerie Queene*, Book III (proem, cantos 3, 11, 12)
Skill of the week: Keeping alive a love of poetry under the pressures of
    scholarship. Prepare and read aloud your favorite passage from the lit-
    erature on the syllabus.

Week 8
Sixteenth-century lyric and early modern interiority
Chaucer's Retraction (as medieval background)
Thomas Wyatt, "Whoso list to hunt," "My galley,"
    "They flee from me," "The Lover Showeth"
William Tyndale, selections from *Obedience*
Edmund Spenser, *Amoretti* 67 and 45
Philip Sidney, *Astrophil and Stella* 1, 15, 61
Mary Sidney, *Psalm 139*
William Shakespeare, Sonnets 20, 55, 147
Skill of the week: Reading for PROSODY. Exercise 6 due.

Week 9
Everyman
Christopher Marlowe, *The Tragical History of Dr. Faustus*
Skill of the week: Reading for ceremony and RITUAL. Exercise 7 due.

Week 10
William Shakespeare, *The Merchant of Venice* (Norton Critical Edition)
Skill of the week: Reading for PLOT. Exercise 8 due.

Week 11
Renaissance lyric
William Shakespeare, Sonnets 129 and 130
Samuel Daniel, "Care-charmer Sleep"
Michael Drayton, "Since there's no help," "Ode to the Virginia Voyage"
Thomas Campion, "There is a garden in her face"
Christopher Marlowe, "The Passionate Shepherd"

Walter Ralegh, "The Nymph's Reply"

Thomas Nashe, "A Litany in Time of Plague"

John Donne, "The Flea," "The Good-Morrow," "The Sun Rising," "The Relic," "Elegy 19," *Holy Sonnets* 7, 10, 14, 18, "Hymn to God My God in My Sickness," *Devotions upon Emergent Occasions*, "Meditation 17"

Izaak Walton, from *The Life of Dr. John Donne*

Ben Jonson, "On My First Son," "To Lucy, Countess of Bedford," "A Sonnet, to . . . Lady Mary Wroth," "Still to Be Neat"

Mary Wroth, "In this strange labyrinth"

George Herbert, "The Altar," "Easter Wings," "Prayer (1)," "The Pilgrimage"

Richard Crashaw, "To the Infant Martyrs," "I Am the Door," "On the Wounds of Our Crucified Lord," "Blessed be the paps," the emblem of the heart/door

Robert Herrick, "Delight in Disorder," "To the Virgins, to Make Much of Time," "His Prayer to Ben Jonson"

Andrew Marvell, "The Coronet," "Bermudas," "To His Coy Mistress," "The Mower to the Glowworms," "The Garden"

Skill of the week: Reading the LYRIC. Exercise 9 due.

Week 12

Renaissance lyric, continued

Skill of the week: Reading for TROPES. Exercise 10 due.

Week 13

John Milton, *Paradise Lost*, Books 1, 4, and 9

Skill of the week: Navigating Milton. Exercise 11 due.

Week 14

Last lecture. Rather than writing an exercise this week, collaborate with your classmates on a review of the course. Apply the skills developed in the exercises to the other texts on the syllabus.

Final examination

The Exercises

Print out two copies of each completed exercise: one to hand to your TA, the other to bring to your section meeting. Your exercises will not be given individual grades, but will count as part of your grade for participation.

Exercise 1: Reading for STYLE

As a technical literary term, "style" describes the compositional habits that shape texts and give them a unity of feel or texture. Style can be broken down into many components: diction, level, syntax, grammar, ornament, and more. Rhetorical theory advises that the style suit the matter. The following exercise approaches *Beowulf* through a focus on grammatical style. In poetry, the weight of meaning can be distributed variously over the elements of grammar. Does the poet stress things and qualities, or actions? Nouns and adjectives, or verbs and adverbs? Use a grammar handbook to review the parts of speech.

Rewrite lines 1557–68 of Heaney's translation of *Beowulf*, conveying the same information but shifting the information around so it weighs differently on the grammar. Do this once for nouns and adjectives, and a second time for verbs and adverbs.

Example, lines 12–14, rewritten with weight on verbs and adverbs: God *comforted* them and *afterward* Shield *fathered* one who *boyishly played* and *prowled nearby.*

Rewritten with the weight of meaning placed mostly on nouns and adjectives: The *late birth* of a *boy-child* for *Shield*—a *cub* in the *yard,* a *comfort* from a *compassionate God* for that *nation.*

Which are the important, textured, eye-catching words? Move them around. Now, which of your "shiftings" sounds most like the poem? On what parts of speech does the *Beowulf* poet place most of the poem's weight of meaning? Write a paragraph on the relation between the poem's "content" and its grammatical style: would you say there's a good fit between the style and the content?

Exercise 2: Reading for THEME
The primary theme of a literary work (say, "the tragic and glorious sacrifices heroes make for their people" in *Beowulf*) is built into many different facets of its composition. Draft a phrase describing a main theme of *Sir Gawain and the Green Knight.* Find passages (list them by line number and brief quotations) in which the poem encodes that theme in (1) an image, (2) a statement, (3) a plot event. Can you find the theme embodied in another important aspect of the poem?

Exercise 3: Reading for IMAGERY
Literary critics usually use the term "image" to describe a moment when the language of a poem appeals explicitly to our visual sense. Images become "key" images when literature makes them a crucial part of a larger structure of visual experience, designs them to encapsulate a central idea or emotion, lavishes enormous verbal ornament upon them, or causes them to shock us with their beauty, violence, or incongruity. Find two images that connect the Pardoner's Prologue with the Pardoner's Tale. Write a paragraph describing the way these images work. Then, in another paragraph, write about the role of imagery in Julian of Norwich's *Showings.*

Exercise 4: Reading for GENRE
Literary "genre" (Chaucer and Spenser would have said "kind") is familiar to all consumers of fiction. Your local video store organizes its wares according to the genres of film: comedy, horror, drama, action, etc. Such categories change over time as writers and filmmakers and others do things differently. Think back on your television experience, and you'll realize you know examples of such historical change. Genre is something

we recognize when we have experienced so many examples that they begin to fall into categories. You may not have read a medieval fabliau, Breton lay, or beast fable before, but the genre of the literary work you're reading is crucial to know. For the record, the Miller's Tale is a "fabliau"—the plural is "fabliaux"—a kind of comic short story built around a dirty practical joke in which certain kinds of characters get punished and others triumph according to a sense of human nature being motivated by physical appetites and competition for scarce resources. The Wife of Bath's Tale is an Arthurian story in the form of a Breton lay, a brief chivalric romance (not a love story, but an adventure) with magical elements that often takes up philosophical questions about love, fate, or power. The Nun's Priest's Tale is a beast fable. You may remember one of Aesop's fables: a clever, quick story with animal protagonists and a human moral that raises ethical questions. Genre embodies not only kinds of characters, settings, styles, and plots, but also sets of values. Genre sets the ground rules, and individual works launch themselves off those rules.

Here's the exercise: Translate the story of one of the three tales we're reading into a one-page version of one of the other two genres. In other words, do one of the following: rewrite the Wife of Bath's Tale as a fabliau or a beast fable, or rewrite the Miller's Tale as a Breton lay or a beast fable, or rewrite the Nun's Priest's Tale as a Breton lay or a fabliau. *Then* write a paragraph explaining how your translation qualifies as an example of the genre by considering at least three main features such as setting, ensemble of characters, ending, values, plot, style, imagery, tone, etc.

Exercise 5: Reading for LEXIS

What kinds of words does a poet use? Specialized vocabularies or jargons develop in the niches of any language-using society. There are words that belong to the technical lexicons of, say, medicine, or Hollywood camera operators, or law, or beauty salons, or skinheads, or physics, though they are nevertheless part of the English language. Dictionaries often identify one of the uses of such words as belonging to that lexicon, while other uses of the word might belong to the culture at large. The lexical affiliations of words provide a palette of meaning for the poet, who can combine different lexicons to produce intricate effects of elevation or comedy or criticism. For instance, a poet can produce a very different result by describing love using medical terms than she can using baseball lingo.

As you're reading the General Prologue, look for the jargons of social niches of medieval English culture. Sometimes Chaucer uses a word that has a specialized meaning in a way that plays that meaning against its normal street use; sometimes the result encourages the reader to take an attitude of praise, sometimes skepticism, sometimes outright disgust. Find an interesting example of a jargon word in the Prologue and explain how it works. Use the *Middle English Dictionary* (U Michigan Press; copy in the reference section of the libraries, online version through Virgo—search for it in "The Middle English Compendium") to try to confirm whether your word is drawn from a specialized lexicon. Can you find other examples of that jargon in the Prologue? You may need evidence from a historical dictionary to clinch your point—because words, as you've probably noticed, change their meaning over time.

Exercise 6: Reading for PROSODY

Find a good literary glossary or encyclopedia and read about meter, rhyme, stanza, and the sonnet (try *The New Princeton Encyclopedia of Poetry and Poetics*; see also the Glossary of Literary Terms in *NAEL*). Write a sonnet in iambic pentameter that imitates (parodies or reveres) something that strikes you as typical of the sonnets we're reading (style? theme? imagery? other patterns or conventions?). Write a paragraph or two describing the feature you find typical and explaining your imitation. Don't be overwhelmed by the dictionaries—we will not be mastering the scanning of poetry in this course, only being introduced to it. What you do need to know: (1) the definitions of the feet and the meters and (2) how to recognize whether something is in iambic pentameter or not.

Exercise 7: Reading for CEREMONY and RITUAL

Fiction depends on our knowledge of the cultural meanings of its primary scenes (for instance, you need to know what "a loan," "a marriage," and "a trial" are in order to understand *The Merchant of Venice*). List the rituals, ceremonies, or cultural practices that *Everyman* relies upon; then do the same for *Dr. Faustus*. Choose one item from your lists, and write a page or two comparing the play's use of it to an earlier text's presentation of a similar cultural practice. For example, compare feasting in *Beowulf* to feasting in *Dr. Faustus*. List the relevant passages. Do a little research into the culture (for example, what are medieval and renaissance banquets like?) to add juicy historical details.

Exercise 8: Reading for PLOT

Literature often has several interwoven plots (i.e., sequences of action). In *The Merchant of Venice*, Shakespeare pairs the story of Portia's marriage with the story of Antonio's debt to Shylock. Write a page or two on a moment where the relation between these two plots is important.

Exercise 9: Reading the LYRIC

Put the lyric poems on our syllabus into groups according to their dominant features—consider aspects of style, theme, imagery, genre, lexis, ritual, and plot. (Some might belong to more than one group.) What are the most important distinguishing features of renaissance lyric? To sharpen your own memory, you might want to consider what distinguishes one poem from the others in its group.

Exercise 10: Reading for TROPES and FIGURES OF SPEECH

Lyric poems often use one or two tropes as a central, organizing principle. As you read the poems, find a good example of a centrally organizing (1) metaphor, (2) simile, and (3) another kind of figure—your choice. Consult the literary terms appendix in *NAEL* and, if necessary, a good dictionary of literary terms to check the definitions of these familiar and unfamiliar tropes (as one's grasp of theory grows more sophisticated, metaphor becomes increasingly complex). Write a paragraph describing the way meaning works in each of your three cases. If you find yourself saying, "It emphasizes the meaning," then you haven't thought enough about it—of course it does! The challenge lies in explaining *how*.

Exercise 11: Navigating MILTON
Write one or two pages using one or more of the exercise skills to begin to analyze *Paradise Lost*.

SIXTEENTH-CENTURY ENGLISH LITERATURE

Course objectives:
- To introduce students to the major authors and issues of sixteenth-century literature in English
- For students to understand the impact of the Reformation, colonial encounters, and a prolonged period of female rule on the literature of the period
- To demonstrate the range of social and cultural perspectives represented in the literature of the period
- For students to appreciate the Elizabethan "golden age" in the context of developments earlier in the century

Week	Author	Title
1	More	*Utopia*
2	Wyatt	all selections
	Howard (Surrey)	all selections
3	in-text topic	Faith in Conflict
4	Ascham	*The Schoolmaster*
	Hoby	*The Courtier*
5	in-text topic	Women in Power
6	Spenser	*The Faerie Queen* (Book I)
7	Spenser	*The Faerie Queen* (Book I, cont.)
8	Ralegh	*Discovery of . . . Guiana*
	in-text topic	The Wider World
9	Sidney	*Astrophil and Stella*
10	Sidney	*The Defense of Poesy*
11	Daniel	sonnets from *Delia*
	Drayton	sonnets from *Idea*
	Spenser	sonnets from Amoretti
12	Marlowe	*Doctor Faustus*
13	Shakespeare	Sonnets
14	Shakespeare	*Twelfth Night*
15	Shakespeare	*King Lear*

EARLY SEVENTEENTH-CENTURY
ENGLISH LITERATURE

Course objectives:
- To introduce students to the major authors and issues of early seventeenth-century literature in English
- For students to understand the "metaphysical" and "cavalier" modes in seventeenth-century literature
- To demonstrate the range of social and cultural perspectives represented in the literature of the period
- For students to understand the cultural background to the English Revolution and the impact of the conflict on writers who lived through it

Week	Author	Title
1	Donne	*Songs and Sonnets*
2	Donne	*Holy Sonnets*, Death's Duel
3	Lanyer	"A Description of Cookham"
	Wroth	*Pamphilia to Amphilanthus*
4	Jonson	*Volpone*
5	Jonson	"To Penshurst," "Ode to Himself"
6	Webster	*The Duchess of Malfi*
7	Bacon	Essays
8	Burton	*Anatomy of Melancholy*
	Browne	*Religio Medici, Hydriotaphia*
9	Herbert	*The Temple* (selections)
	Crashaw	"The Blazing Heart"
	Vaughan	selections
10	Herrick	"Corinna," "The Hock-Cart," "The Vine"
	Carew	"To Saxham," "A Rapture"
	Lovelace	"The Grasshopper"
11	Milton	"Lycidas"
12	Marvell	*Upon Appleton House*, "An Horatian Ode"
	Philips	"Upon the Double Murder"
13	in-text topic	Crisis of Authority
14	Milton	*Paradise Lost*, Books 1–2, 4
15	Milton	*Paradise Lost*, Books 9–10

RESTORATION AND EIGHTEENTH-CENTURY ENGLISH LITERATURE

This course is for students on the third-year undergraduate level; the syllabus assumes a fifteen-week term and three hours of class per week.

Course objectives:
- To introduce students to the major authors and issues of Restoration and eighteenth-century literature
- For students to understand the modes of satire and sentiment in Restoration and eighteenth-century literature
- To demonstrate the range of social and cultural perspectives represented in the literature of the period
- For students to understand the writers' preoccupation with emerging literary values of the era

Week	Author	Title
1	Dryden	"Mac Flecknoe" and "Essay on Dramatic Poesy" (excerpt)
2	Behn	*Oroonoko*
3	Swift	"Verses on the Death of Dr. Swift" *Gulliver's Travels*, book 4
4	Pope	"The Rape of the Lock"
5	Finch	"Nocturnal Reverie," "Introduction"
	Prior	"Epitaph," "A Better Answer"
	Montagu	"Epistle to Mrs. Yonge"
6	Gay	*The Beggar's Opera*
7	Haywood	*Fantomina*
8	Addison and Steele	Essays from *Tatler* and *Spectator*
	Johnson	Essays from *Rambler* and *Idler*
9	Johnson	"Vanity of Human Wishes," *Rasselas*
10	Gray	"Elegy Written in a Country Churchyard," "Eton College"
	Collins	"Ode to Evening"
11	Goldsmith	"The Deserted Village"
	Crabbe	*The Village*
12	Frances Burney	*Evelina* (Norton Critical Edition)
13		*Evelina* (cont.)
	Astell	"Reflections on Marriage" (excerpt)
	Defoe	*Roxana* (excerpt)
14	Boswell	*Journal, Life of Samuel Johnson*
	Burney	Journals and Letters
15	Leapor	"Essay on Woman," "To a Lady"
	Smart	"My Cat Jeoffrey"
	Traditional	Ballads

THE ROMANTIC ERA

This class is for students on the third-year undergraduate level; the syllabus assumes a fifteen-week term and three hours of class per week.

Course objectives:
- To introduce students to the major authors and issues of Romantic literature
- For students to understand the dominant forms of lyric poetry in the period
- To demonstrate the social and cultural perspectives in the literature of the period
- For students to understand the writers' formulation of revolutionary and literary practices and ideals

Week	Author	Title
1	Barbauld	"A Summer Evening's Meditation," "Washing Day"
	Smith	"Written at the close of spring," "To Sleep," "To Night," "On Being Cautioned"
2	Blake	*Songs of Innocence, Songs of Experience* (selections)
	Robinson	"The Poor Singing Dame," "The Haunted Beach"
	Burns	"Tam O'Shanter"
3	W. Wordsworth	"We Are Seven," "Expostulation and Reply," "Tables Turned" "Tintern Abbey," *The Thorn*
4	W. Wordsworth	Immortality ode Preface to *Lyrical Ballads*
	Coleridge	*Biographia Literaria* (excerpts)
5	Coleridge	*The Rime of the Ancient Mariner*, "Kubla Khan," "Frost at Midnight"
6	D. Wordsworth	Journals
	Hazlitt	"My First Acquaintance with Poets"
7	Scott	"Wandering Willie's Tale"
	Edgeworth	"The Irish Incognito"
8	in-text topic	Gothic and the Development of Mass Readership (selections)
9	M. Shelley	*Frankenstein* (Norton Critical)
10		*Frankenstein* (cont.)
11		*Frankenstein* (cont.)
	Austen	*Love and Friendship*
12	P. Shelley	"Mutability," "Ode to the West Wind," "Ozymandias," "England

		1819," "Hymn to Intellectual Beauty," "A Defence of Poetry"
13	Byron	*Don Juan*
14	John Clare	"The Nightingale's Nest," "Pastoral Poesy," "Mouse's Nest," "Clock a Clay"
	Keats	"On First Looking into Chapman's Homer," "When I have Fears," "Why did I laugh," "Bright Star"
15	Keats	"Ode to a Nightingale," "Ode on a Grecian Urn," "Ode on Melancholy," "To Autumn," Letters

---

NINETEENTH- AND TWENTIETH-CENTURY BRITISH LITERATURE

Objectives: To introduce students to significant authors, works, and themes in British and postcolonial literatures of the nineteenth and twentieth centuries. Victorian topics include the Victorian mood, social criticism, Arthurian romance, the woman question, aesthetic issues and the critique of Victorian values, and imperialism. Twentieth-century topics include imperialism, modern poetics, World War I poetry, modernist poetry and fiction, post–World War II poetry, women's issues, and postcolonial literature. The groupings, although not strictly chronological, give students an idea of historical context and literary trajectories.

Weeks 1 and 2: The Victorian Mood: Belief, Skepticism, and Melancholy
John Stuart Mill: from *Autobiography*
Alfred, Lord Tennyson: "Mariana," "The Lotos-Eaters," "Locksley Hall," and selections from *In Memoriam*
Robert Browning: "My Last Duchess," " 'Childe Roland to the Dark Tower Came,' " "Caliban upon Setebos"
Matthew Arnold: "The Scholar Gypsy," "Dover Beach," "Stanzas from the Grande Chartreuse"

Week 3: Social Criticism and the "Condition of England"
Thomas Carlyle: from *Past and Present* ("Democracy" and "Captains of Industry")
Elizabeth Barrett Browning: "The Cry of the Children" and "The Runaway Slave at Pilgrim's Point"
Blue Book material: 1842 Royal Commission on Children's Employment
Charles Dickens: from *Hard Times*

Friedrich Engels: from *The Great Towns*
See also the illustrations of Victorian factory workers in Norton Topics Online.

Week 4: Arthurian Romance
Alfred, Lord Tennyson: "The Lady of Shalott" and *Idylls of the King*
John Ruskin: from *The Stones of Venice* ("The Savageness of Gothic Architecture")
William Morris: "The Defense of Guenevere"
See also illustrations by John Everett Millais and D. G. Rossetti in the color insert to *NAEL* and in Norton Topics Online.

Week 5: The Woman Question
John Stuart Mill: from *The Subjection of Women*
John Ruskin: from "Of Queens' Gardens"
Elizabeth Barrett Browning: *Aurora Leigh*
George Eliot: *Margaret Fuller and Mary Wollstonecraft*
Christina Rossetti: "In an Artist's Studio" and *Goblin Market*

Week 6: Aesthetics, Aestheticism, and the Critique of Victorian Values
John Ruskin: from *Modern Painters* ("A Definition of Greatness in Art" and "The Slave Ship")
Walter Pater: from *The Renaissance* (Conclusion)
Dante Gabriel Rossetti: "The Blessed Damozel"
Oscar Wilde: Preface to *The Picture of Dorian Gray* and *The Importance of Being Earnest*

Week 7: Victorians and Empire
Thomas Babington Macaulay: from "Minute on Indian Education"
Eliza Cook: "The Englishman"
James Anthony Froude: from *The English in the West Indies*
John Jacob Thomas: from *Froudacity*
Rudyard Kipling: "The White Man's Burden" and "The Man Who Would Be King"

Week 8: Imperialism in the Twentieth Century
Joseph Conrad: *Heart of Darkness*
Chinua Achebe: from "An Image of Africa: Racism in Conrad's *Heart of Darkness*"

Week 9: Modern Poetics
Thomas Hardy: "Hap," "The Darkling Thrush"
W. B. Yeats: "The Lake Isle of Innisfree," "No Second Troy," "Easter 1916," "The Second Coming," "Man and the Echo"

Week 10: World War I Poets
Siegfried Sassoon: "They" and "Glory of Women"
Isaac Rosenberg: "Break of Day in the Trenches"
Wilfred Owen: "Dulce Et Decorum Est" and "Strange Meeting"
Robert Graves: from *Goodbye to All That*

Week 11: Modernist Poetry
Ezra Pound: "In a Station of the Metro"
T. S. Eliot: "The Love Song of J. Alfred Prufrock" and *The Waste Land*

Week 12: Modernist Fiction
Virginia Woolf: "Modern Fiction" and "The Mark on the Wall"
James Joyce: "The Dead" and *Ulysses* ("Proteus" and "Lestrygonians")

Week 13: Modern/Postmodern Drama
Samuel Beckett: *Endgame*
Harold Pinter: *The Dumb Waiter*

Week 14: Women in the Twentieth Century
Katherine Mansfield: "The Garden Party"
Virginia Woolf: *A Room of One's Own*
Doris Lessing: "To Room Nineteen"

Week 15: The Empire Writes Back
Derek Walcott: "A Far Cry from Africa"
Seamus Heaney: "Digging" and "Punishment"
Eavan Boland: "That the Science of Cartography Is Limited" and
    "The Dolls Museum in Dublin"
Salman Rushdie: "The Prophet's Hair"

SURVEY OF ENGLISH LITERATURE, BEGINNINGS TO THE PRESENT

(using *NAEL* Major Authors)

This course is aimed at first- or second-year undergraduate students, not necessarily English majors. It is based on a fifteen-week term with three hours of class per week.

Course objectives:
- To survey a selection of major works and authors in the tradition of English literature from the beginnings to the present
- To demonstrate the continuities and discontinuities in considerations of the hero and the modes of writing appropriate for the heroic in the tradition, namely epic, tragedy, and romance
- To raise considerations about the representations of war, religion, suffering, family, and gender in a context of heroism
- For students to reflect on the history of change in ideas about heroism and how modern culture has adapted the formulations of the past

Week	Author	Title
1		*Beowulf*
2		*Beowulf* (cont.)
	Marlowe	*Faustus*
3		*Faustus* (cont.)
4	Milton	*Paradise Lost*
5		*Paradise Lost* (cont.)
6		*Paradise Lost* (cont.)
7	Behn	*Oroonoko*
8	Pope	*The Rape of the Lock*
9	Wordsworth	*Prelude* (excerpts)
10		*Prelude* (cont.)
	Byron	*Don Juan* (excerpts)
11	M. Shelley	*Frankenstein* (Norton Critical Edition)
12		*Frankenstein* (cont.)
13	Yeats	"Adam's Curse," "No Second Troy," "Sept. 1913," "Easter 1916," "The Second Coming"
14	Woolf	*A Room of One's Own*
	Gordimer	*Burgher's Daughter* (outside novel)
15		*Burgher's Daughter* (cont.)

THE RESTORATION AND THE EIGHTEENTH CENTURY: POLITICS OF THE INDIVIDUAL

This class is for students on the third-year undergraduate level; the syllabus assumes a fifteen-week term and three hours of class per week.

Course objectives:
- To introduce students to a range of authors and literary forms of the era, including the developing genre of the novel
- For students to understand the representation of the individual and the emerging sense of individualism in the context of the British enlightenment
- For students to understand the political controversies of the late seventeenth century that spurred the bipartisan politics reflected in eighteenth-century literature
- For students to learn about the foundations of social conflicts in terms of gender, social station, economics, and race in the Restoration and eighteenth century

Week	Author	Title
1	Dryden	*Absalom and Achitophel*
2	Bunyan	*Pilgrim's Progress* (excerpt)
	Butler	*Hudibras* (excerpt)
	Locke	*Essay Concerning Human Understanding* (excerpt)
3	Behn	*Oroonoko*
4	In-text Topic	On Liberty
5	Congreve	*The Way of the World*
6	Astell	"Reflections on Marriage" (excerpt)
	Defoe	*Roxana* (excerpt)
	Montagu	"Epistle to Mrs. Yonge"
	Leapor	"An Essay on Woman" and "An Epistle to a Lady"
7	Finch	"Introduction"
	Swift	"Verses on the Death of . . . Swift"
	Pope	"Epistle to Dr. Arbuthnot" and *The Dunciad*
8	in-text topic	Debating Women
9	Haywood	*Fantomina*
10	Richardson	Pamela (outside novel)
11		*Pamela* (cont.)
12		*Pamela* (cont.)
13	Johnson	*Rasselas*
14	Boswell	*Journal, Life of Samuel Johnson*
	Burney	Journals and Letters
15	Gray	Churchyard elegy
	Prior	"An Epitaph"

THE ROMANTIC ERA: INNOCENCE AND THE CHILD; SIN AND THE OUTCAST

This class is for students on the third-year undergraduate level; the syllabus assumes a fifteen-week term and three hours of class per week.

Course objectives:
- To introduce students to a range of authors and literary forms of the era, including the Romantic novel and autobiographical writings
- To demonstrate the contradictory impulses of Romantic preoccupations with childlike innocence and demonic sinners (as in the Byronic hero)
- For students to understand the literary controversies of the era and the context of political revolution that inspired them
- For students to learn about and discuss the democratic themes and the range of social and cultural perspectives represented in the literature of the period

Week	Author	Title
1	Barbauld	"To a Little Invisible Being," "Washing Day" "The Mouse's Petition"
	Blake	*Songs of Innocence, Songs of Experience* (selections)
2	Baillie	"To a Waking Infant"
	W. Wordsworth	"We Are Seven," "Nutting," *The Prelude* (first two books)
3	W. Wordsworth	Immortality ode
	P. Shelley	"Hymn to Intellectual Beauty"
	Coleridge	"Dejection: An Ode," "Frost at Midnight"
4	Wollstonecraft	*Vindication of the Rights of Woman*
	Mary Hays [or]	*Emma Courtney* (outside novel)
	William Godwin	*Caleb Williams* (outside novel)
5	Hays or Godwin	novel cont.
6	Lamb	"Christ's Hospital"
	Hazlitt	"My First Acquaintance with Poets"
	Hemans	"Casabianca"
7	Austen	*Love and Friendship*
8	Wordsworth	*The Thorn*
	Coleridge	*Rime of the Ancient Mariner*
9	Byron	*Manfred*
10	De Quincey	*Confessions of an Opium Eater*
	M. Shelley	"The Mortal Immortal"
11	P. Shelley	"Defence of Poetry," *Prometheus Unbound*
12	Smith	"To Sleep," "Written in a

		Churchyard," "On Being Cautioned . . ."
	Robinson	"To the Poet Coleridge," "Haunted Beach"
	Hemans	"A Spirit's Return"
	Landon	"Love's Last Lesson"
13	Landon	"Proud Ladye"
	Keats	"La Belle Dame Sans Merci," *Fall of Hyperion*
14	Keats	*Fall of Hyperion* (cont.), Letters
15	Clare	"I Am," "Peasant Poet," "Song," Autobiographical fragments

---

WOMEN AND SEXUALITY IN NINETEENTH-CENTURY BRITISH LITERATURE

Objectives: To familiarize students with the issues and challenges confronting Victorian women through a study of the literary traditions and cultural contexts of nineteenth-century England. The course begins with the theory of separate spheres and moves to issues about the objectification of women, debates about women's rights, cultural problems encountered by middle- and working-class women, prostitution, and independent women of the late century. Literary works include poetry, essays, novels, and short stories by and about nineteenth-century women.

Weeks 1–2: Women, Marriage, and the Theory of Separate Spheres
Coventry Patmore: from *The Angel in the House*
John Ruskin: from "Of Queens' Gardens"
Sarah Stickney Ellis: from *The Women of England*
Dinah Maria Mulock: from *A Woman's Thoughts about Women*
Charles Darwin: from *The Descent of Man* ("Natural Selection and Sexual Selection")
George Meredith: from *Modern Love*
Florence Nightingale: from *Cassandra*
Harriet Martineau: from *Autobiography*
Elizabeth Eastlake: from "Lady Travellers" (in *Norton Topics Online*: The Victorian Age—The Woman Question)

Weeks 2–3: Women as Objects and Subjects
Alfred, Lord Tennyson: "The Lady of Shalott" and selections from *The Princess* ("Come Down, O Maid" and "The Woman's Cause Is Man's)
William Morris: "The Defense of Guenevere"
Robert Browning: "My Last Duchess"
Dante Gabriel Rossetti: "The Blessed Damozel," "Soul's Beauty," and "Body's Beauty"

Christina Rossetti: "In an Artist's Studio"
See also D. G. Rossetti's Portraits of Women (in *Norton Topics Online*: The Victorian Age—The Painterly Image in Poetry) and illustrations by John Everett Millais and D. G. Rossetti in the color insert to *NAEL*

Week 4: The Debate about Women's Rights
Mary Wollstonecraft: from *A Vindication of the Rights of Woman*
John Stuart Mill: from *The Subjection of Women*

Weeks 4 (cont.) and 5: Women as Artists, Writers, and Thinkers
Elizabeth Barrett Browning: "To George Sand: A Desire" and "To George Sand: A Recognition," and from *Aurora Leigh*
George Eliot: *Margaret Fuller and Mary Wollstonecraft* and from *Silly Novels by Lady Novelists*
Virginia Woolf: *A Room of One's Own*

Weeks 6–7: Middle-Class Women as Poets and Writers: Their Stories
Christina Rossetti: *Goblin Market*, "An Apple-Gathering," and "A Triad"
See D. G. Rossetti's illustrations for *Goblin Market* (in *Norton Topics Online*: The Victorian Age—The Painterly Image in Poetry)
Emily Brontë: "I'm Happiest When Most Away," "The Night-Wind," and "Remembrance"
Elizabeth Gaskell: "The Old Nurse's Story"
Charlotte Brontë: *Jane Eyre* (Norton Critical Edition)

Week 8: Working-Class Women
Annie Besant: The "White Slavery" of London Match Workers
Ada Nield Chew: A Living Wage for Factory Girls at Crewe
Henry Mayhew: The Life of a Coster Girl (in *Norton Topic Online*: The Victorian Age—The Woman Question)

Week 9: Prostitution
Anonymous: "The Great Social Evil"
Dante Gabriel Rossetti: "Jenny"
George Bernard Shaw: *Mrs. Warren's Profession*
See William Holman Hunt's *The Awakening Conscience* in the *NAEL* color insert

Weeks 10–11: The New Woman
Walter Besant: from *The Queen's Reign*
Eliza Lynn Linton: from *The Girl of the Period* (*Norton Topics Online*: The Victorian Age—The Woman Question)
Mona Caird: from *Marriage*
Thomas Hardy: *Jude the Obscure* (Norton Critical Edition)

Week 12: Monstrous Women of the Fin-de-Siècle
Bram Stoker: *Dracula* (Norton Critical Edition)

TWENTIETH-CENTURY LITERATURE IN ENGLISH: FROM THE BRITISH EMPIRE TO POSTCOLONIALISM

Objectives: To familiarize students with the literatures, themes, and is-sues relating to twentieth-century British imperialism and its postcolonial aftermath. The course begins with an overview of nineteenth-century attitudes toward imperialism, offering a variety of material that includes high-imperial ideology and criticisms of empire. From there we turn to the twentieth century, where the criticisms become sharper and—in some cases—more self-reflective. The section on language/nation/identity cov-ers a wide range of approaches, in general tending to demonstrate the im-portance of language in shaping the self. This is followed by differing narratives of colonial and cultural encounters, illustrating painful conse-quences. An internalized form of cultural encounter is the theme of the next grouping, which is marked by musings on identity. The course con-cludes with selections focusing on various forms of longing that articulate themselves in terms of history and culture.

Weeks 1–2: The Nineteenth Century: Reflections on Empire
John Ruskin: from *Lectures on Art* (*Norton Topics Online:* The Twentieth Century—"Imperial Duty")
James Anthony Froude: from *The English in the West Indies*
John Jacob Thomas: from *Froudacity*
Edward Tylor: from *Primitive Culture* (*Norton Topics Online:* The Victo-rian Age—Race and Victorian Science)
Benjamin Kidd: from *The Control of the Tropics* (*Norton Topics Online:* The Victorian Age—Race and Victorian Science)
Josephine Butler: from "Our Indian Fellow Subjects" (*Norton Topics On-line:* The Victorian Age—Colonialism and Gender)
Thomas Babington Macaulay: from "Minute on Indian Education"
William Howard Russell: "My Indian Mutiny Diary"
Eliza Cook: "The Englishman"
Joseph Chamberlain: from "The True Conception of Empire" (*Norton Topics Online:* The Victorian Age—Victorian Imperialism: Texts and Contexts; The Civilizing Mission)
T. N. Mukherji: "Observations on the Indian and Colonial Exhibition by the Queen"
Rudyard Kipling: "The White Man's Burden" and "The Man Who Would Be King"

Week 3: The Twentieth Century: Reflections on Empire
Jawaharlal Nehru: *Tryst with Destiny* (*Norton Topics Online:* The Twenti-eth Century—Topics)
Jan Morris: from *Farewell the Trumpets: An Imperial Retreat* (*Norton Top-ics Online:* The Twentieth Century)
George Orwell: "Shooting an Elephant"
J. M. Coetzee: from *Waiting for the Barbarians*

Web Resources (terms, themes, issues): Postcolonial Studies at Emory University and Contemporary Postcolonial and Post-imperial literature in English (*Norton Topics Online:* The Twentieth Century: Imperialism to Postcolonialism; Web Resources)

Weeks 4–6: Language/Nation/Identity
Claude McKay: "Old England" and "If We Must Die"
Hugh MacDiarmid: from *The Splendid Variety of Languages and Dialects,* "A Drunk Man Looks at the Thistle," and "In Memoriam James Joyce"
Louise Bennett: "Jamaica Language" and "Colonization in Reverse"
Kamau Brathwaite: from *Nation Language* and *Calypso*
Ngũgĩ Wa Thiong'o: from *Decolonising the Mind*
Salman Rushdie: from *English Is an Indian Literary Language*
W. B. Yeats: "The Lake Isle of Innisfree"
Brian Friel: *Translations*
Samuel Beckett: *Endgame*

Weeks 7–8: Two Visions of Colonial Conquest
Joseph Conrad: *Heart of Darkness*
Chinua Achebe: from "An Image of Africa: Racism in Conrad's *Heart of Darkness*" and *Things Fall Apart*
Web resource: African history (*Norton Topics Online:* The Twentieth Century)

Week 9: Cultural Encounters
E. M. Forster: "The Other Boat"
Jean Rhys: "Let Them Call It Jazz"
V. S. Naipaul: "One Out of Many"
Paul Muldoon: "Meeting the British" and "The Grand Conversation"

Weeks 10–11: Ambivalence, Hybridity, Identity
James Joyce: "The Dead"
W. B. Yeats: "Easter 1916," "The Second Coming"
Derek Walcott: "A Far Cry from Africa," "The Season of Phantasmal Peace," and "Omeros"
A. K. Ramanujan: "Self Portrait," "Elements of Composition," and "Foundlings in the Yukon"
Nadine Gordimer: "The Moment before the Gun Went Off"

Week 12: History and Memory
Seamus Heaney: "The Grauballe Man," "Punishment," "Casualty," and "Clearances"
Eavan Boland: "Fond Memory," "That the Science of Cartography Is Limited," "The Dolls Museum in Dublin," "The Lost Land"

Week 13: Tradition and Desire
Salman Rushdie: "The Prophet's Hair"

CHAPTER 3

Using Technology in the Classroom

Today's digital environment offers a dizzying array of possibilities for the classroom. From the simple use of email to the more varied applications of electronic texts and PowerPoint presentations, instructors will find much that is valuable for the study of literature. Oftentimes students will be (or will seem to be) more computer-savvy than their instructors, so keeping up with technological advances may appear to be a never-ending task. Yet it's wise to bear in mind that technology should serve the purposes of pedagogy rather than be an end in itself. In the rush to stay current, it's easy to be dazzled by all the bells and whistles, many of which are superfluous to the study of literature. At the same time, today's digital resources offer numerous possibilities for creativity and flexibility in teaching and in developing assignments.

ELECTRONIC COMMUNICATIONS: AN OVERVIEW

Most instructors are familiar with the uses of email. Through email, it's easy to answer student questions, send handouts, post notices, or provide feedback on assignments. But many other alternatives now exist that allow increased control of and flexibility in electronic communication. Discussion logs and chat rooms, for example, are two highly useful ways to stay in touch with students and extend the analysis of course material outside of the classroom. Instructors can access these tools from one of the many online sources or turn to the course-management systems used by an increasing number of colleges and universities. Course-management systems (such as WebCT and Blackboard, which will soon merge) provide an enclosed environment with a variety of technical options, from creating chat rooms to grading and developing assignments. If your institution uses one of these systems, designing your own discussion group or chat room will be simple and you will be able to have students submit assignments online or post papers for review by their peers.

Online Discussion Groups and Chat Rooms

While email is sufficient for individual communications, online discussion groups and chat rooms have several advantages over group email exchanges. Discussion logs can be organized according to particular threads, or topics, for instance, and be cross-referenced for ease of access. Moreover, instructors can decide how much involvement they want. Students can be assigned to one or more small discussion groups that the instructor simply observes, or the instructor can pose questions and be directly involved. In either situation, student participation can be required and graded. This is an excellent way to encourage active critical thinking, foster a more collaborative spirit in the classroom, and help students develop their writing skills. In contrast to discussion groups, chat rooms provide an opportunity for students and/or instructors to engage in real-time exchanges. This is especially useful if you would like to extend your office hours or be available for consultation at a particular time. You might want to collect midterm exams online or talk with students as a group after they have read a particular text, for example. Chat rooms can also be used in lieu of a discussion section following a lecture, facilitated by instructors or teaching assistants, or self-monitored by students.

Electronic Texts

Electronic texts are a valuable resource that can provide additional reading or make accessible documents that would be otherwise unavailable or out-of-print. Numerous Web sites provide access to electronic texts and entire digital archives, ranging in focus from single works, such as the *Electronic Canterbury Tales*, to larger collections of miscellaneous writings, such as those in *Project Gutenberg*. Some sites provide different manuscript versions of texts, allowing students to compare various drafts and trace the process of composition. Other sites, such as *Norton Literature Online* (discussed in a separate section of this chapter and in Chapter 4) and the *Victorian Web*, link archived documents with study material, images, and historical and biographical information on authors and works. Additionally, some texts are available in hypertext format and can be searched for particular words and phrases. While most electronic texts are transcriptions of literary material, digital images of actual pages are also available, which is helpful if you are teaching classes in the history of the book or want to focus student attention on manuscript variations. Although electronic texts in all their guises are undoubtedly useful in the classroom, quality, accuracy, and editorial oversight vary greatly among Web sites, so caution is recommended.

Web Site Development

Many teachers find it beneficial to develop their own Web sites for specific courses, with syllabi, assignments, and links. Rather than giving students hard-copy handouts (which frequently are lost), instructors can place these materials online, saving copying expenses and class time. Colleges and universities often post Web sites or offer classes in Web site development. In addition to creating your own site, you may want to assign students a Web project. Web assignments are particularly successful as group projects. Each group may be asked to work on a specific topic, such as an author biography, historical topic, or cultural issue. Students of Victorian literature, for example, may want to research the topic of the "fallen woman" in connection with a reading of D. G. Rossetti's "Jenny" and then post their findings on a Web site that they develop as a group. The benefit of a Web project is that the public nature of the posting helps students form a professional attitude toward their writing, in addition to teaching them to work collaboratively.

PowerPoint Presentations

PowerPoint presentations offer another valuable—and by now very familiar—technological resource for the literature instructor. The advantage of PowerPoint is that it can be used to link several types of media, such as video, images, text, music, and recorded speech. Moreover, PowerPoint can be combined with electronic texts or Web sites. Thus, you can provide an image of a particular manuscript page, link it to a short video of an author, and follow up with relevant paintings or prints. Students also can be asked to develop their own group presentations on a particular author or work. Such group projects can be enjoyable for students to work on, stimulating creativity and active engagement with the course material.

Plagiarism

With the Internet, students have an ever-expanding supply of potential sources to plagiarize: Web sites, reviews, paper mills, and any number of electronic documents are easily accessible. Yet instructors, too, have the same access and resources as their students. You may use software programs that specialize in detecting plagiarism or go it alone, using search engines to track down suspected unauthorized borrowings. Simply by entering a phrase from the suspected paper in the search box, you will retrieve a number of possibilities that you can sort through. Alternatively, software programs such as Turnitin and MyDropBox.com offer applications packages that not only identify plagiarism but also, like larger course-management systems (with which they are sometimes linked), provide options to help with grading or student peer-group editing.

LIBRARY AND INTERNET RESEARCH

At some point you will want to encourage students to move beyond NAEL and engage in research, perhaps for a final term paper or oral presentation. Research may be focused on a particular author or work or, for upper-division classes, on a historical, social, or theoretical topic. In a research project, students learn to locate articles in scholarly publications and to use critical and contextual material. While all of these activities were engaged in long before the Internet, today they are largely dependent on computerized sources. From articles to books and encyclopedias, most traditional library materials are now either in electronic form or referenced online. Even the novice who wishes only to pull a book off the shelf must learn to navigate the online library catalogue and understand the principles of a basic search.

The Digital Library

Many university libraries have a seemingly endless collection of electronic resources. The largest institutions have slides, newspapers, encyclopedias, bibliographies, indices, journals, vast article databases with numerous full-text articles, databases of literary texts, and special collections available to students and faculty in electronic form. Some of these are especially valuable to the literature student, such as the MLA Bibliography database, which contains citations on books and articles relating to literature, linguistics, and folklore. Other databases, such as Gale, provide critical essays and biographical material on authors and literary works in full-text format. Many institutions now subscribe to the online version of the *Oxford English Dictionary*, an important resource that allows researchers to locate the earliest use of a word and trace its development. Unlike traditional print sources, digital sources are immediately accessible at any time of the day or night and available to multiple users at once.

The Internet

Anyone undertaking research today can tap into the Internet for an amazing selection of source material. For any conceivable topic, literary or otherwise, there is a related Web site, blog, article, or review posted online. Yet while the collection at a college or university library is closely monitored for quality, the Internet offers an indiscriminate assortment of material, from the reliable to the dubious. Despite this drawback, the research benefits of the Internet are numerous. There are many excellent scholarly Web sites that contain faithful transcriptions of literary texts, some with different manuscript versions or searchable formats. Some sites provide biographical information on authors, historical and critical data relevant to particular works, and other items applicable to the study of literature. The *Rossetti Archive*, for example, contains (or will contain when completed) essays, articles, reviews, historical information, and source material relating to the work of Dante Gabriel Rossetti, along with original and later editions of his writing and images of his paintings and drawings. (Please see the separate section in this chapter on *Norton Literature Online*; see also Chapter 4.) Also of interest are radio programs that can be accessed via computer streaming (such as BBC Radio 4, which has an arts and drama section) and that offer interviews with authors or dramatizations of plays and novels. Unlike traditional radio programs, online versions usually have archived materials that can be retrieved for a limited time after airing.

Evaluating Web Sources

Students using the Web for research will need guidance in choosing dependable sources. Anyone can put up a Web site, and online journals vary in quality just as much as print versions. In general, the more documentation, the better; the author's name, credentials, contact information, and institutional affiliation are promising indications. Look for sites supported by respected organizations and scholarly institutions. When choosing articles or book excerpts, give more credibility to those that have undergone a peer-review process or other editorial procedure. Moreover, the article or piece itself should be documented in the same manner as a print source, with full bibliographic information. Articles and books, in particular, should provide a date of posting. Be especially suspicious of anything that is poorly written (with grammatical or spelling mistakes) or that is vague about authorship or organizational affiliation. Finally, check to see if you can find any evaluative comments or ratings; these can sometimes help in determining reliability.

Getting Students Started

Instructors will meet with a wide disparity in computer literacy among students. Although it may seem that most students know quite a bit about technology, some have rarely used a computer, while others can download music but do not know how to search an online library catalogue. Many colleges and universities have library skills–training programs (both online and at the library itself) or lectures that give students a good overview of research methods. If your institution has such a program, you can assign it as part of the research project. In lieu of this, a simple handout is helpful. Bear in mind that once students realize that full-text articles can be retrieved online, they will be reluctant to use print sources. You may have to use a bit of coercion to get them into the library, but it is necessary for students to learn traditional search methods in addition to computerized approaches. Despite the wide availability of online articles and book excerpts (both in the library and on the Web), some sources (especially books) exist only in print form. Students who rely solely on electronic sources may find that their research is seriously distorted.

NORTON LITERATURE ONLINE

Norton Literature Online (NLO) is an extensive network of interlinking Web sites and teaching aids that supplement Norton's literary anthologies and guides. It provides links to sites focused on specific Norton texts, such as *NAEL*, and a General Resources section with information on numerous topics. Instructors wishing to find guidelines on essay writing, research, or documentation, for example, or contextual material such as maps, illustrations, or historical timelines, can use *NLO*. Students can use the glossary flashcards or take some of the quizzes. Without doubt the material in *NLO* will stimulate student interest in literature and provide help in writing and research. While a thorough discussion of *NLO* would require more space than is allotted here, what follows is a brief outline of a few sources that will be of particular interest to *NAEL* users (see also Chapter 4 of this guide).

Norton Topics Online

Norton Topics Online (NTO) is a companion to *NAEL* reached by clicking on the "English Literature" link on the *NLO* homepage. *NTO* contains study material on specific topics, exam and review information, and archived texts and audio recordings. The topics are arranged according to period and are keyed to *NAEL* (see "Connections to *NAEL*"). Each topic contains a series of contextual documents ("Texts and Contexts"), discussion questions ("Explorations"), links to Web resources, and illustrations. The Review section provides short summaries relating to the topics and self-scoring multiple-choice quizzes that can be sent to the instructor. Also in this section, under "Making Connections," is a list of study questions that asks students to compare texts within and across periods and to analyze correspondences between literary texts and cultural or historical issues. These questions can be used on exams or in discussions that place individual readings in a larger framework. Supplemental literary texts and audio recordings can be found in the online archive, arranged according to author. If you are teaching a class in Victorian literature and wish to have students read selections from *Idylls of the King* that are not in *NAEL*, for example, you will find "Pelleas and Ettarre," from the ninth book of the *Idylls*, under the entries for Tennyson. In addition to asking students to read the excerpt from *Idylls*, you can prompt them to listen to a recording of Tennyson reading "The Charge of the Light Brigade," something they can easily find in the Audio Readings section of the archive.

The Norton Resource Library

The *Norton Resource Library* (*NRL*) contains material that can be used either in the classroom or in a distance-learning course. From exam questions to PowerPoint slides, *NRL* has what you need to develop your syllabus, lectures, and assignments. The material in *NRL* can be downloaded and customized. While *NRL* does offer material for instructors in many disciplines, the offerings in English literature include sources specifically keyed to *NAEL*, among them topics relating to the different periods, assignments, syllabi, quizzes, illustrations, and a special section on teaching poetry.

Writing about Literature

NLO's General Resources contains a "Writing about Literature" section that will be especially useful for any English teacher who has ever asked students to write an essay on a literary text. The section covers everything from the various components of the literature essay to developing and documenting a research paper. Individual topics address issues pertinent to the complete novice (such as the purpose and form of a literature essay) or the more advanced writer (understanding the difference between interpretive and evaluative claims, for instance). Also included are sample research essays with annotations, online and print resources for researchers, and an explanation of how to evaluate and work with secondary sources. For lower-division or writing-intensive courses, you may want to make particular units part of the syllabus, while for upper-division courses you may want simply to let students know that this section is available.

Norton Poets Online

Norton Poets Online (under General Resources) connects information about poets and poetry to texts, images, and audio recordings. You can hear Eavan Boland read "That the Science of Cartography Is Limited," for example, after assigning the poem in *NAEL*, and then view her photograph, read an interview with her (through a link to another site), and get a listing of her books, accompanied by short reviews and commentaries. There are links to Web sites, such as *Contemporary Poetry Review* or *Poets.org*, which can help stimulate interest in current poetry trends or provide a place to talk online about poetry. Teachers and students will find this site both instructive and fun.

The Norton History Web Site

Some instructors might want to use the Norton history Web site (under General Resources), which features links to American, world, and English and Western history. Each link provides a student Web site containing historical articles, review guidelines, and multimedia resources. *NAEL* readers will find much material in the English and Western history sections that is relevant to the literature they are studying. All sites include focus questions, summaries, outlines, flashcards, maps, self-scoring quizzes, and suggested research projects. The media section contains links to maps, images, and texts. Given the importance of history in today's approaches to literature, this resource can definitely help students understand the larger picture.

CHAPTER 4

Teaching with Norton's Online Media Resources

What and how we teach will always depend on the media at our disposal. So to a surprising extent will the way we think about the texts we teach and study. Sixty years ago, the rise of the New Criticism was propelled to a significant extent by the entry of large numbers of students into American universities by way of the GI Bill; growing pressure on limited library resources encouraged a sharper focus on the "text itself." Today, we are less likely to view literary works as autonomous objects than as works embedded in rich historical and cultural contexts. Drawing upon the media resources now available, instructors have an unprecedented opportunity to make these contexts—textual, visual, and auditory—a vital part of their students' learning experience. A range of online multimedia collections supplementing *The Norton Anthology of English Literature* (NAEL) exists to provide you and your students with the resources you need.

The Internet has already transformed the nature of teaching and learning and will continue to do so. Many of your students will naturally turn to the Web as their primary research tool. Students tend to see Web-research as both easier and more creative than going to the library. Unfortunately, the results aren't always pretty. Most instructors will have encountered all too many examples of inappropriate Web use. Misuse of the Internet can take several forms (listed here in descending order of severity):

1. **Outright plagiarism.** Copying text from Web sites or purchasing prewritten essays from online services. The former can often be detected with a Google search. For guidance on catching and stopping the more pernicious forms of plagiarism, you might consult a site such as "Plagiarism and the Web" (wiu.edu/users/mfbhl/wiu/plagiarism.htm).

2. **Dubious "sources."** It can be tough convincing students that information culled from idiosyncratic blogs and the like carries less authority than scholarly studies.

3. **Outdated material.** A remarkable amount of nineteenth- and early-twentieth-century criticism and literary biography, now out of copyright, has been posted to the Web. The assumption that the Internet will lead you to the most up-to-date material can be dangerous!

Nonetheless, the Internet has the capacity to transform learning and teaching in wonderful ways. By making the resources of *Norton Literature Online* an integrated part of your course, you will be helping your students discover the best of the Web, while avoiding its pitfalls.

Norton Literature Online (*NLO*; wwnorton.com/literature) is the gateway to a range of learning and teaching materials designed specifically for use with *NAEL*. If the technology can be brought into the classroom or lecture hall conveniently, you might offer a guided tour of the site during the first week of classes; if not, students can easily explore *NLO* on their own. From the main page, they will be able to access various helpful general resources, including a detailed guide to writing about literature, a glossary of literary terms, a selection of maps and timelines, and clear guidelines on citation. With instructor input and advances in technology, these resources will continue to develop and expand. We hope to add a new feature to *NLO* every year.

NLO is the portal to three online repositories tailored to suit the needs of your English literature course. These are *Norton Topics Online* (*NTO*), the *Norton Online Archive* (*Archive*), and the *Norton Resource Library* (*NRL*). The first two may be accessed by students using the free registration code they receive with their new copy of *NAEL*. Students with used books may purchase a registration code online for $5. *NRL*, which includes password-protected materials, is for instructor use only.

The following table gives a quick overview of the contents of each of these sites.

Norton Literature Online (NL0)	Norton Topics Online (NTO)	Norton Resource Library (NRL)
Gateway to all of Norton's literature sites	Twenty-eight Topics— four per period— prepared by the *NAEL* editors	An online source of instructional content to use and adapt for your course
Gallery of General Resources, including: • Writing about Literature • Glossary of Literary Terms • Elements of Literature review quiz • Timelines • Maps • Music • History • Author Portrait Gallery • Citation guidelines • Norton Scholar's Prize essays • Norton Literature in the News • Norton Poets Online • The Favorite Poem Project Two search engines covering Norton's literature sites and the Web	• Annotated Texts and Contexts grouped by Topic • Over 1,000 illustrations • Over 300 Explorations to stimulate critical thinking and generate paper topics • Hundreds of annotated links to related sites • Cross-references and Connections to *NAEL* • Comprehensive search engine • Review materials, including self-grading multiple-choice quizzes based on the period introductions The *Norton Online Archive* including texts, audio readings, and musical selections	• 49 Class Units—7 per period—each consisting of 3 topics • Brief, student-friendly introductions to each literary period • Activities, including essay topics and short writing assignments • Sample syllabi • 30-question quizzes for each period • Extensive links to NTO and other Web resources

The correct citation of Internet sources such as Norton's is often confusing for students and instructors alike. *NLO* contains clear guidelines on citing electronic resources. By consulting these guidelines *before* the first essay is due, students can save themselves (and you) a good deal of trouble later on. You may wish to reinforce this message by showing students how to reference sites like *NLO* and *NTO*. Where a student refers to an *NLO* feature in an essay, the reference (MLA style) should read as follows:

> "Glossary of literary terms." *Norton Literature Online.* [Date posted or last updated.] Norton. [Day Month Year of access] <http://www.wwnorton.com/college/english/literature/general-resources/glossary/glossary_a.htm>.

A reference to a text in *NTO* should look like this:

> Southey, Robert. "The Curse of Kehama." *Norton Topics Online: The Romantic Period.* Ed. Jack Stillinger and Deidre Lynch. [Date posted or last updated.] Norton. [Day Month Year of access] <http://www.wwnorton.com/nael/romantic/topic_4/southey.htm>.

NORTON TOPICS ONLINE

Since its introduction in 1998, *Norton Topics Online* has become a valued resource for undergraduates, graduate students, and academic researchers. *NTO* is a compendium of textual, visual, and audio materials that supplements and extends the offerings of the print anthology. With annotated links to hundreds of other excellent sites, *NTO* makes an ideal home base for the literary Web explorer. It also features quizzes and review materials for student use.

At the heart of *NTO* lie the Topics. Like the various thematic clusters in *NAEL* itself (some of which appeared on *NTO* before migrating to the print volume), the twenty-eight online Topics (four per period) present a selection of short and middle-length texts organized around a historical or literary theme. Some of them supplement and extend the thematic clusters in *NAEL*—e.g., the online Topic "Dissent, Doubt, and Spiritual Violence in the Reformation" supplements and extends the print section "Faith in Conflict." Others, like "*Paradise Lost* in Context," are designed to enrich understanding of a single major text. Featured for every period are Topics focused on global Englishes—that is, texts that originate in and reflect the intersection of the cultures of the British Isles and the rest of the world (examples include "Emigrants and Settlers" for the Early Seventeenth Century, "Romantic Orientalism," and "Twentieth-Century Irish Writers"). Each Topic features an Overview as well as explanatory headnotes for the individual texts.

The best way to introduce students to *NTO* is to include two or three Topics as part of the primary reading on your syllabus. Each Topic Overview should take only about half an hour to read, but students will need to devote at least two hours to reading and viewing a Topic in its entirety. In addition to reading assigned material, students should be encouraged to browse the site and explore what interests them. The Topics are designed to encourage intellectual adventurousness and self-study. Once they are familiar with the structure and contents of *NTO*, the more diligent students will naturally turn to it as a resource to supplement each week's reading.

NTO offers far more than a selection of texts. The site harbors over a thousand images, including illuminated manuscripts and early woodcuts, paintings by Dürer, Blake, and Dante Gabriel Rossetti, and photographs of Victorian factory life and twentieth-century warfare. Visual images help students grasp the "feel" of a historical period and can also provide the basis for comparisons with literary works (e.g., the expulsion from Paradise as portrayed by Milton and Masaccio). The thumbnail images on the site can be enlarged with a click, making them suitable for in-class presentation.

Each Topic includes a selection of links to other sites on the Web. The links are annotated and the sites have been vetted for academic quality. Although we regularly check and update the links on all Norton Web sites, it is inevitable that instructors and students will occasionally encounter broken links. Should this occur, please email the emedia editor at Norton (EConnell@wwnorton.com) and report the fault.

Finally, each Topic features ten or more "Explorations," questions and assignments that encourage students to meditate on historical themes and the contexts of literature. Many of them will prove useful for classroom discussion or in-class writing assignments. Others can serve as the starting point for research papers, prepared presentations, or textual analyses. Students will also find them useful in formulating their own questions about the texts they have read. Note that a further selection of questions, designed specifically for use as assignments, is available in the Assignments section of the *Norton Resource Library* (see below).

In addition to the twenty-eight Topics, *NTO* features a Review section for each period. Students will probably discover and use this portion of the site without prompting from you. The review materials include a summary of the introduction to each historical period; these summaries will help students grasp key facts and themes and solidify their understanding, though the summaries should certainly not be used in lieu of the period introductions in the book. This part of the site also features self-grading multiple-choice quizzes, with roughly thirty questions per period, based on the period introductions. All quiz results will be stored in the password-protected Norton Gradebook. Students can access the Gradebook to review their own results, and instructors can access all the results and sort them by section, chapter, book, student name, and date.

Students should be encouraged to use the textual and contextual resources in *NTO* in conjunction with the general resources on *NLO*. A student interested in the audio materials in the *Archive* (see below) would also be interested in *NLO's* musical offerings. A student who is curious to know what Milton looked liked would find his portrait in the "Author Portrait Gallery." Someone looking for guidance about how to write a good essay inspired by one of *NTO's* Explorations might look to *NLO's* "Writing about Literature" section. She might then enter her subject into the *NLO* search engine and find useful material about it on one of the other literature Web sites (e.g., "The Emergence of the Personal in the European Renaissance," available on *The Norton Anthology of World Literature* site, wwnorton.com/nawol).

NORTON ONLINE ARCHIVE

Housed within *Norton Topics Online* but existing as a distinct resource is the *Norton Online Archive*, a sizable compendium of texts and audio materials. The *Archive* houses more than 150 public-domain texts and will continue to expand in scope and size. By spring 2007, the *Archive* will include all public-domain texts trimmed from *The Norton Anthology of English Literature* over seven editions. The *Archive* includes a Publication Chronology that lists over 1,000 texts and the edition in which each was introduced, dropped, and sometimes reintroduced to *NAEL*. As such, the chronology and the archive of texts present a unique window on the teaching of English literature over four decades. These are carefully edited Norton texts, with glosses and notes, which may be downloaded and printed. The *Archive* enhances your freedom in constructing a course, allowing you to keep teaching a well-loved text or to season your syllabus with a dash of the unexpected.

The *Archive* is also home to audio materials, which you and your students can download and listen to using a program like Real Audio. These materials are of two sorts, readings of texts in *NAEL* and samples of music from the historical periods. The readings, which include Seamus Heaney reading from his translation of *Beowulf* and passages of Chaucer with Middle English pronunciation, are perfect for listening to in the classroom. Many students find that *hearing* poetry makes an enormous difference to their appreciation of it. Audio performances also provide another opportunity to discuss how context affects meaning. In what ways can a performer shape an audience's experience of a poem? How does the experience of listening in a group differ from the experience of reading silently and alone?

Like the images in *NTO*, the music in the *Archive* helps students get a feel for the culture and atmosphere of different historical periods and for what is at stake in the transition from one period to another.   Many students will find it easier to grasp and describe the thematic and stylistic differences between medieval and Renaissance song, or between Classical and Romantic music, than to articulate how literary forms change from one period to another.

THE NORTON RESOURCE LIBRARY

Course-delivery programs such as WebCT and Blackboard are becoming increasingly popular, flexible, and easy to use. Many instructors now use these or similar programs to deliver assignments, cluster review materials, administer quizzes, and engage students in online discussion and debate. The materials in the *NAEL* section of the *Norton Resource Library* (wwnorton.com/nrl/) are designed to provide ready-made and adaptable content for a course-delivery program. However, they are also well-suited for use on a course Web site or in a conventional classroom (e.g., as handouts).

Unlike *NTO* and the *Archive*, *NRL* is geared for the instructor, not the student. While the site offers open access to some sample materials, other pages require a password (which you will receive after completing a short form online). You can thus rest assured that students do not have access to certain types of material before you are ready for them to view it.

NRL is not designed to nudge you into adopting a generic, one-size-fits-all literature course. You can download what you want, leave what you don't want, and customize everything to suit the specific needs of your syllabus. The resources available for adoption and adaptation include links to literary Web sites for each period, sample syllabi, and multiple-choice quizzes. Unlike the quizzes on *NTO*, these are password-protected, so the choice of when to spring them on the class is left to you.

The primary content of *NRL* consists of Class Units and Assignments. For each historical period there are seven or eight Class Units. Although not all courses keep the same pace, a Class Unit is supposed to reflect roughly a week of instruction. The units focus on specific texts or authors (e.g., Chaucer, Spenser, Browning), on literary genres or movements (e.g., medieval drama, modernism), and on historical or cultural developments (e.g., the Civil War, the origins of feminism, the postcolonial condition). Each unit has a reading list of *NAEL* and *NTO* texts and contains three Topics, which offer introductions to particular themes (e.g., "Spenser's View of Ireland," "George Eliot and the Woman Question"). These topics can be made available to students either before the day of instruction, as a means of preparation, or afterward, to assist in review.

Each Class Unit is accompanied by several suggested Assignments, topics for various kinds of writing. Some of the questions require an extensive response (e.g., an essay), while others are suitable for briefer (pre-class or in-class) written exercises. The Assignments can also be used as discussion topics in the Forum section of your course site—or, for that matter, for face-to-face discussion in the classroom itself.

A SAMPLE SYLLABUS

The following syllabus, for a yearlong English literature course covering Anglo-Saxon poetry to postmodern drama, demonstrates how the textual, visual, and audio resources of Norton's online collections can enhance the teaching of core material from the print anthology. Of course, no instructor will take advantage of all the options for every week. For one thing, *NRL* and *NTO* make it easy to assign an essay every week—but your students are unlikely to thank you if you do!

Fall Semester: Volume 1 (A, B, C)
The Middle Ages (4 weeks)

Week 1

The Dream of the Rood
The Wanderer
The Wife's Lament

Literary contexts: Selections from the "Linguistic and Literary Contexts of *Beowulf*" in *NTO* will help students grasp Anglo-Saxon language and culture.

Audio: Expose students to the sound and rhythm of Old English poetry— readings of *The Dream of the Rood, The Wanderer,* and *The Wife's Lament* are available in the *Archive*.

Visual: *NTO* features a range of images of Anglo-Saxon artifacts and manuscripts; note also the link to further treasures from Sutton Hoo under "Web resources."

Activities: The Explorations section provides several questions suitable for essays (e.g., Exploration 4, on the theme of isolation in Germanic poetry).

Week 2

Sir Gawain and the Green Knight

Literary Contexts: For an alternative view of *Gawain*, introduce students to "The Wedding of Sir Gawain and Dame Ragnelle," from *NTO* "King Arthur—Romancing Politics." (This text is also an analogue of *The Wife of Bath's Tale,* to which they will be turning next week.) Use the selection from Ramón Lull's *The Book of the Order of Chivalry,* in "Medieval Estates and Orders," to help students grasp Gawain's ideal of knighthood.

Audio: Listen with your students to Marie Borroff's reading of the first stanza of *Sir Gawain* in the *Archive*.

Activities: The *Norton Resource Library* provides a discussion starter (in the Class Unit "Legendary Histories of Britain") on "*Gawain and the Green Knight* in Context," emphasizing the contrast between late-medieval chivalry and the Anglo-Saxon warrior ideal. The *NRL* Assignments section includes three questions on the poem suitable as themes for discussion or topics for in-class writing.

Week 3

Geoffrey Chaucer
  The Canterbury Tales
    The General Prologue
    The Wife of Bath's Prologue and Tale

Literary Contexts: You might consider using the *Franklin's Tale*, available in the *Archive*, as an additional or alternative main text. The selections in *NTO* "Medieval Estates and Orders" can be used to highlight the ideology underlying Chaucer's depiction of social types—notice in particular the "Old Woman" from the *Romance of the Rose*, whom Chaucer reinvents as the Wife of Bath. *NTO* "The First Crusade" can be used to give students a sense of what is really at stake in the military adventures of the Knight as described in the *General Prologue*.

Audio: Readings from the *General Prologue* and the *Wife of Bath's Prologue* are available in the *Archive*.

Visual: Visual contexts for the Canterbury pilgrimage on *NTO* include the martyrdom of Thomas Becket and a Canterbury pilgrim's badge.

Activities: Use the NRL unit "Chaucer's *Canterbury Tales*." The NRL Assignments section provides a range of questions for essays on the *General Prologue* and the *Wife of Bath's Tale*. If you are assigning the first essay around now, remind students to consult "Writing about Literature," which is included in *NLO's* "General Resources."

Week 4

The York Play of the Crucifixion
Everyman

Literary Contexts: You might consider using *The Chester Play of Noah's Flood*, available in the *Archive*, as an additional or alternative text.

Audio: Medieval drama has links with both religious liturgy and bawdy popular culture. Listen with your students to Hildegarde of Bingen's *O Pastor Animarum* and the well-known "Cuckoo Song," and consider how the traditions they represent are blended in the mystery plays.

Activities: NRL provides a unit on "Staging Miracles" and a range of writing exercises in the Assignments section. Send your students to *NLO's* "Glossary of Literary Terms" for explication of words like *allegory* and *personification*. Since this week concludes your survey of the Middle Ages, you might want to assign the medieval quiz on *NTO*. Finally, since you will be turning to Spenser and Johnson before the end of the semester, point students to the "Making Connections" section of *NTO* as a way of preparing for comparative essays further down the road.

The Sixteenth Century,
The Early Seventeenth Century
(7 weeks)

Week 5

Edmund Spenser
  The Faerie Queene
    A Letter of the Authors
    Book 1, selections
    Book 2, Canto 12

Literary Contexts: Especially if your course will develop a postcolonial emphasis in later periods, consider assigning passages from Spenser's *View of the Present State of Ireland*, available as part of the "Island Nations" cluster in the Sixteenth Century section of *NTO*. With an additional cluster on "Renaissance Exploration," *NTO* offers a detailed introduction to England's cultural and military expansion in the Renaissance.

Audio: Part of Spenser's project in *The Faerie Queene* is to develop and expound a specifically Protestant aesthetic sensibility. To help students think about the difference between Catholic and Protestant aesthetics, have them listen to Guillaume de Machaut's "Agnus Dei," followed by Thomas Tallis's Post-Reformation "Benedictus" (both in the *Archive*). Tallis's mass is still in Latin, of course, but students should note the more somber and restrained tone and the concern to make the words comprehensible.

Visual: In the print volume, Uccello's *St. George and the Dragon* offers an alternative vision of Book 1's climactic confrontation, while Gheeraert's provocative portrait of Captain Thomas Lee, in Irish garb, raises issues of ethnicity and assimilation in Ireland. On *NTO*, the woodcut of "The Pope as Antichrist riding the Beast of the Apocalypse" can be used to explicate the many-headed beast that appears in Book 1, canto 8; and "Island Nations" features a contemporary English caricature of a barbaric Irish feast.

Activities: *NRL* has a unit on Spenser's *Faerie Queene*; topics on "The Kingdom of Our Own Language" and "Reading Book 1" will help students grapple with the style and the stakes of a text that many find off-putting. There's also a topic in *NRL* on Spenser and Ireland, and all three topics have writing activities. In *NTO*, Exploration 1 under "Island Nations" provides guidance for interpreting the racial politics of Spenser's *View* alongside passages of *The Faerie Queene*.

Week 6

William Shakespeare, *Twelfth Night*

Literary Contexts: The Early Seventeenth Century section of *NTO* includes a cluster of texts dealing with cross-dressing (under "Gender, Family, Household")—working with these is an ideal way of shedding light on the interwoven problems of dress, gender, sex, and sexuality in the play.

Audio: The play begins with Orsino listening to music—the music in the *Archive* will let you expose your students to the Elizabethan "food of love" with madrigals by Dowland and Gibbons, as well as Campion's "Fain would I wed" (also in the print anthology). The *Shakespeare Songbook* includes samples of many more songs, among them "Hold thy Peace" and "O Mistress Mine" from *Twelfth Night*.

Visual: In the print anthology, Hilliard's miniature of a "Young Man" surrounded by the flames of love contextualizes Orsino's love melancholy as a fashionable stance. The *NTO* cluster on cross-dressing features caricature woodcuts of Hic Mulier, the Man-Woman, and Haec Vir, the Womanish Man.

Activities: The *NRL* unit on "William Shakespeare" includes two topics relevant to the play, and the Assignments section features a writing exercise on "Cross-Dressing, Convention, and Controversy in *Twelfth Night*." As you move on from the Sixteenth Century, "Making Connections" gives early notice of parallel themes to be explored in Congreve (week 12).

Week 7

Aemilia Lanyer, "The Description of Cookham"
Ben Jonson, "To Penshurst"
Thomas Carew, "To Saxham"

Literary Contexts: Under "Gender, Family, Household" in *NTO*, the letters of Robert Sidney and the diary of Anne Clifford give some insight into the domestic lives of the families celebrated in the "great house" poems of Lanyer and Jonson.

Visual: "Country house" poetry appeals to the visual imagination, but it helps if students have some idea of what to imagine. *NTO* features images of Penshurst Place; Lady Sidney of Penshurst and her children; the "Great Picture" of the Clifford family, praised by Aemilia Lanyer; and Knole, the country estate of Anne Clifford after her marriage.

Activities: *NRL* offers a good discussion starter on "The Country House Poem" (in the "Utopias" unit), along with four topics for short essays on this theme (under Assignments).

Week 8

John Webster, *The Duchess of Malfi*

Literary Contexts: At the heart of this play lie the twin problems of widowhood and remarriage. *NTO*'s "Gender, Family, Household" topic includes a cluster of texts on the theory and practice of early modern matrimony, as well as an eye-opening advice book for widows.

Audio: The complex harmonies of Gabrieli's Sonata XVIII give a taste of the music being enjoyed in the courts of Italy during this period.

Visual: Tour's painting *The Penitent Magdalen* (in the print volume) and the skeletal emblem of Death (*NTO*) can be used to spark reflection on the early seventeenth century's obsession with mortality, so evident in Webster's play.

Activities: The *NRL* unit "Marriage, Madness, and Melancholy" is designed for use with this play, especially when read in conjunction with the selections from Elizabeth Cary's *Tragedy of Mariam*. The Assignments section includes four topics for short comparative essays.

Week 9

Thomas Hobbes, *Leviathan* (all selections)
Katherine Philips, "Upon the Double Murder of King Charles"
Andrew Marvell, "An Horatian Ode"
From "Crisis of Authority"
    Lucy Hutchinson, *Memoirs of Colonel Hutchinson*
    Gerrard Winstanley, *A New Years Gift*
    Edward Hyde, Earl of Clarendon, *The History of the Rebellion*

Literary Contexts: The *NTO* section on "Civil Wars of Ideas" has a cluster of texts devoted to the execution of Charles I. Other voices of the war, such as that of the ranter Abiezer Coppe, are available in the Archive.

Visual: Whereas Van Dyck's portrait *Charles I on Horseback* (in the print volume) captures the glamour of absolute monarchy, the engravings of the trial and execution of Charles I (*NTO*) depict the collapse of that ideal. *NTO* also makes available the ideologically fraught frontispieces of Charles's *Eikon Basilike* and Hobbes's *Leviathan*.

Activities: *NRL* provides a unit on "The World Turned Upside Down," with suggested topics for writing on Marvell's and Philips's representations of regicide. An additional eleven Explorations to stimulate class discussion or provide the basis of essay assignments are available on *NTO*.

Weeks 10–11

John Milton
  Paradise Lost
    Books 1–4
    Books 8–10
    Book 12, lines 552–end

Literary Contexts: *NTO* "*Paradise Lost*: Texts and Contexts" features a range of literary and theological responses to the Genesis narrative, invaluable for locating Milton's emphases and measuring the extent of his orthodoxy. Students interested in exploring the complex character of Milton's Satan may wish to consult the opinions of Blake, Shelley, and Coleridge, clustered in the Romantic section of *NTO*.

Visual: In addition to the paintings of episodes from the Genesis story included in the print anthology, *NTO* offers "Adam and Eve: A Gallery of Renaissance Images," featuring the works of Masaccio, Dürer, and Cranach, among others.

Activities: The *NRL* unit "John Milton and *Paradise Lost*" is complemented by essay questions on Milton's poem and its literary contexts. *NTO* offers eleven additional Explorations on *Paradise Lost*, suitable either for writing assignments or for group work.

The Restoration and the Eighteenth Century (4 weeks)

Week 12

John Bunyan, *The Pilgrim's Progress* (all selections)
William Congreve, *The Way of the World*

Literary Contexts: The innovative *NTO* topic "A Day in Eighteenth-Century London" provides a glimpse of how Congreve's characters might spend their days, including visits to the coffeehouse in the afternoon and the playhouse in the evening.

Visual: Hogarth's riotous engravings are included among a range of depictions of London on *NTO*. But are they images of "so reformed a town" (Congreve) or of Bunyan's "Vanity Fair"?

Activities: Prime your class with the *NRL* topic "Restoration Visions: Congreve and Bunyan." Several Explorations for *NTO*'s "A Day in Eighteenth-Century London" bear on Congreve's play.

Week 13

Aphra Behn, *Oroonoko; or, The Royal Slave*

Literary Contexts: The *NTO* topic "Slavery and the Slave Trade in Britain" offers both a historical overview and a range of pro- and anti-slavery writings from across the period, vital for putting the complex politics of Behn's story in context.

Audio: Almost exactly contemporary with *Oroonoko*, Dido's lament from Purcell's opera *Dido and Aeneas* offers a parallel tragic treatment of the death of an African ruler and gives additional insight into the sensibilities of Restoration audiences. Thomson's "Ode: Rule Britannia," with its insistence that Britons never will be slaves, can also be stirred into the mix at this point.

Visual: NTO provides a substantial collection of contemporary representations of the "middle passage" and of slave mutinies and punishments; also included are abolitionist and pro-slavery images.

Activities: The NRL unit "Slavery and Freedom" includes two topics on Behn, with another on writers of African origin. Note under "Assignments" the short-essay topics on Behn's royalist politics and representations of the "middle passage."

Week 14

Alexander Pope, *The Rape of the Lock*

Literary and Visual Contexts: Selections from the NTO topic "A Day in Eighteenth-Century London" will help illuminate the glittering, superficial world of Pope's poem.

Activities: The question of the poem's genre is introduced in the NRL topic "Satiric Modes: Burlesque and Mock Heroic"; an accompanying Assignment challenges students to consider twenty-first-century generic parallels.

Week 15

Thomas Gray, "Elegy Written in a Country Churchyard"
Oliver Goldsmith, *The Deserted Village*
George Crabbe, *The Village*

Literary Contexts: As you shift from eighteenth-century London to rural life, point your students to Pope's "Epistle to Miss Blount" (in the *Archive*), which draws the contrast between country and city with wit and poignancy. The "Poems Answering Poems" section on the *Norton Anthology of Poetry* site (wwnorton.com/college/english/nap/dialogue_poems. htm) will give your students tools for considering the relationship between Goldsmith and Crabbe.

Audio: Use the reading of Gray's "Elegy" in the *Archive*.

Activities: The NRL unit "The Country and the City" offers an extended contrast of the villages of Goldsmith and Crabbe that can be used as the basis for an in-class writing assignment or debate. Remember, as you reach the end of the Eighteenth Century, that both NTO and NRL feature multiple-choice quizzes.

Spring Semester: Volume II (D, E, F)

The Romantic Period (5 weeks)

Week 1

From "Literary Gothicism and the Development of a Mass Readership"
Horace Walpole, from *The Castle of Otranto*
William Beckford, from *Vathek*
Ann Radcliffe
from *The Romance of the Forest*
from *The Mysteries of Udolpho*
Matthew Gregory Lewis, from *The Monk*

Literary Contexts: Supplement this week's reading with selections from the *NTO* topic "Literary Gothicism," including Jane Austen's satire of the mode in *Northanger Abbey.*

Visual: Gothicism venerates spectacle as well as problematizing the role of the viewer. Illustrations from the stories of Beckford, Radcliffe, and Lewis will help students come to grips with this important aspect of the genre.

Activities: Check out the twelve Explorations accompanying the *NTO* topic.

Week 2

From "The French Revolution and the 'Spirit of the Age' "
Edmund Burke, from *Reflections on the French Revolution*
Mary Wollstonecraft, from *A Vindication of the Rights of Men*
Thomas Paine, from *The Rights of Man*
William Wordsworth, Preface to *Lyrical Ballads*

Literary Contexts: The *NTO* topic on the French Revolution supplements and provides fresh perspectives on the *NAEL* section, with texts including Shelley's apocalyptic "Queen Mab."

Visual: Illustrations by Blake, Gillray, and Delacroix are among the images featured on *NTO*. Note the maps of *ancien regime*, Revolutionary, and Napoleonic France under "General Resources" on *NLO*.

Activities: The *NRL* unit on the French Revolution is supplemented by five topics for essays or discussion; eleven additional Explorations are featured on *NTO*.

Week 3

William Wordsworth
"Lines Composed a Few Miles above Tintern Abbey"
"Resolution and Independence"
"I wandered lonely as a cloud"

Dorothy Wordsworth, from *The Grasmere Journals*
Samuel Taylor Coleridge
  "This Lime-Tree Bower My Prison"
  "Frost at Midnight"
John Keats, "Ode to a Nightingale"
John Clare, "The Nightingale's Nest"

Literary Contexts: With *"Tintern Abbey,"* Tourism, and Romantic Landscape," *NTO* sheds light on how changing perceptions of the natural world lie behind Romantic nature poetry.

Audio: Poets were not the only Romantic artists interested in exploring a new relationship to the natural world. Let your students listen to how Schubert's "Die Forelle" (The Trout) seeks to convey a musical understanding of the sounds of a moving brook.

Visual: The landscape paintings of Claude Lorrain and aquatints by William Gilpin are among images of "romantic landscape" featured on *NTO*.

Activities: The *NRL* unit on "The Romantics and the Natural World" has topics on Wordsworth, Keats, and Clare, supplemented by a range of writing assignments.

Week 4

Thomas de Quincey
  Confessions of an English Opium Eater
    Introduction to the Pains of Opium
    The Pains of Opium
George Gordon, Lord Byron
  Selections from *Childe Harold's Pilgrimage*
  Manfred

Literary Contexts: The *NTO* topic "Literary Gothicism" includes a cluster of texts on "The Satanic and Byronic Hero" that can help students grasp the elements that went into the construction of the most notorious of Romantic celebrities.

Activities: You may want to use materials from the *NRL* unit "The Byronic and Satanic Hero," as well as the assignment that invites students to consider how the genre shapes the representation and reception of the Byronic hero.

Week 5

Percy Bysshe Shelley
  "A Defence of Poetry"
  "Ode to the West Wind"
  "A Song: 'Men of England'"
  "England in 1819"

"To Sidmouth and Castlereagh"
Mary Wollstonecraft, from A *Vindication of the Rights of Woman*

Literary Contexts: More of Shelley's verse is featured in the *Archive*, as well as in the NTO topic "The French Revolution."

Audio: The *Archive* features an anonymous musical setting of "Men of England," fulfilling Shelley's wish that the song serve as a hymn to the labor movement. Listen too to the reading of Anna Laetitia Barbauld's "The Rights of Woman," and invite students to compare its politics with Wollstonecraft's.

Visual: Both Shelley's portrait and that of the French "Liberty" are featured on NTO—in light of Wollstonecraft's treatise, students may wish to consider what is at stake in the conventional portrayal of liberty as female.

Activities: NRL has a unit on "The Radical Shelleys" and several Shelley assignments, including one designed to guide students through a close reading of "Ode to the West Wind." Before moving to the Victorian period, assess students' knowledge of the Romantics with a quiz from NTO or NRL.

The Victorian Age (5 weeks)

Week 6

Thomas Carlyle, "Captains of Industry"
Elizabeth Barrett Browning, "The Cry of the Children"
"Industrialism: Progress or Decline?"

Literary Contexts: The NTO topic "Industrialism" supplements the print cluster of the same title, with texts by Elizabeth Gaskell, among others.

Visual: Photographs and engravings of factory life and poverty in London and the northern milltowns are featured among the illustrations on NTO.

Activities: NRL features a unit designed to complement the Victorian thematic clusters in the anthology and online. An interesting creative writing exercise is included among the assignments, and there are twelve Explorations on NTO.

Week 7

" 'The Woman Question': The Victorian Debate About Gender"
George Eliot
   "Margaret Fuller and Mary Wollstonecraft"
   "Silly Novels by Lady Novelists"
John Stuart Mill, from *The Subjection of Women*

Literary Contexts: The *NTO* topic "The Woman Question" brings the voices of Charlotte Brontë, George Gissing, and Eliza Lynn Linton into the debate and features Henry Mayhew's descriptions of female laboring life.

Visual: From fashion plates to satirical cartoons, *NTO* offers a fascinating range of Victorian illustrations of and for women.

Activities: *NRL*'s unit "The Woman Question" is designed for use with the *NAEL* and *NTO* clusters, highlighting issues such as the relationship between gender and class, the ambiguities of George Eliot, and the rise of the New Woman. There are eight assignments of varying complexity, as well as the usual range of *NTO* Explorations.

Week 8

Robert Browning
   "Porphyria's Lover"
   "My Last Duchess"
   "The Bishop Orders His Tomb at Saint Praxed's Church"
   "Andrea del Sarto"

Literary Contexts: The *Archive* features a range of poems by Browning, including the popular "Home Thoughts from the Sea" and "Two in the Campagna."

Activities: *NRL* has a unit on Browning; an assignment invites students to consider how his poetry appeals to, represents, and plays with the senses.

Week 9

Alfred, Lord Tennyson
   "Mariana"
   "The Lady of Shalott"
Dante Gabriel Rossetti, "The Blessed Damozel"
Christina Rossetti
   "In an Artist's Studio"
   "Goblin Market"
John Ruskin, from *Modern Painters* ["Of the Pathetic Fallacy"]

Literary Contexts: The *NTO* topic "The Painterly Image in Poetry" is designed to complement reading of Ruskin and the Rossettis in particular.

Visual: Some half-dozen works by Dante Gabriel Rossetti are featured on *NTO*, along with Turner's *Slave Ship*, which Ruskin found "too painful to live with."

Activities: *NRL* has a unit on "The Painterly Image" and other units on Tennyson, the Rossettis, and Ruskin and Pater. There are three essay questions in the Assignments section, in addition to the Explorations on *NTO*.

Week 10

George Bernard Shaw, *Mrs Warren's Profession*
Oscar Wilde, *The Importance of Being Earnest*

Literary Contexts: The *NRL* discussion of Shaw's play features a link to his forthright and eloquent "Author's Apology" (for *Mrs Warren's Profession*). Alternatively, if you wish to assign the (apparently) lighter *Pygmalion*, the full text can be accessed by way of the NTO topic "Twentieth-Century Irish Writers."

Audio: For a bit of light relief, have students listen to "If You're Anxious for to Shine in the High Aesthetic Line" (in the *Archive*), W. S. Gilbert's parody of Wildean aestheticism from the operetta *Patience*.

Activities: The *NRL* unit "Drama of the 1890s" will help students understand how Shaw's play responds to the "Woman Question" and how both Shaw and Wilde make anxious comedy out of the contradictions of the English class system. The Assignments include a question on *Mrs Warren's Profession* for classroom or forum debate and a creative writing exercise. Since this is the final week on the Victorian period, give students a quiz from *NTO* or *NRL*.

The Twentieth Century (5 weeks)

Week 11

Joseph Conrad, *Heart of Darkness*
Chinua Achebe, "An Image of Africa: Racism in Conrad's *Heart of Darkness*"

Literary Contexts: The *NTO* topic "Victorian Imperialism" (in the Victorian section) can help contextualize Conrad's novel.

Visual: The gallery of maps (under "General Resources" on the *NLO* homepage) includes several that illustrate the partition of Africa.

Activities: The *NRL* unit features separate topics on Conrad's novel and Achebe's response, with accompanying essay questions under Assignments.

Week 12

Thomas Hardy
    "She Hears the Storm"
    "Channel Firing"
    "In Time of 'The Breaking of Nations' "
    "He Never Expected Much"

From "Voices from World War I"
  Siegfried Sassoon, "The Rear-Guard"
  Isaac Rosenberg
    "Louse Hunting"
    "Returning, We Hear the Larks"
  Wilfred Owen
    "Apologia Pro Poemate Meo"
    "Dulce et Decorum Est"
  May Wedderburn Cannan, "Rouen"
  David Jones, *In Parenthesis* (both selections)

Literary Contexts: Jessie Pope's jingoistic songs encouraging men to enlist and Sassoon's "Soldier's Declaration" against the war are among the texts in the *NTO* topic "Representing the Great War."

Audio: The *Archive* features a reading by Jon Stallworthy of Owen's "Dulce et Decorum Est."

Visual: Photographs of gas warfare and life in the trenches are among the illustrations on *NTO*. Also included are images of postwar memorials and ceremonies, such as the laying of wreaths at the Cenotaph. Under "General Resources" on *NLO*, several maps depict the eve, course, and aftermath of the conflict.

Activities: The *NRL* unit "Voices of World War" includes a topic on World War I, with an assignment inviting consideration of whether the "war poets" constitute a school or movement.

Week 13

T. S. Eliot, *The Waste Land*
Virginia Woolf, "The Mark on the Wall"
James Joyce, from *Ulysses*
Edith Sitwell, "Still Falls the Rain"

Literary Contexts: The *NTO* topic "The Modernist Experiment" includes Eliot's sympathetic and revealing review of a piece of musical modernism, Stravinsky's *Rite of Spring*, together with manifestos by exponents of Vorticism and Futurism. There is more on modernism in the "War and Modernity" topic on *The Norton Anthology of American Literature* site (wwnorton.com/naal/vol_D/topic.htm).

Audio: The *Archive* includes a recording of Sitwell reading "Still Falls the Rain."

Activities: The *NRL* unit "Literary Modernism" features topics on Eliot, Woolf, and Joyce. The assignments include a stream-of-consciousness writing exercise and topics for a short essay contrasting Woolf and Joyce.

Week 14

W. B. Yeats
  "Down by the Salley Gardens"
  "The Lake Isle of Innisfree"
  "The Second Coming"
  "Easter 1916"
  "Leda and the Swan"
  "Sailing to Byzantium"
  "Under Ben Bulben"

Literary Contexts: The *NTO* topic "Imagining Ireland" includes the "Easter 1916 Proclamation of an Irish Republic," which lies behind Yeats's poem. The topic also includes an excerpt from Sean O'Casey's *The Plough and the Stars*, which responds to the Easter Rising in very different terms.

Audio: In the *Archive,* Yeats himself can be heard reading "The Lake Isle of Innisfree." Also featured is Benjamin Britten's musical setting of "Down by the Salley Gardens."

Activities: Several Explorations for *NTO* "Imagining Ireland" require students to ponder the relationship between a historical event (the Easter Rising) and literary responses to that event (by Yeats and others).

Week 15

Samuel Beckett, *Endgame*
Tom Stoppard, *Arcadia*

Literary Contexts: *Arcadia*'s central themes of landscape and the picturesque can be explored with reference to the *"Tintern Abbey*, Tourism, and Romantic Landscape" in the Romantic period section of *NTO*.

Activities: The *NRL* unit "The Challenge of Postmodernism" includes separate topics on Beckett and Stoppard and, under Assignments, a writing exercise that asks students to consider *Endgame* in relation to the history of the drama.

•   •   •

With a final essay and/or exam just ahead, remind students one last time about the useful review materials on *NTO* and the guidance on writing and citation in *NLO*'s "General Resources."

CHAPTER 5

The Middle Ages to ca. 1485

INTRODUCING THE PERIOD

Welcome to the word-hoard. The treasures bequeathed to us by the oldest writers of English and the ancient Celtic poets of England and its neighboring lands are handsome and can quickly enthrall students raised on the *Lord of the Rings, Star Wars,* Harry Potter, and a thousand video games and novels that still trade in the heroic mode. Here they can find beauty, brave acts that determine the fates of peoples, the desolation of wars, the celebration of hard-won alliances, and alien worlds very much like ours where stories and words are an evolving, slippery, precious legacy of real people's kin and customs—a fragile achievement that glistens like the great hall of the Spear-Danes in a dark world.

The strengths of medieval poetry lie in its powerful storytelling, moments of riddling wit, moral and political challenges, incantatory patterns of sound, surreal landscapes, and piercing invasions of the supernatural. These strengths are the teacher's best allies. Reading aloud can cast the spell and help one to discover the particular susceptibilities of one's audience. The Online Archive has an audio section full of resources, but don't neglect the power of your own living voice to transport your students to the past and bring these poems to life. The familiarity they have with romance and epic is a key to unlocking plots and their patterns of emotions and ideas. Once students believe in and feel for the people—Julian, the Geats, Mak, the Gawain poet, Bede, the Wife of Bath, or whatever historical or fictional figures feature in your lectures—then they may care about the histories of their languages, customs, politics, and lands. The students of this century may feel at home in the knowledge that the early history of what is "English" is vexed by migrations, wars, religious conflicts, a wild mix of languages and peoples, and frequently changing rulers. Studying how people of another age used language to shape such a world is perhaps one of the more important things that can be done in college. What will this generation come to think of its literary inheritance? What will your students do with the word-hoard as they make it their own?

Pagan and Christian

Except for a runic alphabet, the Germanic peoples did not acquire the art of writing until after their conversion to Christianity, which for England began in 597 with a mission sent by Pope Gregory the Great to the southeastern kingdom of Kent. We owe most of our knowledge of that conversion to Bede's *Ecclesiastical History of the English People*, which also provides our first written record of an English poem, Cædmon's *Hymn*, in the chapter from which the first selection in NAEL has been translated. Bede, an English monk, tells the story, traditional in his monastery, of how an illiterate cowherd, tending the monks' cattle, was miraculously granted the gift of poetry. Religious works—biblical narratives, saints' lives, allegories, homilies, and sermons—make up the great majority of works that have been preserved from the Anglo-Saxon and, indeed, from the entire medieval period. The predominance of religious writings is natural enough, because the earliest manuscripts were produced and preserved by the Church, where literacy thrived. Yet Christianity did not do away with preliterate traditions of Germanic poetry, but rather used them for its own purposes. A good way, then, to approach the literature of Anglo-Saxon England is to discuss the ways in which the poetic forms and themes of the Germanic invaders were also "converted" to the service of Christian poetry.

In the year 797, the English scholar Alcuin, whom the emperor Charlemagne had recruited to run his palace school, wrote a letter to the bishop of Lindisfarne, a great monastery off the northeast coast of England, in which he asks the rhetorical question, "Quid Hinieldus cum Christo?" (What has Ingeld to do with Christ?). Ing was a Germanic deity (in *Beowulf* the Danes are twice referred to as "friends of Ing"), and Ingeld is king of the Heatho-Bards (*Beowulf*, lines 2032–69), the tribe involved in a feud with the Danes that will probably result, though we can only infer this, in the burning of Heorot. In Alcuin's question, "Ingeld" stands for "heroic poetry," which, Alcuin has learned, was being recited to the monks. One is reminded of the third line of *Beowulf*: "We have *heard* of those princes' heroic campaigns." For Alcuin, the answer to his question is, of course, "Nothing whatsoever!" For us, as students of Anglo-Saxon literature, the answer is, "A lot."

Our knowledge of pagan Germanic mythology and heroic literature is limited and comes to us through archaeology and through literary sources like *Beowulf* in which the pagan world of a distant past has already been filtered through the imagination of Christian authors. Alcuin's letter shows that the *Beowulf* poet could certainly have heard oral poems—perhaps even in a monastic dining hall. He adopted the verse form and probably much of his narrative material from oral poems. *Beowulf* describes bards performing poems in the mead hall, but few scholars today believe that the long work, which survives in the unique manuscript that has come down to us, is a transcription of a poem that was ever performed extemporaneously.

The Legend of Arthur

Arthurian literature evolved out of a mixing of history and romance in narratives that catered to the tastes and ambitions of the French barons who ruled England in the twelfth century. Historically, "Arthurian Britain" was the Roman province Britannia, whose people fought against the Anglo-Saxon invaders after the Roman legions had been withdrawn in the fifth century. After they had been conquered, the Britons told stories in which their defeat was transformed into the overthrow of a legendary kingdom whose greatest ruler had been on the verge of conquering Rome itself before he was betrayed at home. The selections from Geoffrey of Monmouth, Wace, and Layamon trace that kingdom from a prophecy of its foundation by descendants of the survivors of Troy, to its zenith, to the beginning of its downfall, and finally, to a myth of its future restoration. One can already see in these brief selections the paradigm of medieval tragedies of Fortune, the rise and fall of princes, which anticipates the cyclical themes that students will encounter in *Sir Gawain and the Green Knight* and in Malory's *Morte Darthur*. The last line of Layamon's *Brut* tells of Merlin's prophecy that "Arthur once again would come to aid the English," showing that the legendary king of the Britons became a national hero of the very people whose ancestors he had fought against.

Later kings of England invoked the Arthurian legend for their own political purposes. For Edward III's proposal to reestablish an order of Knights of the Round Table, see the *Norton Topics Online* selection from Adam Murimuth's *Chronicle* under "King Arthur." Also at *NTO* is the image of an oak round table, eighteen feet in diameter, probably made for Edward I around 1255. Henry VIII had the table painted with heraldic insignia to assert the Tudor claims of Arthurian ancestry. His daughter Elizabeth I was endowed with Arthurian magic by poets such as Edmund Spenser, and many succeeding English monarchs have fancied an association with an idealized Arthurian chivalry.

Medieval Sexuality

The idealization of sexual love between a man and a woman is not a motive of Anglo-Saxon literature. The closest one comes is *The Wife's Lament*, which is not about romantic love but about the pain of exile and the separation of wife and husband on account of feuds and hatreds that are never explained. Sexual love is an important subject for medieval romance—according to one distinguished critic, the Middle Ages invented romantic love; or, more precisely, it invented that mode of eroticism that one historian called "amour courtois," translated into English as "courtly love."

Courtly love has been seen as the other side of the coin of medieval antifeminism, because it idealizes women but emphasizes, in that very act, their difference from a male standard. Scholars have used the phrase to designate a set of literary conventions in which the lady is wooed, usually at a distance, by a knight who fights in her honor, devotes himself to her, and suffers pallor, chills and fever, insomnia, anorexia, and other symptoms that, he insists, will be his death if he does not obtain her "mercy." This notion of love as service uses metaphors of slavery (he is her thrall), religion (he worships her and prays to her), and politics (he petitions, commits treasons; she is a tyrant) to make women into objects of erotic worship. Romances present such love as extramarital, perhaps because wealthy families usually arranged marriages according to the dictates of rank and property rather than sexual attraction. The third point of the triangle seems to be included in dominant stories like that of Arthur, Lancelot, and Guinevere, in which the bond between Lancelot and Arthur is often treated with erotic or quasi-erotic seriousness.

Chaucer often treats courtly love with tongue in cheek. Hende Nicholas claims to be dying of love in *The Miller's Tale* (lines 172–73), and Chaucer parodies the lover's complaint in "Complaint to His Purse." There are similarly irreverent treatments of doctrines of love and lovers in *Lanval*, *The Wife of Bath's Tale*, and *Gawain*, where the ladies take the initiative and the lovers are passive or "daungerous." Popular love songs like "Alison" and "My Lief Is Faren in Londe" use the motif of unrequited, distant, or betrayed love. These poems are short, but in conventional romances the woes of long-suffering lovers often run on for hundreds of lines. In Middle English writings, eroticism can be found not only in the love worship knights have for women, but also in bonds between men and in medieval spiritual devotion.

Literature and the Medieval Church

Students have vastly differing amounts of knowledge about the Bible, Christian teachings, and the history of the Church. The literature of the period often assumes some familiarity with the doctrines, hierarchy, religious orders, rituals, sacraments, holidays, and many other features of medieval religion. Of course, the teaching of the period need not be constrained by supplying arcane information, much of which is provided in the notes. In many ways the literature itself will teach modern readers about religion, as it was originally intended to teach both clergy and lay readers during the Middle Ages.

There were many different kinds of medieval faith and worship, and the literature shows how the Church was changing over the many centuries in this period. In the best literature, students may feel a tension between the religious and secular aims of both medieval authors and their characters: for example, in the Christian poet's admiration for Beowulf's heroism and his compassion for the good pagans who possess no knowledge of the redemption; in the Wife of Bath's lament, "Allas, allas, that ever love was sinne!" (line 620); in Sir Gawain's reluctant acceptance of the green girdle so that he may live; and in Lancelot's joining a religious order after the fellowship of good knights has been destroyed. To explain the purpose and institutions of monastic life, excerpts from *The Rule of St. Benedict* have been included among the "Medieval Estates and Orders" selections in *NTO*.

"And pilgrimes were they alle"

Both clerics and laypeople went on pilgrimages throughout the Middle Ages, but by the end of the fourteenth century, pilgrimages had become such a popular and, to a considerable degree, commercial activity that they were condemned by reformers. An example of that is the passage from Passus 5 of *Piers Plowman*. Inspired by a revivalist sermon preached by Repentance,

> A thousand men then thronged together,
> Cried upward to Christ and to his clean mother
> To have grace to go to Truth—God grant that they might!
> But there was no one so wise as to know the way thither,
> But they blundered forth like beasts over banks and hills
> Till they met a man, many hours later,
> Appareled like a pagan in pilgrims' manner. (lines 510–14)

The man bears the pilgrim's traditional staff, bowl, and bag, but his costume is absurdly decorated with souvenirs acquired from the different shrines he has visited so that instead of a Christian he resembles a "pagan" (Middle English *paynim*, usually referring to a Saracen). Asked if he has ever heard of a saint called Truth, this professional pilgrim is at a loss. At this point Piers Plowman makes his entry into the poem and gives the seekers after Truth allegorical directions that lead through the Ten Commandments and fundamental Christian and moral doctrine. Offered pay by the pilgrims, Piers says, "I wouldn't take a farthing's fee for Saint Thomas's shrine" (line 358).

You could use this passage to introduce the idea of pilgrimage and to point out the very mixed characters and motivations among the "sondry folk, by aventure yfalle / In felaweshipe, and pilgrimes were they alle" (lines 25–26), gathered at the Tabard Inn to seek "Saint Thomas's shrine." Less obviously than Langland, Chaucer, too, is satirizing the profane aspects of his pilgrims in *The General Prologue* and throughout *The Canterbury Tales*, but that is not to say that the secularism and realism of his work excludes a religious and allegorical level. Both as a whole and in the individual prologues and tales, these poems exhibit a familiar tension between the spiritual and the worldly.

Christ's Humanity

The visual representation of Christ in the Middle Ages can strike modern readers and viewers as strange—sometimes beautiful and moving, sometimes lurid and repulsive. Many modern readers are unused to so bodily, visual, and intensely emotional an account of suffering divinity. After the destruction of images and the banning of religious plays in the sixteenth century, Protestant culture has, for example, often felt uneasy with close-up visual representation of the bodily Christ. Teaching this topic could be an occasion to interest students in the texts produced by an unfamiliar intersection of theology, literature, art, and drama.

One might begin with images of the Crucifixion, and ask students to think about how such images invite their audience to respond conceptually and emotionally. Do they suggest their audience is complicit in the violence done to Christ, or should react angrily against those perpetrating that violence (whether Romans or Jews)? In the context of those responses, a teacher could supply some pertinent theological background, by way of introducing St. Anselm's (d. 1099) theory of the Atonement, which placed the emphasis very much on Christ as suffering human rather than triumphant God. From that theological humanization of Christ derived a powerful movement, known as "affective piety," which was given extensive and various expression throughout the entire later medieval period in Europe. Within the terms of this cultural movement, one responded to Christ's suffering emotionally, or affectively, by making oneself imaginatively present at the events of the Crucifixion. The art designed to provoke these responses was, accordingly, intensely visual and bodily. One might also introduce students to the sacramental side of this concentration on the body of Christ, by sketching the history of the Feast of Corpus Christi: here the Eucharistic Host was, as Christ's actual body, placed at the center of a major festival.

Simple but potent examples of "affective piety" would be some of the lyrics (e.g., "Ye that passen by the weye"). More complex examples might be drawn from Margery Kempe: Kempe's pilgrimages to holy sites, for example, produce intense emotional responses. Almost all forms of bodiliness have a theological resonance in Kempe's experience; certainly all forms of bodily suffering produce in her, by metonymic extension from her focus on Christ's physical suffering, an impassioned response. One might consider those chapters in which Kempe's family relations are treated (her care for her incontinent husband, for example) in this light. One might also ask students to think about how familial bodily relations inflect, in their turn, Kempe's visionary experience with her "husband" Christ. Anti-Semitism is sometimes the flip side of this often uncritical, free-flowing emotional response: consideration of Kempe's vision of the passion-sequence might involve thinking about how empathy with Christ can produce an unreflecting hatred of those who are imagined as his torturers.

Affective piety need not, however, provoke unthinking hatred of those inflicting pain on Christ. *The York Crucifixion Play* provokes an audience urgently to scrutinize how its own daily "work" might inflict pain, and might not measure up to the "works" of mercy demanded by Christ. Asking students to consider the dramatic presentation of the cross in that play (now you don't see it, now, suddenly and powerfully, you do) focuses the question of the audience's own ongoing complicity in Christ's ongoing suffering.

Affective piety was not, however, the only tradition in which Christ's humanity could be presented. In Passus 18 of *Piers Plowman*, readers are asked to think about, not merely to witness, the Crucifixion and Atonement. The Crucifixion, indeed, is treated briefly (if movingly); what takes center stage are characters debating the possibility of the Atonement. The so-called Four Daughters of God, Christ, and Satan: each group stages a debate about the contradictory claims of justice and mercy in the salvation of humanity. In these debates, Christ's humanity is stressed: Christ *needed* to see what humanity had suffered in Hell, just as Christ would not have "suffered" (in the sense of "allowed") his "half-brothers" to suffer without coming to their redemption. The word "stage" here is suggestive, since it underscores the theatricality of Langland's scene, which would provide fertile comparison with the York Crucifixion. Some of the lyrics, too (and particularly "What is he, this lordling, that cometh from the fight?"), provide revealing comparison with Langland's presentation of Christ as conquering hero storming Hell.

Julian of Norwich offers an understanding of Christ's humanity that is all her own. Instructors might begin by showing how Julian sets her vision in the context of Christ's suffering (Chapter 3). But whereas other writers in the tradition of affective piety might stop there, Julian goes much further. Reflection on the body of Christ produces a theological vision of all embodiment, the world itself, reduced to the size and fragility of a hazelnut. Informed by Julian's confidence in Christ's "courteous" preservation of the body, however, her visions do not do away with the body. On the contrary, Christ's maternal nature preserves and cares for sinning, wounded humanity.

In short, Christ's humanity as a topic allows instructors to explore an intersection of theology and literature from many perspectives. It might also provoke students to think about new medieval audiences and readers, given the high profile of women writers, and their claim to authority not via texts or their position in the Church, but via direct vision of the Godhead as a human body.

The Cult of the Virgin and Affective Piety

Medieval literature, as is often remarked, reveals two diametrically opposed stereotypes of women: one represented by Eve, who caused the Fall, and the other by Mary, sometimes referred to as the second Eve (as Christ is the second Adam), who bore humanity's Savior. The Latin *Ave*, the angel's salutation to Mary in the Annunciation, it was noted at that time, is *Eva* spelled backward; and as the Fall was associated with Eve's sexuality, so salvation was associated with Mary's virginity. The cult of the Virgin developed at the same time as the cult of chivalry. In Nativity scenes in art and drama, Mary appears as a simple maiden in a medieval version of the pastoral. In the final scene of the *Second Shepherds' Play*, she speaks kindly to the shepherds after they make their humble but symbolic offerings to the Christ Child, which "lies full cold" (line 1078) in the stable. She also presents a majestic figure as "the high Queen of heaven (line 647). One of the "five fives" symbolized by Sir Gawain's pentangle are her five joys, and therefore, says the poet, her image is fittingly portrayed on the inside of Gawain's shield (lines 646–49). Gawain is in "Great peril . . . / Should Mary forget her knight" (lines 1768–69).

The cult of the Virgin in the late Middle Ages is especially associated with highly emotional expressions of religious feeling. Poetry, drama, and art depicted the physical torment of Christ on the cross and the grief of Mary with a vividness meant to generate powerful feelings of empathy in readers and spectators. When Margery Kempe visited Mount Calvary, she could visualize "in her ghostly sight the mourning of our Lady, of St. John and of Mary Magdalene." She falls to the ground, spreads her arms, writhes, and cries out loudly. This is the first of her chronic outbursts of violent weeping that alienate her fellow pilgrims and others for the rest of her life. In the Passion plays and in the lyric "Ye That Pasen by the Weye," Christ on the Cross asks the spectators to pause and contemplate his wounds. But affective piety was not always or primarily expressed through an outpouring of grief. It could also be an expression of joy as it is in the *Shepherds' Play* when the Angel sings the *Gloria in excelsis* and as in lyrics like "I Sing of a Maiden" and "Adam Lay Bound," which celebrate the Mother of Christ in vernacular song.

Women, the Religious Life, Antifeminism

Although only men could become priests, from early Christian times the convent was an option for women, though mainly women of the aristocracy, who chose to lead a spiritual life. The Abbess Hilda founded the community at Whitby where she presided over both monks and nuns. The miracle of Cædmon's gift is first reported to her, and she gives the orders for testing whether it comes from God. The most likely candidate for the authorship of the lays of Marie de France is Marie, abbess of Shaftesbury, who was a half-sister of Henry II. Instead of the communal life of the convent, women might also decide to become "enclosed" spiritual leaders like Julian of Norwich or the three well-born sisters for whom the *Ancrene Riwle* was written in the early thirteenth century.

The medieval Church, which required its priests, monks, and other officials to be celibate (with uneven success), used the antifeminist literature it inherited from the ancients to persuade men to renounce women. Preachers and others promulgated the view that women, and wives in particular, were promiscuous, luxury-loving, extravagant, loose-tongued, proud, quarrelsome, deceitful, domineering, and guilty of every other vice or annoying disposition men could think of. Even pleasure in sexual relations between husband and wife was doctrinally considered sinful. The Wife of Bath's fifth husband has an anthology of antifeminist literature, which includes most of Chaucer's sources for the *Wife of Bath's Prologue*, and she reminds us that the misogyny of male writers is motivated by vested interests. Antifeminist attitudes even erupt into romance on occasion: after Sir Gawain learns from the Green Knight how he has been taken in by the lady, he tries to comfort himself with a bitter catalog of men who have been betrayed by women, starting with Adam (lines 2415–28). This is treason against the love-service imperatives of chivalry to which Gawain seems to return. Still, the presence of the lady's ugly double, Morgan le Fey, suggests that the antifeminist and courtly images of woman are mysteriously connected.

Romance and Religion

After Lancelot's death, in Malory's account, his nephew Sir Bors, his brother Sir Ector, and two other knights go to the Holy Land where they fight many battles against the infidels, "and there they died upon a Good Friday for God's sake." Malory's late reference to the crusades is a reminder that romance and religion are never far apart in medieval literature. Although in a different key, *Sir Gawain and the Green Knight* also concludes with confession and repentance. The breaking up of the Round Table is already foreshadowed in the French prose romances and in Malory by the Quest for the Holy Grail, which is the only one in which Lancelot fails absolutely. On chivalry as an order, like a religious order, and its social and religious obligations, see the selections from William Caxton's translation of Ramón Lull's *Book of the Order of Chivalry* in NTO under "Medieval Estates and Orders." Chaucer's *Troilus and Criseyde* ends with Troilus's ghost condemning "the blinde lust, the which that may not laste"; and the narrator advises the young people in his audience to set their hearts on the love of Christ instead of "worldly vanitee" that "passeth soone as flowres faire." In the *Retraction*, which follows *The Canterbury Tales*, the author asks Christ to forgive him for his writings of "worldly vanitees" and prays for grace "of verray penitence, confession, and satisfaccion."

The Social Spectrum of Medieval Literature

In early poetry and history, though not in devotional literature, the main characters tend to belong to the aristocracy, and the rest of the world is largely ignored. But in the later Middle Ages the others, who constitute the great majority of men and women, make their presence felt. In the fourteenth century, rebellions broke out against the feudal nobility in France and England, which were quickly suppressed but left their mark on history and literature. During the English "Uprising of 1381" (known to earlier historians as "The Peasants' Revolt"), the rebels chanted the epigram, "When Adam delved and Eve span, / Who was then a gentleman?" In *NTO* (in the Middle Ages, go to "Medieval Estates and Orders"), you can see letters circulated by leaders of the uprising to incite their followers and excerpts from a vitriolic satire (John Gower's *Vox Clamantis*) portraying the rebels as animals attacking their masters.

For medieval social theory of the "three estates," go to "Medieval Estates and Orders" in *NTO*, especially the English monk Aelfric's *Those Who Pray, Work, and Fight*. Most of the human characters in *Beowulf* belong to the warrior elite (those who fight); the "others" are monsters, though even they are imagined with genealogies like those of lords. The knights and ladies of medieval romance also inhabit an aristocratic world in which we rarely see anyone else who is not a servant, but it is a gender-inverted world in which the knights profess themselves to be the servants of all noble ladies. Strength, courage, wisdom, generosity, and loyalty to kin still define the noble hero, but a new badge of class in romance is courtesy. There are elaborate exchanges of courtesy in *Beowulf*, but they involve gifts rather different from "the polished pearls of impeccable speech" (line 917) that the company at Sir Bertilak's castle expect to fall from Sir Gawain's lips.

The social spectrum is wider in *The Canterbury Tales*. Chaucer begins *The General Prologue* by telling us who the pilgrims are, specifically their "condicioun," "degree," and "eek in what array that they were inne" (lines 35–41). To the narrator, these categories all designate rank, profession, and what we now call class. The reader soon notices that the portraits describe not just the social and professional but also the moral and spiritual "condicioun" of the pilgrims. The group is diverse indeed, though it does not include royalty, anyone of elite status, or any of those living in abject poverty. In the opening of the poem, Chaucer describes pilgrimage as politically representative, as its participants come from every shire in England. One of his goals is to suggest how individuals come together to make up a society, and the voting, agreements, and legal language of *The General Prologue* give us an early picture of the idea of social contract. Langland's *Prologue* to *Piers Plowman* begins with an overview of a busy society made up of lively occupational roles. The mystery cycles, which were performed annually for all comers in major towns, were organized by occupation and portray the lives of medieval commoners in the course of telling their biblical stories.

NOTES ON MEDIEVAL GENRES

Old English Epic

The earliest epic poems celebrated the deeds of heroes in a warrior society. Before epic was ever written down, it was composed extempore by professional bards or singers who drew on a stock of traditional verse formulas (on oral-formulaic poetry, see the headnote to Caedmon's *Hymn*). The Germanic tribes before their conversion to Christianity had such an epic tradition, of which only a few vestiges survive.

Germanic epic seems to ignore classical conventions. Little enough of the poetry survives, in any case, for us to deduce generic conventions with any assurance. The alliterative verse form and recurrent formulas indicate that there was a large body of heroic legends, which were performed by oral poets like the *scop* in *Beowulf*, who performs the creation hymn, the Sigemund panegyric complimenting Beowulf, and the Finnsburg episode. The genealogy of the Danish kings, the ship burial, the attack on the hall, the sea crossings, the feasts, the dragon fight, and the beasts of battle are probably all versions of set pieces common to Germanic epic. We modern readers have to piece together the tradition from a few fragments that have survived and from *Beowulf* itself, which is the most complete witness we have of early Germanic heroic poetry. Nor can we take for granted that this poet has passed on the stories in the form that they came down to him. The *Beowulf* poet has shaped his materials to show the world of pagan antiquity from the point of view of his own Christian culture.

The Battle of Maldon (included in the Archive), though very late in the period, probably comes as close as any surviving heroic poem to the form of a short heroic lay. The contrast between the cowards who flee when their leader is slain and the brave men who fight to the death to avenge their lord is the heart of the tradition. Almost a third of the poem is given over to the loyal retainers who utter variations of the same speech, culminating in the eloquent lines of Birhtwold. Wiglaf makes the same kind of speech after Beowulf's other retainers have fled from the dragon fight. There is a strong ethical and hortatory imperative in these Old English epics, expressed in the formula "Swa sceal man don" (So must one do).

Epic always claims to be based on history—that is the point of the "We have heard" formula and the genealogy of the Danish kings with which *Beowulf* begins. The hero's fights with a man-eating monster, a troll-hag at the bottom of a tarn, and a flame-breathing dragon introduce epic motifs that *Beowulf* and the *Odyssey* share with later romance. The selections grouped together as "Legendary Histories of Britain" contain (1) a foundation myth told as a sequel to Virgil's *Aeneid*; (2) a court scene with an insulting challenge and heroic response followed by a counsel of war; and (3) a prophetic dream of disaster. All these are conventional epic motifs. See the discussions below of *The Dream of the Rood* and *Judith* for the use of epic motifs and formulas in Anglo-Saxon Christian poetry.

Further Resources

NORTON ONLINE ARCHIVE

The Battle of Maldon

Audio:
Birhtwold's speech (read by Robert Fulk)

Romance

Epic, History, and Romance

The word "romance," as explained in the historical introduction, originally referred to works written in the French vernacular. In particular, it appeared in the titles of several long twelfth-century French poems that today we might think of as "historical romances" but which their original readers or listeners probably regarded as ancient histories, retold not in Latin but in their native language as poetry. The French *Roman de Troie* was translated into Latin prose as the *Historia Destructionis Troiae* ("History of the Destruction of Troy"), which ironically came to be considered the scholarly original from which the *Roman* had been translated. Wace's *Roman de Brut* is a very free adaptation of Geoffrey of Monmouth's Latin prose *History of the Kings of Britain*. Most people continued to regard Geoffrey's work as authentic history until the seventeenth century. Through intermediate English works such as Holinshed's *Chronicles*, it provided materials for Shakespeare and Spenser. While there is no watertight method of distinguishing epic from history and history from romance, some structural features may help us to perceive differences. Epic will be focused on the heroic exploits of a single person or group (e.g., respectively, *Beowulf* and *The Battle of Maldon*). History, or chronicle, may accentuate the exploits of a great king or queen, but will have a wider historical purview than the acts of that monarch. Thus Geoffrey of Monmouth's *History of the Kings of Britain* does celebrate Arthur, but the work begins long before and extends beyond Arthur's reign. Romances, by contrast, tend to focus on individual knights or ladies and their trials in combat, exile, or love. They often hold out the prospect of a happy ending, even if (as in the case of Thomas's *Tristran*) they fail to deliver that ending. Supernatural marvels may appear in all three story types.

The "romance" elements in Latin, French, and English literature owe a great deal to Celtic stories of love and magic. Geoffrey of Monmouth claimed to have translated his *History* from an ancient Welsh book, which probably never existed, but he unquestionably obtained much of his material from Welsh oral tradition. *The Exile of the Sons of Uisliu*, from Old Irish, is another example of the rich Celtic literature that influenced medieval romance. This tale became a favorite of the Celtic Revival at the end of the nineteenth century. Derdriu is a tragic heroine, an Irish Helen whose passion for "a game young bull," for whose love she rejects an old royal one, brings about a great war between Ulster and Connaught.

Chivalric Romance

In France during the latter half of the twelfth century, King Arthur's court became the center for the most characteristic form of romance associated with the Middle Ages, the romance of chivalry. Its protagonist is a knight who typically rides out alone in search of adventures or on a quest, which is often a rescue mission on behalf of a fellow knight or lady in distress. Worthy knights are praised and wicked knights condemned by the standards of a moral code and a code of manners called chivalry. The word designates the honorable deeds and behavior of a knight (*chevalier, caballero, Ritter*), especially in war and tournaments on his *cheval* (horse). A knight's adventures serve as tests not only of his strength and courage but also of his character and courtliness. Nobility, wealth, good looks, and military prowess are qualities with which the romance hero is often endowed by birth, although in some romances a knight from the lower nobility and of humble means rises to high rank through feats of arms and a great marriage. Often a knight, though nobly born, must nevertheless achieve true "gentilesse" (*Wife of Bath's Tale*) through overcoming his shortcomings and failures in the course of his adventures. Truth, religious faith, loyalty, and humility are the most important qualities in which the protagonists of romance are tested, qualities that are probed and defined by fresh perspectives in different stories.

Further Resources

NORTON TOPICS ONLINE

Medieval Estates and Orders: Making and Breaking Rules
    Ramon Lull, *from* The Book of the Order of Chivalry
    From The Romance of the Rose [The Advice of the Old Woman]

King Arthur: Romancing Politics
    Chrétien de Troyes
    Yvain or the Knight with the Lion
    The Knight of the Cart
    The Prose Vulgate Cycle
    The Prose Lancelot
    The Quest for the Holy Grail
    The Death of Arthur
    The Wedding of Sir Gawain and Dame Ragnelle
    William Caxton, *Preface to* Morte Darthur
    Eustache Deschamps, The Nine Worthies

Allegory

Allegory is a mode of reading as well as a mode of writing. Both pagan and Christian interpreters attributed allegorical meaning to the myths about the Greek and Roman gods, which neither could accept literally. Throughout the Middle Ages and the Renaissance, the stories in the

Bible, although accepted as true history, were also thought to contain hidden spiritual truths, in the mode of both typology and allegory. In a typological interpretation, Old Testament stories and characters are taken to be types, foreshadowings, and concealed prophecies of events and characters in the New Testament. The same story could be given both an allegorical and a typological meaning. The release of the people of Israel from Egyptian bondage, for example, could be interpreted allegorically, as the liberation of the soul from sin, and also typologically, as a prefiguration of Christ's deliverance of the patriarchs and prophets from Hell—a story in the apocryphal Gospel of Nicodemus, known as the "Harrowing of Hell," which is retold at the end of *The Dream of the Rood* and in Passus 18 of *Piers Plowman*.

Trained in this tradition of biblical interpretation, the religious writers of the Middle Ages naturally used allegory as a way of moral instruction in their own narratives. They might relate biblical episodes in such a manner as to bring out their doctrinal meaning, or they might devise original narratives intended to be read simultaneously as enjoyable stories and as allegories of Christian teachings. Allegory reaches into lyric, where its power comes from its ability to crystallize many meanings in an image or phrase (see Chaucer's "Truth").

Not all medieval allegory was religious. *The Romance of the Rose* is a dream allegory of love. Several of the early parts of *Piers Plowman* are taken up with political allegory of corruption in church and state. In the Renaissance, writers like Spenser and Milton were influenced by medieval allegories and combine secular and theological issues in interesting ways. Other later, humanist writers like Ben Jonson use allegory in the dramatic masque as a vehicle for political praise.

The Dream Vision

Allegories often were put into the frame of a dream that the narrator, an Everyman figure, relates to his audience. In *The Dream of the Rood*, the story of the Crucifixion, as told by the personified Cross, is the pattern of the Christian life: by taking up the Cross and undergoing suffering and death for the Lord, the dreamer, who was "stained with sins, wounded with wrongdoings" (1.19), may be transformed and come "where the Lord's folk are seated at the feast, where bliss is eternal" (1.21).

Will, the more individualized dreamer-narrator of *Piers Plowman*, is both the author, William Langland, and an allegorical personification of the obdurate human will, seeking, questioning, and resisting the knowledge that leads to salvation. The climax is reached with Will's vision of the Crucifixion and the Harrowing of Hell, which may be compared with the account of the Old English poet in *The Dream of the Rood*.

Personification Allegory

The Confession of the Seven Deadly Sins in *Piers Plowman* (excerpts from which are included in the Archive) is an example of a personification allegory in which the sins are personified as allegorical agents who describe themselves and act out their natures. The clearest example of personification allegory in the period is the morality play *Everyman*, in which nearly all the characters are personifications. Yet the play's success depends not only on the way in which Everyman's story unfolds the steps of repentance, confession, and satisfaction, which lead to salvation, but on the realistic and very human behavior of the friends who abandon Everyman when they learn what journey he is about to take.

The Literal and the Allegorical

There are many varieties and shadings of allegory, and students should understand that a consistent relationship between literal and allegorical levels of meaning is not to be expected. The Field of Folk in the Prologue to *Piers Plowman* is an allegorical representation of the world, but the description of the folk is also a satire of different trades and professions, and the episode ends with a realistic market scene where vendors cry out their wares. The tavern scene in Passus 5 (included in the Archive), in which Glutton, on his way to confession, is enticed into a drinking party, although an allegory, is also the most graphic picture we have of medieval London lowlife.

One is tempted to read parts of *The Canterbury Tales* as intentionally allegorical. Pilgrimage was a traditional metaphor for the journey of life, and the idea that the pilgrims are a representative group, exemplifying the virtues and vices on the human pilgrimage, is latent from the opening lines with their imagery of spring, of life renewed, and of the blessed martyr's healing power (lines 1–18). *The Pardoner's Tale*, with its unholy trinity of villains and the mysterious old man, who may symbolize sin and death (lines 404–16, 423–61), seems to invite us to look for allegorical meaning. But allegorical interpretations have not garnered critical consensus, and formally the story is best characterized as a moral exemplum, calculated to frighten people into giving their money to the Pardoner. The Introduction to *The Parson's Tale*, with its symbolic setting and the Parson's offer to show the pilgrims the way to the "Jerusalem celestial," is one moment where the poem invites us to interpret the entire work allegorically, but it is a glimmer, never sustained (see especially n. 1).

Satire

A course on satire can work with solely medieval texts or it can begin there and move through writers like Ben Jonson to the eighteenth century and beyond. The *Prologue* and the earlier steps of Langland's *Piers Plowman*, which deal with the marriage of Lady Meed, participate in a genre of writing that modern scholars call "estates satire." On the classification of society into "estates," i.e., classes and professions, see "Medieval Estates and Orders," in *NTO*, where you will find examples of estates satire in two works by Chaucer's contemporary John Gower. *The General Prologue* to *The Canterbury Tales*, although its narrative structure, style, and irony are very different from Gower's, has affinities with estates satire; comparison with Gower and with Langland provides a literary context for Chaucer's prologue to pilgrimage and helps bring out its special qualities. Estates satire is aimed at all estates and professions—barons, knights, lawyers, doctors, merchants, etc.—but much of its sharpest criticism targets those who abuse the Church—bishops, priests, monks, nuns, friars, and laymen employed by the Church, such as summoners and pardoners.

As one may see by reading Langland, Gower, and other contemporaries of Chaucer, Chaucer's criticism of the Church was neither bold nor harsh, and he was certainly no reformer. Students will have no difficulty responding to his irony. What is more difficult to convey to them—and reading just a little bit of Gower makes this easier—is an appreciation of the special qualities of Chaucer's irony: its artfulness, humor, sympathy, and avoidance of a judgmental righteousness. Chaucer the pilgrim narrator presents *all* his fellow pilgrims, not just the good Parson, Plowman, and Knight, as the most wonderful group of people in the world; each is in some respect the best of his or her kind. The narrator's lack of discrimination invites readers to discover for themselves that most of the pilgrims are flawed and that several are, indeed, rascals who are admired chiefly for their consummate charlatanism. Yet the resulting irony need not cancel out the effect of the narrator's delight in and affection for the pilgrims. By reserving judgment, Chaucer leaves critics and students free to disagree about the effect of individual portraits. In many cases there is a delicate balance between satire and sympathy that, depending on the reader, could tilt either way.

Further Resources

NORTON TOPICS ONLINE

Medieval Estates and Orders: Making and Breaking Rules
   Aelfric, Those Who Pray, Work, and Fight
   John Gower, *from* Vox Clamantis, Books 3 and 4
   John Gower, *from the* Mirour de l'Omme

Lyric

Old English Elegy

Elegy is one of the most ancient and persistent forms of lyric verse, and many of the most moving poems in *NAEL* are in the elegiac tradition. Although it is really a didactic poem, we call *The Wanderer* an "elegy" because it laments the passing of the speaker's lord and companions and of the emblems of the heroic world: the horse, the joys of the mead hall, the shining cup, all of them fleeting in the dark, storm-battered world that is passing too.

Readers like to think that the "frost-cold sea" and winter storms in *The Wanderer*, so typical of Old English poetry, describe the actual experience of a tough seafaring people, and perhaps they do. But the gloomy, threatening land and seascapes also reflect the inner state of the exile in a crumbling world, where all of us are wanderers in search of a new lord. That is to say that descriptions of nature in Old English poetry are often symbolic and reflect homiletic themes. Outside the fragile court civilization, represented by the mead hall and its joys, lies a dark wilderness, the habitation of evil. Grendel is also a wanderer, a stalker of the borderlands, but he recognizes no human lord or law. His dwelling place, the mere, resembles the entrance to Hell as it is described in an Old English homily. We are brought to see the natural world as a battleground between good and evil.

Middle English Lyrics

In this edition of *NAEL*, Middle English lyrics have been collected in two sections: Middle English Incarnation and Crucifixion Lyrics, which forms part of the thematic cluster "Christ's Humanity," and Middle English Lyrics, which contains lyrics of a secular character as well as religious lyrics on other themes. These poems demonstrate a continuity with Renaissance song, and reading them together with Campion, for instance, taps into students' vast knowledge of our contemporary song. Chaucer's "Troilus' Song," excerpted from a long narrative poem, is an early translation of Petrarch and a wonderful companion to the early-modern love lyric with its Petrarchan and Chaucerian themes.

Further Resources

NORTON ONLINE ARCHIVE

In Praise of Brunettes
The Appreciative Drinker
A Charm Against the Night Goblin
The Blacksmiths
Earth Took Earth
Spring Has Come with Love
The Henpecked Husband
A Bitter Lullaby

Audio:
The Cuckoo Song ("Sumer is ycomen in") (performed by the Hilliard Ensemble)

Drama

Medieval drama is so various and interesting that it fascinates students on its own. It also sharpens the critical responses of students in Renaissance drama courses, where it can provide the perfect introduction. The headnote on the mystery plays emphasizes the festive and communal character of the plays, which dramatized episodes in the Bible. In performance, the town itself becomes an extension of the stage, just as, in a medieval painting of the Nativity, the spires of an anachronistically contemporary city may appear in the background. Biblical shepherds speaking broad Yorkshire dialect and swearing by Christ's Cross also break down the historical and psychological distance between the far-off biblical event and the audience surrounding the pageant. Thus the Nativity and Crucifixion plays brought home the meaning of Christ's incarnation and sacrifice to the medieval audience.

A contemporary account describes the wagon on which the mystery plays were presented as a "Theater . . . very large and high, placed upon wheels," while another calls it "a high place made like a house with two rooms, being open at the top: [in] the lower room they apparelled and dressed themselves; and in the upper room they played." The spectators stood (or milled around) on all four sides of the wagon, which meant that actors were always aware of their audiences. The actors did not confine themselves to playing on the wagon: they acted scenes or entire plays in front of it. This playing space, the *platea*, was unlocalized. There was no realistic scenery of the sort we are used to; the wagons were, however, rather elaborately decorated, and some had machinery for God or angels to ascend or descend. A favorite wagon decoration was the "hell mouth," into which Satan and his fellow devils gleefully shoved lost souls. Costumes were rich, according to surviving financial records.

During the Reformation, the mystery cycles fell into disrepute. To the Protestant mind, such things as God in a gold mask, the impersonation of Christ, and the farcical elements in the mystery plays were blasphemous. The allegorical morality play did not, at least, break the commandment against graven images of God, though in them the farcical element was at times more pronounced. In this respect, *Everyman* is not a typical morality because it lacks the low comedy routines in which the demons and the so-called vice figures conventionally tempted the hero to commit sin. Yet it makes a rich comparison with Marlowe's *Dr. Faustus*, and is emotionally powerful in the classroom on its own or as background for the Renaissance.

Further Resources

NORTON ONLINE ARCHIVE

The Brome Play of Abraham and Isaac
The Chester Play of Noah's Flood

AUTHORS AND WORKS

Bede

Caedmon's Hymn

This beautiful devotional poem is wonderful to compare with the description in *Beowulf* of the poet singing of creation in shining Heorot. Its mood of awe resonates with moments of Julian of Norwich's *Showings* and a number of later lyric poems. The mystery plays also creatively rewrite Bible stories, as does Milton's *Paradise Lost*. The headnote to Bede's account of Cædmon's *Hymn* discusses the concept of oral-formulaic poetry. Cædmon's *Hymn* provides instructors and their students with a relatively simple text to demonstrate how an oral-formulaic poem works and enables them to read a few lines in Old English. A splendid performance of the *Hymn*, accompanied by a harp reconstructed from instruments probably used by Anglo-Saxon bards, is available in the audio section of the Online Archive.

Further Resources

NORTON ONLINE ARCHIVE

Audio:
Caedmon's *Hymn* (read by J. B. Bessinger, Jr.)

The Dream of the Rood

This is the poem that most clearly illustrates the "conversion" of the heroic to the Christian. Christ is portrayed as a "young Hero," the Crucifixion as a "great struggle," the personified Cross as a loyal retainer who "must stand fast" with its lord and undergoes death and burial with him. But, like its lord, the Cross is ultimately resurrected in glory and holds out that promise to the weary and sin-stained dreamer who is instructed to "tell men of this vision." The language and motifs of the heroic ethic are applied to teaching the new doctrine whose lesson is to suffer and endure rather than to take vengeance. Yet the poem ends on a note of triumph with a reference to the Harrowing of Hell as a warlike rescue mission in which the souls of the patriarchs and prophets are liberated from captivity by the Devil. (Christ's descent into Hell is a part of medieval Christian doctrine, based on apocryphal sources, which students need to have explained.) The last words, "þær his eþel wæs" (where his homeland was), touch on an important allegorical theme in Old English and later Christian literature (e.g., Chaucer's poem "Truth," lines 17–21), poignantly elaborated in *The Wanderer*. We are all wanderers on earth, separated from our true Lord, and exiled from our native land, which is in Heaven.

Beowulf

Beowulf is the oldest and finest example of Germanic heroic literature. Its poet was an antiquarian, fascinated by the artifacts, customs, and beliefs of his pagan ancestors, which he re-created with solemn magnificence. The ship burial of Shield, the eponymous founder of the Danish dynasty (lines 26–52), was vividly documented by the discovery of an early Anglo-Saxon king's funeral ship at Sutton Hoo in East Anglia in the 1930s. If images of the Sutton Hoo treasure, now housed in the British Museum, can be obtained, they make splendid illustrations for the opening of *Beowulf* (try your art department's slide library or search online). Like the *Odyssey, Beowulf* is an exciting adventure story with fights against monsters. Its hero personifies the values of the distant heroic world at its best. But the Christian poet, though he admires those values, represents them as limited and ultimately, like Beowulf himself, doomed. Notably, the religion of these peoples, although pagan, is not basically polytheistic. Hrothgar's *scop* sings a creation hymn reminiscent of Cædmon's, and characters, while they sometimes speak of a deterministic *Wyrd* or Fate (e.g., lines 455, 573), have a concept of a just ruler of all things (e.g., lines 1724–26). Yet the values of the characters are governed by the duty of blood vengeance. The Danes' troubles at the hands of the Grendel family are expressed in the language of a feud. The horror of Grendel's assaults is magnified by the fact that the Danes are incapable of killing the monster or exacting compensation from him; Grendel's mother takes revenge for her son by slaughtering Hrothgar's most beloved retainer. The poet's treatment of the feud ethic is clearest in the "digressions." These include the scattered reminiscences of the wars between the Swedes and the Geats, which, after Beowulf's death, forebode the annihilation of the Geats by the vengeance of their traditional enemies; the Finnsburg episode about the feud of the Danes with the Frisians and Jutes; and the allusions to the feud between the Danes and the Heatho-Bards. The feud mentality is graphically portrayed in Beowulf's speech about a political marriage, contracted to make peace, between Hrothgar's daughter and the Heatho-Bard king Ingeld, whose father has been slain in a feud with the Danes (lines 2020–69). Beowulf foresees how the feud is likely to break out afresh at the wedding banquet when a bitter old warrior will egg on a young man to take blood vengeance on some Dane in the wedding party wearing plundered Heatho-Bard trophies. The Christian poet's allusion to the flames that will destroy the great hall Heorot and the description of the funeral fires that consume the corpses at Finnsburg and finally Beowulf's body (lines 1107–25, 3143–47) foreshadow the apocalyptic fire that awaits the world and all heroic endeavor. Similarly, the gold treasure that acted as security for human heroism and political alliance is, in the end, subject to decay (2754). The earliest English epic we have is already an elegy for epic values, as it questions the warrior code. Later writers of epic will also raise serious objections to values inherent in the genre—Spenser to conquest, Milton to military strength.

Old English Alliterative Verse

Through the use of traditional poetic formulas, cast in meters such as the Homeric Greek hexameter and the Anglo-Saxon alliterative line, professional singers of tales were able to improvise performances of long narrative poems. Although Seamus Heaney's translation of *Beowulf* does not consistently observe the strict rules governing the meter of Old English poetry, many of his lines can serve as good examples of the relation of metrical stress and alliteration:

> The *fó*rtunes of wár *fá*vored Hróthgar (line 64)
>
> the híghest in the *lá*nd, would *lé*nd advice (line 172)
>
> and *fí*nd *frí*endship in the *Fá*ther's embráce (line 188)

Heaney's reading in the Online Archive will also introduce students to the rhythms of alliterative verse. Ask your students to look up *alliteration* in the Literary Terminology appendix, under "Rhetorical Figures: Figures of Speech," where they will also find iambic pentameter lines in later English poetry that have a beat and movement like those in Old English alliterative poetry. Alliteration comes more naturally to Germanic verse because in Germanic languages stress normally falls on the initial syllable. Many traditional English expressions made up of alliterative doublets will already be familiar to students. For example, "laid down the law" and "safe and sound" are phrases that occur in Heaney's translation.

Quick Read

- Genre: *Beowulf* is heroic, a highly wrought literary epic; the story of a hero upon whose actions hang the fates of whole peoples.
- Imagery: Light/dark, the made/the wild, the great halls shining, full of feasting and treasure-giving; the gold treasures and arms; Grendel's arm, Aeschere's head.
- Favorite Topoi: Epithets, kennings (often linking bodies with architecture or the wild with the made), a few luscious epic similes, lines 1197, 1605.
- Speech Acts: Insults, speeches of praise, and what Heaney calls the "formal boast," which is competitive but is also a public vow to undertake responsibilities (e.g., line 632).
- Style: Paratactic, appositive, proleptic; grammatically it stresses things and substance over verbs; sober in tone; digressions imply comparisons.
- Key Passages: Grendel's view of Heorot, lines 86ff.; Beowulf's speech to Hrothgar imagining his death at Grendel's hands, 442; the "hall-session" fight between Beowulf and Grendel, 767; the found sword melting, 1605, and the ecphrasis of its hilt, 1688; the lament of the keeper of the hoard, 2247; the epic simile for King Hrethel's misery, 2444; the corrupting treasure, 2754; Beowulf's funeral, 3134.

Teaching Clusters

Pagan and Christian. *Beowulf* develops significantly through scenes of feasting, which seem to represent good government and the happy results of civilization. These scenes compare well with feasting in such works as *Sir Gawain and the Green Knight*, *Dr. Faustus*, and "To Penshurst." The poem's representation of the heroic can be contrasted with those in, for example, *Sir Gawain and the Green Knight*, *Morte Darthur*, *The Faerie Queene*, and *Paradise Lost*.

Discussion Questions

1. Compare the opening funeral with the concluding one.
2. Does your emotional experience of the poem conflict with your understanding of its themes?
3. How does the significance of gold treasure change as the poem progresses?
4. What does it mean to say there are monsters?
5. What does architecture represent in the poem?
6. Why use an epithet? A kenning?
7. What is the role of art, including poetry, in the poem?
8. Is there a tension between the values of these warrior peoples and the suggested Christianity of the poet?
9. How would you film a key scene?

Further Resources

NORTON ONLINE ARCHIVE

Audio:
From Beowulf, translated and read by Seamus Heaney
    Prologue, Building of Heorot, Arrival of Grendel, lines 1–98
    The Fight with Grendel, lines 710–823
    The Last Survivor's Speech, lines 224lb–70a
    Beowulf's Funeral, lines 3137–82

NORTON TOPICS ONLINE

The Linguistic and Literary Contexts of *Beowulf*
    Widsith
    The Saxon Genesis
    Genesis B
    The Vatican Genesis
    The Prose Edda
    Grettir's Saga

Judith

As observed in the headnote, *Judith* is the other text preserved in the unique *Beowulf* manuscript, and if you assign *Beowulf*, it is interesting to ask what these two very different works have in common that appealed to their Anglo-Saxon audience. An answer to that question brings into focus the relationship between "Pagan and Christian" in the surviving corpus of Anglo-Saxon poetry. The story of Judith will be unfamiliar to most students, and *Judith* is not technically a "Christian" poem. The point needs to be made, however, that for Anglo-Saxon and later medieval interpreters and audiences, the Hebrew Bible would have been an inseparable part of one and the same Scripture, prefiguring truths that would be fully revealed only in the New Testament. Quite naturally, Anglo-Saxon poets were especially drawn to the heroic stories of the Old Testament, especially those in which the Hebrews defend themselves against foreign invaders as the English around that time had been fighting off the Vikings. Other biblical Anglo-Saxon poems include an *Exodus* and a *Genesis*. The latter begins not with the Creation but with the War in Heaven, based on both Jewish and Christian commentary and exegesis of Genesis. The fallen angel Satan, disguised as the serpent, seeks revenge for his own fall from Heaven by bringing about the fall of humankind. This is wonderful to compare to *Paradise Lost*. For an excerpt, see *Norton Topics Online*, "The Linguistic and Literary Contexts of *Beowulf*."

Judith is one of the strong women in biblical story, like Moses' sister Miriam. Miriam's triumphal song, "Sing ye to the Lord, for he has triumphed gloriously; the horse and his rider hath he thrown into the sea" (Exodus 15:21), is believed to be the most ancient text preserved in the Hebrew Bible. For a specific point of comparison with *Beowulf*, you might focus on Judith departing with the head of Holofernes (a favorite scene in art) and Beowulf emerging from the mere holding Grendel's head. Here is one instance where Anglo-Saxon and Judeo-Christian traditions strike a common chord of grisly satisfaction.

King Alfred

Preface to the Pastoral Care

The Preface to the *Pastoral Care* is not a work of fiction, but a fascinating political document on reading and education. It is a key text in Anglo-Saxon literary and cultural history, and will shed light, one way or another, on virtually all the other Anglo-Saxon texts in the anthology. In literary history, it is a manifesto of sorts for a translation program of key texts into English, and stands at the head of the rich tradition of Old English prose. For cultural history, it is significant in a variety of ways: (1) it reveals the close conceptual connection between power (both political and military) and learning; (2) it underscores the fragility of learning and memory in Anglo-Saxon culture, given the vulnerability to attack from outside; (3) the text expresses enormous confidence in the project of translation. So far from it being the case that learned languages should be the preserve of the learned alone, Alfred has no hesitation in planning to translate learned texts into vernacular languages for a wide, albeit male readership, as learning moves westward from Israel to Greece, Rome, and the westernmost reaches of Europe; (4) translation of texts is insufficient: Alfred also plans an educational reform in order to guarantee the usefulness of the translations; and (5) finally, one might stress the fact that Alfred clearly makes a personal investment in the spread of learning: this is not a dry government missive, but a text informed by the passionate and personal commitment to learning by the king himself.

The Wanderer *and* The Wife's Lament

The transitoriness of the world and the human condition are also expressed in the Old English lyrics called elegies, of which *The Wanderer* is an outstanding example. Heroic poems most often treat the deeds of a band of warriors, whether in victory or defeat, but another theme of heroic poetry is that of exile, in which a hero is outlawed or banished from the community of warriors. Sigemund, whose adventures are referred to in one of the inset songs in *Beowulf* (lines 883–96), is such a hero. The isolation of the narrators and the bleak landscapes and seascapes of *The Wanderer* and *The Wife's Lament* focus on the inner world of the exile, where all men and women are searching for a new lord or the one from whom they are separated.

The Anglo-Saxon Chronicle

As pointed out in the headnote, the *Chronicle* was begun in the Anglo-Saxon period but was continued at Peterborough into the twelfth century. The "Obituary of William the Conqueror," compared with King Alfred's Preface to his translation of the *Pastoral Care*, can provide dramatic insight into the effects of the Norman Conquest. Alfred's efforts—to restore the learning that in Alcuin's time had made England a light to other nations and also to make that learning available in the vernacular—contrast sharply with William's raw exercise of power, as seen by the English chronicler, especially the king's cruel enforcement of the game laws. Although no doubt the chronicler expresses English bias against the Conqueror, his rhyme serves as a covert protest against Norman feudalism. See the Online Archive for other selections from the *Chronicle* on Norman usurpation of English monasteries and the breakdown of law and order under King Stephen.

Further Resources

NORTON ONLINE ARCHIVE

The Anglo-Saxon Chronicle
  [Henry of Poitou Becomes Abbot of Peterborough]
  [The Reign of King Stephen]

Thomas of Britain and Marie de France

Both of these authors illustrate the assimilation by Anglo-Norman poets of Celtic tales that would ultimately shape the forms and themes of medieval romance in both English and other European literatures. You may want to treat their works individually, compare them with one another, or discuss them in connection with *Sir Gawain and the Green Knight* and Malory's *Morte Darthur* as examples of early-medieval romance and of Arthurian literature in particular. In those connections, you also have access with Norton Topics Online, "King Arthur," to selections from Chrétien de Troyes, another founder of medieval romance, and to Malory's principal source, the French *Prose Vulgate Cycle* of Arthurian romance.

The Tristran romances, among which that of Thomas is the most influential, are the first to develop the conflict of loyalties in which the best knight becomes the passionate lover of his lord's lady. Much of the plot revolves around the knight and lady arranging meetings and avoiding detection. Indeed, the passion is to a great extent fueled by overcoming the inevitable times of separation and the brevity of the encounters. Marie's brief lay *Chevrefoil* poignantly captures that brevity and intensity. Nowhere is the intensity of the love that joins the lovers more powerfully expressed than in the conclusion of Thomas's poem, where the final union is consummated by death. You may want to compare Thomas's handling of the deaths of Tristran and Isolt with the deaths of Guinevere and Lancelot at the end of Malory's *Morte Arthur*, where death follows the separation of the lovers after the death of Arthur.

Lanval

Medieval romance, of course, is not inevitably adulterous and does not always end tragically. A few romances, of which Marie's lay *Lanval* is perhaps the best example, resolve in a happy ending—not, however, in the conventional Arthurian world. Inevitably, the illustrious reputation of Arthurian chivalry was not always viewed with complete seriousness. In *Lanval*, Arthur is introduced as "the brave and courtly king" and his knights are the best "in all the world." Your students can have a good time discussing how Marie's dry wit proceeds to undercut this conventional estimate of Arthur and his court. Arthur neglects the foreign knight Lanval and turns out to be an uxorious husband trying to pacify his queen, who plays the part of Potiphar's wife (Genesis 39:7–23). Disorder in his kingdom is not so much caused by ravaging Scots and Picts (lines 7–8) as by petty jealousies within Camelot itself; the knights are not portrayed in war or in tournaments but in well-bred social activities and in a comical trial by jury that keeps getting interrupted. In this romance, it is not the knight who rescues the lady, but the lady who rescues the knight, who is last seen riding off seated behind her on her "milkwhite horse." A later ballad about a minstrel called Thomas Rhymer, who is abducted by "the Queen of fair Elfland" mounted on a "milk-white steed," spells out alternative endings:

"O see ye not yon narrow road
  So thick beset with thorns and briars?
That is the path of righteousness,
  Though after it but few inquires.

"And see ye not that braid, braid road
  That lies across that lily leven?
That is the path of wickedness,
  Thou some call it the road to heaven.

"And see not ye that bonny road
  That winds about the ferny brae?
That is the road to fair Elfland
  Where thou and I this night maun gae."

Further Resources

NORTON ONLINE ARCHIVE

Marie de France, Fables
  The Wolf and the Lamb
  The Wolf and the Sow

Ancrene Riwle (Rule for Anchoresses)

The author tells us in a preface addressed to the sisters (an abridged text of the preface is available in *NTO*) that the rule was written at their request. The selection illustrates the mutual influence of the forms of medieval religion and romance. The anchoress's cell is by no means safe from the temptations of the world but is like a castle besieged by enemies. That topos generates the author's allegory of the Christ-knight who comes to the defense of a lady who dwells in a "castle of clay" (i.e., the body). Like the proud mistresses in romances, the lady is hard of heart and rejects the love of the knight who fights for her and finally dies for her sake. The parable concludes with an allegory of the crucifix as a shield raised in our defense.

Further Resources

NORTON TOPICS ONLINE

Medieval Estates and Orders: Making and Breaking Rules
  From the Introduction to Ancrene Riwle

Sir Gawain and the Green Knight

The poet of *Sir Gawain and the Green Knight,* writing late in the fourteenth century in the northwest of Britain, takes stock of a romance tradition that was already three hundred years old in his time. He begins where Geoffrey of Monmouth did with Aeneas, framing his poem at the beginning and end with references to "the books of Brutus' deeds" (lines 1–26 and 2523). Although the poet evokes the legendary history of Britain, he also clearly recognizes his story as what we have come to call "romance" by calling it an "adventure," "a marvel," one of Arthur's "wonders," "a tale of derring-do." Yet, in another way, he sets his story in the fourteenth century through his elaborate descriptions of contemporary costume, armor, and architecture. The moral questions it raises about the meaning of chivalry are also pertinent to the age in which he was living.

The military value of the heavily armored knight on horseback was declining in the late fourteenth century because of the tactical use of the longbow and the introduction of gunpowder. Nevertheless, although the actual usefulness of the knight on the battlefield was diminishing, the cult of chivalry was celebrated more spectacularly than ever in heraldry, ceremony, and spectacle. Edward III and his people were passionately fond of tournaments and pageantry. He did not carry out his plan of founding a new order of the Round Table, but he did establish the Order of the Garter, which remains the highest honor the English monarchy can bestow. When Arthur's knights adopt the green girdle as their badge of honor, either the poet himself or the scribe was reminded of the motto of the Garter, "Hony Soyt Qui Mal Pense," which is inscribed below the text in the unique manuscript of the poem.

In the New Year's Day celebration at Arthur's court, at the beginning of the story, the poet observes the gay entertainment of the youthful court— the jousting, the dancing, the laughter, the exchange of gifts, and the games—with an amused eye, much as Marie de France had viewed the knights and ladies celebrating Saint John's Day. The Green Knight mocks that scene when he playfully asks the king to grant him a "game," which challenges the court's reputation for chivalry. Gawain's "adventure" is, therefore, a test not only of his own knighthood but of the court and, in a larger sense, of the worth of chivalry itself. The essence of chivalry is supposedly truth, as proclaimed by the pentangle on Gawain's shield. In fourteenth-century English, *truth* meant not only truthfulness but "troth," or fidelity. Very much aware of that, Gawain is anxious to demonstrate his fidelity by keeping what he thinks will be his fatal appointment at the Green Chapel. But as it turns out, his "troth" will be tested in ways he does not expect. The poet passes cursorily over Gawain's adventures on the way to keep his appointment on New Year's Day, but he makes us feel Gawain's isolation and the winter hardship, not just of the knight sleeping in his armor but of the birds "That peeped most piteously for pain of the cold" (line 747). On Christmas morning, the action shifts from the winter wilderness to the bedroom, where the hero thinks he is defending himself against the advances of the lady; she counters his resistance by mockingly questioning his reputation as a lover. Can this be the Gawain she has heard so much about? When Gawain comes to face what he believed all along to be the real test, he does not realize, nor do most readers, that the real test is already over and that he has, at least partly, failed it. But Gawain will be absolved, and the failure will bring him to humility instead of the polite modesty that he professed in accepting the Green Knight's challenge. Instead of actually dying under the Green Knight's ax, Gawain is, in a sense, reborn—with a new awareness of his vulnerability to pride and self-deception, which he now recognizes as a potential pitfall of the chivalry to which he aspired.

Gawain *and French Prose Romance*

In the second of the bedroom scenes in *Sir Gawain and the Green Knight*, the lady teasingly reproaches Gawain for his reluctance to make love to her as a knight is supposed to do:

> And name what knight you will, they are noblest esteemed
> For loyal faith in love, in life as in story;
> For to tell the tribulations of these true hearts,
> Why, 'tis the very title and text of their deeds,
> How bold knights for beauty have braved many a foe,
> Suffered heavy sorrows out of secret love. (lines 1512–17)

The *Gawain* poet's original audience might well have shared the lady's surprise at her knight's coyness if they had read about Gawain's amorous adventures in the thirteenth-century French prose romances, which were to become the sources of Sir Thomas Malory's *Morte Darthur*. In Malory, when the recently slain Gawain appears to Arthur in a dream to warn his uncle not to engage Mordred in battle, he is accompanied by "a number of fair ladies" for whom he has done battle "in righteous quarrels." In Tennyson's *Idylls of the King*, Sir Bedivere, in the same context, makes Gawain's reputation as a philanderer more explicit: "Light was Gawain in life, and light in death / Is Gawain, for the ghost is as the man" (lines 56–57). In contrast, the young Gawain appears virginal in the anonymous English poet's romance. His only lady seems to be Mary, whose image is painted on the inside of his pentangle shield. The poet probably intended the surprise; in any case, Gawain's maneuvers to counter the lady's advances are part of the comedy.

Gawain and *Beowulf*

Like the *Beowulf* poet, the *Gawain* poet was an antiquarian in regard to language and style. Unlike *Beowulf*, *Sir Gawain and the Green Knight* does not dress up its warriors in ancient armor. Its characters do not hold pre-Christian beliefs, although some critics have seen vestiges of primitive fertility cults in the Green Knight. A comparison between these works helps bring out the cultural gap between Germanic epic and medieval romance. The *Beowulf* poet can still imagine and sympathize with a deeply flawed heroic society that is nevertheless capable of brave and generous actions worthy of being remembered with admiration, love, and compassion. But it is a bleak world threatened within and without by forces of evil. Even the lighter moments in *Beowulf* have their dark underside.

While Heorot celebrates Beowulf's victory over Grendel with feasting and the singing of heroic lays, we can sense tensions that will eventually bring the great hall down in flames. The treasure Beowulf wins from the dragon, which he is eager to view as he lies dying, cannot save him or his people. It will be returned to the earth "as useless to men now as it ever was" (line 3168). There is plenty of irony in *Beowulf* but hardly any humor. The tone remains elevated and somber throughout. In contrast, the romance is filled with light comedy. There is a threatening air in the Green Knight's speech and appearance at Camelot, but there is also a grotesque humor when he holds up his severed head "and it lifted up its lids" (line 446). Wit is at work when the poet disdains to describe Gawain's heroic battles with serpents, wolves, wild men, and giants during his journey north only to bathetically expatiate, instead, upon the weather: "if the wars were unwelcome, the winter was worse, / When the cold clear rains rushed from the clouds" (726–27). In the Christmas celebration at the castle, one may feel a slight queasiness when the traditional boar's head is carried in (line 1616) if one happens to think of Sir Gawain's bargain with the Green Knight. The plot suggests that the source of civilization, with all its shining lights and glorious costumes pledged against what is dark and brutal, lies in the heroism not of strong arms, but of good manners, wit, and elegance.

The Alliterative Tradition in Middle English

Despite vast changes in the English language and in literary and poetic forms following the Norman Conquest, poetry in Middle English never entirely lost touch with the Old English alliterative tradition. The principal examples of Middle English alliterative verse in *NAEL* are *Sir Gawain and the Green Knight* and *Piers Plowman*.

Not only did the *Gawain* poet and his audience respond to the alliterative beat of the old Germanic epic (though the line had been greatly modified since Anglo-Saxon times), but they must still have understood many archaic words that belonged to the poetic diction of the *Beowulf* poet. The effect of the vocabulary is, of course, lost in translation, but a look at the Middle English of the opening stanza of *Sir Gawain and the Green Knight* gives a fair sample of this poet's word-hoard, which you may want to pause over briefly with your students. In line 1, "Sege" (siege), "assaut" (assault), "sesed" (ceased) are French loan words; in line 2, "borgh" (city, -burgh), "brittened" (crumbled), "brondes" (brands), "askes" (ashes) are Germanic. The form of "askes" is Scandinavian, reflecting the influence of Danish settlement in the north of England, as do "tulk" (man), "biges" (builds), "bonkkes" (banks), "wrake" (revenge), "blunder" (strife), "skete" (swiftly), and "skyfted" (shifted). In part, the archaisms of the poem can be attributed to its regional dialect. But it is also clear that the *Gawain* poet, like the *Beowulf* poet, was fond of old and obscure words and deliberately played with the greatly increased lexicon that English, by the end of the fourteenth century, had acquired through Scandinavian, French, and Latin borrowings.

Quick Read

- Genre: Arthurian chivalric romance, but with a surprisingly chaste Gawain.
- Prosody: Part of the alliterative revival in Middle English of the fourteenth century; long stanzas of long lines plus the end-rhymed bob and wheel.
- Style: Ornate long lines, affected archaisms, courtly indirection and wit, shifts of tense and of tone.
- Imagery: Color (especially green) and the lack of it; the castle like a cut-paper centerpiece for a party table (801); long examples of effictio: the elaborate description of the appearances of the Green Knight (136), Gawain (566), and Lady Bercilak together with Morgan le Faye (941).
- Ritual and Ceremony: Feasts, courtly dialogue, masses, contracts, kisses, hunting.
- Key Passages: *Translatio imperii*, 1; ecphrasis of Gawain's shield, 619; Gawain's tribulations en route, 718; the game proposed, 1105; the dressing of the deer, 1327; the kisses redelivered, 1388, 1639, 1936; the Green Knight's revelation, 2338; Gawain's public interpretation of his belt, 2505.
- Key Words: Truth/troth, courtesy, dress (both persons and slain animals are "dressed").

Teaching Clusters

The Legend of Arthur and **Medieval Sexuality.** Chaucer's *Wife of Bath's Tale* is another Arthurian romance that takes sexual misbehavior (which it characterizes more gravely as rape) as an opportunity to think about ethics and class politics, but from a quite different perspective that makes a good comparison.

Discussion Questions

1. What does the opening, about nation-building, have to do with the rest of the poem?
2. The kisses Gawain delivers to Lord Bercilak are more than perfunctory; what does queer eroticism contribute to the poem?
3. Articulate a theme in Gawain and find it epitomized in one or more striking images.
4. Why is it a girdle and not some other article of clothing—a glove, a sock, a necklace?
5. Why are the images of truth (the pentangle) and chastity (Mary's face) painted on a shield and not, instead, some other article of arms?
6. Manners—eating, dressing, talking—carry a heavy weight of meaning in the poem. How are they reflected in its form (the feast topos, the passages of *effictio*, or description, the dialogues)? What do they mean?

7. Antithesis is a major feature of the double *effictio* at line 941, yet the descriptions of the two women are deliberately enmeshed. So?
8. What role does the feminine play in Gawain's identity?
9. The interlacing of the hunting and bedroom scenes follows a romance plot convention and is a prominent feature of the poem. How are we invited to respond?
10. What qualifies one to be a hero like Gawain in this poem? Compare the poem's depiction of heroism to the heroic in other literary works.

Further Resources

NORTON ONLINE ARCHIVE
Pearl

NORTON TOPICS ONLINE

King Arthur: Romancing Politics
   Chrétien de Troyes
   Yvain or the Knight with the Lion
   The Knight of the Cart
   The Prose Vulgate Cycle
   The Prose Lancelot
   The Quest for the Holy Grail
   The Death of Arthur
   The Wedding of Sir Gawain and Dame Ragnelle

Geoffrey Chaucer

The Canterbury Tales

Chaucer's great poem seems designed for classroom use because it readily falls into such interesting and self-sufficient units and because there are so many ways those units can fit with others on your syllabus. *The General Prologue* is itself a catalog of portraits that can be pillaged according to the needs of your course. You might want to be sure to cover the pilgrims whose tales you assign, but it is also interesting to assign others, or to assign the Wife, for instance, after reading her tale, so that the story is not reduced to dramatic characterization. One might strive instead for social variety or for degrees of satire (from the idealized Parson to the vicious Pardoner). Similarly, no logic insists that you assign any particular tale. The tales chosen here are digestible in length and vocabulary, wonderfully various in genre, style, and topic, and fun. A creative exercise asking students to translate the matter of one tale into the genre of another (fabliau to romance, for instance) can clarify both textual details and the vivid emotional and intellectual effects that Chaucer can produce.

The General Prologue

The famous opening passage of *The General Prologue* draws all of nature and all of England together in the great annual movement of physical and spiritual rebirth. You might ask your students about the syntax of the first sentence of *The General Prologue* (a tour de force of eighteen lines). Why should the movements of nature be set into the same sentence as processes of culture? Why should the natural and animal world be set into the subordinate clause, while the religious practice occupies the main clause? Why should "corages" rhyme with "pilgrimages" at the sentence's shift from subordinate to main clause? Lines 19–42 provide a rich comparison and contrast with lines 1–18: if in the first sentence Chaucer presents the world of cosmic necessity, happening every year in the cycle of nature, in the second sequence he presents instead a world of chance and human agreement, all seen from a specifiable, individual perspective.

The final sequence of *The General Prologue* offers rich reflections on the status of literature and the way in which literature is produced. The literary competition proposed by the Host takes place "by the way," on the road to Canterbury (i.e., within the shadow of higher purposes). The most the winner will receive is a free meal (rather less in value than the eternal life promised by the pilgrimage). The competition is designed to produce no more than "comfort" (i.e., pleasure) by a mixture of "sentence" and "solace," by which the Host means a mixture of literary meaning and literary pleasure. It is significant that everyone agrees to participate in the competition: the tale-telling is itself a contractual event, with a leader chosen by consent. This apparently democratic society does nevertheless respect social distinctions and hierarchies: the Host asks the Knight to draw the first lot; and by chance the Knight draws the lot that permits him to speak first, thus preserving a social hierarchy, even if that hierarchy will be disrupted immediately after *The Knight's Tale* by the Miller.

Ideal and Satiric Portraits in the Prologue

Three portraits—those of the Knight, the Parson, and the Plowman—establish a standard; when measured against it, all the others fall short in varying degrees. The Parson and his brother, the Plowman, are presented as admirable examples of two worthwhile occupations. Some critics have argued, on the basis of what actually happened on the Crusades in which the Knight participated, that Chaucer is also satirizing him as a mercenary. On the other hand, it is possible to think that Chaucer viewed warring on the frontiers of Christendom, just as Malory still did a hundred years later, as righteous wars in contrast with the French wars (from the mid-fourteenth to the mid-fifteenth centuries) or the Wars of the Roses (1455–85)—wars among Christians in which Chaucer and Malory had actually participated.

Other pilgrims are portrayed more or less critically, though sympathetically. The Prioress is not guilty of serious abuses of her office. The satire is mild and based mainly on her ladylike qualities, such as her impeccable table manners, which are not necessarily attributes that make her an ideal Mother Superior of a convent. It has been pointed out that a few phrases in the portrait—"simple and coy," "yën greye as glas," "mouth . . . softe and reed"—are conventional features of heroines in medieval romances. She bends a few rules, for example, by keeping pet dogs, which she spoils by feeding them the finest bread, and perhaps even by leaving her convent to go on a pilgrimage at all. A delicate ambiguity hovers around her spirituality. Does the *Amor* engraved on her brooch emblematize spiritual love, as her office requires, or is Chaucer hinting at her attachment to worldly things?

In the portraits of the Monk and the Friar, which, with the portrait of the Prioress, make up a group portrait of the regular clergy, i.e., those subject to a *regula* or rule, the abuses become increasingly serious and the satire increasingly sharp. As a huntsman and inspector of monastic properties, the portly monk is hardly ever in his monastery, and he condemns the rule of Saint Augustine, bidding a monk to stay in the cloister, as out of date. "How shall the world be served?" he asks rhetorically (line 187). Are monks supposed to be serving the world, and how is *this* monk serving it?

Several double-entendres about the Monk's hunting hint broadly that he does not keep his vow of chastity. In the case of the Friar, his seemingly charitable arrangements for many a marriage of young women "at his owene cost" suggest that these women were victims of his seductions (lines 212–13). He can well afford to set them up because the income from his licensed begging for charity exceeds what he turns over to his house. His worst abuse is that of the sacrament of confession, which he in effect sells to its consumers in return for a healthy donation.

The Summoner and Pardoner are laymen employed by the Church. The one is a corrupt bailiff who hauls persons before an ecclesiastical court for moral offenses if they do not buy him off; the other exchanges pardons and indulgences for "donations" (as well as doing a brisk business peddling fake relics) to obtain forgiveness for sins from the heavenly judge. It was the institution of pardons and indulgences that perhaps more than any other abuse of religion provided ammunition for the Protestant Reformation.

In each portrait, iconographical attributes are mixed with details that achieve a sense of verisimilitude. Chaucer manages to create lively personalities at the same time that he deftly deploys abstraction, symbol, and near-allegory. The tone of each portrait varies exquisitely, though students are often tempted to read them all as dryly satirical once they catch wind of Chaucer's sophistication.

The Host seems to manipulate the drawing of straws so that the Knight, the highest-ranking pilgrim, will tell the first tale. With *The Miller's Prologue*, however, the lower-ranking pilgrims begin to assert their social identities. We soon get into clashes—between the Host and the

Miller, the Miller and the Reeve, the Host and the Parson, the Wife of Bath and the Pardoner, the Wife and the Friar, the Pardoner and the Host—which have been described as social comedy.

Teaching Clusters

The General Prologue is a natural analogue to Langland's opening description of the fair field of folk. Any extended portrait, such as the ornate passages of physical description in *Sir Gawain and the Green Knight*, also bears comparison to Chaucer's portraits here. The opening and closing of the *Prologue*, when considered as a meditation on the constitution of society, might be compared with scenes of social contract from the Middle Ages to the present.

Quick Read

- Genre: Estates satire, literary portraiture, catalogue.
- Key Words: Worthy; felawshipe, accord, and other legal and commercial words, especially in 31–41 and 763 to the end.
- Style: Note the shift from the luxurious, high-style opening to a plainer discursive mode as the plot begins to move; a credulous tone, language that leans toward characters as if attracted to their worlds and values.
- Theme: What makes a community or society?
- Ritual and Ceremony: The (social) contract.
- Characterization: A careful mix of abstraction and verisimilitude; a wide social range (though no royal or aristocrat appears, and there is no representative of the large population of the very poor).

Discussion Questions

1. Does Chaucer draw on different vocabularies for his different portraits?
2. Does Chaucer draw on different values within each portrait? Where do they come from?
3. Describe the stylistic shifts that shape the lines before the portraits begin.
4. What vision of England does this group suggest?
5. Are you surprised when the long opening sentence gives "pilgrimages" as the object of folks' longings? What does the poem invite you to expect? Why would it do that?
6. Choose a portrait that is particularly visually evocative, and describe Chaucer's appeals to the eye.
7. What role does Chaucer suggest for the poet?

The Miller's Tale

Although Chaucer slyly pretends that the Miller's fabliau is "a cherles tale," the narrative voice is not that of the drunken Miller but that of the poet satirizing the courtly affectations of the costume, manner, speech, and behavior of the petit bourgeois characters. The wooing of both Nicholas and Absolon satirizes the typical language and gestures of courtly lovers, and of course Alison, whom they are pursuing, is not a lady. The genre of *The Miller's Tale* is fabliau (plural *fabliaux*): a short, funny, often bawdy narrative in low style, imitated and developed from French models. These are narratives in which those who win do so not through virtue (as in a moral exemplum) or through virtue coupled with high birth (as in romance). Winners are instead the clever, and often the young and attractive clever. Fabliaux are stories about material gain and bodily comfort for the winners, and the reverse for losers. Such "justice" as they represent is concerned only with getting even, or, to use Chaucer's term, "quiting." Their narrative style is streamlined, focusing as it does on those objects that will be used (e.g., tubs and hot pokers). They are unembarrassed about mentioning bodily parts unmentionable in romance. These stories are, in short, materialist, representing a world of material facts and needs to be exploited by the clever.

Teaching Clusters

The mystery plays include religious materials and comedy together in an urban setting and were a source for Chaucer. As Chaucer of course intended, reading other of his tales next to the Miller's (e.g., the Nun's Priest's, which exhibits a different sort of skepticism about learning) can clarify the tale's strategies and style. The blazon of Alison is perfect against the blazons of *Sir Gawain and the Green Knight*, or in conjunction with many Renaissance lyric poems (e.g., Campion's "There is a garden in her face").

Quick Read

- Genre: Fabliau with lots of allusions to Bible stories, perhaps by means of the mystery play.
- Setting: Oxford, with well-described urban architecture: the house with a shot-window (small casement) onto the street, the barn, the church, a smithy; university buildings do not appear.
- Key Words: Versions of "privee" appear some fourteen times (plus its near synonym "derne"), meaning secret, arcane, intimate, unknown, private, clandestine, discreet, stealthy, and the like, comically tying together the specialized scholarly knowledge of Nicholas, sexual behaviors, notions of manners, theological mysteries, marriage, town gossip and publicity, and perhaps even the privy.
- Lexis: Some romance words of mock-delicacy collide with salty terms for body parts like "ers," "queynte," "buttok," "haunche-boon," "hole."
- Key Passages: The blazon of Alison, lines 125–62; Absolon's aubade, 590; sexual euphemism, 444–48.
- Tropes: Nice puns on "queynte" (167–68, a rime riche); "berde," during the famous kiss (629, 634).

Discussion Questions

1. Can we compare the fabliau's vision of the human body to that of the romance?
2. What is the religious material doing in this dirty story?
3. Are all the characters punished at the end? According to poetic justice, where does each of their faults lie?
4. What view of the "private" does the story present?
5. Does it matter that the story is set in Oxford? Why don't we see any university buildings?
6. What, exactly, do Alison and Nicholas enjoy?
7. Compare the fabliau's vision of sexuality to that of the romance.

The Wife of Bath's Prologue

Sexual ideology, economic independence, and marital power are the crucial concerns of the Wife of Bath. Her *Prologue* deals with her stubborn refusal to let herself be exploited by a society where women have no education and few liberties under the law, and where rich old men acquire young girls as property. The most important of the antifeminist sources the Wife's fifth husband alludes to in the tale's prologue is Saint Jerome's *Epistle against Jovinian* (see the headnote). Relevant excerpts from the latter can be found in a useful volume, *Chaucer: Sources and Backgrounds*, edited by R. P. Miller. Excerpts from the speech of the Old Woman, a character in Jean de Meun's part of the *Romance of the Rose* who was a model for the Wife of Bath, may be found in *NTO*.

The Wife of Bath is a controversial character on the pilgrimage. She is mocked and patronized in her *Prologue* by the Pardoner and the Friar. The Clerk dedicates an ironic envoy to her at the end of his tale. A character in *The Merchant's Tale* cites her as an authority on the miseries of getting married. She has been interpreted by some scholars as an incarnation of the sins of the flesh and the scourge of husbands. Perhaps the more common tendency today is to regard her as a proto-feminist heroine who is fighting against and, to a degree, triumphing over a patriarchal system that considers women fair game for disparagement and violence. You and your students can argue for or against either of these views in class, or you may prefer the position that Chaucer is, as so often, trying to have it both ways. However, it is difficult not to sympathize with the resentment the Wife feels toward the men she married and the clerks who wrote diatribes demonizing women, and difficult not to admire her intellectual audacity, her courage, her will, her staying power, and her love of life.

Teaching Clusters

Medieval Sexuality and the Social Spectrum of Medieval Literature.
The Wife of Bath's Prologue verges on what we later call dramatic monologue and bears comparison with Chaucer's other great prologue of this kind, the Pardoner's. Some of its themes reappear in the *Nun's Priest's*

Tale, especially questions about literary authority and interpretation. Any text that raises issues about sexual ideology and its regulation by social institutions benefits from juxtaposition with the Wife's logic.

Quick Read

- Genre: Antifeminist satire (or a critique of antifeminist satire?).
- Verse-form: Rhyming pentameter couplets.
- Characters: A wife and her five husbands: three old, plus two young.
- Sections: Lines 1–168: the Wife's defense of multiple marriages, in which she deploys the learned argument of men against learned male authorities. Lines 199–508: the Wife's remembrance of how she exploited her first four husbands. Lines 509–834: the Wife's narration of her fifth marriage, with Jankyn, in which the matrimonial struggle is different from her previous marriages in two ways. She loves Jankyn (a dangerous position for the Wife to be in), and he is learned himself, taking particular pleasure in stories drawn from the antifeminist tradition about wicked wives.
- Thesis: "Experience, though noon auctoritee / Were in this world, is right enough for me / To speke of the wo that is in mariage." In fact, the Wife draws liberally on both textual authority and her own personal experience to speak of the woe and the intense competitiveness of marriage.
- Style: The Wife uses learned language when it suits her and, in the narration of her marriages, the down-to-earth, urban language of fabliaux.

Discussion Questions

1. Is the Wife an example of the antifeminist tradition, or is she a counter to it?
2. Or, to put the same question another way, does the *Wife of Bath's Prologue* belong in Jankyn's book of wicked wives, or does it effectively tear the antifeminist tradition apart?
3. How does the Wife manipulate argument and textual authority? Is she justified in manipulating texts and argument in the way she does?
4. Does the Wife expose power relations that are inevitable in marriage?
5. Is the Wife capable of imagining any alternative to the exercise of absolute power by either husband or wife in marriage?
6. How acute is the Wife about why so few stories of good wives exist?
7. Is the *Prologue* simply about one woman's history, or is it also about how literary tradition is determined by structures of power?

The Wife of Bath's Tale

The Wife of Bath's Tale is an elegant Arthurian romance of a kind folklorists call the "loathly lady" tale, which students may recognize from the *Shrek* films. It includes the motif of the fairy bride and the inversion of gender roles that are important in *Lanval* and is wonderful to read on its own as well as in conjunction with the Wife's *Prologue*. When they read it first, students are able to see the brilliance of the tale apart from its uneven role in characterization. The tale includes a long sermon (given as pillow talk) on the topic of true "gentilesse" (nobility, qualifying to be upperclass, niceness). It's helpful to prepare your students by alerting them to its beginning, end, and themes before they read, so that they don't drown in it. They may be surprised by its argument if they subscribe to modern prejudices about medieval worship of hierarchies.

Teaching Clusters

Medieval Sexuality and the **Legend of Arthur.** *Lanval* makes a good partner to the Wife's *Tale*. As a feminist Arthurian romance, the *Tale* nicely accompanies (and exposes) *Sir Gawain and the Green Knight* and Malory's *Morte Darthur*, which both view women rather unsympathetically. The rape makes it a good counterpart to Gower's *Tale of Philomena and Tereus*. Spenser's Britomart, the heroine of her own Arthurian romance, reinforces Chaucer's feminism when, in the House of Busirane, she investigates the ways that literary discourses of love constrain and contort women's sexuality.

Quick Read

- Genre: Breton lay; brief Arthurian romance in loosely iambic pentameter couplets; while the long didactic sermon is untypical of romance, it does expand on issues central to the genre.
- Primary Sections: First half of the poem is public, roaming widely; second half takes place in bed.
- Topics: What women want; the nature of true class (gentilesse), what makes a good marriage, what makes beauty.
- Key Words: "Lere" (916, 988, 1000), gentilesse, list/lust/liking/pleasance, maistrye.
- Structuring Images: Midas's ears.
- Set-pieces: The Midas exemplum (956–88); sermon on "gentilesse" (1115–82); on poverty (1183–1212); on age and ugliness (1213–22).

Discussion Questions

1. What about those ass's ears? What does "beastliness" represent in this poem?
2. What *do* women want? (Technically, this is a romance *demande d'amour*—a question for discussion.)
3. What makes the lady beautiful?
4. Does she give up her "maistrye" at the end or retain it?
5. "Maistrye" over what? Can more than one person "have" it in a relationship?

6. What does the knight learn? Does he earn his happy fate?
7. Does this change your understanding of medieval ideas of social order or class?
8. Compare this Guinevere to those in *Sir Gawain and the Green Knight* and Malory.
9. Why does Chaucer include the faery dance of beautiful ladies?
10. Would it change the poem if the bachelor knight were named "Gawain"? (He is, in a wonderful parallel version of the story, available in *NTO, Sir Gawain and Dame Ragnell.*)
11. Why is the second half of the poem set in bed? Compare it to the bedroom scenes in *Sir Gawain and the Green Knight.*
12. In this story, what kind of crime is rape?
13. Why should the hard-headed bourgeois Wife choose a romance about aristocrats ending happily ever after for her tale?

The Pardoner's Tale

The Pardoner is a confidence man, a vice figure whose monologue reveals his tricks. The literary confession seems oddly appropriate to an agent of the Church's sacrament of penance, except that he boasts rather than expressing regretful penitence, and then tries his just-revealed tricks on his audience, the other pilgrims. The Pardoner's text dramatizes philosophy's "liar's paradox" (can a liar tell the truth?), bringing it into a theological and administrative arena with high stakes for the medieval Church (can a valid sacrament of penance include a sinful Pardoner?). In literary terms, students can pose a similar question with regard to satire, Chaucer's mode here: Does satire's portrayal of vice cause us to reform, or teach us to do worse?

This text opens up under many different approaches. Like *The Wife of Bath's Prologue*, the Pardoner invites us to interpret speech psychologically as a revelation of self (something Chaucer probably learned by translating the *Roman de la Rose*). The tale, particularly the mysteriously symbolic figure of the Old Man, can be read as expressing the Pardoner's despair and secret longing for absolution; the Old Man's apostrophe to his mother the earth, the sexual aggression of the Host, and the kiss of peace at the end can be read, with or without *The General Prologue* portrait of the Pardoner, for their sexual suggestiveness. The queerness of his body resonates with the image in his sermon text "*Radix malorum est cupiditas*" ("Cupidity is the root of evil"), where the "root" of avarice issues in evil, just as the tree at the center of the tale issues, as the Old Man predicts, in the death of the three rowdies. Sexual perversions of various kinds were excoriated in medieval doctrine because they were practices that did not "bear fruit." Botanical images suit the sermon, which claims that death entered the world through Adam's eating of fruit and which is organized around the three "sins of the mouth," gluttony, gambling, and false oaths. The mouth and the digestive system create an important theme here, linking actions like speaking, eating, and kissing to the sermon and serving as the occasion for lots of disgust. The sermon's main exemplum is a tour de force, a brilliant short story whose plotting bears close attention (and is borrowed by John Huston's 1948 *The Treasure of the Sierra Madre*, starring Humphrey Bogart). Rhetorical approaches that ask how the Pardoner's speech has the power to fleece his audience can be extended, too, into asking how Chaucer affects us with this portrayal.

Teaching Clusters

Literature and the Medieval Church and its means of salvation. Chaucer's use of disgusting images of consumption and the body makes this text a good comparison to Julian of Norwich's different appeals to disgust. *The Wife of Bath's Prologue* is a fruitful comparison if the two are treated as psychological portraits or if the question of the use and abuse of religious doctrine and sexual ideology is raised. Comparison with Passus 5–7 of *Piers Plowman* will produce rich reflection on the idea of pardon.

Quick Read

- Genre: Literary confession, inserted sermon with exempla, sales pitch, monologue, anticlerical satire.
- Theme: Just as the man says "*Radix malorum est cupiditas*," his sermon goes on to preach against the three sins of the mouth.
- Rhetoric: Apostrophe—a sudden turn to address an absent person or inanimate object and a reflection of the Pardoner's scorn for and reliance upon others.
- Style: Bombastic, taunting, allusive, exclamatory, fast "ordinary" speech.
- Key Word: Entente (115, 120, 135, 144, and more).

Discussion Questions

1. How does Chaucer craft our responses to the Pardoner? When are we drawn to him; when do we recoil?
2. What is the relation between the prologue and the tale?
3. Find some images that help to bind the poem together and explain their significance.
4. Does the Pardoner's exposé of his own vice invite us to be better or worse?
5. How can we assess sexual orientation six centuries gone?
6. If we say the Pardoner is a homosexual, how does that affect our reading of the poem?
7. What is the quest vowed by the three "riotours"? (To kill Death.) Is it wrong to imitate Christ?
8. What are the different registers of tone employed by the Pardoner?
9. Work out the significance of the "turd-shrine" at the end of the poem.
10. How does the old man who longs for death affect us?
11. Is this poem a criticism of the Church?

The Nun's Priest's Tale

The Nun's Priest tells a rhetorically ornate and accomplished tale about chickens. The tale centers on a household that consists entirely of females with one exception: the rooster Chauntecleer. Chauntecleer rules the roost, that is to say, his seven hens who are "his sustres and his paramours." His favorite wife is "faire damoisele Pertelote." Chauntecleer and Pertelote have a few romance trappings—Chauntecleer's colors and martial bearing have chivalric associations and are blazoned; Pertelote's sententious words on what all women desire (lines 92–97) suggest that she, like Sir Bertilak's lady, has read romances. But the academic argument that she has with Chauntecleer, in which she refutes the epic and tragic intimations he sees in his dream by diagnosing its cause as indigestion, makes her sound more like the Wife of Bath arguing with one of her husbands. In his rebuttal of Pertelote, Chauntecleer behaves like a clerk, overwhelming her with a long string of authorities on dream lore. But though he appears to trump her, he submits to her charms and pays for his arrogance—or his affection?—with a close call.

In moralizing his fable, the Nun's Priest, who is the Prioress's confessor but her social inferior, momentarily strays into the standard antifeminist narrative:

> Wommenes conseils been ful ofte colde,
> Wommanes conseil broughte us first to wo,
> And made Adam fro Paradis to go,
> Ther as he was ful merye and wel at ese.

Then he quickly recovers:

> But for I noot to whom it might displese
> If I conseil of wommen wolde blame,
> Passe over, for I saide it in my game—
> Rede auctours where they trete of swich matere,
> And what they sayn of wommen ye may heere—
> Thise been the cokkes wordes and nat mine:
> I can noon harm of no womman divine. (lines 436–46)

Antifeminism is just one of the many kinds of medieval writing that Chaucer sends up in *The Nun's Priest's Tale*. Others include dream lore, philosophy, epic, proverbs, scriptural exegesis, bestiaries, and, of course, fables. The narrator almost buries the tale under sententious commentary that parodies the habit of medieval preachers and poets to find multiple meanings and morals in everything. Parody does not exclude affection for the works that are being parodied. Part of the tale's charm lies in Chaucer's delight in the pretensions of the kinds of language he is employing. There is some danger that students will find some of the parody more tedious than amusing. The verses quoted above about "wommenes conseil," for which the tale disclaims all responsibility, are plain enough.

Other passages, like the musings about predestination (lines 414–31)—
whether Chauntecleer's fate is a case of simple or conditional necessity—
may be harder to digest. Tell your students that if they cannot "bulte it to
the bren" like the priest they "need nat han to do of swich matere." The
point here is to hear the voices, not to follow the logic. The speakers are,
after all, chickens. This is a good poem to "act" out loud—one might divide a class into groups and practice speeches—because to dramatize it
you have to figure out what the speech acts are. Is this speech a stretch of
nagging, a bid for reconciliation, or an angry refusal? Is this one a concerned warning, a dominating putdown, or an expression of affection?
And so forth.

Teaching Clusters

Animal poems, rhetoric, and moral exemplum. The poem is interesting
to compare with other beast fables (Henryson's, for example), with poems
that raise issues about textual authority and interpretation (the *Wife of
Bath's Prologue*), with dream visions (*Piers Plowman*), and with portrayals
of heterosexual couples and power (e.g., the *Wife of Bath's Tale*).

Quick Read

- Genre: Beast fable, mock-tragedy (the fall), comic short story.
- Lexis: Fancy, Latinate, technical dream theorizing.
- Favorite Topoi: Blazon of Chauntecleer, apostrophe, exemplum,
  epic simile.
- Style: High style comically unsuited to low matter, characters,
  action.
- Theme: Interpretation—of dreams, of authority, of stories.

Discussion Questions

1. What does the poem suggest about literary interpretations and
   criticism?
2. Why does Chauntecleer translate "mulier est hominis confusio" (line
   344) the way he does?
3. What are the values upheld by the beast fable as a genre? How does
   Chaucer demonstrate or correct those values?
4. Why explore grave philosophical issues in a fiction about chickens?
5. Why not write this one in an Aesopian plain style?

The Parson's Introduction and Chaucer's Retraction

Although *The Canterbury Tales* remains unfinished and Chaucer was in
the process of revising it, creating new tales and links, reassigning tales
already written to different tellers, and inventing a roadside incident that
introduces a new teller (the Canon's Yeoman), *The Parson's Tale* was at
some time put in place to be the final story to "knitte up wel," as the Host

calling on him says, "a greet matere." In effect, the Parson takes over from the Host as the leader of the pilgrims and abandons storytelling for spiritual guidance. His "tale" turns out to be a sermon on the seven deadly sins, a work Chaucer may have translated at an earlier time as he did the other philosophical and religious prose works he cites in his Retraction. That is not to say that the Parson's Introduction does not retain an element of comedy in the Parson's rejection of the "Rum-Ram-Ruf" of alliterative verse and rhyme. But clearly the road to Canterbury here takes a new and final turn.

Teaching Clusters

First, you may want to recall the Parson's portrait in *The General Prologue* and his altercation with the Host in *The Man of Law's Epilogue*, where he rebukes the Host for swearing and, in a very different tone, is put down by the Host, who sarcastically calls him a Lollard (lines 12–15).There are many opportunities for comparing Chaucer's treatment of the Parson with Langland's persistent angry anticlericalism shown in his *Prologue* (lines 83–86) and Piers Plowman's altercation with a priest in Passus 7.

Quick Read

- Genre: Sermon.
- Key Words: Sentence, fable, draf/whete, feste, pilgrimage.
- Form: Poetry vs. prose as media for doctrine.
- Setting: Sunset.

Discussion Questions

1. How would you compare and contrast Chaucer and Langland in their treatments of clerical abuses in their time?
2. Compare Chaucer's "Retraction" at the end of *The Canterbury Tales* with "The Dreamer Meets Conscience and Reason" from Langland's C-text. Langland writes of his life in London "Among lollers . . . and illiterate hermits." Chaucer probably ended his days dwelling among monks in Westminster Abbey. Could one argue that the Parson's *Prologue* is Chaucer's version of the encounter with Conscience and Reason?
3. Compare the conclusion of the *Canterbury Tales* with the conclusion of Julian of Norwich's *Book of Showings*. In the Parson's *Introduction*, does Chaucer, in his way, declare, "Love is our Lord's meaning" as Julian does in ending her work?

Troilus's Song

Courtly or Petrarchan love in both medieval and sixteenth-century literature revolves around an idealized love for a seemingly unattainable woman. In one typical conceit, the lady is a distant star; the lover, the storm-tossed ship that tries to steer by the star. The single best example of this kind of love in *NAEL*'s Middle Ages is "Troilus's Song," printed with Chaucer's lyrics. These elegant stanzas are a translation of one of the sonnets in Francis Petrarch's famous lyric sequence, which also inspired the sixteenth-century sonnets by Wyatt, Surrey, Sidney, Spenser, Shakespeare, and others. Chaucer wrote them for his great tragedy *Troilus and Criseyde*, where they are said to have been composed by Troilus to describe his conflicting emotions after he falls in love with Criseyde. In the fifteenth century, the stanzas were printed in some manuscripts in the way they are here, as a separate love poem. Full of paradox, pathos, and complaint, soaked in logically intricate imagery, this lyric inaugurates an Englishing of Petrarchan love poetry that fueled the explosion of the genre in the next centuries.

Teaching Chaucer in Middle English

Some users of *NAEL* prefer to teach Chaucer in translation because they believe there is not adequate time to teach Chaucer in Middle English. (A separate Norton booklet, in which all the Chaucer passages in the anthology are supplied in both the original language and interlinear translation, is available.) Other teachers believe that students stand to gain greater pleasure and knowledge by encountering even a limited number of the selections in *NAEL* in the original rather than by reading more of his works in translation. Students love to hear Chaucer read aloud; even if the instructor is not a specialist, it is well worth the effort to master a few passages to read to the class. The classic requirement that students memorize the first 18 lines of the *General Prologue* can be a good way to start, because it gives them rough and ready practice in pronunciation. It's not difficult to do, and many alumni have been heard to recite these lines with enduring pleasure.

A systematic presentation of Middle English is available in the *NAEL* introduction to the Middle Ages. One can always refer back to it; but to start with, students are probably just as well off coping with the glosses and notes and listening to the readings in the audio section of the Online Archive. You can obtain recordings of the Chaucer selections in *NAEL* in Middle English from the Chaucer Studio, Department of English, Brigham Young University, Provo UT 84602-6218, at a moderate price. You may request a printed catalog or view the catalog at English.byu.edu/Chaucer/. There are a number of good pronunciation tutorials online as well.

A few general points about Middle English's principal differences from Modern English can be helpful.

ME Phonology

1. Pronounce the long vowels the way you would in modern European languages—Spanish, French, Italian, German.
2. Pronounce consonants that have become silent, such as the *g* in *g-nat*; the *k* in *k-night*; the *l* in *fol-k*.
3. In combination with the vowels *a, o, u,* the letters *gh* had the sound of *ch* in the name of the German composer *Bach*; in combination with *e* and *i,* the letters *gh* had the sound of *ch* in the German noun *Licht* (light). If you have trouble with those sounds, you can leave them silent as in modern *thought* and *lit* (past participle of the verb *to light*), or they can be pronounced with the sound of *k,* in which case Middle English *nought* (not) sounds like *knocked* and Middle English *light,* like *licked,* pronounced at the back of the throat.
4. Pronounce *-e* as an unstressed syllable at the end of words, *unless* it would spoil the meter. This gets easier as one develops a feeling for the proper number of syllables in the line. The final *-e* is normally suppressed before words beginning with a vowel or *h.*

ME Grammar

1. The second-person singular pronoun is *thou* (nominative), *thee* (objective). The second-person plural pronoun is *ye* (nominative), *you* (objective). In Middle English the singular forms of address are familiar as in Spanish and French *tu,* German *Du;* the plural forms are formal as in *usted, vous, Sie.* In Chaucer the social distinction between these forms is often important in dialogue. For example, in *The Miller's Prologue* the Host addresses the lordly Monk as *ye,* but the churlish Miller as *thou* (lines 10, 27). Chauntecleer and Pertelote, being an aristocratic couple, address one another as *ye* and *you.*
2. The third-person singular feminine form (*her*) is *hir(e), her(e).*
3. The third-person plural possessive form (*their*) is like the feminine singular *hir.*
4. The third-person plural objective form (*them*) is *hem.*
5. A few nouns form their plural with *-n,* most frequently *yën* (eyes).
6. The ending *-st* in verbs is a sign of the second-person singular. The ending *-th* is usually a sign of the present-tense, third-person singular, but it also occurs in all persons of the present-tense plural and in the plural imperative. In the indicative, these endings remain standard in Shakespeare and in the King James translation of the Bible.
7. The plurals of verbs in the third person and infinitive may end in *-n.*
8. The prefix *y-* often marks the past participle. In later periods, the prefix was used (especially by Edmund Spenser) to give the style an archaic effect.
9. Sentence structure is more flexible than in Modern English. One will often find the subject or verb at the end of a sentence.

Pronouncing Middle English makes it much easier to understand it on the page. Students gain a good deal of confidence from having read some Chaucer in the original and are thereby better prepared for the language of Spenser, Shakespeare, and Milton.

Further Resources

NORTON ONLINE ARCHIVE

The Canterbury Tales
  The Franklin's Tale
    The Introduction
    The Prologue
    The Tale
  The Merchant's Tale
    The Introduction
    The Tale
    The Epilogue
  The Tale of Sir Thopas
    The Introduction
    The Tale
  From The Knight's Tale ["A Thoroughfare Full of Woe"]
  From The Monk's Tale
    [The Definition of Tragedy]
    [The Tragedy of Pierre de Lusignan]
  From The Parson's Tale [The Remedy Against Lechery]
From Troilus and Criseyde ["This Worlde that Passeth Soone . . ."]

Audio:
From The Canterbury Tales
  General Prologue, lines 1–18 (read by J. B. Bessinger, Jr.)
  General Prologue, the Miller, lines 547–68 (read by Alfred David)
  The Miller's Prologue (read by V. A. Kolve)
  The Miller's Tale, lines 163–98 (read by Alfred David)
  The Man of Law's Epilogue (read by V. A. Kolve)
  The Wife of Bath's Prologue, lines 1–29 (read by Marie Borroff)
  The Pardoner's Tale, lines 428–61 (read by Alfred David)
  The Nun's Priest's Tale, lines 337–66 (read by Alfred David)

John Gower

The Tale of Philomena and Tereus

Scandal and gore, horror and feminist threat: this is a cautionary tale, told by the confessor Genius to the rather meek confessing lover Amans in order to warn him not to become a sexual predator. It stands on its own as a gripping plot (see synopsis below) that probes the relation between trauma and voice (as did Gower's source, Ovid's *Metamorphoses* 6.426–676). Birdsong—because of its artistry long a figure for poetry—is here a music that can be made (like the tapestry) out of tragedy, rage, and violent desire. The confessional frame story turns that topic into a meditation on gender and sexual behavior. The issues of sexual violence and its representation are likely to be hot ones; you might take advantage of that and talk about whether sexual violence has a role in art (the art of the tapestry, of the birdsong, of the poem), and whether the purpose of art has anything to do with trauma. Where does metamorphosis fit in? Read the passage on the rape in class and notice the tropes used: poetic language metamorphoses its objects. What's the purpose of this poem's peculiar effects? Gower's surprising mix of the courteous and the horrific is a large part of the power of his tale. How does the poem move us and why? Here the discussion questions (below) that concern our moral responses to the characters and the action might be effective. One might ask students to compare this narrative of rape and/or female violence with others in the anthology (e.g., *Judith*; *The Wife of Bath's Tale*). One might also invite students to read and compare this narrative with its Ovidian source (*Metamorphoses* 6.426–676).

Teaching Clusters

Rape, violence, and power relations between the genders; the conditions in which narrative about marriage is produced. Genius's tale is a perfect, short counterpart to the tale told by Chaucer's Wife of Bath, which includes a rape, moral and bodily transformations, and a concern with women's voices. Gower is interested in the ability to speak; Chaucer emphasizes the ability to listen (the Wife's partial deafness is a result of her husband smacking her on the ear; the rapist knight must learn to hear women's desires).

Spenser's Masque of Cupid episode (*Faerie Queene*, Book 3, "of chastity," cantos 11–12) is another good partner in the classroom, because it shares Gower's stress on sisterhood in the face of male violence and is equally interested in the role trauma (particularly rape) plays in the creation of art (the tapestries, etc.). *Judith* provides another scene of female violence, but one with a political context. Gower's poem is full of well-wrought complaints (plaints, pleyning), a lyric form especially loved by early English writers; other examples of the complaint are "The Wife's Lament" and Chaucer's "Complaint to His Purse" and "Troilus's Song."

Other ways in which Gower resonates with our Chaucer selections: the theme of adultery is treated comically rather than tragically in the *Miller's Tale*; greed is treated viscerally by the Pardoner; and Chaucer's retraction sets up a literary version of a confession. *Piers Plowman* also includes a number of fictional confessions: see those of Envy and Gluttony. Another way of throwing Gower's poem into relief would be to compare it with other strong appeals to horror: to move her readers Julian of Norwich uses arresting and even disgusting images, which she juxtaposes with opposite evocations of care and sweetness. *Everyman* uses horror with a clear, effective purpose. Shocking and gruesome events suddenly punctuate Malory's courteous narrative.

Quick Read

- Prosody: Running iambic tetrameter couplets.
- Genre: Ovidian metamorphosis, confessional dialogue.
- Cast: Genius and Amans, Philomena and Progne (sisters, daughters of King Pandion of Athens), Tereus (king of Thrace, a knight, husband of Progne), Ithis (the son of Tereus and Progne).
- Plot Synopsis: Tereus rapes his wife's sister, cuts out her tongue. When Philomena reveals this by weaving a tapestry to send to her sister, Progne kills Ithis and serves him to his father in a stew. All three are changed into different birds by the gods.
- Key Passages: Philomena's internal complaint, 110–38; Progne's prayer of complaint to Cupid and Venus, 276–97; her petition to Apollo, 301–15; her public accusation of her husband, 370–82.
- Themes: The role of art in trauma and its transformative powers; sexual crimes, womanhood, and public speech.
- Tropes: The rape itself generates lots of linguistic ornament: the metaphor of fire that becomes the epic simile of 77–87, the simile (the wolf) in 88 and another extended simile (the goshawk) in 99–104. The tongue-shearing has him as a lion (139) and a hound (156), and Philomena as a bird (155).
- Key Words: "Preie" (5), un/kind (un/natural), virginitee, and lots of words for sounds people make: "chitre" (the jargon of birds, 155, 466), speke, plain, cry, sing, tell, rede, weep, moan, and more.
- Morals and Thesis Statements: Genius states theme, 3–5; Progne: proper remedy for such things isn't weeping, 247–48; Philomena on love, 446–50, full of oxymorons.

Discussion Questions

1. What is the effect of Progne's vengeful acts on our feelings for her?
2. Does she act according to "kind" (nature)?
3. Does it matter that the characters are royal? What difference does it make?
4. Why does the tale have Philomena weave a tapestry rather than (honestly!) write a letter?
5. What's the role of art (stories, tapestries) in the experience of trauma?

6. What's the purpose of the poem's appeals to our senses and even to our viscera?
7. In what sense are the surreal transformations into birds "true"?
8. Why does Tereus become a lapwing and not, say, the goshawk or wolf of the similes?
9. What's the relation between the two forms Gower uses here: Ovidian narrative and confessional dialogue?
10. What is the meaning and importance of voice in the poem?

William Langland

The Vision of Piers Plowman

The challenge of teaching *Piers Plowman* is both cultural and formal. In both respects, this mysterious and magnificent text is exceptional. Culturally, *Piers Plowman* might, on a superficial reading, confirm prejudices about pre-Reformation, Catholic culture as being authoritarian and capable of only didactic poetry. In Passus 1, for example, the figure personifying the Church talks down to and berates the poem's protagonist, Will (both a proper name and a personification of the human will). Holy Church promises to explain and contain the "field full of folk" that we have witnessed in the Prologue. She gives very high profile to the value of "Truthe," by which she means God as the ultimate justice; truth-telling; and fidelity in social relations, or "troth." It might be a good pedagogic strategy to begin with that sequence of Prologue and Passus 1, by way of confirming cultural pre-judgments. Once such judgments are confirmed, however, the rest of the selection here undoes such convictions: it turns out to be the humble laborer, Piers Plowman, who offers to lead the pilgrimage to Truthe. And that pilgrimage itself turns out to be no such thing: the real pilgrimage consists of staying at home and helping one way or another in the hard labor of producing food. Even in the ploughing, social and religious order breaks down: the Knight cannot enforce order, and the loafers quickly relapse into a rebellious sloth, rejecting both the Knight and Piers Plowman. The only true authority is exercised by Hunger. Perhaps the most spectacular disruption of any authoritarian, priest-dominated version of religious experience comes with Piers's tearing of the Pardon sent by Truthe. Faced with a complacent and condescending priest, Piers tears the pardon, and places his faith wholly in God's mercy. Pardon from Truthe, or God as justice, is no pardon at all (how can justice forgive?); in the act of tearing the document, Piers declares his faith in a higher, merciful version of "truthe," beyond justice. In short, the poem begins by confirming, but quickly questions received ideas about pre-Reformation religious culture. One could surprise students by revealing that. One could also read the moving biographical passage from the C-Text included in *NAEL*: Will plausibly represents himself as the poet, and he is anything but an official figure. On the contrary, he lives and works on the economic and moral margins.

Formally, *Piers Plowman* is very fluid. It may help students to offer them the basics of the poem's formal units: *Piers* is a linked sequence of eight visions, which together imagine a reformation both of individual Christians and of the entire Church. The poem is also divided into "passus" (steps); in some cases a passus constitutes an entire vision, while in others a vision is made up of a sequence of passus. In short, the passus boundaries mark a smaller break, and the vision boundaries a larger break in the narrative argument of the poem. The word "argument" is used advisedly, since, although the poem does contain powerful sequences of narrative, its overall structure is conceptual. The poem expresses, indeed, a creative tension between poetic narrative on the one hand and analytical argument on the other.

Teaching *Piers Plowman* successfully involves transmitting a sense of both that linking argument and the areas of sustained narrative coherence. Of course students will respond to the imaginative narrative more readily, but they will reap a richer harvest from the poem if they can also understand its argument. The passages chosen here are simultaneously poetically powerful and conceptually coherent. Once the "argument" concerning the fragmentation of "truthe's" meanings, as sketched above, has been made, then students might better appreciate the force of individual narratives. These sequences, for example, repay close attention for their poetic power: the social energies represented in the Prologue; Holy Church's intensely lyrical account of Truthe in Passus 1; the frightening power of Hunger in Passus 6; and enigmatic tearing of the Pardon in Passus 7. Each of these is poetically powerful, and together they exemplify Langland's understanding of profound religious experience as grounded in material labor and need. Religion for Langland is anything but abstract theology alone.

The other continuous passage of *Piers Plowman* represented here is Passus 18, in which Will witnesses the Crucifixion and so-called Harrowing of Hell. This is one of Langland's great sequences of self-contained narrative, and it is included in the "Christ's Humanity" section.

In addition to internal focus on the Langland texts here, one might ask students to compare the Prologue of *Piers Plowman* with that of *The Canterbury Tales*. Langland seems much more authoritarian and dismissive. Early on, for example, he powerfully criticizes pilgrims and their lying tales, which is the very matter that generates the entire *Canterbury Tales*. Closer inspection, however, reveals in Langland a fascination with the teeming energies of urban, profit-driven activity and occupations. One could also compare Langland's treatment of pardon with the representation of pardons and pardoners in Chaucer's *Pardoner's Tale*.

The dreamer Will, at once poet, everyman, and model of human desire (or will), is at the center of *Piers Plowman*. For Will, the answer to his many questions comes with a dream vision of the Crucifixion and the Harrowing of Hell (Passus 18), which is the doctrinal and emotional climax of the poem and, for many readers, the single most moving piece of Middle English religious poetry.

The images of romance blend with those of the Bible. The dreamer's vision of Christ's entry into Jerusalem "As is the nature of a knight that draws near to be dubbed" (line 13), like *The Dream of the Rood*, allegorizes the Crucifixion as a battle, only here the imagery is that of a tournament in which the prize is humanity's salvation. Christ rides to the combat barefoot, armed only in the flesh of His incarnation, to win His spurs in a joust with the Devil, who claims his entitlement to all human souls by right of the sin of Adam and Eve. As in medieval drama, Hell is portrayed as a castle, from which the Christ-knight liberates the imprisoned souls of the saved. As knights in romance tournaments sometimes conceal their identities, so Christ's humanity also serves as a disguise. The disguise here is a trick to catch the Devil, justified by the Devil's trick in disguising himself as a serpent to betray Adam and Eve into sin. The dreamer asks Faith "what all this affair meant, / And who was to joust in Jerusalem" (lines 19–20). The speaker in William Herebert's lyric asks what amounts to the same question—"What is he, this lordling, that cometh from the fight"—of the Christ-knight returning in blood-red garment from battle, and the Knight himself answers, "Ich it am . . . / Champioun to helen mankinde in fight." For the same romance image of Christ as the champion of a lady, with yet another twist, see *Ancrene Riwle*.

Teaching Clusters

Satire; religious allegory; biblical narrative in a local setting. *The Second Shepherds' Play* provides a perfect comparison with *Piers Plowman* for the way in which theological questions are embedded in the painful material realities of hunger and poverty. The mystery plays generally offer rich comparative material for *Piers*, insofar as they set biblical narrative in a specifically contemporary setting. One might also ask students to compare the Prologue of *Piers* with Chaucer's *General Prologue*: how and why does each author criticize society? The other Chaucer text that will repay comparison with *Piers* is *The Pardoner's Tale*, since both Langland and Chaucer lay grievous charges against ecclesiastical practice in these texts. Langland's presentation of Christ's humanity is very different from that of either Julian of Norwich or Margery Kempe, but the comparison is rewarding. You might also compare *Piers* with much older material, such as *The Dream of the Rood*, where Christ is also presented as a heroic figure. See also the lyric "What is he, this lordling that cometh from the fight?"

Quick Read

- Genre: Mixed! Langland uses dream vision; sermon; estates satire; satire against the abuse of money; ecclesiastical satire; para-biblical narrative.
- Prosody: Alliterative verse, used with less metrical precision than *Sir Gawain and the Green Knight*, and more lexical freedom.
- Style: Langland is capable of the pungently materialist poetics of satire, and the elevated style of psalmic aspiration.
- Text Divisions: Passus (steps); visions.

- Focus of Interest: Langland deals with the whole of society in the Prologue and Passus 1; in what remains of the First Vision (Passus 2–4) he broaches corruption from legal and economic perspectives; in the Second Vision (Passus 5–7) he broaches corruption from an ecclesiastical, penitential perspective. Passus 18 provides a solution of sorts: a confirmation that Christ will modify the strict law of Truthe, or justice, that had seemed both so necessary and so austere in Passus 1–7.
- Key Word: Truthe.

Discussion Questions

1. What is Langland's topic, the individual or the Church? Or both?
2. Is theology separate, for Langland, from questions of law and economics?
3. Is Langland a rigid conservative rejecting the urban and money-driven world with which he is faced?
4. Why should Langland's poem be so fluid formally?
5. What is the status of the narrator, Will? Is he reliable?
6. Why should the poem's spiritual hero, Piers, be a plowman?
7. Why should Langland go to such lengths to set Christ within a specifically fourteenth-century world?
8. Is Langland's anger at the corruption of the world matched by his pity for the pain of sinners?
9. Does Langland believe in the possibility of works contributing to salvation?

Further Resources

NORTON ONLINE ARCHIVE

Piers Plowman
  Passus 5 [The Confession of Envy]
  Passus 5 [The Confession of Gluttony]

Middle English Incarnation and Crucifixion Lyrics

In "I Sing of a Maiden", the Virgin chooses the "King of alle kinges" (lines 3–4) as a lady might choose a lover. Her power is a function of her purity: virginity is the force that enables the weak to control the strong. This short lyric may help a modem reader sense the mystery and idealism that surrounded virginity in chivalric culture.

In the four-line lyric "Sunset on Calvary," the feeling is all the stronger for being greatly compressed. In this poem, the sympathy of the natural world for its Creator is conveyed by the sun setting behind the wood (the woods in the background but also the wood of the Cross). However, the setting sun also holds the promise of its rising and, therefore, of the Resurrection, which is one of the joys of the Virgin.

Julian of Norwich

The powerful mix of "homely," or ordinary, friendly language with arcane, complex theological concepts and the paradoxical melding of disgusting imagery with exhortations to comfort and joy make Julian's writings unforgettable. Students often need help following and acknowledging the complex emotional pattern of the work: severe revulsion at the vivid images of wounds and suffering, the proffered happiness of Julian's interpretation, the comfort of the domestic imagery, and the awe at the cosmic in juxtaposition with the trivial. They may need to be reassured that she intended us to feel initial disgust at the image of Jesus as our mother, nursing the reader with blood to be sucked from the wound in his side. It seems good to resist allowing students to "normalize" these images by thinking of them as banal medieval commonplaces, and to encourage them, instead, to explore Julian's brilliance in fashioning power and meaning. Comparison of this devotional text with texts that are primarily literary in intention can help students see how our literary approaches are designed to elicit particular kinds of (sometimes reverential, but nondevotional) meaning, kinds that are illuminating but often go against the text's embodied intentions.

Teaching Clusters

Renaissance religious poetry makes a good counterpart to Julian's paradoxes and gender bends: sexualized eroticism and preparations for death in Donne's famous lyrics, Crashaw's lactation in "To the Infant Martyrs" and "Blessed be the paps which Thou hast sucked" and body-part mixing in "On the Wounds of Our Crucified Lord," Herbert's "homely" diction and architectural theological propositions in *The Temple*, and Milton's paradoxical conceptions of the deity in *Paradise Lost*, especially the creatively gendered apostrophe to the spirit in the opening lines of the poem (17–22). Modernism reprises spiritual paradox and offers a whole new group of texts for comparison, especially T. S. Eliot's. He quotes Julian in *Four Quartets*.

Quick Read

- Genre: Mystical, theological prose.
- Structuring Images: The showings themselves; the bleeding head as rain falling off the roof-eaves, pellets, herring scales; Mary annunciate; the lord as clothing; creation as a tiny ball the size of a hazelnut; imagery is surreal, fragmentary, emotionally powerful, and paradoxical.
- Style: Iterative, expansive, discursive.
- Ritual: Julian receives the last rites at the opening of the text, when she dies only to be brought back.
- Tropes: Familial kinship is a primary mode of understanding God here; paradox is both a theological and an emotional tool of the text.

- Diction: Ordinary, plain speech; "speaking" here seems to be the rehearsal of the movement of the soul in prayer or in understanding.
- Thesis Statements: All shall be well (chapter 27); love was his meaning (chapter 86).

Discussion Questions

1. Does it matter that Julian was a woman?
2. Describe the spatial imagination of the text.
3. Is there a connection between the text's spatial imagination and the fact that Julian was enclosed?
4. How do Julian's interpretations of her visions compare to the way literary critics unpack images?
5. How many kinds of paradox can you find in the text?
6. Is it fruitful to describe Julian's discourse in terms of privacy and publicity?
7. Can you discern a gender politics to her work?
8. What is the meaning of pain in Julian's writings?
9. How are the mental and the emotional experiences of this writing related?
10. Is this "autobiography"?

Further Resources

NORTON ONLINE ARCHIVE

From The Book of Margery Kempe [A Visit with Julian of Norwich]

Margery Kempe

The Book of Margery Kempe survived in a single manuscript that was not recovered until the 1930s. Kempe's vision of Jesus, who appears to comfort her after she has suffered a nervous breakdown, is quite different from that of Julian of Norwich. Kempe sees Christ as "most beauteous" and "most amiable," dressed in a mantle of purple silk and sitting on the side of her bed. He addresses her as "Daughter," reproaches her for having forsaken him, then ascends slowly until he disappears in the heavens. Unlike Julian, whose interpretation of her vision is original but who lived the accepted life of a religious recluse, Kempe wrote fairly conventional religious texts, but the life she lived was radically different. She was controversial, and—as she tells us—she aroused intense hostility among both churchmen and laymen, although many, most notably Julian of Norwich, supported her. Kempe is remarkable for her struggle to make herself independent and to lead a holy life in the world rather than in a convent or anchorage. She is constantly negotiating her freedom—with her husband, freedom from continuing to have sexual relations with him and to go on pilgrimage to Jerusalem; with the archbishop of York, freedom to speak her conscience. These arguments she wins by a combination of courage and cunning. Late in her life, she negotiates with God not to be burdened with the nursing of her husband, who has become senile and incontinent, so that she may not be interrupted in her prayers and other religious observances. This time she does not get her way. She accepts the Lord's will "that thou be free to help him at his need in my name." And she resigns herself to her husband's care, reflecting,

> how she in her young age had full many delectable thoughts, fleshly lusts, and inordinate loves to his person [body]. And therefore she was glad to be punished with the same person and took it much the more easily and served him and helped him, . . . as she would 'a done Christ himself.

Teaching Clusters

The obvious comparative text is Julian of Norwich. One might also compare the domestic presentation of spiritual experience with *The Second Shepherds' Play* or *Everyman*. Margery is also a loner, and students might find it fruitful to discuss loners: Chaucer's Pardoner and Langland's Will would be obvious places to start.

Quick Read

- Genre: Autobiography.
- Form: Prose.
- Characters: Margery Kempe; everyone else a bit player.
- Locale: Huge spaces, from England to Jerusalem.
- Style: Margery's text is intensely visual at points, focused as it is on bodily experience (her own, her husband's, and that of Christ). It also gives very high profile to direct speech.
- Key Words: Weeping, ghostly, comfort, compassion.

Discussion Questions

1. Why should Margery be the first writer of autobiography in English? What are the conditions of autobiography?
2. Is Margery the mistress or the victim of her text?
3. What is the style of Margery's text? What is the effect of its being written in prose?
4. How do the social forms of Margery's society (particularly related to marriage) inform her spirituality?
5. Is this text a form of therapy?
6. What is the function of conversation in this text?
7. What is the importance of pilgrimage for Margery?

Further Resources

NORTON ONLINE ARCHIVE

The Book of Margery Kempe
  [Her Pride and Attempts to Start a Business]
  [A Visit with Julian of Norwich]
  [Examination before the Archbishop]

The York Play of the Crucifixion

As the final selection in the "Christ's Humanity" cluster, *The York Play of the Crucifixion* provides an excellent opportunity to reflect back on what we mean by "humanity," not just the humanity assumed by Christ in his incarnation but the humanities of those who encounter him in the very different visionary experiences of Julian of Norwich and Margery Kempe, portrayals of actual witnesses of the Crucifixion such as the Jews and Longinus in Passus 18 of *Piers Plowman*, and, in this play, the common soldiers who have the dirty job of crucifying Christ. The playwright has portrayed them with a gallows humor, first in the pride they take in their grisly task, then gradually in their growing panic as everything goes wrong. Do these wretched creatures offer a test of our own humanity? Are we supposed to laugh as their smug confidence breaks down and they start blaming one another for the unexpected difficulties they encounter in nailing Christ to the cross and then raising it? Should we despise them for their angry mocking after they finally manage to set the cross in place? Imagine yourself and your students as Margery Kempe witnessing in her imagination the buffeting, scourging, and mocking of Jesus by the Jews. In the play, the soldiers' anger and malice rise as they begin to blame the sloppiness of their work on the trickery of this "warlock." Will the audience hate and despise them as Margery Kempe does the Jews? The play leads up to the single stanza spoken by Jesus, bidding "All men that walk by way of street" to regard his suffering and, implicitly, like the Father to "Forgive these men" and seek forgiveness for their own sins.

Teaching Clusters

Most relevant, of course, are the other texts in "Christ's Humanity." Comparison with the Anglo-Saxon *Dream of the Rood* brings out the stark contrast between the Jesus of the York play and the heroic figure Christ, whose suffering is projected upon the cross that bears him, and who liberates the patriarchs in a triumphant raid on Hell and reenters Heaven, "where his home was." During the Reformation in England, performances of the mystery plays came to be suppressed (see headnote). Contrast with the sixteenth- and seventeenth-century religious lyrics is also revealing. There you may wish to note the personal and private meditations in which poets like Donne ("Hymn to God in My Sickness") and Crashaw ("On the Wounds of Our Crucified Lord") privately contemplate Christ's sufferings on the cross. These meditations offer a clear contrast to the public spectacle evoked by drama of the kind we see in the York play.

Quick Read

- Genre: Mystery or Corpus Christi play; climax of the Passion sequence.
- Author: "York Realist"?
- Verse Form: Twelve-line stanza, in each of which all four soldiers speak among each other except for two stanzas (lines 49–60 and 253–64) in which Jesus speaks to "my Father" and "All men."
- Key Words: "Work(s)"

Discussion Questions

1. Imagine that you are directing a performance. Are the characters of the four soldiers developed and differentiated in any way? How would you direct them to play and speak their parts?
2. Are there significant silences when the action seems to freeze?
3. Compare the Crucifixion play with the image of the Crucifixion from Lapworth Missal in *NAEL* (C6). What attitudes toward the Crucifixion are the playwright and the illuminator seeking to evoke from the audience and the user of the missal? Do these works have anything in common?
4. Compare the soldiers in the Crucifixion play with the shepherds in *The Wakefield Second Shepherds' Play*. As different as the subjects are, can you see similarities in the way the playwrights make use of minor characters in dramatizing the Nativity and the Passion?

Mystery Plays

The Wakefield Second Shepherds' Play

Like the religious lyric, the religious drama was a machine for turning distress and sorrow into sudden gladness, and comedy into solemnity and awe. There is no better example of this than *The Second Shepherds' Play*. One must remember that the plays were performed as part of the celebration of major religious feasts, Corpus Christi and Whitsuntide, when the weather was most likely to be at its best. The shepherds make their entrances complaining of the bitter cold, the insolence of "these gentlerymen" (line 26) who exploit them, and the miseries of married men. Their sour mood is at odds with the holiday season, and although one can sympathize with much of their grumbling, it also has its comic side. The ingenious comic plot of the false Nativity, with much slapstick like the tossing of Mak in a blanket, consumes 80 percent of the play. Much of the hilarity comes from the declarations made by the deceivers, which turn out to be true in odd ways. For instance, Gill swears (771) that she'll eat her own child if she has beguiled them, which is awful. But she means it—she plans to eat the sheep her husband stole, and is wrong to do so. Yet in that wrong lies the possibility of redemption, because in the Eucharist a Christian does eat the Lamb of God, which is the Nativity child in the cradle.

When the Angel sings, the mood magically changes. You and your students may have seen the annual Christmas special *Charlie Brown's Christmas*, which has the same tonal structure. Charlie Brown is trying to organize the children to rehearse the school Christmas play, but they pay no attention to him, preoccupied with their usual activities. All is comic noise and confusion until Linus begins to read from the text, "And there were in the same country shepherds abiding in the field, keeping watch over their flock by night," and wonder prevails. The theme throughout the play is poverty, and how Christianity offers itself especially to the poor.

This play takes the civic responsibilities of its genre to mean addressing political issues like the enclosure of common land for farming by the gentry, taxation, hunger, children, men's and women's hard work. Language itself is presented as a class marker and a potential disguise. The political topics issue in the opening *complaints*, which are transformed to *hymns* by the end, as Christian doctrine steps in to transform the raw material of political dissent (Gill's feminist complaint at 598 ff. makes another) into religious awe and sung, social harmony.

Teaching Clusters

Literature and the Medieval Church. The play is wonderful next to *The Miller's Tale*, *The Nun's Priest's Tale*, and any other comic text. The scenes treating poverty in *King Lear* make it a rich partner. It is interesting to pair the *Second Shepherds' Play* with *Everyman*, both to show the difference in genre and to compare the handling of religious doctrine and audience response. One might take the lyric complaints from the opening scenes and compare them to various lyric complaints by Renaissance authors, or take Gill's complaint as a counterpart to *The Wife of Bath's Prologue*.

Quick Read

- Genre: Mystery play or pageant.
- Prosody: Thirteen-line stanzas rhyme abab abab cdddc.
- Setting: Bethlehem (bedlam) is a short walk from where they are, yet they seem to be in Yorkshire (Wakefield is a town in the north of England, in Yorkshire).
- Primary Sections: Shepherds make complaints, an important lyric genre of the period; Coll: the weather is awful and husbands (i.e., farmers) and shepherds are oppressed by the gentry, 1–78; Gib: the weather is awful and married men are henpecked, 79–156; Daw: the weather is awful and wages stink, 170–247; they sleep, Mak steals the sheep and it's discovered, 274–905; shepherds sleep again and the angel appears and they visit the stable with gifts, 905–1087.

- Key Words: Grace (452, 1084) curious technical terms for singing, which represents social harmony.
- Structuring Images: The sheep; food for hungry poor folk and the Eucharist.
- Style: Witty, punchy, hip-hoppy (the rhyme series), loose but well crafted.

Discussion Questions

1. What is the role of music and singing in the play?
2. Is there any symbolism in the gifts the shepherds offer the child?
3. Why bring the sacrament of the Eucharist into the Nativity story? Why not baptism or marriage or something more suitable?
4. Are the conditions about which the shepherds and Gill complain improved during the play?
5. Is this a play of social criticism, or does it reinforce class stratification?
6. How would you stage the play?
7. Compare the play to other rewritings of the Nativity story in popular culture. (*Fat Albert's Christmas Special* is a good one to use.)

Sir Thomas Malory

If Sir Thomas Malory of Newbold Revell is, as most scholars believe, the "knight prisoner" who wrote *Morte Darthur* (see headnote), his criminal record may be a sign of the disruptions that the Wars of the Roses brought upon the feudal nobility in the late fifteenth century. The dying out of the old order helps to explain Malory's passionate nostalgia for chivalry, especially the chivalry of his hero Sir Lancelot. Sir Ector's eulogy for Lancelot could be read as an elegy for chivalry itself.

Morte Darthur

Lancelot and Guinevere are the most famous pair of lovers in medieval literature. Their liaison first appears in Chrétien de Troye's unfinished romance *Lancelot* and was greatly elaborated in the French prose romances of the thirteenth century. Reading of Lancelot's and Guinevere's first kiss, Francesca tells Dante in the *Inferno*, she and her brother-in-law Paolo looked at one another and "That day we read no further." Malory omits the tale of the first kiss (an image of that scene from a French *Lancelot* manuscript is available in *NTO*)—for him the love of Lancelot and Guinevere is a given on which he ultimately blames the destruction of the Round Table.

As Malory treats the affair, it is remarkably free of romantic longing and passion. He is far more interested in the dangers that Lancelot undergoes rescuing the queen from perilous situations than he is in their trysts. Malory opens the last book of *Morte Darthur* with a conventional reference to spring as the season "when every lusty heart flourisheth"—the same topos that begins *The Canterbury Tales*. Here, however, the coming of spring sets up a tragic irony: "so this season it befell in the month of May a great anger and unhap that stinted not till the flower of chivalry of all the world was destroyed and slain." Warned by his nephew, Sir Bors, of the risks of visiting the queen on the night they are betrayed, Lancelot replies that the queen has sent for him and he will "not be so much a coward" as to refuse her invitation. When they are together, Malory professes not to know "whether they were abed or at other manner of disports."

The most passionate declarations of their love take place after the end of the affair, when she has become a nun and he a priest. A vision instructs Lancelot that, for remission of his sins, he must hasten to Guinevere's convent, where he will find her dead, and that he must bury her beside King Arthur. He learns from the nuns that she had known of his coming and had prayed aloud as though making a public confession: "I beseech Almighty God that I may never have power to see Sir Lancelot with my worldly eyes." Seeing her face in death, Sir Lancelot "wept not greatly, but sighed. . . . And when she was put in the earth Sir Lancelot swooned and lay long still." Reproached by a hermit that he is displeasing God by such excessive grief, Lancelot replies that his sorrow is not "for any rejoicing of sin" but for his fault and pride. The measure of his repentance is also the measure of his love for both Guinevere and Arthur. Thereafter, Lancelot barely takes nourishment and shrivels away until he is dead. Malory goes so far as to imply that he has become a saint, for the head of the monastery has a vision of Lancelot being taken into heaven by angels, and his body gives off a sweet odor.

Teaching Clusters

The Legend of Arthur. Malory is also interesting to compare as a prose writer with Margery Kempe and Julian of Norwich, among others. The many Arthurian stories your students are likely to know already are, of course, profitable for discussion.

Quick Read

- Genre: Chivalric Arthurian romance(s) knit together by Caxton into one large prose work divided into chapters that correspond roughly to episodes; in mode, tragic, elegaic, chroniclelike; yet the romance issues of identity, women's desires, rich clothing and furnishings, fine courtly etiquette are suppressed to a low murmur.
- Tone: Never dry, but terse and often plodding, which can muffle Malory's curious tendency to hyperbole (so many knights seem to be "the most worshipfull" or "the most traitorous").
- Style: A syntax as full of parataxis as Hemingway's; few poetic embellishments; limited, repetitive vocabulary; understatement together with hyperbole; formulaic treatment of virtue and vice; stoic reporting of pain and misery.
- Themes: Honor and worship; the nation and the nature of kingship; male fellowship.

- Imagery: The prose is not very visually descriptive; the exceptions are the supernatural moments—the sword held by the arm coming up out of the lake, the barge of ladies that take the dying Arthur away, the funeral processions.
- Speech Acts: Malory directly reports speeches that tend to be complaints, accusations, vows—most create, reaffirm, or sever alliances among characters.

Discussion Questions

1. Compare Malory's sense of the national significance of women's desires with the treatment of the same question in *The Wife of Bath's Tale* or *Sir Gawain and the Green Knight*.
2. What makes one honorable in Malory?
3. Is there an ethical difference between the "good" knights and the "bad" knights?
4. What is the role of religious reference in Malory? (See the passage where Guenevere vows to be martyred.)
5. What is the role of dreams in Malory? (Compare with *The Nun's Priest's Tale*.) What is the significance of the image of Excalibur being received into the lake by the arm? Why do you think it has persisted in so many later works?
6. Is Malory a good writer? Where does his power lie, and where his weakness?
7. What does the text seem to want us to think about?
8. Knowing other versions of Arthurian legends, were you surprised at the style, texture, or values of Malory's?

Further Resources

NORTON TOPICS ONLINE

King Arthur: Romancing Politics
   The Prose Vulgate Cycle
      The Prose Lancelot
      The Quest for the Holy Grail
      The Death of Arthur
   William Caxton, Preface to *Morte Darthur*

Robert Henryson

The Cock and the Fox

Whoever enjoys *The Nun's Priest's Tale* from *The Canterbury Tales* will also take pleasure in this imitation written about a century later by Robert Henryson. Henryson's works, especially his *Testament of Cressid*, which is a sequel to Chaucer's *Troilus and Criseyde*, testify that by the end of the fifteenth century a literary canon, of which Chaucer was revered as pro-genitor, was now established in Britain. Few of Chaucer's many followers captured his spirit, especially his humor, as successfully as Henryson. Henryson is more overtly a moralist than Chaucer, and the *Moralitas* at the end of the fable spells out its lesson with more gravity. But he shares Chaucer's gift for endowing animals with human personality. An original twist in Henryson's version of the fable is the introduction of speeches individualizing three of Chauntecleer's wives after the fox makes off with him; in these speeches the wives voice their different opinions about the rooster as a husband and lover. Each wife represents an antifeminist stereotype, and one of them is clearly a sister of the Wife of Bath. The fable is short, and if you assign the *Nun's Priest's Tale*, your students will probably appreciate Henryson and enjoy wrestling with his Scots dialect after Chaucer's by-then-familiar Southeast Midland.

Teaching Clusters

Henryson's fable was obviously inspired by and begs for comparison with Chaucer's *Nun's Priest's Tale*. Here the satire is less on the world of learning expounded so amusingly and at such length by Chauntecleer and the Priest narrator than on the debate of the three hens regarding the rooster's fate. Henryson's fables, with their *Moralitas* spelling out the lesson, are more truly in the tradition of Aesop's fables. You might compare this one with two of Marie de France's fables in the Online Archive: "The Wolf and the Lamb" and "The Wolf and the Sow." But *The Cock and the Fox* can also contribute to a cluster on the theme of marriage—most notably including *The Wife of Bath's Prologue*, the marriage of Margery Kempe (Book I.11, 35–36), More's *Utopia* [Marriage Customs], Bacon's "Of Marriage and the Single Life," and Defoe's *Roxana*.

Quick Read

- Genre: Beast fable, allegorical exegesis (Moralitas).
- Verse Form: The seven-line stanza called "rhyme royal"—see Chaucer's lyrics and the "Literary Terminology" appendix.
- Dialect: Scots as opposed to Chaucer's East Midland (see notes).
- Debate: Chauntecleer's hens discuss his character and fate.

Discussion Questions

1. Why do you think Henryson eliminated Chauntecleer's dream, which plays such an important part in *The Nun's Priest's Tale*, and how does that omission change the fable? Is there a true moral to be gleaned from Henryson that evades us in Chaucer?
2. Efforts have sometimes been made to draw the character of Chaucer's Nun's Priest, who doesn't receive a separate portrait in the *General Prologue* and speaks only a few lines, from the tale he tells. Whether or not the speaker there is in fact a dramatic character or Chaucer

himself, how would you compare him with the narrator of *The Cock and the Fox?*

3. Compare *The Cock and the Fox*, lines 36–77, with *The Nun's Priest's Tale*, lines 464–501. Without deciding which author offers a more seductive temptation, describe how the author's own style and character emerge in these passages. In Henryson's case you have just one tale to go on. But drawing on other passages in Chaucer, how does this one exhibit his particular style and humor?

Everyman

Everyman is a late and not very typical example of a medieval morality play, a genre that is generally full of slapstick comedy with clowns personifying vices. In moralities, the theme of salvation is played out not, as in the mystery cycles, through the history of the world from the Creation to Judgment Day, but as an allegory of the day of judgment that comes in the life of every human being. Death makes a chilling appearance in the first scene. There is comedy in the way Everyman's kindred and friends abandon him, but the last part of the play is sober and intent. The personification allegory enacts the steps every person must take to gain salvation. First he or she must gain Knowledge, which leads to Confession. When Everyman performs penance by scourging himself, Good Deeds, which had been too feeble to rise, is finally able to get up and accompany Everyman to the grave while his personal qualities desert him one by one. The doctrine of the play is interesting inasmuch as it insists that not grace alone but good works, however faint, are essential for salvation.

Teaching Clusters

Literature and the Medieval Church. Allegory. Marlowe's *Dr. Faustus* makes a superb partner to *Everyman*, as it too leans heavily on the sacrament of penance, includes an allegorical play with the seven deadly sins, and creates a surreal, oppressive crisis of temporality. *Piers Plowman* is interestingly different in its uses of personification allegory.

Quick Read

- Genre: Morality play, personification allegory, also calls itself a "treatise," *not* a tragedy: his soul ascends at the end.
- Verse Form: Very irregular rhythm and rhyme. Uses couplets, quatrains, tail-rhymes, rhyme royal stanzas, octaves, and stanzas of 5, 6, or 7 lines. Very motley.
- Characters: Seventeen characters, listed in the *dramatis personae* table; if they double, it requires ten actors. The personifications are of varying types: some interior, some exterior.
- Key Passages: Lines 1–462: Everyman deserted by fellowship, kin, cousin out of fear; 462–771: Good deserts him too. Everyman

has shame. Good Deeds and Knowledge lead him to Confession, and then Eucharist and Extreme Unction are administered off-stage (three sacraments, only one of which is personified). 772–921: Beauty, Strength, Discretion, and 5-wits are scared off by the grave; Knowledge remains while Everyman and Good Deeds go into the grave. Angel speaks about his Soul going to heaven and Doctor gives the moral.

- Plot: The plot is pageantlike, run by a succession of characters. The main action is simply death and the three sacraments helping it along. The plot is described as a pilgrimage, but there are no towns or landmarks to make a "horizontal" map for us. It becomes, as the Parson says of the *Canterbury Tales* effort, a pilgrimage to the celestial Jerusalem that is heaven.
- Thesis: "Man, in the beginning / Look well, and take good heed to the ending" (10–11).
- Speech Acts: The play is largely made up of promises and betrayals.
- Key Words, Images, Tropes are identical: Reckoning and other commercial terms, account, the account book. This commercialism is in tension with the thesis about material goods, yet this is not surprising: medieval penitential manuals often use a commercial lexicon.
- Style: Not aureate; not what's spoken on the street, either, but a kind of common sermon mode—trying a bit for formality, but not at the expense of friendliness.
- Themes: Accounting, judgment, "how transitory we be," "given" vs. "lent" in 161–62.
- Space: Confession lives in the House of Salvation; the grave ("this cave," 792) is vivid, but the play is set in a rather bleak and Beckett-like landscape.

Discussion Questions

1. Compare Everyman's appeals to our disgust with those of Julian of Norwich or Chaucer's Pardoner.
2. What is the significance of the book (a stage property) to the larger purposes of the play?
3. Whom would you cast in a current production?
4. Compare Beauty to Marlowe's Helen.
5. Create a set for the play.
6. Does the play require a Christian audience to be powerful?
7. To what extent can great art be didactic?
8. What is the most moving moment of the play?

The Middle Ages:
Texts in the Norton Online Archive
by Authors Not in *NAEL*

The Battle of Maldon
An Old English Riddle [The Bow]
Sir Orfeo
The York Play of the Crucifixion
The Brome Play of Abraham and Isaac
Medieval Lyrics
    In Praise of Brunettes
    The Appreciative Drinker
    A Charm Against the Night Goblin
    The Blacksmiths
    Earth Took Earth
    Spring Has Come with Love
    The Henpecked Husband
    A Bitter Lullaby
Lludd and Lleuelys
From *Aucassin and Nicolette* [Aucassin Renounces Paradise]
"The Land of Cockaigne"
"Ubi Sunt Qui Ante Nos Fuerunt"
["The Last Journey"]
["A Change in Perspective"]
Boethius, *from* The Consolation of Philosophy
    [Triumph Over the World]
    [Fortune Defends Herself]
William Caxton, *Preface to* Morte Darthur
Dante, Fortune an Agent of God's Will
François Villon, The Ballad of Dead Ladies

CHAPTER 6

The Sixteenth Century
1485-1603

INTRODUCING THE PERIOD

Our image of the sixteenth century is dominated by two great figures, Queen Elizabeth and William Shakespeare. Four centuries after their deaths, in parts of the world they never visited or perhaps even heard of, the faces of both remain instantly recognizable. To a remarkable extent, the age of Elizabeth and Shakespeare has come to stand for a timeless and essential "Englishness." In your course, students will become more familiar with the major writers of the Tudor era, but they may also find them less familiar—more strange—than they had expected. While films like *Elizabeth* and *Shakespeare in Love* present the luminaries of the period as modern individuals in Renaissance garb, the texts in the anthology give access to a strange, sometimes disturbing, and endlessly fascinating culture.

The Tudor era marks the start of something new in the history of English literature, but the start of what exactly? You might begin by explaining that there are two different terms for what seems to have begun in the sixteenth century: "the Renaissance" and "the Early Modern Period." The term "Renaissance," which was first used in the nineteenth century (as in Walter Pater's *The Renaissance*), draws attention to the period's conscious break with medieval culture. It applies to the revival of Greek and Roman culture that began in Italy during the fourteenth century and spread to England in the late fifteenth and sixteenth centuries. Because the term means "rebirth," it implies that classical learning in the Middle Ages had become moribund. Of course, the Middle Ages, and especially its monastic institutions, had in fact preserved and transformed much of the inherited Latin culture. Few medieval scholars, on the other hand, knew any Greek; and many of the key Greek texts and some by Latin authors had not been available to them. The revival of Greek and the addition of new (old) texts to the classical canon (especially the editing and translating of the Greek New Testament) had enormous influence. Sidney regarded himself as a pioneer in a new age of English literature. His *Defense of Poesy* makes a display of the author's familiarity with Greek and Latin literature; with condescending praise, he wonders that Chaucer "in *that misty age* could see so clearly" while "we in *this clear age* go so stumblingly after him" (emphasis added).

The term "Early Modern," used in linguistics for the stage of the language that came right after Middle English, is also used to refer to an era of sweeping cultural change. The emphasis here is on the relationship between the sixteenth century and our own present. This was an era in which many of the seeds of the modern world were being sown—seeds of such phenomena as the market economy, the individual subject, and the centralized state. Whereas the idea of the Renaissance attunes our ears to the new, sometimes brashly confident tone characteristic of the era, the notion of early modernity draws our attention instead to tensions, ambiguities, and conflicts between residual and emergent ideologies.

The extraordinary revolution in literature that took place after 1580 did not come in response to any decisive historical event. It is instead best understood as resulting from the confluence of many different currents (humanism, Protestantism, the Italian Renaissance, the exploration of the New World, the decline of magic, the centralization of state power, etc.) in the minds of writers attuned to their culture. Spenser, Marlowe, and Shakespeare could not have been as innovative as they were had they not been masters of a kind of cultural alchemy. In their works, disparate materials—some new, some old—were blended together and transformed into gold. To bring out the peculiar blend of innovation and tradition characteristic of this era, it is useful to compare a famous later-sixteenth-century text with a predecessor. Marlowe's *Doctor Faustus*, a play to which students almost always respond favorably, can be instructively paired with the late medieval morality play *Everyman*. Shakespeare's *King Lear* and Spenser's *Faerie Queene*, with their source in the twelfth-century legends of Geoffrey of Monmouth, can be compared with some of the medieval texts grouped under "Legendary Histories of Britain."

TEACHING CLUSTERS

Reformation and Conflicts of Faith

Teaching the themes and conflicts of the English Reformation to students today means starting more or less from scratch. Many will be unclear even on the nature of the division between Catholicism and Protestantism, let alone the finer points of Calvinism, Lutheranism, and the Anglican compromise. This should be seen as an opportunity rather than an obstacle. The In-text Topic "Faith in Conflict," consisting of short selections from Tyndale, Calvin, Foxe, Hooker, and others, provides a basis for exploring the most important debates and outcomes of the Reformation. These selections illustrate the point that the Reformation was not a single event, but rather a series of ruptures and conflicts on every level of society. "Faith in Conflict" also emphasizes the crucial role played by literature and literary problems in the events of the Reformation. One of the central conflicts was over who should be allowed to read a certain book, and in what language. Above all, the Reformation proved to people of all faiths the extraordinary power of the English language when allied with a relatively new invention, the printing press. In addition to texts from the Reformation era, this cluster includes Elizabethan literary works that in different ways contribute to—or struggle to escape from—the conflict of faiths.

Identity, Performance, and Disguise

In the sixteenth century, power and status were closely bound up with costumes, symbols of authority, and visible signs of rank—the fetishism of dress. Clothing in this culture, as in ours today, was used as a marker of identity, but to a remarkable extent it could also appear to determine both gender identity and social rank. While dramatists indulged in metatheatrical games of disguise and revelation, ambitious young men self-consciously played out the role of the Renaissance courtier, a role which for many involved the writing of poetry. Social theorists have pondered the extent to which power was a species of performance. This cluster groups together texts from across the century, and from a range of genres, united by a common and quintessentially Tudor obsession with the metaphor of the world as stage.

Love and Subjectivity

This cluster allows you to explore a range of texts dealing with love, sex, desire, and the self, often in relation to wider cultural themes. If it was an accident that English poets discovered Petrarch's love poetry shortly before the beginning of a half century of female rule, it was an accident with profound consequences for English literature. The existence of a reigning queen—especially a virgin queen whose marital intentions were a matter of anxiety—unquestionably heightened the fascination of courtiers and poets with the Petrarchan themes of the power of eros and the erotics of power. Courtly and popular writers alike in this period were intrigued by the theme of desire and its relation to subjectivity. To love was to lay claim to a private self, independent of and unreachable by the otherwise pervasive networks of power, deference, and obligation. Writing about sex in this period ranges from the delicately ornamental and spiritualized to the frankly physical. In spite of the often draconian spiritual and legal penalties attending proscribed sexual activity, the Elizabethans were remarkably open to the expression and praise of sexual desire, including homoerotic desire.

New Worlds

The sixteenth century saw the first English literary responses to the discovery of the New World across the Atlantic, and the first English attempts to explore and settle there. As More's *Utopia* and many later texts show, writing about the New World provided an opportunity for commenting on affairs closer to home. Rife as they sometimes are with racism and xenophobia, sixteenth-century travelers' tales often manage to leave the impression that other societies may be better—wiser, more just, or more noble—than English society. In addition to texts dealing with the Americas, this cluster is also the place for texts that seek to imagine different societies or worlds, such as Spenser's Faerieland. Nor should it be forgotten that in a period of rapid and drastic religious, cultural, and economic change, England itself could appear to many of its inhabitants to have become a New World.

The Representation of Power

Few monarchs have made a more forceful impression on their subjects and on the minds of latter-day historians than Henry VIII and his daughter Elizabeth, whose combined reigns covered more than eighty years of the sixteenth century. In addition to Elizabeth, three other women—Lady Jane Grey, Mary Tudor, and Mary Queen of Scots—ruled in England or Scotland during this period. All of these individuals attracted intense interest, and many texts of the period represent them directly or allegorically. Others, such as Shakespeare's plays, employ fictional or historical rulers for their meditations on the nature and practice of power. In no other period, perhaps, has power been so closely tied to spectacle. There is room in this cluster for fiction and nonfiction, for works of drama, prose, and poetry, all focusing on the fascinating, threatening, and sometimes strangely vulnerable image of royalty.

AUTHORS AND WORKS

John Skelton

John Skelton was a one-off. There is no poet remotely like him in *NAEL,* and indeed there was no one very much like him in his own time. Yet, in spite of his uniqueness, part of the value of teaching Skelton is his capacity to shed a distinct light on the subsequent literary history of the sixteenth century. From one point of view, he can be seen to represent the irreverent, convivial spirit of "merry old [Catholic] England," which the Reformation despised and did its best to eradicate. Conversely, he can be seen as a proto-Reformer, levelling sharp and witty criticism at the social and spiritual corruption of early Tudor society.

The Tunning of Elinour Rumming

Quick Read

- Form: Comical/satirical verse.
- Summary: The excerpt describes the atmosphere in the alehouse kept by Elinour Rumming and her peculiar brewing practices, involving chicken dung.
- Themes: The lives of the common people; drink; merry-making.
- Key passages: "I learned it of a Jew / When I began to brew, / And I have found it true," lines 49–51; "sweetly together we lie / As two pigs in a sty," lines 74–75.

Teaching Suggestions

Students who have studied medieval literature previously will recognize elements of Middle English in Skelton's language. Those who have not may need more help in grasping the general sense. The verse form, commonly called Skeltonics, will strike some as delightful and others as plain silly. You can help them to see that it is more than mere doggerel by emphasizing the versatility of Skelton's style. You might point in particular to lines 66–71, where the whole course of a sexual encounter between husband and wife, from foreplay to sleep, is recounted by way of six breathless rhymes on "ony." You may also wish to raise the question of to what extent Skelton is criticizing, and to what extent celebrating, the lives and actions he describes.

Teaching Clusters

The Skelton selections in *NAEL*, all concerned in different ways with love and sexuality, fall naturally into the **Love and Subjectivity** cluster. Skelton's attitudes will form a marked contrast with texts from later in the period. Post-Reformation writers may spiritualize sex, decorate it, or debase it, but none of them quite match Skelton for cheerful frankness. Perhaps the closest parallel is found in another early Tudor text, *Utopia*, where More writes approvingly of the custom of men and women being displayed naked to one another before marriage, so that they will know what they are getting in the bargain.

Discussion Questions

1. Identify aspects of Skelton's work that seem medieval in character. Are there other aspects that seem to point to a more modern sensibility?
2. Is Elinour Rumming a popular heroine, or a symptom of a corrupt and decadent society?

3. How do the "Skeltonics" contribute to the effect of "The Tunning of Elinour Rumming"?
4. What resemblances and what differences do you perceive between Elinour Rumming and Chaucer's Wife of Bath?

Further Resources

NORTON ONLINE ARCHIVE

Upon a Dead Man's Head
To Mistress Margaret Hussey
From Colin Clout [The Spirituality vs. the Temporality]

Sir Thomas More

Thomas More rose from relative obscurity to become both a leading European intellectual and Chancellor of the realm, and died on the block as the most famous victim of Henry VIII's Reformation. The selections in NAEL give a glimpse of the breadth and shape of his extraordinary career. Utopia, which will occupy the bulk of students' attention, reveals More in the guise of Renaissance humanist, questioning the very foundations of social life with acumen and provocative wit. The excerpt from The History of King Richard III offers a glimpse of More the statesman, while "A Dialogue Concerning Heresies" (in the In-text Topic "Faith in Conflict") shows his later emergence as a passionate religious controversialist.

Utopia

Among the most enduringly controversial texts in English literature, More's Utopia still provokes heated debates. Written for an international audience of humanist intellectuals, Utopia purports to describe a distant civilization, but its real focus is on the ills of contemporary Europe. In book 1, the returned traveler Raphael Hythloday counters More's suggestion that he "devote . . . time and energy to public affairs . . . by joining the council of some great prince" with sarcastic remarks about kings and their counselors and with a devastating critique of European society and government. Pointing up the greed, arrogance, ignorance, and cruelty that riddle societies such as England's, Hythloday asserts that only through the abolition of private property and the introduction of common ownership can society be made just. In book 2, Hythloday describes the imaginary commonwealth of Utopia (More coined the name from the Greek for "no place"), which he claims has solved the problems that so beset England and every other European nation. The text is to some extent ironic, but it nonetheless issues an urgent call for sweeping social transformation. More could not yet have foreseen the English Reformation, which would cost him his life and radically transform English society—though not along Utopian lines.

Quick Read

- Form: Political treatise/dialogue.
- Summary: The traveler Raphael Hythloday criticizes the injustice and hypocrisy that prevail in European kingdoms, advocating instead the Utopian model, which dispenses with both kingship and private property. The second speaker, "More," remains skeptical.
- Organization: Two books. The first is devoted to the debate between More and Hythloday over whether enlightened intellectuals should seek employment as royal counselors or remain aloof from public affairs. The second consists of Hythloday's description of Utopia.
- Themes: The just society; private property; the role of the intellectual; the value of religion.
- Key Passages: "Your sheep . . . that used to be so meek and eat so little. Now they are becoming so greedy and wild that they devour human beings themselves, as I hear," 531; "Nothing in the world that fortune can bestow is equal in value to a human life," 533; "There is no place for philosophy in the councils of kings," 541; "I am wholly convinced that unless private property is entirely done away with, there can be no fair or just distribution of goods, nor can the business of mortals be happily conducted," 544; "If you know one of their [Utopian] cities, you know them all, for they're exactly alike," 548; "consider how large a part of the population in other countries exists without doing any work at all," 552; "Anyone who takes upon himself to leave his district without permission, and is caught without the governor's letter, is treated with contempt, brought back as a runaway, and severely punished. If he is bold enough to try it a second time, he is made a slave," 557; "they hold gold and silver up to scorn in every conceivable way," 558; "Anyone who thinks happiness consists of this sort of [physical] pleasure must confess that his ideal life would be one spent in an endless round of hunger, thirst, and itching, followed by eating, drinking, scratching, and rubbing," 565; "everyone may cultivate the religion of his choice, and strenuously proselytize for it too, provided he does so quietly, modestly, rationally, and without bitterness towards others," 580; "the Utopians all believe that after this life vices are to be punished and virtue rewarded; and they consider that anyone who opposes this proposition is not even one of the human race. . . . The man may not argue with the common people on behalf of his opinion," 581; "Now isn't this an unjust and ungrateful commonwealth? It lavishes rich rewards on the so-called gentry, goldsmiths, and the rest of that crew, who don't work at all, are mere parasites, or purveyors of empty pleasures. And yet it makes no provision whatever for the welfare of farmers and colliers, laborers, carters, and carpenters, without whom the commonwealth would simply cease to exist," 587.

Teaching Suggestions

NAEL now includes the full text of *Utopia*, including the prefatory material and illustrations from early editions. Reading the full text will permit students to discover that *Utopia* is much more than an early example of science fiction. It is in book 1 that More's concern with pressing "real life" problems—the stance of the humanist intellectual toward monarchical government, the fair distribution of goods, the system of crime and punishment—comes to the fore. Many of these problems are as pertinent today as in More's time, and of a kind that undergraduates find easy to engage with. What good is academic theory in relation to political realities? Is it better to remain aloof and idealistic, or to try to change the system from within? Should government aim to deter crime through harsh penalties or prevent it by looking to the root economic causes?

Utopia is not a didactic political treatise but an imaginative dialogue. Book 1 is a long conversation with several participants, and book 2, while narrated mostly by Hythloday, includes a closing response by another speaker (More). Students should be encouraged to consider the significance of the text's multiplicity of voices. The main speakers are the traveler Raphael Hythloday and someone named Thomas More—but is this "More" always to be identified with the author of the work? Is it significant that "More" in Latin can also connote "fool"? What should we make of the fact that More, at the time of writing, was himself considering whether he should pursue a career as a counselor to power, or preserve his integrity as an unaligned intellectual?

Almost all open-minded readers of book 2 will feel that the description of Utopian society offers a mixture of the genuinely utopian (in the modern sense) and the chillingly repressive. The social evils and injustices that beset the England and Europe of book 1 are largely banished from the state of Utopia. Yet this is a state that punishes unauthorized travel with slavery, repeated adultery with death, and oversees almost every aspect of its citizens' lives. Some students may, in fact, respond to Utopia as though it were a darkly ironic dystopia. But did More write with an ironic intention? Would Utopia have seemed as repressive and joyless to his intended audience as it does to some of us? Do the problems entitle us to ignore or dismiss its very real advantages over early modern society, or indeed our own?

Some of the unsettling aspects of Utopian life may be examples of humanist humor. For example, should we take seriously the Utopian practice of having bride and groom inspect one another naked before the wedding to reveal any defects? Hythloday thinks it foolish, though the Utopians, for their part, are "amazed" at the folly of Europeans in disallowing this custom. More may be remembering a passage in *The Wife of Bath's Prologue* in which she claims that her old husband complains that men have the right to inspect every article or animal before they purchase it, except for a wife (lines 288–98). It may also be relevant that Plato, whose *Republic* is the great model for More's ideal commonwealth, in all seriousness commends a similar practice in *Laws VI*. Whatever one thinks of Utopian customs, they force readers to think about the customs of their own country.

Teaching Clusters

As a description of a New World civilization (albeit an imaginary one), *Utopia* clearly has a place in the **New Worlds** cluster. The text inaugurates a tradition of self-reflective travel writing whereby descriptions of the farthest-flung corners of the globe could reveal new and sometimes uncomfortable truths about the English themselves. *Utopia's* ideal civilization can be contrasted with the idealization of the "noble savage" in texts such as Montaigne's "Of Cannibals" (in *NTO*) or the Virginia voyage of Amadas and Barlowe.

Given More's own crucial and tragic role in the English Reformation, he has an obvious place in the cluster on **Reformation and Conflicts of Faith**. The latter part of book 2 of *Utopia*, dealing with religious customs, would work well here, together with "A Dialogue Concerning Heresies." *Utopia* is also relevant to the theme of **Identity, Performance, and Disguise**—in Utopia, one of the chief guarantees of good behavior is the awareness that one is under constant observation by one's peers. All public life becomes a kind of play-acting. More was himself a courtier, and intensely aware of the imperative to engage in the kind of social performance analyzed by Castiglione.

Discussion Questions

1. What is the relationship between book 1 and book 2? What light does each shed on the other?
2. How should we read "More's" rejection of Utopian communism in the last paragraph? Do his reasons seem valid?
3. What do Utopian uses of gold (e.g., for chamberpots) suggest about the nature of economic value?
4. Why does More make slavery so essential to the functioning of Utopian society?
5. Why does More set Utopia in the New World?
6. What is the importance of the scene in Cardinal Morton's table, remembered by Hythloday, in relation to the book as a whole?
7. Is it useful to distinguish between "More," the speaker in the dialogue, and More the author of *Utopia*?
8. How would the Utopians resolve the vexing problems of modern urban life, such as the fair distribution of parking spaces?

Sir Thomas Wyatt

Thomas Wyatt has a towering significance in literary history as the poet who introduced the sonnet form—and the preoccupations of Petrarchan poetry—into English. Like his many Elizabethan successors and imitators, Wyatt writes of the pangs of love, portraying the lover as the victim of both an intemperate passion and an ideal but cruelly indifferent mistress. The lover is exalted and suffers by turns, is tossed between hope and despair. Yet Wyatt's knotty and vigorous style differs markedly from the smoother lines of Surrey, Sidney, and Shakespeare. His path-breaking work is also less typical of the English Petrarchan tradition in that the poet's despair and bitterness tend to predominate, a feature also seen in original poems like "They flee from me." Later sonneteers, like Petrarch himself, cling more stubbornly to the hope of transcendence.

They flee from me
The Lover Showeth How He Is Forsaken . . .

Quick Read

- Form: Lyric (two versions of the same poem, from different sources).
- Summary: The poet complains that he has been inexplicably forsaken by his lover, whose former sexual openness he recalls.
- Themes: Love; loss, memory; mutability.
- Key Passages: "When her loose gown from her shoulders did fall, / And she caught me in her arms long and small, / Therewithall sweetly did me kiss / And softly said, 'Dear heart, how like you this?' " ("They flee from me," lines 11–14). Notice the difference between the two conclusions: "But since that I so kindly am servèd / I fain would know what she hath deservèd" ("They flee from me"); "But since that I unkindly so am served / How like you this, what hath she now deserved?" ("The Lover Showeth").

Teaching Suggestions

Wyatt is not always an easy poet for modern readers to like. There is no question that he spends much of his time complaining about women and feeling sorry for himself. Yet it is worth stressing that in the courtly atmosphere in which Wyatt moved, love and power were inevitably intertwined, and it is frequent in Wyatt's poetry for the personal to shade into the political. Thus, "Whoso List to Hunt" appears to include a reference to Henry VIII's courtship of Anne Boleyn, while "Who list his wealth and ease retain" includes a painful memory of her execution. The gender politics of "Divers doth use" are also worth close examination. The poem is clearly critical in different ways of both men and women. Wyatt claims that unlike most men (and unlike the persona who speaks in many of his other poems), he is content for women to change their minds in love relationships because this is their "kind" (nature). There is certainly a strong element of misogyny in the poem, but it arguably presents a more complex and balanced view of gender relations than is usual in Petrarchan verse. Similarly, the different conclusions of "They flee from me" and "The Lover Showeth," in one of which the lover complains of being treated "kindely" and in the other "unkindly," suggest rather different perceptions of women's nature and gender politics.

Teaching Wyatt gives you a perfect opportunity to get students thinking about poetic form (specifically, the sonnet) and the practice of translation. You can stimulate discussions of both by comparing Wyatt's translations of Petrarch with the originals (or, rather, with modern literal translations), and in some cases with translations by Wyatt's younger contemporary, Henry Howard, Earl of Surrey.

"The long love that in my thought doth harbor" is based on Petrarch's Sonnet 140, a literal English translation of which appears below. Compare Surrey's version of the same sonnet ("Love, that doth reign and live within my thought"):

> Love, who lives and reigns in my thought and keeps his principal seat in my heart, sometimes comes forth all in armor into my forehead, there camps, and there sets up his banner.
>
> She who teaches us to love and to be patient, and wishes my great desire, my kindled hope, to be reined in by reason, shame, and reverence, at our boldness is angry within herself.
>
> Wherefore Love flees terrified to my heart, abandoning his every enterprise, and weeps and trembles; there he hides and no more appears outside.
>
> What can I do, when my lord is afraid, except stay with him until the last hour? For he makes a good end who dies loving well.*

"Whoso list to hunt" is based on Petrarch's Sonnet 190. Herewith a literal translation:

> A white doe on the green grass appeared to me, with two golden horns, between two rivers, in the shade of a laurel, when the sun was rising in the unripe season.
>
> Her look was so sweet and proud that to follow her I left every task, like the miser who as he seeks treasure sweetens his trouble with delight.
>
> "Let no one touch me," she bore written with diamonds and topazes around her lovely neck. "It has pleased my Caesar to make me free."
>
> And the sun had already turned at midday; my eyes were tired by looking but not sated, when I fell into the water, and she disappeared.

"My galley" is based on Petrarch's Sonnet 189. A literal English translation follows:

> My ship laden with forgetfulness passes through a harsh sea, at midnight, in winter, between Scylla and Charybdis, and at the tiller sits my lord, rather my enemy;

---

*This and the two other translations from Petrarch are reprinted by permission of the publisher from *Petrarch's Lyric Poems*, translated and edited by Robert M. Durling (Cambridge, MA: Harvard UP, 1976). Copyright © 1976 by Robert M. Durling.

each oar is manned by a ready, cruel thought that seems to scorn the tempest and the end; a wet, changeless wind of sighs, hopes, and desires breaks the sail;

a rain of weeping, a mist of disdain wet and loosen the already weary ropes, made of error twisted up with ignorance. My two usual sweet stars are hidden; dead among the waves are reason and skill; so that I begin to despair of the port.

Teaching Clusters

As the founder of the English Petrarchan tradition, which had such a huge impact on Elizabethan attitudes to love, Wyatt seems indispensable to **Love and Subjectivity**. His bitter and cynical attitudes toward love and women make a compelling contrast both with his contemporary Surrey and with later sonneteers such as Sidney, Spenser, Drayton, and Daniel. Shakespeare, by contrast, is heir to some of Wyatt's embittered attitudes. Poems like "Whoso list to hunt" and "Who list his wealth and ease retain," which glance at the omnipresent and sometimes brutal power of Henry VIII, would work well in the cluster on **The Representation of Power**.

Discussion Questions

1. What attitudes toward women are prominent in Wyatt's poetry? Can Wyatt be described as a "love poet"?
2. Compare Wyatt's and Surrey's translations of Petrarch's Sonnet 140. How do they differ from each other, and from the original Italian poem?
3. Two versions of the poem "They flee from me" are given. The first is from a manuscript. The second is from *Tottel's Miscellany*. Have students compare the scansion of lines 2, 3, 4, 5, and 16. What is the difference? Which do they prefer and why?
4. Is "Divers doth use" misogynistic or respectful in its attitude to female "kind"—or is it both?

Further Resources

NORTON ONLINE ARCHIVE

Like to the Unmeasurable Mountains
Lux, My Fair Falcon
Tangled I Was in Love's Snare
In Spain
And wilt thou leave me thus?

Audio:
They flee from me (read by James Knapp)

Faith in Conflict

Trying to read the literature of the later sixteenth century without a basic grasp of the English Reformation and its cultural ramifications is like reading Victorian literature without knowing what is meant by words like "railroad," "empire," and "factory." Confessional conflicts shaped the culture and politics of the later Tudor era to an extraordinary extent. Studying the "Faith in Conflict" topic will give your students the tools to understand crucial aspects of Marlowe, Shakespeare, Donne, and Milton, and to unlock the chief mysteries of Spenser's *Faerie Queene*.

The English Bible

The four different versions of 1 Corinthians 13 illustrate what was at stake in the debate over translating the Bible and may also allow you to open up a discussion of the problems inherent in the task of translation. No language precisely matches another in the sense and connotation of every word. Variant translations are thus inevitable, and in periods of ideological strife are apt to become a focal point of conflict. This is the case with Tyndale's controversial choice of "love" instead of "charity" in 1 Corinthians 13, and also with his translation of Latin *ecclesia* (a loan word from the Greek for "assembly") as "congregation" rather than as "church." (Such instances drove Thomas More to complain that Tyndale, by his own stated principles as a translator, might as well translate the word "world" as "football.")

Students are apt to be perplexed by the opposition of the pre-Reformation church to biblical translation. The key point to be stressed is that this opposition was not based on hostility to the word of God, but on the fear that the scriptures would be dangerously misinterpreted by unschooled laypeople. In the preface to his translation of the Pentateuch (included in *NTO*), William Tyndale recognized that the central debate was over the rights and duties of textual interpretation. In the context of a literature course, his words have a resonance that goes beyond the question of biblical translation:

> A thousand books had they liefer to be put forth against their abominable doings and doctrine, than that the scripture should come to light. For as long as they may keep that down, they will so darken the right way with the mist of their sophistry, . . . and with wresting the scripture unto their own purpose clean contrary unto the process, order, and meaning of the text, and so delude them in descanting upon it with allegories, and amaze them expounding it in many senses before the unlearned lay people (when it hath but one simple literal sense whose light the owls cannot abide), that though thou feel in thine heart and art sure how that all is false that they say, yet couldest thou not solve their subtle riddles.

Anne Askew

In addition to introducing important issues relating to the Eucharist, lay preaching, and individual conscience, "The First Examination of Anne Askew" is not without literary interest and dramatic force. One of the most important woman writers of the sixteenth century, Askew struggled and succeeded in making her voice heard through preaching during her life and in print after her death. Like her predecessor Margery Kempe and her successor Anna Trapnel (see the Norton Online Archive), she was bold and sometimes witty in answering the religious authorities, who accused her of heresy. Askew was less fortunate in her fate than Kempe and Trapnel, but like them she left a record of her examination, which survived her. She may in addition have been the author of the ballad "I Am a Woman Poor and Blind" (in *NTO*), which remained widely popular for at least a century after her death.

Book of Homilies

It is important to convey that opponents of the English Reformation included not only lofty figures like Thomas More but thousands of ordinary people of all social classes, appalled by changes that included the dissolution of monasteries and abbeys and the seizure of church property. The "Homily Against Disobedience," sternly instructing the faithful that "all sins possible to be committed against God or man be contained in rebellion," serves as a reminder that resistance to the Reformation was not swiftly snuffed out. That its inclusion in the *Book of Homilies* followed the Northern Rebellion of 1569 is also a reminder of the link between religious and regional tensions: in the middle decades of the century a string of rebellions pitted the north and west of England against London and the southeast, as well as Catholics against Protestants. The first and greatest of these was the Pilgrimage of Grace (1536–37); Norton Topics Online contains several remarkable documents of the Pilgrimage, including the "Pilgrims' Oath and A Song for the Pilgrims of Grace" (reminiscent of Skelton):

> Alack, alack!
> For the Church sake,
> Poor commons wake,
>   And no marvel!
> For clear it is,
> The decay of this,
> How the poor shall miss
>   No tongue can tell.

Teaching Suggestions

In most cases, your students will include individuals from a range of religious faiths, together with those professing none. In order to avoid misinterpretation and offense, it may be best to begin by stressing that you will not be dealing with the true nature of Protestantism, Catholicism, or Christianity, but rather with the images Protestants and Catholics constructed of themselves and one another. Not all Catholics were drawn to religious images—Thomas More, a martyr for the Catholic faith, banishes images from his Utopia. Not all Protestants were content to drink in the official doctrine of the *Book of Homilies*—the radical reformers known as Puritans despised the Church of England as little holier than that of Rome. For the purposes of a literature course, however, the chief task is to come to grips with contemporary cultural perceptions of the Reformation, and responses to it in the second half of the sixteenth century—including, above all, Spenser's *Faerie Queene*.

Teaching Clusters

Most or all of the texts gathered under "Faith in Conflict" are essential for the teaching cluster on **Reformation and Conflicts of Faith.** They are well suited, among other things, to provide a solid foundation for interpreting the religious allegory of *The Faerie Queene*. Foxe's account of the execution of Anne Askew looks ahead to the account by the same author of the death of Lady Jane Grey, and to the later execution of Mary Queen of Scots (who sought the status of a Catholic martyr). Selections dealing with the confrontation between tradition and innovation—notably those commenting on the power of the printing press, and the Pilgrimage of Grace texts in *NTO*—are suitable for **New Worlds.**

Discussion Questions

1. What seem to be the key differences between the different translations of 1 Corinthians 13? Do these linguistic differences reflect religious or ideological differences? What other factors might be involved in differing translations?
2. Why was Tyndale's choice of the word "love" over "charity" in 1 Corinthians 13 so controversial?
3. Compare Anne Askew with Kempe and/or Trapnel as an example of a woman inspired to speak publicly about her religious convictions. What similarities are there, and what important differences?
4. Compare the authorial voice in "The First Examination of Anne Askew" with that in "I Am a Woman Poor and Blind" (*NTO*). What signs suggest that these are or are not the work of the same hand? What aspects of Askew's beliefs and her sufferings are emphasized in each?
5. Compare "A Song for the Pilgrims of Grace" with the "Homily Against Disobedience" in terms of the vocabulary, rhetoric, and imagery they have in common. What is the significance of these similarities in texts coming from opposite ends of the religious divide?

Further Resources

NORTON ONLINE ARCHIVE

Translations of the Twenty-Third Psalm
A Latin-English Psalter
Thomas Sternhold and John Hopkins's Psalm-Box
The Bishop's Bible
The New English Bible
John Foxe, *from* Acts and Monuments
John Hooker, Of the Laws of Ecclesiastical Polity
  From the Preface [On Moderation in Controversy]
  From Book 1, Chapter 8 [On the Scope of the Several Laws]
  Book 1, Chapter 10: The Foundations of Society
  From Book 1, Chapter 12 [The Need for Revealed Law]
  From Book 1, Chapter 16 [Conclusion]
An Exhortation Concerning Good Order and Obedience to
  Rulers and Magistrates
William Shakespeare, *from* Troilus and Cressida
  [Ulysses' Speech on Degree]

NORTON TOPICS ONLINE

Dissent, Doubt, and Spiritual Violence in the Reformation
  The Bible
  William Tyndale, Preface to his 1530 Old Testament Translation
  Edward Hall, *from* The Union of the Two Noble and Illustre Families
    of Lancaster and York [Buying and Burning Bibles]
  Martyrdom
  A Ballad of Anne Askew ["I Am a Woman Poor and Blind"]
  John Frith on the Eucharist
  The Pilgrimage of Grace
  Robert Aske, The Pilgrim's Oath
  Robert Aske, [On Abbeys]
  A Song for the Pilgrims of Grace

Roger Ascham

The Schoolmaster

Quick Read

- Form: Prose treatise on education.
- Summary: In the two excerpts, Ascham shows how to train pupils in
  a good Latin style through double translation and condemns English
  aping of decadent Italian manners.
- Themes: Decorum; style; Englishness.
- Key Passages: "a true choice and placing of words, a right ordering
  of sentences, an easy understanding of the tongue, a readiness to

speak, a facility to write, a true judgment both of his own and other men's doings, what tongue soever he doth use," 642; "these be the enchantments of Circe brought out of Italy to mar men's manners in England: much by example of ill life but more by precepts of fond books," 644; "I know when God's Bible was banished at the court and *Morte Darthur* received into the prince's chamber," 645.

Teaching Suggestions

Ascham's description of what constitutes a good style or "decorum" in a language is an excellent introduction to the social and literary ideals of the Elizabethan period. It might allow for some discussion of how the role of the poet overlaps with that of the courtier. Ascham's account of the evils of Italian culture is entertaining; you might wish to draw parallels with fears about immigration and cultural influence in more recent eras. One of the main points you can draw out from the passage on the Italianate Englishman is the extraordinary influence Ascham attributes to books in shaping (or corrupting) human nature. This perception of the power of the book was widespread in the period, and is reflected in particular in Edmund Spenser's *Faerie Queene*, with its professed aim "to fashion a gentleman."

Teaching Clusters

In spite of his anti-Italian prejudices, Ascham's "decorum" is closely linked to Castiglione's courtly ideal of "grace." A good place for the selections from *The Schoolmaster* is alongside Hoby's translation of Castiglione in the cluster **Identity, Performance, and Disguise.** As noted above, it also serves as a prelude to Spenser's project of fashioning a gentleman in *The Faerie Queene.*

Discussion Questions

1. Why and how does Ascham draw a link between facility in Latin composition and a more general ideal of human excellence?
2. How do Ascham's perceptions of Italian corruption sort with your own perceptions of the "Italian Renaissance"?
3. What, for Ascham, links together contemporary Italian literature with the fifteenth-century English book *Morte Darthur*?

Further Resources

NORTON ONLINE ARCHIVE

From Toxophilus [Comeliness]

Henry Howard, Earl of Surrey

Wyatt and Surrey provided models for an explosion of aristocratic English lyric poetry, influenced by classical and Continental lyric genres. Wyatt introduced the Petrarchan or Italian sonnet to England, but it was Surrey who adapted it to the "English" or "Shakespearean" sonnet form. He exercised an even greater influence over the Elizabethans through his innovation, in his translation of Virgil's *Aeneid*, of unrhymed iambic pentameter, or blank verse. It works well to teach Surrey in tandem with Wyatt, and with an eye to their influence on poets who come later in your course. The differences between Surrey and Wyatt are also worth attention; in both style and mood, Surrey's sonnets are smoother and sweeter than those of his older contemporary.

Love, that doth reign and live within my thought

Quick Read

- Form: Sonnet (an "English" sonnet, though with one rhyme repeated between the second and third quatrains: *abab cdcd ecec ff*).
- Summary: A translation of Petrarch's Sonnet 140, on the trials of (personified) love.
- Themes: Love, desire, pain, death.
- Key Passages: "she that taught me love and suffer pain," line 5; "Sweet is the death that taketh end by love."

Teaching Suggestions

In discussing Surrey's stylistic innovations, you might draw attention to the fact that the English language, in which stress normally falls on the initial syllable, is rich in alliteration but poor in rhyme. Although Surrey demonstrated in "The soote season" that it is possible to compose a sonnet using just two rhymes, the "English" sonnet (of which "Th'Assyrians' king" is a good example) has seven rhymes (*abab cdcd efef gg*) and is consequently much easier to write. The division of the sonnet into multiple quatrains also allows for more complexity in terms of the development of a theme.

Surrey's "Love, that doth reign and live within my thought," like Wyatt's "The long love that in my thought doth harbor," is a translation of Petrarch's Sonnet 140, and can be fruitfully compared with both (see "Teaching Suggestions" under Wyatt). There is a world of difference in sense and feeling between Wyatt's stern conclusion, "For good is the life ending faithfully," and Surrey's more romantic "Sweet is the death that taketh end by love." The sonnet is also useful for illustrating such common Petrarchan themes as the pain of love, and the use of martial imagery to describe the trials of the lover.

Teaching Clusters

Surrey fits naturally alongside Wyatt in the cluster on **Love and Subjectivity**. He is closer in spirit and style to the Elizabethan sonneteers Sidney, Spenser, Drayton, and Daniel. Shakespeare, by contrast, is heir to some of Wyatt's embittered attitudes. "Th'Assyrians' king," describing a monarch enslaved to fleshly pleasure who is both like and unlike Henry VIII, could be included under **The Representation of Power**.

Discussion Questions

1. What perceptions of masculinity are prominent in Surrey's poetry? Does Surrey's masculinity differ from Wyatt's?
2. What does Surrey achieve through the innovation of blank verse in his translation of Virgil's *Aeneid*?
3. Compare Wyatt's and Surrey's translations of Petrarch's Sonnet 140. How do they differ from each other, and from the original Italian poem?

Further Resources

NORTON ONLINE ARCHIVE

Set Whereas the Sun Doth Parch the Green
The Fourth Book of Surrey
Give Place, Ye Lovers, Here Before
From The Second Book of Virgil [Hector Warns Aeneas to Flee Troy]

Sir Thomas Hoby

Castiglione's The Courtier

The skills required by sixteenth-century power seekers and politicians were in some ways not so different from those in use today. Yet in the sixteenth century, service at court was not only a means to wealth and power but also a code of conduct, an art, and a style to be learned, cultivated, and written about. Castiglione's *The Courtier* (1528) is the classic expression of the Renaissance courtier ideal.

Quick Read

- Form: Prose dialogues, translated from the Italian of Castiglione.
- Summary: In the two excerpts, the courtiers discuss the mysterious quality of personal grace and the nature of love.
- Themes: The court; grace; self-fashioning; love; spirituality.
- Key Passages: "[U]se in everything a certain Recklessness, to cover art withal," 647; "love is nothing else but a certain coveting to enjoy beauty," 648; "Whereupon doth very seldom an ill soul dwell in a beautiful body. And therefore is the outward beauty a true sign of the

inward goodness . . . ," 650; "Think now of the shape of man, which may be called a little world . . . ," 650; "let us climb up the stairs which at the lowermost step have the shadow of sensual beauty, to the high mansion place where the heavenly, amiable, and right beauty dwelleth . . . ," 658.

Teaching Suggestions

If students remember one thing from their encounter with Castiglione, it should probably be *sprezzatura*, the word Hoby translates as "Recklessness." Difficult to define with a single English word, *sprezzatura* refers to that studied social grace that comes across as though it were completely natural. Castiglione is one cornerstone of the Elizabethan obsession with the intertwining of art and nature, found especially in Spenser and Shakespeare. The long discussion of the "ladder of love" has at its heart the Neo-Platonic doctrine that the appreciation of earthly (especially female) beauty is a stepping-stone to love and to spiritual beauties. Bembo's long passages of exposition are of central importance, but you may also wish to draw attention to the way other characters dispute, complicate, or ironize his doctrines.

Teaching Clusters

The discussion of courtly "Recklessness" has a key role to play in the cluster **Identity, Performance, and Disguise**, alongside Ascham's definition of "decorum." With its insight into the essentially dramatic nature of courtly and political life, it could also be included under **The Representation of Power**. The section on the "ladder of love" would work well as part of **Love and Subjectivity**, especially as a prelude to Sidney's *Astrophil and Stella*, where the poet (especially in Sonnet 71) describes how remarkably difficult it is to move beyond the rung of physical desire.

Discussion Questions

1. Is there a modern equivalent for the ideal of *sprezzatura*? In what public figure or celebrity today might that ideal be embodied?
2. How and why is the possession of "grace" so important to success in the role of Renaissance courtier?
3. Is the Neo-Platonic ideal of the ladder of love, as expounded by Bembo, sensual or anti-sensual? Is the doctrine favorable to women, or inherently misogynistic?
4. What difference does it make that *The Courtier* takes the form of dialogues between actual Italian courtiers, rather than that of a single-voiced didactic treatise?

Further Resources

NORTON ONLINE ARCHIVE

From The Courtier, Book II (Love)

Women in Power

There is ample reason to include writings by and about the "four queens" of sixteenth-century Britain in your literature course. The careers of all of these women have given rise to enduring popular fascination, and some of your students will already have encountered them in films or fictionalized biographies. Teaching the selections gathered under "Women in Power" means bringing both women's writing and the representation of women into central focus, while also shedding light on the public spectacle of monarchy, in a way that will prove useful when you turn (for instance) to Shakespeare's plays.

Mary Tudor

Whatever preconceptions your students may have about "Bloody Mary," the texts gathered in *NAEL* reveal a woman struggling deftly and desperately to survive in the shifting political and religious climate of the mid-sixteenth century, and a ruler capable of both overcoming and exploiting her perceived weaknesses as a woman—someone, in other words, not so very different from Elizabeth I.

The Oration of Queen Mary in the Guildhall

Quick Read

- Form: Political speech.
- Summary: Queen Mary rallies the people of London to resist Wyatt's rebellion (which sought to block her marriage to Philip II of Spain).
- Themes: Female rule; marriage; motherhood.
- Key Passages: "I am your queen, to whom at my coronation, when I was wedded to the realm and laws of the same (the spousal ring whereof I have on my finger which never hitherto was, nor never shall be left off)," 667; "I cannot tell how naturally the mother loveth the child; for I was never yet the mother of any; but certainly, if a prince and governor may as naturally and earnestly love her subjects, as the mother doth the child, then assure yourselves that I, being your lady and mistress, do as earnestly and tenderly love and favor you," 667.

Teaching Suggestions

The three documents associated with Mary Tudor (her desperate letter to her father, the account of her coronation, and her speech in the Guildhall) can very easily be taught alongside similar texts associated with her younger sister, Elizabeth (the verses written under imprisonment, the coronation, the early speeches dealing with the theme of marriage). Many of the metaphors for rule that would become so closely associated with Elizabeth—the queen as married to her country, and as mother of her people—are already present in Mary's royal rhetoric. The chief difference, perhaps, lies in a certain reticence or reserve upon the part of Mary when in the public eye. In her coronation ceremony, she is almost always a mute recipient of honors rather than an active participant (notice especially her place having to be taken by a stand-in in the remarkable communal bath).

Lady Jane Grey

The tragic figure of Lady Jane Grey became better known to many through the film biography *Lady Jane*, starring Helena Bonham Carter. Although the film is filled with specific inaccuracies, it does paint a reasonably good general picture of the period. The Jane who emerges from the documents gathered in *NAEL* is more complex and rather less sweet-tempered than the movie heroine.

A Letter of the Lady Jane to M.H.

Quick Read

- Form: Prose letter.
- Summary: The imprisoned Lady Jane bitterly denounces her former tutor, Thomas Harding, for abandoning the Protestant faith to save his life.
- Themes: Religion; integrity; martyrdom.
- Key Passages: "Yea, when I consider these things, I cannot but speak to thee, and cry out upon thee, thou seed of Satan, and not of Judah, whom the devil hath deceived, the world hath beguiled, and the desire of life subverted, and made thee of a Christian an infidel," 670; "Be constant, be constant; fear not for pain; / Christ hath redeemed thee, and heaven is thy gain," 672.

Teaching Suggestions

Although Lady Jane Grey was, in her historical career, almost always the passive victim of other people's plots, the texts gathered here reveal a teenage woman as strong-willed as she was highly educated. She never learned the art of tactical self-abasement that, at different points, probably saved the lives of both Mary and Elizabeth (see, e.g., Mary's letter to her father, Henry VIII). In her prison writings, where she prepares herself for martyrdom, she seems less comparable to her royal cousins than to the resolute Anne Askew. You might compare Foxe's description of her "words and behaviour . . . upon the scaffold" with his similar account of the execution of Askew. To what extent is Foxe forcing Jane in her last moments to conform to a literary-martyrological pattern? To what extent did Lady Jane, like Mary Queen of Scots, rehearse for the role of martyrdom?

Mary Queen of Scots

The career of Mary Queen of Scots was, by the standards of any age, scandalous, melodramatic, and tragic, and remains endlessly fascinating. For the purposes of a literature course, an additional source of interest lies in determining where, if anywhere, it is possible to locate Mary's personal voice.

Casket Letter Number 2

Quick Read

- Form: Prose letter, purportedly translated from French.
- Summary: Mary addresses her lover (presumably Bothwell), for whom she is making a bracelet, complains of life with her ill husband, Darnley, and makes apparent reference to a plot to murder him.
- Themes: Adultery; murder.
- Key Passages: "Alas! And I never deceived anybody; but I remit myself wholly to your will. And send me word what I shall do, and whatever happen to me, I will obey you. Think also if you will not find some invention more secret than physic . . . ," 678.

Teaching Suggestions

Your students can easily be brought to enjoy and involve themselves in the mystery of the "Casket Letters," which no sleuth has ever been able to solve. Are they Mary's own damning love-letters to Bothwell (translated by her prosecutors from the French)? Are they forgeries designed to implicate her in adultery and murder? One possibility is to divide the class into two groups representing the two sides of the question (with perhaps a third group acting as jury), and have them debate the authenticity of the letters. What kinds of evidence are relevant in determining authorship? How can we define, and detect, a personal "voice"?

Mary's 1568 letter to Elizabeth, which can more reliably be called her own, also reveals a struggle to craft a voice that will win the sympathy of her suspicious cousin. (The letter should be considered together with Elizabeth's earlier, hostile letter to Mary in 1567 [694].) Mary attempts to appeal to Elizabeth both as a fellow queen and as a woman. Her complaint that "I am in a pitiable condition, not only for a queen, but for a gentlewoman; for I have nothing in the world, but what I had on my person when I made my escape . . ." recalls, perhaps intentionally, Elizabeth's claim in an early speech that "I am endued with such qualities that if I were turned out of the realm in my petticoat, I were able to live in any place of Christendom" (694). Mary, in other words, can be seen to be holding up a mirror in which Elizabeth can recognize herself; the English queen, however, saw Mary rather as the threatening other—a psychological as well as a political threat.

Elizabeth I

Elizabeth was at least as well educated as most of her male courtiers. As we might expect from the one-time pupil of Roger Ascham (as, of course, was Lady Jane Grey), she had mastered classical rhetoric and the complex of linguistic and social values Ascham called "decorum": "a true choice and placing of words, a right ordering of sentences, an easy understanding of the tongue, a readiness to speak, a facility to write, a true judgment both of his own and other men's doings, what tongue soever he doth use" (642). The poems Elizabeth wrote in English, such as "The doubt of future foes" and "On Monsieur's Departure," are personal in tone, revealing her understanding of her own and others' doings, while testifying to her constant anxiety over appearances and public opinion. Her "Golden Speech" and "Speech to the Troops at Tilbury," by contrast, are propaganda pieces in which the queen expertly manipulates the emotions of her auditors. The stirring address to the English troops awaiting the Spanish invasion helps us understand the veneration in which she was held by her people.

The Passage of Our Most Dread Sovereign Lady Queen Elizabeth through the City of London to Westminster on the Day Before Her Coronation

Quick Read

- Form: Prose report of public event.
- Summary: Richard Mulcaster describes Elizabeth's progress through the city on her way to be crowned, with signs that presage the success of her reign.
- Themes: Queenship; public spectacle; the crowd; religious faith.
- Key Passages: "If a man should say well, he could not better term the City of London that time than a stage wherein was showed the wonderful spectacle of a noble-hearted princess toward her most loving people," 689; "when her grace had learned that the Bible in English should there be offered, she thanked the City therefore, promised the reading thereof most diligently, and incontinent commanded that it should be brought. At the receipt whereof, how reverently did she with both her hands take it, kiss it, and lay it upon her breast, to the great comfort of the lookers-on!" 690.

Verse Exchange Between Elizabeth and Sir Walter Ralegh

Quick Read

- Form: Verse epistles in heroic couplets.
- Summary: Ralegh denounces Fortune for robbing him of the queen's favor; Elizabeth teasingly rebukes Ralegh for imagining that her love is subject to fortune and assures him of her continuing regard.
- Themes: The court; love and power; fortune.
- Key Passages: Ralegh: "Sorrow, henceforth, that shall my princess be— / And only joy that Fortune conquers kings," lines 16–17; Elizabeth: "Ah, silly Pug, wert thou so sore afraid?" line 1; "Ne chose I thee by fickle Fortune's rede, / Ne she shall force me alter with such speed / But if to try this mistress' jest with thee," lines 13–15.

Teaching Suggestions

Early and late, a quality that emerges consistently from Elizabeth's writings, and which you can highlight using the texts in *NAEL*, is the self-conscious engagement in performance. Even in the brief "Verses Written with a Diamond" she refers to herself in the third person—"*Quod* Elizabeth the prisoner"—as if she were the audience to the quasi-theatrical spectacle of her imprisonment. The theatricality comes across clearly in Mulcaster's account of her coronation progress. It is worth pointing out that, at the time Mulcaster compared London to "a stage," there were no permanent public stages in England. Elizabeth's spectacles were in a sense a model for the public theater that would take shape in the course of her reign.

As we know from both her public life and her private verses, Elizabeth knew her Petrarch well. Lines such as "I am and not, I freeze and yet am burned" from "On Monsieur's Departure" are classically Petrarchan. (Compare that line with the last line of Chaucer's "Troilus's Song," which is the first translation of one of Petrarch's sonnets into English.) In court, Elizabeth was accustomed to receiving adulation in language similar to that addressed to the Petrarchan mistress. Ralegh writes to her in the voice of the despairing lover, and Elizabeth reassures him by dismissing her anger as a "mistress' jest." Foreign ambassadors, noble courtiers, and members of Parliament all participated in Elizabeth's cult of love, showering her with extravagant compliments. You might draw attention to the remarkably revealing comment of Sir John Harrington, quoted in the headnote: "We all loved her, for she said she loved us" (687).

The young Elizabeth shared with the others in this section both royal disfavor and the threat of execution. Like Mary Tudor, she saw herself as both bride and mother of her country. Like Lady Jane Grey, she played the role of Protestant heroine. Like Mary Queen of Scots, she repeatedly raises in her writings questions of personal authenticity and "voice." The scope and complexity of her career and writings can best be conveyed when she is taught alongside one or all of her fellow British queens.

Teaching Clusters

The writings by and about all four women could lie at the heart of **The Representation of Power**; the accounts of Mary's and Elizabeth's successive coronations are particularly relevant to *King Lear*, which begins with an equally ritualized scene of de-coronation. Several of the selections— including Grey's letter to Harding, Foxe's account of her execution, Mary's Guildhall speech, Elizabeth's embrace of the English Bible, and the martyrdom of Mary Queen of Scots—would work perfectly within the cluster on **Reformation and Conflicts of Faith**. Texts that raise the issue of voice, such as Mary Queen of Scots's "Casket Letters," are suitable for **Identity, Performance, and Disguise**, while poems by Elizabeth such as "On Monsieur's Departure" and the verse exchange with Ralegh have a place in the cluster on **Love and Subjectivity**.

Discussion Questions

1. Compare the account of Mary's coronation with Mulcaster's description of Elizabeth's progress through London. What similarities and differences do you see in the behavior of the royal sisters?
2. What metaphors for queenship does Mary employ in her speech at the Guildhall? As the first female ruler of England for several centuries, does she present a coherent and compelling image of what it means to be a queen?
3. Compare Foxe's account of Lady Jane Grey's execution with his description of the martyrdom of Anne Askew, and/or with the account of the death of Mary Queen of Scots. To what extent is each of these women presented as a martyr for her faith?
4. What reasons do we have for thinking the "Casket Letters" are or are not the authentic writings of Mary Queen of Scots?
5. To what extent is it possible to "know" Mary Queen of Scots (or Elizabeth) through the writings attributed to her?
6. Compare the tone of Elizabeth's early speeches to Parliament (1560s) to that of the "Golden Speech" (1601). How has she changed, if at all?
7. In her speech to the troops at Tilbury, Elizabeth claims to have the body "of a weak and feeble woman" but "the heart and stomach of a king." Elsewhere, however, as in her exchange with Ralegh, she uses her femininity to her advantage. Do these strategies of self-presentation contradict each other? Which strategy seems more successful?
8. What signs do you see in the writings of any of these powerful women of concern for the lot of women in general?

Further Resources

NORTON ONLINE ARCHIVE
Letter to Henry III, King of France

Audio:
When I Was Fair and Young (read by James Knapp)

Sir Arthur Golding

Ovid's Metamorphoses

Quick Read

- Form: Translation in rhyming couplets of Ovid's Latin poem.
- Summary: The excerpt describes the decline of human society from the idyllic golden age to the present iron one (by way of the ages of silver and brass).
- Themes: The good society; mythology; the origins of evil.
- Key Passages: "There was no fear of punishment, there was no threatening law / In brazen tables nailèd up, to keep the folk in awe," lines 105–6; "men began to bound / With dowls and ditches drawn in length the free and fertile ground / Which was as common as the air and light of sun before," lines 151–53.

Teaching Suggestions

In addition to offering a glimpse of how Elizabethans (including Shakespeare) read their Ovid, the excerpt on the Four Ages allows you to make two vital points about the Elizabethan worldview. The first is that it was quite possible for Elizabethans to view many of the developments we think of as signifying "progress" as being instead symptoms of an irreversible decline. Naval exploration and advances in agriculture and mining are all, for Ovid and Golding, features of the brutal and corrupt "iron age"; in the bygone "golden" era, by contrast, human societies were simple, peaceful, and apparently communistic. Much as More's *Utopia* criticizes the English, so this description of the Golden Age entails a sharp critique of "civilized" norms: "There was no man would crouch or creep to judge with cap in hand, / They livèd safe without a judge, in every realm and land" (lines 107–8).

This leads to the second point, which is that this classical vision of primitive simplicity had a powerful influence on how sixteenth-century English people responded to non-European cultures. Contemporary accounts of encounters with Native Americans, some of which are included in *NAEL* and others in Norton Topics Online, constantly draw explicit or implicit comparisons between these "simple" societies and the legendary "Golden Age." Thus, Ralegh's *Discovery*, Amadas and Barlowe's *Voyage*, Drayton's "Ode," and (looking ahead) Marvell's "Bermudas," all of which discover features of the Golden Age in the New World. A dark irony is involved in the use of Ovid's Golden Age as a model for travelers' descriptions of newly discovered lands. One of the central features of the Golden Age according to Ovid was that people never undertook sea voyages: "The lofty pinetree was not hewn from mountains where it stood, / In seeking strange and foreign lands, to rove upon the flood" (lines 109–10). If Europeans rediscover the Golden Age by voyaging, it is also such voyaging that must bring the Golden Age to an end.

Teaching Clusters

Both for its influence on English perceptions of the New World and for its vision of how one age succeeds another, the passage from Ovid has a clear place in the New Worlds cluster. Direct references to the Golden Age occur in both Drayton's "Ode" and Amadas and Barlowe's *Voyage*.

Discussion Questions

1. Compare Ovid's description of the Golden Age with the description of New World lands and/or peoples in Ralegh's *Discovery*, Amadas and Barlowe's *Voyage*, Drayton's "Ode," or Marvell's *Bermudas*. What similarities do you see, in both general mood and specific detail? What do the similarities suggest?
2. How do you read the assertion that there was no private property in the Golden Age?
3. How compatible is Ovid's narrative with the Judeo-Christian story of the Fall from Paradise, as recounted in Milton's *Paradise Lost* or in any of the various Fall stories gathered in Norton Topics Online (see topics on *Paradise Lost* and the seventeenth century)?

Edmund Spenser

Even more than most of his contemporaries, Spenser was immersed in the political and religious controversies of his time, and this makes studying his works in their historical and cultural contexts more than usually urgent—and more than usually rewarding. Spenser's poetry is the response to an exceedingly complex cultural situation by an even more complex mind. His works are examples of how politics can influence literature, but they also suggest the power of literature to shape our responses—for better or for worse—to events, ideas, and people.

The Shepheardes Calender

The Shepheardes Calender is a dialogue in praise of poetry and a complaint about the way it has been neglected in England. By making his poetic debut with a pastoral, Spenser was declaring, as would Milton in "Lycidas," that he was working his way up to the epic, which classical genre criticism held to be supreme in the hierarchy of literary forms. In the *Calender*, Spenser was already cultivating an archaic diction, drawn from Chaucer, which was supposed to highlight the native Englishness of his verse.

Quick Read

- Form: Pastoral lyrics.
- Summary: Two shepherds, Piers and Cuddie (the latter possibly a representation of Spenser), discuss the sources of poetic creativity and the poet's social role,

- Organization: Twelve eclogues, one for each month of the year, with "notes" by the mysterious "E.K."
- Themes: The role of the poet; the pastoral tradition.
- Key Passages: Piers: "Cuddie, the prayse is better, then [than] the price, / The glory eke much greater than the gayne," lines 19–20; Cuddie: "But ah Mecaenas is yclad in claye, / And great Augustus long ygoe is dead: / And all the worthies liggen wrapt in leade, / That matter made for Poets on to play," 61–64.

Teaching Suggestions

Once they get past the quaint pastoral milieu and the medievalized diction, students should have little difficulty warming to this poem, which considers the perennial problem of the sources of artistic creativity and concludes, charmingly, that they are to be found in drink. If you are teaching the October eclogue as a prelude to *The Faerie Queene*, you may wish to draw special attention to Spenser's youthful experimentation with antique terms, and to the central passage (lines 55–78) where Cuddie compares the lot of poets in Augustan Rome to the situation they encounter in contemporary England. Virgil's progression from pastoral to epic (from the "Oaten reede" to "warres and deadly drede") is an implicit model for the aspiring English poet, yet a similar career path seems impossible under present English circumstances. There are no patrons willing to support patriotic and virtuous verse. A poet of talent must either compromise himself—to "rolle with rest in rymes of rybaudrye"—or simply "wither." Yet this pessimistic note is to some extent countered by the poem's conclusion, with its praise of wine.

The Faerie Queene

Quick Read

- Form: Verse epic/romance.
- Summary: The knights of the Faerie Queene, embodying virtues such as Holiness, Temperance, and Chastity, pursue their quests, opposed by allegorical monsters and aided at crucial moments by Prince Arthur.
- Organization: The unfinished poem consists of six books, each composed of twelve cantos, which are in turn composed of varying numbers of nine-line stanzas. Each canto is headed by a quatrain summarizing the action.
- Themes: The career of the soul; conflicts between Protestantism and Catholicism; the reign of Elizabeth I; Ireland; gender and sex; identity and disguise.
- Key Passages: "The generall end therefore of all the booke is to fashion a gentleman or noble person in vertuous and gentle discipline"; the monster Error's "vomit full of bookes and paper was, / With loathly frogs and toades, which eyes did lacke," book 1, canto 1,

stanza 20; Archimago: "An aged Sire, in long blacke weedes yclad . . . Simple in shew, and voyde of malice bad," 1.1.29; Redcrosse's wet dream: "nigh his manly hart did melt away, / Bathèd in wanton blis and wicked joy," 1.1.47; the description of the evil Lucifera sounds oddly like Queen Elizabeth: "A mayden Queene, that shone as Titans ray, / In glistring gold, and peerelesse pretious stone," 1.4.8; of Duessa: "Her neather parts, the shame of all her kind, / My chaster Muse for shame doth blush to write," 1.8.48; the temptation of Despair: "Die shall all flesh? What then must needs be donne, / Is it not better to do willinglie, / Then linger, till the glasse be all out ronne? / Death is the end of woes: die soone, O faeries sonne," 1.9.47; Sir Guyon in the Bower of Bliss: "But all those pleasant bowres and Pallace brave, / Guyon broke downe, with rigour pittilesse . . . And of the fairest late, now made the fowlest place," 2.12.83.

Teaching Suggestions

Teaching *The Faerie Queene* to undergraduates involves a number of special challenges, the first and most unavoidable of which is posed by the language. Ben Jonson complained that "Spenser writ no language." Yet for students to whom Early Modern English may sound as archaic as Middle English, Spenser's pseudo-Chaucerian language is unlikely to present a special problem. He requires fewer glosses than Chaucer and may, in some respects, be easier than other Renaissance texts because in *The Faerie Queene* Spenser was trying to revive what he felt to be the homeliness of his beloved Chaucer's native tongue. Like so much else about the poem, the language has political significance. Spenser's nationalism has a linguistic side, and, in opposition to the Latinizers of English speech, he was demonstrating that the ancient forms of English were adequate for celebrating the past and present glories of the country. Students should be reassured that if they stumble over strange terms like "ycladd," they are in the same boat with Spenser's first readers. Educated Elizabethans would have found the language of his poems intelligible, but would have recognized its distinctiveness and occasional difficulty. It is for this reason that Spenser's works, unlike those of his contemporaries, are reproduced in their original spelling.

From the point of view of the syllabus-planner, the greatest problem with Spenser is length. One has to make a decision whether to teach Book 1 of *The Faerie Queene* as a unified whole or to excerpt a few colorful episodes such as the Redcrosse Knight's encounters with Error, Archimago, Duessa, and Despair. If one chooses the former course, it is remarkable how little can be easily cut out (perhaps the Corceca-Abessa-Kirkrapine episode and some of the allegory of the House of Holiness).

Whichever parts of *The Faerie Queene* are assigned, it is a good idea to begin very slowly and carefully, demonstrating how complex are the meanings that come to accrue to names like Errour or Archimago or Malacasta, and how complex and confusing is the moral landscape. For example, one might ask the students to pick out the clues in Book 1, canto 1, stanza 7, that tell us that this is not a healthy place (it is not identified as "Errours den" until stanza 13), or to say what is fishy about the holy hermit we meet in stanzas 29 and 30 (he is not named until stanza 43; by then, we have penetrated his disguise, but the name helps us to understand his allegorical role).

As Spenser makes clear in the letter to Sir Walter Ralegh that prefaced the first edition of the poem, the whole work is to be understood as "a continued allegory, or dark conceit." If you have not spent much time on allegorical reading up until this point, it is worth taking some time to explain what is involved in this mode of reading, and to stress that it is more flexible and fertile than one might first suppose. Some of the characters in Book 1, such as Despair and Contemplation, are allegories in the simplest sense, personifications of abstract states. (Yet even they have distinctive, idiosyncratic qualities—and why do they look so much alike?) In most other cases, the relationship between a character and its allegorical significance is more complex. Redcrosse—who spends much of Book 1 being weak, lustful, misguided, and despairing—can hardly be considered an allegory of holiness, but rather of something like the will-to-be-holy. It is only in the conclusion of the book, and then only arguably, that he achieves his apotheosis as a personification of holiness.

Except for explaining that the Faerie Queene is Elizabeth, Spenser does not unpack the pervasive political and spiritual allegory, which must have fascinated his Elizabethan audience. He left it to his readers to work out most of the allegorical identifications for themselves, expecting them to be familiar with the religious and political controversies springing from the Reformation. (If it is any comfort to the modern reader, the glosses that Elizabethan readers scrawled in the margins, sometimes identifying characters in the poem with actual people, vary wildly and often seem absurd; but the general outlines of the allegory would have been clear enough to Spenser's contemporaries.) With the help of the notes, which explain the meanings of the characters' names and their associations, the instructor can show how the first book allegorizes the history of the Church of England (Una) in its rivalry with the Roman Catholic Church (Duessa). Spenser sees this history from a militant Protestant perspective, based on an interpretation of the Book of Revelation (chapter 17) in which the Whore of Babylon stands for the Roman Catholic Church. The separation of Redcrosse from Una early in the book and his disastrous partnering with Duessa represent the centuries of separation Protestants saw between the original Christian church and the rule of the Roman Church in England before the English Reformation.

Spenser's first book also embodies a reinterpretation, again from a Protestant point of view, of holiness. Catholicism celebrated the monastic (contemplative) life above the active and held virginity to be a higher state than marriage (see, for example, *The Wife of Bath's Prologue*). Spenser does not by any means reject the contemplative life, but he suspects monasticism of hypocrisy, and in the figure of the Redcrosse Knight he asserts the active life of Christian warfare as necessary and holy. The evil wizard Archimago, masquerading as a hermit, declares to Redcrosse that holiness has nothing to do with "warre and worldly trouble" (1.1.30). Despaire tells Redcrosse that all his "great battels" will only increase his sin and his punishments (1.9.43). But the true hermit Contemplation refutes Archimago and Despaire in telling Redcrosse that the knight cannot be admitted to the heavenly city until "thou famous victorie hast wonne" (1.10.60). In the betrothal of Redcrosse and Una, after the victory over the dragon, Spenser celebrates the renewed union between holiness and the True Church, which for him was the Church of England.

The Middle Ages had a doctrine of two symbolic cities: Babylon, the city representing wickedness, and Jerusalem, the heavenly city, which is not the Jerusalem on earth but the heavenly Jerusalem, the goal of every wandering Christian soul. For Spenser, however, there are three symbolic cities: Babylon, the wicked city identified by Protestants with Rome; Jerusalem; and, between the two, Cleopolis (famous city, Spenser's name for London), which, Contemplation tells Redcrosse, is "for earthly frame, / The fairest peece, that eye beholden can" (1.10.59). Cleopolis thus becomes the symbolic city of earthly wealth, power, and fame, which are no longer to be despised, allied with the One True Church in creating a better world on earth. As the capital city of the English nation, Cleopolis is also the home of the empire just coming into being.

In this connection, one should remember that Spenser was writing the greater part of *The Faerie Queene* in Ireland, where he served an oppressive and often brutal colonial regime. The 1580s and 1590s were troubled years in Ireland, with low-level guerrilla resistance by the native Irish alternating with full-scale rebellion. A succession of English lord deputies in Ireland experimented with various methods of pacifying the country. Spenser himself contributed to the debate over how Ireland could be finally conquered and fully controlled in his unpublished prose tract "A View of the Present State of Ireland" (an excerpt is in *NTO* under "Island Nations"). In the "View," Spenser endorses both military domination and strategic use of famine as a means of pacifying—or eliminating—the troublesome natives. He also condemns the practice of English settlers having sexual contact with Irish women, which, he believed, would lead to cultural contamination. The temptations of Book 2's Bower of Bliss, where the witch Acrasia turns men into swine, resonate with the threat Spenser believed was posed to Englishness itself by Irish temptresses.

In addition to the probable colonial allegory, the scene in the Bower— Acrasia, veiled in transparent silk and stretched out beside the sleeping young man on a "bed of roses"—has analogues in many Renaissance paintings of semi-nude Venuses in repose. The Bower is a good example of the heavily charged eroticism of other Elizabethan works. Spenser had the problem of making sexual fantasy seem at the same time both sensually seductive and morally repelling. How well did he succeed? In stanzas 74 and 75 he has written one of the loveliest *carpe diem* lyrics in the language. Spenser was certainly not puritanically against sex; indeed, he celebrates it in the epithalamion written for his own wedding. He regards sex as divinely ordained for the ends of wedded love and procreation. He does object to voyeurism and sexual exploitation. This, arguably, is what he condemns in the Bower of Bliss and still more searchingly in the sinister masque of Cupid at the House of Busyrane (Book 3, cantos 11–12).

An element sometimes neglected in Spenser, but one that can be a great help in getting students to read him, is his humor. Too often Spenser is pictured the way Milton saw him, as "our sage and serious poet." But Spenser's undoubted seriousness is continually relieved by a sly and whimsical fantasy: the dragon Errour vomiting ink and books and papers, the Lion licking Una's feet, the giant Orgoglio deflating to an empty bladder. Many students who have taken part in the vogue of fantasy books, magazines, and games will discover much in Spenser that touches a familiar and cherished chord.

Teaching Clusters

An encyclopedia of Elizabethan obsessions (albeit from the perspective of one rather unusual man), The Faerie Queene can be included in any teaching cluster. It is largely a question of which passages one chooses to assign. All of Book 1, with its allegorical history of the struggles of the English church, can serve as crown to the cluster on the **Reformation and Conflicts of Faith**. Equally, the imaginary milieu of Faerieland, which Spenser likens (in a passage not in NAEL) to "th'Indian Peru," makes this a suitable text for the **New Worlds** cluster.

If you would rather not assign Book 1 or prefer to assign only brief selections from it, the Bower of Bliss and the selections from Book 3 could make for an absorbing unit in the **Love and Subjectivity** cluster. Such a unit would teach well in relation to Shakespeare's sonnets, which are preoccupied with similar themes of love and time. Yet another option is to focus on the various representations of female rule and authority in the poem—all of them arguably reflections of Queen Elizabeth, though some (e.g., Lucifera in 1.4 and Acrasia in 2.12) are far from flattering. These selections could be taught in relation to **The Representation of Power**.

Discussion Questions

1. How should we interpret the crowded and slightly comical scene at the beginning of Book 1? What is the significance of the battered state of Redcrosse's shield? Of Una's ass? Her lamb? The dwarf? Are there elements of this scene that do not have an allegorical role?
2. Why is Error's vomit full of books?
3. Why does Archimago use sexual dreams and visions to work the separation of Redcrosse and Una? What do Redcrosse's responses to his series of dreams and visions reveal about him?
4. To what extent is there a right reading of the poem's allegory? To what extent is its interpretation left up to the reader? Why are all the characters not given obvious allegorical names like Error and Despair?

5. Is the poem as enthusiastic in its praise of Queen Elizabeth as Spenser promises in his letter to Ralegh? What signs are there of coded criticism? How should we interpret the apparent resemblance between Elizabeth and Lucifera?

6. Compare Spenser's representation of the Seven Deadly Sins in the House of Pride with Langland's portraits of Envy and Gluttony in *Piers Plowman*. In what ways does Spenser's procession resemble Renaissance painting? (You might look at some books of Renaissance art in the library.) Is the procession just for show, or does it have a meaningful function in Book 1?

7. What does Spenser mean when he describes Duessa's genitals as "the shame of all her kind" (1.8.48). Should we understand her "kind" as women or as witches? Compare Fradubio's description of "her neather partes" at 1.2.41.

8. How should we interpret Guyon's destruction of the Bower of Bliss at the end of Book 2? Does Spenser wholly endorse the razing of an environment whose beauty he has praised in such loving detail?

9. As the selections from Book 3 make clear, Spenserian "chastity" means both more and less than mere sexual abstinence. How would you define it?

10. Is Cuddie in *The Shepheardes Calender* a transparent spokesman for Spenser-the-poet. Are there points where Spenser may be seeking to ironize or undercut Cuddie's uncompromising creative principles?

Further Resources

NORTON ONLINE ARCHIVE

The Faerie Queene
  Book II, Canto VII: The Cave of Mammon
  Book III
    Proem
    Canto 1
    Canto 2
    Canto 3 [The Visit to Merlin]
    [Canto 4 *Summary*]
    Canto 5 [Belphoebe and Timias]
    [Cantos 7 and 8 *Summary*]
    [Cantos 9 and 10 *Summary*]
  Book VII: The Mutabilitie Cantos
    Canto VI
    Canto VII
    Canto VIII, unperfite
A Hymn in Honour of Beautie
Amoretti
  Sonnet 15 ("Ye tradefull merchants, that will weary toyle")
  Sonnet 35 ("My hungry eyes through greedy covetise")
  Sonnet 37 ("What guyle is this, that those her golden tresses")

Sonnet 59 ("Thrise happy she, that is so well assured")
Sonnet 65 ("The doubt which ye misdeeme, faire love, is vaine")
Sonnet 68 ("Most glorious Lord of Lyfe, that on this day")
Sonnet 70 ("Fresh spring the herald of loves mighty king")

Sir Walter Ralegh

Like Sir Philip Sidney, Ralegh aspired to the complex and versatile ideal of the Renaissance courtier: poet, statesman, soldier, lover, and discoverer. Yet even before his long imprisonment and eventual execution, Ralegh's voice was almost always gloomier and more introspective than that of the young and sparkling Sidney. A participant in massacres in Ireland and the New World, a victim of intrigue at court, Ralegh knew too well the dark side of the courtier ideal.

The Lie

Quick Read

- Form: Lyric.
- Summary: The poet instructs his soul to "give the lie"—to accuse of lying and thereby challenge to a duel—a series of representatives of corruption and hypocrisy.
- Themes: Personal integrity; the corruption of society.
- Key Passages: "Say to the court it glows / And shines like rotten wood; / Say to the church it shows / What's good, and doth no good. / If church and court reply, / Then give them both the lie," 7–12; "Stab at thee he that will, / No stab thy soul can kill," 77–78.

Teaching Suggestions

"The Lie" is typical of Ralegh in that it adopts a stance of defiance and contempt toward the society in which he is, at the same time, striving to get ahead. In his writings, at least, Ralegh could not easily adapt himself to the servile role of the Petrarchan courtier/lover. Even in his verse exchange with Queen Elizabeth (in the In-text Topic "Women in Power"), he disdains the approach of the abject lover, preferring instead to denounce Fortune and (half-explicitly) the queen for being subject to it. The unusual tone of Ralegh's verse and its peculiar power derive in part from the fact that he was a realist—and a bit of a cynic—moving in an atmosphere of glittering illusions. This point can be extended and deepened in a discussion of "The Nymph's Reply to the Shepherd," wherein Ralegh rejects the captivating visions of Marlowe's "Passionate Shepherd to His Love," reminding him that worldly delights "Soon break, soon wither, soon forgotten— / In folly ripe, in reason rotten" (453, lines 15–16).

The discovery of the large, rich, and beautiful Empire of Guiana

Quick Read

- Form: Travel narrative.
- Summary: Ralegh describes his expedition to Guiana in South America and urges an invasion to conquer the fabled golden city of Manoa.
- Themes: Exploration; conquest; domination.
- Key Passages: "Every stone that we stooped to take up promised either gold or silver by his complexion," 924; "Guiana is a country that hath yet her maidenhead, never sacked, turned, nor wrought, the face of the earth hath not been torn, nor the virtue and salt of the soil spent by manurance, the graves have not been opened for gold, the mines not broken with sledges, nor their images pulled down out of their temples. It hath never been entered by any army of strength, and never conquered by any Christian prince," 925.

Teaching Suggestions

As an account of exploration in the New World and a tract in favor of imperial expansion, *The Discovery* is best taught in conjunction with some of the texts in "The Wider World" and/or *Norton Topics Online* "Renaissance Exploration, Travel, and the World Outside Europe." You may wish to stress the violent sexual imagery that Ralegh uses in arguing for the penetration of Guiana's "maidenhead." Is this an attempt to position England as the aggressive military phallus, compensating for anxieties about female rule? How does Ralegh expect the Virgin Queen to whom the tract is addressed to respond to the imagery of rape?

Teaching Clusters

The Discovery will work well alongside other colonial encounter narratives in the **New Worlds** cluster. The Guiana expedition was not Ralegh's only colonial project—he had a main hand in organizing the Virginia voyages of the 1580s, represented in *NAEL* by Amadas and Barlowe and Hariot. A good place to situate Ralegh's other writing, much of which comments directly or obliquely on the life of the court, would be under **Identity, Performance, and Disguise.** "The Lie" purports to see through the very kinds of shallowness, hypocrisy, and double-dealing that practiced courtiers might wish to pass off as courtly "grace."

Discussion Questions

1. Is "The Nymph's Reply to the Shepherd" simply realistic in its rejection of fragile illusions, or does it slip over into being defeatist and cynical?
2. How does the uncompromising integrity of "The Lie" sort with the shape of Ralegh's own career under Elizabeth?
3. Is Ralegh's use of the imagery of rape and loss of maidenhead in the

account of Guiana a calculated move, or is it more likely to be the expression of unconscious desires? How would Elizabeth respond to this passage?
4. How does Ralegh describe natural phenomena in his description of Guiana?

Further Resources

NORTON ONLINE ARCHIVE

A Report of the Truth of the Fight About the Isles of the Azores . . . Walsinghame

The Wider World

A notable feature in many accounts of first encounters between Europeans and New World peoples is the sense of wonder experienced on both sides. Both peoples found themselves suddenly exposed to utterly strange, sometimes incomprehensible societies and ways of life. The Europeans, of course, relied to a large extent on preexisting stereotypes (the noble or ignoble savage) and often saw just what they expected to see. Nevertheless, such preconceptions were liable to be overturned (e.g., when the Eskimo in the account of Frobisher's voyage indignantly denies the charge of cannibalism).

Hariot's Report on Virginia, 1585

Thomas Hariot's *Brief and true report of the new-found land of Virginia* is among the most complex, ambiguous, and unsettling of Elizabethan travel narratives. Hariot reports with satisfaction that the Algonkians regarded the English as favored by God and that their priests "through conversing with us . . . were brought into great doubts" about their own religion. But this incitement to doubt worked both ways: Hariot's observations have serious implications for European beliefs as well. For instance, his description of how the Algonkian priests control the "common and simple sort of people" with false tales of torments after death in a place called Popogusso raises unsettling questions about the Christians' belief in hell.

Teaching Suggestions

These short texts work best when taught in conjunction with Ralegh's *The discovery of . . . Guiana*. Ralegh organized the expedition that brought Amadas and Barlowe to Virginia, and he was Hariot's friend and patron. (Interestingly, both men were accused in whispering campaigns of Satanism and/or atheism, possibly because of their interest in New World religions.) You might focus your teaching of these texts around the moment of encounter, noting the different ways Europeans and Native Americans are seen to perceive and respond to one another. In Frobisher's voyage, the Inuit people of Baffin Island are seen as savage beasts and immediately suspected on no evidence of cannibalism, a charge they vehemently deny. Drake and Barlowe, by contrast, encounter hierarchical societies whose structure they assume to be not unlike their own, with a "king" at the top and a network of power relations spreading outward and downward from that point. Hariot is perhaps more capable than the others of grasping the genuine difference of Native American culture, yet he too always seems to have one eye on England, whose own customs and beliefs can never be seen in quite the same way after the encounter.

Descriptions of the lands and peoples of America often invoke visions of unspoiled Paradise or the "Golden Age," modeled on Ovid's Four Ages (see the passage from Ovid's *Metamorphoses* translated by Sir Arthur Golding). Arthur Barlowe describes the people of Virginia as "most gentle, loving, and faithful, void of guile and treason, and such as live after the manner of the golden age." Similarly, Michael Drayton in his "Ode. To the Virginia Voyage" praises Virginia as "Earth's only paradise" and describes its inhabitants as those to whom "the golden age / Still nature's laws doth give." The idea of the Golden Age is related to that of the noble savage; for a deeper understanding of both, point your students toward Montaigne's brilliant essay "Of Cannibals" (*Norton Topics Online*, "Renaissance Exploration").

The account of Frobisher's voyage can help your students think more deeply about practices of representation. The Eskimo captive taken onboard ship first mistakes a painting of another Eskimo, captured the previous year, for a living being and then concludes (so the writer imagines) that the English are magicians who can "make men live and die at our pleasure" (931). This fablelike anecdote projects onto the New World savage a set of ideas about representation, artifice, and magic that are in fact pervasive throughout English Renaissance literature. You may be able to refer back to the story of the Eskimo and the portrait on a number of occasions—for instance, when discussing Faustus's conjuring of Alexander and his paramour, or Hero's floral veil "Whose workmanship both man and beast deceives" (Marlowe, *Hero and Leander*, line 20).

Teaching Clusters

These selections form the heart of the **New Worlds** cluster. They are best taught as a group and benefit from being read alongside Ralegh's *Discovery . . . of Guiana* and Drayton's "Ode." Other excellent companion pieces include More's *Utopia*, which first proposes the theme of the New World as the site of alternative and possibly superior ways of life, and Montaigne's "Of Cannibals." Hariot's report from Virginia would make for an interesting unit in the **Reformation and Conflicts of Faith** cluster, suggesting how the spirit of questioning released by the Reformation could ultimately appear to threaten religion itself.

Discussion Questions

1. Compare the qualities that Montaigne in "Of Cannibals" finds admirable in the Brazilians with the qualities that Barlowe describes in the Virginians and with those that characterize the people of Ovid's "Golden Age."
2. Of the various encounter narratives, which, if any, seems to you to involve a genuine response to and observation of New World peoples, rather than a projection of European assumptions? How do you make this judgment?
3. Why, when Barlowe insists that the Algonkians are gentle people of the Golden Age, do the English voyagers remain so fearful of violence?
4. In what ways can Hariot's *Brief and true report of the new-found land of Virginia* be read as offering an implicit analysis of English customs and beliefs?
5. Where else in literature, or in contemporary culture, have you encountered the idea of the "noble savage"?
6. Try to imagine how the appearance of Amadas and Barlowe, or Drake and his crew, would have affected the indigenous inhabitants of the area. Try retelling the encounter narrative from the indigenous perspective.

Further Resources

NORTON ONLINE ARCHIVE

Hakluyt's Voyages
    A Brief and True Report
    The Course Which Sir Francis Drake Held
    An Extract of Master Ralph Lane's Letter
John White, The Wife and Daughter of a Chief

NORTON TOPICS ONLINE

Renaissance Exploration, Travel, and the World Outside Europe
    Arthur Barlowe, The First Voyage Made to Virginia
    George Peckham, *from* A True Report of the Late Discoveries
    Jean de Léry, *from* History of a Voyage to the Land of Brazil
    Michel de Montaigne, *from* Of Cannibals
    Andrew Borde, *from* The first book of the Introduction of Knowledge
        From Purchas His Pilgrims, The Second Part
    Ralph Fitch and Peter Mundy, Observations of India

John Lyly

Euphues: The Anatomy of Wit

- Form: Prose fiction.
- Summary: In the excerpt, Euphues, a young gentleman of Athens, takes up residence in Naples and displays a mixture of admirable and decadent qualities. It is, however, difficult to pick out the storyline from the dense web of stylistic ornaments.
- Themes: Human nature; literary style.
- Key Passages: "As therefore the sweetest rose hath his prickle, the finest velvet his brack, the fairest flower his bran, so the sharpest wit hath his wanton will, and the holiest head his wicked way" (944–45).

Teaching Suggestions

The chief point in teaching this excerpt from the popular *Euphues* is to provide a sense of the kind of literary style Elizabethans appreciated in the decade before the emergence of Spenser, Shakespeare, and Marlowe. Today, the ornate style that became known as "euphuism," with its ponderous comparisons and self-conscious amplifications, strikes most readers as tedious, artificial, and a bit silly. Yet while many later Elizabethan writers mocked the excesses of euphuism, they did not reject the aesthetic impulses out of which it sprang. The euphuistic love of extended comparisons, of delicate natural images, and of artificiality for its own sweet sake are all evident, for instance, in the opening lines of *Twelfth Night*:

> If music be the food of love, play on,
> Give me excess of it that, surfeiting,
> The appetite may sicken and so die.
> That strain again, it had a dying fall.
> O, it came o'er my ear like the sweet sound
> That breathes upon a bank of violets,
> Stealing and giving odor.

Teaching Clusters

Symptomatic of the Elizabethan obsession with style and modes of public discourse, *Euphues* would work nicely in the cluster on **Identity, Performance, and Disguise.**

Discussion Question

1. Try rewriting a piece of relatively plain prose—say, a weather forecast or newspaper editorial—in the style of *Euphues*.

Further Resources

NORTON ONLINE ARCHIVE

Cupid and My Campaspe

Sir Philip Sidney

The Countess of Pembroke's Arcadia

Sidney's fiction is a curious crossing of two favorite Renaissance genres, pastoral and romance. The text also serves Sidney as a frame for many of his lyrics. It is the source of the Gloucester-Edmund-Edgar plot in *Lear*. Sidney keeps up an elevated tone in the narrative and the rhetorical speeches and soliloquies of his characters. The prose is studded with extended comparisons and elaborate digressions, but lacks the ponderous stiffness of Lyly's euphuism.

Quick Read

- Form: Prose fiction, with inset lyrics.
- Summary: In the excerpt, the king and queen both fall in love with the young man, who has disguised himself as an Amazon in order to woo their daughter.
- Themes: Gender, disguise, romance, chivalry, honor.
- Key Passages: "A lamentable tune is the sweetest music to a woeful mind" (950).

Teaching Suggestions

The plot of the *NAEL* selection reads much like one of Shakespeare's romantic comedies. The king and queen both fall in love with the young man, who has disguised himself as an Amazon in order to woo their daughter. This excerpt works well when taught alongside *Twelfth Night*—Gynecia's pursuit of "Zelmane" is in some ways comparable to Olivia's pursuit of "Cesario," and her longing for doleful love songs recalls Orsino at the start of the play. There is, however, an element of cruelty and misogyny in Sidney's depiction of Gynecia that has no immediate parallel in Shakespeare.

Astrophil and Stella

Sidney's Astrophil was, for the later Elizabethan, the paradigmatic Petrarchan lover, and *Astrophil and Stella* the model sonnet sequence. The voice of the young male lover who narrates the sequence can still sound fresh and engaging, though it may also strike some readers as unduly artificial and slightly chilly.

Quick Read

- Form: Sonnet sequence, with inset songs.
- Summary: Astrophil, or Star-Lover, woos and pines for Stella (Star); the relationship is often seen as reflecting that of Sidney with Penelope Rich.
- Themes: Love, poetic inspiration, authenticity, individual desire vs. public duty.

- Key Passages: "'Fool,' said my Muse to me, 'look in thy heart and write,'" Sonnet 1, line 14; "Reason, thou kneel'dst, and offered straight to prove / By reason good, good reason her to love," Sonnet 10, lines 13–14; "So while thy beauty draws the heart to love, / As fast thy Virtue bends that love to good; / 'But, ah,' Desire still cries, 'give me some food,'" Sonnet 71, lines 12–14.

Teaching Suggestions

Whether teaching a large clutch of the sonnets or just a small handful, you will have opportunities to draw attention to the tensions and contradictions that run through the sequence. In the first sonnet, Astrophil is commanded by the Muse to "look in thy heart and write" (line 14), and the sequence purports to be the direct expression of an individual's inner state. Yet it is also exquisitely and self-consciously conventional; to write from the heart was, in Sidney's time, already a Petrarchan cliché. The speaker claims to be in the very throes of love, yet he is as prone to ratiocination as to romantic passion, and tends to approach courtship as a logical puzzle to be cracked (e.g., Sonnets 10, 52). Sonnet 71, weighing Neo-Platonic theory against the imperatives of lust, can be read as a response to Bembo's doctrine of the "ladder of love" in Castiglione's *The Courtier*. If *Astrophil and Stella* is taught as a dramatic sequence and not just as a series of miscellaneous sonnets, it can be interesting to compare Sidney's persona of the "Star Lover" with the speaker in Shakespeare's sonnets and with the female speaker in Lady Mary Wroth's sonnet sequence (in the Early Seventeenth Century section of *NAEL*).

The Defence of Poesy

The Defence of Poesy is both a theoretical treatise, which displays a great deal of humanist learning, and a survey of "Poetry in England," which bestows somewhat patronizing praise on Chaucer and some of Sidney's contemporaries, notably Spenser and his *Shepheardes Calender*. The substantial selection from *The Defence* is difficult for students to master on their own, but with some help from the teacher it can be a valuable aid in explaining Renaissance poetic theory—the hierarchy of genres, for example, and especially the humanistic idea that poetry has a high moral purpose. *The Defence* clarifies Spenser's grand plan for *The Faerie Queene* as set forth in his letter to Ralegh. It also makes for a poignant comparison with what Chaucer says about his works in the *Retraction*.

Teaching Clusters

The sonnet sequence *Astrophil and Stella*, which betrays at least as much interest in what it is like to be a lover as in the beloved, will fit very well in the cluster on **Love and Subjectivity**. That Sidney, in the grip of a different convention, was capable of writing very differently about love is demonstrated by the passage from *The Countess of Pembroke's Arcadia*.

Yet both texts could also be included in the cluster on **Identity, Performance, and Disguise**, and this might prove the more revealing choice. The passage from *Arcadia* involves the literal disguise of Zelmane, but also suggests in various ways that love is a self-conscious performance (e.g., in Basileus's song). In the sonnets, Sidney weaves complex webs around identity and role-play, looking into his heart for the authentic language of love and finding there a ready-made conventional vocabulary. The same cluster would be a good home for *The Defence of Poesy*.

Discussion Questions

1. How does Sidney appear to feel about his characters in the passage from the *Arcadia*? How do the ornate stylistic devices shape our response to the action?
2. What is the role of music and song in the passage from the *Arcadia*?
3. How if at all can terms like "authenticity" or "real feelings" be applied to the conventional love relationship delineated in *Astrophil and Stella*?
4. What are the chief characteristics distinguishing Sidney's sonnets from those of his predecessors, Wyatt and Surrey? Are they all equally "Petrarchan"?
5. How does Sidney write about public life and responsibilities in *Astrophil and Stella*?
6. On what grounds does Sidney insist in *The Defence of Poesy* that poetry is superior to both history and philosophy?

Further Resources

NORTON ONLINE ARCHIVE
The Nightingale
Thou Blind Man's Mark
Leave Me, O Love
Ring Out Your Bells
From Astrophil and Stella
   7 ("When Nature made her chief work, Stella's eyes")
   39 ("Come Sleep! O sleep the certain knot of peace")
   61 ("Off with true sights, oft with uncallèd tears")
   64 ("No more, my dear, no more these counsels try")
From The Countess of Pembroke's Arcadia
   [The Absent Urania]
   [The Country of Arcadia]
An Apology for Poetry

Fulke Greville, Lord Brooke

Caelica

Quick Read

- Form: Sonnet.
- Summary: The poem describes the nightmares and frightening visions that come in the darkness, attributed to devils but in fact the product of "hurt imaginations."
- Themes: Psychology; dreams; demonology.
- Key Passages: "And from this nothing seen tells news of devils, / Which but expressions be of inward evils," lines 13–14.

Teaching Clusters

The nature of apparitions was a flashpoint of Reformation controversy. Catholics insisted that the souls of the dead really could return from Purgatory as ghosts, to warn the living or request their aid. Protestants retorted that such specters could only be devils in disguise. Greville appears to endorse a third possibility, namely that such apparitions are psychological rather than supernatural in origin. This sonnet is worth teaching in the cluster on **Reformation and Conflicts of Faith**, especially if you will be assigning larger works dealing with devils, witchcraft, or apparitions, such as Marlowe's *Doctor Faustus*, Shakespeare's *King Lear* (the visions of Tom o' Bedlam), or, for that matter, *Hamlet*.

Discussion Question

1. What does Greville mean by "hurt imaginations"? Does the phrase suggest madness, guilt, or both?

Further Resources

NORTON ONLINE ARCHIVE

From Mustapha [Chorus Sacerdotum]

Mary (Sidney) Herbert, Countess of Pembroke

Psalms 52 and 139

Quick Read

- Form: Free translations of two biblical psalms.
- Summary: Psalm 52 threatens God's vengeance on a "tyrant"; Psalm 139, with its more intricate stanzas, describes an individual's relationship with the Lord.
- Themes: Faith; divine justice.

- Key Passages: Psalm 52: "Thinks't thou to bear it so? / God shall displace thee: / God shall thee overthrow, / Crush thee, deface thee," lines 17–20; Psalm 159: "Each inmost piece in me is thine: / While yet I in my mother dwelt, / All that me clad / From thee I had. / Thou in my frame hast strangely dealt," lines 43–47.

Teaching Suggestions

For educated women in the sixteenth century, translation was the chief means of entering the textual sphere while preserving gender decorum. Mary Herbert's psalm translations are quite free, giving her ample opportunities for both formal and verbal creativity. They should probably be taught alongside more literal translations of the two psalms in question. The King James version of Psalm 52 is below:

> 1 Why boastest thou thyself in mischief, O mighty man? the goodness of God endureth continually. 2 The tongue deviseth mischiefs; like a sharp razor, working deceitfully. 3 Thou lovest evil more than good; and lying rather than to speak righteousness. Selah. 4 Thou lovest all devouring words, O thou deceitful tongue. 5 God shall likewise destroy thee for ever, he shall take thee away, and pluck thee out of thy dwelling place, and root thee out of the land of the living. Selah. 6 The righteous also shall see, and fear, and shall laugh at him: 7 Lo, this is the man that made not God his strength; but trusted in the abundance of his riches, and strengthened himself in his wickedness. 8 But I am like a green olive tree in the house of God: I trust in the mercy of God for ever and ever. 9 I will praise thee for ever, because thou hast done it: and I will wait on thy name; for it is good before thy saints.

Teaching Clusters

As an exercise in translating scripture, these psalms have a place alongside the section on biblical translation in the cluster on **Reformation and Conflicts of Faith.** It is worth asking what William Tyndale would have said about these very free renderings of the originals! Alternatively, since these poems raise the question of when and how it was possible for a woman's voice to make itself heard in the public sphere, another good choice would be **Identity, Performance, and Disguise.**

Discussion Question

1. What might have made biblical translation attractive to a woman writer like Mary Herbert? What are the advantages and the limitations of this literary mode?

Further Resources

NORTON ONLINE ARCHIVE

Psalm 58 (*Si Vere Utique*)

Samuel Daniel

Delia

Quick Read

- Form: Sonnet sequence (3 excerpts).
- Summary: Sonnet 33 looks forward to old age, when the beloved will repent her scorning of the poet; Sonnet 45 is a prayer for quiet sleep; Sonnet 46 promises the preservation of the beloved's youth and fame by means of Daniel's poetry.
- Themes: Love; the passage of time; death; poetry; immortality.
- Key Passages: Sonnet 33: "Thou mayst repent that thou hast scorned my tears / When winter snows upon thy golden hairs," lines 13–14; Sonnet 46: "Let others sing of knight and paladins / In agèd accents and untimely words," lines 1–2.

Teaching Suggestions

Daniel was, according to Ben Jonson, "no poet." Yet for many, *Delia* is among the best of Elizabethan sonnet sequences. His themes, the loss of youthful beauty and the preservation of such beauty through poetry, are shared with Shakespeare. Daniel was aware of contemporary currents in poetry, and the dismissal of "knight and paladins . . . agèd accents and untimely words" in Sonnet 46 is a conscious swipe at Spenser's *Faerie Queene*. Sonnet 45, with its longing for untroubled sleep, works well alongside Greville's sonnet from *Caelica*, on nightmare.

Teaching Clusters

Together with his fellow Elizabethan sonneteers, Sidney, Spenser, Drayton, Barnfield, and Shakespeare, Daniel belongs in the cluster on **Love and Subjectivity**.

Discussion Questions

1. That youthful beauty will fade but can be preserved in poetry is among the most conventional of sonnet sentiments. What does Daniel do to breathe life into this tired notion?
2. Is the opening sneer at Spenser in Sonnet 46 mere poetic rivalry, or are there deeper issues at stake?

Further Resources

NORTON ONLINE ARCHIVE

From Delia, Sonnet 34 ("When winter snows upon thy golden hairs")
From Musophilus [Imperial Eloquence]

Michael Drayton

Ode. To the Virginian Voyage

Quick Read

- Form: Ode.
- Summary: The poem wishes success to the expedition of the Virginia Company of 1606, imagining the New World as an earthly paradise.
- Themes: Colonial expansion; the golden age.
- Key Passages: "To get the pearl and gold, / And ours to hold, / Virginia, / Earth's only paradise," lines 21–24; "In kenning of the shore . . . Let cannons roar / Frighting the wide heaven," 49–54.

Teaching Suggestions

Drayton's praise of Virginia as "Earth's only paradise" where the "golden age" still prevails bears comparison with Barlowe's report that the people of Virginia are "most gentle, loving, and faithful, void of guile and treason, and such as live after the manner of the golden age." One source for Drayton's vision of the New World is Ovid's description of the Golden Age in *Metamorphoses*, translated by Arthur Golding; another source, clearly, is the biblical Garden of Eden. The idealization of New World societies did not of course prevent the English from seeking to conquer them— even as he praises the native way of life, Drayton exhorts the English voyagers to "Let cannons roar."

Drayton's sonnets are well-crafted and work well alongside Daniel's or Shakespeare's. In "To the Reader of These Sonnets," Drayton strikes a flamboyant anti-Petrarchan pose, proclaiming that his theme is not love but his own shifting mental state. Yet, in Sonnet 6, he returns to the classic theme of beauty's transience and its immortalization through (his) verse. Sonnet 61, with its simple personifications of Love, Faith, and Innocence, can work as an introduction to the allegorical mode, in preparation, for instance, for a reading of *The Faerie Queene*.

Teaching Clusters

As a Petrarchan sonneteer, Drayton finds a home in the cluster on **Love and Subjectivity**. "Ode. To the Virginian Voyage" sheds a useful light on the nonfiction texts in the **New Worlds** cluster, especially those dealing with Virginia (though the voyages of Amadas and Barlowe and of Hariot occurred some twenty years before the expedition to which Drayton refers).

Discussion Questions

1. Does the information Drayton displays about the New World in "Ode. To the Virginian Voyage" seem to derive mainly from travelers' accounts or more ancient sources?

2. What does Drayton mean by saying, "My muse is rightly of the English strain, / That cannot long one fashion entertain" ("To the Reader," lines 13–14)?

Further Resources

NORTON ONLINE ARCHIVE

Idea
   37 ("Dear, why should you command me to my rest")
   50 ("As in some countries far removed from hence")

Christopher Marlowe

Marlowe was a legend (though not a very nice one), in his own time, and remains one today. Early in the twentieth century the sensational details about his death were discovered; these and testimony against Marlowe implied that he had been employed in the queen's secret service. The comments on Marlowe by the government spy Richard Baines and the Puritan Thomas Beard (among the documents provided in *NTO*) have been used to suggest that characters like Tamburlaine and Faustus are projections of Marlowe's own radical skepticism and his hunger for knowledge and new experience. It has sometimes been fashionable to represent him in the guise of one of his own "over-reaching" protagonists, or as a near-abstract nihilistic force. Yet Marlowe was surely more complex and more human than this suggests. While appearing to defy the most hallowed religious, political, and sexual mores, he could be rigidly conservative in his outlook, even a snob. As one student once demanded, "What kind of 'rebel' pulls strings with the Privy Council to get his M.A.?"

Hero and Leander

Quick Read

- Form: Unfinished epyllion (short erotic epic).
- Summary: The progress of the love affair between Hero, virgin priestess of Venus, and Leander, who swims the Hellespont to reach her.
- Themes: Mythology; love; sexuality.
- Key Passages: "Her kirtle blue, whereon was many a stain, / Made with the blood of wretched lovers slain," lines 15–16; Leander's remarkable ignorance of sex: "Albeit Leander, rude in love and raw, / Long dallying with Hero, nothing saw / That might delight him more, yet he suspected / Some amorous rites or other were neglected," lines 545–48; Neptune and Leander, lines 668–77.

Teaching Suggestions

Marlowe's epyllion is playfully erotic—and homoerotic—but it is far from being pornographic (even in the sense that Shakespeare's *Venus and*

Adonis arguably is). Marlowe has his tongue firmly in his cheek throughout the poem, and the urge to laugh is often the strongest response to
the various sexual encounters. The opening description of Hero's dress
(lines 9–36), ornamentally stained with the blood of lovers and adorned
with an impossible menagerie of burbling artificial birds, sets the tone for
the poem as a whole. Marlowe is attempting something close to modern
magic realism here, and at the same time sending up the classical tradition, and teasing, rather than rewarding, the prurience of his readers. The
passage in which Leander is wooed by an amorous Neptune is worthy of
close attention. Here, Marlowe artfully engineers the reader's complicity
in Neptune's homosexual seduction. Leander's naive heterosexual mindset—"I am no woman, I"—is ironized in a way that encourages the reader,
as well as Neptune, to smile knowingly.

The Passionate Shepherd to His Love

Quick Read

- Form: Lyric.
- Summary: The shepherd woos his love with promises of various gifts,
  some simple and others luxurious or exotic.
- Themes: Mythology; love; sexuality.

Teaching Suggestions

This is perhaps the most famous love poem of the century. Its fame
rests largely on its mixture of passion and delicacy; each of the gifts the
shepherd promises is exquisitely imagined and instantly visualized. Marlowe's poem inspired many replies, among them Ralegh's ("The Nymph's
Reply to the Shepherd") and Donne's ("The Bait"). A comparison of these
can make a good topic for discussion or for a paper. You could also invite
your students to write a reply to Marlowe's shepherd in the style of some
other seventeenth- or eighteenth-century poet. An audio recording of the
poem is available in the Archive. Sir Ian McKellen's film of *Richard III*
opens with a musical rendition of the poem, sung in the style of the
1930s.

Doctor Faustus

Quick Read

- Form: Dramatic tragedy.
- Summary: The learned Faustus sells his soul to the devil in exchange
  for magical powers, and after various unrewarding adventures is at
  last dragged down to hell.
- Themes: Knowledge; power; magic; demonology; redemption.
- Key Passages: "A sound magician is a mighty god. / Here Faustus, try
  thy brains to gain a deity," scene 1, lines 62–63; "'Tis magic, magic

that hath ravished me," 1.110; "Faustus: How comes it then that thou art out of hell? Mephastophilis: Why this is hell, nor am I out of it," 3.75–76; "Was this the face that launched a thousand ships, / And burnt the topless towers of Ileum? / Sweet Helen, make me immortal with a kiss," 12.81–83; The stars move still, time runs, the clock will strike, / The devil will come, and Faustus must be damned. / O I'll leap up to my God! Who pulls me down?" 13.67–69.

Teaching Suggestions

Marlowe's drama contains many elements that are obviously derived from the medieval morality play. It is therefore instructive to compare this play with the late medieval play *Everyman*. The characters in *Everyman*, including the title character, are all personifications in a continued allegory. In most respects Faustus is anything but an "everyman." In the opening scene he is already the most learned man in the world, having mastered all the arts and sciences but one, the forbidden art of black magic for which he makes his pact with the devil. Yet Faustus is also like Everyman inasmuch as he must eventually make his reckoning with God, and in this, as the least educated groundling watching Marlowe's play would realize, Faustus remains stubbornly ignorant of the essential knowledge that Knowledge gives to Everyman at the end of that play. The whole point of *Everyman* is to teach him and thereby the audience the doctrine of Confession and Penance, which brings him to salvation, the standard conclusion of the morality play. Throughout Marlowe's play, Faustus is repenting his bargain but is afraid of breaking it. For the first audience of *Faustus*, there must have been suspense as the final scene proceeded. The speech of the Old Man in the B Text, printed on page 596, seems to encourage the hope that Faustus will, after all, pronounce the saving words. Like Everyman, Faustus desperately begs for time, "A year, a month, a week, a natural day" (13.64). The stage effect of the striking clock emphasizes the urgency. Even if one already knows the outcome, the trap door opening with smoke pouring from it comes as a shock. The old morality play has turned magnificently into a new tragedy.

Marlowe's achievement in *Doctor Faustus* is both astonishing and unprecedented. Yet though the play owes much to Marlowe's unique personality, poetic gifts, and career, it cannot be understood in isolation from the larger cultural context. "The Magician, the Heretic, and the Playwright" (NTO) provides a range of contextual materials and aids for teaching and studying Marlowe's play. Here students can discover that the story of Faustus was not Marlowe's sole invention but came from a German narrative about an actual historical figure. The German book was translated into English as *The Damnable Life and Deserved Death of Doctor Faustus*. This text is the immediate source of Marlowe's play. The powerful fears aroused by a figure like Faustus, and the legends associated with his name, are inseparable from widespread anxieties about sorcery and magic. This was the era when witch-hunting was at its height, especially in Scotland, England's northern neighbor. *News from Scotland,* a pamphlet printed in London in 1591, describes the chilling case of Doctor Fian, a man accused, brutally tortured, and finally executed for witchcraft. Doctor Fian, like Doctor Faustus, was believed to have made a pact with the devil.

Teaching Clusters

Marlowe's works can be taught within several different clusters. *Hero and Leander* and "The Passionate Shepherd" clearly belong within the cluster on **Love and Subjectivity,** and the element of homoeroticism in the former makes it a good companion piece for Shakespeare's sonnets and/or Barnfield's. With its themes of diabolical temptation and divine punishment, *Doctor Faustus* could be situated in the **Reformation and Conflicts of Faith** category. However, especially if taught alongside the late-medieval *Everyman,* it could also work very well in **New Worlds,** illuminating the transition from one kind of theater to another. Although potentates are peripheral figures in *Faustus,* Marlowe's fascination with the attainment and exercise of power makes the cluster on **The Representation of Power** another good possibility.

Discussion Questions

1. Why does *Hero and Leander* open with a long description of the heroine's dress? How does the fantastical nature of the dress shape our expectations of what is to come?
2. What is the connection between eroticism and laughter in *Hero and Leander?* How is the reader encouraged to view the rather fumbling sexual adventures of the characters?
3. Compare Marlowe's "Passionate Shepherd to His Love" with the responses by Ralegh and/or Donne. To what extent in either case is Marlowe's shepherd really answered?
4. Does it seem to you that Faustus is really beyond hope of the redemption he begs for in his last hour of life, or is it rather that he has still failed to repent?
5. What are the most significant differences between the passages from the A and B texts of *Doctor Faustus* (*NAEL,* pp. 595–96).
6. What is the role of the comic scenes in *Faustus?* Is it likely that they are by the same author as the rest of the play?
7. What do you make of Faustus's exploits as a magician? Could they be more spectacular or satisfying? What accounts for his gradual descent down the social ladder?

Further Resources

NORTON ONLINE ARCHIVE

Audio:
The Passionate Shepherd to His Love (read by James Knapp)

NORTON TOPICS ONLINE

The Magician, the Heretic, and the Playwright:
Faustus, Marlowe, and the English Stage
    Richard Baines to the Privy Council
    [One Christopher Marly]
    Thomas Beard, *from* The Theatre of God's Judgments
    [A Conjurer and Seducer of the People]
    Christopher Marlowe, The Final Scenes of the B-Text of *Doctor Faustus*
    The . . . Damnable Life and Deserved Death of Doctor John Faustus
    [Faustus's Final Night]
    News from Scotland
    [The Torture and Execution of the Doctor Fian]
    Christopher Marlowe, Scene 9 of the B Text of *Doctor Faustus*
    ["I'll Have His Head"]
    Reginald Scot, *from* The Discoverie of Witchcraft
    ["The Decollation of John Baptist"]

William Shakespeare

Sonnets

Shakespeare's sonnets have acquired the popular reputation of being the most beautiful and profound love poems ever written. Students who come to the sonnets aware of this reputation are likely to come away disappointed, especially when they move beyond a few well-known favorites (or see these favorites in the context of the sequence as a whole). Published a decade after the end of the Elizabethan sonnet craze, Shakespeare's sequence falls outside the main stream of the Petrarchan sonnet production represented in NAEL by Sidney, Spenser, Daniel, and Drayton (all of whom are more interested in writing "love poems" than Shakespeare appears to be). In their frequent bitterness and disillusionment, Shakespeare's sonnets bear comparison with Wyatt's path-breaking productions. In their marked homoeroticism, they can be compared to the sonnets of Richard Barnfield.

Quick Read

- Form: Sonnet sequence.
- Summary: For those who accept that the sequence has a coherent plot, it appears to involve "Two loves . . . of comfort and despair," the first for a fair-haired young man, the second for a dark lady. The

poet's relationship with the young man, whom he initially idolizes, is increasingly marked by suspicion and disillusion, while the relationship with the dark lady is, from the beginning, tainted with deceit, lust, and self-loathing.

- Themes: Love; beauty; the immortality of poetry; trust and betrayal; gender.
- Key Passages: "And all in war with Time for love of you, / As he takes from you, I ingraft you new," Sonnet 15; "do thy worst, old Time: despite thy wrong, / My love shall in my verse ever live young," Sonnet 19; "A woman's face with Nature's own hand painted / Hast thou, the master mistress of my passion," Sonnet 20; "Such civil war is in my love and hate, / That I an accessory needs must be / To that sweet thief that sourly robs from me," Sonnet 35; "That time of year thou mayst in me behold / When yellow leaves, or none, or few, do hang / Upon those boughs which shake against the cold / Bare ruined choirs, where late the sweet birds sang," Sonnet 73; "heaven in thy creation did decree / That in thy face sweet love should ever dwell; / Whate'er thy thoughts or thy heart's workings be," Sonnet 93; "When in the chronicles of wasted time / I see description of the fairest wights, / And beauty making beautiful old rhyme / In praise of ladies dead and lovely knights," Sonnet 106; "My love looks fresh, and death to me subscribes, / Since, spite of him, I'll live in this poor rhyme, / While he insults o'er dull and speechless tribes: / And thou in this shalt find thy monument, / When tyrants' crests and tombs of brass are spent," Sonnet 107; "Th'expense of spirit in a waste of shame / Is lust in action," Sonnet 129; "My mistress' eyes are nothing like the sun," Sonnet 130; "To win me soon to hell my female devil, / Tempteth my better angel from my side, / And would corrupt my saint to be a devil / Wooing his purity with her foul pride," Sonnet 144; "For I have sworn thee fair, and thought thee bright / Who art as black as hell, and dark as night," Sonnet 147.

Teaching Suggestions

The first question readers tend to ask about the sonnets—what do they tell us about Shakespeare the man?—is not necessarily the most interesting or fruitful. The identities of the young man and the dark lady, if these people ever existed, are likely to remain wrapped in obscurity for all time. (Shakespeare, while repeatedly promising to eternalize the young man's fame, never bothers to tell us his name.) In the past it was common to insist that the intense love the poet expresses for the young man was purely conventional and safely nonerotic. The texts of a few poems would seem to cast doubt on such a notion—notably the punning Sonnet 135, in which "will" seems to designate not only "Will" Shakespeare but a friend ("my will") whose name is also William, perhaps the mysterious Mr. W. H. on the title page of the original edition of the sonnets. Inevitably, the sonnets have generated much fruitless speculation on what they reveal about Shakespeare's personal life. However that may be, they are powerful love poems in which the ideal of eternal love, "an ever-fixed mark / That looks on tempests and is never shaken" (116), is, in fact, shaken by age, suspicion, jealousy, shame, lust, and betrayal.

Shakespeare could write in the Petrarchan vein, but in Sonnet 130 he sets out to ridicule Petrarchan conventions, in particular the trite and sometimes silly conceits employed to exalt the mistress's beauty. Hair, for instance, was commonly compared to fine golden wire, as it is in Spenser's Sonnet 37, though Spenser too takes issue with the convention: "What guyle is this, that those her golden tresses, / She doth attire under a net of gold . . . ?" Although Shakespeare's Sonnet 130 can be read on its own as a witty exercise, the so-called Dark Lady of his sonnet sequence is the very antithesis of the Petrarchan mistress. Whatever the nature of the poet's love for the young man, this idealized male love is contrasted with sheer lust (powerfully analyzed in Sonnet 129) for the dark mistress. Not only does she consort with the speaker, but she seduces his friend—presumably the young man of the first part of the sequence (Sonnet 144). Unlike the cruelly chaste Petrarchan mistress, the Dark Lady tempts and corrupts. In the context of the Petrarchan tradition, these powerful but disturbing poems strike a bitterly discordant note.

Although Shakespeare's sonnets provide plenty of fodder for discussions of desire, gender, and sexuality, there is no need to neglect their formal brilliance. In fact, few works reward close reading so well. You might lead your class through a close analysis of Sonnet 15. With regard to the dominant metaphors, point out that there are two, one being that people are like plants ("men as plants increase"), the other that the world is like a stage ("this great stage presenteth not but shows"). Although the two metaphors initially appear quite distinct, with Shakespeare shifting abruptly from botany to the theatre in line 3, and back to plants in 5, they move closer together and eventually merge. The weird hybrid beings who "vaunt in their youthful sap" in line 7 are somehow both actors and trees.

Point out as well how Sonnet 15 repeatedly forces the reader to go back and reread lines with a new understanding of their grammar. On first reading "When I consider everything that grows," we assume that the sentence will have a "when/then" structure—that is, that Shakespeare is about to tell us what happens when he considers everything that grows. But the second line, "Holds in perfection but a little moment," shows us our mistake. "Holds" is a verb, and the subject of the verb can only be "everything that grows." This discovery forces us to revise our understanding of line 1, to go back and add in a silent "that"—"When I consider [that] everything that grows holds in perfection. . . ." This mental operation is shared by virtually everyone who reads the poem, though it may happen so rapidly that we hardly notice it. The same thing happens again in the couplet: "And all in war with time for love of you, / As he takes from you, I engraft you new." Here, we begin by assuming that the subject is "all," only to discover four words from the end that the subject is in fact "I," and "all" is really an adverb (as in, "I'm all shook up"). It is on the basis of effects such as these that the critic Stephen Booth has written that "sonnets like number 15 . . . do not merely describe inconstancy, but evoke a real sense of inconstancy from a real experience of it."

The Plays

If your course covers several literary periods, you will probably not have time to teach both *Twelfth Night* and *King Lear*. The choice between them is difficult but will to some extent be dictated by the structure of the course. If you are stopping, temporarily or permanently, at the end of the sixteenth century, then *Twelfth Night* makes a satisfactory and uplifting conclusion to a course. If you are carrying on into the seventeenth century, then the pessimistic Jacobean *Lear* is a good choice. Teaching either play on its own or both together, you will have the opportunity to introduce students to themes and conflicts that were central to Shakespeare's culture and to his art: conflicts between custom and innovation, between men and women, between social classes, and between appearances and inner truth.

Twelfth Night

Quick Read

- Form: Dramatic comedy.
- Summary: The twins Viola and Sebastian are separated in a storm. Dressed as a boy, Viola enters the service of Duke Orsino and woos Olivia on his behalf. Olivia falls in love with "Cesario" (Viola), and the Duke also seems drawn to him. Viola's twin Sebastian appears and is mistaken for Cesario by Olivia, who marries him. Viola's true sex can be revealed, and she marries the Duke. In a subplot, Olivia's humorless steward Malvolio is baited and tormented by other members of her household.
- Themes: Gender; desire; identity; music.
- Key Passages: Orsino: "That instant was I turned into a hart, / And my desires, like fell and cruel hounds, / E'er since pursue me," 1.1.20–22; Olivia: "Why, what would you?"; Viola: "Make me a willow cabin at your gate / And call my soul within the house . . . ," 1.5.254–56; Viola: "O time, thou must untangle this, not I. / It is too hard a knot for me t'untie," 2.2.39–40; Sir Toby: "Art any more than a steward? Dost thou think, because thou art virtuous, there shall be no more cakes and ale?" 2.3.106–8; Orsino: "There is no woman's sides / Can bide the beating of so strong a passion / As love doth give my heart; no woman's heart / So big, to hold so much. They lack retention," 2.4.92–95; Viola: "She never told her love, / But let concealment, like a worm i' the bud, / Feed on her damask cheek," 2.4.110–12; Malvolio: "'M.O.A.I.' This simulation is not as the former, and yet to crush this a little, it would bow to me, for every one of these letters are in my name," 2.5.131–33; Feste: "To see this age!

A sentence is but a cheverel glove to a good wit, how quickly the wrong side may be turned outward," 3.1.11–13; Viola: [aside] "Pray God defend me. A little thing would make me tell them how much I lack of a man," 3.4.288–89; Sebastian: [to Olivia] "So comes it, lady, you have been mistook. / But nature to her bias drew in that. You would have been contracted to a maid . . . ," 5.1.257–58; Malvolio: "I'll be revenged on the whole pack of you," 5.1.373; Orsino: ". . . Cesario, come— / For so you shall be while you are a man; / But when in other habits you are seen, / Orsino's mistress, and his fancy's queen," 5.1.380–83.

Teaching Suggestions

Twelfth Night is a delicate and sparkling comedy, which still holds the stage with remarkable success. (There has been more than one recent film version that you might consider screening for your class.) Yet this play is far from being an insubstantial confection. In the merciless punishment of Malvolio, amounting to something close to torture, the relationship between comedy and cruelty is impossible to ignore. The play also raises some profound issues of identity—how, in both a philosophical and a social sense, do we know who we are? In Twelfth Night, these questions tend to center around the problem of gender identity. The play manages to suggest both that gender is a matter of biological fact and that, conversely, it is no more essential than the clothes one wears.

At the end of Twelfth Night, even though Viola's sex has at last been revealed, Orsino continues to call her Cesario. He will do so, he explains, until she resumes her feminine attire, for only then will she be transformed back into a woman. Is Viola/Cesario at this moment in the play a man or a woman? Is gender a matter of biology or of dress? The question is made still more complex by the fact that, on the Shakespearean stage, the actor playing the part was a boy. Where Orsino sees a woman playing a man, the audience would see a boy playing a woman playing a man. This must have required a large measure of mental agility on the part of the audience, who would simultaneously have to remember that Cesario was Viola, and forget that Viola was an adolescent male actor.

In Twelfth Night there are ambiguities of rank as well as of gender. Olivia, a countess, rejects Duke Orsino but is eager to marry Viola disguised as the duke's servant Cesario. In the end she is happy to settle for Viola's twin brother, while Orsino gets Viola. The exact "estate" of Viola and Sebastian is never entirely clear, but Shakespeare takes pains to establish that they are wealthy gentlefolk. In act 1, scene 2, Viola gives the Captain gold and tells him that she wishes to conceal her rank, promising to pay him "bountifully" to assist in her disguise. Furthermore, she addresses him by the familiar "thou" and he addresses her by the respectful "you." Thus she would seem to be, if not an equal, at least an eligible mate for Duke Orsino, and her brother for Countess Olivia. Sir Andrew Aguecheek, whose chief claim to knighthood is "three thousand ducats a

year," is, however, a ridiculous suitor for Olivia's hand. And the very notion of an unequal union is mocked in the subplot, where Malvolio falls
into Maria's trap by believing that Olivia is in love with him. Malvolio is
put in his place; still, the comedy suggests that such grand illusions are
not outside the realm of possibility for less vain and more sophisticated
suitors. Sir Toby, we learn, has married Maria in reward for her successful
plot to humiliate Malvolio. Class barriers are growing permeable.

King Lear

Quick Read

- Form: Dramatic tragedy.
- Summary: Lear, king of Britain, in a very ancient period, resolves to
  divide his kingdom among his three daughters on the basis of how
  much they profess to love him. The youngest, Cordelia, refuses to
  take part and is banished, but is pitied and married by the king of
  France. Having given away his power, Lear is maltreated by his two
  elder daughters, Goneril and Regan. He goes mad and wanders
  in the wild. Meanwhile, the good Earl of Gloucester is tricked by
  his bastard son Edmund into banishing his good son Edgar, and
  Gloucester's eyes are subsequently put out. Cordelia returns from
  France with an army, and the characters converge on the field of battle, where Lear and his daughter are defeated. The deceptions of Edmund, Regan, and Goneril are revealed, leading to their deaths, but
  not before Cordelia has been murdered in prison. At the end of the
  play, Lear enters carrying her dead body and dies with his eyes fixed
  upon Cordelia's face.
- Themes: Love; loyalty; nature; fate; madness; isolation.
- Key Passages: Lear: "Nothing will come of nothing, speak again";
  Cordelia: "Unhappy that I am, I cannot heave / My heart into my
  mouth. I love your majesty / According to my bond; nor more nor
  less," 1.1.90–93; Edmund: "Thou, nature, art my goddess; to thy
  law/ My services are bound," 1.2.1–2; Gloucester: "These late
  eclipses in the sun and moon portend no good to us. Though the wisdom of nature can reason it thus and thus, yet nature finds itself
  scourged by the sequent effects. Love cools, friendship falls off,
  brothers divide . . . and the bond cracked 'twixt son and father,"
  1.2.103–9; Fool: "Can you make no use of nothing, uncle?" Lear:
  "Why, no, boy; nothing can be made out of nothing"; Fool: [to Kent]
  "Prithee, tell him, so much the rent of his land comes to,"
  1.4.127–31; Lear: "How sharper than a serpent's tooth it is / To have
  a thankless child!" 1.4.284–85; Lear: "O, reason not the need! Our
  basest beggars / Are in the poorest thing superfluous. / Allow not
  nature more than nature needs, / Man's life's as cheap as beast's,"
  2.4.262–65; Lear: "Poor naked wretches, whereso'er you are, / That

bide the pelting of this pitiless storm, / How shall your houseless heads and unfed sides, / Your looped and windowed raggedness, defend you / From seasons such as these? O, I have ta'en / Too little care of this!" 3.4.29–34; Lear: "Thou art the thing itself; unaccommodated man is no more but such a poor bare, forked animal as thou art. Off, off, you lendings! come unbutton here," 3.4.103–5; Lear: "Down from the waist they are Centaurs, / Though women all above. / But to the girdle do the gods inherit. / Beneath is all the fiends' . . . ," 4.6.122–25; Gloucester: "O, let me kiss that hand!"; Lear: "Let me wipe it first; it smells of mortality," 4.6.131–32; Edmund: "Yet Edmund was beloved. / The one the other poisoned for my sake, / And after slew herself," 5.3.239–41; Lear: "Thou'lt come no more, / Never, never, never, never, never! / Pray you, undo this button. Thank you, sir. / Do you see this? Look on her, look, her lips, / Look there, look there!" 5.3.307–11.

Teaching Suggestions

If you are moving on from *Twelfth Night*, you might begin by stressing that the fetishism of dress is also a dominant theme in *King Lear*, though here the determining power of clothing is considered in regard to the fictions of social class rather than those of gender. Lear is first moved to a recognition of common humanity by the sight of Edgar/Poor Tom, and his immediate reaction is to try to strip off his own clothes: "Thou art the thing itself; unaccommodated man is no more but such a poor, bare, forked animal as thou art. Off, off, you lendings! come unbutton here" (3.4.103–5). Later, in a moment of lucidity-in-madness, the king declares: "Through tattered gowns small vices do appear; / Robes and furred gowns hide all" (lines 161–62).

Although it is one of the last selections in the Sixteenth Century section of *NAEL*, *King Lear* properly belongs to the early seventeenth century and to the reign of Elizabeth's successor, James I. In its themes and in its somber mood, the play reveals the precariousness of the Tudor and Stuart establishments and the gloom that seems to have overtaken the country at the turn of the century. *Lear* calls into question all the familial, social, and political bonds that had been invoked to rationalize and justify the Tudor monarchy in the sixteenth century. More fundamentally, the play comes close to shattering the faith in nature on which the whole social order was supposed to rest.

The anxious questioning and generalized pessimism of *Lear* reflect wider social processes and ideological tensions. Shakespeare lived and wrote in an era when one very old and well-honored social system was gradually and uneasily giving way to another. According to the traditional values upheld in the play by Lear and Gloucester, one's position in society rested on the relatively intangible bases of rank, lineage, and loyalty; people were supposed to remain in the station to which they were born. But in Shakespeare's lifetime traditional assumptions were increasingly being called into question by new social forces—forces associated in the play with Edmund, Goneril, and Regan—and by the rise of early capitalism. Real authority now seemed to lie not in fuzzy concepts like social rank but in how much power—most fundamental, economic power—one could bring to bear. In one traditional set of terms, then, King Lear's aspiration to remain a king while giving up his power makes perfect sense. But in the coldly pragmatic terms of the emergent society, it is patently absurd.

The ideological debate in *King Lear* does not refer directly to "economics" or "society" but rather to "nature." The word recurs constantly in the play. Both Edmund and Lear refer to nature as a goddess, but with opposing meanings. When Edmund declares, "Thou, nature, art my goddess; to thy law / My services are bound," he means that he is not bound by worn-out old ideas of custom, legitimacy, and loyalty. In "nature," Edmund worships the sort of chaotic social forces unleashed by the market economy (and his prayer foreshadows such modern clichés as "It's a dog eat dog world"). On the other hand, when Lear cries out, "Hear, Nature, hear! dear goddess, hear!" he invokes a traditional conception of nature as upholding the innate authority of fathers and of kings. It is not clear which version of nature is responsible for the storm that batters Lear and his companions in act 3. Perhaps in the storm, nature is revolting against the unnatural cruelty of Goneril and Regan; or perhaps the natural world is simply mocking all human appeals to hierarchy, reason, and morality.

Teaching Clusters

Shakespeare is said to be universal, so where in your course could he belong but everywhere? His works could find a home in almost any cluster. The sonnets can clearly be associated with the productions of Sidney, Spenser, Daniel, Drayton, and Barnfield under the rubric of **Love and Subjectivity**. Yet Shakespeare's suspicion that love is a species of duplicitous performance (as in Sonnet 138, "When my love swears that she is made of truth") and the fascinating puzzle over the real identities of the protagonists make **Identity, Performance, and Disguise** an equally strong option. **Identity, Performance, and Disguise** is also the natural grouping for *Twelfth Night*—indeed, the comedy is the ideal culmination of this cluster.

Depending on your emphasis in teaching *King Lear*, it could find a place in several groupings. Although it contains no explicit reference to the Christian religion, the play has many affinities with the themes explored in **Reformation and Conflicts of Faith**, such as the relationship between human beings and the divine ("as flies to wanton boys are we to the gods"). The ravings of Tom o' Bedlam are derived from a contemporary scandal involving Jesuit exorcists; this aspect of the play could be worth bringing out if your syllabus also includes Marlowe's *Doctor Faustus* and/or Fulke Greville's sonnet on diabolical visions. Because it marks the transition from Elizabethan to Jacobean, *King Lear* could also work as part of the **New Worlds** cluster. The most compelling choice is probably **The Representation of Power**, which cluster this tragedy would serve to crown.

Discussion Questions

1. Explicate one of Shakespeare's sonnets both as a separate poem and as part of the sequence. You will want to read a few of the sonnets that precede and a few of those that follow your choice. Do other poems in the sequence clarify the meaning? Instructors may want to specify the sonnet or provide a limited choice.
2. Compare Shakespeare's Sonnet 20 with Sonnet 11 from Richard Barnfield's *Cynthia*. How do these poems go about expressing the nature of homoerotic desire?
3. Why does Sonnet 15 shift so perplexingly between metaphors proper to botany and others belonging to the theater? What is the relationship between actors and plants?
4. What attitudes to women are apparent in the "Dark Lady" sonnets?
5. Why, at the conclusion of *Twelfth Night*, does Duke Orsino insist on continuing to call Viola "Cesario"?
6. Compare Olivia's pursuit of Viola (a woman disguised as a boy) in *Twelfth Night* with Gynecia's pursuit of Zelmane (a man disguised as a woman) in Sidney's *The Countess of Pembroke's Arcadia*. How does each writer portray the older female wooer? How does each deal with the undercurrent of homoerotic desire?
7. To what extent do "clothes make the man" in *Twelfth Night*? And in *King Lear*?
8. How are we meant to feel about the escapades of Sir Toby Belch and his cronies, especially their treatment of Malvolio? Do our attitudes toward them change in the course of the play?
9. How many distinct references to "nature" can you spot in *King Lear*? What different meanings are assigned to the word? Are they complementary or conflicting? Does any one sense seem to predominate throughout or at the end?
10. The original Lear story concluded with a victory for Lear and Cordelia. Why did Shakespeare change the ending?
11. Gloucester: "As flies to wanton boys are we to the gods; they kill us for their sport," 4.1.37–38. Is this the final message of *King Lear*?
12. *King Lear* was produced during the period when King James was pursuing the union of Scotland and England into the kingdom of Great Britain. How does Shakespeare's tragedy appear to comment or reflect upon this political project?

Further Resources

Thomas Campion

Campion is among the best-known of Elizabethan poets, though he is remembered today not primarily as a poet, but as a composer. It is certainly worth having your students listen to some of his songs; numerous recordings are available, including "Fain Would I Wed" in the Norton Online Archive. Of the lyrics in *NAEL*, "Fain Would I Wed" deserves particular attention, both because of the excellent rendition by Dame Janet Baker available in the archive, and because of its remarkably easy-going approach to both sexual and religious scruples. The "bloodless sickness" of line 3, sometimes known as "green sickness," was a recognized medical condition in the sixteenth century; afflicted young women were thought to be in danger of wasting away through sexual longing, and the cure—as seen in Shakespeare's *Two Noble Kinsmen*, among other places, was sexual intercourse. The cure of "quickness" in line 4 refers not only to liveliness but also to pregnancy. More shocking still, to some listeners, is the maid's intention to join "some holy order"—that is, to become a Catholic nun. She concludes, however, by resolving to produce children—presumably, given the title, within wedlock.

Teaching Clusters

Love and Subjectivity is the best grouping for Campion's songs. They are especially worth teaching under this heading if your syllabus includes the Bower of Bliss episode in *The Faerie Queene*, with the inset song to the "Virgin Rose" (Book 2, canto 12, stanzas 74–75).

Further Resources

NORTON ONLINE ARCHIVE

When Thou Must Home to Shades of Underground
What If a Day
Never Love Unless You Can
Rose-cheeked Laura
Think'st Thou to Seduce Me Then

Audio:
Fain Would I Wed (sung by Dame Janet Baker)

Thomas Nashe

A Litany in Time of Plague

Quick Read

- Form: Lyric.
- Summary: A farewell to life in the face of inevitable mortality.
- Themes: Life's brevity; death.
- Key Passages: "I am sick, I must die. Lord have mercy on us!" (the conclusion to each stanza).

Teaching Suggestions

The plague of 1592–93, a severe but not extraordinary outbreak, killed well over 10,000 Londoners, a significant proportion of the urban population. Nashe's somber lyric reflects the omnipresence of death at this time, yet its theme is not just bubonic plague but the inevitability of death in general. If you are moving on into the seventeenth century, you can draw the connection between "A Litany in Time of Plague" and works by such mortality-obsessed early-Jacobean authors as John Donne and John Webster. It is also worth noting that, grim though it is, the poem ends on an uplifting note: "Heaven is our heritage, / Earth but a player's stage; / Mount we unto the sky." Nashe was certainly no Calvinist; heaven, in this version, appears to be the common destination of humanity, when the play is over.

Teaching Clusters

The fact that the song is identified as a litany, and that it carries echoes of the late-medieval theme of the *Danse Macabre*, makes **Reformation and Conflicts of Faith** one good option. However, noting how the song concludes by describing this world as "a player's stage" and implicitly dismisses worldly fame and high degree as so much play-acting, you might prefer to include this text in the **Identity, Performance, and Disguise** cluster.

Discussion Questions

1. What view of the universe is implicit in Nashe's pronouncement "All things to end are made"?
2. Compare the depiction of death in Nashe's "Litany" with that in the play *Everyman*, written roughly a hundred years earlier. Does the English Reformation appear to have altered responses to this most unchanging of human conditions?

Further Resources

NORTON ONLINE ARCHIVE

From Pierce Penniless, His Supplication to the Devil
　[The Defense of Plays]
　An Invective Against Enemies of Poetry
From The Unfortunate Traveler, or The Life of Jack Wilton
　[Roman Summer]
Spring, the Sweet Spring

Richard Barnfield

Cynthia

Quick Read

- Form: Sonnet sequence (2 excerpts).
- Summary: Sonnet 9 recounts how Venus created Ganymede, the beautiful boy lover of Zeus, from the blood of Diana; in Sonnet 11, the poet reveals to a male friend that he is in love with him, by showing him the face of his love in a magic glass (in fact a mirror).
- Key Passages: "He opened it: and taking off the cover, / He straight perceived himself to be my lover," lines 13–14.

Teaching Suggestions

As the headnote remarks, Barnfield's sonnets lie at the far end of a homoerotic spectrum that includes works by Shakespeare, Marlowe, and Spenser. Barnfield is therefore best taught in conjunction with one or more of those poets. It is tempting to save Barnfield as a surprise, to be brought out at that moment when, in teaching Shakespeare's sonnets, a student objects that the instructor is imposing a modern "gay" reading on the Elizabethan text. It is a common though ill-founded assumption that the expression of homoerotic desire was off-limits in Elizabethan England, and that therefore Shakespeare can't have really meant it that way. Barnfield's Sonnet 11 makes clear just how much in the way of explicit homoeroticism a sonneteer could get away with without (as far as we know) having to fear censorship or punishment.

In leading the class through the two sonnets, you might want to draw attention to their visuality. Both, in different ways, lead up to the triumphant unveiling of the beloved boy/man in the final line. In Sonnet 9, the boy is literally assembled (from blood, crystal, and snow) over the course of the poem. In 11, it is the beloved's own face that in the final line suddenly fills the field of vision.

Teaching Clusters

Barnfield probably belongs in the cluster on **Love and Subjectivity**, alongside his fellow Elizabethan sonneteers. His sonnets will resonate with Marlowe's *Hero and Leander*, featuring the erotic encounter of Leander and Neptune. Indeed, Sonnet 9 probably owes much to Marlowe's gaudy, slightly surreal classicism. Sonnet 11 should be read alongside Shakespeare's sonnets to the young man, notably Sonnet 20.

Discussion Questions

1. What is signified or suggested by the mingling of snow and blood in Sonnet 9?
2. How should we imagine the reaction of Barnfield's friend in Sonnet 11 to seeing his own face in the mirror?
3. Compare these sonnets with Shakespeare's Sonnet 20, addressed to a "master mistress." How does each poet go about describing or defining homoerotic desire?

The Sixteenth Century
Texts in the Norton Online Archive
by Authors Not in NAEL

Lyrics
  The Queen Champion Retires
  The Shepherd's Consort
  Weep You No More, Sad Fountains

Back and Side Go Bare, Go Bare
In Praise of a Contented Mind
Though Amaryllis Dance in Green
Come Away, Come, Sweet Love!
Thule, the Period of Cosmography
Madrigal ("My love in her attire doth show her wit")
The Silver Swan
Constant Penelope Sends to Thee
William Bullein, A Dialogue Against the Pestilence
Sir John Davies, Orchestra
Sir John Cheke, Our Own Tongue Clean and Pure
Edward Dyer, My Mind to Me a Kingdom Is
Richard Edwards, Amantium Irae Amoris Redintegratio Est
George Gascoigne
   Gascoigne's Lullaby
   Woodmanship
   The Lullaby of a Love
   Farewell with a Mischief
Hakluyt's Voyages
   A Brief and True Report
   The Course Which Sir Francis Drake Held
   An Extract of Master Ralph Lane's Letter
Hugh Latimore, Sermon of the Plowers
Martin Marprelate
   Hay Any Work for Cooper
   Church Government
George Peele, Fair and Fair
Philip Stubbes, The Anatomy of Abuses
Chidiok Tichborne, Tichborne's Elegy
Isabella Whitney, Will and Testament

CHAPTER 7

The Early Seventeenth Century 1603–1660

INTRODUCING THE PERIOD

And new philosophy calls all in doubt;
The element of fire is quite put out;
The sun is lost, and the earth, and no man's wit
Can well direct him where to look for it.
And freely men confess that this world's spent,
When in the planets and the firmament
They seek so many new; they see that this
Is crumbled out again to his atomies.
'Tis all in pieces, all coherence gone;
All just supply, and all relation:
Prince, subject; father, son, are things forgot,
For every man alone thinks he hath got
To be a phoenix, and that there can be
None of that kind of which he is, but he.

These lines from John Donne's *Anatomy of the World* (205–18) introduce several of the themes, moods, and perceptions that characterize the literature of the early seventeenth century and help mark the break between the Elizabethan and Jacobean periods. The sense Donne conveys of a world that has severed its links with the past and fallen under the spell of bewildering innovations is particularly worthy of emphasis, given that both students and instructors may at times be inclined to wonder what exactly is new and different about early-seventeenth-century literature. More than any other division between literary periods, the line dividing literature written under the Tudors from that written under the first Stuarts can seem artificial, a matter of convenience rather than a useful critical tool. The fact that the careers of major authors such as Shakespeare and Donne span the Elizabethan-Jacobean divide makes it easy for the teacher to effect the transition from one era to the next without much fuss.

Nevertheless, there are good reasons to draw attention at the outset to what is new and distinctive in Jacobean literature. Students find periodization a useful aid in grasping long-term historical change—reference to some sort of dividing line, however arbitrary, makes it much easier to grasp the huge gulf that lies between the worlds of More and Milton. Moreover, as the lines from Donne's *Anatomy* indicate, the subjects of James VI and I were themselves acutely aware of the break their society had made with its recent past. Early-seventeenth-century literature is suffused with the sense of a people, or rather a new confederation of peoples, entering into new and uncharted waters. The challenges to the old social order leading up to the English Revolution and beyond are recognizable both in the rise of the individual ("every man . . . a phoenix") and in the development of new and subversive forms of class consciousness. Like many members of his society, Donne scanned these new developments with a sense of distinct unease for the future. It is perhaps this peculiar wonder at new worlds balanced against pessimism and nostalgia for a stable past that is most distinctive of the period and has the capacity to make its literature seem especially relevant to students today.

The notion of the human being as a self-interested, self-seeking individual operating in a society composed of other such individuals is now so familiar that students may find it difficult to understand how in the early seventeenth century this perspective on society could be regarded as both new and profoundly unsettling. Many will be inclined to argue that this is simply a matter of human nature. If you are in the midst of a survey course, you will be able to point out that there is little or no equivalent in the periods you have studied previously to the type of villain delineated in *King Lear* and *The Duchess of Malfi*, or to the sudden intrusion of the private individual into Milton's *The Reason of Church Government Urged Against Prelaty*. When reading political texts such as Hobbes's *Leviathan* and Milton's *Areopagitica*, many of whose assumptions students will be inclined to accept as givens, point out that these are foundational texts that did much to shape the ideas about human nature and society they now seem to reflect. To study early-seventeenth-century literature and culture is to some extent to study the developments that culminated both in Hobbes's vision of the state of nature as that of "war of every man against every man" and in Milton's ideal individual questing after truth within the free market of ideas.

Another point that must be born in mind in any comparison between this period and the century that preceded it is that the early seventeenth century witnessed both a major increase in literacy and the massive growth of the print trade. The number of books being published annually more than doubled between 1600 and 1640; and in the civil war and the

Interregnum, with the rise of the newsbook and the temporary collapse of censorship, the number of titles published exceeded the total printed before that period. These massive cultural shifts allowed for the entry of a chorus of previously excluded voices into the literary sphere. Not only were there many more writers than before, but also there were many more kinds of writers, and more kinds of writing. This era saw the entry of women in significant numbers into the fields of authorship and publication. Nine women writers are represented in the Early Seventeenth Century section of NAEL, almost a third of the total. This period saw the emergence, from Ben Jonson onward, of the professional author as a (relatively) respectable member of early capitalist society. And it is also in this era that we begin to hear, if still only faintly and unclearly, the voices of the laboring poor. Faced with such sudden abundance, no anthology and no survey course can hope to represent all the different kinds of writers and writing. Recognizing this inevitable fact, the beginning of this section of your course may be a good time to present your students with the question of canon formation, the drawbacks and advantages of literary canons, and the ways they are continually being transformed and remade.

The events known to some as the English Revolution, to others as the English Civil War(s), and to the less Anglocentrically minded as the War of the Three Kingdoms, continue to challenge and divide historians. For the teacher of literature, the challenges posed by this period can be even more daunting, because the time you have to introduce students to the history of the conflict is extremely limited. On the other hand, opportunities abound to teach important aspects of the great struggle through the texts in NAEL. Few if any of the poets and prose writers who lived and wrote in the tumultuous years 1640 to 1660 were successful in avoiding politics, even if they wished to do so. Many were actively involved in contemporary struggles or served as (paid or voluntary) propagandists. Others sought to distance themselves from the disasters of the age; but the events that impinged, often painfully, on their personal and public lives inevitably left traces in their prose and poetry.

The old observation that there are no winners in war is particularly apt in regard to the internecine conflicts of the middle seventeenth century. Almost every writer who lived through the middle decades of the seventeenth century was deeply affected by the English Revolution and its aftermath. Some took up arms in defense of the old order; others used their pens to justify rebellion and regicide. Almost all had the experience of watching their cause go down to apparently absolute defeat. The consequences of defeat may be traced in terms of shattered careers, crises of faith, and, frequently, brilliant poetry.

TEACHING CLUSTERS

Debate, Dissent, and Revolution

The idea that literature (and poetry above all) should rise above and remain aloof from tawdry political squabbles would have struck most seventeenth-century writers as distinctly weird. This is the great age of overtly and passionately politicized literature. This cluster finds its center in the conflict of 1640–60, but reaches back to chart how writers found and honed their oppositional (and loyalist) voices in the first decades of the century. Just as the political struggles of the period could never be reduced to a single issue or cause, so there is room in this cluster for texts engaged in a range of debates and conflicts—over religion, free expression, the distribution of wealth, and the relationship between the sexes.

Faith, Devotion, and Doubt

The era of Donne, Herbert, Crashaw, and Milton produced some of the greatest devotional poetry of all time—poetry that retains the power to move and challenge readers of all faiths and none. The influence of the Calvinist doctrine of predestination—far more widespread than is sometimes believed—prompted intense introspection, a searching of the soul for signs of grace or reprobation. This was also an age of radical doubt, not in the sense of atheism, perhaps, but of relentless questioning of received truths about the relationship between God and his creation. This new spirit of inquiry could take the form of religious radicalism in the burgeoning of separatist sects, or, equally, the scientific scrutiny of nature and social systems. That Milton should have found it necessary in *Paradise Lost* not merely to praise his Creator but "to justify the ways of God to man" is a sign of his anything but orthodox times.

The Material World

The early seventeenth century was also the era of the Scientific Revolution, the age of Kepler, Galileo, Bacon, Harvey, and Hooke. The profound otherworldliness of much seventeenth-century writing is matched by, and sometimes interwoven with, a new fascination with the material world. Scientists and philosophers, many of whose works are gathered in the Intext Topic "Forms of Inquiry," sought the material causes of everything from the movement of the stars to the phenomenon of mental illness (melancholy) and the structure of human society. Also participating in this cultural shift are those (male) poets who wrote with startling directness and not a little cynicism about the physical act of sex.

Writing Women

This cluster encompasses both writing by women in the period—of which there was more, at least in terms of what has survived, than from all previous centuries combined—and writing about women. The latter sometimes took the form of conservative and misogynistic attacks on the growth of female freedom. Almost for the first time, women's voices were heard in rebuttal to such attacks, and on various other matters of political and social urgency. Even the major writers of the period who have earned a reputation for misogyny (including Donne and Milton) were required to represent women as participants in dialogue and partners in life, rather than as mere objects of male desire and authority.

Style

The period that includes the works of Donne, Jonson, Bacon, Browne, Herbert, Vaughan, Marvell, and Milton is ideal for talking about style. Some eras have a dominant style, and it takes a trained ear to distinguish a sonnet of Sidney's from one by Daniel or Drayton, or Pope's couplets from Dryden's. What is remarkable about the early seventeenth century is the number of excellent writers composing in very distinctive styles. Students can be initially resistant to thinking and talking about style—they think they do not know what it is or take it to be a particularly arcane and difficult branch of knowledge and are afraid of looking foolish. Nevertheless, even students who are convinced they have no ear for poetry can learn a great deal about style by comparing and contrasting the poets and prose writers of the seventeenth century.

AUTHORS AND WORKS

John Donne

Donne's literary productions are extraordinarily diverse, and he himself discouraged readers from seeking for a common thread, preferring to make a distinction between the restless and libidinous "Jack Donne" of his younger years and the more sage and serious "Dr. Donne," Dean of St. Paul's. Yet many key concerns, favorite metaphors, and idiosyncratic habits of thought run through the whole corpus of Donne's writings, from early to late. Time allowing, it is worth letting students sample Donne at all ages and in all guises, from "Satire 3" to "Death's Duel."

Songs and Sonnets

The lyrics collected as Donne's *Songs and Sonnets* are not necessarily all products of his youth, though their subjects are almost exclusively secular and amorous. Donne has acquired a reputation as a great love poet, but this requires not looking too closely at the peculiarity of these lyrics.

The mistress is always nameless and entirely lacking in distinguishing mental or physical features. The desire for union to which the poet repeatedly returns is also a desire for common annihilation. Donne is, arguably, in love with love, but this is at least in part because in his eyes love looks so much like death.

The Flea

Quick Read

- Form: Lyric.
- Summary: Donne draws his beloved's attention to a flea that has sucked both their bloods, and develops from this theme a series of arguments for their having sex now.
- Key Passages: "We are met, / And cloistered in these living walls of jet. Though use make you apt to kill me, / Let not to that, self-murder added be, / And sacrilege, three sins in killing three," lines 14–18.

The Sun Rising

Quick Read

- Form: Aubade (a poem in which lovers greet the coming of dawn).
- Summary: The poet berates the sun for interrupting their love-making, and develops a view of their bedroom as a world in itself.
- Key Passages: "Look, and tomorrow late, tell me, / Whether both th'Indias of spice and mine / Be where thou left'st them, or lie here with me," lines 16–18; "She is all states, and all princes I, / Nothing else is," lines 21–22.

The Bait

Quick Read

- Form: Lyric.
- Summary: A response, like Ralegh's "The Nymph's Reply to the Shepherd," to Marlowe's "The Passionate Shepherd to His Love," drawing a series of at once humorous and sensuous parallels between seduction, poetry, and angling.
- Key Passages: "There the enamored fish will stay, / Begging themselves they may betray," lines 7–8.

Teaching Suggestions

In many of the *Songs and Sonnets*, Donne turns his back with ostentatious indifference on his culture's normative codes and values. In "The Canonization," for instance, he scornfully tells a friend, "Take you a course, get you a place, / Observe His Honor, or His Grace" (lines 5–6), but chooses for himself the role of the lover isolated from politics, commerce, and society. Often he declares that he and his lover are capable of replicating, containing, or obliterating the rest of the world: "She is all states, and all princes I, / Nothing else is" (lines 21–22). In these defiant verses, Donne makes a show of rejecting the society that had already rejected him. In "The Canonization," which probably celebrates his ruinous (in career terms) marriage, the lovers are willing to die (with a sexual pun) as one person and to be preserved "in sonnets" through which they will be worshipped as saints by future lovers. In the poem at least, love triumphs over difference in class and wealth. Yet Donne's desire to overmaster or efface the world is frequently matched by his desire, in poems such as "The Good-Morrow," "A Valediction: Forbidding Mourning," and "The Ecstasy," to efface his own individuality in the Neoplatonic union of lovers' souls. Also in "The Canonization" he declares, "The phoenix riddle hath more wit / By us: we two being one, are it" (lines 23–24)—the phoenix, which elsewhere symbolizes the self-made, self-serving individual, here becomes an emblem of the surrender of individuality. (The audio section of the Online Archive features musical settings of several of Donne's poems.)

Both in the interest of grasping Donne's achievement and in preparation for what is to come (e.g., Herbert, Crashaw, or Vaughan—"the Metaphysical Poets"), this is a good time to talk about figurative language and the idea of the "conceit." The conceit as Donne and his followers employ it (sometimes called "the metaphysical conceit") is a far-fetched, intellectualized, and unusually elaborate comparison. The best poem to use in introducing the concept of the metaphysical conceit is probably Donne's "A Valediction: Forbidding Mourning," with its comparison of the lovers' souls to the legs of a compass:

> If they be two, they are two so
>   As stiff twin compasses are two;
> Thy soul, the fixed foot, makes no show
>   To move, but doth, if th' other do. (lines 25–28)

What makes this conceit metaphysical is not only its unlikeliness at first glance, but also the multileveled quality of the comparison. The lovers are like parts of a compass because, though distinct, they together form a single entity; because the one that is fixed sympathetically leans toward the one that moves; because one part grows "erect" (line 32) when joined to its fellow; because the fixity of one ensures the other's fidelity and eventual return.

Teaching the *Songs and Sonnets* also invites a discussion of literary history and trends in criticism. With the rapid shift in intellectual and aesthetic fashions following the Restoration, Donne was one of several major poets suddenly relegated to the status of footnotes in literary history. Those who excelled at metaphysical wit were now seen as clever but difficult, arrogant, and offensive. In *A Discourse Concerning the Original and*

Progress of Satire, John Dryden condemned Donne because "he affects the metaphysics . . . and perplexes the minds of the fair sex with nice speculations of philosophy, when he should engage their hearts, and entertain them with the softnesses of love." Samuel Johnson amplified these criticisms, coining the phrase "metaphysical poets" for all those, such as Abraham Cowley, who shared Donne's perceived faults. If you will be using volume 2 of *NAEL* later in the course, you have the opportunity at this point to assign T. S. Eliot's "The Metaphysical Poets," among the most important and influential pieces of twentieth-century criticism. Even if your students do not have volume 2, or if Eliot's essay seems too difficult or time-consuming to assign in its entirety, it is still worthwhile quoting a few passages to give the students a sense of how and why Donne, Crashaw, Herbert, and Vaughan were rescued from literary obscurity. Eliot is much more forgiving than Dryden and Johnson of the metaphysical conceit: "the elaboration . . . of a figure of speech to the furthest stage to which ingenuity can carry it." More memorable and significant is his assertion that these were the last poets to "feel their thought as immediately as the odour of a rose," before the infamous "dissociation of sensibility," which set in under the influence of Milton and Dryden. It is not, of course, necessary to endorse all of Eliot's sometimes dubious historical claims, nor need you worry that students will swallow his argument hook, line, and sinker. What Johnson and Eliot offer are simply conflicting perspectives that students may enjoy testing against examples of seventeenth-century verse. They also offer radically different (but not mutually exclusive) ways of describing the transition from the literature of the early seventeenth century to that of the Restoration—as triumph of good taste, or as dissociation of sensibility.

Satire 3

Quick Read

- Form: Satire (after the manner of Persius).
- Summary: Donne examines the difficulty involved in determining which version of Christianity, imagined as a mistress, is the true religion, and derides those who in one way or another shun this personal responsibility.
- Key Passages: "Is not our mistress, fair Religion, / As worthy of our souls' devotion / As virtue was to the first blinded age?" lines 5–8; "Mirreus, / Thinking her unhoused here, and fled from us, / Seeks her at Rome; there, because he doth know / That she was there a thousand years ago. / He loves her rags so, as we here obey / The statecloth where the prince sate yesterday," lines 43–48; "On a huge hill, / Cragged and steep, Truth stands, and he that will / Reach her, about must, and about must go, / And what the hill's suddenness resists, win so; / Yet strive so, that before age, death's twilight, / Thy soul rest, for none can work in that night," lines 79–84.

Teaching Suggestions

A bit of biography is essential here. This poem was written while Donne was engaged in the painful process of leaving the Roman Catholic Church, the church of his fathers and of his martyred uncle and brother. Like all those who came to the Church of England early or late in the sixteenth century, Donne ultimately had to break the bond 'twixt son and father. (The Reformation, among other things, gave official backing to the idea that one thousand years of fathers could be wrong.) Yet in the satire Donne retains some reverence for tradition: "ask thy father which is she, / Let him ask his; though truth and falsehood be / Near twins, yet truth a little elder is" (71–73). We should not be too hasty to read this as an affirmation of Catholicism, however, for Protestants also insisted that they represented the original and oldest form of the church, from which Catholics had deviated in more recent times. At any rate, Donne has more respect for those who follow their ancestors than for those lazy or conformist souls who let others—"a Harry, or a Martin" (line 97)—choose their faith for them. "Fool and wretch, wilt thou let thy soul be tied / To man's laws, by which she shall not then be tried / At the last day?" (lines 93–95). This reference to the Last Judgment is useful in getting across the point that though this satire does advocate honest inquiry, it never for a moment suggests that all religions are equally valid. Anticipating the possibility of being tortured for his faith, Donne asserts "unmoved thou / Of force must one, and forced but one allow; / *and the right . . .*" (lines 69–71, italics added). The sufferings one may have to endure for getting it right on earth are as nothing to those that the afterlife threatens for those who get it wrong.

Holy Sonnets

Just as many of Donne's most amorous poems are full of theologically informed conceits (for instance, the suggestion in "The Flea" that killing the insect in which three bloods are mingled would constitute sacrilege against the Trinity), so his devotional verse is distinguished by the use of daringly erotic images. "Holy Sonnet 18," for instance, pursues the traditional image of the Church as "bride of Christ" into dangerous territory:

> Betray, kind husband, thy spouse to our sights,
> And let mine amorous soul court thy mild dove,
> Who is most true and pleasing to thee then
> When she is embraced and open to most men.
> (lines 11–14)

Similarly, "Holy Sonnet 13" imagines Christ as a mistress who might just be seduced with the right pick-up line ("This beauteous form assures a piteous mind"). "Sonnet 14" calls on God to penetrate and "ravish" Donne's heart in terms that are unmistakably sexual.

Some students may find this shocking or simply weird, while others will assume that the erotic passages represent an anti-religious countercurrent in Donne's poetry. Donne is in fact writing in a very well-established tradition of eroticized devotion, which also inspired Richard Crashaw. To correct the impression that Donne is perverse or less than holy-minded in these sonnets, you might have students check out Crashaw's "To the Noblest & Best of Ladies, the Countess of Denbigh" and/or "The Flaming Heart." In addition, you might send them back to some of the medieval works gathered in the cluster on "Christ's Humanity," such as the lyric "I Sing of a Maiden" or the erotic visions of Margery Kempe.

Meditation 17

In this meditation, part of a series of "Devotions" composed after a serious illness, Donne famously responds to the tolling of the passing bell with the recognition that "No man is an island. . . . Any man's death diminishes me, because I am involved in mankind; and therefore never send to know for whom the bell tolls; it tolls for thee." Without denigrating the meditation or denying its sincerity, it is worth drawing attention to the ways in which it carries forward some of the egocentric and nihilistic preoccupations of Donne's profane poetry. While Donne here stresses his participation in humanity, he does so to deepen and sharpen his own introspection, turning another's affliction into his own "gold." Even this limited form of identification with another, which in an older work such as *Everyman* is simply taken for granted, is achieved by Donne only by means of strenuous mental effort. Donne's self-absorption finds its ultimate expression on his deathbed, where, as Izaak Walton records, he had himself painted in his own winding sheet and contemplated that image.

Teaching Clusters

Donne's works can be at home in several different teaching clusters. The religious poetry and "Devotions" are an essential component of the cluster on **Faith, Devotion, and Doubt.** *An Anatomy of the World,* with its lament at the collapse of old spiritual certainties, fits into the same category. Yet when, in the *Anatomy,* Donne complains that "new philosophy . . . calls all in doubt," he is referring to advances in science; there is scope, then, for including this poem in the cluster on **The Material World,** along with some of the *Songs and Sonnets,* such as "The Flea," which dwell on the materiality of bodily substances and the sexual act. Others of the *Songs and Sonnets,* in which the mistress is at once so present and so absent, would fit into **Writing Women.**

Especially if you are going on to teach some or all of the major "metaphysical poets"—Herbert, Crashaw, Vaughan, Cowley, and Traherne—Donne's poems make a good starting point for the cluster on **Style.** The focus here would be partly on the metaphysical conceit, but also on Donne's relaxed attitude toward the rules of prosody, for which, Ben Jonson insisted, he "deserved hanging."

Discussion Questions

1. How should we interpret the anonymity and apparent featurelessness of the woman—or women?—to whom Donne addresses the *Songs and Sonnets*?
2. How is the female body represented in Elegy 20, "To His Mistress Going to Bed?" How does Donne represent male desire?
3. How is the reader meant to respond to the blending of sacred and sexual elements in Donne's religious poetry? And in his love poetry?
4. "Nothing else is" ("The Sun Rising"): why are references to nothingness and annihilation so prominent in Donne's love poetry?
5. What attitudes toward Catholicism, the religion Donne abandoned, are apparent in poems such as "The Canonization" and "The Relic"?
6. What makes the conceit in a poem like "A Valediction: Forbidding Mourning" successful or otherwise?
7. Why does Donne appear so anxious about modern life in *An Anatomy of the World*?
8. What aspects of Donne's religious prose are most reminiscent of his profane (or religious) poetry?

Further Resources

NORTON ONLINE ARCHIVE

Meditation XI
Twicknam Garden
To the Countess of Bedford
The Curse
Lover's Infiniteness
The Storm
Elegy I: Of Jealousy
Elegy IV: The Perfume
Paradoxes and Problems
   Paradox VI: That It Is Possible to Find Some Virtue in Women
   Problem II: Why Puritans Make Long Sermons
   Problem VI: Why Hath Common Opinion Afforded Women's Souls?
Sermon LXVI: On the Weight of Eternal Glory
Sermon LXXVI: On Falling Out of God's Hand
A Nocturnal upon St. Lucy's Day, Being the Shortest Day
The Blossom
A Lecture upon the Shadow
Holy Sonnet 17 ("Since she whom I loved hath paid her last debt")

Audio:
Go and Catch a Falling Star
Break of Day (music by William Corkine)
A Hymn to God the Father (music by John Hilton)
—performed by Susan Bender, Neil Gladd, and Myrna Sislen

NORTON TOPICS ONLINE

Emigrants and Settlers
    John Donne, *from* A Sermon . . . Preached to the Honorable
    Company of the Virginia Plantation, 13 November 1622

Izaak Walton

The Life of Dr. John Donne

Quick Read

- Form: Biography/hagiography.
- Summary: Walton describes Donne's preparations for death, provides an admiring summation of his character, and looks forward to seeing his body reanimated.
- Themes: Mortality; the good death; sainthood.
- Key Passages: "He brought with him into that place his winding-sheet in his hand, and having put off all his clothes, had this sheet put on him, and so tied with knots at his head and feet, and his hands so placed as dead bodies are usually fitted, to be shrouded and put into their coffin, or grave. Upon this urn he thus stood, with his eyes shut, and with so much of the sheet turned aside as might show his lean, pale, and deathlike face. . . . In this posture he was drawn at his just height; and when the picture was fully finished, he caused it to be set by his bed-side, where it continued and became his hourly object till his death. . . ." (1310)

Walton's biography of the saintlike Donne reflects the poet's constant preoccupation with death. Students can discuss whether posing for his own *memento mori* is a mark of Donne's humility or his egoism. The remarkable closing passage, describing the dissolution of Donne's body to "a small quantity of Christian dust" and vowing "But I shall see it reanimated" (1313) has a quiet force and grandeur to match Donne's own *Meditations*.

Teaching Clusters

You will naturally teach Walton in company with Donne's religious writings. This probably means the cluster on **Faith, Devotion, and Doubt**, though Walton's preoccupation with the fate of the body after death—a preoccupation he shares with the Donne of "Death's Duel"—makes **The Material World** another good option.

Discussion Questions

1. To what extent is Walton making Donne out to be a saint? Are there any limits to his admiration?

Further Resources

NORTON ONLINE ARCHIVE

Donne Takes Holy Orders

Aemilia Lanyer

Salve Deus Rex Judaeorum

In spite of the off-putting Latin title, this is a text whose message students will instantly grasp and warm to. Whereas more recent advocates of women's equality have tended to ground their arguments in reason rather than scripture, Lanyer derives her feminist principles directly and explicitly from the Gospels. Although she stops short of proclaiming women's full equality with men—basing her argument instead in part on women's weakness—Lanyer's place in the history of feminism remains underrated.

Quick Read

- Form: Devotional poem, with dedicatory verses and a prose epistle.
- Summary: In the excerpts, Lanyer dedicates her poem to the queen, urges her female readers to maintain solidarity in the face of male criticism, and expounds a theological argument against the male domination of women.
- Themes: Women's rights; female friendship; faith; the Bible.
- Key Passages: "Some forgetting they are women themselves, and in danger to be condemned by the words of their own mouths, fall into so great an error, as to speak unadvisedly against the rest of their sex. . . . [R]efer such points of folly to be practiced by evil disposed men, who forgetting they were borne of women, nourished of women, and that if it were not by the means of women, they would be quite extinguished out of the world, and a final end of them all, do like vipers deface the wombs wherein they were bred . . . ," "To the Virtuous Reader," 1316; "If Eve did err, it was for knowledge sake; / The fruit being fair persuaded him to fall," "Eve's Apology," lines 53–54; "Then let us have our liberty again, / And challenge to yourselves no sovereignty. / You came not into the world without our pain; Make that a bar against your cruelty," 81–84.

The Description of Cookham

In "The Description of Cookham," Lanyer recalls with gratitude and affection her reception there by the countess and her daughter. Like Jonson's poems, "Cookham" is dotted with classical allusions. The fact that the poem is a nostalgic leave-taking of the place also gives it a feeling of sadness.

Quick Read

- Form: Country-house poem.
- Summary: Lanyer concentrates more on her noble hosts than on the house itself, affirming their undying friendship while lamenting their separation.
- Themes: The social order; landscape; patronage; female friendship.
- Key Passages: "The very hills right humbly did descend, / When you to tread on them did intend. / And as you set your feet they still did rise, / Glad that they could receive so rich a prize," lines 35–38; "To this fair tree, taking me by the hand, / You did repeat the pleasures which had passed, / Seeming to grieve they could no longer last. / And with a chaste, yet loving kiss took leave, / Of which sweet kiss I did it soon bereave," 162–66.

Teaching Suggestions

One of the most rewarding ways to study the social order through literature is by focusing on the peculiarly seventeenth-century genre of the country-house poem. Assigning Lanyer's "Description of Cookham," the first such poem to be published, and following it with Jonson's "To Penshurst," Carew's "To Saxham," and Marvell's *Upon Appleton House*, can be a remarkably effective way of shedding light on the complex questions of patronage, class, aristocratic display, the social order, and the rural economy. At the same time, of course, you will be able to draw various distinctions among them. (Since these distinctions include gender, it is worth reminding students that Lanyer is not the only one of these three poets who "has" gender.) To enhance this part of your course, the Norton Topic Online "Gender, Family, Household" includes a selection of texts and images relating to the country house, focusing on the households of the Cliffords, Lanyer's patrons, and the Sidneys at Penshurst.

Some students have trouble warming to the "country-house" genre, both because the ostensible subject matter sounds rather banal, and because the relationship of poet to patron seems mercenary and antithetical to the (romantic) spirit of poetry. While this latter charge may be fair enough in some cases, it certainly does not apply to "The Description of Cookham, where the delicate, difficult relationship between Lanyer—a socially and economically marginal figure—and her noble female patrons is a central theme. The attempt to gloss over the difference in degree and resultant relationship of dependence with the rhetoric of female friendship is only partially successful, as Lanyer herself acknowledges: "Unconstant Fortune, thou art most to blame, / Who casts us down into so low a frame / Where our great friends we cannot daily see . . ." (lines 103–5). The passage in which Lanyer and Lady Anne Clifford exchange a kiss mediated by a tree (lines 157–78) is especially worth focusing on.

Teaching Clusters

All of the selections from Lanyer could easily be included in the cluster on **Writing Women**, on the basis of not only their authorship but also their pervasive concern with female friendship and the state of women. Lanyer is the first female voice of the new century, and the herald of an expanding tradition that will encompass Wroth, Cary, Speght, Philips, and Cavendish. "Eve's Apology in Defense of Women" would also work well in the **Faith, Devotion, and Doubt** cluster, especially if you will be going on to look at other versions of the Fall, such as Rachel Speght's (in Norton Topics Online) and, of course, Milton's.

Discussion Questions

1. What are the grounds of Lanyer's defense of Eve and of women? Is it accurate to regard her as an early feminist?
2. How does Lanyer's version of the Fall accord with the account in the biblical Book of Genesis (chapters 1–3)?
3. How does Lanyer represent her own relationship to the estate of Cookham and its noble residents?
4. How is the natural world depicted in "The Description of Cookham," in itself and in relation to the human masters of the estate?
5. What similarities and what differences do you find between Lanyer's "Cookham" and Jonson's "Penshurst"? Is gender important to understanding the differences between these poems?

Ben Jonson

The Masque of Blackness

Quick Read

- Form: Masque.
- Summary: The daughters of Niger, played by the ladies of the court, including Queen Anne, are brought into the presence of the sun-king, James, whose radiance can wash them white.
- Themes: Cosmic order; race; gender; royalty.
- Key Passages: "It was her majesties will to have them blackamoors at first," 1327; "in their black the perfect'st beauty grows," line 44; "For were the world, with all his wealth, a ring, / Britannia (whose new name makes all tongues sing) / might be a diamond worthy to enchase it, / Ruled by a sun, that to this height doth grace it. / Whose beams shine day and night, and are of force / To blanch an Ethiop and revive a corpse," 136–41.

Teaching Suggestions

The challenge and hopefully the pleasure of teaching this text is that it involves introducing students to an entirely unfamiliar literary genre. It is important to make it clear from the outset that the masque is not simply a kind of play. It differs not only in the emphasis on music, dance, and spectacle, but also in the relationship between the performers and the audience. The central focus of the masque is not anything or anyone on the stage, but the King, who watches the entertainment. Though James was not required to take an active role, he is the real protagonist of *The Masque of Blackness*, under whose influence black skin turns to white. The involvement of court ladies and gentlemen as performers and dancers alongside professional actors further blurs the line between stage and audience, witness and spectacle.

The Masque of Blackness, the first of the twenty-four masques Jonson wrote, is short and well worth assigning. The elaborate description of sets, makeup, costumes, and music and the preciosity of the dialogue will give students an impression of what these events were like, and also help them to see what Puritans found objectionable about the Jacobean court. The appearance of the ladies of the court, at the queen's direction, in blackface as African beauties was doubtless intended to be exotic. Jonson gave this a mythological explanation out of Ovid: the Ethiopians were turned black when Phaëton drove the sun's chariot too close to the equator but now are instructed to seek out Britannia, where the more temperate sun (that is, King James) will restore their original whiteness. The racial and gender politics of this entertainment are immediately apparent, and well worth exploring. (For more on the masques, see "Inigo Jones and Costumes of the Masques" under "Civil War of Ideas" in the Early Seventeenth Century section of *NTO*.)

Volpone

Quick Read

- Form: Dramatic comedy.
- Summary: Like all of Jonson's plays, *Volpone* has a complex and intricate plot, full of twists and turns. Volpone is an old trickster who, with the help of his servant Mosca, extorts gifts from a succession of fools who hope to inherit his wealth when he dies. He subsequently disguises himself as a mountebank and spots Celia, Corvino's wife, whom he attempts to seduce. In the latter part of the play, the dupes plot against Volpone and he against them, while Mosca seeks to betray his master to his own advantage. In the end, all are punished by the law, saving the virtuous characters Celia and Bonario. See Jonson's own acrostic summary of *"the Argument"* (1336).
- Themes: Greed; corruption; hypocrisy; the city; the law.
- Key Passages: Volpone [to his gold]: "Hail the world's soul, and mine!" 1.1.3; "I glory / More in the cunning purchase of my wealth, / Than in the glad possession, since I gain / No common way," 1.1.30–33; Politic Would-Be [speaking of Stone, the court jester]: "I knew him one of the most dangerous heads / Living within the state,

and so I held him . . . He has received weekly intelligence, / Upon my knowledge, out of the Low Countries, / For all parts of the world, in cabbages," 2.1.65–70; Corvino [attempting to prostitute his wife Celia]: "Honor? Tut, a breath. / There's no such thing in nature; a mere term / Invented to awe fools. What is my gold / The worse for touching? Clothes for being looked on? / Why, this's no more," 3.7.38–42; Volpone's song: "'Tis no sin love's fruits to steal, / But the sweet thefts to reveal. / To be taken, to be seen, / These have crimes accounted been," 3.7.179–83; Mosca: "Sell him for mummia; he's half dust already," 4.4.14; Mosca: "So, now I have the keys, and am possessed. / Since he will needs be dead afore his time, / I'll bury him or gain by him," 5.5.12–14.

Teaching Suggestions

Whereas Jonson's masques are operatic spectacles to entertain the court, comedies like *Volpone* are sardonic satires of bourgeois greed and lust. Jonson was deeply influenced by classical models, but there is nothing musty or antiquarian about *Volpone*. The play is attuned to the pulse of London commercial life, thinly disguising its immediate topicality with the exotic Venetian setting.

Volpone makes an excellent companion piece to Shakespeare's *King Lear*. Written a year or so later, *Volpone* is arguably the more pessimistic play, in spite of its also being a successful comedy. Shakespeare and Jonson both protest in different ways against the rise of a commerce-driven society in which personal interest knows no higher law. Both draw on contemporary fascinations, such as demonic possession and exorcism, for theatrical effect (compare Edgar in *Lear*, act 4, scene 1, with Voltore in *Volpone*, act 5, scene 12). But whereas Shakespeare's play presents us with several heroic models of fidelity and fortitude struggling against the current of a foul society, Jonson offers only Celia and Bonario, whose goodness is more or less proportional to their lack of effectiveness and personality. These characters rarely engage students' sympathies as do Cordelia and Kent, and this is probably because they do not engage Jonson's. Although he scorns and satirizes the society that spews up the likes of Volpone, Jonson seems incapable of imagining a viable alternative; instead, his imagination is drawn, almost against his will, to the ever-expanding frontiers of commodification, in an age when even old corpses had a market value. As Mosca says of Corbaccio in act 4, scene 4, "Sell him for mummia; he's half dust already." (Jonson is not the only author to latch onto the strange trade in mummy dust as an emblem of the new market economy; Bosola in *The Duchess of Malfi* mentions it [lines 4.2.112–13], and Sir Thomas Browne is magnificent on the subject: "The Egyptian mummies, which Cambyses or time hath spared, avarice now consumeth. Mummy is become merchandise, Mizraim cures wounds, and Pharaoh is sold for balsams" [*Hydriotaphia*].)

To Penshurst

Quick Read

- Form: Country-house poem.
- Summary: Penshurst is presented as a model of the ideal social order, where human beings live in harmony with a subservient nature and one another, in a scene presided over by benign nobility.
- Themes: The social order; landscape; patronage; nobility.
- Key Passages: "Thou art not, Penshurst, built to envious show / Of touch, or marble . . . but stand'st an ancient pile, / And these [other houses] grudged at, art reverenced the while," lines 1–6; "Thou hast thy ponds, that pay thee tribute fish, / Fat aged carps that run into thy net," 32–33; "Here no man tells my cups; nor standing by, / A waiter, doth my gluttony envy," 67–68; "Now, Penshurst, they that will proportion thee / With other edifices, when they see / Those proud ambitious heaps, and nothing else, / May say, their lords have built, but thy lord dwells," 99–102.

Teaching Suggestions

The best-known of country-house poems teaches well on its own, and still better in company with other examples of the genre, such as Lanyer's "Description of Cookham," Carew's "To Saxham," and Marvell's *Upon Appleton House.* (Note also the range of images and texts relating to the Sidneys and Penshurst in "Gender, Family, Household" [*NTO*].) Students are always amused by the extravagance of images such as that of "Bright eels that . . . leap on land, / Before the fisher, or into his hand" (37–38). It doesn't take a trained Marxist critic to detect something fishy about such passages, in which the authority of the Sidneys is naturalized to the extent that nature itself bows down before them. Yet Jonson should not be mistaken, even here, for a mere servile flatterer. The glorification of Penshurst involves an explicit comparison with the mass of country houses and noble families who do not measure up to its high standard. Whether or not it is the case that the walls of Penshurst were "reared with no man's ruin, no man's groan; / There's none, that dwell about them, wish them down" (46–47), the same clearly cannot be said for the majority of stately homes in Jacobean England.

"To Penshurst" should also be read in relation to Jonson's evolving conception of himself as a laureate poet. Rather than flattering either king or commoner, Jonson understood his role to be the expression of the highest and best values of his society. Where his contemporaries appeared to fulfill or embody those values, he would praise them. Where they fell short, they would be told of it. In late poems such as the ode on Cary and Morison, "To the Memory of My Beloved, The Author, Mr. William Shakespeare," and "Ode to Himself," Jonson presents himself as the keen-sighted and unbiased judge of what is fair and foul in others, and himself. These poems can be used to open a discussion of what, for Jonson and his society, constitutes the good individual and the good life. What qualities does Jonson appear to value most highly in human beings? Of what faults is he most critical? Does Jonson hold himself to the same standards as others? Whence does he derive his authority to act as arbiter and judge?

Teaching Clusters

Jonson was, in some respects, the leading literary voice of official England for the first three decades of the seventeenth century. As such, his works provide an excellent way of launching the cluster on **Debate, Dissent, and Revolution**. In many ways, Jonson's masques and poems embody the values the Puritans and political radicals would react against. (In this context, you might wish to follow *The Masque of Blackness* with the selection from Prynne's *Histriomastix*, attacking masques, in *NTO*.) It is important, however, not to present Jonson as the pliant stooge of absolutism. The critical elements in the *Masque*, "To Penshurst," and a number of the poems are themselves a contribution to early Stuart debate and dissent.

The relentless materialism and commodification displayed in *Volpone* make the play highly suitable for **The Material World**. Selections from Jonson's poetry would be well placed in the cluster on **Style**, especially if you will be going on to look at works by members of the so-called Tribe of Ben. Here you will have an opportunity to indicate how Jonson's followers both imitated him and rebelled against his model, and how they explicitly acknowledged his tutelage. Carew's "To Ben Jonson" offers a vision of the laureate-as-lawgiver with his "just chastising hand," but blames Jonson for taking offense at reasonable criticism. Herrick's "His Prayer to Ben Jonson" is shorter and more playful, lightly twitting Jonson for his former Catholicism by invoking him as "Saint Ben" and, kneeling at his altar, offering him a lyric—this poem—and candles.

Discussion Questions

1. What does "blackness" signify in *The Masque of Blackness*? Are its connotations entirely negative?
2. What signs if any of criticism of the monarch can be detected in *The Masque of Blackness*?
3. Why are the representatives of virtue in *Volpone* so bloodless and uninspiring in comparison to the many representatives of vice?
4. Does *Volpone* present any alternative to the rapacious world of corruption and commodification it depicts?
5. Look at Jonson's "love" poetry—e.g., *A Celebration of Charis* and "My Picture Left in Scotland." Do you see any resemblances to love poetry you've previously encountered? How does Jonson represent desire, or any personal emotion? Jonson writes of love for his dead son in "Of My First Son"—what kind of personal feelings are articulated here?
6. In "To Penshurst," Jonson represents what appears to be an ideal com-

munity. What is included in that ideal, and what has Jonson omitted in order to create it?

7. Is "To Penshurst" better described as a celebration or a coded criticism of the English aristocracy?

8. How well does Jonson's image of himself as a poet in "Ode to Himself" match up with the poetry he writes?

Further Resources

NORTON ONLINE ARCHIVE

It Was a Beauty That I Saw
An Elegy
Gypsy Songs
[The Vision of Delight]
An Ode: High-Spirited Friend
Songs from Vision and Delight
On Don Surly
To William Camden
To Penshurst
In the Person of Womankind (In Defense of their Inconstancy)
Slow, Slow, Fresh Fount
Epitaph on Elizabeth, L. H.
A Celebration of Charis in Ten Lyric Pieces
    5. His Discourse with Cupid
    6. Claiming a Second Kiss by Desert
Though I Am Young
Pleasure Reconciled to Virtue

NORTON TOPICS ONLINE

Civil Wars of Ideas: Seventeenth-Century Politics,
Religion, and Culture
    Inigo Jones and Costumes of the Masques

Emigrants and Settlers
    The Irish Masque at Court

Mary Wroth

The Countess of Montgomery's Urania

Quick Read

- Form: Prose romance.
- Summary: In the excerpt, the sorrowing Urania enters a mysterious cave where she discovers first a sonnet and then a man, Perissus, who agrees to tell her the cause of his woes.
- Key Passages: "Not to find least respite from her sorrow, which so dearly she did value, as by no means she would impart it to any,"

1454; "what devilish spirit art thou, that thus dost come to torture me? But now I see you are a woman, and therefore not much to be marked, and less resisted," 1456.

Pamphilia to Amphilanthus

The sonnet sequence of Sidney's niece Mary Wroth may be read both as a tribute and as a response to her uncle's. *Pamphilia to Amphilanthus* is particularly interesting for the way it at once carries forward and critiques Elizabethan, Petrarchan, and male assumptions, transforming the traditional relationship between an ardent lover and his cold beloved into a woman's charged dialogue with her own desire.

Quick Read

- Form: Sonnet sequence.
- Summary: In some respects a traditional Petrarchan sonnet sequence from a female perspective, *Pamphilia* is marked by its introspective, somber tone; "Love," a capricious and sometimes cruel figure, is a much more prominent character than the shadowy Amphilanthus.
- Themes: Love; pain; secrecy.
- Key Passages: "Like to a ship, on Goodwin's cast by wind, / The more she strives, more deep in sand is pressed, / Till she be lost; so am I, in this kind, / Sunk, and devoured, and swallowed by unrest . . ." (sonnet 68, lines 5–8); "In this strange labyrinth how shall I turn? / Ways are on all sides, while the way I miss" (sonnet 77, lines 1–2).

Teaching Suggestions

Students are unlikely to find Mary Wroth's sonnets immediately enjoyable. They do not read as easily as those of the major Elizabethan sonneteers; nor do they deliver the anticipated punchline in the closing couplet. In fact, they often lack closing couplets—Wroth used a number of rhyme schemes, but none of the sonnets in NAEL are in the familiar "English" form inaugurated by Surrey and perfected by Shakespeare. Among her favored schemes (in sonnets 1, 16, and 68) is *abba abba ccdeed*. The unusual progression of rhyming sounds, together with the often heavy use of enjambment, tends to slow down the experience of reading, to rob it of a clear sense of trajectory and culmination, and to introduce an element of recursiveness. Wroth's sonnets can be compared to the "strange labyrinth" of which she writes in Sonnet 77. If students initially find her style alienating or turgid, you can help them to see that the effect is appropriate to the subject of the sequence, an intensely private and often painful journey into the heart's interior, with no end in sight. A further metaphor for Wroth's poetic practice is provided by the passage from *Urania*, which follows the sorrowful heroine's movement from the outside light into the interior of a dark and secret cave, a journey again marked by the recitation and reading of sonnets.

Teaching Clusters

Wroth can be a key figure in the **Writing Women** cluster. Differing in almost every respect (class, themes, mode, mood, and style) from her contemporary Aemilia Lanyer, she teaches well alongside her. The sonnets would also be at home in the **Style** cluster; her somber refashioning of the Petrarchan tradition makes her in some ways closer to Milton than to either Sidney or Donne.

Discussion Questions

1. In what ways do Wroth's sonnets resemble sonnets you have encountered previously (e.g., by Donne, Shakespeare, and others), and how do they differ? Is Petrarch's influence apparent?
2. In what ways, if any, is Wroth's poetic voice gendered female?
3. What is the intended effect of the interweaving of prose and poetry in *Urania*?

John Webster

The Duchess of Malfi

Quick Read

- Form: Dramatic tragedy.
- Summary: The widowed Duchess secretly marries her servant Antonio, against the counsel of her brothers, the Cardinal and Ferdinand. The marriage clearly has the blessing of playwright, audience, and all the decent characters in the play but precipitates the tragedy. The brothers pursue vengeance that leads finally to the Duchess's death. They are in turn punished through the agency of their penitent tool, the melancholy malcontent Bosola.
- Themes: Death; desire; widowhood; madness.
- Key Passages: Antonio: "'Tis great pity, / He should be thus neglected; I have heard / He's very valiant. This foul melancholy / Will poison all his goodness," 1.1.68–71; Duchess: "This is flesh and blood, sir; / 'Tis not the figure cut in alabaster, / Kneels at my husband's tomb," 1.3.156–58; Ferdinand: "Damn her! That body of hers, / While that my blood ran pure in't, was more worth / Than that which thou wouldst comfort, called a soul," 4.1.119–21; Duchess: "I am Duchess of Malfi still," 4.2.127; Ferdinand: "Cover her face; mine eyes dazzle: she died young," 4.2.245; Ferdinand: "When I go to hell, I mean to carry a bribe; for, look you, good gifts evermore make way for the worst persons," 5.2.39–40; Antonio: "I do love these ancient ruins. / We never tread upon them but we set / Our

foot upon some reverend history," 5.3.9–11; Ferdinand: "Like dia-
monds we are cut with our own dust," 5.5.71; Malateste: "How came
Antonio by his death?" / Bosola: "In a mist: I know not how; / Such a
mistake as I have often seen / In a play," 5.5.91–94.

Teaching Suggestions

The general laugh that greeted the introduction of "Webster"—a nasty
boy with a grisly imagination—in showings of the film *Shakespeare in
Love* demonstrates that this playwright's notoriety is more widespread
than one might have guessed. Webster stands for Jacobean tragedy, and
Jacobean tragedy is understood to be violent, bloody, macabre, passionate,
and spectacular. Students will be gratified to find all these assumptions
confirmed in *The Duchess of Malfi*, but they will also find something
deeper and more complex than the horror show they may have been
prepared for. The figure of the Duchess, who may initially be seen as
self-indulgent, evolves under the pressure of torment and temptation to
madness to an almost saintlike figure, whose apotheosis, paradoxically, involves an affirmation of her earthly, secular role: "I am Duchess of Malfi
still," 4.2.127. Even the villainous characters in the play are capable of
moments of startling moral clarity. The question of Bosola's moral redemption adds fascination and paradox to the ending of the play.

The play is full of references to bodies and bodily substances. Blood,
particularly that of the Duchess, is a constant preoccupation. In Bosola's
case, the significant fluid may be black bile, an excess of which was
thought to bring on melancholy. The significance of melancholy in the
play is worth bringing out, especially if you will be going on to teach Burton's *Anatomy of Melancholy*. Although standard humor theory taught
that it was but one of four possible imbalances in the human constitution,
melancholy in many seventeenth-century works seems rather to be the individual's response to an imbalanced society. Like the Fool in *King Lear*,
the melancholic man has a kind of license to speak truth to power. Thus
in Webster's *Duchess of Malfi*, Ferdinand sees Bosola as wearing an advantageous "garb of melancholy" (1.2.185), rather than as suffering from a
psychological malady. If Bosola's melancholy "poison[s] all his goodness"
(1.1.71), it also allows him—as it allows Hamlet, and Jacques in Shakespeare's *As You Like It*—to voice penetrating criticisms of the world he inhabits and the behavior of his betters.

The Duchess of Malfi makes an especially good match with Cary's *The
Tragedy of Mariam*, of which two scenes are included in NAEL (the complete text is available in the Norton Online Archive). There are a number
of significant parallels in the plots of these two plays, both of which explore issues of marriage, female independence, and female choice, jealousy, murder, and madness. Both also have in common an extremely
pessimistic vision of society, in which the good can do little or nothing to
struggle against the power of the self-willed, sadistic, and corrupt. Of
course, there are also important differences between the two plays, which

can form the basis for student discussions and essays. What are the relative advantages and disadvantages of the stage-play and the closet drama as instruments of social analysis and comment? Students will be inclined to imagine actresses playing both title roles: does it make a difference that the Duchess of Malfi was played by a boy and Mariam by no one at all? What similarities can be detected between the two problematic characters of Bosola and Salome? Is it reasonable to associate any of their controversial pronouncements with the views of Webster and Cary? What are the wellsprings of evil and tragedy in Webster's Italy and Cary's Judea?

Teaching Clusters

The play's intense preoccupation with bodies, blood, tombs, and corpses makes it a good candidate for the cluster on **The Material World**. You will wish to point out that alongside the fascination with the body as doomed to death and corruption—"Thou art but a box of wormseed," Bosola tells the Duchess—is an equally strong concern with the fate of the soul (note the accumulating references to hell in the final scenes). Burton's *Anatomy of Melancholy* and Browne's *Hydriotaphia, or Urn-Burial* both pick up on facets of the play's focus on the human body.

The extraordinarily powerful characterization of the Duchess—a part it is hard to imagine a Jacobean boy actor performing—makes this play suitable for the **Writing Women** cluster. This would be a particularly attractive option where *The Duchess* is taught alongside Cary's *Tragedy of Mariam*.

Discussion Questions

1. What is Bosola's function in the play? Where does he fit on its moral scale?
2. How is the idea of "melancholy" important to Bosola's character, and to the tragedy as a whole?
3. What is the significance of the singing and dancing madmen (act 4, scene 2)? What does this scene suggest about Renaissance perceptions of madness? What other characters in the play might be considered "mad," and why?
4. What are the sources of evil in *The Duchess of Malfi*? Can evil ever be defeated, or contained? What hope, if any, is offered in the play's conclusion?
5. What explanations does the play seem to offer for Ferdinand's intense obsession with his sister's body and blood?
6. Compare the representation of women and their choice of sexual partners in *The Duchess* and Cary's *Tragedy of Mariam*? What differences in perspective and sympathy do you detect?

Elizabeth Cary

The Tragedy of Mariam

The Tragedy of Mariam is the first example of a published drama by a female author, and some features of the heroine's situation closely resemble Elizabeth Cary's own difficult marriage to a domineering and "very absolute" husband. In addition, *Mariam* is a closet drama, a form that allowed the author to develop complex ideas and characters and to experiment with perspectives in ways that would not be possible (for political or practical reasons) on the stage.

Quick Read

- Form: Closet drama.
- Summary: Mariam, having been relieved at news of her tyrannical husband Herod's death, despairs at the news of his imminent return. The jealous and unbalanced Herod condemns her to death; Mariam goes to execution secure in her virtue and integrity, though regretting her pride.
- Themes: marriage; jealousy; suffering; the lot of women.
- Key Passages: Chorus: "'Tis not enough for one that is a wife / To keep her spotless from an act of ill: / But from suspicion she should free her life, / And bare herself of power as well as will," 3.3.100; Mariam: "Had I but with humility been graced, / As well as fair I might have proved me wise: / But I did think because I knew me chaste, / One virtue for a woman might suffice," 4.8.35–38; Mariam: "'tis my joy, / That I was ever innocent, though sour," 4.8.43–44.

Teaching Suggestions

The two excerpted scenes from the play both center on the question of whether Mariam's undoubted chastity is or should have been sufficient to protect her from her husband's jealousy. Mariam has been unable to restrain her tongue or conceal her scorn for the husband she despises, but she has not betrayed him sexually. The Chorus in 3.3, with its implicitly male perspective on the case, takes her to task for imperfect obedience. Mariam on the verge of death acknowledges her fault but remains confident in her innocence.

The play has a number of interesting and provocative parallels with Webster's *The Duchess of Malfi*, and they teach well together. See "Teaching Suggestions" under Webster.

Teaching Clusters

With its female author and female protagonist, embattled and defiant in similar ways, *Mariam* is right at home in the **Writing Women** category. Webster's *Duchess of Malfi* makes a good companion piece, as do the controversial pieces by Swetnam and Speght (focusing partly on women's domestic role) gathered under "Gender Wars." If you are teaching a larger chunk of the play by means of the Web site, the piercingly negative depiction of the monarch Herod makes the play suitable for the cluster on **Debate, Dissent, and Revolution.**

Discussion Questions

1. Both the Chorus and Mariam herself analyze the causes of her downfall. Are their analyses similar? What differences do you see?
2. How does the play distinguish between spiritual virtue and social decorum? Can they be easily disentangled?

Further Resources

NORTON ONLINE ARCHIVE

The Tragedy of Mariam (complete text)

The Gender Wars

Joseph Swetnam

The Arraignment of Lewd, Idle, Froward, and Unconstant Women

Quick Read

- Form: Prose tract.
- Summary: An attack on women, particularly for their failure to remain subservient to men.
- Themes: Gender; women's failings; scriptural teachings about women.
- Key Passages: "She [Eve] was no sooner made, but straightway her mind was set upon mischief, for by her aspiring mind and wanton will she quickly procured man's fall," 1545; "there are divers women whose beauty has brought their husbands into great poverty and discredit by their pride and whoredom," 1546.

Rachel Speght

A Muzzle for Melastomus

Quick Read

- Form: Prose tract.
- Summary: A response to Swetnam, condemning Swetnam's ignorance and bad style as well as his argument, and correcting his account of woman's creation and purpose.
- Themes: Gender; misogyny; the creation story; women's equality with men.

- Key Passages: "The emptiest barrel makes the loudest sound, and so we will account you," 1546; "Many propositions have you framed, which, as you think, make much against women, but if one would make a logical assumption, the conclusion would be flat against your own sex," 1546–47; "in the image of God were they both created; yea and to be brief, all the parts of their bodies, both external and internal, were correspondent and meet for each other," 1548.

Teaching Suggestions

Swetnam was a late, unschooled, and somewhat incoherent contributor to the centuries-old *querelle des femmes*. Rachel Speght was a remarkably sharp and unabashed teenager who became the first English woman to respond under her own name to this kind of misogynist attack. Swetnam was obviously overmatched, yet many students will be puzzled by the apparent tentativeness of Speght's response. She gaily takes him to pieces as a bad scholar and a foolish curmudgeon, but when it comes to refuting his argument she is less robust, acknowledging, for instance, that Eve's creation was subsequent to Adam's and that her sin was greater. As with Aemilia Lanyer, she is forced to work with the material of Genesis 1–3, and turn it to feminist advantage where possible. This unit can be rounded out with Lanyer's more forthright "Eve's Apology." Swetnam's attacks also shed light on *The Duchess of Malfi*, in which the Cardinal, Ferdinand, and Bosola mouth much the same sort of misogynist rhetoric.

Teaching Clusters

This pair of texts has a key role in the **Writing Women** cluster. Swetnam's and Speght's references to the biblical story of the Fall should be compared with Lanyer's, and in combination they survive as excellent background—and/or counterpoint—to Milton's treatment of the Genesis story in *Paradise Lost*. Viewing this range of texts as a polemical exchange on the subject of the Fall makes the cluster on **Faith, Devotion, and Doubt** another strong option.

Discussion Questions

1. What are the foundations of Swetnam's antifeminist argument? Is there a coherent argument here at all?
2. Compare Speght's reading of the Genesis story with Lanyer's in *Salve Deus*. What differences in argument or emphasis are apparent?

Further Resources

NORTON ONLINE ARCHIVE

Morality's Memorandum
From A Dream

Forms of Inquiry

Situated between the age of explorations and the Enlightenment, the early seventeenth century was also an age of discovery. The range of works gathered in this section attests to the many modes of self- and social analysis in this era. It is not necessarily an instance of a radical epistemic break with the past, but rather of an intensification of certain preoccupations and the development of a range of styles to accommodate them. There is a growing interest in empiricism in this period, but most of the authors collected here remain primarily interested in the (moral, practical, political) uses of knowledge about self and society, rather than in amassing information of any kind for its own sake.

Francis Bacon

Essays

Quick Read

- Form: Essays.
- Summary: Bacon employs the form of the short essay to explore a range of issues, from "Truth" to "Masques and Triumphs"; the style is always terse and analytical, though in their late (1625) versions the essays are longer and more openly didactic.
- Key Passages: "Truth may perhaps come to the price of a pearl, that showeth best by day, but it will not rise to the price of a carbuncle, that showeth best by various lights. A mixture of a lie doth ever add pleasure," 1552; "He that hath wife and children hath given hostages unto fortune," 1553; "I like a plantation in a pure soil; that is, where people are not displanted to the end to plant in others. For else it is rather an extirpation than a plantation," 1558.

New Atlantis

Quick Read

- Form: Utopian prose fiction.
- Summary: European travelers discover the island of Bensalem, whose inhabitants are devoted to science; in the excerpt, they learn the secrets of Solomon's House, a scientific society or institute.
- Key Passages: "The end of our foundation is the knowledge of causes, and secret motions of things; and the enlarging of the bounds of human empire, to the effecting of all things possible," 1570; "we have consultations, which of the inventions and experiences which we have discovered shall be published, and which not: and take all an oath of secrecy, for the concealing of those which we think fit to keep secret; though some of those we do reveal sometimes to the State, and some not," 1572.

Teaching Suggestions

Useful knowledge is the one goal of the scientists of Solomon's House in Bacon's *New Atlantis*. Rather than seeking to enlarge the bounds of learning per se, they are set on "the enlarging of the bounds of human empire, to the effecting of all things possible." (In this they make for a sharp contrast with the Laputans in Swift's *Gulliver's Travels*, theoretical mathematicians whose contempt for practical knowledge prevents them from being able to build proper houses.) Although Bacon made little contribution to the experimental sciences he praised, his approach to social and philosophical questions in the *Essays* was nothing if not utilitarian. Beginning with "Of Studies," you can use Bacon's works to get your students thinking about ways of reading and the uses of learning in the seventeenth century (and today). Who is the implied reader of Bacon's *Essays*? What can this reader expect to gain from studying them? How is Bacon's style designed to influence the way the information he provides will be absorbed and deployed?

Bacon's *Essays* may be contrasted both with the works of other prose writers and with each other. Changes in his style—a relaxation of his austere, aphoristic manner, a comparative smoothness and expansiveness—can be traced in comparing the 1597 and 1625 versions of "Of Studies." Essays new in the 1625 edition can be compared with those introduced in 1597 or 1612.

Robert Burton

The Anatomy of Melancholy

The extracts from *The Anatomy of Melancholy* in NAEL are designed to give students a sense of the style and matter of Burton's magnum opus (they cannot, of course, do more than hint at its extraordinary range and sheer mass). Burton crams his work with dizzying numbers of citations, giving all equal weight and leaving little or no room for reasoning outside the box of his bibliography. As he acknowledges in his preface, "Democritus Junior to the Reader," his is a "roving humour" that seeks "to have an oar in every man's boat, to taste of every dish, and sip of every cup." Melancholy offers Burton a means of organizing his boundless interests and erudition around a broad and infinitely capacious subject. Yet if Burton represents himself as a descendant of the "laughing philosopher" Democritus, his treatise draws the reader into a weirdly dark and supremely melancholic world, in which all sources of knowledge and all modes of living seem equal, and equally mad. As he promises in another part of the preface, not included in NAEL:

> thou shalt soon perceive that all the world is mad, that it is melancholy, dotes; that it is (which Epicthonius Cosmopolites expressed not many years since in a map) made like a fool's head . . . a crazed head, *cavea stultorum*, a fool's paradise . . . a common prison of gulls, cheaters, flatterers, etc., and needs to be re-

formed. [The map referred to here appears on the cover of *The Norton Shake-speare* (1997).]

While Burton represents himself as standing amused and apart from it all, the prurient misogyny of the passages of *Love Melancholy* reveals this member of an all-male academic society in a more unsettling light.

You can teach Burton simply as the supreme example of a certain kind of early modern scholarship, perhaps contrasting him with the rather different scholarly style of Sir Thomas Browne. The *Anatomy* is especially valuable, however, if you are teaching other texts focusing on melancholy, such as Webster's *Duchess of Malfi* and Milton's "Il Penseroso."

Sir Thomas Browne

Religio Medici

Quick Read

- Form: Prose treatise.
- Summary: An exposition of the author's religious beliefs, largely orthodox but distinctively expressed.
- Themes: Reason vs. faith; confessional conflict; heresy.
- Key Passages: "Neither doth herein my zeal so far make me forget the general charity I owe unto humanity, as rather to hate than pity Turks, infidels, and (what is worse) Jews," 1583; "We have re-formed from them [Catholics], not against them . . . and therefore I am not scrupulous to converse and live with them, to enter their churches in defect of ours, and either pray with them or for them," 1583; "In philosophy, where truth seems double-faced, there is no man more paradoxical than myself, but in divinity I love to keep the road; and, though not in an implicit, yet an humble faith, follow the great wheel of the church, by which I move," 1585; "We carry with us the wonders we seek without us: there is all Africa and her prodigies in us," 1587; "all things are artificial, for nature is the art of God," 1588; "thus was I dead before I was alive. Though my grave be England, my dying place was Paradise, and Eve miscarried of me, before she conceived of Cain," 1589.

Hydriotaphia, or Urn-Burial

Quick Read

- Form: Prose treatise.
- Summary: Prompted by the example of some anonymous Roman (actually Anglo-Saxon) cremation urns unearthed in Norfolk, Browne in the excerpt contemplates the impossibility of achieving an immortal memory on earth, and recalls the true immortality that is promised in the next life.

- Themes: Death; memory; oblivion; immortality.
- Key Passages: "The iniquity of oblivion blindly scattereth her poppy, and deals with the memory of men without distinction to merit of perpetuity. Who can but pity the founder of the pyramids?" 1591; "Egyptian mummies, which Cambyses or time hath spared, avarice now consumeth. Mummy is become merchandise, Mizraim, cures wounds, and Pharaoh is sold for balsams," 1592; "To live indeed is to be again ourselves, which being not only an hope but an evidence in noble believers, 'tis all one to lie in St. Innocent's churchyard as in the sands of Egypt: ready to be anything, in the ecstasy of being ever, and as content with six foot as the *moles* of Adrianus," 368.

Teaching Suggestions

Browne's *Religio Medici* and *Hydriotaphia*, although not written to serve a specifically religious function, are learned meditations on topics such as faith, death, and dissolution, executed in elaborate and sonorous prose that is meant to give pleasure as well as instruction. Students should be encouraged to read some of Browne's marvelous sentences aloud, and to consider what Virginia Woolf meant when she said, "Few people love the writings of Sir Thomas Browne, but those who do are of the salt of the Earth." Browne wears his learning more lightly than Burton, and trusts to it less. Browne's famously well-crafted sentences seem designed to help him run rings around his own reason. "In philosophy, where truth seems double-faced, there is no man more paradoxical than myself." In matters of religion, Browne's eagerness to subordinate reason to faith leads him to declare that "there be not impossibilities enough in religion for an active faith." He is glad not to have lived in the age of miracles, for "then had my faith been thrust upon me." His antipathy to dull proof contrasts sharply with Hobbes's determined pursuit of it.

Thomas Hobbes

Leviathan

The selections from *Leviathan* cover both physical science and political theory. Today, these subjects belong to entirely different spheres of learning, but for Hobbes they are closely linked. The selection from the Introduction (1596) can be used to help make this clear. Hobbes's argument here is that life, properly considered, "is but a motion of the limbs" guided by "some principal part within." If this is so, then we cannot deny the quality of life to the State, wherein the various limbs (individuals or institutions) are guided by the sovereign, "an artificial soul." Hobbes is withering in his scorn for those who do not share his scientific outlook. The chief fault of universities, he argues, is "the frequency of insignificant speech" (1597). Some students and instructors may be tempted to agree! The selections on the state of nature and the commonwealth are sufficient to provide a basic grasp of Hobbes's political theory. For Hobbes, freedom of choice and transcendent justice are illusions. The state of nature—before, that is, the establishment of laws and sovereignty—is a state of war with every man against every other man, a war in which the stronger prevails rather than truth or justice. The only protection lies in surrendering one's freedom and submitting to the restraint of laws held in common in a society—"that great Leviathan called a Common-Wealth or State." Insofar as this philosophy counsels absolute subjection of the individual to the head of state, it is a royalist view. Yet Hobbes's perception that initial choice of sovereign was essentially pragmatic and arbitrary did not sit well with royalist doctrine of the divine right of kings. In his time, he pleased few readers, yet his influence was nonetheless immense.

Hobbes's exceptionally clear style and his hostility to all ambiguity help grant his work the air of pure ratiocination that we associate with modern philosophy. At times, however, we catch notes of the aphoristic style honed by the young Bacon half a century before.

Teaching Clusters

Many of Bacon's *Essays* are well-suited to the **Debate, Dissent, and Revolution** cluster. They are particularly attractive as launching pads for the study of various seventeenth-century themes and modes. For instance, "Of Plantations" can be read alongside such colonial texts as Marvell's "Bermudas" as well as those grouped in the *Norton Topic Online* "Emigrants and Settlers." "Of Masques and Triumphs," with its ambiguous meditation on court entertainments, teaches well alongside Jonson's *Masque of Blackness*. The section "Solomon's House" could initiate a survey of early modern versions of Utopia, reaching back to More's seminal text and forward to such disparate texts as Gerrard Winstanley's proclamation of Digger communism in "The True Levellers' Standard Advanced," Milton's description of Eden, and Margaret Cavendish's *The Blazing World*. (Thomas Traherne's vision of a wondrous world without private property as seen through a child's eyes in *Centuries of Meditation* and *Wonder* [1756] also merits consideration as a version of Utopia.)

In the **Writing Women** cluster, the essay "Of Marriage and Single Life" could be the starting point for a wide-ranging survey of the literature of the period organized around the theme of marriage. Such a survey might cover Webster's *Duchess of Malfi*, Cary's *Tragedy of Mariam*, Suckling's "A Ballad upon a Wedding," Philips's "A Married State," Cavendish's *A True Relation*, and finally, Paradise Lost. (*Norton Topics Online* offers even more resources that provide historical background and conflicting contemporary views about marriage and the social order.)

Burton, Browne, and Hobbes teach well together as part of **The Material World**. Burton and Hobbes both, in different ways, derive social truths from material causes (internal in the former case, external in the latter). Browne ponders the material and dematerializing force of entropy in human history. All three of these writers could equally be considered in the cluster on **Style**; Hobbes and Browne in particular wrote a distinctive kind of sentence that they considered integral to their very different philosophical projects.

Taught singly, Browne could be well-placed in the **Faith, Devotion, and Doubt** category. Hobbes has a clear role to play, alongside the texts in "Crisis of Authority," in the cluster on **Debate, Dissent, and Revolution.**

Discussion Questions

1. What does Bacon mean when he compares truth to a pearl, rather than a diamond? What positive aspects does he see in lying?
2. Compare Bacon's 1597 essay "Of Studies" to the final version of 1625. How have his style and approach changed? Has his argument changed substantially?
3. What does Bacon mean by "Idols"?
4. In what ways does Burton's *Anatomy of Melancholy* embody or perform the malady it purports to diagnose?
5. How does Browne depict the conflict between faith and reason in *Religio Medici*?
6. What, if anything, is at stake politically in Browne's argument in *Hydriotaphia* that the perpetuation of an earthly memory is doomed to failure?
7. What kind of discourse is Hobbes condemning when he refers to "the frequency of insignificant speech"?
8. Does justice have a place in Hobbes's theory of the social contract?

Further Resources

NORTON ONLINE ARCHIVE

From The Anatomy of Melancholy
  Exercise Rectified
Leviathan, *Part I, Chapter 5*, Of Reason and Science
John Aubrey, The Life of Thomas Hobbes
Abraham Cowley, To Mr. Hobbes
Sir William Davenant, The Author's Preface to . . . Mr. Hobbes
Thomas Hobbes, The Answer to Sir Will Davenant's Preface . . .

George Herbert

George Herbert is among the greatest and most devout religious poets of the seventeenth or any other century. His surviving poetry is entirely devoted to religious subjects, in particular the subtle movements of the sometimes doubtful soul and the boundless mercy of God. Herbert's verse was part of a private conversation carried on with God; there is no evidence that during his lifetime it circulated even in manuscript.

Affliction (1)

In this partly autobiographical poem, Herbert traces a very different career course from those followed by Donne and Jonson. Like so many of his poems, this one is a dramatic monologue in which the poet's silent interlocutor is God. In contrast to Donne and Jonson, Herbert was born into a distinguished family and began life with brilliant prospects. A graduate of Trinity College, Cambridge, he obtained election to the Public Oratorship of the university, a post that, as the headnote points out, "would have been a step toward a career at court or in public service" (1606). The "service brave" Herbert originally anticipated ("Affliction" [1609, line 2]) was nominally dedicated to God and perhaps aimed at an ecclesiastical career; however, the "joys," "benefits," and "glorious household stuff" (lines 2, 6, 9) are a courtier's rewards. Herbert's complaints about the disappointment of his hopes and ambitions through illness and the death of patrons lead to a crisis and then a sudden reversal at the end, characteristic of his poems:

> Well I will change the service and go seek
>   Some other master out.
> Ah, my dear God! though I am clean forgot,
> Let me not love thee, if I love thee not.

Jordan (1) and (2)

In the two poems entitled "Jordan," Herbert attempts to define what Christian poetry—or at least, his own—should be. "Jordan (1)" scorns the standard romantic and erotic subjects of contemporary verse as "fictions only and false hair." Herbert's poetry will instead be devoted to "*My God, My King.*" In "Jordan (2)," he seeks for the appropriate poetic style to suit his divine subject. Having experimented with "quaint words" and grandiose conceits, he hears the voice of a friend (the Holy Spirit) whisper:

> There is in love a sweetness ready penned:
> Copy out only that, and save expense. (lines 17–18)

The couplet intentionally recalls the conclusion of Sonnet 1 of Sidney's *Astrophil and Stella*: "'Fool,' said my Muse to me, 'look in thy heart and write.'" Herbert turns this conventional sentiment to holy use, concluding that true devotional poetry will be content simply to reflect an experience of God's love, rather than resorting to artificial technical effects.

Teaching Suggestions

The "Jordan" poems provide an excellent way of introducing Herbert's conception of himself as a poet (you might make a point of contrasting these poems with Jonson's various poems about writing poetry, such as "Ode to Himself"). The curious fact is that while Herbert purports to scorn quaint conventions and artificial technical effects, his poetry abounds in self-conscious artifice and technical virtuosity. In addition to being among the most devout of poets, he is also among the most playful and experimental. In poems like "The Altar" and "Easter Wings," he crafts "shaped verses" whose visual forms on the page reflect their subject matter. In "Denial," he lets the first five stanzas, in which the speaker laments his distance from God, trail off without a concluding rhyme; when a rhyme is finally heard at the end of the final stanza, it signals the final "chime" or meeting of the speaker's mind with God.

As these examples indicate, Herbert's formal games and experiments were by no means frivolous. Rather, his goal was a poetry absolutely devoted to God—a poetry that expressed devotion in its *form* as well as its content. Herbert is loved by many today, yet his poems will not be to everyone's taste. Whether your students warm to his work may depend on whether they find his technical flourishes effective or merely pretentious and distracting.

Teaching Clusters

Herbert's technical virtuosity, combined with the tone of humble and devout simplicity that characterizes some of his poems, and the sharp ear for vernacular speech exhibited in others, make him an ideal poet to discuss with reference to **Style**. Like Donne, he is a master of the metaphysical conceit, yet his images are typically more homely, and not infrequently economic (as when, in "Redemption," he likens God's covenant with his people to a lease binding a tenant to a landlord). **Faith, Devotion, and Doubt** is another category where a taste of "Holy Mr. Herbert" would seem nothing less than essential.

Discussion Questions

1. Does Herbert ever write as "simply" as he claims to do in "Jordan (1)"?
2. What kind of images does Herbert seem to favor for his conceits? Is there a common thread?
3. How does Herbert represent the voice of God in his poetry?
4. What might have drawn Herbert to "shaped verses" (e.g., "Easter Wings" and "The Altar")?
5. What are the implications of Herbert's representation of God as a landlord in "Redemption"?

Further Resources

NORTON ONLINE ARCHIVE

Temptation
Anagram
Hope
Sin's Round
Love Unknown

Aaron
The Altar
Redemption
Easter Wings
Jordan (1)
The Collar
The Pulley
The Flower
Love (3)

Henry Vaughan

The World

Quick Read

- Form: Lyric.
- Summary: A vision of heaven as a tranquil shining ring, beneath which the world and its sinful inhabitants whirl about; while a few rise up and are saved, most fail to take notice of the bliss above their heads.
- Themes: Salvation; sin; earthly temptations; election.
- Key Passages: "I saw eternity the other night, / Like a great ring of pure and endless light," lines 1–2; "The weaker sort slight, trivial wares enslave / Who think them brave / And poor, despised Truth sat counting by / Their victory," lines 42–45; "this ring the bridegroom did for none provide / But for his bride," lines 59–60.

Teaching Suggestions

"The World" provides an excellent way of introducing Vaughan in relation to Herbert, noting both similarities and key differences. Vaughan is like Herbert in his deep religious devotion, and his attention to the details of worldly life; the voice that whispers to him in the poem's conclusion is a recognizable Herbertian touch. But whereas Herbert concentrates on his day-to-day relationship with God, Vaughan is almost always focused on the last days or the afterlife, where he will at last know his Creator. The beloved things of this world—from the lover's lute to the miser's pelf—are not, as they might have been for Herbert, figurative keys to unlock a heavenly treasure, but dross to be shunned and transcended.

Almost all of the Vaughan poems in NAEL focus one way or another on visions of return, escape, or transcendence. Like Traherne (and later Wordsworth), Vaughan associates childhood with a closeness to God— "looking back, at that short space / [I] Could see a glimpse of His bright face" ("The Retreat," lines 9–10). The poem concludes by wishing for a death that will also be a return to the earliest state of infancy. "Regeneration" and "They Are All Gone into That World of Light" conclude in similar ways with the desire for death and heaven. "The Waterfall," a complex poem, elaborates the ways in which a river can offer a glimpse of eternal mysteries—yet, in a move typical of Vaughan, the poem concludes by rejecting the earthly object as unworthy of the celestial thing it signifies: "thou art the channel my soul seeks, / Not this with cataracts and creeks" (lines 39–40).

Teaching Clusters

For many of the same reasons that apply to Herbert (alongside whom Vaughan is probably best taught), these poems are well-suited either to the cluster on **Style** or to that on **Faith, Devotion, and Doubt.** In the latter cluster, Vaughan's depiction of the holiness of childhood in "The Retreat" is ideal preparation for Traherne's poem "Wonder."

Discussion Questions

1. What does childhood signify in "The Retreat"? Should "Regeneration" also be considered a poem about childhood?
2. How does Vaughan write about death?
3. What spiritual meanings does Vaughan find in running water in "The Waterfall"?

Further Resources

NORTON ONLINE ARCHIVE

The Book
Peace
Man
A Rhapsody
I Walked the Other Day (To Spend My Hour)

Richard Crashaw

Richard Crashaw wrote to shock. His poems are full of bizarre and disturbing images, of wounds that are at once mouths and eyes ("On the Wounds of Our Crucified Lord"), of murdered infants drinking milk from the stars ("To the Infant Martyrs"), of nature reversed so that a mother sucks sustenance from her son ("Luke 11"). At times his poems seem to verge on blasphemy, but this is the farthest thing from his intention. Crashaw shocks the reader in order to jolt him or her out of the normal patterns of thought and perception. The grotesque is a battering ram against the mundane, opening up a path to the divine.

The Flaming Heart

Quick Read

- Form: Lyric.
- Summary: Crashaw describes a picture of St. Teresa and the Seraph, arguing that the inspirational Teresa should in fact be represented as the dart-bearing angel, for her ability to set the hearts of believers on fire.
- Themes: Sainthood; suffering; divine ecstasy.
- Key Passages: "Why man, this speaks pure mortal frame, / And mocks with female frost love's manly flame," lines 23–24; "in love's field was never found / A nobler weapon than a wound," lines 71–72; "By all thy brim-filled bowls of fierce desire, / By thy last morning's draft of liquid fire; / By the full kingdom of that final kiss / That seized thy parting soul, and sealed thee his," lines 99–102.

As both "The Flaming Heart" and "To the Noblest and Best of Ladies" demonstrate, Crashaw often expresses spiritual devotion in explicitly erotic terms. Shocking as this may seem to both religious and secular readers today, there are many precedents for this in English literature, including Margery Kempe's visions of marriage and intimacy with Christ and John Donne's plea to God, in "Holy Sonnet 14," to "ravish" him. Yet the closest parallels for Crashaw's brand of erotic devotion come from the European continent. A convert to Catholicism, Crashaw was much influenced by the autobiography of the sixteenth-century Spanish mystic St. Teresa of Avila, in which she describes the ecstatic trances she was plunged into by visits of the Holy Spirit. In Bernini's statue of *Saint Teresa and the Seraph*, Teresa's writhing body and the dart the angel is about to plunge into her have unmistakable sexual connotations. Crashaw could not have seen Bernini's statue, but his thoughts are running along similar lines in "The Flaming Heart," which begins by suggesting that the saint and the seraph should change places. An image of Bernini's masterpiece, available in *Norton Topics Online*, makes an excellent teaching aid.

Teaching Clusters

Crashaw's almost exclusively religious subject matter and his spiritual shock tactics make his poetry suitable for the cluster on **Faith, Devotion, and Doubt**. The erotic spirituality of "The Flaming Heart" and "To the Noblest and Best of Ladies" makes these poems work especially well alongside Donne's similarly daring—if less extreme—*Holy Sonnets*. These poems could also be introduced into the cluster on **Writing Women**. The "Sacred Epigrams," with their hair-raising conceits, will be at home in the **Style** category.

Discussion Questions

1. Why does Crashaw employ such shocking images in his "Sacred Epigrams"? Do they draw the soul to wonder, or are they merely repellent?
2. Why does Crashaw argue that Teresa should be represented as the Seraphim? Does his argument seem feminist or misogynistic?
3. How does Crashaw write about bodily fluids (blood, milk, tears)? What meaning do these substances appear to have for him?

Further Resources

NORTON ONLINE ARCHIVE

Luke 7
On Our Crucified Lord, Naked and Bloody

Robert Herrick

Corinna's Going a'Maying

Quick Read

- Form: Lyric.
- Summary: An invitation to join in the custom of "bringing in the May," made urgent by a reminder of time's passage and youth's brevity.
- Themes: Youth; time; *carpe diem*.
- Key Passages: "Come, let us go while we are in our prime, / And take the harmless folly of the time. / We shall grow old apace, and die / Before we know our liberty," lines 57–60; "Then while time serves, and we are but decaying, / Come, my Corinna, come, let's go a-Maying," lines 69–70.

Teaching Suggestions

Although it is less explicitly an invitation to sexual intercourse than some other poems of the genre, "Corinna" exemplifies the Cavalier spirit of *carpe diem*, inviting comparison with Carew's "A Rapture." Much of the imagery is unashamedly erotic and indeed pagan. Yet Herrick, like Herbert, was a parish priest. As a preface to your discussion of "Corinna," you might read your students this excerpt from Philip Stubbes's *Anatomie of Abuses*:

> Against May, Whitsunday, or other time all the young men and maids, old men and wives, run gadding over night to the woods, groves, hills, and mountains, where they spend all the night in pleasant pastimes. . . . And no marvel, for there is a great Lord present amongst them, as superintendent and Lord over their pastimes and sports, namely Satan, prince of hell. But their chiefest jewel they bring from thence is their Maypole, which they bring home with great veneration, . . .

this Maypole (this stinking idol, rather) which is covered all over with flowers and herbs. . . . And then fall they to dance about it, like as the heathen people did at the dedication of the Idols, whereof this is a perfect pattern, or rather the thing itself. I have heard it credibly reported . . . , by men of great gravity and reputation, that of forty, three-score, or a hundred maids going to the wood over night, there have scarcely the third part of them returned home undefiled.

Norton Topics Online offers more examples of Puritan social critique, including selections from the irrepressible William Prynne, who was sentenced to have his books burned and his ears cropped for implicitly comparing the queen to a whore because she took part in masques and pastorals; see "Styles of Belief, Devotion, and Culture" under "Civil Wars of Ideas" in the Early Seventeenth Century section.

The Hock-Cart, or Harvest Home

In this poem, Herrick, who deliberately courts Puritan disapproval with his praise of superstitious or quasi-Catholic practices such as blessing the cart and kissing the sheaves (line 19), represents his rural revelers as the backbone of English society. After drinking their Lord's health, they drink "to the plow (the common-wealth)" (line 39). The phrase closely echoes a remark by Robert Cecil in the House of Commons in 1601, which is in turn indicative of a broad stream of conservative thought: "I do not dwell in the Country, I am not acquainted with the Plough: But I think whosoever doth not maintain the Plough destroys this Kingdom."

Yet particularly in its final lines, "The Hock-Cart" draws attention to the operation of power in the commonwealth maintained by the plow. "And you must know, your Lord's word's true, / Feed him ye must whose food fills you" (lines 51–52). The last part of the poem, with its reiteration of *must* and the emphasis on pain (line 54), draws surprisingly frank attention to the coercion by which the social order is maintained and raises the question of how and by whom wealth and food are produced in this society.

The Bad Season Makes the Poet Sad

Written in the middle to late 1640s, this poem refers to the years before the civil wars and the flight of Henrietta Maria as a "golden age" (line 7). Concluding with a line translated from Horace's first ode to his patron Maecenas, Herrick associates this golden age with the reign of the emperor Augustus (and thus anticipates the "Augustan" spirit of the Restoration). Although the poem was written before the execution of the king, the golden age of the prewar years already seems infinitely remote and— except in wishful fantasy—all but irrecoverable.

Teaching Clusters

Although England's civil troubles only intrude occasionally into Herrick's poetic world (as in "The Bad Season"), his erotic, quasi-pagan extravagance can always be attributed at least in part to a wish to taunt the

Puritans. As such, **Debate, Dissent, and Revolution** would be an appropriate category for much of his verse. It would be tempting to follow Herrick with Milton's "Lycidas," which lambasts the corruption of the Anglican clergy—Herrick was very much the kind of bad shepherd Milton had in mind. The frank eroticism of a poem like "The Vine," which leaves the poet alone in bed with his erection, makes it suitable for the cluster on **The Material World**; "The Vine" would be well accompanied by Carew's "A Rapture."

Discussion Questions

1. How, if at all, does Herrick accommodate the erotic and pagan themes of poems like "The Vine" and "Corinna" in his clerical profession?
2. Why, in the last lines of "The Hock-Cart," does Herrick remind the laborers of their "pain"?
3. What attitudes toward Ben Jonson are evident in Herrick's poem to Jonson, and in his verse more generally?
4. Is there more to the politics of "The Bad Season Makes the Poet Sad" than appears on the surface?

Further Resources

NORTON ONLINE ARCHIVE

An Ode for Him
Discontents in Devon
Upon a Child That Died
Oberon's Feast
The Pillar of Fame
His Grange, or Private Wealth
Upon His Spaniel Tracy
To Lar
The Lily in a Crystal
To Blossoms
To the Water Nymphs Drinking at the Fountain

Audio:
To the Virgins, to Make Much of Time
(music by Thomas Ravenscroft, performed by the Hilliard Ensemble)

Thomas Carew

A Rapture

Quick Read

- Form: Lyric.
- Summary: The poet urges Celia, married to another, to have sex with him and journey to an erotic utopia, the "Love's Elysium."

- Themes: Sex; honor, conventional morality; class-consciousness.
- Key Passages: "The giant, Honor, that keeps cowards out, / Is but a masquer, and the servile rout / Of baser subjects only bend in vain / To the vast idol, whilst the nobler train / Of valiant lovers daily sail between / The huge Colossus' legs," lines 2–8; "My rudder with thy bold hand, like a tried / And skilful pilot, thou shalt steer, and guide / My bark into love's channel, where it shall / Dance, as the bounding waves do rise or fall," lines 87–90; "Like and enjoy, to will and act is one; / We only sin when Love's rites are not done," lines 113–14.

Teaching Suggestions

There are relatively few poems by Carew in *NAEL*, but almost all of them can make a valuable contribution to your course, exemplifying a range of Caroline/Cavalier attitudes and genres. "A Rapture" is among the most daring erotic poems of the first half of the century, and also one of the most rhetorically complex. Carew's swings between idealization of the lover and the sexual act and cynicism about both (the last word of the poem is "whores") are fascinating to chart. That the poet's lust is inflected by class consciousness is worthy of remark. As the reference to the "nobler train" (6) sailing deftly through Honor's legs indicates, Carew was conscious of libertinism—or at least the perception of libertinism—as belonging to an aristocratic code.

"An Elegy upon the Death of the Dean of Paul's, Dr. John Donne" and "To Ben Jonson" shed light on how the works of these two early-seventeenth-century poetic masters were received by the next generation. The poem to Jonson is explicitly a response to "Ode to Himself," and Carew demonstrates his absorption of and adherence to Jonson's values not only by praising him, but by taking him to task: "Why should the follies then of this dull age / Draw from thy pen such an immodest rage / As seems to blast thy else-immortal bays, / When thine own tongue proclaims thy itch of praise?" (23–26). Carew's relationship to Jonson can also be explored through his country-house poem, "To Saxham." An unusually short example of the genre, but covering many of the main themes of "To Penshurst" (including the self-sacrificing fish, 27–28), "To Saxham" can be read as a kind of digest or epitome of country-house poetry and values.

Teaching Clusters

"To Saxham" should of course be read in conjunction with other country-house poems, by Jonson and perhaps Lanyer and Marvell. This could mean categorizing it under **Debate, Dissent, and Revolution** or, alternatively, under **Style.** The latter cluster is the best place for the poems to Donne and Jonson, which deal explicitly with their influence as literary and moral teachers. "A Rapture," with its fairly precise detailing of a sexual act that is to be valued in itself (or which is transcendent only in that it transports the lovers to a purely sexual Elysium), could go in a different cluster, **The Material World.**

Discussion Questions

1. Comparing Carew's elegy for Donne with his poem to Jonson, how does he regard each poet? How has each influenced him?
2. For what does Carew criticize Jonson in "To Ben Jonson"?
3. Who is the intended audience of "A Rapture"? Is its success as a seduction piece threatened by the coarse closing reference to "whores"?
4. In what ways does Carew's "To Saxham" depart from its chief model, Jonson's "To Penshurst"?

Further Resources

NORTON ONLINE ARCHIVE

Song ("Give me more love, or more disdain")
The Second Rapture
Disdain Returned
Song ("Persuasions to Enjoy")

John Suckling

A Ballad upon a Wedding

Quick Read

- Form: Mock-rustic ballad.
- Summary: A country yokel describes to his friend "Dick" (possibly Lovelace) an aristocratic wedding he has witnessed, concluding with knowing speculation about what transpired in the bridal chamber.
- Key Passages: "At Charing Cross, hard by the way / Where we, thou know'st, do sell our hay, / There is a house with stairs," lines 7–9; "At length the candle's out, and now / All that they had not done, they do: / What that is, who can tell? / But I believe it was no more / Than thou and I have done before / With Bridget and with Nell," lines 127–32.

Teaching Suggestions

Suckling's "Ballad" makes a good counterpoint to Carew's "Rapture." Whereas Carew strives to imagine a sexual experience reserved for the nobility alone, Suckling emphasizes the universal and leveling quality of sexuality. When the country yokel recognizes at the end of this poem that sex is the same for lords and laborers, the social order seems to wobble very slightly. Like Herrick's "The Hock-Cart," however, the poem allays any doubts it may raise by virtue of its exuberant confidence in the vitality and timelessness of the old order. Read one way, poems like these cynically celebrate the power of the aristocracy to pull the wool over the eyes of rural laborers by means of spectacle. Read another, they celebrate the games and festivities that bind the aristocracy and the rural poor together, in opposition to Puritans and the urban middle classes. Part of the point of Suckling's ballad is that his rural speaker has ventured as far as Charing Cross in London, the heart of mercantilism and Puritanism, and, thanks to witnessing the wedding, come away ideologically unscathed. ("Styles of Belief, Devotion, and Culture" in the *NTO* Early Seventeenth Century section "Civil Wars of Ideas" offers texts that will allow deeper examination of issues of social order.)

Teaching Clusters

As a quintessential Cavalier, Suckling has a natural home in the cluster on **Debate, Dissent, and Revolution**. In such a context, one would wish to emphasize the implicit politics of "A Ballad upon a Wedding." Alternatively, the identification of sexuality as the common denominator in "A Ballad" and the refusal to romanticize desire—which this poem shares with "Out Upon It!"—make the cluster on **The Material World** another strong option.

Discussion Questions

1. Does "A Ballad upon a Wedding," with its reference to the universality of sex, subvert class divisions, or shore them up?

Further Resources

NORTON ONLINE ARCHIVE

A Song to a Lute

Richard Lovelace

Lovelace can be and is often thought of as the quintessential Cavalier, yet in several ways he differs from his fellow royalists and proclaimed libertines Suckling, Carew, and Herrick. Many of his poems respond not only to Puritan provocation but also to the experience of crushing defeat. Lovelace consequently invests traditional Cavalier preoccupations—honor, sex, and alcohol—with a new spiritual and inspirational significance.

The Grasshopper

Quick Read

- Form: Lyric.
- Summary: Drawing on Aesop's fable of the careless grasshopper and improvident ant, the poet audaciously takes sides with the grasshopper and vows to live by the ideals of summer (the interrupted reign of Charles I) even in the winter of the interregnum.
- Key Passages: "We will create / A genuine summer in each other's

breast; / And spite of this cold time and frozen fate / Thaw us a warm seat to our rest," lines 21–24; "Thou lord of all that seas embrace, yet he / That wants himself is poor indeed," lines 39–40.

Lovelace's *Lucasta* was published in 1649, a year after Herrick's *Hesperides* and after Parliament had crossed the bridge of regicide. "The Grasshopper" and "To Althea, from Prison" reveal the response of this quintessential Cavalier to the destruction of his cause, a response that is almost paradoxically optimistic and life-affirming. Whereas for Herrick there can be no joy until the wished-for and still-conceivable return of the golden age, Lovelace in prison creates a golden world in miniature out of the elements of love, friendship, wine, and unbending royalism. Students tend to respond very warmly to "To Althea"; "The Grasshopper," with its comparatively complex rhythms and close-clustered allusions, is more difficult, but involves the finest statement of the Cavalier ideal. For Lovelace, at least, this ideal never boils down to defiant hedonism, but requires self-knowledge and fidelity to the truth found in the heart: "Though lord of all that seas embrace, yet he / That wants himself is poor indeed," lines 39–40.

Teaching Clusters

The civil war and its defeats were the formative experience behind Lovelace's poetry, which consequently has a clear place in the cluster on **Debate, Dissent, and Revolution.** Lovelace can be taught alongside Suckling, Herrick, and perhaps Carew in this category, with an eye to both his participation in and evolution from the prewar Cavalier ideal.

Discussion Questions

1. In what ways do Lovelace's Cavalier values differ from those of Cavaliers like Suckling and Carew? Is Lovelace closer to the spirit of Ben Jonson?
2. How does Lovelace go about adapting the fable of the ant and the grasshopper to describe the plight of royalists in the aftermath of the civil war?

Further Resources

NORTON ONLINE ARCHIVE

The Snail

Edmund Waller

The chief reason for teaching the selections by Waller would be as preparation for the shift in poetic taste and style following the Restoration. The Augustans greatly admired the smoothness and balance of Waller's verse. "The Story of Phoebus and Daphne Applied" is especially illustrative of Waller's appeal to the ensuing period; the poem is in heroic couplets, the favored Augustan form, and concludes with an ironic epigram of the sort Dryden or Pope would have appreciated: "He catched at love, and filled his arms with bays" (20).

Teaching Clusters

Style is the category in which to include Waller. Students may turn with relief to the easiness of his style after the jaggedness, elusiveness, or obscurity of many of his contemporaries.

Further Resources

NORTON ONLINE ARCHIVE

Of the Last Verses in the Book
On a Girdle
Of English Verse

Abraham Cowley

Cowley's "Ode: Of Wit" is worth teaching both for its efforts to define a key poetic concept, wit, and also for its own sparkling wittiness. Cowley is also important in that he would come to symbolize the mannerisms, and the excesses, of the so-called metaphysical poets. In his *Life of Cowley*, Samuel Johnson would complain of the extravagance of Cowley's metaphysical conceits:

> The most heterogeneous ideas are yoked by violence together; nature and art are ransacked for illustrations, comparisons, and allusions; their learning instructs, and their subtlety surprises; but the reader commonly thinks his improvement dearly bought, and, though he sometimes admires, is seldom pleased.

The "Ode" gives plenty of evidence of what Johnson calls the ransacking of nature and art for comparisons—in one stanza we find wit compared to false London wares (9), an ancient Greek painting (12), an object seen in magnifying glasses (14), and a shooting star (16). Yet Cowley was himself aware of the kind of criticisms Johnson would later make. Whatever wit may be, it is not "upon all things to obtrude / And force some odd similitude" (53–54).

Teaching Clusters

As with Waller, **Style** is the right cluster for Cowley. The "Ode" can be introduced after or in the course of explaining the importance of the metaphysical conceit in Donne's poetry. Johnson's *Life of Cowley* is useful in shedding light on this poet and the metaphysicals generally, but students should be reminded that Johnson's ideas about style are the product of a very different (neoclassical) age.

Discussion Questions

1. Does Cowley's "Ode: Of Wit" bring us any nearer to an understanding of what "wit" is? To what extent is it possible to define something by declaring what it is *not*?

Further Resources

NORTON ONLINE ARCHIVE

The Wish
To Mr. Hobbes
To the Royal Society

Katherine Philips

Upon the Double Murder of King Charles

Katherine Philips never shied from controversy. As a teenager, she wrote a witty poem against the institution of marriage. As a royalist married to a prominent member of Parliament, she denounced Parliament's execution of Charles I.

Quick Read

- Summary: The poem responds angrily to the execution of Charles I, and still more to posthumous attacks upon his character (the second murder).
- Themes: Justice; royalism; regicide.
- Key Passages: "Slander must follow treason; but yet stay, / Take not our reason with our king away," lines 23–24; "Christ will be King, but I ne'er understood, / His subjects built his kingdom up with blood," lines 29–30.

Teaching Suggestions

The bitterly witty and rhetorically complex "Upon the Double Murder of King Charles" satirizes attempts to justify regicide: "He broke God's laws, and therefore he must die, / And what shall then become of thee and I?" (lines 21–22). Although Philips claims that she "think[s] not on the state" (1) and that her anger is provoked only by the needless slanders heaped on "the dying lion" Charles (10), her disgust at the regicide itself is abundantly clear. Philips's straightforward position makes for an interesting comparison with Marvell's apparently more complicated one in "An Horatian Ode," discussed below.

The poems written to the female friends she dubbed "Lucasia" and "Rosania" (Philips herself was "Orinda") are distinctive and interesting works. Lines like "There's a religion in our love" ("Friendship's Mystery," line 5) and "thus we can no absence know" ("To Mrs. M. A. at Parting,"

19) should remind students instantly of Donne's *Songs and Sonnets*. There is a homoerotic element in these poems, but the emphasis is on the transcendent nature of the love between female friends—sufficient, Orinda declares, to "teach the world new love, / Redeem the age and sex, and show / A flame fate dares not move" ("To Mrs. M. A.," 50–52).

Teaching Clusters

"Upon the Double Murder of King Charles" belongs in the **Debate, Dissent, and Revolution** cluster, and makes an excellent contrast with Marvell's "Horation Ode." An expanded unit on regicide would also include the accounts of Charles's trial and execution in the In-text Topic "Crisis of Authority." The rest of Philips's works have a key role to play in the cluster on **Writing Women**. Her keen interest in female friendship bears comparison with Aemilia Lanyer's attempt to exalt such friendship as transcending class barriers in "The Description of Cook-ham." It also looks forward to the friendship between the Empress and the Duchess of Newcastle in Cavendish's *Blazing World*.

Discussion Questions

1. What should we make of Philips's insistence in the opening line of "Upon the Double Murder of King Charles" that "I think not on the state . . ."?
2. What kind of sources does Philips draw upon to frame a poetic language of female friendship?

Andrew Marvell

The Mower Poems

Teaching Suggestions

Almost all of Marvell's lyric poetry is, one way or another, linked to the sense of nostalgia. Yet Marvell's nostalgia is not so much for a particular moment in his own or the nation's past as for a lost sense of wholeness and integration. One way or another, Marvell and his poetic personae can rarely escape the longing to go back to the way it was before—before the civil war and regicide, before sex, before the Fall, before there were other people in the world.

The sense of lost wholeness is particularly acute in Marvell's mower poems: "The Mower Against Gardens," "Damon the Mower," "The Mower to the Glowworms," and "The Mower's Song." In all of these, the mower laments the loss of an integrated natural world, in which there was no division or disjunction between his mind and the organic environment around him. In "The Mower Against Gardens," the blame is laid on the invention of gardening, which has tainted and adulterated nature, stealing the flowers from the fields "Where Nature was most plain and pure" (line 4). Practices such as grafting and hybridization have robbed the botanical world of its Edenic innocence, which is now to be found surviving only in the fields.

In the other three mower poems, the blame for breaking the state of innocent union between man and nature is blamed on the coming of a woman, Juliana. As he tells the glowworms, who seek to guide him on his way at night: "Your courteous fires in vain you waste, / Since Juliana here is come, / For she my mind hath so displaced / That I shall never find my home" (lines 13–16). Similarly, in "The Mower's Song" he complains that thoughts of Juliana have fatally disrupted his communion with the fields: "For Juliana comes, and she, / What I do to the grass, does to my thoughts and me" (23–24; 29–30). The mower is bitter because the meadows, rather than loyally reflecting his own anxious and lovelorn state, continue to grow "more luxuriant still and fine" (8), covering themselves with flowers. He therefore resolves to lay waste to the fields with his scythe: "And thus ye meadows, which have been / Companions of my thoughts more green, / Shall now the heraldry become / With which I shall adorn my tomb" (25–28).

It is a curious feature of the mower poems that the mower himself, who mourns nostalgically for the innocent world of nature, often plays a key role in destroying that world. In "The Mower's Song" he vengefully lays waste to the meadows. In the mowing scene in *Upon Appleton House* (see below) one of the mowers accidentally kills a small bird hidden in the grass, which becomes a symbol for the innocent lives lost in the civil war. In a similar moment at the end of "Damon the Mower," the mower with his mind on Juliana accidentally cuts his own ankle: "And there among the grass fell down / By his own scythe the mower mown" (79–80). This is a small reenactment in the meadows of the original fall of humankind, and the loss of Eden.

Upon Appleton House

Quick Read

- Form: Country-house poem.
- Summary: Marvell recalls the history of the Nunappleton estate, including that of the dissolved Catholic convent that once possessed the site; he recounts its present appearance under his patron, Fairfax, who has retired from public life following the regicide; the sight of a party of mowers brings a dismal reminder of the civil war; Marvell seeks to hide himself from such thoughts in Appleton's woods and gardens; the thought of his beautiful and virtuous pupil Maria Fairfax recalls him to himself, and gives him hope for the future.
- Themes: Landscape; the civil wars; duty; retirement.
- Key Passages: "Oh thou, that dear and happy isle / The garden of the world ere while . . . / What luckless apple did we taste, To make us mortal, and thee waste?" stanza 41; on the mowed field: "The world

when first created sure / Was such a table rase and pure; / Or rather such is the toril / Ere the bulls enter at Madril," stanza 56; "How safe, methinks, and strong, behind / These trees have I encamped my mind; / Where Beauty, aiming at the heart, / Bends in some tree its useless dart," stanza 76; "'Tis not, what it once was, the world, / But a rude heap together hurled; All negligently overthrown," stanza 95.

Teaching Suggestions

Vastly longer than other examples of the country-house genre, *Upon Appleton House* nonetheless carries forward and probes the themes that characterize "The Description of Cookham" and "To Penshurst." The harmony with nature experienced on the estate, its superiority to and implicit lesson for the outside world, the relationship of the poet with the host family, and that family's distinctive virtues are all explored in mellow, meditative depth. Readers find it difficult to respond to the poem as a whole, given its length and wandering structure. However, if you break it up into manageable sections, students will find much to ponder and discuss. The historical episode in which Fairfax's ancestor abducts Thwaites from the convent (stanzas 29–34), the description of the modern Fairfax's slightly comical fort-shaped garden (stanzas 36–46), and the disturbing account of the mowers (48–57) are all worth dwelling on in some detail. These episodes, singly and in combination, raise significant ethical and philosophical questions. How should we understand the contrast between the headstrong violence of the elder Fairfax and the passive retirement of his descendant, Marvell's patron? What exactly do the brutal mowers, whom Marvell at one point terms "Israelites" (49) and who subsequently embrace that term (51), signify?

An Horatian Ode

Quick Read

- Form: Ode.
- Summary: The ode recounts the rise of Cromwell, the execution of Charles I, and Cromwell's more recent military victories.
- Themes: The great man; historical causation; justice; regicide.
- Key Passages: "'Tis madness to resist or blame / The face of angry heaven's flame; / And if we would speak true, / Much to the man is due," lines 25–28; "*He* nothing common did or mean / Upon that memorable scene, / But with his keener eye / The ax's edge did try; / Nor called the gods with vulgar spite / To vindicate his helpless right; / But bowed his comely head / Down, as upon a bed," 57–64; "The same arts that did gain / A power must it maintain," 119–20.

Teaching Suggestions

Marvell's famous account of the execution of King Charles in the central stanzas of "An Horatian Ode" (lines 53–72) is easier to follow but more difficult to grasp than Katherine Philips's "Upon the Double Murder of King Charles." Marvell is concerned with achieving a balanced judgment—or at least the appearance of such a judgment—and these stanzas are particularly finely balanced, breaking in the middle with "While," "But," "But," "So," "And yet" (lines 55, 59, 63, 67, 71). The politics and sympathies of this poem have been and continue to be disputed, and the poem provides an excellent theme for a classroom discussion or debate. It will be important to point out, however, that the implied question "Cromwell or Charles?" already excludes a range of alternative political positions; there is no room in "An Horatian Ode" for the voices of Levellers, Diggers, or Fifth Monarchists, all active in 1650 and all opposed to Cromwell's rule as well as to kingship.

Teaching Clusters

"An Horation Ode" is a centerpiece of the cluster on **Debate, Dissent, and Revolution**. It can be taught alongside both Philips's "Upon the Double Murder" and the journalistic accounts of the regicide gathered under "Crisis of Authority." *Upon Appleton House*, taught as a country-house poem in the company of Lanyer, Jonson, and Carew, would do well in the same category. Alternatively, **The Material World** would be an interesting choice for *Appleton House*, together with the mower poems and lyrics such as "A Dialogue Between the Soul and the Body" and "To His Coy Mistress." These poems are marked by a contradictory longing to be again truly integrated with the natural, physical world and an equally marked longing to be rid of that world entirely.

Discussion Questions

1. How does Marvell's *Upon Appleton House* relate to, and challenge, the genre of country-house poetry? What are the poem's central themes?
2. Is *Appleton House* unequivocal in its commendation of the estate and its master, Thomas Fairfax?
3. Look at "The Definition of Love" and "To His Coy Mistress." What do love and sexuality signify to Marvell? How are women, and women's bodies, represented here? What similarities or differences do you find between these poems and Cavalier love lyrics?
4. What do gardens signify in Marvell's works? (Poems you might choose to focus on include "The Garden," "The Mower Against Gardens," and "The Picture of Little T. C. in a Prospect of Flowers.") Are "gardens" the same as "nature"?
5. How does Marvell's representation of the English garden compare with his depiction of a colonial Eden in "Bermudas"?
6. How does Marvell describe regicide in "An Horatian Ode"? Does he sympathize with the king or celebrate his death? Compare Marvell's response to regicide with that of Katherine Philips in "Upon the Double Murder of King Charles."
7. Compare the representation of Oliver Cromwell in Marvell's "Horatian

Ode" with that in Milton's sonnet "To the Lord General Cromwell" and Clarendon's "Character of Cromwell." How do these writers want us to think of Cromwell? How do their versions of the man vary?

Further Resources

Norton Online Archive

Mourning
On *Paradise Lost*

Crisis of Authority

This special section brings together writings by men and women who experienced the English Revolution in very different ways. All took risks and suffered losses as a result of the stances they took during and after the war. The selections in this section focus on the hugely important and divisive issue of authority. Read in conjunction with further selections in the Online Archive—by the Leveller John Lilburne, the Fifth Monarchist Anna Trapnel, and the Ranter Abiezer Coppe—they provide a rounded introduction to the various parties and "voices" that contended for power (or at least a hearing) in the middle decades of the seventeenth century. The selections in this cluster have full headnotes to assist students in grasping the political and cultural background and the key issues at stake.

Reporting the News: The Trial and Execution of Charles I

The trial and execution of Charles I by the victorious Parliament and army were traumatic events for the war-torn nation. They were also, in more than one sense, dramatic events. At a time when the public performance of plays was banned, accounts of the king's trial in Parliament and his last words on the scaffold were published in a form closely resembling the scripts of plays. You might wish to play up the dramatic aspect of these newspaper reports, especially if you are teaching them in conjunction with Marvell's "Horatian Ode," where Charles is described as a "royal actor" on a "tragic scaffold" (lines 53–54). The "characters" in the news accounts of Charles's trial and execution can be seen as participants in a deadly drama, presenting themselves both to the public and to posterity. How does Charles seem to have understood his "role," before and after being sentenced to death? How did those involved in determining and carrying out the sentence present themselves and seek to justify their actions?

Political Writing: Filmer, Milton, and Winstanley

The three very different versions of the origins of political authority included in this section should be read alongside the selections from Hobbes's *Leviathan* for a good overview of the diversity of political opinions on this crucial question. Filmer and Hobbes are both royalists, but they differ sharply from each other. The conservative Filmer finds the origins of monarchy in the God-granted authority of fathers over their children: "if we compare the natural rights of a father with those of a king, we find them all one, without any difference at all but only in the latitude or extent of them" (524). For Hobbes, by contrast, sovereignty is a human invention whereby societies escaped the brutal "state of nature." This is to say that both Filmer and Hobbes trace the origins of sovereignty to the earliest state of humanity, but whereas for Filmer this means the divinely ordained order in the Garden of Eden, for Hobbes it consists in savage primitivism and chaos.

Milton and Winstanley, both opponents of monarchy, are equally opposed to one another. Milton, in his account of the origins of sovereignty, sounds deceptively like Hobbes: "falling among themselves to do wrong and violence, and foreseeing such courses must lead to the destruction of them all, they agreed by common league to bind each other from mutual injury, and . . . to ordain some authority" (526). The key difference is that Milton does not follow Hobbes in seeing this contract as forever binding; rather, the source of sovereignty in the popular will is evidence of "the liberty and right of freeborn men to be governed as seems to them best" (528). Winstanley, the communist, goes further than Milton in identifying "kingly power" not merely with misused sovereignty but with sovereignty *per se.* Winstanley is at the opposite political extreme from Filmer, yet curiously like him in that he believes it possible to restore the political order that prevailed in the Garden of Eden. For him, this means radical egalitarianism and the abolition of private property: "the common land is my own land, equal with my fellow-commoners, and our true property, by the law of creation" (533).

Students should be encouraged to approach each text with certain basic questions in mind. What, for each writer, is the ultimate source of political power? How does God intercede in human affairs, if at all? What is the role of the individual in shaping history? How would each writer respond to Milton's call for freedom of thought and a free press in *Areopagitica*? Answers to these questions could form the basis for essays or a less formal assignment.

Writing the Self

The selections in this part of "Crisis of Authority" will allow you to initiate a discussion of how different voices compete to be heard in the public sphere. Three of the writers included here are women; several espouse positions and spring from backgrounds that in the past would almost certainly have barred them from appearing in print. The breakdown of censorship, the challenges to traditional authority, and the blossoming of debate in the 1640s created conditions in which all of these voices could compete for a hearing. They did not, of course, compete on a level playing field—groups like Dorothy Waugh's Quakers lacked almost all of the cultural and economic resources available to the traditional leaders of opinion. Yet from the aristocrat Clarendon to the persecuted maidservant Waugh, the common thread in these selections is their remarkable forthrightness and confidence in laying controversial views before the general public.

Teaching Clusters

"Crisis of Authority" is the heart of the **Debate, Dissent, and Revolution** cluster. As noted above, the texts in the section on political writing should be read in company with Hobbes to provide a full overview of the political spectrum. The newspaper reports of the trial and execution of Charles I make an ideal complement to Philips's "Upon the Double Murder of King Charles" and Marvell's "Horatian Ode." The latter also makes a good counterpoint to Clarendon's biography of Cromwell. Both Marvell and Clarendon are seeking the ideal of a balanced view (or a balanced tone), but they arrive at very different conclusions.

The prominence of religious themes and implicit or explicit references to Eden in the texts by Filmer, Milton, and Winstanley make these texts suitable for the cluster on **Faith, Devotion, and Doubt**. They could be included in an extended survey of visions of Eden, from Lanyer's in "Eve's Apology" to Milton's in *Paradise Lost*. The selections by Hutchinson, Halkett, and Waugh would be valuable components of the cluster on **Writing Women**, revealing both the range of women's political views and the new confidence born of the conflict.

Discussion Questions

1. Do the reports of the trial and execution of Charles I read as objective accounts? Can you detect the writer's bias or sympathies?
2. Compare the news account of the execution with Marvell's account of it in "An Horatian Ode"? Where do the accounts correspond and where do they differ?
3. What does the Garden of Eden mean for Filmer? For Milton? For Hobbes?
4. How would Hobbes counter Milton's argument that the choice of sovereign resides with the people?
5. Do any of the writers in the section on "Political Writing" take into account women or women's rights?
6. What ideas of the proper role of women emerge from Lucy Hutchinson's *Memoirs*? Is Hutchinson a feminist in any sense?
7. Compare Clarendon's description of Cromwell's character with Marvell's in "An Horatian Ode." Where do they differ and where do they agree? Is one view more balanced than the other?

Further Resources

NORTON ONLINE ARCHIVE

Abiezer Coppe, A Fiery Flying Role
Anna Trapnel, Anna Trapnel's Report and Plea
John Lilburne, The Picture of the Council of State
Lucy Hutchinson, *From* Memoirs of Colonel Hutchinson
Edward Hyde, Earl of Clarendon, The Character of John Hampden
Gerrard Winstanley, The True Leveler's Standard Advance
The Freeing of the English Israelites

NORTON TOPICS ONLINE

Civil Wars of Ideas

Thomas Traherne

Wonder

Quick Read

- Form: Lyric.
- Summary: Traherne recalls the ecstatic—and clear-sighted— innocence of his childhood, when he looked with wonder on the common objects of this world.
- Themes: Childhood; innocence; the true nature of the world.
- Key Passages: "I within did flow / With seas of life like wine; / I nothing in the world did know / But 'twas divine," lines 21–24; "Proprieties themselves were mine, / And hedges ornaments," lines 57–58.

Teaching Suggestions

Traherne's ebullience and enthusiasm for childhood may make him seem naive to some readers. He is not. The theology espoused in "Wonder" and its prose companion piece from *Centuries of Meditation* is idiosyncratic and, in its own cheerful way, quite radical. The first line of "Wonder"—"How like an angel came I down!"—will inevitably remind readers of Vaughan's "Retreat," which begins "Happy those early days! when I / Shined in my angel infancy." But the real gulf between Traherne and Vaughan opens up in the second line of "Wonder": "How bright are all things here!" For Vaughan, the glory of infancy lies in its nearness to heaven, and its untaintedness by the earth; thinking back to the time "before I understood this place" (line 3), the only wish Vaughan can formulate is to die, so as to regain that innocence again. Traherne, by contrast, insists that the infant does understand this place, in a way that corrupted adults generally fail to do. The earth really is, or can be, a place of holy wonder and magnificence. The task of the mature Christian is to regain the clear-sightedness of the childhood. The last stanza of "Wonder" is particularly challenging, numbering private property among the delusions into which the divine vision of childhood has not yet fallen.

Teaching Clusters

Like his predecessors among the metaphysical poets—Donne, Herbert, Vaughan, Crashaw, and Cowley—Traherne's works are suitable either for the cluster on **Style** or for **Faith, Devotion, and Doubt.** In either case, it makes sense to teach Traherne together with Vaughan, who comes closest to his idealization of childhood yet differs from him utterly in his appreciation of the things of this world.

Discussion Questions

1. What are the political implications of the last stanza of "Wonder," in which hedges and strongboxes (the signifiers and guardians of private property) are re-imagined as beautiful ornaments (and, as such, common property)?
2. How does Traherne's vision of childhood differ from Vaughan's in "The Retreat"?

Further Resources

NORTON ONLINE ARCHIVE

On News

Margaret Cavendish

The Blazing World

Quick Read

- Form: Prose utopian romance.
- Summary: A noble earth woman finds her way into an alternative world, home to various hybrid species, where she meets and marries the emperor, and rules virtuously; she is subsequently introduced by spiritual means to the Duchess of Newcastle (Cavendish), who wishes for a world of her own to rule.
- Key Passages: "Though I cannot be Henry the Fifth or Charles the Second, yet I endeavour to be Margaret the First; and although I have neither power, time nor occasion to conquer the world as Alexander and Caesar did; yet rather than not to be mistress of one, since fortune and the fates would give me none, I have made a world of my own, for which nobody, I hope, will blame me, since it is in everyone's power to do the like," 1781; "But, said she, women and children have no employment in church or state. 'Tis true,' answered they; but although they are not admitted to public employments, yet are they so prevalent with their husbands and parents that many

times by their importunate persuasions they cause as much, nay, more mischief secretly, than if they had the management of public affairs," 1782; "I have made my Blazing World, a peaceable world, allowing it but one religion, one language, and one government," 1785.

Teaching Suggestions

The Blazing World falls within the category of utopias, yet because it is also a royalist romance, it differs markedly both from More's *Utopia* and from most subsequent works in the genre. Cavendish's protagonist, the empress, is a benign despot, ruling a society in which rebellion is not only prohibited but unimaginable. No one in this world can desire to alter their social station because they—be they bear-men, worm-men, or spider-men—are genetically programmed for their particular social function: "each followed such a profession as was most proper for the nature of their species" (1781). Yet *The Blazing World* cannot be easily dismissed as a reactionary fantasy either. Cavendish's attention to the political and cultural status of women, though not always feminist in tone, reveals an independent and ambitious mind struggling with a remarkable degree of success to escape the limited roles her society and upbringing had marked out for her.

Cavendish was widely scorned for what were perceived as her pretensions, and her husband was mocked for encouraging and financing her ventures into print. In the slyly witty "The Poetess's Hasty Resolution," she mocks her own ambition in rushing into print, yet concludes in the confident expectation that readers will "Wipe off my tears with handkerchiefs of praise" (line 24). Still more subtle and intriguing is her description of her motives for and manner of writing in *A True Relation of My Birth, Breeding, and Life*. Here, her anxiety about the public reception of her work is overmastered by recourse to sheer bravado: "it is true, that 'tis to no purpose to the readers, but it is to the authoress, because I write it for my own sake, not theirs" (1779). Yet this triumphant declaration of self-sufficiency is immediately followed by a recurrence of the fear that she will be forgotten or, worse, confused with another wife.

Teaching Clusters

Cavendish's wide-ranging interests make her works suitable for a number of different clusters. She is a good choice to crown the cluster on **Writing Women**—like other women writers of the period, she propounds a mixture of feminist and antifeminist positions. Like Mary Wroth and Elizabeth Cary, she possessed a high social station; unlike these predecessors, she had the full support of her husband. These combined advantages allowed her to express her views with an unusual degree of freedom.

As a royalist utopia produced in the aftermath of exile, *The Blazing World* works well in the cluster on **Debate, Dissent, and Revolution**, especially if you want to make a transition to the literary politics of the

Restoration era. Still another option would be to include Cavendish's scientific utopia, initially published together with her *Observations upon Experimental Philosophy*, in the cluster on **The Material World**.

Discussion Questions

1. How does Cavendish register the pressures brought to bear on a female author in *A True Relation of My Birth, Breeding, and Life*?
2. Why does Cavendish choose to inhabit the Blazing World with hybrid species like the bird-men and the bear-men?
3. What attitudes toward women, and particularly toward women in power, are evident in *The Blazing World*?
4. What, for Cavendish and her readers, is the value of being able to create a world of one's own?

Further Resources

NORTON TOPICS ONLINE

Restoration and Eighteenth Century: The Plurality of Worlds
    Margaret Cavendish, A World in an Eare-Ring

John Milton

We often think of the mid-seventeenth century—roughly 1530 to 1570—as the "age of Milton." This is precisely how he seems to have thought of it himself. What is remarkable about Milton, early and late, is his overriding certainty of his destined role not only as the greatest poet of his time, but as spokesman and interpreter for and to his nation and his age. That such unreasonable confidence should be so amply rewarded by history is, depending on one's perspective, either infuriating or inspiring.

The first question when it comes to teaching Milton in a survey course must inevitably be "how much?" Along with ample selections of Milton's early verse, the sonnets, and a sampling of the prose writings, *NAEL* includes the full text of *Paradise Lost*. Although there can be no substitute for the poem in its entirety, you may well be constrained by other commitments to teaching only a few books, along with some of the shorter works. It is still possible to give students a fulfilling experience of the poem, if not a full one, and you will have the comfort of knowing that they have the whole poem in their possession if they find themselves hooked, as more than a few will be.

Il Penseroso

This early poem is especially worth teaching if your syllabus also includes Burton's *Anatomy of Melancholy* or Webster's *Duchess of Malfi*, in which the melancholy of Bosola is a key factor. "Il Penseroso" is paired with a poem in praise of mirth, "L'Allegro," but its greater length suggests Milton's preference for "staid Wisdom's hue" (line 16)—that is, in terms of humor theory, the dark complexion brought on by black bile. That the poet appears to regard his dominant humor as a matter of choice does not mean that his melancholy is merely figurative; rather, in common with much modern science, Milton believes that the constitution of the body will follow, as well as determine, the constitution of the mind. He or his speaker opts for melancholy because he regards it as a pleasurable state, which in this account it does seem to be. Il Penseroso's melancholy will not prevent him from attending plays, reading Chaucer's *Canterbury Tales*, or dissolving into religious "ecstasies" (line 165).

Lycidas

Quick Read

- Form: Pastoral elegy.
- Summary: The elegy mourns the death of Milton's fellow shepherd (poet) Lycidas (Edward King), contemplates the value of art in the face of mortality, and denounces the corrupt and ineffective Laudian clergy.
- Themes: Death; poetry; immortality; the clergy; prophesy.
- Key Passages: "Comes the blind fury with abhorred shears / And slits the thin-spun life. / 'But not the praise,' / Phoebus replied, and touched my trembling ears," lines 75–78; "The hungry sheep look up, and are not fed / But swol'n with wind, and the rank mist they draw, / Rot inwardly, and foul contagion spread, / Besides what the grim wolf with privy paw / Daily devours apace, and nothing said," lines 125–29.

Teaching Suggestions

Although ostensibly an elegy for Edward King, "Lycidas" tells us much more about Milton than it does about King. Milton seizes on the fact that King was something of a poet to make him into a kind of alter ego. Confronting the fact of King's untimely death, he confronts the possibility of his own—a possibility made the more horrible by the fact that he has yet to fulfill his destiny as a poet. The plants mentioned in the opening lines—laurel, myrtle, and ivy—are all symbols of the poet's craft. Milton represents himself as having to pluck them too early, before they are ripe, and while his own fingers are still rude and untrained. As in the sonnet "How Soon Hath Time," Milton in "Lycidas" is preoccupied with the passage of time and his own frustratingly slow ripening as a poet.

The poem initially proceeds along predictable pastoral lines, reminiscent of much Elizabethan poetry. Milton and King are described as two singing shepherd boys, making harmonious music as they tend their flocks. But the elegy is subjected to repeated and dramatic interruptions, first by Phoebus Apollo, who reassures Milton that fame is immortal, and then by St. Peter, "the Pilot of the Galilean lake" (109). Peter laments King as a rare good minister in a Church of England otherwise full of corrupt, self-serving clergy. This develops into a risky, full-scale attack on the Laudian church, whose ministers look after themselves while leaving the people of England to expire in spiritual darkness. In the last lines the focus shifts to the poet himself, and it ends with the promise that he is bound for higher things: "At last he rose, and twitched his mantle blue: Tomorrow to fresh woods, and pastures new" (192–93). The conclusion of the poem indicates that Milton, having come to terms with the threat of mortality, has reaffirmed his calling as a poet. He is now ready to embark on his next great work—whatever that may be.

Readers differ over to what extent "Lycidas" works as an elegy, and to what extent it is supposed to work. Are all the anxieties raised about mortality, fame, and time truly resolved by the end of the poem? Is unity really reestablished after the disturbing interruptions of Apollo and St. Peter? Are these disruptive voices at odds with the poem's message, or do they contribute to a larger, organic whole? How would we read the poem differently without the headnote added in 1645 (seven years after the poem's initial publication), boasting of the downfall of the corrupt clergy, and claiming for the poet the status of prophet?

The Reason of Church Government Urged Against Prelaty

Milton's discussion of his epic projects in *The Reason of Church Government* is essential in preparing the way for *Paradise Lost*. Compared to the poets who flourished in the earlier decades of the century, Milton comes across as extraordinarily confident, indeed arrogant, in his calling. His sense of poetic vocation, already fully developed in "Lycidas," leads him to inform the (no doubt perplexed) readers of *The Reason of Church Government* of his determination "to fix all the industry and art I could unite to the adorning of my native tongue . . . to be an interpreter and relater of the best and sagest things among mine own citizens throughout this island in the mother dialect."

Milton speculates here about the epic poem he has had to defer because "Time serves not now." The outbreak of the civil war had put his plans for writing an epic on hold as Milton threw himself into the task of helping to create a free society. King Arthur had occurred to him as someone "in whom to lay the pattern of a Christian hero." When after the Restoration he wrote *Paradise Lost*, however, he pointedly dismissed the traditional heroic subject matter of epic and romance, "fabled knights / In battles feigned," in favor of Christian virtues: "the better fortitude / Of patience and heroic martyrdom / Unsung" (lines 30–33).

Areopagitica

Quick Read

- Form: Political speech (published rather than orally delivered).
- Summary: An argument against censorship before publication, with a vision of England's coming role in spiritual history.

- Key Passages: "Books are not absolutely dead things, but do contain a potency of life in them to be active as that soul was whose progeny they are," 1816–17; "as good almost kill a man as kill a good book; who kills a man kills a reasonable creature, God's image, but he who destroys a good book kills reason itself," 1817; "I cannot praise a fugitive and cloistered virtue, unexercised and unbreathed, that never sallies out and sees her adversary," 1817; "Behold now this vast city: a city of refuge, the mansion house of liberty, encompassed and surrounded with his protection; the shop of war hath not there more anvils and hammers waking, to fashion out the plates and instruments of armed justice in defence of beleaguered Truth, than there be pens and heads there, sitting by their studious lamps, musing, searching, revolving new notions and ideas wherewith to present, as with their homage and their fealty, the approaching Reformation: others as fast reading, trying all things, assenting to the force of reason and convincement," 1822.

Teaching Suggestions

This pamphlet is the key document for insight into the idealism and high hopes of the young Milton at the outset of the revolution. He wrote to oppose the censorship law enacted by Parliament. The argument is based on the premise of humankind's God-given freedom to seek truth and to choose right moral action. "[W]hen God gave [Adam] reason," Milton writes, "he gave him freedom to choose, for reason is but choosing; he had been else a mere artificial Adam, such an Adam as we see in the motions [puppet shows]." Censorship and hierarchy deprive people of the freedom to choose and, therefore, freedom of conscience and of expression are essential if moral choices are to have any meaning. *Areopagitica* envisions a reformed utopian society—"a noble and puissant nation rousing herself like a strong man after sleep"—united "into one general and brotherly search after truth." The nationalism of *Areopagitica* is evident in its invocation of England as a new Israel, the spearhead and bastion of the Reformation. (See also the political sonnets, "On the New Forcers of Conscience under the Long Parliament," "To the Lord General Cromwell," and "On the Late Massacre in Piedmont.")

It will also be important for students to grasp what *Areopagitica* is *not* saying; like Donne's "Satire 3," it is often read anachronistically in the light of modern liberal notions. Milton is not arguing against all censorship, but against barring books from publication—if, in the open field of public judgment, they are found wicked, they may be condemned and banned. Works whose evil is already well known—that is, treatises of "popery and open superstition" (1825)—will not benefit from Milton's doctrine of toleration. These caveats are not intended to expose Milton as a hypocrite, but to place his text in the context of its times, in which it was nonetheless among the most powerful calls for freedom of the press.

Paradise Lost

Quick Read

- Form: Epic.
- Organization: Twelve books.
- Summary: The whole poem tells of Satan's expulsion from Heaven, his vengeful tempting of Eve, and the expulsion of the first people from Paradise. BOOK 1. Satan and his fellow rebels awake in Hell, build the palace of Pandemomium, and sit in council. BOOK 2. The fallen angels debate how best to retaliate against or appease God. Satan embarks for the newly created earth to seek revenge. At the gates of Hell he meets Sin and Dearg. BOOK 3. Satan's journey is observed from Heaven. The Son offers to sacrifice himself to redeem humankind from the sin into which Satan will lead it. BOOK 4. Satan reaches the Garden and plots to make Adam and Eve sin by eating of the Tree of Knowledge. On his first attempt to seduce Eve in her sleep, he is apprehended by the angel Gabriel. BOOK 5. Raphael dines with Adam and Eve, and tells them the story of Satan's rebellion in Heaven. BOOK 6. Raphael tells of the war in Heaven, and the expulsion of Satan and the rebel angels by the Son of God. BOOK 7. Raphael tells of the creation of the world in six days. BOOK 8. Adam tells Raphael of his own creation and meeting with Eve. BOOK 9. Satan returns in the guise of a serpent and tempts Eve to eat the forbidden fruit. Learning what she has done, Adam consents to eat as well. They fall victim to lust, shame, and mutual recrimination. BOOK 10. Satan returns in triumph to Hell, but he and his devils are transformed into snakes. Adam and Eve bemoan their state. BOOK 11. The angel Michael tells Adam and Eve that they must depart from Paradise. First, he reveals to Adam the future of humankind. BOOK 12. Michael continues his revelation, including the coming of Christ. Hand in hand, Adam and Eve depart from Paradise.
- Key Passages:

> That, to the height of this great argument,
> I may assert Eternal Providence,
> And justify the ways of God to men. (1.24–26)

> The mind is its own place, and in itself
> Can make a Heav'n of Hell, a Hell of Heav'n . . .
> Better to reign in Hell than serve in Heav'n. (1.254–63)

>   who would lose,
> Though full of pain, this intellectual being,
> These thoughts that wander through eternity,
> To perish rather . . . ? (2.146–49)

Hail holy Light, offspring of Heav'n firstborn,
Or of th'Eternal coeternal beam
May I express thee unblamed? (3.1–3)

                  I made him just and right,
Sufficient to have stood, though free to fall. (3.98–99)

Me miserable! which way shall I fly
Infinite wrath and infinite despair?
Which way I fly is Hell; myself am Hell;
And in the lowest deep a lower deep,
Still threat'ning to devour me opens wide,
To which the Hell I suffer seems a Heav'n. (4.73–78)

Evil be thou my good . . . (4.110)

For contemplation he and valor formed,
For softness she and sweet attractive grace,
He for God only, she for God in him. (4.299–301)

                  nor turned, I ween,
Adam from his fair spouse, nor Eve the rites
Mysterious of connubial love refused:
Whatever hypocrites austerely talk
Of purity, and place, and innocence,
Defaming as impure what God declares
Pure, and commands to some, leaves free to all.
Our Maker bids increase; who bids abstain
But our destroyer, foe to God and Man?
Hail wedded Love, mysterious law . . . (4.741–50)

I alone seemed in thy world erroneous to dissent
From all: my sect thou seest, now learn too late
How few sometimes may know, when thousands err. (6.145–48)

But who I was, or where, or from what cause,
Knew not; to speak I tried, and forthwith spake,
My tongue obeyed and readily could name
Whate'er I saw. (8.270–73)

            when I approach
Her loveliness, so absolute she seems
And in herself complete, so well to know
Her own, that what she wills to do or say,
Seems wisest, virtuousest, discreetest, best:
All higher knowledge in her presence falls
Degraded; Wisdom in discourse with her
Loses discountenanced, and like Folly shows;
Authority and Reason on her wait,
As one intended first, not after made
Occasionally . . . (8.546–56)

Since first this subject for heroic song
Pleased me long choosing, and beginning late;
Not sedulous by nature to indite
Wars, hitherto the only argument
Heroic deemed chief mastery to dissect
With long and tedious havoc fabled knights
In battles feigned; the better fortitude
Of patience and heroic martyrdom
Unsung . . . (9.25–33)

Forth reaching to the fruit, she plucked, she eat.
Earth felt the wound, and nature from her seat,
Sighing through all her works gave signs of woe,
That all was lost. (9.780–84)

Should God create another Eve, and I
Another rib afford, yet loss of thee
Would never from my heart; no no, I feel
The Link of Nature draw me: flesh of flesh,
Bone of my bone thou art, and from thy state
Mine never shall be parted, bliss or woe. (9.911–16)

Teaching Suggestions

Paradise Lost can be a great pleasure to teach precisely because students typically expect not to like or even understand it, and are delighted to find themselves doing both. Students generally find as well that they know much more of the story than they think they do. A drawback to this, however, is that some are inclined simply to conflate the plot of Paradise Lost with "the Bible story" and Milton's religious views with "Christianity." A good way of countering this is to point out that many of the most memorable events in the poem, including the "great consult" in Hell (Books 1–2) and Eve's delighted discovery of her reflection in the water (Book 4), have little or no basis in scripture. Moreover, Milton's mature theology, often implied in the epic poem and revealed in his unpublished Christian Doctrine, was unorthodox on a number of points; most notably in the poem, Christ is not coequal and coeternal with the Father, as all churches taught, but merely "of all creation first" (3.383).

Paradise Lost is the greatest example of the epic genre in English. The difficulty with teaching it as such is that you may not have had much occasion to mention the epic up until this point in the course (unless you have covered The Faerie Queene and emphasized its epic qualities). Providing students with a few examples of epic conventions (in a lecture or on a handout) will prove more effective than simply listing the standard features of an epic poem. Contemporary translations of Homer and Virgil were almost always in rhyme, which Milton abhorred, so you may prefer to use modern unrhymed translations (available in Norton Topics Online) to give students a sampling of epic statements and invocations. Alternatively, let them hear the magnificent opening of Dryden's Aeneid:

> Arms, and the man I sing, who, forced by fate,
> And haughty Juno's unrelenting hate,
> Expelled and exiled, left the Trojan shore.
> Long labors, both by sea and land, he bore,
> And in the doubtful war, before he won
> The Latian realm, and built the destined town;
> His banished gods restored to rites divine,
> And settled sure succession in his line,
> From whence the race of Alban fathers come,
> And the long glories of majestic Rome.
> O Muse, the causes and the crimes relate;
> What goddess was provoked, and whence her hate;
> For what offense the Queen of Heaven began
> To persecute so brave, so just a man;
> Involved his anxious life in endless cares,
> Exposed to wants, and hurried into wars!

More examples of epic conventions can be drawn from within NAEL. The first twelve lines of Pope's The Rape of the Lock can also be compared with the first sixteen lines of Paradise Lost. Similarly, the brief passage from Henry Howard's translation of Virgil offers a perfect example of an epic simile, and the opening of The Faerie Queene can be referred to for a largely self-explanatory example of beginning in medias res. Armed with a few such examples, students will be in a better position to appreciate the neatness and audacity with which Milton reinvents such tired epic conventions as the descent into the underworld.

Of the poem's many important themes, one that never loses its resonance is that of free will. The Restoration left Milton, as he wrote, "fall'n on evil days, / . . . In darkness, and with dangers compassed round" (Book 7, lines 25–27). Yet while this once-influential man had been reduced to powerlessness and marginality, the inalienable freedom of the will to choose one's own destiny remained his essential theme. "Here at least we shall be free," Satan declares (Book 1, lines 258–59), without realizing that Hell is what he has freely chosen. Freedom of choice also brings about the Fall of the first human couple. Milton elaborates the story of the Fall in Genesis by inventing the scene in which Eve, to prove her independence, wants to leave Adam to work in the garden alone. Adam tries to persuade her to stay but cannot force her to remain at his side: "God left free the will; for what obeys / Reason is free" (Book 9, lines 351–52). Unlike Lanyer in "Eve's Apology," Milton is unwilling to excuse Eve on grounds of her ignorance and the serpent's cunning and makes her reject Adam's warning. But he also makes her more generous than Adam in accepting responsibility for the Fall. The quiet ending stresses once again their mutual freedom of choice:

> Some natural tears they shed, but wiped them soon;
> The world was all before them, where to choose
> Their place of rest, and Providence their guide:

> They hand in hand with wand'ring steps and slow,
> Through Eden took their solitary way.

Teaching Clusters

It is possible to include a surprising amount of Milton's work in your course and at the same time do justice to the length and variety of his career by interspersing his shorter works throughout the weeks or months you spend teaching this period. Thus "On Shakespeare" might be introduced in the **Style** cluster in company with Jonson's "To the Memory of My Beloved," prompting a discussion of how Shakespeare's reputation developed in the seventeenth century (Dryden's comparison of Shakespeare and Jonson could also have a role here). "L'Allegro" and "Il Penseroso" could be used in **The Material World** alongside other texts dealing with melancholy and humors (*The Duchess of Malfi* and/or Burton's *Anatomy*). In the **Faith, Devotion, and Doubt** cluster, "On the Morning of Christ's Nativity" makes for an obvious yet interesting pairing with Crashaw's "In the Holy Nativity of Our Lord God." *Lycidas* could be taught alongside Donne's *An Anatomy of the World*, another poetic response to a premature death, or as a way of introducing the religious conflicts of the middle part of the century. In the cluster on **Debate, Dissent, and Revolution**, *Areopagitica* will work well alongside "Crisis of Authority." Milton's political sonnets can also be introduced as a discussion of the Revolution, and "To the Lord General Cromwell, May 1652" makes for a great comparison with Marvell's "An Horatian Ode." (Alternatively, the sonnets can serve as the culmination of a survey in the **Style** cluster charting the development of the form from the classic Elizabethan sequences, through the works of Donne, Wroth, and Herbert.) Many other linkages between Milton and other and earlier writers are possible. Proceeding in this way, you will find you have been able to cover a great deal of Milton's work before "arriving" at the destination of *Paradise Lost*.

When you reach Milton's epic, there will still be plenty of opportunities to draw connections with texts you have covered earlier on. The poem is so multifarious that all or large portions of it can work as part of any cluster, **Faith, Devotion, and Doubt** being only the most obvious choice. As part of the **Writing Women** cluster, the question of Milton's sexism or otherwise in his portrayal of Eve can be explored more fruitfully where representations of Eve by near-contemporary women writers are available for comparison. Lanyer's "Eve's Apology in Defense of Women," which turns the story of the Fall to feminist account, presents a very different image of Adam and Eve from that found in *Paradise Lost*, and Book 9 in particular. Another seventeenth-century woman's version of the Fall is Rachel Speght's *A Muzzle for Melastomus*. Similarly, Milton's first description of Adam and Eve in Book 4 can be situated within a debate about marriage going back to Webster's *Duchess of Malfi* and Cary's *Mariam* at the beginning of the period and including Milton's own notorious *Doctrine and Discipline of Divorce* (extracts of which are in *Norton Topics Online*).

Discussion Questions

1. How does "On the Morning of Christ's Nativity" (and/or the early sonnets "On Shakespeare" and "How Soon Hath Time") reflect the young Milton's sense of vocation? What signs are there that he feels called to be a poet? What does he consider a poet to be?
2. Milton's "L'Allegro" and "Il Penseroso" praise diametrically opposed approaches to life. Which approach, if either, does the poet seem to prefer, and why? Is there a serious purpose behind this apparently playful exercise?
3. What kind of poem is "Lycidas"—that is, what is its genre (or genres)? Consider how Milton in this poem—and in the headnote added in 1645—lays claim to the power of prophecy. What does this suggest about his conception of the poet's role?
4. How does Milton justify the intrusion of personal material into his polemic *The Reason of Church Government*?
5. How extensive is Milton's call for liberty of the press in *Areopagitica*? What are its significant limitations?
6. What is the significance of the images Milton chooses to describe the awakening nation in *Areopagitica*?
7. To what extent is Milton's Satan a sympathetic character? When does he cease to be so? Did Milton have a conscious intention here, or was he, as Blake later said, "of the devil's party without knowing it"?
8. How, compared with other seventeenth-century writers such as Lanyer and Speght, does Milton depict the Fall? Does he attribute more or less culpability to Eve than do the two women writers?
9. How does Eve's account of her awakening and first encounter with Adam in Book 4 sort with Adam's version of the same events in Book 8?
10. Milton's voice is heard in the openings of Books 1, 3, and 9. How does he present himself as a religious—and at the same time epic—poet? What significance does he apply to his own blindness?

Further Resources

NORTON ONLINE ARCHIVE

At a Solemn Music
When the Assault Was Intended to the City
A Book Was Writ of Late Called *Tetrachordo*
Lawrence, of Virtuous Father Virtuous Son
Of Education
Comus
To My Friend, Mr. Henry Lawes, on His Airs
Paradise Lost: The Arguments
Samson Agonistes
Samuel Johnson, *Lives of the Poets* [Milton: "L'Allegro," "Il Penseroso"]

CHAPTER 8

———

The Restoration and the Eighteenth Century 1660–1785

INTRODUCING THE PERIOD

The complicated religious and political history of the years 1660 to 1785 poses a stumbling block for new readers, but the literature embraces the details of religion, politics, philosophy, and cultural events as it does for no other era, and so it is necessary to have at least a cursory understanding of them. A brief review of history or periodic historical mini-lectures will help clarify puzzling issues and allow the students to appreciate the poetry and prose more fully. Teachers should make some allowances for transmitting historical information at appropriate times; the headnotes and introductions in *NAEL* provide a good base, and the online counterparts can provide important supplements of text and image. There are several good historical references listed in the bibliography that teachers might assign as supplementary reading. Excerpts from some writers included in *NAEL*, like Pepys, Locke, Newton, Astell, Boswell, and Burney, provide documents of the history and culture as well. Additionally, by providing a list of topics and a starting bibliography, teachers could assign historical annotations, brief writing assignments, or presentations that explain some aspect of the history related to the text at hand. The students can teach the others what they have researched.

Students (and new instructors!) may be initially dismayed by the density of heroic couplets, the most popular poetic line of the period. Invest the time early in the course or at the start of the section for a training session in couplets, and it will pay great returns down the road. The headnote to Alexander Pope and the literary terminology appendix offer a good start. You may want to supplement student reading with additional material from a good handbook, such as Perrine's *Sound and Sense* (11th edition). Students first need to work through the highly stylized poetic diction, epigrammatic style, and compression and inversion of language in the balanced and antithetical structure so that they can paraphrase the meaning of a poem. Often students coming from modern and contemporary poetry do not expect the lines to behave according to grammatical norms, and so they don't read with such norms in mind. The fact is, most of the poetry of the period is written in sentences and tells a story; recognizing this will help students come to its meaning and give them a sense of mastery and pleasure. However, it is crucial that they get some training in unpacking the language. Sometimes it is difficult simply to identify the subject, verb, and object. One exercise that works well is to have each student take a couplet and paraphrase it out loud. A particularly long poem like *Absalom and Achitophel* or *The Rape of the Lock* gains much from this. Move from student to student (giving them a chance to figure out which couplet will be theirs), and have each one read a couplet and offer a paraphrase. It's harder than it sounds and very effective. In addition to learning the meaning of the poem, the students benefit by reading slowly, taking risks, getting immediate feedback, practicing their skills, and learning that paraphrase is not a science but an art. After paraphrase becomes second nature, you can move onto other poetic devices and higher levels of interpretation.

Another exercise for reading comprehension is the ungraded identification quiz. Provide an unidentified excerpt from an assigned poem, one that is important to the whole and is readily recognized, and ask the students to identify it and write four to five sentences on its meaning and significance. Review the results as a group, focusing on a detailed reading of the multiple levels of interpretation. If you do this on a regular basis, students will begin to read for significant passages on their own.

Satire may also pose challenges for new readers. Satire is the dominant mode of literary expression through 1740 and continues to have a vital presence thereafter. Consequently, it is crucial to provide some context and tools of analysis for this slippery mode so that students can enjoy the range of ideas expressed in it. Again, references listed in the bibliography will provide good background for neophytes, and some, like Dustin Griffin's *Satire: A Critical Reintroduction*, are accessible to undergraduates. Often students mistake the tone of satire as a personal expression of hatred, anger, or revenge, and while this is not always wrong, it tends to overlook the public significance of satire that Restoration and eighteenth-century audiences understood. One way to convey this public function is to suggest parallels from today's popular culture, such as *Saturday Night Live, The Daily Show,* or the writings of Dave Barry, Erma Bombeck, or William Safire. These contemporary works regularly employ parody, hyperbole, understatement, mock-idioms, fictional personae, sarcasm, irony, lampoon, and many other satiric devices. Moreover, they are popular because people enjoy them and sometimes learn from them, just as Restoration and eighteenth-century audiences enjoyed and learned from the satires of their day. Because much of the classicism of this neoclassical age manifests itself through imitation and parody, the satires of the period provide good opportunities for illustrating literary relationships, intertextuality, and allusion. Small groupings of texts that belong to a parodic family can be taught together to illustrate the effects. For example, after teaching the epic *Paradise Lost*, one can teach the mock-epic *The Rape of the Lock* and the domestic mock-epic "Washing-Day" by Anna Letitia Barbauld (in the Romantic section of *NAEL*), drawing out specific Miltonic inheritances and tracing the shifts in cultural contexts from cosmos, to beau monde, to soap bubbles. This sequencing also has the benefit of demonstrating that parody can be both a compliment and a criticism. Surely Pope wouldn't "mock" Milton! Would Barbauld? Through such discussions, satire becomes a more playful field of meaning and rich signification.

One student assignment that brings home the lessons of satire is the imitation. Challenge students to write a modern-day imitation of a poem from the eighteenth century, and it will almost always involve satire. Good choices might be "Mac Flecknoe," "Description of a City Shower," or the exchange on "The Lady's Dressing Room" by Swift and Lady Mary Wortley Montagu.

These pedagogical challenges—history, the couplet, and satire—come with the territory of this literature, but with preparation they can become areas of significant achievement for the students.

TEACHING CLUSTERS

The Public Sphere and Civil Society

Texts to be taught under this rubric include representations of politeness, sociability, urban growth and development, gender relations in public spaces, domestic tourism and travel, theatre, coffeehouses, libraries, and salons. They respond to demographic changes in the shift to urban centers like London or spa cities like Bath and Bristol, the beginnings of a shift away from dominant rural life, as well as a rapid population growth. They also take up discussion of philosophical questions about human nature and proper behavior in civil society. The public sphere of coffeehouses and theatres provided the space for a community to share information and develop codes of politeness to govern their interactions. Men and women shared these spaces and negotiated various terms of power and pleasure within them.

Texts: "Mac Flecknoe," Pepys's *Diary*, Rochester's amorous lyrics, *Oroonoko*, *The Way of the World*, essays from *The Spectator*, *The Rape of the Lock*, *Fantomina*, *The Beggar's Opera*, Boswell's *Life of Johnson*, Gray's "Elegy," *The Deserted Village*

Norton Topics Online: "A Day in Eighteenth-Century London" and "Trade, Travel, and Expansion of Empire" provide excellent background information, texts, and illustrations to supplement this cluster.

Authorship and Literacy: New Readers, New Writers, New Forms

With the tremendous rise in literacy that occurred in the seventeenth century, more readers began to demand more material to read. The burgeoning book industry filled the need, and new writers became gainfully employed in the marketplace of ideas. Texts included under this rubric essentially fall into two categories, although there is considerable overlap. In the first category, the texts are the products of innovation. New writers such as women, middle- and laboring-class writers, and non-white authors take up the pen and participate in the republic of letters. New literary forms such as the periodical essay and the novel emerge. The second category responds to the novelty with advice, criticism, and satire. Works in this category take authorship as their subject and inaugurate the field of literary criticism. Tensions between tradition and originality take the form of the debate between the Ancients and the Moderns, the high and low, true wit and dullness, the poets and the hacks.

Texts: "Mac Flecknoe," Dryden's essays, *The Pilgrim's Progress*, *Oroonoko*, Finch's "The Introduction," *Verses on the Death of Dr. Swift*, essays from *The Spectator*, Pope's *An Essay on Criticism*, *Epistle to Dr. Arbuthnot*, *Dunciad*, "Epistle from Mrs. Yonge," Leapor's "An Epistle to a Lady," *The Beggar's Opera*, *Rasselas*, Johnson's essays, *The Life of Johnson*, Burney's journals and letters, Gray's "Elegy," popular ballads

Explorations in Science and Nature

Dramatic developments in science spurred by Bacon, Boyle, Newton, and others set the background for a culture of curiosity and intense observation of the natural world. Not surprisingly, such findings lead to questions about the role of human beings in nature and the universe, which of course intersected with the heated religious controversies of the seventeenth century. Enlightenment thinkers placed humankind at the center of their investigation but debated the significance of "man" and his rational capacities. Cartesian dualism provided the philosophical grounding for a mind-body split that authorized the rational and spiritual subordination of the passions. However, it was Locke's empirical views of human understanding and the role of the senses that came to dominate in the eighteenth century. The literature of the period nonetheless attests to the fervor surrounding the investigation of fundamental ideas of cognition, sense, understanding, and the world at large. Texts included under this rubric include representations of changing views of science, nature, human nature, curiosity, sentimentality, exploration, world travel, and empire.

Texts: *Essay Concerning Human Understanding*, Newton's Letter, *Satire Against Reason and Mankind*, *Oroonoko*, "Nocturnal Reverie," books 3 and 4 of *Gulliver's Travels*, "Inkle and Yarico," "Vanity of Human Wishes," *Rasselas*, *The Life of Samuel Johnson*, Burney's letters and journals, Thomson's *Autumn*, Gray's "Elegy," "Ode to Evening," "My Cat Jeoffrey," *The Deserted Village/The Village*, *The Task*

Norton Topics Online: "Plurality of Worlds" and "Trade, Travel, and Expansion of Empire" provide excellent background information, texts, and illustrations to supplement this cluster.

Politics of the Individual

The political upheavals of the seventeenth century led to the establishment of partisan politics that divided along fairly clear lines by the early decades of the eighteenth century. Tories were associated with landed wealth, Anglicanism, and the monarchy, and Whigs were associated with trade, commerce, low-church dissenters, and progressive reform. The question of proper authority was key to both. Locke's contract theory of government assumed that all men were born free and exchanged their liberty for a safe, civil society headed by a legitimate authority. It soon became clear that only certain men, namely white, property-owning men of education, were free and that women, children, laborers, and slaves did not have the ability to make contracts. The literature that falls under this rubric investigates the troubled emergence of the individual in discourses on slavery and marriage. The political discourses also inspired new expressions of autonomy, as seen in the emergence of evangelicalism—which authorizes individual experiences of religious salvation—as well as new forms such as biography, which narrates the development of an identity. Other works, such as those focusing on the noble savage or primitive literatures, recall an idealized state of nature and grace antecedent to civilization.

Texts: *Absalom and Achitophel*, *The Pilgrim's Progress*, *Essay Concerning Human Understanding*, *Hudibras*, *Oroonoko*, *The Way of the World*, *Some Reflections on Marriage*, *Roxana*, Finch's "The Introduction," Prior's "An Epitaph," *Verses on the Death of Dr. Swift*, "A Modest Proposal," "Epistle for Mrs. Yonge," Leapor's "An Epistle to a Lady," *Rasselas*, *The Life of Samuel Johnson*, In-text Topic on "Liberty," Gray's "Elegy," *The Deserted Village/The Village*

Norton Topic Online: "Slavery and the Slave Trade" provides excellent background information, texts, and illustrations to supplement this cluster.

AUTHORS AND WORKS

John Dryden

Because Dryden is the most important literary figure of the last four decades of the seventeenth century, most courses will include his work. Whether you are doing a large selection of Dryden or a single poem, some historical context should be stressed, because Dryden was a creature of his environment, a modern commentator, and a poet who aimed to please his audience. His success with the heroic couplet influenced later poets such as Pope and so helped to set the standard poetic line of the following century. His literary criticism, although frequently occasional and directed to his own work, was greatly admired and likewise set the standard for taste in elegant, simple, refined writing that was nonetheless muscular, flexible, and precise. For these reasons, the guide highlights three of Dryden's works: *Absalom and Achitophel*, "Mac Flecknoe," and excerpts from his prose criticism.

Absalom and Achitophel

Dryden's superb satire functions as both art and politics, and it provides a perfect seventeenth-century example of media spin. One can approach the work as a brilliant piece of poetry, admiring its energetic couplets and detailed satiric portraits, and at the same time one can use the work to introduce students to the beginnings of partisan politics in Britain. Dryden wrote the piece to influence public opinion on the Exclusion Crisis, and more specifically the judgment of Shaftesbury, a crisis that precipitated the development of the Whig and Tory parties. The representation of Shaftesbury's view of government, with allowances for satire and partisanship, reflects the Whig interests in parliamentary control of the succession of the crown and toleration for dissenting Protestant religions; while the poet's voice—particularly in lines 753–810—represents the Tory response to these democratic impulses and their belief in traditional forms of monarchy and hierarchical authority. When you draw students' attention to the legitimacy of both perspectives, again with allowances for satire, modern equivalents of slanted representations of politics will frequently come to mind.

Quick Read

- Form: Varronian satire—an indirect satire that uses narrative to convey a serious issue in a pleasant way—in heroic couplets and heroic idiom. Mixed with dramatic forms of dialogue, personal satiric portraits, panegyric, and a brief elegy.
- Allegory: Based on the biblical story of Absalom's rebellion against his father, King David, in 2 Samuel 13–18. Assigning this as additional reading can be beneficial. David stands in for Charles II; Absalom for the Duke of Monmouth; Achitophel for Shaftesbury;

Jerusalem for London; Jesubites for Catholics; Sanhedrin for Parliament.

- Key Passages: Opening comic treatment of Charles's promiscuity, 1–10; analysis of the Popish Plot, 45–149; temptation scene, 230–476; portrait of Zimri, 545–68; the poet's address to Israel, 753–810; Charles II's speech, 939–1025.
- Themes: Personal ambition corrupts even the best of men; unregulated passions authorize rebellion and mob rule (democracy), while rationality endorses established authority and stability; flattery is delusive and persuasive, while satire provides corrective truth.
- Potential Pedagogical Challenges: The poem is long, over a thousand lines of heroic couplets and full of dense political and religious allusions.

Teaching Suggestions

It is helpful to provide a set of reading questions or key passages that outline the poem *before* the students read so as to ground their understanding of the long work. In class, a close reading of the opening five couplets will provide students a chance to analyze Dryden's technique and to appreciate the humor within the serious political commentary. Assigning a couplet per student to paraphrase out loud will facilitate this close reading. This is especially important if this is the first work of the section or course on Restoration and eighteenth-century literature. Spend time addressing the biblical allegory, the comic tone, the touchy political issues of the king's promiscuity and lack of legitimate heirs, and Dryden's technical mastery (cohesion achieved through alliteration and assonance, movement of the caesura, confident rhythms and rhymes, playful imagery). Contrast these lines with more dramatic conversational lines in the temptation scene, or the masterful antithesis in the portrait of Zimri. The temptation scene can be profitably compared to Milton's temptation scene between Satan and Eve, illustrating the stylistic differences and similarities as well as the politics underlying each.

Dryden's skill as a dramatist is in evidence particularly in the dialogue between Absalom and Achitophel (230–476). With preparation, students may be able to do a dramatic reading of the scene. In any event, it should be read out loud to emphasize Dryden's control over the range of emotions and changing opinions conveyed through natural-sounding conversation. Reading Dryden's criticism with *Absalom and Achitophel* provides an excellent opportunity to discuss the technical aspects of satire as well as Dryden's ability to criticize his own work. Dryden's criticism of satire is nicely excerpted in the passage from *Discourse on the Origin and Progress of Satire*, in which he comments directly on the portrait of Zimri or Buckingham. Dryden's literary relationship with the subject of his satire parallels that in "Mac Flecknoe" (in this case Buckingham was a leading author of *The Rehearsal*, a very popular play that lampooned Dryden and gave him the everlasting nickname Bayes).

Teaching Clusters

Absalom and Achitophel belongs most clearly in the **Politics of the Individual** cluster, because of its direct engagement with political affairs of the Exclusion Crisis and the way it anticipates the partisan politics of Whigs and Tories. The poem sides with Charles II and the conservative investment in the established authorities of the monarch and the Church of England. Dryden reserves his harshest language for Presbyterians and other sectarians from the civil wars and Commonwealth. His satire contrasts well in this respect with Butler's *Hudibras*, both in style and in tone. For a more positive view of dissenting religion, one can assign Bunyan's *Pilgrim's Progress*, which also offers contrasts on the use of allegory in literature. Dryden's king is a mild and benevolent father figure; good subjects are compliant, obedient, and rational. It is interesting to contrast this view of authority with Dryden's song from *Marriage à la Mode*, which expresses a desire for rebellion in the form of adultery. The dangers of democracy surface later in the century in Burke's conservative response to the French Revolution (*NAEL*, Romantic period).

Discussion Questions

1. What tricky issues did Dryden confront in writing this poem about Charles II and his illegitimate son? What strategies did he use? How successful are they?
2. What motivates Achitophel? Why does he need Absalom?
3. Why does Absalom change his mind and join Achitophel?
4. Note the description of Achitophel's confederates. What do they have in common? What makes the satire in this section so effective? (The portrait of Zimri is the chief example.)
5. Note the description of Charles II's loyal followers. What do they have in common? How does this differ from the earlier portraits? What are the differences between satire and panegyric? Which makes better reading?
6. What is Charles II's message in his speech? Why does Dryden put it in the poem at that point?
7. Evaluate the closing lines of the poem. Why does Dryden end it so equivocally?
8. Where are the women in the poem? Why don't they play a role?
9. Almost one hundred years after the publication of *Absalom and Achitophel*, Samuel Johnson said that this best-seller continued to be so well known he didn't need to describe it for his readers. How can you account for the continuing popularity of the work?
10. How does the poem function as "spin"? What contemporary parallels can you find? How do they compare with Dryden's work?

Mac Flecknoe

Dryden's compact mock-epic is a delight to teach because it can be sheer fun. In it Dryden raises insult to an art form by giving purely elegant expression to the adolescent impulses of rivalry, name-calling, scatology, and personal attack. The sophistication of the heroic tone at the start and the subtlety of Dryden's irony may initially misguide students, and so you will want to clue them in to the humor without killing it through explication. Because the poem has a clear narrative, having the students read for the story is a good start. However, the satire depends on recognizing the ironic parallels to the story, and so you will want to address the relationship between the coronation of Shadwell as the Prince of Dullness and Ascanius's rise in the empire of Rome. If you have already taught *Absalom and Achitophel*, then you may want to explore the parallels between literary kingdoms and political kingdoms and what the poem implies about proper authority. But don't let the ironic parallels interfere with the full appreciation of Dryden's portrait of Shadwell and his visually rich coronation scene. In fact, focusing on the senses of sight, sound, touch, and smell may be a good way to bring out the humor of the poem.

Quick Read

- Form/Style: Mock-epic in heroic couplets. Begins in heroic idiom and moves into less lofty language. Includes parody and lampoon.
- Parallels: Flecknoe is compared to Aeneas, and Shadwell—the satiric target—is compared to Ascanius on the occasion of his taking over the empire for his father; Roman Empire parallels the Empire of Dullness; numerous parallels drawn to Restoration and Renaissance drama.
- Key Passages: Opening three couplets establish ironic parallel; Flecknoe's speech identifying Shadwell as his successor, 7–63; the location of Shadwell's coronation, 64–93; the coronation, 94–138; Flecknoe's prophecy and departure, 139–217.
- Key Images: Shadwell's "genuine night" and "goodly fabric," 21–27; the city of London, 64ff.; Shadwell's throne, 74–93; the "mangled poets" littering the streets, 98–107; Shadwell's coronation garb, 120–29; "the yet declaiming bard" falling through the trap door, 211–17.
- Potential Pedagogical Challenges: Very few! This is a great work to teach. Some students may be alienated by the personal attack and view Dryden as "mean."

Teaching Suggestions

The closing image of the "yet declaiming bard" falling through the trapdoor can be a useful way to imagine Dryden's art; he creates a series of trapdoors through which the reader falls. The first of these is in the opening six lines, where the only indication that we are dealing with a satire comes with the single word "Nonsense." Thus the heroic idiom leads the reader to expect dignity until the word "Nonsense" places our expectations in the absurd. Through a series of inflations and deflations (in imagery, in rhetoric, in scenes or actions), Dryden humorously deflates the

reader's expectations. These funny deflations gain through plentiful allusions and metaphors throughout the poem. Thus, when Flecknoe claims
to be preparing the way for Shadwell's "greater name," the allusion to
John the Baptist suggests that Shadwell is Christ, but the echoes of his
name ring through "Pissing Alley," and it is the fish that come to the call,
as they do to the human excrement that floats on the surface of the
Thames. Dryden's poem is vibrantly attuned to sight, smell, and sound,
and students should be encouraged to imagine the coronation scene using
the details that Dryden provides.

The allusions need not distract the students very much, particularly
those to Shadwell's own plays. The footnotes will clarify the literal meaning in the poem and any comprehension beyond that is a bonus. The criticism of dramatists might be introduced here through the excerpts from
"Essay on Dramatic Poesy." One can comment on how the poem illustrates the coterie audience and competitive field of the Restoration theatre, especially if you attend to the origin and circulation of the poem in
manuscript. The success of the satire, however, is that it rises above the
conditions of its origin. The poem also raises issues of literary value that
come to dominate the era, and so the poem can be used as a vehicle to introduce Restoration and eighteenth-century poetry or theatre. In addition
to being an excellent example of Dryden's vigorous couplets, the poem's
emphasis on *dullness* as an ironically celebrated ideal suggests the culture's preoccupation with sharp wit and keen, intelligent literature. What
Flecknoe praises in Shadwell is actually what the elite culture deplored:
plagiarism, verbosity, word play. Dryden implies (and demonstrates
through his own brilliant poem) that good literature is original without
being irrational, subtle without being boring, imitative without being slav-
ish, heroic without being bombastic.

Teaching Clusters

"Mac Flecknoe" teaches well as part of the **Authorship and Literacy:
New Readers, New Writers, New Forms** group. As explained above, the
poem can demonstrate the literary values of Dryden's age, and so it will
compare with works such as Pope's *Essay on Criticism* and Addison's
essays on *Paradise Lost* and the "Pleasures of the Imagination." Read
together, these works can provide students with a sense of what
eighteenth-century readers looked for in good literature. Most particularly, "Mac Flecknoe" anticipates the mock-epic satire on the grub-street
writers of the next era in Pope's *Dunciad*. That pairing offers opportunities to discuss contrasts in couplet style and types of satire, and it also
provides insight into the cultural changes that transpire between the coterie writing public of Restoration London and the increasing commercial
production of literature in the 1720s and 1730s.

Dryden's portrayal of the city of London in the description of the place
for Shadwell's coronation also makes the poem a good choice for the cluster on the **Public Sphere and Civil Society**. Dryden's image of the

streets choked with the unread and unbought work of poets compares with Swift's catalog of detritus that chokes the street in "Description of a City Shower"; the mangled limbs of poets suggests a level of violence akin to Gay's London in *The Beggar's Opera*. This wasteful, undignified environment contrasts with Dryden's vision of London in *Annus Mirabilis*, which might be usefully alluded to here. His proud description of London pairs with Addison's orderly vision of the Royal Exchange in *The Spectator*.

Discussion Questions

1. What is the occasion of the poem? (What does it commemorate?)
2. How would you summarize the narrative of the poem?
3. In what sense is Shadwell Flecknoe's son?
4. If Flecknoe's speech identifying Shadwell as his successor (lines 15–26) should be complimentary, what do the lines suggest about Shadwell? About Flecknoe?
5. Where does Dryden place the coronation and how does he describe it? What is the significance of this environment?
6. What does the "yet declaiming bard" prophesy about his successor?
7. How does Dryden treat his fellow Restoration playwrights in the poem? What is the significance of this? How does he treat earlier playwrights? What is the significance of this?
8. If satire aims to correct vice, what does "Mac Flecknoe" aim to correct?
9. What does the word "dullness" imply in the poem?
10. "Mac Flecknoe" is a poem that uses the political concerns over proper succession to illustrate a problem in the literary kingdom. What parallel (metaphor) does Dryden construct? What are the implications of the comparison?

An Essay on Dramatic Poesy and Other Criticism

Dryden's "Essay on Dramatic Poesy" provides an important link in survey courses that span the earlier and later periods because it focuses on the dominant genre of the Renaissance—plays—while it introduces and influences the dominant mode of the later periods—prose. Dryden's ideas on drama and the writing of plays give important insight into the world of Restoration theatre and how its denizens perceived the great writers of the past, but they also enable him to demonstrate a new, clean, flexible prose style that would come to characterize the easy, conversational prose of the Enlightenment.

Quick Read

- Form: Prose essay in dialogue form. Excellent summary in notes.
- Excerpts from "Essay": (1) Elements of bad writing—good introduc-

tion to the new literary values of the Restoration. (2) Defines wit through the example of the ancients; compares with modern writer, Cleveland. (3) Describes the strengths of Shakespeare and Jonson— the Homer and Virgil of English dramatic poetry.

- Excerpt on Heroic Poetry: Why heroic literature calls for bold language; defines wit as the proper alignment between thought and expression.
- Excerpt on Satire: The art of fine raillery as "a vast difference betwixt the slovenly butchering of a man, and the fineness of a stroke that separates the head from the body, and leaves it standing in its place" (2131). Praise for his portrait of Zimri.
- Excerpt from Preface to Fables: Praise for Chaucer's good sense, originality, breadth. Justification for Chaucer's "musicality."

Teaching Suggestions

Excerpts from Dryden's criticism can best be read alongside his own works to offer critical insight, but they also make good companions to the works by authors he addresses. For instance, you might want to teach the excerpt on Shakespeare and Jonson when teaching the drama of the Renaissance. Similarly, the excerpt on wit and Cleveland may elucidate the poetry of the metaphysical poets; compare this with Johnson's Life of Cowley, which also addresses metaphysical wit. Dryden's treatment of satire will provide some terms by which to discuss the effectiveness of any given satire. Likewise, his discussion of heroic poetry can add depth to a discussion of Milton's epic and the mock-epics that follow in its wake. His treatment of Chaucer, which was fairly innovative at the time, offers a glimpse into the historical conditions of literary taste.

Dryden's prose writing can also be valued for its style. Toward this end, the idea of wit may be applied to his own writing. He consciously adapted a style to fit the expression of his thoughts; in his criticism he favored an easy, conversational style, informed by wide reading but without pedantry.

Teaching Clusters

The critical writings most obviously fall into the cluster on **Authorship and Literacy: New Readers, New Writers, New Forms.** Samuel Johnson's label for Dryden as "the father of English criticism" speaks both to his founding a new form of writing and to his influence on the prevailing taste of the age. It is interesting to find echoes of Dryden's criticism in Swift and Pope and, of course, Johnson. Dryden's criticism of bad poetry—for example, "he creeps along with ten little words in every line, and helps out his numbers with for to, and unto, and all the pretty expletives he can find"—receives new, compressed expression in Pope's couplet in An Essay on Criticism: "While Expletives their feeble Aid do join, / And ten low Words oft creep in one dull Line." In addition to influencing poetry, Dryden's essays also serve as antecedents to the prose criticism by

Addison and Johnson in the periodical press. Finally, what Dryden said concisely about the relative values of Shakespeare and Jonson, Samuel Johnson would enlarge on in his famous *Preface to Shakespeare*.

Discussion Questions

1. What are the characteristics of bad poetry?
2. How does Dryden define wit?
3. As the headnote suggests, Dryden did not feel obliged to maintain an opinion simply because he once expressed it in writing. Can you find evidence of any changing opinions in these excerpts?
4. How does Dryden's view of Jonson in the "Essay on Dramatic Poesy" inform his treatment of Shadwell—who claimed to be Jonson's literary heir—in "Mac Flecknoe"?
5. Would you characterize Dryden's prose criticism as fair? Why or why not?
6. How does Dryden's treatment of earlier authors in his prose criticism compare with his treatment of contemporary authors in the verse satire "Mac Flecknoe"?
7. What are the dominant characteristics of Dryden's prose style? How does it compare with that of other writers from his era (see excerpts from Pepys, Bunyan, Locke, and Newton)? How does it compare with the prose of Johnson?

Further Resources

NORTON ONLINE ARCHIVE

Epilogue to The Conquest of Granada, II
Prologue to The Tempest
Epilogue to Tyrannic Love
Song from The Indian Emperor
Song from An Evening's Love
To the Pious Memory of . . . Mrs. Anne Killigrew
The Secular Masque
The Preface to Fables Ancient and Modern
  [In Praise of Chaucer]

Samuel Pepys

The Diary

Both of Pepys's diary entries provide rich, vivid social history for students of the Restoration and eighteenth century. The entries record actions more than thought or reflection, and so they read quickly. They offer informative nonfiction counterparts to other representations of the London fire of 1666 and clandestine sexual behavior both within and outside of marriage.

Quick Read

- Form: Prose diary entries from 1666 and 1668; first-person account not intended for public.
- Summary of excerpt on the London fire: Describes the progress of the fire with minute geographical detail and comments on the behavior of people trying to escape. Also records interactions with leaders: King Charles II, James Duke of York, and the Lord Mayor of London.
- Summary of excerpt on the Deb Willet Affair: Records Pepys's sexual interactions with the serving girl, Deb Willet, and the angry, emotional response of his wife; Pepys's continued pursuit of Deb after she is moved to another situation; Pepys's uncertain reconciliation with his wife.
- Potential Pedagogical Challenges: Treatment of Deb Willet and the philandering of Pepys, although coded in Spanish, is explicit and may be offensive.

Teaching Suggestions

Reading the section on the fire in London is a gripping experience and a bracing alternative to Dryden's panegyric on the city and the king in *Annus Mirabilis*. Teaching this with a map of London would be instructive. Teaching the Deb Willet affair provides an interesting counterpart to the sexual repartee of Restoration comedy and the libertine verse of Rochester and Behn. It represents the cultural standards for sexual behavior most explicitly in the conditional toleration of male promiscuity and the sexual access to females of the serving class. Compare Dryden's representation of Charles's promiscuity in *Absalom and Achitophel* and his representation of adultery in the song from *Marriage à la Mode*. The representation of serving girls as sexual objects anticipates a scene from Eliza Haywood's *Fantomina* and the revolutionary treatment of the subject in Richardson's 1740 novel of letters, *Pamela*.

To convey a sense of the genre of life writing, and perhaps to offset Pepys's sexism, you might assign students to write Mrs. Pepys's version of the Deb Willet affair or an entry from Deb Willets's journal treating her interactions with Pepys. Students may be referred to the fictional work *The Journal of Mrs. Pepys: Portrait of a Marriage*, by Sara George (1999). With a focus on life writing, the selections from James Boswell's journal and Frances Burney's diary make excellent reading companions.

Teaching Clusters

The excerpt on the fire of London can begin the cluster on the **Public Sphere and Civil Society** because of its detailed representation of the geography of the city, its inhabitants, and the great concern people (or is it just Pepys?) have for their "goods." One gets the sense of traveling through the city and the utility of the Thames for movement. Pepys was both an acquisitive and a social person, and the excerpt highlights the "things" of daily life as well as a sense of the rhythms of social exchange. This nonfictional representation will provide good balance to Addison and Steele's representation of the city and its inhabitants in *The Spectator*. One could also teach Daniel Defoe's *Journal of the Plague Year*, which has affinities in style and content with Pepys's diary, as a good pairing.

Discussion Questions

1. Look at a seventeenth- or eighteenth-century map of London. What parts of the city did the fire consume?
2. What are Pepys's principle concerns in reviewing the progress of the fire? What emotions does he experience and why?
3. What conditions make the fire's progress so extraordinary?
4. Why don't people attempt to extinguish the fire? What role does Pepys play in controlling the fire?
5. What happens when the fire (or fear of the fire) reaches Pepys's own house? What are his principle concerns?
6. With regard to the Deb Willet affair, how does Pepys feel about Deb? How do you know? What can we tell about her feelings for him?
7. How does Pepys regard his wife? What is her reaction to walking in on her husband being intimate with Deb? What does he do in response?
8. What does Pepys's prolonged agony over (and persistence in) the affair suggest about his character? About his marriage?
9. Why does Pepys write these entries? What do they record? What is their value for contemporary readers?

John Bunyan

The Pilgrim's Progress

Like *Paradise Lost* and Lucy Hutchinson's *Memoirs*, *Pilgrim's Progress* reveals the response of a boldly eloquent Puritan to the experience of defeat. The Vanity Fair episode offers a devastating allegorical depiction of English society and its treatment of dissenters after the Restoration. Though Bunyan writes within the age-old tradition of Christian allegory, he is a keen observer of contemporary England, with its emerging consumer society. Yet, like the older Milton, Bunyan found himself less concerned with the reformation of the commonwealth than with the transformation of the human soul. In a hostile society, the individual is often required to seek the path to salvation unaided and alone.

Quick Read

- Form: Allegorical prose narrative; dream vision; journey.
- Major Characters: Christian, Obstinate, Pliable, Faithful, Hopeful, and Ignorance.
- Important Images: Wicket gate; City of Destruction; the book Christian reads; Christian's burden; Slough of Despond; Vanity Fair; River of Death; certificate.
- Themes: Salvation is a difficult, personal journey requiring sacrifice and faith; reading (the Bible) is the guide to salvation; Christian is the "every person" of religious life.
- Style: Homely imagery; dense biblical allusion; biblical rhetoric.

Teaching Suggestions

The simplicity of the prose narrative allows students immediate access, and so much of the teaching of this text can take place through discussion. The excerpts allow for connection to earlier Christian allegories in a long survey course, in particular *Everyman* or *The Faerie Queene*. Bunyan's depiction of Vanity Fair directly influences nineteenth-century novels, including of course Thackeray's *Vanity Fair*, for which it serves as a controlling metaphor. Teaching this segment in concert with the novel can provide historical and literary context for Thackeray's art. *Pilgrim's Progress* was a children's classic loved by Maggie Tulliver in George Eliot's *The Mill on the Floss* and the March sisters in Louisa May Alcott's *Little Women*, many chapter titles of which are taken from Bunyan's allegory. One can discuss the reasons for its popularity and how its meaning changes in the new literary expressions. For a course or section focused on Restoration and eighteenth-century literature, the sarcastic allusion to "Bunyan's works" as entertainment in Congreve's *Way of the World* suggests the dynamic of literary conflict between the serious moral work of dissenters and the light, amoral wit of libertine culture. Discussion that draws out the contrasts will help the students appreciate the complexity of the time period.

The difficulty of Christian's journey and the abuse he meets may be suggestive of parallels with today's culture of religious controversy, and so may help to open the text to non-Christian readers. If you focus on the journey metaphor and Christian's reactions to the obstacles he meets, the text can be read in more secular and literary ways.

Teaching Clusters

Politics of the Individual. The excerpts from *Pilgrim's Progress* highlight the mindset of a religious dissenter in the late seventeenth century, and as such can provide a literary alternative to the representation of the "losers" in the Restoration (compare, for example, Dryden's representation of dissenters as hypocrites and rebels in *Absalom and Achitophel*). Dissenters believed in the political republic and the freedom to pursue independent

Christian forms of religion outside of state control. The Anglican view dominated after the restoration of the king and state religion, and at various times dissenting preachers and congregations were legally harassed and abused. Of course, one should ask students to consider how Christian's journey represents the individual's struggle against temptations of the world, but you could also ask the students to consider what it means that Christian pursues his journey alone with only the aid of his book. What or who authorizes Christian's journey/salvation?

Authorship and Literacy: New Readers, New Writers, New Forms. The role of reading, a personal and frequently isolated activity, also plays a role in this text. If reading the Bible independently guides Christian to the Celestial City, then others, too—particularly newly literate groups like laborers and women—could pursue independent spiritual fulfillment. Furthermore, reading works like *Pilgrim's Progress* replicated the spiritual experience by making the allegory applicable to the individual reader of the text. Bunyan's incredibly popular story was meant to teach people how to reach salvation.

The Public Sphere and Civil Society. This cluster might include the section on Vanity Fair as an alternative representation of urban growth. Here the pilgrims are seen by inhabitants of the city as uncouth, strange, and foreign, Even their language seems different. This could be an allegory for the dissenting experience, but it also represents the sophisticated world of urban wealth and trade as dissolute and corrupt.

Discussion Questions

1. What is the significance of Christian's burden? What is the City of Destruction?
2. Why do people resist what Christian has learned in his book?
3. What book does Christian read? Why is the act of reading so important?
4. What is the allegorical significance of the "journey"? Where does Christian come from and where does he go? How does this compare with other journeys of literature?
5. Do you need to know the Bible in order to understand Bunyan's allegory? Why or why not?
6. Evaluate the categories of items sold at Vanity Fair. Can you name modern allegorical equivalents?
7. What is the purpose of the certificate? Why does Ignorance fail to gain entrance into the Celestial City? Where does he go?
8. How is this story an allegory for religious dissent?

Further Resources

NORTON ONLINE ARCHIVE

From Grace Abounding to the Chief of Sinners

John Locke

The Epistle to the Reader from An Essay Concerning
Human Understanding

It is, perhaps, a useful pedagogical irony that Locke's passage on "clear
and distinct ideas" is confoundedly confusing. He had to change the
wording to "determined" in order to be clear! Locke's essay had tremendous influence on the development of British Enlightenment thought,
and so students will be curious to read a selection. Like the *NAEL* selection from Newton, it provides some intellectual context for the literary developments, and in particular it is useful if you are establishing a theme
or teaching cluster around ideas of individualism. The excerpt demonstrates the Enlightenment impulse to break down complex thoughts into
accepted truths so as to establish a common ground or understanding in
argument or conversation. Significantly, the complex thought that Locke
attempts to break down here is complex thought.

Quick Read

- Form: Essay; letter to the reader.
- Style: Humble, conversational, and philosophically abstract.
- Themes: Learning is pleasurable; received opinions are less important than thinking for oneself; effective communication relies on language appropriate for ideas.
- Important Concepts: Each reader will experience the essay uniquely;
  determined ideas are fixed objectively in the mind and are the basis
  of truth or knowledge.
- Important Images/Points: Hawking after ideas; the origin of the
  essay; changing "clear and distinct" to "determined" in order to be
  clearer.

Teaching Suggestions

Focusing on the "genre" of the letter to the reader will help open the
text for discussion. Consider that this information is directed at the new
reader and potential critic of Locke's *Essay*. His strategies are aimed at
minimizing negative judgment and encouraging a specific form of reading, one that asks the reader to verify the truth of the text according to his
or her own experience. Locke's ideal is for the reader to think for himself
(or herself). Ask students to consider why this would be important for the

writer of *An Essay Concerning Human Understanding*, and also why it might be threatening.

Locke's explanation for the origin of the essay also merits discussion. First you might ask the students to consider what topic his friends met to discuss and how they handled the disagreement of ideas. Locke's solution appears simple and radical. He considers the soundness of their individual opinions based on the capacities of their understandings. The scene of "conversation" is one that eighteenth-century literature would take up repeatedly, and the lessons for establishing common understandings would derive from Locke. See, for example, *The Spectator*, *Rasselas*, and many other works.

Enjoy the irony of Locke's having to clarify "clear and distinct ideas." What does his explanation suggest about the problems he encountered after the first editions of the essay? What do his changes attempt to do? It might be helpful to think about how this conceptual problem illustrates the linguistic difficulty he is trying to eliminate.

In all cases, the information in the *NAEL* headnote is necessary for understanding some central concepts and the historical importance of Locke's writings.

Teaching Clusters

Politics of the Individual. For those teaching a course focusing on the rise of the individual or secularism, this excerpt illustrates the turn away from divine authority toward individual authority. Locke looks to the understanding, or the individual's mind, to ratify the acceptability of ideas rather than to divine or ecclesiastical authority. His *Essay Concerning Human Understanding* would become involved in heated controversies over such questions of authority, but his empirical view would eventually win over the majority. For a refutation of Lockean ideas, see Mary Astell's preface in the In-text Topic on "Liberty."

Explorations in Science and Nature. Locke's *Essay* also plays a key role in changing ideas of human nature. Taken together with the information in the headnote, the excerpts will help explain the eighteenth-century fascination with cognition, scientific inquiry, and rational argument. For those teaching a course or section that focuses on developing ideas of the aesthetic, the excerpt from Locke provides a simple introduction to the process of the mind that would evolve to accommodate aesthetic judgment. In this way, the excerpt pairs nicely with Addison's essay on "Pleasures of the Imagination." The excerpt from Locke would also work well when training students to write their own papers. His emphasis on original thinking as opposed to received opinion is pertinent. His focus on the problems of communication stemming from poorly chosen language may lend credence to your efforts to get students to be more precise and accurate in their language.

Discussion Questions

1. How does Locke represent his *Essay* in the letter? Why does he represent it in this way?
2. What suggestions does he give to the reader of his *Essay*? What does he hope the reader will take away from the reading?
3. How did the *Essay* originate? How did it evolve? What do the conditions for writing the *Essay* tells us about its content?
4. Whom does he exclude from his intended audience for the *Essay* and why?
5. What does he hope to contribute to the "commonwealth of learning"?
6. What is a determinate idea? What is a determined idea? How will an understanding of such ideas in appropriate language end many disputes?
7. How are Locke's ideas in this excerpt "radical," "individualistic," or threatening?
8. Based on the texts in the *Norton Topic Online* "Plurality of Worlds," how would Locke's ideas fit into the context of scientific inquiry at this time?

Isaac Newton

Nature and *nature's* laws lay hid in night,
God said, Let Newton be, and all was light.

Pope's couplet captures a sense of the wonder and respect Newton inspired in the poets of the following generation. Newton is himself the subject of many poems, and his scientific findings—particularly those on light—influenced many, many more. While the ordering of the natural world into mathematical laws and observable phenomena earned the scorn of later Romantic poets, it is a mark of the Enlightenment that poetry found science its proper object.

A Letter of Mr. Isaac Newton . . . Containing His New Theory about Light and Colors

Teaching the excerpt from Newton's letter on the principles of light and color provides intellectual context for the later poetic praise, and it helps students re-create a sense of the excitement created by Newton's discoveries. It requires an effort of imagination—but one that is well worthwhile—to recapture the pious wonder with which readers first greeted Newton's revelation that even colors obeyed divine laws.

Quick Read

- Form: Letter published by the Royal Society.
- Style: Clear, scientific method.
- Major Concepts: Light refracts into separate rays of color, each color

has a corresponding refractability; whiteness is a composite of color; light may be a substance.

Teaching Suggestions

As with Locke's epistle, teaching the excerpt from Newton will be useful if you are developing a particular theme, in this case that of nature, science, curiosity, exploration. It provides an excellent opportunity for interdisciplinary discussion with students studying physics or other sciences. One way to engage the students is to ask them to consider what it would mean for a society to be delivered this information by Mr. Newton; what perceptions would it be displacing? On a more conceptual level, Newton's excerpt illustrates the epistemological revolution of the seventeenth century that allowed for the emergence of modernity. His text follows clear scientific experimental methods based in mathematical precision and verifiable results. Understanding the natural laws of the universe meant that mystery, superstition, and legend gave way to empirical knowledge. It meant that the earth and the universe were knowable.

Teaching Clusters

Exploration in Science and Nature. Any unit dealing with this cluster should include the excerpt from Newton if only as intellectual context. The excerpt can be explored for its empirical method as well as the discoveries it announces. It expresses the genuine scientific imagination that Pope celebrates in *An Essay on Man*, that Thomson incorporates in the excerpt from *Autumn*, and that Swift mocks in the third book of *Gulliver's Travels*. The Romantic poets would attempt to recapture the magic and superstition of the natural landscape (Robinson's "The Haunted Beach," Coleridge's *Rime of the Ancient Mariner* and "Kubla Khan") as would the gothic novel (see *NAEL*, The Romantic Period), but even in their retreat from Newtonian science, these authors and texts register the impact of Newton's work.

Discussion Questions

1. What is the significance of Newton's breakdown of color as individually refractable rays of light?
2. Why is his discovery of whiteness as the composite of all color "the most surprising and wonderful"?
3. How would you describe his method of experimentation?
4. How would you describe his style of reporting the experimentation and results?
5. What would it mean for a scientific community to hear the results of Newton's experiments with light for the first time? For information on the scientific community and the popularization of science, see *Norton Topics Online* "Plurality of Worlds."
6. How do you account for the popular impact of Newton's discoveries in optics?

7. What role does light play in poetry (as image, as metaphor, as theme)?
   Examine Pope's *Essay on Criticism*, for example. How might Newton's
   discoveries change the role of light in poetry?

Samuel Butler

Hudibras

The excerpt from *Hudibras* provides a good opportunity to illustrate the
connection between form and function in poetry. The burlesque form,
which is not heavily represented in this section of *NAEL*, is a low form of
satire, and Butler clearly vented his own antipathy toward Presbyterians
and Independents in the poem. Teasing out the allusions through the
footnotes will provide students with a sense of the history to which the
poem responds. You might direct the class to an analysis of the tetrameter
couplets and the rough rhymes focused around the question of why or
how the lines are an appropriate vehicle for the burlesque. Taking the
analysis one step further, you can bring the class to understand why the
burlesque is appropriate for Butler's unruly emotional response to the former rulers.

Quick Read

- Form: Narrative poem; burlesque or travesty in tetrameter couplets.
- Style: Rough cadences, inelegant rhymes, some doggerel.
- Key Passages: Description of the knight, Sir Hudibras (15–42); his
  learning in languages, rhetoric, mathematics, philosophy (45–186);
  attack on Presbyterians (187–228).
- Key Metaphors: Religion as a prostitute; "holy text of pike and gun"
  (194).

Teaching Suggestions

Reading the poem aloud will facilitate a discussion of the form and
function of the lines. Encourage students to memorize and recite a few
couplets themselves. These lines also are easy to imitate and so make a
good model for an imitation assignment. In order to understand the context of the poem, students will need to read the headnote, which provides
essential background. Also, you might encourage the students to read the
poem through without the footnotes the first time, and then read it again
more slowly paying attention to the footnotes. The passage breaks down
nicely into three sections that can be analyzed through discussion questions: the description of the knight, his learning, and the final attack on
Presbyterians. Throughout, Butler represents religion as something deliberately unreligious through a variety of metaphors that merit discussion.
Also, the knight's responsibility in his role as landlord and magistrate, although subtly introduced in the opening section, motivates some of the
hostility and so might be addressed. As a travesty, the poem contrasts with

Dryden's "Mac Flecknoe," and a study of the differences in style, tone, and subject will make a nice illustration of the different forms and functions. Also, Byron's playful lines from *Don Juan* make for a later contrast.

Teaching Clusters

Politics of the Individual. As the earliest and most vociferous representation of the Presbyterians and Independents immediately after the Restoration, the poem illustrates nicely the connection between religion and politics that energizes much of the literature in this cluster. Dryden's "Mac Flecknoe" shares mildly this Tory/Whig dynamic, but it is much more visible in his *Absalom and Achitophel*. Swift's "Tale of Tub" directly addresses issues of religious difference and so comments on the historical development of the controversy after *Hudibras*. See also Blake's poems on religious hypocrisy, such as "All Religions Are One" and "There Is No Natural Religion."

Discussion Questions

1. How does Butler describe Hudibras's behavior as a magistrate or "domestic knight"?
2. What does Sir Hudibras's learning consist of?
3. Explain the relationship between his learning and his religion (see lines 187–88).
4. What is the point of a holy text of "pike and gun"? To what extent is this an accurate depiction of Presbyterianism?
5. How do Butler's rhymes reflect the broad humor of the poem? Why is this an appropriate form for burlesque?
6. What fuels the hostility of the poem?
7. Does the significance of the poem rise above its context? Cf. "Mac Flecknoe."

John Wilmot, Second Earl of Rochester

Epitomizing the Restoration in so many ways, Rochester is both a conspicuous figure in the literature (most notably the rake of licentious Restoration comedies) and a ventriloquist for vibrant Restoration characters in his own writing. He is usually brilliant, and he is always acting a part. Whether you choose to teach his obscene libertine poems ("The Disabled Debauchee," "The Imperfect Enjoyment") or his philosophical paradox poems ("Upon Nothing," *A Satire against Reason and Mankind*), be certain to emphasize that the speaker of the poem is a character and not an authentic expression of Rochester himself. Moreover, prepare the students for the ways in which the constructed surface of the poem gives way to an underlying play in meaning. Rochester is having fun with the reader!

A Satire against Reason and Mankind

The key to understanding this poem is the technique of paradox, or an apparent contradiction that is nonetheless somehow true. The value of the paradox is its ability to shock, and Rochester is particularly well practiced in outraging his audiences. The central idea that the poem responds to is the theological argument that humankind's superiority is based on the divine attribute of *reason*, and this view is most succinctly stated by the interlocutor in lines 60–71. Rochester asserts that reason makes humans inferior to beasts. One way to teach the poem is to ask students to follow Rochester's poetic arguments for and against reason in order to determine in what way the paradox can be true. However, Rochester is tricky. The meaning of words such as "sense" and "reason" shifts throughout the poem.

Quick Read

- Form: Formal verse satire in heroic couplets; imitation of Boileau's *Satire VIII*.
- Style: Energetic, interruptive, elegant (note: this is not an obscene poem).
- Key Passages: Opening proposition on preferring to be an animal, 1–7; reason as the *ignis fatuus* of the mind, 12–24; the reverend interlocutor, 46–71; defense of "right reason," 98–111; human baseness compared to beasts, 115–67; addition—portraits of courtier, priest, bishop, 179–215; the ideal man, 216–25.
- Themes: Reason is used to justify the corruption of humanity; right reason is the proper use of one's sense/senses; human beings are more bestial than animals; animals are more humane than humans.

Teaching Suggestions

Begin teaching the poem by addressing the speaker's misanthropic attitude in the opening lines. Throughout, it will be important to address the complicated metaphors Rochester constructs. In particular, pay attention to the *ignis fatuus* lines (foolish fire, will-o-wisp). From these lines, the students can see that reason—that is, false reason—strays from sense or instinct. The shocking image of the "reasoning engine" huddled in the dirt (29) resonates with the themes of mortality from "Upon Nothing" and illustrates for Rochester the quintessential end of humankind's divine rationality. The presence of the interlocutor is part of the formal tradition of verse satire in which another voice enters the poem to offer an alternative view. Ask the students to describe how the "formal band and beard" is characterized by his speech. The satirist's reaction to the reverend is explosive; the pious hypocrisy of the religious perspective provokes the satire on the baseness of humanity that follows. Students are usually drawn to the passage on "right reason" because it appears to state the standard for the poem—instinct guides reason. However, students should be sure to evaluate the logical conclusion of such a standard (that beasts are at least as wise as human beings), a standard with which the speaker appears to be comfortable. The poem's ambiguously hopeful ending also merits discussion. Generically, the poem compares well with Pope's *Epistle to Dr. Arbuthnot* and Johnson's *Vanity of Human Wishes*, other formal verse satires.

Caution should be used in teaching the obscene poems. While they illustrate vividly the libertine ethos of the period and they intersect well with the Restoration sex-comedies like Congreve's *Way of the World*, the language and themes may be inappropriate for classroom discussion. One way to minimize the sense of sexism in "The Imperfect Enjoyment" (and also to contextualize "The Disabled Debauchee") is to teach Aphra Behn's poems together with Rochester's. Her "Disappointment" deals with a sexual encounter that fails because of a man's lack of performance (see also "The Reasons that Induced Dr. Swift . . ." by Lady Mary Wortley Montagu). These poems by Rochester and Behn were intended to shock, and they belong to a genre dating back to Ovid's *Amores* (and, in English, at least as far back as Thomas Nashe's *The Choice of Valentines*, written in the 1590s). With these points established, it is possible to focus on the important differences between the two poems. Rochester's sexual imagery is harsh and violent, whereas Behn writes an ironic version of the pastoral. Behn emphasizes her empathy with the nymph Cloris, while Rochester's poem is male-centered ("Corinna" seems to disappear halfway through the poem, leaving the poet alone with his disobedient penis). On the other hand, both works have interestingly ambiguous titles. If you and your students are sufficiently comfortable with the material, there are grounds here for an interesting debate over which lover experiences "Imperfect Enjoyment" and which "Disappointment."

Teaching Clusters

Explorations in Science and Nature. Rochester's *Satire* puts into question the very nature of humanity and its place on the scale of being, and so it teaches well in this cluster. The lines on fear (139–56) resonate with Hobbes's state of nature, and the general misanthropy of the poem anticipates the fourth book of *Gulliver's Travels*, which also deals explicitly with the idea that beasts are more reasonable than human beings.

The Public Sphere and Civil Society. Rochester's amorous lyrics are anything but civil, and they demonstrate the standard against which eighteenth-century men could estimate their own gallantry toward the ladies. However, Rochester's obscene poems tend to be frank representations of sexual interest along with playful renderings of gendered conventions, conflicts, pains, and pleasures. They share a sense of shock-value with Swift's "Dressing Room" poems, but they also anticipate some of the female-authored responses to Swift.

Discussion Questions

1. What tone does Rochester set in the opening lines of A Satire?
2. How is reason an *ignis fatuus*—or foolish fire—of the mind, and what is the significance of putting reason at odds with sense, the "light of nature"?
3. What does the image of the "reasoning engine" huddling in the dirt signify, and why might this be blasphemous?
4. What is false reason in the poem? What is right reason?
5. In what ways are human beings less reasonable than animals?
6. Why is fear so powerful a motivator in the poem? What does this suggest about human nature?
7. The speaker categorically condemns human beings: "Most Men are Cowards, all Men should be Knaves" (169). To what extent is the speaker a confirmed misanthropist? What are his reasons?
8. Evaluate the closing image of the ideal man. What qualities must this man possess? What is the significance of these traits? In the end, how much hope does the speaker have for meeting such a man?
9. In what sense is this a satire? How does it compare with other satires of the age?
10. Compare Rochester's style and language in this poem with that of his shorter lyrics. How do they differ? Why is the style appropriate for this poem?

Aphra Behn

Oroonoko

The easiest way to center a class on this hybrid prose narrative is to focus on the character of Oroonoko. It was, after all, the character who inspired Behn's audience and went on to new lives in dramatic reproductions and abolitionist poetry. It is Oroonoko who physically carries the story from Coramantien to Surinam and so structurally and thematically connects the divergent parts of the narrative. Because the text is so teachable and illustrates seventeenth-century ideas and genres so well, the text will probably be included in a number of different types of courses. With that in mind, three levels of treatment are recommended: the cursory, the intermediate, and the detailed. Cursory treatment focuses on the character of Oroonoko with an emphasis on the tragic end. Intermediate treatment can develop the character of Oroonoko in the two halves of the novel, the romance of Coramantien and the tragedy of Surinam, and the thematic continuities and discontinuities. In full detailed treatment, the class should address Oroonoko's character in the two halves of the novel, the thematic continuities and discontinuities, and the narrator's relationship to the character and related issues of composition and genre. There are many additional aspects of the novel that you may or may not want to take up—for instance, Tory politics or historical representations of empire and slavery—but this model will provide a good starting place.

Quick Read

- Form: Hybrid prose narrative (biography, memoir, travel narrative, romance, nouvelle/novel, political allegory).
- Main Characters: Oroonoko, the royal slave; Imoinda, his wife; the King of Coramantien, Oroonoko's grandfather; Trefry, Oroonoko's master; William Byam, deputy governor; Banister, Oroonoko's executioner; the narrator (Behn).
- Key Themes: Nobility is innate, not a product of culture; art and sophistication are corrupt; native simplicity is ideal; love and honor are the overriding concerns of the hero; death is more honorable than slavery; idealism cannot survive in the real(istic) world.
- Key Passages (Cursory): Description of Oroonoko, 2187; Oroonoko visits Imoinda in the otan, 2195; Oroonoko's mourning and heroic valor, 2197–98; Oroonoko's capture, 2200; Oroonoko "endured no more of the slave but the name," 2205; reunion with Imoinda, 2217–18; Oroonoko needs liberty, 2209; Oroonoko incites other slaves to rebel, 2217–18; Oroonoko concedes the slaves are dogs, 2220; Oroonoko's humiliation/revenge, 2221; Oroonoko kills Imoinda, 2223; Oroonoko's self immolation, 2226; Oroonoko's execution, 2226.
- Key Passages (Intermediate): Oroonoko meets Imoinda, 2188; the otan, 2188; Imoinda's "lie" and punishment, 2197; the middle passage, 2201–03; Oroonoko meets other slaves, 2203–04; description of Clemene, 2206–07; Imoinda's pregnancy, 2205, 2216; Oroonoko's heroic hunting, 2211+; visits the "Indian" village, 2213–15; Byam seeks rebel slaves, 2218; Imoinda shoots Byam, 2219; Oroonoko is whipped, 2220; the use of Oroonoko's body as warning, 2226.
- Key Passages (Detailed): Narrator's truth claims, 2183; naming of Caesar, 2205; narrator's assuring Oroonoko's "liberty," 2207; narrator "entertains" Oroonoko and Imoinda, 2208; fear of Oroonoko, narrator as babysitter, 2209+; narrator flees during insurrection, 2221; Trefry "protects" Oroonoko, 2222; narrator's departure from the sick room, 2225; narrator's closing hope, 2226.

Teaching Suggestions

At the cursory level, the focus relies on concepts of the heroic. This may tie the story into discussions of *Paradise Lost* and earlier epics, and it also ties into discussions of heroic literature of the seventeenth century (see the excerpt from Dryden's criticism on heroic poetry). Restoration audiences were fascinated with the heroic, as demonstrated by the defense of Virgilian and Homeric epics, the popularity of heroic tragedy on stage, and the formation of heroic idioms such as the iambic pentameter couplet. Begin by showing (or asking) how Behn constructs Oroonoko as the heroic ideal. Examine Oroonoko's conflict between love and honor (first in the otan and second in remaining a slave while he is with Imoinda). Focus on the paradox of the Royal Slave and the logic of the tragic end. Why must Oroonoko revenge himself upon Byam? Oroonoko's honor leads him to sacrifice Imoinda and ultimately to endure stoically his dismemberment and execution. For today's students, the concept of honor might resonate with elements of masculine codes of behavior and add meaning to the violence and tragic choices of the story's conclusion.

With the intermediate treatment, the heroic ideal is developed further through analysis of the romance elements of the Coramantien scenes and the realism of the Surinam section. At this level, the class should discuss Imoinda's character and her role in the two halves of the story. In Coramantien, her beauty and virtue inspire Oroonoko to heroic deeds (sex and war), but in the end her unborn child and physical vulnerability motivate his destructive behavior. The exaggerated language of romance, although entirely conventional for Behn, may seem strange to students. The extravagant language and actions of the lovers can provide a pedagogical moment to discuss the linguistic difficulty of conveying extreme or unbelievable emotions. Are we meant to believe that Oroonoko lies prostrate with grief for days? If not, what are we meant to believe? In tension with this, of course, is the text's detailed representation of the natural world of Surinam and the graphic depiction of physical violence (the visit to the Indian village, Imoinda's dead body, Oroonoko's self-immolation, his execution). The two modes of writing may reflect the theme that the ideal cannot survive in the real(istic) world. The focus may prompt good discussion of both style and themes in the novel.

With the full detailed treatment, the class focuses on a third character, the narrator, and the meta-narrative details she includes about the writing of the story. Beginning with the narrator's truth claims, you can introduce additional subjects like the gender of the author and the rise of the novel. The entire opening section provides ample illustration of the generic instability (or hybridity) of the text. It is memoir, biography, travel narrative; ironically her truth claims call into question the story's fictional status and consequently its frequent association with the novel. By addressing the narrator, however, you also introduce important issues of colonialism, race, and slavery. Not only does colonialism provide the occasion for Behn's visit to Surinam and thus for meeting Oroonoko, but colonialism also of course relies directly on slavery, which brings Oroonoko to the colony. Colonialism obviously shapes the plot of the story, but it also influences the way the story is told, the construction of the characters, and the thematic significance of the conclusion. Colonialism also informs the gender conflicts of the story, in particular the way the narrator absents herself from the scene of Oroonoko's rebellion and violence. This attention to gender then reflects back on the character of Imoinda and the narrator's treatment of her race and status.

The *Norton Topics Online* treatment of slavery will be useful for historical context in particular if students bring to class assumptions about slavery based on nineteenth-century American abolitionist texts. The slave trade for England was in its infancy during the period about which Behn writes, and her ideas of slavery were influenced by the economic and cultural advantages gained by colonialism.

Teaching Clusters

The Public Sphere and Civil Society. Behn's treatment of love and the natural gentility of Oroonoko and Imoinda might be treated in this cluster. The representation of the native inhabitants of the colony, what she calls the "Indians," includes a version of the noble savage. Note: Oroonoko is not a noble savage; he is extremely refined and was educated in European culture. The view of the colonies as a rich supplier of commodities also contributes to this cluster. In this way, the novel would pair well with Addison and Steele's essays, especially "Inkle and Yarico."

Authorship and Literacy: New Readers, New Writers, New Forms. *Oroonoko* illustrates both the new writer (a woman!) and new forms (see above). Behn's representation of herself throughout the text is ambivalently humble. Her fame and the popularity of her hero suggest an influence on later writers that would make the text a good choice for this cluster. It would pair well with Finch's "Introduction," as well as Haywood's prose fiction, *Fantomina*.

Explorations in Science and Nature. Behn's treatment of the natural world in the Surinam sections of the narrative belongs in this cluster. Her opening description of the colony's natural resources, the story of Oroonoko's exploits with the tigers and eels, and the visits to the "Indian" villages highlight the age's fascination with the exotic but real world beyond England's borders. In this way, the novel would pair well with *Rasselas*.

Politics of the Individual. Given Behn's Tory politics and the story's harsh treatment of commonwealth men, some readers have seen Oroonoko as a political allegory. As Caesar, Oroonoko represents the beleaguered Charles II; as martyr, Charles I. As the noble slave, however, he might best represent the conflicts that the current king, James II, faced as political struggles over religion, sovereignty, and proper authority boiled to a head in the Glorious Revolution. In this reading, Oroonoko's heroic refusal to be enslaved or to suffer humiliation serves as an idealized portrait of the sovereign's dignity, and his execution is an extreme expression of passive obedience.

Discussion Questions

1. In what sense is Oroonoko heroic? What are his dominant characteristics? How does he compare with other heroes of literature?
2. How does the novel represent slavery? What are Oroonoko's attitudes

toward slavery? The narrator's? Compare this with representations of slavery in the *Norton Topic Online* "Slavery and the Slave Trade."

3. Why is Oroonoko suffered to be a slave in name only? Why is this insufficient for him?
4. How does the story portray the love between Oroonoko and Imoinda? Why can't their love survive in Surinam?
5. Why does Oroonoko kill Imoinda? In what sense is his action justified? In what sense can it never be justified?
6. In what sense does Oroonoko become "exemplary" in the conclusion of the novel? What is he a symbol of?
7. Evaluate the grim violence that lies just beneath the surface of civility in the story, in particular in the execution of Oroonoko. What role does this grisly scene play? Is it appropriate? Why or why not?
8. Evaluate the narrator's self-representation. How do you explain the contradictions between the adoring biographer, the humble female pen, and the colonist who conveniently disappears when Oroonoko needs her?
9. In what ways does colonialism shape the story? See information on trade and expansion in *Norton Topics Online*.
10. How does Behn represent political power (either in Coramantien or in Surinam)? What is the basis of authority? What is an abuse of authority?

William Congreve

The Way of the World

Congreve's comedy reads like a modern-day soap opera, except that it is very polished and very witty. Because the plot is so complicated, and its pleasures rely less on surprise than on execution, it may be wise to give students a complete plot summary broken down by act before they read the play. The summary of relationships provided in the headnote offers essential information, and it can be used as a model for the summary here suggested.

Quick Read

- Form: Play in prose; comedy of manners.
- Main Characters: Mirabell (whom all the women love) and Millamant (who eventually marries Mirabell); Lady Wishfort (the controlling rich widow to whom everyone except Mirabell is related); Mrs. Fainall (Wishfort's daughter); Mr. Fainall (the villain); Mrs. Marwood (Mr. Fainall's mistress); Foible (servant to Wishfort).
- Key Scenes: Mirabell and Millamant's contract scene (Act 4); Fainall's negotiation for divorce (Act 5); revelation of Mrs. Fainall's deed of trust (Act 5).
- Key Themes: Lawful love is unfashionable; money is the prime mover; true wit and true love find their mark.

- Potential Pedagogical Challenges: This is a long and complicated play of talking and dense metaphorical wit; it requires slow reading.

Teaching Suggestions

Because of the complicated plot, it may help to develop a plot outline highlighting the real and intended (or hoped for) relationships between the characters. Part of the fun of the play relies on the overturning of expected hierarchies, such as outwitting the mother/rich widow by disguising a footman as her paramour. As suggested in the headnote, the dialogue needs to be appreciated for its polished gems of wit, but after careful reading the play ought to be brought to life through dramatic reading or staging. Drawing on the modern parallel of soap operas or celebrity gossip, ask students to imagine appropriate casting for the play. Who should play Mirabell? Who should play Fainall? Ask them to consider why the best actor of the time was assigned the role of the villain and not the hero. Who would play the many leading ladies? The first three acts may be slow, and so I recommend focusing on the fun and dramatic fourth act to stage or read aloud. The character of Sir Wilfull should be played with gusto!

Teaching Clusters

The Public Sphere and Civil Society. Congreve's play represents the moralized version of Restoration comedy, the "reformed" stage. References in the prologue to "so reformed a town" and to the entertaining reading of Lady Wishfort's closet (Act 3) suggest the tensions between the puritanical impulses of the 1690s and the Restoration libertine ethos that the play mildly represents through the adulterous Fainall and the prior history of Mirabell. The play could be taught with other literary treatments of the fashionable world, such as The Rape of the Lock, some of the Spectator essays, Fantomina, and Hogarth's painting sequence Marriage à la Mode.

Politics of the Individual. The cynical machinations that move the plot forward in The Way of the World have base self-interest at their core, and so a cluster on individualism might include this play. However, the play's concern with marriage and the proper bounds of behavior of married persons also works well with this cluster, especially if the section focuses on liberty and the circumscription of the wife's behavior in marriage. In this way, the play teaches well with Astell's and Defoe's excerpts, Wortley Montagu's "Epistle from Mrs. Yonge," and sections of Rasselas.

Discussion Questions

1. What is a reformed rake? What about Mirabell's behavior suggests that he is reformed?
2. Why is Lady Wishfort considered so repulsive? Why is she so powerful?

3. Why does Millamant read Suckling and Waller in Act 4? What does it mean that Mirabell can cap her verse?
4. What are Mirabell and Millamant actually negotiating in the contract scene of Act 4?
5. What appears to motivate the precipitous coupling of the other characters in the play (for example, Sir Rowland and Lady Wishfort)?
6. What is the significance of the class inversions in the play (for example, Waitwell becoming a knight and wooing a lady; Lady Wishfort becoming the "property" of her servant)?
7. Compare Fainall's negotiations for a divorce settlement in Act 5 with the marriage contract scene in the previous act. What values are expressed in each? What does this say about the characters involved? What values appear to win out in the end?
8. Why does Mirabell return the deed of trust to Mrs. Fainall?
9. Examine the illustrations of theatres in the *Norton Topic Online* "A Day in Eighteenth-Century London." How might the design of the theatre affect the staging and acting of this play?

Further Resources

NORTON ONLINE ARCHIVE

Love for Love

Mary Astell

Some Reflections upon Marriage

Astell's prose is a refreshing change from the dominant male-authored views of marriage in the Restoration, and it compares well with other satires of the period. While Dryden, Rochester, and Congreve represent women and marriage as burdens to male freedom, Astell provides the view of marriage from the perspective of women. It was, in fact, women who literally gave up their liberty (and rights) upon marriage, and no amount of flattery in courtship changed that fact. Astell's underlying message to women in the essay is to wake up and see marriage for what it really is before they decide to accept a "monarch for life." The excerpts here demonstrate her range of argument, addressing the reasons for male choice in marriage partner through the requirements of a proper wife. They also reveal her command of different styles and tones, from logical argument to devastating sarcasm to aphoristic wit.

Quick Read

- Form: Excerpted prose essay, satirical.
- Main Points: Men choose wives poorly, based on irregular appetites; women are educated solely to find a husband; women ought to be educated in philosophy so as to conform their minds to resignation

and subservience; marriage is a poor lot for women, but proper subservience will qualify them for heaven.

- Key Aphorism: "Thus, whether it be wit or beauty that a man's in love with, there's no great hopes of a lasting happiness; beauty, with all the helps of art, is of no very lasting date; the more it is helped, the sooner it decays; and he, who only or chiefly chose for beauty, will in a little time find the same reason for another choice" (2286).
- Key Aphorism: "A husband indeed is thought by both sexes so very valuable, that scarce a man who can keep himself clean and make a bow, but thinks he is good enough to pretend to any woman" (2286–87).
- Key Aphorism: "And for this reason 'tis less to be wondered at that women marry off in haste, for perhaps if they took time to consider and reflect upon it, they seldom would" (2288)

Teaching Suggestions

Students may take issue with Astell's representation of marrying for love, and this disagreement can provide a useful way to introduce similarities and differences between marriage then and now. Supplemental reading on marriage law—an appropriate excerpt from Blackstone's *Commentaries on the Laws of England* (1765–69), chapter 15, regarding marriage and divorce, for example—would illustrate the absolute conditions of marriage for women. As put by *The Lawes Resolution of Women's Rights* in 1632, all women were understood as married or to be married and as such were subsumed into the political authority of their husbands. Divorce with the ability to remarry was virtually unheard of, although some husbands could "put their wives away" for the crime of adultery (and this is suggested in *The Way of the World*). With these understandings, students may come to see why Astell wants men and women to choose their spouses very carefully.

Teaching Clusters

Politics of the Individual. This excerpt belongs in any course focusing on marriage and liberty because it highlights the absolute power relations between husband and wife. While Astell focuses on the rewards of heaven to be gained by living a virtuous life of servitude, she does not mince words in any romantic way about love and marriage. Astell's views are echoed in other works on marriage, such as Defoe's *Roxana*, Wortley Montague's "Epistle from Mrs. Yonge," and sections of *Rasselas*. Her reference to women as the slaves of men resonates with many other protofeminist evaluations of marriage and ties into the debates over individual freedom and slavery. See her lively preface to the fourth edition excerpted in the In-text Topic on "Liberty."

Discussion Questions

1. At what point is it appropriate, according to Astell, to consider money in marriage decisions? Why?
2. Why is marrying for love as doomed to failure as marrying for money?
3. If wit is so fashionable (cf. *The Way of the World*), why does Astell criticize it?
4. Why don't women "choose" a spouse? How is it different today?
5. What do you suppose would be Astell's argument for a good choice in marriage partner? (This is not included in the *NAEL* excerpts, but students may be able to interpolate the answer; i.e., good moral character, equality of mind, status and wealth.)
6. Examine the tone of Astell's comments on flattery. What does her sarcasm suggest about the routine modes of courtship? (See *The Way of the World* and *Fantomina* for examples.)
7. Why should women be educated to something other than finding a husband?
8. In her final paragraph, how does Astell describe the purely good wife? What compensation does such behavior merit?
9. How does Astell's wisdom and advice play in modern times? What remains the same? What changes have made it obsolete?

Daniel Defoe

Roxana

In many ways, Roxana's arguments against marriage sound a modern note, and students will find them appealing. The expression of sexual liberation and independence of fortune have decidedly feminist themes. However, students ought not to be misled by Roxana's rhetoric, which even she admits runs away from her. Her motivations for not marrying are, first, financial pragmatism in the face of property laws in marriage and, second, when the Dutch merchant obviates the first, saving face. The eloquent defense of women's independence is feigned.

Quick Read

- Form: Prose narrative; fictional biography.
- Main Characters: Roxana; the Dutch merchant.
- Themes: Ambition corrupts and leads you from your true interest; lies beget lies; arguments for sexual equality are morally expedient.
- Key Points: Husband acquires the wife's property upon marriage; husbands have the ability to give up that control; marriage is customary, ordained by heaven, and essential for creating legitimate offspring; women's place in marriage is unequal to men's.

Teaching Suggestions

If you set aside the framing narrative for a moment, the debate over the pros and cons of marriage for women is of genuine interest. Ask the students to examine the arguments for each side and to consider the legitimacy of each position. You could even stage a debate, but I wouldn't recommend making this men against women because the issues today are less gender-based than value-based. For example, Roxana demands the ability to control her own finances, which legally she will be unable to do in marriage. Today financial arrangements in marriage are a matter of personal choice and cultural expectations, not sex-specific law. Some women may enjoy the idea of eating "the fat" and drinking "the sweet" of their husband's labor; others may find this repulsive. The question of sexual freedom outside of marriage similarly reflects different sets of cultural values that cannot be anticipated along strictly gendered lines. If your goal is to learn about the conditions of marriage in the eighteenth century, then a review of this debate will serve the purpose. However, to appreciate the complexity of Defoe's representation, one must return to the framing device and assess Roxana's motives for making a case that she really didn't believe.

Teaching Clusters

Politics of the Individual. Roxana's claim that marriage rendered a wife "at best, but an upper servant" and that it deprived a woman of her "liberty, estate, authority" places this excerpt clearly in the cluster on politics and the individual. Although she doesn't believe in them, Roxana voices the terms of debate over marriage current in her society. People who criticized the laws of the institution, and more centrally, the customs of marriage, commonly viewed women as "slaves," and in this way the text teaches well in discussions on liberty of the individual. Roxana even speaks of marriage as a contract, echoing the language of Locke's views of contractual government. The excerpt teaches well (and borrows from) Astell's writings as well as Finch's "Introduction," Wortley Montagu's "Epistle from Mrs. Yonge," and sections of *Rasselas*.

Discussion Questions

1. What is Roxana's principal objection to marrying the Dutch Merchant? Why doesn't she acknowledge this?
2. What arguments does she make against marriage in general?
3. What arguments does the Dutch Merchant offer to counter these?
4. What role does procreation play in their respective arguments?
5. Where Roxana has law on her side of the argument (the laws are against women), the Dutch Merchant offers affection, religion, and custom as inducements to marry. What does this alignment of reasons suggest about relative motivations for marriage?
6. How accurate is the Dutch Merchant's picture of the wife of leisure? How persuasive is his enticement?

7. Why does Roxana imagine such extremes of poverty in marriage? How persuasive is her fear?
8. How does Defoe's representation of the pros and cons of marriage play in modern times? What objections to marriage remain? What inducements? What has changed?
9. As the headnote to Astell suggests, "to question the customs and laws of marriage is to question society itself, its distribution of money and power and love." What is Defoe's point in this fictional representation? If this is social criticism, what is being criticized?

Further Resources

NORTON ONLINE ARCHIVE

The History and Remarkable Life of the Truly Honorable Col. Jaques
A True Revelation of the Apparition of One Mrs. Veal

Anne Finch

A Nocturnal Reverie

In a series of calm, meditative, descriptive adverbial clauses, Finch draws out a single sentence into a fifty-line poem. The idea behind the poem is deceptively simple, and the imagery so gentle and captivating that the reader hardly realizes Finch is using the same poetic line as Dryden and Pope. The nocturnal world in its peaceful harmony and imaginative freedom offers the speaker (and the soul) profound respite. The closing couplets reassert an order and rationality that places the poem squarely in its Augustan context.

Quick Read

- Form: Landscape poem, meditation, in iambic pentameter couplets.
- Key Images: Zephyr, 3; Philomel, 4; catalogue of flowers, 13–16; Salisbury, 19; "tyrant man," 38; "free soul," 43.
- Key Passage: Closing four lines.

Teaching Suggestions

Reading the poem aloud slowly, ask the students to attend to the sense imagery in the first forty-six lines. You might even suggest that they close their eyes as you read so that they can imagine the scene. The poem moves from aural images, to faint visual images, to olfactory images, as the speaker walks the landscape at night. Ask the students to attend to the title and work through the images and their significance in order to appreciate why the soul finds itself (herself) in harmony with this landscape. The last four lines of the poem return the speaker to the rational world of daylight and so set up a series of parallels that the poem puts into question. In its two-part structure, the poem neatly introduces several tensions typical of Augustan literature, but with a twist. Here the emphasis of the poem lies on the night, the imagination, the senses, the natural world, the darkness, the feminine. The change in tone, rhythm, and sound of the final lines is so sudden and marked that it underscores the difference of the values being reasserted in daylight.

Because of Wordsworth's attention to the poem (see headnote), many readers want to call it "pre-Romantic." While this may help create some useful continuities in a survey course, attention should be paid to the way Finch adopts the typically Augustan poetic style: the couplet form, the use of poetic diction, conceits, elision, inversion, personification, gendered abstractions, paradox. In this way, it may be interesting to compare the poem with Pope's lines, perhaps in *Eloisa to Abelard*, which explore some of the same tensions. The poem may be taught with "The Introduction" by drawing attention to the parallels between the role of the female writer and the feminine presence in "Nocturnal Reverie." See other poems by Finch in the In-text Topic "Debating Women" and the *Online Archive*.

Teaching Clusters

As a landscape poem that focuses on intense observation of the natural world, "Nocturnal Reverie" belongs in the **Explorations in Science and Nature** cluster. Because it questions the human placement in the natural world, it would be taught well with some of the later landscape poetry by Cowper, Crabbe, and Goldsmith. Of course, "Nocturnal Reverie" pairs well with some of the Romantic landscape poems, particularly Charlotte Smith's sonnets and Wordsworth's "Tintern Abbey." An entire segment of nighttime poetry might also include the excerpt from Thomson's *Autumn* on night, Gray's "Elegy," Collins's "Ode to Evening," the excerpt from Cowper's *The Task*, Smith's "To Night," Wordsworth's "It is a beauteous evening," and Keats's "Ode to a Nightingale" and "Bright star."

"The Introduction" can be taught in either the cluster on **Authorship and Literacy: New Readers, New Writers, New Forms** or the one on **Politics of the Individual**. In the former, the poem serves as a veritable statement of the female author's conflicts in the public forum of print (and might help explain part of the impulse toward coterie manuscript culture), and in the latter the poem's emphasis on the misogynist customs of her society offers insights into the problems of female liberty.

Discussion Questions

1. How is the poem punctuated? What effect does the punctuation have on the meaning of the poem?
2. What sense is highlighted in the opening lines? Why is this appropriate? What senses are highlighted in lines 7–12? Why is this appropriate?
3. Why is the soul "to a composedness charmed" in this landscape?

4. What is feminine in this landscape? (Pay particular attention to the figures of Philomel, Salisbury, the gendered soul.) What is the significance of the emphasis on the feminine?
5. In what sense is "man" a "tyrant"? Over whom or what?
6. How does the sound of the final four lines differ from that of the rest of the poem? What does this change in sound signify?
7. What parallels do the final lines construct? What is the significance?
8. Evaluate the paradox that darkness brings clarity.

Further Resources

NORTON ONLINE ARCHIVE

On Myself

Matthew Prior

An Epitaph

Writing amusing epitaphs was something of a fad in the eighteenth century, and one can begin this class with the question of genre. Why would this "genre"—and Prior's representation of it—appeal to a culture that valued the Horatian goals of pleasure and instruction? What is amusing or instructive about an epitaph? By fulfilling the impulse to memorialize the dead, an epitaph offers the occasion to summarize a person's life. As satire, the epitaph provides the opportunity to showcase the failings of that life through decorous irony and then to apply the implicit lessons to humanity in general.

Quick Read

- Form: Satirical epitaph, in iambic tetrameter couplets.
- Characters: Jack and Joan.
- Themes: The middle way may prevent vice but does not secure virtue; as you live so you shall die.

Teaching Suggestions

The concept of irony will be central to teaching this poem. Prior's irony works on the level of genre (this is not how one would want to be remembered) and on the level of moral ideals. While eighteenth-century moral writing often touted the *via media* as virtuous, astute satirists like Prior, Swift, and later Johnson saw the limitations of the practice of moderation. As Johnson would have Nekayah explain in *Rasselas*, " 'Nature sets her gifts on the right hand and on the left.' . . . There are goods so opposed that we cannot seize both, but by too much prudence, may pass between them at too great a distance to reach either." Swift explores the limitations of a purely rational life in book 4 of *Gulliver's Travels*. In "An Epitaph," Prior exposes the moral bankruptcy of people who appear to be perfectly decent. Explore how the memorial to this stable couple gradually changes from stanza to stanza, as Prior builds a case for their selfish lack of concern for others.

As an epitaph, the poem might feature in a cluster of works that highlight death and memorials, such as Swift's *Verses on the Death of Dr. Swift*, the section on the Struldbruggs in *Gulliver's Travels*, Leapor's "Epistle to a Lady," Johnson's "On the Death of Doctor Levet," Gray's "Elegy," Wordsworth's "Extempore Effusion," and Shelley's *Adonais*.

Teaching Clusters

By raising the implicit moral that we all owe something to the society in which we live, something more than paying the poor tax, Prior's poem plays into the themes of a cluster on **Politics of the Individual**. As the country moved toward a parliamentary government, where laws, taxes, and rights regulated the interactions of society, Tory satirists tended to lament the passing of older social ties of community. Sauntering Jack and Idle Joan represent the moral passivity of people concerned only with their own welfare. Prior's "epitaph" serves as a public exposure of such a meaningless life.

Discussion Questions

1. How would you describe the life of Jack and Joan? What makes them an appropriate subject for a poem?
2. What does the poem praise about them? What does the poem censure? How do you know?
3. When does prudence become selfishness?
4. How might Jack and Joan appear in their community?
5. In what sense is the poem an "epitaph" for Jack and Joan? What does it memorialize?
6. What lessons does the satire offer for humanity in general?
7. Why is the genre of the epitaph particularly effective in relating truths about the way we live our lives?

Further Resources

NORTON ONLINE ARCHIVE

A True Maid

Jonathan Swift

Clearly one of the most important writers of the era, Swift is a supreme ironist whose writings remain as well known today as anyone's works from the period. His prose satire is frequently excerpted, and *Gulliver's Travels* has passed into iconicity through numerous reproductions in story, film, and artifact. The poetry, though less read, is also important. The guide will highlight three of Swift's works: *Verses on the Death of Dr. Swift*, book 4 of *Gulliver's Travels*, and "A Modest Proposal."

Verses on the Death of Dr. Swift

What prompts a person to write his own epitaph? Swift's verses on his death are both an example of the satirist turning his craft on himself and a witty analysis of his impact on culture. In the poem he employs the tools of defamiliarization and satiric personae, but he offers a far more personal statement than in his other more famous works. The poem consequently teases us with insights into the author himself.

Quick Read

- Form: Mock elegy in iambic tetrameter.
- Style: Lively, conversational, irreverent.
- Key Passages: Rochefoucauld's maxim, 1–38; Pope's couplets, 45–52; importance of Swift's irony, 55–66; predictions of Swift's death, 71–146; reactions of friends, 205–42; satire on the print culture, 253–98; self-portrait, 307–484; Swift's satire, 455–74.
- Themes: We find something in the adversity of our friends that does not displease us; death is our common fate; we survive in the memory of those whose lives we touch.

Teaching Suggestions

The opening passage of Swift's *Verses* presents a negative view of human nature that students respond to quite passionately, some in agreement and some in shock. Allow students to consider the paradox of enjoying a friend's misfortune and question what it means for Swift to open his epitaph in this way. What are we to expect by way of a memorial to himself if he has such a low view of human nature? This maxim allows him to imagine the benefit his misfortune will bring to others, and it is through this lens that he views his decline and death. While he ironically presents the predictions of his death and the various responses of his friends, enemies, and culture at large, he also gives us genuine insight into his values—literary, moral, political. For example, his lines on Pope's couplets are an accurate assessment of Pope's strengths, and you can use these lines to teach the difference between Pope's tightly compressed iambic pentameter and Swift's loose, conversational tetrameter couplets. By suggesting the virtues that raise his envy, he tells the reader what he values in his own writing, and in this way the poem can serve as a commentary on his other works. His satire on grief is a hilarious understatement of his friends' value for him, but the most significant part of the poem lies in the "impartial portrait" drawn by an observer. Like the moment when the projector drops his mask in "A Modest Proposal," this section contains Swift's most straightforward presentation of his sentiments.

In particular, the lines on "too much satire in his vein" may help students understand the intentions behind Swift's intense satire.

Teaching Clusters

The emphasis on a writing culture and the writing relationships Swift formed throughout his life makes this poem a good choice for **Authorship and Literacy: New Readers, New Writers, New Forms.** His representation of the print shop a year after his death offers a view of Grub Street akin to that in Dryden's "Mac Flecknoe" and Pope's *Dunciad*.

In the impartial portrait, Swift includes a detailed account of his political motivations and the strong sense of liberty that motivated his defense of Ireland. In this way, the poem teaches well with other works on liberty in the **Politics of the Individual** cluster. As a mock epitaph, the *Verses* parallel Prior's "An Epitaph," but typically Swift takes the joke to elaborate extremes.

Discussion Questions

1. What does Rochefoucauld's maxim suggest about Swift's view of humanity?
2. Note the use of different voices in the poem. How does Swift use this technique? What is the effect?
3. How do the various groups respond to news of Swift's death?
4. Why does Swift include the people he does? Who is missing?
5. What happens to the author a year after his death? To what extent is this an accurate picture of Swift's fate?
6. What do we learn about Swift in the "impartial" character? What does he value about himself?
7. How "impartial" is the character Swift gives us?
8. If Swift is really a misanthropist, then why does he devote so much energy to preserving the dignity of the race?
9. What do the verses tell us about Swift's ideas on satire? To what extent is this a helpful commentary on his own writing?

Gulliver's Travels

Swift's best-known work during his lifetime and thereafter, *Gulliver's Travels* is a brilliant satire on many levels. The descriptions of Lilliput, Brobdingnag, and Laputa satirize different aspects of eighteenth-century English society—its politics, its wars, its new science. But increasingly the satire also focuses on the human animal. Physically, the Lilliputians appear charming and delicate—like toys—to Gulliver, and he seems repulsive to them. Only gradually does he come to see their pride, pettiness, and meanness. In Brobdingnag, these conditions are exactly reversed, and Gulliver's own pride and nastiness emerge in his offer to make gunpowder for the king. Harder questions are raised by the great and controversial fourth book. Here, for once, Swift's point of view is not entirely clear. The account of Gulliver's travel to the land of Houyhnhnms challenges our most fundamental and cherished views of human nature. While Swift's contemporaries enjoyed the earlier books for their satire, the figure of the debased Yahoo as an analogue for the human being deeply disturbed them. Commentary over the years has helped readers acquire a more complete understanding of Swift's troubling representation of virtue and vice, and the fourth book stands alone well as an excellent representative of Swift's complex prose satire.

Quick Read: Book 4

- Form: Prose satire, fictional travel narrative, fable.
- Style: First-person account; empirical rhetoric; clean, simple, descriptive sentences.
- Key Passages: Chapter 1, encountering the Yahoos and Houyhnhnms; chapter 3, Gulliver assimilates; chapters 4–6, Gulliver's narrative of England; chapter 7, Gulliver's decision to remain with the Houyhnhnms; chapter 9, General Assembly; chapter 10, Gulliver's banishment; chapter 11, Captain Pedro de Mendez; chapter 12, Gulliver reconciled to his Yahoo family.
- Key Terms: Satiric fable or narrative: the journey to the Houyhnhnms; satiric persona: Gulliver; defamiliarization: presenting the familiar through a lens of distortion in order to see it in a new way.

Teaching Suggestions

Teaching *Gulliver's Travels* demands some attention to the formal aspects of satire. Most definitions of satire will include the following elements: distortion through verbal pictures, an attitude of censure, and wit or humor, all intended to improve humanity or expose vice. For *Gulliver's Travels*, the primary mode of distortion is through the fictional travel narrative or fable, in this case Gulliver's journey to the land of the Houyhnhnms. In this imaginative story, we read about speaking horses and incoherent brutish humans. The fiction includes details that distort reality in a way that calls attention to their meaning. We ask, what is the significance of the race of virtuous Houyhnhnms and vicious Yahoos? What does it mean for Gulliver to be at first amazed at this world and gradually to acclimate and internalize its values, even after he returns to the "normal" world of England?

Swift also relies on the technique of defamiliarization—as he does throughout *Gulliver's Travels*—a method of representing the everyday world and its values in such a way as to render them unfamiliar and consequently worth evaluating. Here the value of reason is owned by horses, who in the "normal" world are brutes, and vice is embodied in animalist humans, who are supposed to be rational creatures. By characterizing all the actions of the Houyhnhnms as governed by reason, Swift highlights the virtue of reason and also, incidentally, its limitations. By rendering vice in the figure of a debased human being, Swift highlights the repulsiveness of behaviors characterized by selfish brutality. He also uses this technique to great effect in having Gulliver recount the history of and current political situation in England. What happens to common notions of war or government when Gulliver explains them to beings governed solely by reason?

Finally, the character of Gulliver is another significant medium for Swift's satire. By creating this fictional voice, Swift removes himself from the work and adopts a persona through which he can criticize his world. This technique gives the satirist a great deal of imaginative freedom, but it can pose difficulties for the reader. As a full, developed character, Gulliver operates according to the strengths and weaknesses of his character. We receive information through his judgment and understanding, and so the reader needs to be attuned to the limitations of this vision. What character flaws or blindspots impede Gulliver's judgment? When do we believe Gulliver? When does Gulliver himself become the object of satire?

Teaching Clusters

Because it questions the very nature of humanity, the fourth book of *Gulliver's Travels* teaches well in the cluster on **Explorations in Science and Nature**. It treats in greater detail the issues raised by Rochester in *A Satire against Reason and Mankind* and challenges the more optimistic views of humanity represented in Addison's "On the Scale of Being" and Pope's *Essay on Man*. As a fictional travel narrative and a proto-novel, the text teaches well next to *Oroonoko*; one might compare the rhetoric of empirical observation used in both narratives and the different effects achieved. Similarly, the fictional travel narrative and the concern with exotic locales anticipate Johnson's *Rasselas*, and later Mary Shelley's *Frankenstein*.

Discussion Questions

1. What is Gulliver's reaction to being considered a Yahoo? Why is this significant?
2. Evaluate the notion of "saying the thing that is not." What role does language play in the Houyhnhnm world?
3. What is the point of Gulliver's account of war and law in England?
4. Why does Gulliver decide to never lie again and never to return to human society?
5. How is the society of the Yahoos (described in chapter 8) different from (inferior to) the society of the Houyhnhnms?
6. What does reason dictate regarding reproduction, death, and art?
7. What does the Grand Assembly debate and conclude? To what extent is this a valid response to the problem?
8. What is the significance of Pedro de Mendez?
9. Are the purely rational Houyhnhnms really ideal beings?
10. What are Gulliver's limitations as a narrator? What has he really learned from the virtues of the Houyhnhnms?

11. Examine the illustration of Gulliver in the land of the Houyhnhnms in the *NAEL* color insert. How does this picture comment upon the text?

A Modest Proposal

Succinct, memorable, and brutally clear, Swift's famous essay may already be familiar to your students, but even if your students have read it for another class, the powerful work of this master ironist merits repeated attention. On one level, it is a superb example of irony and controlled rage. On another level, it documents the colonial history of Ireland and the desperation of its inhabitants. On yet another level, it sounds a chord of humanitarianism that continues to be significant in this world of haves and have-nots.

Quick Read

- Form: Satiric prose essay, mock proposal.
- Key Techniques: Persona of projector, irony.
- Key Passages: Mathematical reckoning of population, 2463; "a young healthy child . . . is at a year old a most delicious, nourishing, and wholesome food," 2464; food proper for landlords, 2464; six advantages gained, 2466; "let no man talk to me of other expedients . . ." 2467.

Teaching Suggestions

Because the proposal to sell one-year-old infants as flesh like so many pigs for market is patently outrageous and taboo, students will readily see the irony of Swift's satire. In some ways, this essay teaches itself, but you can aid your students by analyzing the techniques that Swift uses to achieve his effects. As with *Gulliver's Travels*, Swift adopts a persona with definite limitations in judgment. You can address the same questions on persona here: What character flaws or blindspots impede the projector's judgment? When do we believe the projector? When does the projector himself become the object of satire? One can explore the assumptions behind the projector's reckoning of so many human souls in monetary terms, particularly within a context of slavery and colonialism. Ask the students to gauge their sympathy for the projector's cause (if not his solution) throughout the piece, and spend time analyzing the list of actual expedients that Swift ironically introduces at the end. What keeps Ireland from adopting these more humane expedients?

Teaching Clusters

Politics of the Individual. Because this essay addresses the issues of colonial control, it will teach well in the cluster on politics. Swift's projector, although ironic, nonetheless raises relevant issues in the discussion of human cargo and the moral implications of trafficking in human flesh. As such it teaches well with other treatments of slavery, such as *Oroonoko*, the excerpt from Equiano's *Interesting Narrative*, and Johnson's "A Brief to Free a Slave."

Discussion Questions

1. In what sense does the essay make literal the metaphor that the English are devouring the Irish? What is the relationship between the metaphoric devouring and the literal starvation of the Irish people?
2. Swift lets the mask of the persona slip at several points in the essay: where does Swift's genuine sentiment emerge?
3. Discuss the brutality of the imagery (for example, "dressing them hot from the knife"). To what extent is this effective? Why?
4. Why is the comparison between the economic state of Ireland and the cannibalism of infants appropriate?
5. What is the moral purpose of Swift's satire?
6. Who is Swift's audience for the satire?
7. Are there modern parallels for which the satire would be applicable?

Further Resources

NORTON ONLINE ARCHIVE

An Argument against the Abolishing of Christianity in England
A Tale of a Tub

Addison and Steele

Essays from The Spectator

At the end of the eighteenth century, Jane Austen wrote, "Now had the same young lady been engaged with a volume of the *Spectator*, instead of [a novel], how proudly would she have produced the book and told its name" (*Northanger Abbey*, published posthumously in 1818). *The Spectator* apparently achieved its goal of becoming the Socrates of polite society; however, the style and contents of its pages would not remain in vogue past the start of the nineteenth century. Reading Addison and Steele's periodical essays offers a glimpse into the changing social world of the period and provides much information on its morals, values, and interests. The *Spectator*'s popularity during the eighteenth century and its influence over the literate masses make it especially important.

Quick Read

- Form: Periodical prose essays.
- Style: Informal, brief, "middle style," humor, satire.
- Topics: Men's social club, improving society, female constancy, benefits of world trade, literary criticism, imagination, metaphysics.
- More *Spectator* essays are available in the Norton Online Archive.

Teaching Suggestions

The brief essays are easy to teach individually to accompany certain clusters or topics, but if you teach them independently as a group the following collaborative exercise can help draw out some of the social dynamics created around the new form of the popular periodical essay.

The Club: Ask students to form small groups of no more than five or six members and to imagine they make up a reading club that meets at a coffeehouse or drawing room of a prominent lady of fashion. One of the chief activities is sharing the daily paper and discussing it. Recall that the *Spectator* imagines there are twenty readers for every one of the *Spectator* issues sold. Ask them to imagine they are part of the audience addressed by the *Spectator* in number 10 and to discuss the issues or topics that speak most to their imagined character. You might target the essay "Inkle and Yarico" because it raises issues about gender, love, capitalism, and empire that might be particularly interesting or accessible. The essay on dueling, which is available in the archive, is another important social document that raises issues of masculine honor and violence. You can provide simple discussion questions to guide the small-group work or let them handle it in their own way. After allowing time for independent discussion, bring the class together in a general discussion to evaluate what they learned in the exercise. You might gear this discussion toward questions about who or what the students identified with, or if the works seemed alien to them, you might address what the essays tell them about a culture so different from our own.

Teaching Clusters

The "Spectator's Club" and "Aims of the Spectator" belong in the **Public Sphere and Civil Society** cluster. In many ways, these are the documents that made possible a cluster on these topics! The "Inkle and Yarico" essay can be taught in **Explorations in Science and Nature** as a moral tale of love and empire, and so it pairs well with *Oroonoko* and *Rasselas*. Likewise, the essay on "The Pleasures of the Imagination" can help to amplify the significance of Newton's and Locke's excerpts on light and understanding. The last essay, on "The Scale of Being," also is appropriately taught along with Locke and anticipates the deist appreciation in Pope's *Essay on Man*. It offers a nice contrast to Rochester's and Swift's attacks on human reason. The essays of literary criticism (on wit, on *Paradise Lost*) can be taught as documents in the **Authorship and Literacy: New Readers, New Writers, New Forms** cluster; indeed, as examples of a new form, all of the periodical essays can be taught in this context, and they pair well with Johnson's *Rambler* and *Idler* essays and later nineteenth-century prose essays by Lamb and Hazlitt.

Discussion Questions

1. Who are the members of the *Spectator* club?
2. What does this membership suggest about the organization of Addison and Steele's society? Who is missing? Why?
3. What are the *Spectator*'s goals? What does it mean to be the Socrates of the tea table?
4. Why are female readers particularly likely to benefit from the essays?
5. What do the essays teach you about eighteenth-century London life?
6. How would you evaluate the political implications of the celebration of the Royal Exchange? Are there modern parallels?
7. In what sense is trade an extension of empire? (Compare the problems for Ireland expressed in Swift's "A Modest Proposal.") See *Norton Topic Online* "Travel, Trade and Expansion of Empire" for more information and illustrations.
8. Why is Addison so interested in determining true, false, and mixed wit? What is at stake in the discussion?
9. Why does Addison choose *perception* as the foundation of consciousness in a living creature and therefore a key to its placement on the scale of being? See *Norton Topic Online* "Plurality of Worlds" for more information and illustrations.
10. In the end of the essay on the scale of being, Addison claims that no creature deserves as much attention as "man." Why? What are the implications of making "man" the central focus? What evidence do you see for this shift (from deity to man) in the literature of the age?

Further Resources

NORTON ONLINE ARCHIVE

Addison: Pary Patches (*Spectator* 81)
Steele: The Trial of the Petticoat (*Tatler* 116)
Steele: The Gentleman; The Pretty Fellow (*Tatler* 21)
Steele: Dueling (*Tatler* 25)
Addison: Sir Roger at Church (*Spectator* 112)
Addison: Sir Roger at the Assizes (*Spectator* 122)

Alexander Pope

Like Swift and Dryden, Pope stands as one of the most important writers of the era, and so the guide will highlight three of his works: *An Essay on Criticism, The Rape of the Lock,* and *Epistle to Dr. Arbuthnot.* Pope's mastery of poetic language and form requires attention, and so time should be spent in class addressing the characteristics of Pope's style and the strategies for unpacking and appreciating the wit and music of his poetic lines. In particular it will be helpful for you to introduce or emphasize the following techniques: parallelism, balance, antithesis, elision, syntactical inversion, personifications, abstractions. The headnote will provide some good starting points for attending to his use of sound. Also recommended, the excerpt from Johnson's *Life of Pope* provides insight into Pope's methods of composition and his poetic practice.

An Essay on Criticism

This is an excellent poem to use to introduce Alexander Pope's art as well as the Augustan era itself. Because its subject is critical thinking about poetry, the students may have a difficult time at first, but with some guidance it can become an important work for illuminating the literature of the whole period. This would be a good candidate for selective excerpting for in-class close reading. If you provide an overall summary of the poem's parts beforehand (several are available on the Web), the students will be able to focus closely on shorter pieces while appreciating the whole. Before the students read the poem, challenge them to find the most quotable lines, such as "A little learning is a dangerous thing" and "For fools rush in where angels fear to tread"!

Quick Read

- Form: Imitation of Horace, the art of poetry (or criticism) in iambic pentameter couplets, three parts.
- Style: Conversational language, well-read ease.
- Key Phrases: "And mark the point where sense and dullness meet," 50–51; "Nature methodized," 89; "Nature and Homer were, he found, the same," 135; "And snatch a grace beyond the reach of art," 155; "A little learning . . . ," 215–16; "True wit is Nature to advantage dressed," 297; "To err is human, to forgive divine," 525; "For fools rush in where angels fear to tread," 625.
- Key Themes: Bad criticism is worse than bad poetry; Nature is the best guide; Pride is the greatest flaw in judgment and human nature.
- Potential Pedagogical Challenges: It is long; the couplets are compressed.

Teaching Suggestions

After reviewing the structure and main points that Pope makes in the essay, break down key passages for close reading and practice unpacking the meaning of the couplets. What Pope apparently creates with such ease is quite difficult for students to appreciate at first. Taking the opening eight lines, examine the basic idea he advances and explore the use of parallelism, particularly in the third couplet. Note the way that the couplet form creates a natural binary between lines Pope also uses the caesura to create a subset of binaries within the line. Students tend to have a difficult time with "this" and "that" and the way Pope (and others) use the pronouns to create a shorthand for continuing the ideas of the previous couplets. Pope tends to match the antecedents with mathematical precision. More than anything, it is crucial to get the students to feel as though they *can* understand these lines, and so reading and interpreting together as a class is immensely useful.

To examine an important conceit, take the opening lines of part 2, where Pope introduces the central problem of pride. Much time can be profitably spent on the section where Pope describes the importance of variety in versification (337–83); these couplets end with an encomium to Dryden and especially his poem *Alexander's Feast*. The lines on sound being an echo to sense are frequently excerpted and for good reason. Pope memorably illustrates the sound devices that he criticizes. These are excellent tools for teaching students to attend to the sound of poetry.

Another common stumbling block in teaching Pope's couplets is the use of inversion. Be sure to take some good examples and illustrate for the students how the syntax operates. For example, "Envy will merit, as its shade, pursue" (466) should be understood to say that envy will pursue merit as its shade. The meaning is complicated also by the use of abstraction and metaphor. Similarly, "Blunt truths more mischief than nice falsehoods do" (573) should be read as "Blunt truths do more mischief than nice falsehoods," a line that illustrates the use of antithesis with blunt truths and nice falsehoods.

Teaching Clusters

Clearly Pope's *Essay on Criticism* belongs to a cluster on **Authorship and Literacy**. It takes as its object the training of critics in a new era of refined taste. The work alludes to a burgeoning practice in literary criticism, which in fact would take place during Pope's lifetime. The *Essay* teaches well with Dryden's "Mac Flecknoe," which also discusses through irony the literary values that Pope highlights. Together the two pieces are complimented by the excerpt from Johnson's *Life of Pope*, which offers some contrasts with Dryden.

Discussion Questions

1. Pope seems to be as much concerned with the moral qualities of the critic as his literary qualifications. Why? To what extent might these be connected?
2. What is Pope's attitude toward "the rules" in this poem? What is his attitude toward originality?
3. What role does Nature play in the work of great writers like Homer? What role should it play for critics?
4. Whom does Pope include in his catalogue of great writers and critics? What is the significance of this list?
5. What are the primary aesthetic values expressed in this piece?
6. How do Pope's couplets complement the aesthetic ideas expressed?
7. Evaluate the poet's self-reference in the closing lines of the poem. What purpose does it serve?

The Rape of the Lock

In *The Rape of the Lock*, Pope tells a classic story in a delightful way. Although the psychological dimensions of Augustan poetry are often underplayed in favor of figures of logic and intellectual or moral themes, Pope lavishes attention on his characters and their world(s) in this poem and creates a compelling psychological drama that engages the students. Pope's richly visual and charmingly musical poem illustrates how the language of poetry constructs a psychological environment for the narrative. An initial focus on the beauty, emotions, and eros that emerge from the details and sounds of the poem will allow for a more meaningful discussion of Pope's satire and mock-epic form. Once you bring the students into Belinda's bedroom or the elegant rooms of Hampton court, they will be more able to discuss the question of what is trivial and what is grand. In the end, it is not at all certain that Pope himself was not ensnared by the beauty of the lock he created. Once they care about the aborted affair between Belinda and the Baron, they will be ready to discuss the numerous comparisons between Pope and Milton, Virgil, and Homer.

Quick Read

- Form: Mock-epic, heroic couplets, five cantos.
- Key Characters: Belinda, Ariel, the Baron, Umbriel, Clarissa, Thalestris, Sir Plume.
- Key Passages: Invocation, 1.1–10; Belinda's dream, 1.105–15; arming of Belinda, 1.121–48; Baron's sacrifice, 2.35–46; Guardian sylphs, 2.55–136; Hampton court, 3.1–24; game of ombre, 3.25–100; severing the lock, 3.125–54; Cave of Spleen, 4.16–88; Clarissa's speech, 5.9–34; the battle for the lock, 5.53–112; ascension of the lock, 5.123–40.
- Key Themes: Trivial beauty has immense power; beauty will fade but merit will endure; poetry secures beauty's everlasting fame.

Teaching Suggestions

There are many ways to approach Pope's most famous work, but in all of them attention to his couplet form will be paramount. See above for strategies to teach the style of Pope's poetry. *The Rape of the Lock* benefits from slow, close reading if the students are not yet familiar with the poetic form. Beginning with the invocation, you can focus on the literal meaning of the lines, then their purpose as invocation. Finally, you might compare this to Milton's invocation or other epic invocations in order to establish the ways in which the poem functions as mock-epic.

While the opening establishes the poem's subject as trivial, it will become apparent to students as you explore the texture of the poem created by the details (e.g., white curtains, noontime, silver watch, downy pillow) that the subject is equally attractive. Throughout the poem, bear in mind the tension between the poet's gentle mockery of the fashionable world and its gender conventions and the poet's fascination with and beguilement by the sensuous beauty of the same. It is helpful to show illustrations of the work. Aubrey Beardsley's 1896 drawings are particularly interesting and readily available online. The key passages generally involve a significant parody or borrowing from Homer, Virgil, or Milton (and there are many more in the poem), and like the invocation their meanings can be teased out on three levels: literal meaning in the narrative; poetic or symbolic function; satiric implications of the parody.

The figure of Clarissa generally prompts great discussion because she provides the scissors as well as the moral of the poem. As a moral, Clarissa's speech carries with it the same ironic potential as the dismissal of female beauty as trivial. After all, nobody listens to Clarissa. The final lines of the poem undermine Clarissa's moral as well, because Pope's tribute to beauty is not transient but enduring.

Teaching Clusters

The Rape of the Lock may serve as a centerpiece in any cluster discussing gender issues, in particular **The Public Sphere and Civil Society**. From the opening dedication throughout the description of the sylphs and the Cave of Spleen, Pope's poem condescends to women and engages the worst stereotypes for women of his day. However, his representation of men, and those in particular who pay gallant service to the ladies, is hardly complimentary. (In this, of course, he implicates himself as the flattering poet.) Also, the poem provides exquisite details on courtship rituals and the social interactions between the sexes in public places and so offers much matter for discussion. The poem would teach well with the In-text Topic on "Debating Women" and would also complement many domestic novels, in particular *Evelina* by Frances Burney or *Emma* by Jane Austen, both of which narrate sympathetic and satirical portraits of their beautiful and flawed heroines.

Discussion Questions

1. What social and literary functions does the dedicatory letter serve?
2. What are the dominant characteristics of our hero and our heroine? How does Pope convey these to us?
3. What is the effect of scale in Ariel's speech in Canto 2? To what extent do we identify with Pope's machinery? For information on the impact of scientific discoveries, such as the telescope and the microscope, on the impressions of scale, see *Norton Topic Online* "Plurality of Worlds."
4. What happens in the moment of hubris when Belinda wins the game of Ombre? What is the significance?
5. What is the moral in Clarissa's speech? How effective is her delivery?
6. What social commentary does Pope make through the mock battle that ensues?
7. How is the conflict resolved? To what extent is this an example of deus ex machina?

8. How does Belinda achieve the immortal status that the poet claims?
9. What features of heroic style does Pope borrow from the epic? How does his use of epic convention compare with Milton's?
10. To what extent is the poem about proper sexual behavior? What does the cutting of the lock symbolize?

Epistle to Dr. Arbuthnot

Pope's famous verse epistle offers students a primer on the ethics of satire in the early eighteenth century. Because Pope makes himself the subject of the poem, students also learn about the poet; however, it is important to emphasize that Pope's self-representation is filtered through various theatrical postures, as mentioned in the introduction. The energetic and passionate couplets of this satire contrast nicely with the urbane control of *An Essay on Criticism* and the sensuous beauty and gallant banter of *The Rape of the Lock*. Together the selections in *NAEL* demonstrate the incredible stylistic range of Pope's couplets.

Quick Read

- Form: Verse epistle, satire, also dialogue, in iambic pentameter couplets.
- Key Passages: Opening (pestered by other writers), 1–68; "No creature smarts so little as a fool," 83–108; "Why did I write," 125–34; portrait of Atticus (Addison), 193–214; tribute to John Gay (on patrons), 249–70; immoral satire, 283–304; Sporus (Hervey), 305–33; Pope's self-portrait, 334–77; tribute to his parents, 380–413.
- Key Themes: Writing is a form of madness; satire ought to be informed by righteous anger and not spare its targets; the moral satirist is a virtuous son and friend.

Teaching Suggestions

The energy and interruptive style of the opening lines of the poem make it ideal for dramatic reading in class. This strategy also emphasizes the theatrical nature of Pope's self-representation. Not surprisingly, Pope's themes in this epistle resonate strongly with the work of his friend, Swift, especially in the *Verses Written on the Death of Dr. Swift*. A comparison of the two self-portraits would be revealing. Also, Pope's insistence that he spared the names of his enemies (in the advertisement to the original) compares well with Swift's claims for his own satire. Why is this an important point for the satirists?

The poem's memorable satirical portraits of Addison and Hervey raise problems for Pope's claims to universal satire. However, they compare well with Dryden's portraits, in particular Zimri in *Absalom and Achitophel*. It would be interesting to read Dryden's prose on the art of personal satire to judge Pope's success. Pope expresses his own standard for satire in the poem, however, and it is important to read the lines on immoral satire in order to appreciate what he attempts to do in this poem.

Students generally find Pope's self-representation of particular interest in his tribute to his parents. Explore these closing lines for the moral significance they imply for the satirist. How does being a good son qualify Pope to be a good satirist?

Teaching Clusters

Along with Swift's *Verses on the Death of Dr. Swift,* and his own *Essay on Criticism,* Pope's *Epistle to Arbuthnot* belongs in the cluster on **Authorship and Literacy: New Readers, New Writers, New Forms.** Pope's satire functions on one level as a disciplinary gesture; he lashes bad writers and bad satirists in particular. His implicit values set the standard for ethical satire in his age and so stand as a critique of the Grub Street culture he disdains. In this way, the poem also teaches well with *The Dunciad* and the literary criticism of Dryden and Johnson.

Discussion Questions

1. Why are Bedlam and the Mint appropriate homes for the authors Pope wants to flee?
2. What is an appropriate target of satire according to the speaker in this poem?
3. What motivates the speaker (Pope) to write? (See lines 125–34 in particular.)
4. What moral virtues does the speaker claim?
5. Why does Pope include the portrait of Atticus in this poem? What is the target of his lash here?
6. What does it mean to break "a butterfly upon a wheel"? Why does he do it anyway?
7. What voices or postures does Pope adopt in this poem?
8. To what extent is Pope's self-representation accurate? Why would this be important?
9. How do Pope's tone and style in this poem compare with the tone and style of *An Essay on Criticism? The Rape of the Lock?* Why is the style appropriate for this poem?

Further Resources

NORTON ONLINE ARCHIVE

Elegy to the Memory of an Unfortunate Lady
The First Satire of the Second Book of Horace Imitated
The Universal Prayer
Epistle to Miss Blount
    [The Carnation and the Butterfly]
Ode on Solitude

Eliza Haywood

Fantomina

There is a wonderful irony in placing Haywood immediately following Pope in *NAEL*. Her unlearned, female-centered, and extremely popular prose narratives represent much of the new literary world Pope despised. His naming her in the *Dunciad* as a prize for hack publishers symbolically placed her in the canon of Dunces, but unlike Shadwell in Dryden's anti-canonical poem, Haywood has been resurrected and legitimately placed in the anthology of English literature. She is here on the strength of her storytelling and her psychological portraits of passionate women in a paradoxical world that insisted on female chastity and male promiscuity. *Fantomina* is a blend of literary currents, reflecting Haywood's experience in the worlds of theatre and print culture. Like other works by Haywood, it was wildly popular and so it tells us something of what the increasing numbers of new readers wanted to read.

Quick Read

- Form: Seduction narrative, prose.
- Main Characters: Fantomina and Beauplasir.
- Roles that Fantomina Plays: Fantomina, Celia, Widow Bloomer, Incognita.
- Themes: Man's passion fades after consummation; men are inconstant lovers, women are hopelessly constant; indulging desire/vanity leads to ruin.
- Key Concepts: Liberty, honor, constancy.

Teaching Suggestions

What makes a nice girl want to play at being a prostitute? Curiosity? Desire? Liberty? *Fantomina* begins with this scenario, appropriately staged in a playhouse, and follows a highly improbable plot that seems designed to satisfy female sexual fantasy. While the students may readily accept the character's motivation for changing her identity to keep her lover, they probably will question her ability to do so. It may be helpful to draw attention to the connections between the story and conventions of the stage: Haywood creates a female protagonist who makes conspicuous use of costumes and acting in order to keep Beauplasir's interest. The narrator even explains that Beauplasir is always fooled because of Fantomina's superior acting skill. As with other literary genres that rely heavily on convention—such as romance or gothic—it may be interesting to consider what these exaggerated behaviors stand in for. What is the symbolic significance of Beauplasir's repeatedly falling for the same woman in a different disguise? As noted in the introduction, the author was at one time both a playwright and an actress herself. For illustrations of and information on eighteenth-century playhouses, see *Norton Topic Online* "A Day in Eighteenth-Century London."

While the story suggests that Fantomina needs to remake herself continually in order to preserve Beauplasir's passion, it also indicates that she takes great pride and pleasure in being able to do so. The story might also be discussed in terms of gender and subjectivity, especially in response to such a claim as Pope's in his "Epistle to a Lady": "Most women have no character at all." Does Haywood pattern her story on the same idea, or does she challenge Pope's view by granting women the power to deceive in the guise of many characters? Fantomina's role-playing also raises questions about class, status, and gender as sources of identity in the early eighteenth century.

In the end, Haywood reasserts the dark consequences for young women who indulge their vanity and sexual desire, and the abrupt and troubling conclusion of *Fantomina* merits discussion. To what extent is Fantomina's exposure inevitable? To what extent is her downfall biologically determined? What are the implications for ending it this way? For an example of how eighteenth-century discussions of nature and science intersected with questions of human nature and gender, see Haywood's *Female Spectator*, excerpted in *Norton Topic Online*, "The Plurality of Worlds."

Teaching Clusters

Fantomina belongs in the cluster on **The Public Sphere and Civil Society** because of its attention to playhouses and its focus on gendered interactions in that public sphere. It teaches well with other early prose fictions, particularly Defoe's *Roxana*, which raises arguments about the power of mistresses and that of legitimate wives. As in *Roxana*, the female protagonist's transgressive sexual conduct highlights the repressive social limitations for women. But because of its theatrical focus, the fiction also works well with Restoration plays such as Congreve's *Way of the World* or *Love for Love* (in the Norton Online Archive). As a portrait of destructive female passion, it compares well with Pope's *Eloisa to Abelard*.

Discussion Questions

1. What elements of Fantomina's initial behavior toward Beauplasir lead to his confusion about her status?
2. Why is Beauplasir's "constancy" so important to Fantomina? What motivates her elaborate plans to captivate him?
3. Haywood uses the language of triumph and victory as well as slavery and liberty. In what sense is the relationship between Beauplasir and Fantomina a battle? In what sense is either enslaved?
4. What is the distinction between virtue and reputation? Why is the latter more important in this story?
5. Why does Beauplasir believe Fantomina "in the end . . . would be in reality the thing she so artfully had counterfeited"? What determines the authentic self? Is it different for men than for women?
6. How does Beauplasir's behavior to Fantomina change depending on

the class or status she assumes? What does this tell us about the gendered and class structures and social conventions of the time?

7. What happens when Fantomina's mother arrives in town?
8. What is the significance of Fantomina's giving birth to a daughter? Why do Fantomina and her mother reject Beauplasir's offer to take the child?
9. Why do you think this story was popular?

Lady Mary Wortley Montagu

Epistle from Mrs. Yonge to Her Husband

The strong passions expressed in this poem immediately engage the reader and parallel other imitations of Ovid's *Heroides*, like Pope's *Eloisa to Abelard*, but because this is based on a true story, the historical and biographical interest is also high. Divorce was extremely rare in England, and this poem fictionalizes the response of a real woman who went through the public humiliation of a divorce trial. The poem allows students to glimpse what was at stake for an unhappily married woman and how the reality of divorce in the eighteenth century differs from the reality now. It also demonstrates the permissive sexual ideology of the upper classes, which students schooled in post-Victorian literature tend not to expect.

Quick Read

- Form: Imitation of Ovid, heroic epistle in iambic pentameter couplets.
- Key Passages: Opening to her husband, 1–8; injustice of marriage laws, 9–37; synopsis of her affair and divorce, 38–58; justification, 59–68; sarcastic adieu to husband, 69–80.
- Key Personages: Mary Yonge, speaker; William Yonge, addressee; Sir Robert Walpole, Yonge's patron.
- Themes: Women have the same sexual needs as men, but the laws prevent them from fulfilling them; marriage laws are unjust; the husband is cruel for enacting the laws.

Teaching Suggestions

This poem works well in a discussion of marriage and gender in eighteenth-century literature, and some background information on marriage laws ought to be provided. See suggestions in the Mary Astell entry. Teaching this poem with Astell's and Defoe's excerpts on marriage can help set an informed context. You might approach the poem as the expression of a woman confined in the type of marriage described by Astell or Defoe and unable to break the bonds. It is important, however, to recognize the privilege associated with the upper classes in that Mrs. Yonge assumes the right to carry on affairs of her own just as Lady Walpole had done. (Also recognize that Astell would hardly condone Mrs. Yonge's response to her husband's infidelity.) In this way, the poem shares themes with *Fantomina*, whose protagonist is also a lady of the upper class. This ideology differs from that expressed in middle-class novels, particularly after 1740.

The poem also makes an interesting comment on gender and authorship, especially if you read it next to Pope's imitation of Ovid. Ask the students to compare the two works and discuss the differences. In particular you might address why one chooses a legendary couple and another a contemporary scandal; how one voices passionate conflict and continuing love while the other sustains anger and hatred. You could frame the discussion around what techniques each poet uses to construct the voice of the abandoned woman. You also might contrast the objectives for writing the poems.

Teaching Clusters

Lady Mary's poem chiefly belongs in the **Politics of the Individual** cluster because of its critique of marriage law and its defense of the sexual equality of women. However, because of its being the product of a female pen and clearly concerned with female issues, it might also teach well in **Authorship and Literacy: New Readers, New Writers, New Forms**.

Discussion Questions

1. What is the subject of the speaker's complaint?
2. How does the poem represent the unequal treatment of male and female infidelity? Why?
3. According to the poem, how are the laws of marriage unfavorable to women?
4. How does the speaker represent her own "tender crime"?
5. In what sense is the speaker "abandoned" (59)? How does this compare with other speakers in the *Heroides* or its imitators?
6. What does the speaker hope for her husband in the end? In what sense is this poetic justice?
7. What objectives are met by writing this poem?
8. How do you account for its not being published until 1972?

Debating Women—Arguments in Verse

The poems of this section have been nicely grouped into a dialogue that students will readily follow. Because the discussion mainly turns on women—their characters, flaws, typical behaviors—you might want to begin with the question "Why women and not men?" Is there something about the age that made women the subject of such scrutiny? If so, how do the poems reflect their historical contexts? If not, what makes the idea of women so inherently interesting as to merit such attention in verse?

The poems break down into nice pairings, with the exception of Mary Leapor's poems. Indeed Leapor's poems ought to be taught on their own, and suggestions for doing so follow. The introduction to the section sets up some important distinctions between the work of Swift and that of Pope, the only two male voices heard here, and these observations can be put to use in contrasting the poems. For example, you can ask the students to see how Swift's attitude toward Celia in "The Lady's Dressing Room" differs from his attitude toward Strephon. Similarly, one should evaluate if Pope constructs "woman" as a product of nature or of custom. Ultimately, readers may feel more comfortable with either Pope or Swift, and you can tease that reaction into a reasoned response by turning back to the poetry and identifying what causes the comfort/discomfort.

The responses by the female writers help to balance the misogyny of Swift's and Pope's poems, but students should not expect revolutionary sentiments here. Remember that these women lived in a world that sanctioned the subordination of women to men in every way. The women are empowered by the relatively recent belief in the rational equality of women and their great potential for education. You might ask students to examine what claims the poems make on behalf of women (if, indeed, they make any) and how they justify or defend those claims.

Discussion Questions

1. What is "custom" in these poems? How does it differ from "nature"?
2. Compare the different modes of satire, for example, of Swift and Lady Mary, or of Pope and Ann Finch. Do men use satire in different ways than women?
3. Are terms like *Juvenalian* or *Horatian satire* useful in discussing these poems? Why or why not?
4. What role does education play in the construction of women in these poems?
5. If this a debate, what is being debated?

Mary Leapor

An Essay on Woman

As a plebian poet and a woman, Leapor is an important representative voice to include in eighteenth-century survey courses. As a witty and sophisticated poet who responds to Alexander Pope, the greatest poet of her lifetime, she merits close attention. The two poems included in NAEL offer original, earthy images taken from her everyday working world, but their themes, methods, allusions, and aspirations tie them closely to more elite poetry. In terms of gendered debates, they provide an important perspective on the ways in which the category of "woman" is developed through class identity.

Quick Read

- Form: Verse satire in iambic pentameter couplets.
- Style: Popeian influence, relaxed cadence with sharp sarcasm and homely imagery.
- Key Passages: Character of "woman," 1–14; change at marriage, 15–18; Sylvia and Pamphilia (beauty and wit), 19–38; Cordia (avarice), 39–48; Mira's wish, 49–52; fate of women (slave at large), 53–60.
- Key Themes: Women receive hyperbolic praise before marriage and ceaseless criticism thereafter; the characters of women are formed for this; even wealth cannot promise happiness.

Teaching Suggestions

This poem adopts the Horatian essay form of satire to address a general theme, in this case the character of woman. Formally it alludes to Pope's harsh satire "Of the Characters of Women: An Epistle to a Lady," and so one way to teach the poem is to compare the tone, imagery, and techniques of satire in the two poems. For example, one might structure the comparison around the central question of what each poem targets for reform: while Pope lashes the vain and vapid characters of many immoral women, Leapor implicates the conditions of women's customary life (i.e., marriage). Another good point of comparison is the ideal versions of womanhood each poem sets up. For Pope it is his friend and her perfectly amiable character, but in Leapor the tentative wish she expresses for herself (lines 49–52) offers the only sense of an ideal alternative to woman's cruel fate.

Students of working-class backgrounds or first-generation college students tend to respond positively to Leapor's colorful version of eighteenth-century life; it provides a wonderful contrast to the elite imagery of Behn, Pope, Haywood, and others. This is especially true of her "Epistle to a Lady," which offers an autobiographical picture of the mixed benefits of learning for the laboring class poet. Several of the illustrations in the *Norton Topic Online* "A Day in Eighteenth-Century London" reflect working or laboring class life, but much of it is satirical or negative. Similarly, many representations of the servants and farm laborers in the literature are dismissive or functional. For a fuller representation of serving- and laboring-class identity, see Tobias Smollett's *Humphry Clinker*.

Teaching Clusters

Like all the works in this topic, Leapor's "Essay on Woman" can be taught in the **Politics of the Individual** cluster, but her poems also belong in the **Authorship and Literacy: New Readers, New Writers, New Forms**, particularly because they are so reflective of her own experience as a writer. The emphasis on death in "Epistle to a Lady" links it interestingly with other poems on death, such as Johnson's "On the Death of Dr. Robert Levet" and Gray's "Elegy."

Discussion Questions

1. How would you summarize Leapor's rather cynical appraisal of womankind in the opening lines? How does her perspective as a young laborer affect the representation?
2. How does Hymen (line 15) change the character of woman? Whose perspective is the poem targeting for its satire here?
3. What is the effect of invoking Artemesia, the poet's patron?
4. How do the tone and subject of the satire shift after line 20?
5. What is the fate of Sylvia and Pamphilia? How are they emblematic of the fate of womankind?
6. What advice does the poem offer to the material-minded reader? How does this fit in with other moral satires of the era?
7. How does the poet represent herself in lines 49–52, and what are the implications?
8. Examine the closing lines and Leapor's use of the image of woman as a "slave at large" (60). What is particularly poignant about Leapor's perspective on this metaphor?

John Gay

The Beggar's Opera

Gay's play teaches easily and well on many levels. It serves as a good introduction to the workings of eighteenth-century theatre with the meta-theatrical framing of the Beggar and the Player and the mock-opera satire. The bold characters and uninhibited behaviors of Gay's underworld are engaging and fun to act out or imagine, and they provide a peek into the seedy side of London life and criminal justice. The light but pervasive irony created through parallels between high and low society offers pungent social and moral criticism that rises above the historical circumstances of the play's extraordinary debut.

Quick Read

- Form: Mock-opera (the original), three-act play in alternating prose and song.
- Key Characters: Macheath, Polly and Lucy, Mr. Peachum, Lockit.
- Key Themes: The higher sort of people have crimes in the same degree as the low and ought to be punished for them; high life and low life share the same manners, motivations, desires, and fears; self-interest is the prime motivator of human behavior; an opera must end happily.
- Key Scenes: Beggar and Player (Introduction); satire on marriage, 1.7–10; honor among thieves, 2.1–2; betrayal of Macheath, 2.6; po-

litical criticism of Peachum and Lockit, 2.10; of all animals of prey, man is the only social one, 3.2; poisoning scene, 3.7–10; dance of the prisoners, 3.12; Macheath's reflections, 3.13; Macheath's wives, 3.15; Player and Beggar change the ending, 3.16.
- Teaching Aids: Painting of scene by Hogarth (insert); recording of airs; video of stage productions.

Teaching Suggestions

Gay's play can be discussed as a satire on three levels: formal, political, and social. By addressing the first, you can engage students in the history of theatre. See *Norton Topic Online* "A Day in Eighteenth-Century London" for illustrations and essays on theatre. The craze for Italian opera was at its height when Gay introduced the homegrown ballad opera based in the criminal underworld of London. The introduction of the Beggar and Player as well as scene 3.16 explicitly refer to this "taste of the town." For Pope's satirical description of the Italian opera, see *The Dunciad*, 4.45–60. Properties of the opera that Gay inverted include the use of foreign language; lavish, pretentious spectacle; subjects of myth, legend, or ancient history; themes of heroic love and villainy; high-born heroes and heroines; the recitative (lack of dialogue); conventional, quaint similes; a stock prison scene; division of leading roles for ladies; the castrato; a poisoning attempt; arias; and the unjustified happy ending. Look for the ways in which Gay played on the audience's expectations for opera and the implications of his many inversions.

Throughout the play, Gay draws explicit parallels between leaders and the gangs of thieves and between leaders and the gangs of courtiers or politicians. From the opening air, where Peachum compares his employment with that of a lawyer and a statesman, through the constant references to Macheath as the "Great Man," a common name for Walpole, Gay targeted political corruption in his play. This political satire is most explicit in the relationship between Lockit and Peachum—for example, in their initial scene together, 2.10.

The social satire of the play targets sexual mores and self-interest in staged parallels between high and low society. Note the use of formal language among the confederates, who call themselves gentlemen or fine ladies. The opening act focuses on the "ruin" of Polly, who has married Macheath in secret; Mrs. Peachum is given some excellent one-liners in a satire on marriage. The satire works primarily by inverting our social expectations: marriage is ruin; sexual dalliance is profitable.

This play should come to life in the classroom in some form. Recordings of the airs will help to demonstrate how Gay used popular tunes to replace the sophisticated arias of traditional opera. An excellent recording of the stage production with Roger Daltrey playing Macheath is also available. Ask the students to watch clips of the film with their books open because they may have difficulty understanding the accents. You also might want to stage some scenes on your own. In addition to the players themselves, ask your musically inclined students to produce the airs, and other students to research and present props or scenery.

Teaching Clusters

Gay's depiction of the London underworld should be taught in the cluster on **The Public Sphere and Civil Society** because of its topsy-turvy view on polite, urban living. In this way, it pairs well with *The Rape of the Lock* and Swift's "Description of Morning." The characterization of Jonathan Wilde as the Thief-taker General (Peachum in the play) would teach well with Fielding's *Life of Jonathan Wilde.*

As the original ballad opera or the mock-opera, this play also might feature in the cluster on **Authorship and Literacy: New Readers, New Writers, New Forms.** The role of the Beggar emblematizes the increased literacy among lower classes, and the satire on opera plays on the untrained taste of the fashionable world. In this way, the play might pair well with other mock-genres, such as "Mac Flecknoe" (mock-heroic), *The Rape of the Lock* (mock-epic), and Gay's own "Trivia," a mock-pastoral, available in the Norton Online Archive.

Discussion Questions

1. What is the significance of the play's title? In what sense is this a beggar's opera?
2. What effect do the ballads have in the play? (It will be helpful to hear the airs if possible either through a recording or the video reproduction.)
3. Evaluate Gay's use of irony in the play. How does the play maintain its light tone despite the dreary situations and cynical behavior?
4. What does the play say about marriage?
5. What does the play say about criminal justice?
6. What does the list of stolen objects (throughout the play) tell us about the society?
7. What is the point of Gay's repeated comparison between high and low?
8. Imagine the effect of the prison dance in Act 3. How would you stage it and why?
9. What is the meaning of Air 67? How does this serve as a central theme of the play?
10. How does Hogarth's illustration of the final prison scene (3.11) comment on the staging of the play? On the moral of the play?

Further Resources

NORTON ONLINE ARCHIVE

The Birth of the Squire. An Eclogue
Recitativo and Air from *Acis and Galatea*

Samuel Johnson

Johnson ushers in a new age in literature, one that he largely defined, and so the guide will detail three works: *The Vanity of Human Wishes*, *Rasselas*, and selections of his prose writings. Johnson's moral seriousness is everywhere apparent in his writings, but unlike Swift and Pope, his satire is tempered by a compassion for human frailty. He combines the Augustan taste for wit with the new mode of sensibility in that he depicts the human condition as fraught with emotions, sensitivity, and complex psychological motivations. His overriding concern is with the capacity of the human mind to deceive itself by ignoring experience and attending to desire or hope. Teaching the excerpts from Boswell's biography of Johnson will add depth and meaning to the reading experience of Johnson's own writings.

The Vanity of Human Wishes

It may be some consolation to students to know that Johnson's own student, David Garrick, found this poem "hard as Greek," but it merits attention for many reasons. It is Johnson's greatest poem, and it suggests the ways in which Augustan literary values persisted even after Pope's death. Most importantly, it offers a sober look at the painful delusions we humans cherish in pursuit of money, fame, and power. It also contains many fine moral maxims.

Quick Read

- Form: Imitation of Juvenal's tenth satire, verse satire in iambic pentameter couplets.
- Style: Stately, pointed maxims, compressed phrases, heavy use of abstraction.
- Key Passages: Opening lines stating intention, 1–20; ambivalence of riches, 21–48; invocation to Democritus, 49–72; uncertainty of political preferment, 73–98; portrait of Wolsey, 99–120; fame of scholars, 135–74; fame of soldiers, 175–254; desire for long life/old age, 255–310; fame of beauties, 319–42; role of prayer, 349–68.
- Key Themes: Human beings ignore or evade the present in pursuit of future fame and glory; power, money, fame do not last; history records numerous instances of the revolutions of fate, the ambition for greatness, and the subsequent loss.
- Potential Pedagogical Obstacle: It is "hard as Greek."

Teaching Suggestions

Because of the difficulty of Johnson's couplets, time should be spent paraphrasing and explaining some of his techniques. As a class, paraphrase the opening lines (1–20), and pay particular attention to Johnson's use of abstraction and metaphor. Ask the students to consider the meaning of "Observation" surveying humankind from China to Peru. What does this noun mean in this role? Breaking down the imagery of "busy scenes of crowded life" and "the cloudy maze of fate" will help students understand the point of Johnson's survey in the poem and give them an appreciation for his principle of universal human nature. We are all alike, according to Johnson, in our ambitions, desires, and flaws, although we are differently circumstanced. One way to analyze the poem is to view the catalogue of historical figures as examples of these different circumstances, all of which illustrate the same general human condition: we ignore or evade the present in pursuit of future fame and glory, which does not last or satisfy us.

Students may especially appreciate the lines on the difficulty of gaining fame through scholarship (135–74). One has to use caution in celebrating the maxim: "And pause a while from letters to be wise" (158), especially if your class falls anywhere near a holiday! The long passage on political leaders offers excellent moral lessons for the revolutions in empire, not to be lost on today's audiences. The final section on the fame of beauties addresses women in particular, and although it is noteworthy that these are the only women (except one princess) who achieve fame in the poem, it is nonetheless a relevant gendered issue. While in no way a proto-feminist, Johnson usually has insight into and compassion for the psychological constraints faced by women of his society.

Teaching Clusters

Although Johnson's *Vanity of Human Wishes* doesn't clearly belong in any particular teaching cluster, its treatment of human nature aligns it with the **Explorations in Science and Nature** category. It will teach best if taught beside *Rasselas*, which explores many of the same themes and is much more accessible. As an adaptation from a classical satire, it would also teach well with Rochester's *Satire on Reason and Mankind*.

Discussion Questions

1. What does the title of the poem mean?
2. What does the poet establish in the opening twenty lines?
3. What role does the invocation to Democritus play? Why Democritus? How does the poem change at this point?
4. What is the point of the catalogue of individuals that follows? What errors or misfortunes does Johnson illustrate through these figures?
5. How does the passage regarding learning (135–64) compare with the treatment of this issue in *Rasselas*?
6. How does the poem represent old age? What are the implications?
7. Who are the women listed in the passage on the fame of beauty (319–42)? How do they compare with the other illustrious personages mentioned in the poem? What does this say about the fame of women?
8. In the ending, does the poet dismiss the usefulness of prayer or does he allow for the benefits of faith?

Rasselas

Rasselas is a delightful philosophical tale about the elusive quest for human happiness. It incorporates many eighteenth-century literary developments, with its developed prose narrative, periodic sentence style, and blend of satire and sentiment. It is set in northern Africa, a context that would have been considered very exotic and which places *Rasselas* within the popular genre of the Oriental tale. Such a setting reflects both the literary tastes of the age and the subject of colonial expansion that persists throughout the era.

Quick Read

- Form: Prose narrative, Oriental tale, philosophic fable.
- Style: Majestic and precise vocabulary, stately periodic sentences.
- Key Characters: Rasselas, Imlac, Nekayah, Pekuah.
- Key Chapters: Chapter 1, the Happy Valley; chapters 8–9, 11–12, history of Imlac; chapter 10, dissertation on poetry; chapters 26–29, marriage debate; chapters 31–32, visit to the pyramids; chapters 40–44, 46, the astronomer; chapter 49, the conclusion in which nothing is concluded.
- Key Themes: I. Happiness is not found in satisfying all one's needs and desires; II. A survey of humanity shows that no choice of life produces unalloyed happiness; III. Engagement in society and variety of experience produce knowledge and prevent despair.

Teaching Suggestions

One way to teach this tale is to address the structure. *Rasselas* breaks down nicely into three sections that develop individual themes:

I. Chapters 1–14 (Happy Valley): Rasselas listens to Imlac's story.

II. Chapters 15–32 (Observational survey—their search for the choice of life): The four characters leave the valley to see the world; they watch.

III. Chapters 33–49 (Engagement—the episodes beginning with Pekuah's capture): The characters learn the value of society and friendship; they become active.

The description of the Happy Valley will seem familiar to students who have read *Brave New World* or other dystopian fiction, but it presents a simple illustration for the philosophical question that Johnson pursues: how do we satisfy this desire for happiness when happiness itself becomes cloying? The introduction of Imlac provides a useful contrast in the parable, and the conversation between Rasselas and Imlac often sounds like a debate between innocence and experience (cf. the angel discoursing with Adam in *Paradise Lost*). The dissertation on poetry in chapter 10 provides important statements on Augustan literary theory, and it is often excerpted in critical anthologies. Keeping with the light ironical tone of the narrative, though, Johnson undercuts Imlac's enthusiasm for poetry with

Rasselas's stark pragmatism. He balances the story nicely with the addition of Nekayah and her lady Pekuah, providing female characters that allow for gendered discussions of experience. In particular, the debate over marriage is remarkable and worth discussing with the class. The visit to the pyramids provides a good opportunity to discuss the value of studying literature of the past. With Pekuah's capture and Nekayah's depression, the story evokes the psychological difficulty of grief and loss, and this is balanced by the demonstration of the importance of social interactions in the episode of the Astronomer. The story of the Astronomer's recovery of reason illustrates the ways in which women became important to society at this time as the mistresses of polite conversation. Students will either delight in the circular ending of the conclusion in which nothing is concluded or find it infuriatingly open-ended. Channel their reactions into a reasoned discussion of the structure of the whole and the implications for structuring it this way.

If time allows, discuss Johnson's ponderous and precise prose style, for which he justly became famous. He brings the balance and antithesis of the couplet form to periodic prose sentences. Unlike his poetry, Johnson's prose is not compressed; on the contrary, it is expansive like the blank verse of *Paradise Lost*. He creates grand symmetrical sentences that hold an idea in suspense until the very end. Try to have students identify the parallel phrases (looking for resemblance or correspondence), for example, in the opening sentence. Try to identify the balance and antithesis in the following examples: "Integrity without knowledge is weak and useless, and knowledge without integrity is dangerous and dreadful." "In the state of future perfection, to which we all aspire, there will be pleasure without danger, and security without restraint." Charting these on the board will be a useful illustration of his style. Take it one step further and ask your students to consider the significance of such parallel structures for the meaning of Johnson's sentences.

Teaching Clusters

While *The Vanity of Human Wishes* is difficult to place in a teaching cluster, *Rasselas* could be taught in many clusters. Regarding **Authorship and Literacy**, Imlac's discussion of poetry makes a good excerpt for literary values. It teaches well with Johnson's other literary criticism, Dryden's critical prose, and "Mac Flecknoe," Pope's *Essay on Criticism*, and even Leapor's "Epistle to a Lady," which discusses the mixed benefits of learning for the working-class poet. As an imaginative and exotic tale of travel, *Rasselas* pairs well with Swift's *Gulliver's Travels* and Behn's *Oroonoko* in the **Explorations of Science and Nature** cluster. Johnson's character Nekayah is one of the most likeable and most intelligent female characters in eighteenth-century literature, and her discussion of marriage and other issues of gender belong in **Politics of the Individual**. In this way, *Rasselas* teaches well with other works on marriage, such as those by Astell and Defoe, and in the In-text Topic on "Debating Women."

Discussion Questions

1. What are the implications of the Happy Valley, its name and setting? Why begin the tale here?
2. What is the effect of contrasting Rasselas's idealism with Imlac's experience of the world?
3. In chapter 10, how does Imlac describe the "business of a poet," and what are the implications of Rasselas's cutting him off at the start of chapter 11?
4. What is the significance of Rasselas's journey to discover the "choice of life"? How does this compare with other journeys in literature?
5. What is the result of the survey? Why is no one completely happy?
6. What does the story tell us about marriage? About the pursuit of knowledge?
7. How does the story of the Astronomer illustrate the value of human relationships? What role do women play in this?
8. What does each traveler plan at the conclusion of his or her journey? Why do they return to Abisinnia?
9. What role do the emotions play in the various episodes? How is this emphasis on the power of emotions different from the treatment of emotions in earlier eighteenth-century literature?
10. What themes does *Rasselas* share with *The Vanity of Human Wishes*? How are their endings different?
11. After reading several accounts of travel in the *Norton Topic Online* "Travel, Trade, and the Expansion of Empire," how do you see *Rasselas* comparing as a representation of the world outside England?

Selections from Other Prose Writings

Johnson's essays, like Dryden's, can be read together as a group or individually to supplement the teaching of other writers, such as Shakespeare, Donne, Dryden, Milton, and Pope. The introduction in *NAEL* gives very clear reasons why Johnson's critical and periodical essays are worth teaching. His prose is often complex and heavy, and it carries a wisdom and grave humor that the young and giddy may not appreciate. Have them read it anyway; it's good for them.

Teaching Suggestions

Whether you teach Johnson's critical or periodical essays alone or as a supplement to another text, you might want to prepare students for the prose style. See *Rasselas* for some suggestions on how to break down the grand periodic sentences. If the students want to call Johnson "wordy" (and they will), you can take the opportunity to demonstrate the difference between precise use of words and excessive or redundant words.

Below are several simple summary statements and some suggestions for pairings:

Rambler No. 4 establishes the exemplary function of literature; the readers of novels are the young and uneducated and therefore novels need to represent the highest standard of morality. References the work of Richardson and Fielding. Good to teach with any novel of the era.

Rambler No. 60 discusses the importance of biography and the need to create interest for the reader while preserving the truth of the life. Can be read with Johnson's own *Lives of the Poets*, Boswell's *Life of Johnson*, or other biographical writings of the era.

Preface to the *Dictionary* with some definitions expresses Johnson's theory on the mutability of language and the attempt to hold off inevitable deterioration by fixing definitions. Definitions are worth reading both for insight into the literature and for humor. Essay will be of interest to all focusing on history of the English language, rhetoric, or literary theory.

Preface to Shakespeare: Johnson claims Shakespeare as the poet of nature but discusses his faults; this is followed by his pragmatic rejection of the unities of time and place. Discussion of *King Lear* is significant. Useful comparison to Dryden's *Essay on Dramatic Poesy*; also could be taught with Shakespeare. Insights on imagination and the stage make this useful for teaching other eighteenth-century drama as well.

Lives of the Poets: Cowley—worth reading with Donne and other metaphysical poets. Johnson defines wit several ways, none of which praises the writings of the metaphysicals. Milton—criticism of *Lycidas* applies to false use of pastoral imagery; criticism of *Paradise Lost* offers a primer on epics that can be broadly applied; the particular criticism offers excellent insight into Milton's poem and its importance to eighteenth-century literature. It is highly recommended that you teach this with *Paradise Lost*. Pope—description of Pope's method of writing and revising makes a good commentary on Pope's poems in progress (*The Rape of the Lock*); the extended comparison between Pope and his master Dryden is affectionate, insightful, and balanced. Good to read with both poets.

Teaching Clusters

All of Johnson's prose essays belong in the cluster on **Authorship and Literacy: New Readers, New Writers, New Forms.** His periodical essays (including *Rambler* 5 on Spring and *Idler* 31 on Idleness) are examples of the new essay periodical made popular by Addison and Steele, and so they can be taught in conjunction with those essays. They anticipate the literary essays of Hazlitt and Lamb in the Romantics. All of his critical writings participate in the response to new readers and new writers and in the burgeoning practice of literary criticism. Specific pairings are mentioned above.

Discussion Questions

1. How would you describe the moral tone of the *Rambler* essays? In what ways do literary concerns reinforce moral ones and vice versa?
2. Is *Rambler* No. 4 a call for censorship? If so, can you see parallels with today's society?
3. How does Johnson define "lexicographer," and what does this tell us about him?
4. To what extent have Johnson's predictions of the deterioration of English come true?
5. In what sense is Shakespeare a poet of nature? (See definition of "nature" in Johnson's *Dictionary*.)
6. What are Shakespeare's faults? What do these tell us about the state of dramatic criticism in the mid-eighteenth century?
7. In what ways is Johnson's Preface indebted to Dryden's treatment of Shakespeare in *Essay on Dramatic Poesy*?
8. How would you describe the tone of Johnson's criticism of the metaphysicals? Is this a fair assessment of their poems? Is this a fair assessment of wit?
9. Evaluate Johnson's criticism of *Paradise Lost*. What are its strengths? What are its weaknesses?
10. How does Pope compare with Dryden in Johnson's assessment? Is this an accurate assessment?

Further Resources

Norton Online Archive

Prayers and Meditations
   Easter Eve, 1761
   Good Friday, 1779, 11 PM
Rambler No. 203: Futurity
Idler No. 58: Expectation of Pleasure
Prologue Spoken by Mr. Garrick
Translation of Horace, *Odes*, Book 4.7
Lives of the Poets
   Milton [*L'Allegro, Il Penseroso*]
   Cowley [Metaphysical Wit]
   [Pope's Intellectual Character. Pope and Dryden Compared.]

James Boswell

The Life of Samuel Johnson

Boswell's famous biography of Samuel Johnson presents an irresistible view of the literary and moral censor of the age as an endearing bundle of human contradictions and fundamental goodness. It is a fascinating read with all the insider knowledge of London literati one could want, and it provides gritty historical representations of such things as eating and drinking in taverns, dress and cleanliness, politics and theatre. Most of all it provides a human context for the moral dictums that Johnson published for his society. It also stands as an extraordinary biographical account.

Quick Read

- Form: Prose biography, includes letters, memoirs, records of conversations.
- Style: Unpretentious, lively prose; often in first person.
- Key Passages: Plan for the biography, 2781–82; Johnson's education, 2783–84; letter to Chesterfield, 2787–90; Boswell meets Johnson, 2790–92; on Smart, 2792–93; Goldsmith, 2793–94; on the social order 2795; meeting the king, 2796–97; fear of death, 2797; dinner with Wilkes, 2800–04; Johnson's death 2807–10.

Teaching Suggestions

Obviously this work complements the teaching of Samuel Johnson's writings and will help students understand the author better and so, perhaps, help them appreciate his writings. It is an excellent text with which to begin a section on the literary world of the second half of the eighteenth century because of its featured appearances by authors included in NAEL: Christopher Smart, Oliver Goldsmith, Edmund Burke, and a host of other significant literary personae. Johnson's views on the social hierarchy and his criticism of America and republicanism may generate discussion of the ways in which ideas of liberty were debated at the time. His own views on death provide a personal context for the moral gravity with which he discusses the subject in "On the Death of Dr. Robert Levet" and Rasselas. This excerpt, along with the narrative of his own death, can be taught well with other discussions of mortality in eighteenth-century literature.

If you are focusing on genre or on life writing, the opening excerpt on Boswell's plan for the life is important to teach because it explicitly outlines the rationale for his methodology. Teaching this with Johnson's Rambler No. 60 essay on biography will provide further insight into the influences on Boswell. Boswell does not attempt in any way to remove himself from the biography, and so one can also discern something of the author in this work. Pairing this with his journal entry on meeting Voltaire, you can develop a discussion of the strengths and limits of the biographer himself, and this may lead to an analysis of his particular view of Johnson. Boswell's was by no means the only view of Johnson among his contemporaries.

Teaching Clusters

The Public Sphere and Civil Society. The many accounts of social interactions and London life in the *Life of Samuel Johnson* make this an excellent text to teach in this cluster. Johnson's own ambivalence toward social graces makes Boswell's portrait of him an interesting commentary on the social practices of the time. This work would teach well with Pepys's journal entries, Addison and Steele's social essays, and Burney's journal entries.

Authorship and Literacy. *The Life of Samuel Johnson* is an excellent example of the new trend in biographical writing and so would fit well with other "lives," such as those written by Johnson himself. It includes a number of conversations on literary values and so also provides insight on the critical attitudes of the culture; in this way, it can be taught with texts such as "Mac Flecknoe" and *An Essay on Criticism*. Because of their insight into the characters of certain writers, excerpts can be taught with the work of Christopher Smart, Oliver Goldsmith, and Edmund Burke.

Explorations in Science and Nature. The excerpts on fear of death and Johnson's own death belong in a discussion of human nature and the contemplation of the hereafter. In this way, the text could be taught with other works that focus on the theme of death, such as Swift's *Verses on the Death of Dr. Swift*, the section on the Struldbruggs in *Gulliver's Travels*, Leapor's "Epistle to a Lady," Johnson's "On the Death of Dr. Robert Levet," Gray's "Elegy," Wordsworth's "Extempore Effusion," and Shelley's *Adonais*.

Politics of the Individual. The excerpts on republicanism and Wilkes represent conservative Tory attitudes toward government and society and so may be taught alongside the texts on liberty in that In-text Topic.

Discussion Questions

1. What principles does Boswell use in assembling his biography of Johnson? To what extent is this consistent with the views that Johnson expresses in *Rambler* 60?
2. Why does Boswell want to write a biography of Johnson?
3. What are some of the inconsistencies in Johnson's character that Boswell develops?
4. Is there evidence that Boswell manipulates Johnson? That Boswell manipulates the facts of Johnson's life?
5. Evaluate Boswell's records of Johnson's conversations. What are the

chief characteristics of Johnson's conversation? Why is it worth recording? To what extent can we rely on this as an accurate record?

6. Does Boswell discuss any of Johnson's flaws? If so, how does he do it?
7. To what extent might this biography be a memorial to Johnson? Does that take away from its legitimacy as a biography?
8. To what extent is this a biography of Boswell? What are the strengths and limitations of Boswell's appearance in the text?
9. How does Boswell's representation of Johnson affect your view of Johnson's writings?

Frances Burney

Selections from the Letters and Journals

The excerpts in *NAEL* demonstrate Burney's expertise in narration, dialogue, and creating a character. They also cover a range of experience—from age fifteen to sixty—and subject matter, from light banter to the excruciating narration of her mastectomy. From gentle irony to intense emotion, Burney's writing conveys humor and realistic human behavior. Like Pepys and Boswell, she brings the eighteenth-century social world to us with personal insight, and her perspective as a woman and a quiet observer brings to light a side of this world that we seldom see in the literature. Here is the embarrassment of a woman denying a suitor; here is Samuel Johnson gossiping in the parlor; here is a woman facing breast cancer. It is riveting and revealing.

Quick Read

- Form: Prose journal entries and letters.
- Style: Elegant, precise irony and emotional, dramatic narration; first-person; some dialogue.
- Key Passages: Writing to "Nobody," 2811; refusing her suitor, 2812–15; conversation with Johnson and Mrs. Thrale, 2815–16; on suicide and immortality, 2818; conversation with the king, 2819–21; breast cancer and mastectomy, 2822–27.
- Pedagogical Warning: The mastectomy letter is particularly detailed and gruesome.

Teaching Suggestions

Burney's journal and letters teach very well on their own, but they also serve as a nice complement to her fiction. Both *Evelina* (1778) and *Cecilia* (1782) fall within the period division of the eighteenth century, and *Camilla* (1796) and *The Wanderer* (1814) belong to the Romantic era. The last has a major character, Elinor Joddrel, who seems modeled on the agreeable infidel from the excerpt. The first entry of Burney's journal often receives attention for the connection between the "nobody" to whom she addresses the journal and the young female "nobody" of her first novel, the heroine Evelina. Evelina represents in some ways the non-identity of unattached women in Burney's society. The details of her unwanted courtship with Barlow also seem to find a place in her fiction, as many of her heroines, particularly Cecilia, have to decline assiduous suitors. The passages on Samuel Johnson in conversation with Mrs. Thrale offer an excellent counterimage to Boswell's public, masculine Johnson of the tavern. Likewise, Burney's encounter with King George III in 1789 presents a dramatic contrast to Johnson's much earlier interview; Burney's empathetic portrait of the ailing king is surprisingly touching. The most significant of the excerpts, however, is Burney's astonishing account of the mastectomy she underwent without anesthesia in 1811. Anyone interested in women's issues or the history of medicine will want to include this dramatic narrative.

Suggested writing assignment: Given the contrasts between the Samuel Johnsons represented by Boswell and by Burney, you can challenge students to write a "day in the life" of Johnson adopting the style of either Boswell or Burney. You might encourage them to take a topic from one of Johnson's essays and imagine a scene that would dramatize the ideas Johnson expresses.

Teaching Clusters

Authorship and Literacy: New Readers, New Writers, New Forms. Burney's journals and letters belong to the new genre of biographical and autobiographical writing, and so would teach well with Pepys's and Boswell's writings, as well as Olaudah Equiano's autobiographical narrative. Additionally, as the leading female novelist of the second half of the eighteenth century, she represents the new writer. Her entries in this case would teach well with works by Aphra Behn, Eliza Haywood, and later Maria Edgeworth, Jane Austen, and Mary Shelley.

Explorations in Science and Nature. Burney's narration of her mastectomy details the entire episode, from before the parade of doctors entered her room and demanded an old mattress for her to lie on through the exhausting agony of a twenty-minute amputation, as well as the emotional trauma resulting from the surgery. As a document on the history of medicine, it can be taught with other scientific works, such as the excerpt by Newton or the poems by Barbauld on Joseph Priestley. The novel *Frankenstein* is a product of the same decade and treats some related themes. For more information on scientific discoveries of the era, including the microscope, see the *Norton Topic Online* "Plurality of Worlds."

Discussion Questions

1. Why does Burney begin a journal? Why does she address it to "Nobody"?
2. What prevents Burney from quickly dispatching Barlow? What do we learn about eighteenth-century courtship from this episode?
3. How does Burney represent her father in the journal and letters? What role does he play in her life?
4. What role do other family members play in Burney's journal and letters? How does she represent them?
5. What is Burney's attitude toward Samuel Johnson? How does her representation of him compare with Boswell's?
6. Why is Burney so surprised by the young, agreeable infidel? What does *infidel* mean in this case?
7. What is Burney's overriding concern in the episode on meeting the king? How does this representation of King George III compare with your knowledge of him from history?
8. Why does Burney write an account of her mastectomy? Why does it take her six months to write?
9. Does Burney's account of her mastectomy read like fiction? Why or why not?
10. What is the value of Burney's account of her mastectomy? What do we learn from it?

Liberty

John Locke, *from* Two Treatises of Government

Mary Astell, *from preface to* Reflections on Marriage

Shaftesbury, *from* Sensus Communis

James Thomson, Rule Britannia

David Hume, Of the Liberty of the Press

Edmund Burke, *from*
Speech on the Conciliation with the American Colonies

Samuel Johnson, A Brief to Free a Slave

Olaudah Equiano, from The Interesting Narrative

Teaching Suggestions

The texts in this section combined with the resources from *Norton Topic Online* "Slavery and the Slave Trade in Britain" form the foundation of a strong teaching block on slavery. Most of the prose excerpts provide historical context on the ways in which Britons conceived of liberty and, by contrast, slavery, both actual and metaphoric. The substantive excerpt from Equiano's *Interesting Narrative* is the most significant text upon which to center the section. His descriptions of the Middle Passage can be supplemented by the pro- and anti-slavery writings online, including descriptions of the Middle Passage by slavers themselves. The illustrations will offer a visual analogue to Equiano's prose descriptions. The poems by Cowper, More, and Blake will supplement other abolitionist writings, particularly from the Romantic era, such as Barbauld's "Epistle to Wilberforce" and Wordsworth's "To Toussaint l'Ouverture" and "September 1st, 1802."

As the only representative voice of Anglo-Africans in this section, Equiano's narrative deserves to be highlighted. (There are additional works by Phyllis Wheatley and Ignatius Sancho in *Norton Topics Online*.) The excerpts focus on two pivotal moments in his history as a slave, the description of the Middle Passage and the purchasing of his freedom. The language of the manumission underscores the deep contradictions of the British commitment to native liberty and offers a profound commentary on Locke's excerpt from *Two Treatises of Government*.

Teaching Clusters

These texts form the backbone of the cluster on **Politics of the Individual**, and they will teach well with earlier works that emphasize the struggle for liberty, such as the excerpts by Astell and Defoe on the status of wives. Also, Behn's quasi-fictional account of slavery in Surinam, in *Oroonoko*, offers an excellent narrative to compare with Equiano's autobiographical work.

Discussion Questions

1. How does Locke define slavery?
2. What arguments does Johnson use for the freeing of a slave? To what extent is this indebted to Locke?
3. What is the meaning of Thomson's line "Britons never shall be slaves"?
4. In what ways are the roles of wives and African slaves similar? In what ways are they distinct?
5. What are some of the many ways these writers understand the term "liberty"?
6. What makes the Middle Passage especially torturous for Equiano? How does his description compare with those of the slave traders in *Norton Topics Online*?
7. How does Equiano gain his freedom? What about this experience might make this a persuasive argument for abolition in England?
8. What role does religion play in Equiano's narrative? How does this compare with the role of evangelical religion in the abolition movement?
9. Based on the excerpts, how would you describe Equiano's character? What are his strengths? What are his weaknesses?

10. How does Equiano's description of slavery compare with Aphra Behn's treatment of it in *Oroonoko*?

James Thomson

Autumn

Thomson's poetry strikes a different note in eighteenth-century poetry because it is in blank verse and not the heroic couplet. This Miltonic line expands to accommodate Thomson's imaginative observation of night-time. Although the line is different, the poem includes many poetic devices typical of Augustan verse—for example, a heavy use of personification and stylized diction, such as "dusky-mantled lawn." The excerpted passages in *NAEL* also reflect the keen interest in Newton's optics and the influence of science and reason on poetry. Thus the poetry draws from two recent poetic traditions and points forward toward the Romantic concerns with nature poetry and landscape.

Quick Read

- Form/Content: Descriptive nature poem; meditation on night sky.
- Poetic Line: Blank verse in iambic pentameter.
- Style: Stately, Miltonic inversions, stylized diction.
- Key Passages: Description of the harvest moon, 1089–1102; aurora borealis, 1109–14; superstition, 1115–32; scientific examination, 1133–37; night confusion, 1138–64; dawn, 1165–71.

Teaching Suggestions

The value of Thomson's poetry becomes clearer by contrast with other work, and so it would be best to teach this excerpt in dialogue with other nighttime poetry, poetry of science, or later nature poetry in blank verse. The inverted syntax and stylized descriptions may seem stilted to students, but the use of blank verse is noteworthy because it allows for an expansive meditation on the effects of nature on the mind. (To appreciate the use of Thomson's blank verse, you might compare a passage from Milton's *Paradise Lost*; the interaction between Satan and Night at the end of book 2 is appropriate.) Thomson's lines contrast the superstitious response to the aurora borealis (1109–14) with the more rational scientific observation of the night sky (1133–37), clearly approving the latter. You can incorporate text and illustrations from *Norton Topics Online* "Plurality of Worlds," which includes information on telescopes and the impact of such discoveries on the general populace. Thomson hints at the sublimity of the night—in complete darkness "a shade immense!"—and this offers an interesting contrast to Anne Finch's treatment of the night as liberating. Note too how dawn brings serene beauty and light for Thomson but chaos for Finch.

Teaching Clusters

This excerpt from Thomson teaches well in the cluster **Explorations in Science and Nature**, and so could be taught with Pope's *Essay on Man* and later poems like Barbauld's on Joseph Priestley. The focus on the moon and nighttime also makes this an appropriate companion for Finch's "Nocturnal Reverie," Gray's "Elegy," Collins's "Ode to Evening," Smith's "To Night," Wordsworth's "It is a beauteous evening," and Keats's "Bright Star." To demonstrate Wordsworth's stylistic departures you might teach this excerpt with Collins's "Ode to Evening" before teaching Wordsworth's "Tintern Abbey."

Discussion Questions

1. What role does the sense of sight or observation play in Thomson's descriptions?
2. What makes blank verse a suitable form for this poem? How would it be different in closed couplets?
3. What effect does the aurora borealis have on the uneducated observers?
4. What role does science play in the poem?
5. What causes the wanderer to get lost in night (1145–64)?
6. What effect does night have on the imagination in this poem? How does this contrast with Finch's representation of night?
7. How does this excerpt compare with other excerpts from Thomson's *Seasons*? (See the Norton Online Archive.)

Further Resources

NORTON ONLINE ARCHIVE

An Ode on Aeolus's Harp
The Seasons
    Summer: Dawn
    Summer: Swimming
    Summer: Evening
    Winter: A Snowstorm

Thomas Gray

Elegy Written in a Country Churchyard

Gray's famous "Elegy" is an appealing and eminently teachable poem that opens up many issues for discussion. As an elegy it raises the question of our mortality and who is remembered after he or she dies. The setting of the poem in a country churchyard and the outsider status of the educated poet create tensions between the rural and the sophisticated that get amplified in the poem's dominant theme: the paths of glory lead but to the grave. As a poet Gray focuses on how we memorialize the dead and why we do so, questions that continue to be relevant today. The tone of melancholy and the emphasis on solitude and contemplation signal new directions in eighteenth-century poetry, and Gray's elegy can demonstrate for students the break from Augustan wit and society and a poetics of introspection and withdrawal.

Quick Read

- Form: Pastoral elegy in iambic pentameter quatrains of *abab*.
- Key Passages: Introduction of poet in churchyard, 1–4; remembering the forefathers, 13–28; paths of glory, 33–36; memorials of the proud, 37–44; graves of unknown/unfulfilled potential, 45–60; poverty's effect on ambition, 61–76; memorials of the "unlettered Muse," 77–92; the poet's death, 93–116; the poet's epitaph, 117–28.
- Key Themes: The paths of glory lead but to the grave; full many a flower is born to blush unseen; rural simplicity contrasted with the dangers of the glamorous world; literacy is a privilege and a responsibility.

Teaching Suggestions

As preparation for reading the poem, ask students to consider the ways our culture memorializes the dead. You can even ask them to read obituaries from local papers or bring in examples of funeral memorials. To glimpse the pomp and pageantry granted to the honored dead, ask students to visit the Web site for Westminster Abbey, the most famous collection of memorials for the dead in Britain. In particular, take the tour of Poets' Corner. This visual information provides a good contrast to the rural hamlet of the poem and will emphasize the significance of Gray's setting. The poem also should be read aloud very slowly; there is a recording of the poem in the online archive, but also encourage your students to read it for themselves. Note the elegiac tolling sound of the alternating rhymes.

The poem begins in a liminal state as night falls on the poet isolated in the landscape; this in-betweeness is emphasized throughout the poem as the outsider, anonymous poet seeks to find an appropriate way to remember those people whose graves surround him. Ask the students to consider in what ways the poet differs from the people he is trying to memorialize. What are his attitudes toward the "rude forefathers" in the opening stanzas? The differences between the poet and the dead whom he does not know create a cognitive gap that the poem tries to breach through sentimental imagery. Ask students to consider the implications of the poet's description of their labor in 25–28. This sentimental imagery gives way to philosophical introspection as the poet considers the mortality of the entire human race, including himself. After he considers the limitations of poverty, he focuses on the dangers of the glamorous world ways that echo Johnson's moral satire, *The Vanity of Human Wishes*. How has his attitude toward the rural inhabitants changed by this point in the poem? His vision of his own death, memorialized by a "hoary headed swain," reverses the dilemma of the opening stanzas and emphasizes the poet's ambivalence toward fame and memory. Although the poem contains many fine lines of moral sentiment, it is far more complicated and ambiguous than appears by quick reading. Careful attention to the shifts in perspective (note the two very different uses of the second person in the poem) and the syntax will yield interesting insights.

Ideas for teaching Gray's "Elegy" are indebted to the scholars in a roundtable discussion at ASECS 2004 dedicated to teaching the poem: Madeleine Marshall, John Sitter, David Fairer, Margaret Doody, and Lorna Clymer.

Teaching Clusters

The Public Sphere and Civil Society. By taking up the theme of the dangers of the pursuit of fame and glory in contrast to the virtues of rural simplicity, the poem participates in the literature of polite society. However, Gray's poem is no celebration of the virtues of landed gentry. In this way, it would teach well with Prior's "Epitaph" and contrast with several of Pope's representations of the civic ideal, for example, in *Windsor Forest*.

Authorship and Literacy: New Readers, New Writers, New Forms. The poem's representation of the effects of literacy ties it into this cluster. The rich ambivalence of Gray's own epitaph would read well against the laboring poet's representation of her own learning in Leapor's "Epistle to a Lady."

Explorations in Science and Nature. As a poem principally set in the rural countryside, the "Elegy" belongs with other nature poems, such as Finch's "Nocturnal Reverie" and Thomson's excerpts from *Autumn*. It also teaches well with the landscape poems by Goldsmith and Crabbe, which investigate the historic changes the English countryside underwent during the century.

Politics of the Individual. Because the poem highlights the huge differences between the rich and the poor, the literate and the illiterate, it might also teach well in this cluster. Again, it would pair well with Leapor's poems, but it also looks forward to the work of other plebian poets, such as Burns and Clare.

Discussion Questions

1. Whom among the dead do we commemorate, and how do we do so?
2. Whose elegy is this? Why is the speaker writing/speaking this elegy?
3. How does the perspective of the outsider poet affect the representation of the rural poor in this poem?

4. As a pastoral elegy, the poem is populated with swains and shepherds. What effect does this pastoral imagery have on the meaning of the poem? (Would it be different if the characters were more realistic?) See Johnson's criticism of *Lycidas* for more information on the pastoral.

5. How does the poem's dominant theme—that we all await the final hour of death—compare with the treatment of the theme in other poems of the era, for example, Rochester's *Satire against Reason and Mankind*, Swift's *Verses on the Death of Dr. Swift*, or Johnson's "Vanity of Human Wishes"?

6. In lines 37–40, whom is the poet addressing and why?

7. What does the poem have to say about the fame of the laboring poor? Do they achieve fame? Why or why not?

8. The last section of the poem focuses on the role of epitaphs—poetry. How does one remember the illiterate? What does the "unlettered muse" write on their gravestones?

9. Who is "thee" in line 93, and what are the implications this address?

10. The poem celebrating the unhonored dead ends with a fantasy of the poet's own memorial, where he envisions his anonymity and marginality but creates his own fame (both in the epitaph and in the poem, which literally made Gray famous). How does this ending illustrate the problems of fame and immortality that the poem tries to work out?

Further Resources

NORTON ONLINE ARCHIVE

Hymn to Adversity

Audio:
Elegy Written in a Country Churchyard (read by Anton Lesser)

William Collins

Ode to Evening

Collins's pretty poem celebrates the coming on of nightfall in the figure of Eve, reminiscent of Milton's character from *Paradise Lost*. The extended personification and quiet lines of natural beauty anticipate Keats's "To Autumn." It is a lovely change of pace in the poetry of the eighteenth century.

Quick Read

- Form: Rhymeless metrical ode.
- Style: Quasi-pastoral.
- Key Images: "chaste Eve," 2; "nymph reserved," 5; "maid composed," 15; "calm vot'ress," 29; "meekest Eve," 42; Fancy, Friendship, Science, rose-lipped Health, 50.

- Key Passages: Poet's address to Eve, 1–8; poet's request "teach me," 15–20; the magic fancy of evening, 21–28; poet to follow evening throughout the seasons, 29–48; poet as Evening's votary, 49–52.
- Key Themes: Evening's magic and beauty inspire the poet's fancy; evening is like a lovely woman; the poet woos her with his hymn.

Teaching Suggestions

Because the poem draws an extended comparison between evening and Milton's Eve, it may be useful to teach a passage or two from *Paradise Lost* with this poem. The descriptions of Eve in Book 4 and in particular her evening worship with Adam (4.610–775) are good illustrations. Be certain to read Collins's poem aloud in full. The lack of end rhyme will perhaps surprise the students, but astute listeners/readers will be able to identify the sources of the poem's music. Note also the way the lines contrast with Milton's bold strains and stately iambic pentameter. As in "Ode on a Poetical Character," Collins writes a poem about the poetic process, the source of inspiration, but in this case the prospect for success is more optimistic. Collins's portrait of Eve is at once an exquisite nature poem and a love song. Ask the students to attend to the personification of evening and the attributes Collins ascribes to it. This poem also presents a good opportunity to discuss issues of gender and beauty, and you might supplement the work with some passages from Burke's *Philosophical Enquiry* that highlight the characteristics of beauty as soft, feminine, smooth, and timid. Notably Burke identifies the effect of beauty as love and affection but not admiration, which is the effect of the sublime.

Teaching Clusters

As a nature poem, this ode teaches well in **Explorations in Science and Nature**, and it could be taught with other poems of evening such as Finch's "Nocturnal Reverie" and Thomson's excerpt from *Autumn*. Because of the extended personification, the poem may teach well with Keats's "To Autumn."

Discussion Questions

1. How would you describe the style of this poem? How does it compare with the blank verse used by Milton?
2. What are the effects of punctuation and fluid syntax in the poem?
3. Who is "chaste Eve" in line 2? What are her characteristics? How or why is this personification appropriate?
4. What mood is created through the imagery of lines 5–14?
5. What is the poet's relationship to Eve? What does he ask of her?
6. What does the poet commit himself to in the final lines of the poem?
7. What does the poem suggest about the role of nature in poetry?
8. In what ways is this poem more optimistic about the poetic process than "Ode on the Poetical Character"?

Further Resources

NORTON ONLINE ARCHIVE

Ode Written in the Beginning of the Year 1746
Ode on the Death of Mr. Thomson

Christopher Smart

Jubilate Agno

Smart's playful lines on his cat Jeoffrey will appeal to those who want to teach the oddities of eighteenth-century literature or to those who will be focusing on animal poems throughout the ages. It is an endearing prayer-poem that accentuates Smart's powers of observation (an eighteenth-century motif) and the limited surroundings upon which he could exercise them.

Quick Read

- Form: Antiphonally arranged prayer.
- Subject: Jeoffrey, a cat.
- Theme: The cat's beauty and ingenuity is a sign of God's providence.

Teaching Suggestions

Samuel Johnson discussed the incarceration of this poet and concluded, "I'd as lief pray with Kit Smart as anyone else," but most members of his society did not agree, and so they had him put in a madhouse. One way to teach this poem is as an exercise in perceptions of sanity. Poetry often blurs the lines of what is real and what is imagined; for example, a metaphor fuses two unlike things to create new meanings, new emphases. Ecstatic poetry, of which this is an example, pushes the limits of understanding even further, and sense gives way to symbol, sound, and excess of feeling. Ask the students to evaluate the poem for its sense. Ask the students to consider the poem for its symbolism. Is the author sane and poetic? At what point do we take the praise of his cat Jeoffrey literally? At what point must we abandon conventional sense and interpret the poem on some other register? What register of meaning would be most explanatory: literary, spiritual, psychological, other?

Teaching Clusters

As a poem that features the powers of observation it might be included in the **Explorations in Science and Nature** and taught with *Rasselas* or Thomson's excerpt from *Autumn*. A playful unit on animals might include Gray's "Death of a Favorite Cat," Barbauld's "The Mouse's Petition," Burns's "To a Mouse," and Blake's "The Lamb" and "The Tyger." The religious tenor and the long lines of the poetry resemble some of Blake's prophecy poems, and so one might teach it with "Marriage of Heaven and Hell.

Discussion Questions

1. In what sense is the cat doing what the poet claims he is doing?
2. What is the tone of the poem?
3. How would you describe the language of the poem? What is the significance?
4. At what point does Jeoffrey become more than a housecat? What does the poem claim for him?
5. Is the poem funny? Do you think it is meant to be so? Why or why not?
6. How does the author feel about Jeoffrey? How do you know?

Further Resources

NORTON ONLINE ARCHIVE

A Song to David

Oliver Goldsmith

The Deserted Village
(with excerpt from George Crabbe's *The Village*)

Few works can be paired so effectively in a course as Goldsmith's *The Deserted Village* and Crabbe's *The Village*. These works can challenge students to think more deeply about the politics of poetry and the ways in which poetic choices contribute to political statements. Both poems convey outrage at the poverty and depopulation of the countryside that happened as a result of enclosures and engrossing, but they represent the people of that countryside in starkly opposed ways. Furthermore, Goldsmith's easy couplets and sentimental imagery were chosen in response to the "affected obscurity" of Collins and Gray and the "tuneless flow of our blank verse, the pompous epithet, laboured diction" of poetry popular in the mid-century. Crabbe, on the other hand, deliberately writes with harsher cadence and uglier imagery to offset Goldsmith's idealization of the rural poor.

Quick Read

- Form: Landscape poem in iambic pentameter couplets.
- Style: Sentimental, pastoral, easy, simple couplets with variety and gentle cadence.
- Key Passages: Memory of Auburn from youth, 1–34; current desolation of countryside, 35–50; wealth and trade, 51–74; poet returns, laments change, 75–112; the sounds of the past are silenced,

113–28; the solitary poor widow, 129–36; portrait of country preacher, 140–92; portrait of country schoolmaster, 193–216; memory of the country tavern, 219–36; pleasures of the rural poor vs. pleasures of the urban rich, 251–64; call to political leaders, 265–86; metaphor of nation to woman, 287–302; image of betrayed country girl in the city, 325–36; emigration, 341–84; apostrophe to luxury, 385–94; apostrophe to poetry, 407–30.

- Key Themes: Luxury is the root of national and domestic destruction; depopulation of the peasantry is a permanent and grave loss.
- Potential Pedagogical Challenge: The poem is long; you may need to prep students for it before they read.

Teaching Suggestions

Because the poems by Goldsmith and Crabbe describe the effects of the historical changes to the British countryside, it may be worthwhile to provide some information regarding these developments. Donald Greene in *The Age of Exuberance* offers a brief, readable explanation, and there are many informative Web sites on enclosures. Suffice to say that technological advances in farming combined with the transition from open-field farming to enclosed farming made it possible to increase the yield of food production in the country significantly, which helped sustain the tremendous population growth over the course of the eighteenth century. However, large landowners took to engrossing commons and other lands to build huge estates for profitable farm production, which forced poorer farmers off the land and depopulated the countryside. The poems focus only on the latter effect. For a literary representation of the positive impact of enclosures for gentleman farmers, see Book 3 of Tobias Smollett's *Humphry Clinker*.

Ask students to examine the way Goldsmith constructs the "poet" of *The Deserted Village* and the inhabitants of the now desolate village. By focusing on the pastoral imagery and the elaborate sentimental metaphors—most notably the comparison of the country to a fallen woman—students will begin to appreciate what motivates Crabbe in his deliberately unsentimental view of the vices of the rural poor. Goldsmith's fantasy of the poet's return to his homeland is both sentimental and gently ironic. Note how this passage contrasts with William Wordsworth's sublime memory of a rural visit in "Tintern Abbey." The image of the poor solitary widow who alone remains in "Sweet Auburn" merits attention, especially as it contrasts with the two portraits of prominent members of his youthful village: the preacher and the schoolmaster. The sentimental representation of the village tavern anticipates the homely realism of such scenes in George Eliot's *Silas Marner*. It is important to stress, however, that despite Goldsmith's sentimentalism, the poem asserts a very direct moral: that the luxury of trade and wealth is seriously damaging the core strength of the country, the bold peasantry. His call to politicians is direct. He envisions a dismal future for the country if it continues on this path:

"I see the rural Virtues leave the Land," and he lists these virtues: Toil, Care, Tenderness, Piety, Loyalty, and Love. Finally, he addresses Poetry as the potential cure for these ills. This suggestion receives a bitter reply in Crabbe's poem: "Can poets soothe you, when you pine for bread, / By winding myrtles round your ruined shed?"

There are several resources for teaching Goldsmith available through *Norton Topics Online*, including links to portraits of Goldsmith, excerpts from other works, and an interesting comparative text by his grandson, Oliver Goldsmith, called "The Rising Village."

Teaching Clusters

Public Sphere and Civil Society. As a representation of the negative effects of luxury, wealth, and trade, these poems serve as a counterdiscourse in an age that celebrated the urbane, refined politeness of *The Spectator* and *The Rape of the Lock*. In this way, the poems teach well with other critiques of urban wealth, such as *The Vanity of Human Wishes* and Gray's "Elegy." They also anticipate the Romantic appreciation for landscape and the emotional investment in touring the countryside, best exemplified in William Wordsworth's poetry and Dorothy Wordsworth's journals.

Explorations of Science and Nature. As landscape poems with an attitude, these works belong in this cluster. They could be taught well with Finch's "Nocturnal Reverie," Thomson's *Autumn*, Gray's "Elegy," Collins's "Ode to Evening," and sections of Cowper's *The Task*.

Politics of the Individual. As political poems that criticize the decisions of the rich against the welfare of the poor, these poems can be taught in this cluster. Note how different the politics look in Goldsmith and Cowper as compared to in Dryden, Swift, and Pope. The edge of satire gives way to pathos, and in this way these poems could be taught effectively with Charlotte Smith's *Beachy Head* and Barbauld's "1811" and "Epistle to William Wilberforce."

Discussion Questions

1. Examine Goldsmith's depiction of women (the solitary poor widow, the betrayed country girl in the city). What roles do they play in the poem? How does he characterize them?
2. Why does Goldsmith choose to present the portraits of the country preacher and schoolteacher? What is significant about their roles in his memory?
3. What role does memory play in this poem? What role does creative invention play?
4. What does the poem say to the political leaders of Goldsmith's country?

5. In the final apostrophe to poetry, what does Goldsmith hope poetry can do?
6. In what ways does Crabbe's poem criticize pastoral representation of the rural poor?
7. According to Crabbe, do the rural poor benefit from poetry? Why or why not?
8. How do the inhabitants of the rural countryside in Crabbe's poem differ from those in Goldsmith's? What is the point?
9. In what sense is Crabbe's portrayal more realistic than Goldsmith's? Which is more effective?
10. The *Norton Topic Online* "A Day in Eighteenth-Century London" includes excerpts and illustrations that highlight fashionable urban life, such as the theatre, Ranelagh, and Vauxhall Gardens. In what way do these poems comment upon these urban amusements?

Further Resources

NORTON ONLINE ARCHIVE

GOLDSMITH
Letters from a Citizen of the World
  Letter XXVI: The Character of the Man in Black;
    With Some Instances of His Inconsistent Conduct
  Letter LXXI: The Shabby Beau, the Man in Black,
    the Chinese Philosopher, etc., at Vauxhall
CRABBE
The Borough
  Letter XXII, The Poor of the Borough: Peter Grimes

William Cowper

The Task

Take a break from the fast pace of the twenty-first century and enjoy the thoughtful, contemplative blank verse of William Cowper. His poetry requires slow reading, deep cleansing breaths, and an alternative perspective. Think of it as eighteenth-century yoga. *The Task* was a favorite of Jane Austen's, which speaks to its clarity and her finely balanced sense and sensibility. Cowper's poem has the moral compass of Johnson's prose and the limpid lines of the best Romantic nature poetry.

Quick Read

- Form: Blank verse, iambic pentameter, landscape poem, meditative verse.
- Style: Clear and distinct imagery; easy, gentle rhythms; simple, everyday diction.

- Key Passages: From Book 1, the river Ouse, 163–80; sounds of nature, 181–209; crazy Kate, 534–56; from Book 3, the stricken deer, 108–33; from Book 4, winter evening, 243–332.
- Key Theme: Contemplating nature restores mental balance.

Teaching Suggestions

Cowper's descriptive poetry is extremely visual and auditory, and so students might find useful parallels by viewing some naturalistic landscape painting and/or hearing birdsong, especially to accompany the first excerpt. The *Norton Topics Online* Romantic section "Tintern Abbey, Tourism and Romantic Landscape" includes some good illustrations, such as the views by Francis Town and the images of Ullswater. As Cowper claims, his "raptures are not conjured up / To serve occasions of poetic pomp." There is a distinct move away from the pastoral tradition to a purer language and more natural description in Cowper's poem. In his words, "The sturdy swain diminished to a boy!" This stylistic move accompanies a thematic shift; whereas previous poems meditated on abstractions such as Fear or Evening, Cowper's poem invites the reader to share the poet's own response to nature. At times he becomes the metaphorical subject of the poem's contemplation, in particular in the excerpt on the stricken deer. At other times he creates vignettes about people who occupy the landscape, such as Crazy Kate, a technique that will be used to great effect by later poets such as Charlotte Smith, Mary Robinson, and William Wordsworth. The poet's humble representation of his own melancholy and the restorative power of nature signals modern preoccupations with the power of the mind and an aesthetic view of nature. His descriptive lines on dusk falling in winter evoke strong parallels with Coleridge's magnificent "Frost at Midnight."

Teaching Clusters

Exploration in Science and Nature. As descriptive landscape and nature poetry, *The Task* belongs in this cluster, but its sympathies lie more squarely with Romantic poetry than with earlier Restoration and eighteenth-century poetry. A study in poetic transitions might begin with some descriptive passages from Milton's *Paradise Lost*, followed by Finch's "Nocturnal Reverie," Thomson's *Autumn*, Collins's "Ode to Evening," Goldsmith's *Deserted Village*, and then *The Task*.

Discussion Questions

1. What about the landscape pleases Cowper/the poet in the opening excerpt?
2. What effect does the landscape have on the viewer? On the reader?
3. How does the story of Crazy Kate exemplify the theme "fancy, too / Delusive most where warmest wishes are"?
4. To whom does the poet compare himself as a stricken deer? What is the significance?

5. Cowper writes of the coming evening, "Composure is thy gift." In what sense does evening compose? How does this excerpt compare with Collins's similar praise in "Ode to Evening" and Finch's "Nocturnal Reverie"?
6. What does the "soul that does not always think" (4.285) do instead?
7. What transition does the poet describe with the snowfall?

Popular Ballads

As indicated in the introduction in *NAEL*, these ballads are difficult to place historically because they were transmitted orally. It is significant that they were recorded and published during this era. A class on popular ballads therefore might address first how these poems represent a common voice, a male or female singer, a musical historian from the past. Second, the class might address what about these poems prompted their publication at this time. Finally, amid the forgeries and fakes of antiquity and the newly inspired ballads of the era, the class might discuss what makes these particular ballads authentic.

Quick Read

- Form: Ballad, variety of (mostly) short-lined stanzaic patterns.
- Key Motifs: Love leads to death; love bridges death; grief lasts a "lang" time.

Teaching Suggestions

The narratives of these ballads are spare and require some inference. Ask the students to take each one and analyze the details to fill out the story. For example, examine the details of "Lord Randall" and discuss what happens before the son returns to his mother. Why does she fear he is poisoned? In what sense is "sick at heart" literally poisoned? Who is correct? The motivation behind "Bonny Barbara Allan" can be similarly inferred from the key fifth stanza. As representatives of the oral tradition, the ballads tell "timeless" stories, and "The Wife of Usher's Well" can be discussed in terms of its iconic image of grief. What does the ballad suggest about the powerful ties between mother and son? Death appears frequently in the ballads, both as that which sets the narrative in motion and as that which concludes it. You might discuss the different ways the poems represent death. For example, the image of a bed recurs. In "The Three Ravens," the birds discuss the non-human response to human death. All the ballads pay tribute to the lasting impact of grief, and thus they suggest the healing power of song throughout the ages.

Teaching Clusters

Paradoxically, these ancient ballads might best be taught in the cluster on **Authorship and Literacy: New Readers, New Writers, New Forms.** A tension emerges in the literature of this cluster between ancients and moderns, a tension that these ballads embody. As anonymous texts from the oral tradition, they share with ancient texts authority and precedence, but as newly published ballads they reflect a change in contemporary taste. In this way, the ballads would teach well with other works that attempt to capture the medieval or traditional literary styles, such as the Gothic literature in the Romantic period. These would also teach well with Scottish poets who adopt the local dialect, such as Robert Burns, Joanne Baillie, and Sir Walter Scott.

Discussion Questions

1. Whose voice is speaking in each ballad? What or whom does it represent?
2. How do these poems fit in with eighteenth-century literature? Why would there be interest in publishing them at this time?
3. What makes these poems "authentic" ballads?
4. How do the ballads represent love? Why is it so fatal?
5. What images or symbols stand in for death in these ballads? Why?
6. What role does grief play in the ballads?
7. What are the chief characteristics of sound in these ballads?

The Restoration and the Eighteenth Century: Texts in the Norton Online Archive by Authors Not in NAEL (also Textual Clusters)

Ignatius Sancho and Laurence Sterne
      Sterne: Reply to Sancho
      Sterne: *Tristram Shandy*, Volume 9, Chapter 6
Richard Brinsley Sheridan
      The School for Scandal
A Grace Beyond the Reach of Art
      Longinus: Genius and the Rules
      Quntilian: When to Break the Rules
      Rene Rapin: Grace Beyond the Rules
      Sir William Temple: The Inadequacy of the Rules
      John Hughes: Curiosa Felicitas
      Roger de Piles: Grace Gains the Heart
      Leonard Welsted: No Precepts Can Teach Grace
The General and the Particular
      Aristotle: Poetry and History Contrasted
      Horace: Character Types in Comedy
      Sir William Davenant: Poetry and History Contrasted
      Anthony Ashley Cooper, Third Earl of Shaftesbury: The General and the Particular in Painting
      Samuel Johnson: The Particular in Biology
      Samuel Johnson: The Simplicity of Grandeur

CHAPTER 9

The Romantic Period
1785–1830

INTRODUCING THE PERIOD

The Romantic period in literature is vibrant, experimental, and filled with emotional extremes. The literature found here encompasses a full spectrum: from Gothic novels and the Byronic hero, to the ecstatic contemplation of beauty in nature, to the celebration of the child and new beginnings, to the stark realizations of fragile, human mortality. There is a tremendous variety of untraditional voices in this section, including a fair number of women writers, peasant or working-class writers, and regional writers, such as native Scottish and Irish who feature the language and culture of their people. This mélange can in some ways be attributed to the "Spirit of the Age," a spirit of renovation, rebellion, and revolution that had its roots in the political and social revolutions of the era. Students will need to know a certain amount of the historical context in order to appreciate the significance of the innovation and democratic impulses of the literature. The introduction to the Romantic period will be crucial for establishing this base of information, and you may want to supplement this with general histories and biographies listed in the bibliography at the back of *NAEL*.

Most of the literature in this section is poetry and much of it is lyric poetry. To teach this period, the instructor must have a good grounding in skills of close reading. Students coming upon the Romantic period in a large survey may breathe a sigh of relief as they read the straightforward diction and the comfortable speaking "I" of the poems. In many ways, the Romantic period set the agenda for the poetry that dominated throughout the twentieth century. Students will immediately assume that the lyric "I" is the poet and that the poem expresses the author's feelings in a specific biographical moment. Certainly Wordsworth's poetry and his Preface to the *Lyrical Ballads* encourage this identification. Students will need to be wary, however, because the poets use the speaking voice of the poem artfully and with self-conscious variations. There is, in fact, a wide range of voices represented in the lyric poems. Even Wordsworth experimented, as is evident from his notes on *The Thorn*. Furthermore, many texts are far more interested in the observation and description of the external referent than in the detailing of poetic subjectivity. In Robinson's "London's Summer Morning," no speaking "I" is in evidence: the poem begins by asking "Who has not wak'd" to the pleasing cacophony of London street life on a hot summer's morning and goes on to describe in rich detail the noise and splendid chaos of the busy city. The "poor poet" appears only briefly and in the third person. Other texts—Blake's dramatic monologues and persona poems in *Songs of Innocence* and *Songs of Experience*, several of Wordsworth's contributions to *Lyrical Ballads*—explore the workings of subjectivities quite distinct from the poet's. Indeed, Blake continually plays with voice and reminds the reader that he is doing so, writing as various prophet-personae (demonic and otherwise) like "the voice of the Bard" ("Introduction," line 1), "The Voice of the Devil" (*The Marriage of Heaven and Hell*), and "The Voice of one crying in the Wilderness" ("All Religions Are One"). Smith's sonnets, wherein the speaking and poetic "I" do merge, are often intensely self-regarding, but what they describe is a longing for the dissolution of subjectivity. Attention to the way a poet constructs the voice of the poem, therefore, is important.

A central aspect of the era's poetic innovation is the use of lyric forms. In the preceding period, poets attended to the traditional hierarchy of genres that placed epic and heroic poetry at the top, and much of the poetic production of that age adopted formal verse genres from ancient Greek and Roman writers. Part of the daring in Wordsworth's Preface and the *Lyrical Ballads* themselves lies in overthrowing that canonical hierarchy of genres and making the lowly lyric the genre of choice. He wasn't the first to write lyric ballads in that era, but he was their most important advocate. New instructors should get a firm grasp of the popular lyric forms used in the period: ballad, song, sonnet, and ode. The simple rhythms and rhyme schemes of the traditional ballad stanza—a tetrameter/trimeter quatrain with *abab* rhyme scheme—are easy for the students to grasp and can become their training ground in scansion and analysis of sound. You can move up the ladder of complexity in lyric genres, focusing on the fourteen-line stanzas of the sonnets and comparing the use made of them by the accomplished sonneteers of the period—Smith, Wordsworth, and Keats. You can introduce the way the sonnet allows for the structuring of ideas in formal patterns: the Shakespearean progression of ideas in the quatrains defined by rhyme (*abab, cdcd, efef*) and concluded by a couplet, or the Petrarchan conflict and resolution in the octave and sestet. For more information on teaching sonnets, see the entry for Charlotte Smith. Finally, spend time on the magnificent odes of the era, the most significant of the lyric genres. Each author adopts his or her own stanzaic pattern in the ode, but they all conform to the ode's general characteristics: a lyric poem devoted to a single theme in exalted language. Teaching suggestions for some of the era's best odes are outlined in the author entries. See the entry on Keats for treatment of the rhyme scheme. Also be certain to provide additional information on the forms if students require greater preparation. The literary terminology appendix in *NAEL* is a good start, but you might want to consult other texts on poetry. These short poems provide excellent opportunities to engage the students in exercises of close readings, analyzing the implications and connotations of language choice, the full range of significance for metaphors, similes, personification, and other devices, as well as the ways in which sound reinforces meaning in the lines. For examples on teaching close-reading techniques, see the entry on Blake. It is often helpful to compare and contrast two poems of the same genre in order to appreciate the differences and to underscore the fact that such differences arise from the poet's decisions.

TEACHING CLUSTERS

Revolution, Freedom, and Rights

The political revolutions of the Romantic era constitute a fundamental context and inspiration for the literature, and so an excellent teaching cluster could be based on **Revolution, Freedom, and Rights**. From the perspective of most Romantic writers, the French Revolution was the most animating event of the age; it promised both practical and political changes and the transformation of "intellectual and spiritual" and imaginative life as well. In addition to representing the revolutions in America, France, and Haiti, authors also saw the political upheaval and transformation as causes (and sometimes even as symptoms) of literary change—whether the latter involves changes in the hierarchy of genres or changes in the identity of the author. In this context, the cluster could consider "Cockney poets" (Keats, Lamb, Hazlitt), "unsex'd females" (Barbauld, Smith, Wollstonecraft), and "the ploughman poet" (Burns). The focus on freedom and rights also translated directly into what Wollstonecraft calls "a revolution in female manners" as well as into the movement for abolition of the slave trade, and so this cluster also includes works of proto-feminism and abolitionist support.

Texts: In-text topic "The Revolution Controversy and the 'Spirit of the Age,'" Burns's "For a' that," Blake's *Visions of the Daughters of Albion*, *Marriage of Heaven of Hell*, and "Little Black Boy," Charlotte Smith's *The Emigrants*, the second half of Wordsworth's *Prelude*, Hazlitt's "My First Acquaintance with Poets," Percy Shelley's *Prometheus Unbound*, "To Wordsworth," and "England in 1819," Keats's *The Fall of Hyperion*,

Austen's *Love and Friendship,* Anna Barbauld's "Epistle to William Wilber-force," Wordsworth's "To Toussaint l'Ouverture" and "September 1st, 1802," Mary Wollstonecraft's *Vindication of the Rights of Woman,* and Barbauld's "The Rights of Woman"

Supplemental novels: Smith's *Desmond,* William Godwin's *Caleb Williams, or, Things as They Are,* Robinson's *Walsingham,* Austen's *Pride and Prejudice,* Burney's *The Wanderer,* Shelley's *Frankenstein*

Norton Topics Online: "The French Revolution" provides important background information, texts, and illustrations for this cluster.

Who Is a Poet, Writing for Whom?

The era's controversies about political authority along with the explosion in literacy rates raised questions about the politics of literacy and about the relationship between literature and popular or mass culture. In the Preface to *Lyrical Ballads,* Wordsworth asks, "What is a poet?" and to the extent that he both redefines the poet as someone who speaks the language of common life and yet dissociates poetry from the popular culture of a new mass audience, the Preface could be a starting point for a cluster on the politics of literacy. This cluster also includes works that feature the problematic figure of the peasant poet, such as Burns and Clare, and the ways in which they are valorized (but also condescended to) for their access to a natural, uncivilized, or uncorrupted language. Similarly, regional literatures such as that by Scott, Edgeworth, Baillie, and Burns also pertain to this group. The cluster questions how regional differences as well as class differences affect Romantic ideas of literary value. For example, one could analyze the ways in which Scotland and Ireland come to be associated with an oral tradition that disappears with the spread of the standard English of print culture. Or one could focus on the value of poetic spontaneity and the figure of the inspired bard/minstrel/improvisatore in contrast to earlier poetic models of mimesis or imitation.

Texts: Barbauld's "Washing-Day," Robinson's "The Poor Singing Dame," Preface to *Lyrical Ballads,* selections of the *Lyrical Ballads,* Coleridge's discussion in *Biographia Literaria* of Wordsworth's claims about rustic life and poetic diction, In-text Topic "The Gothic and the Development of a Mass Readership" (especially the "Essay on Terrorist Novel Writing," Coleridge's review of *The Monk,* and the excerpt from *Biographia Literaria*), Lamb's "On the Tragedies of Shakespeare, Considered with Reference to Their Fitness for Stage Representation" and "Detached Thoughts on Books and Reading," books in Wordsworth's *Prelude* (1, 2, 5), selections from Byron's *Don Juan,* Clare's poems and autobiographical prose fragments, Wordsworth's "Solitary Reaper," Dorothy Wordsworth's journal, Joanna Baillie's "A Winter's Day" and "Woo'd and Married and a,'" Scott's "Lay of the Last Minstrel" and "Wandering Willie's Tale," Edgeworth's

"The Irish Incognito," Blake's Introductions to *Songs of Innocence* and *Songs of Experience*, Hemans's "Corinne at the Capitol," Shelley's "To a Sky-Lark" and *A Defence of Poetry*, and Keats's odes

Supplemental novels: Edgeworth's *Castle Rackrent*, Scott's *Waverley*, Sydney Owenson's *Wild Irish Girl*

Outlaws, Outsiders, and Exiles

A fascination with the mysterious isolated figure, whether outlaw, outcast, or outsider, pervades the literature of the era and provides a locus for a provocative teaching cluster. Included here are the many texts that center on the mental state of a figure exiled from society, haunted by guilt over past transgressions, and defined by those crimes. A study of Byron and the Byronic hero is pertinent, and this cluster could make good use of the online materials on the Satanic hero, under "Literary Gothicism." Under this rubric, one might consider the production of poetry itself in what Percy Shelley calls "The Spirit of Solitude" and the autobiographical impulse in Romanticism as represented by texts such as Wordsworth's *Prelude*. Further, one could examine how women poets engage the topic of poetic ambition through the exiled or isolated figure and their representation of the poet as a quasi-Satanic transgressor. Alternatively, one could teach authors that treat this subject as a dangerous preoccupation and represent it through satire, such as Burns or Austen.

Texts: Coleridge's *Rime of the Ancient Mariner*, Shelley's *Alastor*, *Prometheus Unbound*, and *A Defence of Poetry*; Byron's *Manfred* and *Don Juan*; Wordsworth's *Prelude* (especially the "spots of time" passages in books 1 and 4), *The Thorn*, "Nutting," and "Resolution and Independence"; Lamb's essays; Hazlitt's "My First Acquaintance with Poets"; De Quincey's *Confessions of an English Opium-Eater*; Mary Shelley's "Mortal Immortal" and the introduction to *Last Man*; Barbauld's "Summer Evening's Meditation"; Charlotte Smith's *Elegiac Sonnets* and *Beachy Head*; Mary Robinson's "To the Poet Coleridge" and "The Haunted Beach"; Felicia Hemans's "Corinne at the Capitol"; Burns's "Tam O' Shanter"; Austen's *Love and Friendship*

Supplemental novels: Mary Shelley's *Frankenstein*

Norton Topics Online: "Literary Gothicism" and "Romantic Orientalism" provide useful background, supplemental texts, and illustrations for this cluster.

Gothic Times, Gothic Enchantments, the Revival of Romance

Following an age of reason, when the mysteries of the universe were discovered to be subject to mathematical laws, poets and novelists began to turn back in history to a time of gothic magic in order to re-enchant what science and knowledge had disenchanted. Some Romantic writers thought that a pre-enlightened, medieval past—and the literary forms they associated with that bygone era, such as ballads and narrative romances—allowed more scope and more freedom for the imagination than did the contemporary moment. The literature here shares with the cluster on outlaws a fascination with altered mental states—the mental states of primitives or of the mad or those under the influence of dark, mesmeric powers. The in-text topic "The Gothic and the Development of a Mass Readership," especially the essay by the Aikins, would be a good starting point. Also to be included are the many narrative poems that revive the medieval romance, especially those by Keats. For Keats, romance served as a seductive enchantment even in the poetry that moves beyond it, such as in the odes, and so they would be appropriate here as well.

Texts: Robinson's "Poor Singing Dame," Burns's "Tam O' Shanter," Wordsworth's *Lyrical Ballads*, the Lucy poems, *The Thorn*, Coleridge's *Christabel, Rime of the Ancient Mariner*, Scott's "Wandering Willie's Tale," Byron's *Manfred*, Mary Shelley's "The Mortal Immortal," Felicia Hemans's "A Spirit's Return," Keats's *The Eve of St. Agnes, Lamia*, and the odes, Letitia Landon's "The Proud Ladye"

Supplemental novels: Walpole's *The Castle of Otranto*, Smith's *Emmeline*, Lewis's *The Monk*, Radcliffe's *The Romance of the Forest* or *The Italian*, Scott's *Ivanhoe*; alternatively Austen's *Northanger Abbey*

Norton Topics Online: "Literary Gothicism" and "Romantic Orientalism" include important background information, supplemental texts, and illustrations for this cluster.

Education, the New Child, New Beginnings

The late eighteenth century pioneered new schemes for education and a new literature written explicitly *for* children, and the writers of this era turn to children as both a topic of literature and a putative audience. In this way, the works in this cluster focus on the new rather than the old, on the figure of the child as an emblem of revolutionary hope. The new child becomes a symbol of a transfigured, democratized world, as suggested by Blake's image "Albion Rose" in the color insert. While the literature beholds the world through the perspective of young, untainted eyes, it also presents for the child the values it will need to thrive in the world. In this way, the cluster includes conversations on education, especially as it relates to girls and women, and the significance of nurturing domesticity and maternal bonds.

Texts: Barbauld's "To a little Invisible Being," "Washing-Day," and "The Mouse's Petition," Blake's *Songs of Innocence and of Experience*, Joanna

Baillie's "To a waking infant," Wordsworth's "We are Seven," "Nutting," the first two books of the *Prelude*, maybe the sixth, and especially "Ode: Intimations of Immortality," Coleridge's "Frost at Midnight," Lamb's "Christ's Hospital Five-and-Thirty Years Ago," Hemans's "Casabianca," Wollstonecraft's *Vindication*, Austen's *Love and Friendship*

Supplemental novels: Hay's *Memoirs of Emma Courtney*, Austen's *Mansfield Park* or *Northanger Abbey*, Mary Shelley's *Frankenstein*

Science, Exploration, and Observation of the Natural World

By the end of the eighteenth century, scientific discovery had introduced exciting and alarming facts about human existence that were incorporated in the literature through a new emphasis on the interconnectedness between human beings and other living things. Radical changes to the British landscape leading toward the Industrial Revolution also fueled what we would now call an ecological consciousness, a sensitivity to environment that received further impetus from consideration of very different, un-British natures that had been "discovered" in the South Pacific. Works to be included in this cluster investigate human relationships with animals, plants, and the environment, including scientific and picturesque appreciations. These works reflect the increased interest in domestic tourism and the related art of landscape painting. In terms of later works from the era, the cluster might include representations of technology, such as steam power and railways.

Texts: Barbauld's "Washing-Day," "Mouse's Petition," "An Inventory of the Furniture in Dr. Priestley's Study," and "A Summer Evening's Meditation," Charlotte Smith's *Elegiac Sonnets* and *Beachy Head*, much of Wordsworth, especially "Tintern Abbey," *Michael*, "Steamboats, Viaducts, and Railways," and the *Prelude*, Dorothy Wordsworth's journals, Coleridge's *Rime of the Ancient Mariner*, "This Lime Tree Bower," and "Frost at Midnight," Austen's *Love and Friendship*, Shelley's "Mont Blanc," "Alastor," and *A Defence of Poetry*, John Clare's "The Nightingale's Nest" and "The Mouse's Nest," Keats's odes, Mary Shelley's "Mortal Immortal," Wollstonecraft's *Letters Written in Norway, Sweden, and Denmark*, Joanna Baillie's "Address to a Steam Vessel"

Supplemental novels: Mary Shelley's *Frankenstein*, Austen's *Persuasion*

Norton Topic Online: "Tintern Abbey, Tourism, and the Romantic Landscape" provides useful background information, supplemental texts, and illustrations for this cluster.

AUTHORS AND WORKS

Anna Letitia Barbauld

Washing-Day

Barbauld's deceptively simple poem about domestic drudgery contrasted with poetical whimsy introduces Romantic motifs of childhood, subjectivity, memory, and imaginative power, while at the same time it pays respect to the Augustan poetic tradition and the work of great writers that came before her, namely Shakespeare and Milton. The epigraph itself, taken from As You Like It, captures Barbauld's balanced position between the old and the new, as Shakespeare's words remind us of literature's preoccupation with the human life cycle and the parallels drawn between old age and infancy. Barbauld's poem sets up a number of additional symbolic parallels, primarily between the imaginative play of the mature poet and that of the child of her memory.

Quick Read

- Form: Mock-epic in blank verse.
- Style: "Slip-shod measure," mock seriousness, Miltonic gravity, and homey imagery.
- Key Passages: Invocation of the domestic muse, 1–8; dawn and washer women, 13–14; displaced master, 34–46; shift to first-person memory, 58+; Montgolfier's balloon, 80–86.
- Motifs: Childhood subjectivity; memory as a source of poetry; power of imagination.

Teaching Suggestions

In order to appreciate how the poem pays homage to the past, it is important to discuss the form of mock-epic. (For more on this, see entries on Pope and Dryden.) Following Milton in the use of repetitive phrases for the effect of grandeur, otherwise known as *epanalepsis* ("Cast at the lowering sky, if sky should lower") and Cowper in the use of a humble domestic subject for an epic poem, Barbauld sets a tone of playfulness. The choice of muse that she invokes indicates the sphere of her mock-epic; hers is not Milton's spirit but the "domestic Muse." The opening lines indicate the locale of not only her poem but poetry in general at that time: "The Muses are turned gossips; they have lost / The buskined step, and clear high-sounding phrase." Barbauld's muse occupies the farmyard and fraternizes with children. You can discuss with students what sort of poetic transition Barbauld is describing and how her own poem fits in the context of other Romantic-era poetry.

You can also teach the poem in terms of the gendered issues it raises. Typically in mock-genres, the playfulness raises the subject matter higher than it probably deserves, but it also lowers the dignity of the original tradition. In this way, "Washing-Day" asserts the propriety of writing poetry about women's work. The displacement of the master of the house during the arduous washing activity could be a gendered focus of discussion as well. The students may need to be made aware of the difficulties of washing day in the eighteenth century, an activity that was generally scheduled every five weeks and which put the entire house into service for the elaborate processes of washing, rinsing, drying, ironing, and folding.

The poem turns toward the recognizable Romantic lyric "I" at line 58, and students could profitably examine the ways in which the two halves of the poem compare. The perspective of the child of the poet's memory offers a playful contrast to the feverish work of the women in the first part. The poet's memory leads by seeming whimsy to the play of children blowing soap bubbles, which provides for the provocative comparison with which the poem ends. Time should be spent analyzing what Montgolfier's balloon, which represents the human ability to ascend from the earth, children's soap bubbles, and the poet's own poem have in common. A discussion of the multiple meanings of the word "bubble" will be instructive.

Teaching Clusters

As a poem that articulates a new sphere of poetry, "Washing-Day" could be included in the cluster **Who Is a Poet, Writing for Whom?** It would partner well with Blake's Introductions and poems from *Songs of Innocence and of Experience*, and more provocatively with Hazlitt's "My First Acquaintance with Poets." Of course, this fits in well with the main work of this cluster, Wordsworth's Preface and the *Lyrical Ballads* themselves.

Because of the perspective of the child, "Washing-Day" could also be taught in the cluster on **Education, the New Child, New Beginnings**. The emphasis on Montgolfier at the end ties this loosely to the cluster **Science, Exploration, and Observation of the Natural World**, although Barbauld's poems on Priestley would fit in that cluster much more securely.

Discussion Questions

1. What significance does the parallel between infancy and old age, suggested by the epigraph, have in the poem?
2. What evidence does the poem provide for a shift in patriarchal power in the home during washing day?
3. How do the opening lines of the poem compare with earlier epic or mock-epic invocations? What is the significance of Barbauld's departures?
4. What is the tone of the poem, and what devices does Barbauld use to achieve it?
5. How does the voice of the speaker change at line 58?
6. What is the meaning of lines 78–79: "Then would I sit me down, and ponder much / Why washings were"?
7. How is the power of the imagination represented in the poem?

8. What do soap bubbles, Montgolfier's balloon, and the poem have in common?

9. How does the representation of the child here compare with that in "To a Little Invisible Being Who Is Expected Soon to Become Visible"?

10. In "A Summer Evening's Meditation," what is the significance of sending her mind to roam among "the trackless deeps of space"?

11. Barbauld's relationship to Wollstonecraft is difficult to assess. How do you read her response to Wollstonecraft in "The Rights of Woman," particularly the ambiguous final stanza?

12. How does Barbauld represent slavery in "Epistle to Wilberforce"? To what does she attribute the country's refusal to end the slave trade?

Further Resources

NORTON ONLINE ARCHIVE

Life

Charlotte Smith

Elegiac Sonnets

As explained in the headnote, Charlotte Smith virtually began the revival of the sonnet form in the Romantic period, and her poems had tremendous influence on a generation of Romantic writers. She adopts the fourteen-line form to accommodate a representation of nature as an analogue to psychological states, and this figurative use of the landscape soon became characteristic of Romantic poetry. In a long literature survey, Smith's sonnets can be taught in comparison with the celebrated practitioners of the Renaissance (Shakespeare, Sydney, Spenser, Milton), as well as later sonnet writers Wordsworth and Keats. The sonnets included in *NAEL* also introduce a number of important Romantic motifs and so they can be taught in conjunction with longer Romantic-era poetry if the course features this period.

Quick Read

- Form: Traditional Shakespearean sonnet with variations in second and third quartets.
- Motif: Landscape representing psychological state, "Written at the Close of Spring," "To Night," "Written in the Church-Yard," "The Sea View."
- Motif: Isolated individual in the landscape.

Teaching Suggestions

A focus on the sonnet form, rhyme scheme, and punctuation may be a useful way to begin teaching these poems, particularly if you will be comparing Smith's sonnets with others. Characteristically, the compact poems create a contrast or represent a problem that achieves some resolution, and the rhyme scheme structures the thought of the poem. Ask the students to examine the poems for such "argument" or movement of ideas. For Smith, description is primary, as opposed to metaphor or symbolic action, and this is particularly true in the poems that feature the landscape: "Written at the Close of Spring," "To Night," "Written in the Church-Yard," and "The Sea View." For example, in the traditional Shakespearean sonnet "Written at the Close of Spring," the first quatrain describes the fading flowers of late spring, the second laments the cessation of spring until its renewal the following year, the third compares the cycle of human passion with the seasons, and the final couplet draws the contrast to a sharp and poignant conclusion. Ask the students to compare this formal sequence with the variations Smith employs in the other sonnets and to describe the effects this has on the structure of thought in the poems. Also ask the students to examine her use of punctuation, in particular the dash and the exclamation point, and the effect it has on the structure of ideas.

Smith's sonnets provide a good context from which to compare the use of the sonnet form by other Romantic-era poets, namely Wordsworth and Keats, who both have a number of selections in the text. In doing so, you might note how each author represents the speaking "I" of the poem differently. While all three use the form autobiographically (see Wordsworth's "Surprised by joy" and Keats's "On First Looking into Chapman's Homer" for examples), there are important differences that the students can discern. Also ask students to look for differences in form (Wordsworth favors the Petrarchan or Italian sonnet, while Keats favors the English like Smith) and style (Wordsworth's tend to greater narrative and philosophical speculation—"Composed upon Westminster Bridge," "London, 1802"—while Keats famously uses a sensuous, densely metaphorical and symbolic style—"When I have fears," "Bright star"). At the conclusion of the exercise, you can discuss why the sonnet as a short, personal lyric form appeared so congenial to Romantic-era poets.

Teaching Clusters

The *Elegiac Sonnets* will teach well in the cluster **Science, Exploration, and Observation of the Natural World** because of the intense representation of nature and landscape. As suggested above, these poems will teach well with other sonnets by Wordsworth, Keats, and Shelley, but they also make good companion texts to the *Lyrical Ballads*. The focus on precise detail in the natural landscape underscores the scientific motif, and this is also particularly true of the long poem, *Beachy Head*, which should be taught in this cluster.

"To Sleep" and "On Being Cautioned against Walking" might also be taught in the cluster on **Outlaws, Outsiders, and Exiles** because of their focus on the isolated individual.

Discussion Questions

1. What does the poet conclude about human happiness in "Written at the Close of Spring"? How does this compare with Percy Shelley's representation of the seasonal cycle in "Ode to the West Wind"?
2. How does the poet differ from the peasant, sea boy, or shepherd in "To Sleep," and what is significant about these identities?
3. How does Smith's "Written in the Church-Yard" compare with the representation of that subject in Gray's famous "Elegy Written in a Country Churchyard"? Are there any deliberate echoes?
4. In what sense does the poet describe a longing for the dissolution of the self—of subjectivity—in any of these poems? What is to be gained by this?
5. How does Smith represent the mad or "lunatic" subject in "On Being Cautioned against Walking"?
6. How does Smith adjust the sonnet form to represent her criticism of war in "The Sea View"? What is the tone or attitude in this poem? How does this compare with the representation of war and its effects in *The Emigrants*?
7. In what sense can you categorize these poems as pastoral? What pastoral themes do they engage? How does this compare with similar representations of pastoral subjects and themes in Blake or Wordsworth?
8. Other than the speaking "I" of the poem, what perspective(s) does the poet represent in "The Sea View"?
9. What is the tone of these poems? How is it achieved?
10. Compare Smith's representation of the landscape in these poems with the landscape portraits available in *Norton Topics Online* "Tintern Abbey," and discuss how the mind creates the objects it perceives.

Mary Robinson

The Poor Singing Dame

While the selections from Robinson exhibit a range of form, tone, mood, and subject, and each would teach well in a survey or a Romantic-era course, "The Poor Singing Dame" is the most accomplished and unique of the selections. This poem features an isolated female poet and so provides interesting opportunities to discuss the gendered representation of the production of poetry. It also flirts with the supernatural and suggests that the natural world wreaks vengeance on the sinner. In this way, it shares some motifs with the "Haunted Beach," which has been discussed often in connection with Coleridge's *Rime of the Ancient Mariner*, but its sympathies lie with the victim and not the outlaw figure.

Quick Read

- Form: Narrative lyric in eight-line stanzas of anapestic tetrameter (*ababcdcd*).

- Style: Gothic, romance.
- Key Passages: The hovel and the castle, 1–8; the natural beauty of the hovel, 9–16; the lord hears the woman singing, 17–24; the woman's gay singing throughout the year, 25–32; the lord's envy leads him to imprison the woman, 33–40; she dies and is buried, 41–48; the owls haunt the lord, 49–56; the lord dies unmourned, 57–64.
- Themes: Poetry (song) is a source of pure joy; misery loves company; nature avenges her own.

Teaching Suggestions

Teaching this poem should begin with reading it out loud and enjoying the rhythm and sound. This is particularly important because the sound of the poem contrasts with its tragic action, creating potential irony—or a gap between what the poem says and how it says it. Begin discussion with the setting of the poem and Robinson's description of the natural environment of the hovel—stanzas 1 and 2. Discuss the symbolic contrasts between the castle and the hovel and what they represent as material objects. The contrast (and antagonism) shifts to the occupants of the buildings in the next two stanzas. You might discuss how the song of the old woman operates as both a source of joy and a source of pain and how the symbols of wealth and power (revels, huntsmen, castle-bell) in the poem are removed from the scene of poetic production. Stanzas 5 and 6 focus on the lord's envy and the cessation of poetry or song. Here it would be appropriate to question the motivation of the lord and to speculate on the meaning of the woman's death. Note the way that Robinson describes the natural world in sympathy with the martyred poet. The final stanzas feature the lord's suffering at the hands of nature, and students might discuss why the owls are appropriate vehicles of vengeance. Note also the way that the closing lines describing the position of the two graves reflect the original placement of the two homes in the opening stanza.

Teaching Clusters

Because the poem features a gothic setting of castles and hovels and a romance style of antique simplicity, it fits in the cluster on **Gothic Times, Gothic Enchantments, the Revival of Romance**. With its focus on the female victim, it compares well with Landon's "Proud Ladye" and Keats's "La Belle Dame sans Merci," but it also shares many themes and motifs with Coleridge's "Kubla Khan." The topoi of sin and guilt, but notably not redemption, connect this poem to "The Haunted Beach" and Coleridge's *Rime of the Ancient Mariner*.

Discussion Questions

1. What tone is created by Robinson's use of the anapestic measure? How does this contrast with the tragic narrative? What effect does this contrast between sound and meaning have?

2. Why do the turrets "frown" upon the hovel? What do the dwellings suggest about their inhabitants?
3. In what ways does nature sympathize with the old singing dame? Why?
4. What motivates the lord to silence the old woman? Why doesn't she stop singing?
5. Why does the old woman die? Why does the lord die? How are their deaths different?
6. In what ways might this poem be about the plight of the woman poet in a culture hostile to female authorship?
7. Why is there such a pronounced class difference between the lord and the old singing dame? What is the significance of this gulf in the poem?

Other Discussion Questions on Mary Robinson

1. In "London's Summer Morning" and "January, 1795," how does Robinson convey the essence of the season of summer or winter using only the cityscape and its human inhabitants? Given that Robinson's poems, written in the same year, share certain strategies—both proceed by means of itemization and addition, both use figurative language sparingly—how do they manage to achieve such different effects?
2. How does "To the Poet Coleridge" comment upon "Kubla Khan"? What does it mean for Robinson to identify in Coleridge a new genius in poetry?
3. What information needs to be inferred in "The Haunted Beach"? How does this compare with traditional ballads, such as "Sir Patrick Spens" and "The Wife of Ushers Well," as well as those by Burns and Scott?

William Blake

Songs of Innocence and of Experience

Blake's poems offer the perfect opportunity to analyze poetry as a multimedia event. Three of his illustrations from the volumes are included in the text (the title page to Songs of Innocence, the title page to Songs of Experience, and the watercolor illustration of "The Tyger"). Blake's poetry is intimately connected to his painting and etching. Teaching the poems with the illustrations is important because it re-creates a sense of the original way Blake issued the poems and so helps to create the intended context for them, but it also emphasizes the symbolic and ironic potential of the poetry. Additionally, reading a series of paired poems from the two collections neatly illustrates the "two contrary states of the human soul" and so prepares students for the Romantic predilection for reconciling opposing ideas. In fact, the deceptively simple, enjoyable songs can serve as an excellent way to introduce many Romantic motifs and concerns: new ways of seeing, revolutionary impulse, fascination with the child, glorification of the commonplace, and renovation of minor lyric forms.

Quick Read

- Form: Short lyrics of varied meters, measures, and stanzaic forms.
- Useful Pairings: "Introduction" (*Innocence*) with "Introduction" (*Experience*); "The Lamb" and "The Tyger"; "The Chimney Sweeper" (*Innocence* and *Experience*), "The Divine Image" with "The Human Abstract," "Holy Thursday" (*Innocence* and *Experience*), "Infant Joy" and "Infant Sorrow."
- Pedagogical Aids: Additional watercolors and a portrait of Blake are included in the *Norton Topics Online* for the Romantic period.

Teaching Suggestions

The accessibility of these poems makes them ideal for first classes or classes when students have not prepared any reading. You can read them aloud in class and discuss them immediately. If you have the students read ahead of time, be certain to assign the illustrations as well so that they can begin to analyze the connections. In class, read the "Introduction" from *Songs of Innocence* aloud and have the students look at the title page for the volume. The discussion for each poem can be structured for simplicity and maximum coverage in four or five steps: denotative meaning, form, symbolic or figurative language, dialogue with illustration, dialogue with partner poem. Because the denotative meanings are fairly easy, more time can be spent on the close reading of poetic devices and symbolism. The meaning of the poem's sound should be addressed on the level of form (how does the trochaic meter here sound different from the anapests of "Chimney Sweeper" [*Innocence*] or the iambs of "Divine Image") and symbolic and figurative language (what is the effect of repeating the word "pipe" and "piper"?). The songs make use of a number of effective forms, such as the dialogues and dramatic monologue (see "Infant Joy" and "Infant Sorrow" for an especially dramatic and imaginative use), and so attention should be paid to the different effects of the speaking voices.

The illustrations create a dialogue with the poetry that might be surprising for the students. For example, the illustration of "The Tyger" looks playfully cartoonish (you can show pictures from *Norton Topics Online* to demonstrate Blake's more fearsome creations for contrast). The visual image of the Tyger contrasts with the "fearful symmetry" of the verbal image and so creates a tension you can explore with the students. What might this suggest about the Tyger itself? Is the beast a source of fear or is it a cuddly animal? What might the image suggest about the state of the soul represented in "The Tyger"? *The Songs of Innocence* and *The Songs of Experience* can be read on their own as complete poems, but by reading them in pairs you can develop a fuller sense of the psychological complexity of Blake's artistic vision. You might connect this discussion of "The Tyger" to "The Lamb" and analyze what the two animals symbolize in terms of the human experience. The Tyger, as experience, might embody wisdom, an awareness that brings disillusionment and pain, or cynicism.

The Lamb, as innocence, might embody pure-heartedness, naiveté, or blind orthodoxy.

The most obvious and disturbing contrasts between the two states of the human soul can be seen in the poems that share the same title: the "Chimney Sweeper" and "Holy Thursday" poems. In the first, the same childhood tragedies are canvassed from the different perspectives of a child in a state of innocence and a child in a state of experience. In the second, the image of charity children singing for their benefactors changes from a celebration of humanitarianism to a satire on religious hypocrisy and the gap between haves and have-nots. These two pairs illustrate Blake's social criticism and sharp ironies and so can be used to develop a discussion on social issues of the era as well as literary technique. Blake is one of the few Romantic poets to exploit irony to this degree. (See Byron for another Romantic expert on irony.) Blake invites his readers to draw a moral (perhaps multiple, conflicting morals) from the *Songs*, but he doesn't make it easy for them. For more information on Blake's revolutionary ideas, consult the very informative headnote in *NAEL*.

Teaching Clusters

These poems fit best in the cluster on **Education, the New Child, New Beginnings**. The focus on the subjectivity of children is enhanced by the ambiguous relationship between the *Songs of Innocence* and the *Songs of Experience*, which suggests the third rubric in this cluster—new beginnings. Blake's vision calls for breaking down restrictive moral binaries and establishing a new moral order. These poems could be taught with Blake's *Marriage of Heaven and Hell*, especially the Proverbs from Hell, for which there is a brilliant watercolor illustration available online. As a set of poems that center on the subjective experiences of children, you could teach them with Barbauld's "To a Little Invisible Being," Baillie's "A Mother to Her Waking Infant," Wordsworth's "We Are Seven," "Lucy Gray," or "Nutting," or Hemans's "Casabianca."

Discussion Questions

1. How do the "Introduction" poems represent the practice of poetry? How are they different?
2. What do the title-page illustrations suggest about the content of each volume? To what extent are these pictures accurate predictors of content? To what extent are they symbolic?
3. What does the lamb symbolize in "The Lamb"? How consistent is this symbolic meaning when the image appears in other poems?
4. How does your interpretation of "The Lamb" change after you read "The Tyger"?
5. How is the poem "The Tyger" presented on the page? What is the relationship between the text and the illustration? How does this differ from traditional, standard presentation of poetry as text?
6. What do the *Songs of Innocence*, taken collectively, suggest about

Blake's use of the pastoral? Consider pastoral themes, such as the loss of innocence, the healing power of nature, the triumph of life over death.

7. To what can we attribute the difference between the "Chimney Sweeper" of *Innocence* and the "Chimney Sweeper" of *Experience*? What do the poems suggest about the contrary states of the human soul?

8. Who are the speakers in "Infant Joy"? Why is this significant? (Contrast "Infant Sorrow," available in the Norton Online Archive.)

9. What sort of moral vision do the two volumes of poetry together suggest?

10. Why is the child or a child's subjectivity an appropriate subject of these poems?

Further Resources

NORTON ONLINE ARCHIVE

On Another's Sorrow

Robert Burns

Tam O'Shanter: A Tale

Listening to David Daiches's recording of Burns's charming ghost story ushers you into the ancient world of Scottish lore and bawdy humor. To be sure, there are important educational points to be made, but the musical enchantment of the Scots dialect and jaunty tetrameter couplets will captivate as fully as the mock-heroic idiom and hilarious story will amuse. The poem may also serve as an occasion to discuss the role of the peasant poet, folk myths, and the appeal of Scottish culture in the Romantic era.

Quick Read

- Form: Folk tale in iambic tetrameter couplets.
- Style: Scots dialect, mock-heroic idiom.
- Key Characters: Tam; Meg or Maggie, his horse; Nannie ("Cutty-sark"); Kate, his wife; the poet.
- Places: The Scottish town of Ayr; the river Doon; the haunted church; the kirk of Alloway.
- Key Passages: Opening description of Tam and his wife, 1–32; Tam's drunken delight, 37–58; Tam departs in the rainy night, 69–78; Meg and Tam pass scenes of violent death, 89–96; see kirk alight, 101–13; ghost dance, 115–50; Nannie in her cutty-sark, 163–78; Tam's mistake, 183–89; the chase, 191–218; poet's interruptions/direct address, 33–36; 151–62; 179–80; 201–04; 219–24.

Teaching Suggestions

Reading the Scots dialect can be frustrating for students not used to it, and so it will be imperative to present the poem aurally. Reading it becomes more pleasurable after hearing it, and students will gain a greater appreciation for it. On the surface, the poem is a delightful rendering of the mishaps of a drunken Scottish laborer, but the poem gains depth through the manner of the storytelling. One way to focus discussion is by drawing attention to the role of the storyteller in the poem. The opening section is important because it establishes the poet's role and his relationship to his subject. Burns adopts a mock-heroic idiom by placing the action in an undetermined past (folk myth), by describing mundane events through hyperbole ("Ah, gentle dames! It gars me greet"), and through serio-comic treatment of low subjects, such as getting drunk ("Wi' reaming swats, that drank divinely"). His numerous asides and direct commentary on the story offer additional points of ironic contact. For example, you can ask students what the poet's address to the wives (33–36) contributes to the tale; how does it affect the action or the tone? More centrally, the poet's address to Tam himself (151–62) on his reaction to seeing old women dance in their undies offers the opportunity to analyze the poet's sympathy with Tam. Finally, the poet's closing address to the reader offers a mock moral that playfully puts into question the purpose of poetry.

Teaching Clusters

With the focus on witches, warlocks, and the devil, the tale of "Tam O'Shanter" belongs in the cluster on **Gothic Times, Gothic Enchantments, the Revival of Romance,** and could be taught with other ghost stories, such as Robinson's "The Haunted Beach," Coleridge's *Christabel* and *Rime of the Ancient Mariner,* and Hemans's "A Spirit's Return." Because it shares with Scott's "Wandering Willie's Tale" a Scottish setting and emphasis on folklore, the pair would make a particularly strong component. The playful ironies of Burns's tale make it a good contrast to the more sensational Gothic literature featured in the In-text Topic "The Gothic and the Development of a Mass Readership," such as the excerpts by Beckford and Lewis.

Discussion Questions

1. Where does the poet's sympathy lie in the opening stanza? Why?
2. What generates the conflict between husband and wife in the poem, and why is this important?
3. Evaluate these lines: "Kings may be blest, but Tam was glorious, / O'er a' the ills o' life victorious!" (57–58). What is the style? What is the point? What happens immediately after?
4. What is the effect of the series of similes in lines 59–67 and again in 193–200?

5. How does the poem represent the witches and warlocks of Alloway Kirk? What is significant about them?
6. Why does Tam yell out "Weel done Cutty-sark!" and why does Nannie react the way she does?
7. How serious is the poet's closing moral? What might be implied instead?
8. How does this poem, usually considered Burns's most polished, compare with his other tales and songs? In what sense is this the work of a "peasant poet"?
9. What does the poem say about magic or enchantment? What causes Tam to be "bewitched"?
10. How does this poem reflect Scottish culture? Why might it inspire admiration for such culture among Romantic enthusiasts? Compare the works of Baillie and Scott.

Further Resources

NORTON ONLINE ARCHIVE

Corn Rigs an' Barley Rigs
Willie Brewed a Peck o' Maut
Ae fond kiss
Ye flowery banks

The Revolution Controversy and the "Spirit of the Age"

It is difficult to overstate the influence of the political revolutions of this era on the literature, although that influence has not always been acknowledged. This special section demonstrates how enthusiastically Romantic thinkers were involved in political debate, struggling to realize such abstractions as liberty, justice, and equality in concrete social terms. It may be hard for students to grasp the import of cataclysmic events for a historically distant people, so you may wish to underscore what's already emphasized in the introduction to the section, the extent to which the French Revolution transfixed the Romantic imagination. The prose selections gathered here are concerned with the English controversy about the Revolution. They are conveniently selected to demonstrate the tone of the discourse, and so they lend themselves nicely to an analysis of language and politics or form and function.

Quick Read

- **Richard Price:** From *A Discourse on the Love of Our Country*, supportive of French Revolution, celebratory.
- **Edmund Burke:** From *Reflections on the Revolution in France*, condemns French Revolution, sensational.

- **Mary Wollstonecraft:** From *A Vindication of the Rights of Men*, supports French Revolution, condemns Burke's treatise, indignant.
- **Thomas Paine:** From *Rights of Man*, supports French Revolution, condemns Burke's treatise, matter-of-fact.

Teaching Suggestions

These texts demonstrate the ways in which political-pamphlet wars were about control over language—that is, who owned the correct meaning of key words such as "rationality" or "civility." The way a political statement is made, as Burke knew well, is as important as what the statement is. This point should not be lost on students who are educated on liberal bias or conservative bias in the media and the frantic efforts to put the desired ideological spin on images during a heated political race. One way to focus discussion of these texts is to highlight the dual meaning of "convention" as used by Burke. On the one hand, social and political convention is what binds society and ensures peaceful, stable transitions from generation to generation. On the other, literary conventions are the recognized structures of poetic or rhetorical traditions. Burke draws an explicit parallel between literary and political structures when he quotes Horace on the need for poems to have beauty and to raise affection: "The precept given by a wise man, as well as a great critic, for the construction of poems, is equally true as to states" (157).

The selections here can be analyzed for their method of making a political point. Price puts forth his celebratory ideas in the form of an enthusiastic sermon, speaking to fellow dissenters who share his beliefs. Burke sends a chilling counter-message in an open letter meant to engage the sympathies of upper-class English men and women through emotional rhetoric and appeals to cherished values of chivalry. His lament for the fallen queen is the height of such sensationalism. Wollstonecraft and Paine both respond to the mode of Burke's address, and each of their texts is highly conscious of style. Wollstonecraft repeatedly urges her lack of polish as a political statement, while Paine counters Burke's "incivility" with the ostensible presentation of objective facts. Both Wollstonecraft and Paine, however, are capable of rhetorical excesses of their own, as when Wollstonecraft terms the European gentleman "an artificial monster" and when Paine describes the French government as an "augean stable of parasites and plunderers."

Teaching Clusters

Revolution, Freedom, and Rights. While students can glean some historical information from these texts, the implication that the Revolution had for poets is also made clearer: convention belonged to the past, while innovation, new vision, and hope lay within their own imaginative enterprises. The political arguments authorized their departure from literary authorities. In this way, these texts make a good foundation for the political understanding of Wordsworth's Preface to *Lyrical Ballads* and the *Lyrical Ballads* themselves, not to mention the criticism of his political retreat by Hazlitt and Percy Shelley ("To Wordsworth"). Also included should be Smith's *The Emigrants* and Blake's "Visions of the Daughters of Albion" and "Marriage of Heaven and Hell." For an important, and funny, send-up of this type of anti-authoritarianism, include Austen's *Love and Friendship*. See *Norton Topics Online* "The French Revolution" for more related texts and illustrations, many by Blake.

Discussion Questions

1. How does Price represent the "bloodless" revolution of 1688? How does this compare with Burke's version of those events? How do you account for the difference?
2. How does Burke employ the metaphor comparing the polis to a family? What is the effect?
3. In what ways does Burke appeal to the sensibility of his readers? What sentiments does Wollstonecraft appeal to in her writing? Paine?
4. How does the notion of politeness become politicized in Wollstonecraft's treatise? How does this compare with similar claims made in her introduction to *A Vindication of the Rights of Woman*?
5. Compare Wollstonecraft's use of the term "rational" or "rationality" with Burke's. What does Wollstonecraft imply by it? What does Burke?
6. According to Burke, how will civility and religion protect society from the dangers inspired by the revolution in France?
7. Why does Paine accuse Burke of incivility? How does he counter Burke's representation of France? According to Paine, what is the point of the revolution?
8. How would each of these four writers define a practical notion of liberty?
9. What role do the impoverished or laboring poor occupy in these arguments?
10. How do the political arguments presented here translate into literary arguments? What might they mean for poets such as Blake, Coleridge, Wordsworth, Smith, Clare, or Keats?

Mary Wollstonecraft

A Vindication of the Rights of Woman

Wollstonecraft's landmark analysis of the condition of women is not the first feminist essay, but it certainly is one of the most famous. Wollstonecraft would deploy similar arguments to those she used in *Rights of Men*—that all humans are *by nature* rational beings, that society should not constrain any individual's pursuit of reason and virtue, that the most long-standing social traditions may be the most tyrannical ones—in *A Vindication of the Rights of Woman*. Here Wollstonecraft challenged the commonplace belief that women were less rational and more emotional than men, possessing a weaker ethical sense but greater sensibility. Thus the "prevailing opinion" was that women were designed (by Nature, by God) not for work in the public sphere but to serve men: raising children, managing a household, providing emotional support, and being alluring, seductive mistresses. The selections from *Vindication* included in *NAEL* especially demonstrate Wollstonecraft's claim that women's subjugation results not from their native inferiority, but from social convention and faulty education.

Quick Read

- Form: Essay, political and social analysis.
- Style: Purportedly unpolished and unaffected; lively, witty, rapid accumulation of thoughts in an energetic and unsystematic order.
- Key Concepts: Women are weaker than men but ought to be educated to be morally responsible in their degree; women's inferiority stems from faulty education; middle classes are the most natural state; women's artificial weakness leads to tyranny; women trained only to get husbands will make poor wives; neglected wife makes a good mother; current education of women makes them creatures of sensibility and not intellect.
- Outline: Introduction, statement on style, summary of argument; chapter 2, analyzing how women are represented in literature or educated by authors; chapter 4, criticism of common female behaviors— love of pleasure, vanity, frivolity; sensibility produces contempt, call for education of heart and head.
- Analysis of Authors: Allusion to Burke; Milton (particularly Eve of *Paradise Lost*); Rousseau; Dr. Gregory; Pope.

Teaching Suggestions

In order for students to appreciate the oppression Wollstonecraft identifies in *Vindication*, you should assign and discuss the informative headnote, which provides background on women's legal and social standing at the turn of the century and the extent to which women lacked basic political rights and opportunities for meaningful or well-paid employment. For information on marriage laws, see the entries for Astell and Defoe in this guide.

The Introduction provides a summary of Wollstonecraft's argument and sets out her audience and method. Having students outline the main points here will provide a good overview of her piece. The two chapters excerpted from the longer work provide different evidence or proofs in Wollstonecraft's argument, and you can set them against each other to analyze the various sources of women's apparent inferiority. In chapter 2, Wollstonecraft takes to task many of the male authors who either create influential portraits of women (Milton, Rousseau) or set out to educate women into servile dependence (Gregory). Her approach anticipates methods used by feminist literary critics who analyze the representations of women, and so might present a good opportunity to discuss the connection between cultural representations and the construction of gender. This may prove especially fruitful if you have previously assigned *Paradise Lost*. In chapter 4 she criticizes the types of behaviors women have developed in response to their education and dependence, and she implicates women in their own oppression. For example, she says quite perceptively, but without trying to be indulgent to women, that until women stop accepting the specious praise offered in the form of gallantry, they will not become rational, respectable, and morally independent people. Challenge students to pursue this line of argument in contemporary society and to draw parallels with the arguments that Wollstonecraft makes, but be certain to highlight the many different options available to some contemporary women.

Writing assignment: Compare several Romantic-era texts in their responses to Milton's *Paradise Lost*—Barbauld's "Washing-Day," Wollstonecraft's *Vindication of the Rights of Woman*, Wordsworth's "London, 1802," Lamb's "Detached Thoughts," Byron's *Don Juan*, and Keats's *Fall of Hyperion*.

Teaching Clusters

This selection can be best taught in the cluster on **Revolution, Freedom, and Rights**, particularly since Wollstonecraft's language draws explicit parallels between the state of women and abject slavery. In this way, the *Vindication* could be grouped with anti-slavery writing, such as "Epistle to Wilberforce," Wordsworth's "To Toussaint l'Ouverture," and selections from Byron's *Don Juan*. The essay has direct ties to the writings in the section on the French Revolution, but it also prompts an ambiguous response from fellow female author Anna Barbauld in her poem, "The Rights of Woman." These could be taught together to explore the ways in which each represents "Woman" and the significance of the differences.

Discussion Questions

1. What arguments and rhetorical strategies do Wollstonecraft's *A Vindication of the Rights of Men* and *A Vindication of the Rights of Woman* share? How do the concerns of the former anticipate her analysis of the situation of women?
2. What role do texts by Rousseau, Milton, and Dr. Gregory have in the *Vindication*?
3. What do you make of her assertion that women are also like the rich of both sexes, trained in folly and vice, and soldiers, instructed in gallantry, prejudice, and blind submission to authority? What is the effect of her making such disparate comparisons?
4. How does Wollstonecraft explain the paradox that women's artificial weakness leads to tyranny?
5. Evaluate the "prevailing opinion" that women were created for men.

What implications derive from this opinion? How does Wollstonecraft aim to change it? To what extent are her arguments valid today?

6. How is romantic love used to degrade women? In what sense can passion (i.e., love) be rational according to Wollstonecraft?

7. How important is beauty to women, and why does Wollstonecraft criticize this?

8. What arguments does Wollstonecraft make in favor of expanding women's education? Whom is she trying to persuade?

9. To what extent does Wollstonecraft accept the superiority of men? Why?

10. How does the voice of the writer in *A Vindication of the Rights of Woman* compare with the voice of the writer in *Letters Written in Sweden, Norway and Denmark*? What concerns do the texts share?

Joanna Baillie

A Winter's Day

In the "Introductory Discourse" to her 1798 *Plays on the Passions*, an essay that influenced Wordsworth and Coleridge, Joanna Baillie suggested that ordinary people were in fact more interesting than their aristocratic betters: "those works which most strongly characterize human nature in the middling and lower classes of society, where it is to be discovered by stronger and more unequivocal marks, will ever be the most popular." Wordsworth similarly argued that "the essential passions of the heart" were best displayed in "low and rustic life" (Preface). But Baillie and Wordsworth both disapproved of the pastoral tradition that depicted rustic people as quaint or charmingly primitive. Baillie's narrative poem "A Winter's Day" depicts a day in the life of laboring people in rural Scotland with sympathy and attentiveness, but Baillie glamorizes neither her laborers nor their relationship with the natural world.

Quick Read

- Form: Narrative in blank verse.
- Structure: Rising, 1–84; breakfast, 85–121; morning industry, 122–53; midday activity, 154–79; evening: return to shelter, 180–240; night: friends around the fire, 241–98; bedtime, 299–311.
- Key Passages: Roosters and peasants implicit parallel, 1–23; winter landscape, 66–84; blackbird shot by huntsman, 143–53; the poor old veteran, 186–226 and 270–76; rural society compared with urban dissipation, 281–98.

Teaching Suggestions

Because the poem is structured as a day in the life of a good Scottish peasant family, one way to teach the poem is by noting how it marks time. You can break the poem into four sections corresponding to the time of day: morning, midday, evening, and night. What activities define the parts of the day for the different members of the family? What effect does this representation have? In each of the sections, the peasants correspond to or care for the living creatures of the land, most notably the birds. In this way, Baillie sets up parallels between the animals and the human world. Note, for example, how the cock must leave his comfortable rest with his mate to do his morning duty, just as the husbandman must do the same. Throughout, Baillie uses the images of birds to create significant parallels: the hungry sparrows knocking at the door prefigure the impoverished old soldier who approaches the cottage at evening. The one figure who appears to disrupt the otherwise natural and harmonious—if not lovely or idealized—industry of peasant life is the figure of the gentlemen wielding his fowling piece. Given the parallels between the birds and people in the poem, ask the students to consider what the death of the blackbird means. The soldier's story of war and the image of bullets hissing by his head suggest another parallel with the blackbird. What, then, do we make of the honorable death of his soldier sons? Baillie added lines 281–98 after the first version of the poem was published. While these lines represent the act of evening worship practiced among the Scottish peasants, they also contain a sharp comparison between the purity of peasant life and the dissipation of urban revelries. Given the subtle impressions made by the bird and animal imagery in the poem, you might consider discussing the merits of these relatively heavy-handed lines. Certainly it makes the celebration of Scottish peasantry clearer, and this provides a good opportunity to discuss the relative representation of Scottish peasants in the poems of Baillie and Burns.

Teaching Cluster

Who Is a Poet, Writing for Whom? Baillie's interest in representing the commonplace activity of peasants certainly puts into question the proper subject of poetry, and so this work would properly belong to the cluster that explores these ideas. Along with Wordsworth's Preface to *Lyrical Ballads*, Baillie's own preface to her plays in 1798 sets out a new agenda for literature (see headnote). The poem compares well with Burns's "Holy Willie's Prayer," "To a Mouse," and "To a Louse." Baillie's own poem written in dialect ("Woo'd and Married and a'") would also be appropriate in this cluster in that it focuses attention on the national identity of the poet.

Discussion Questions

1. How does the poem mark the passing of the time of day?
2. How would you describe the style of the poetry? How does this style correspond to Baillie's recommendations for dramatic language—that it should forsake "the enchanted regions of simile, metaphor, allegory, and description" in favor of "the plain order of things in this everyday world"? What makes these lines poetry?

3. What role do the birds—the cocks, redbreasts, sparrows, etc.—play in the poem?
4. What is the significance of the gentleman's killing the blackbird?
5. How does the old soldier's history comment upon a culture used to war?
6. Discuss the addition of lines 281–98. What does the poem gain by it? What, if anything, does it lose?
7. What, according to the poem, makes the rural peasants happier than their urban counterparts?
8. How does this representation of day compare with the hopeful song "Up Quit Thy Bower?"
9. How does Baillie's representation of the Scottish peasant compare with that of Burns or Scott?
10. How does Baillie's representation of the rural countryside (see 66–84 in particular) compare with earlier landscape poems such as Goldsmith's *Deserted Village* or Crabbe's *The Village?*

Maria Edgeworth

The Irish Incognito

Edgeworth's lighthearted tale about the differences between Irish and English culture at the end of the eighteenth century reflects the Romantic concern with marginal identities and evokes the tensions that existed between the dominant and subordinate nations during a period of transition. As a story about trying to live between cultures, "The Irish Incognito" also serves as a parable about "passing," a modern term used to describe how people with one cultural identity act in ways to suggest a different cultural identity. While the nationalistic differences that move the plot of the story may be completely unfamiliar to North American audiences (they probably will not know what an Irish "bull" is), the psychological conflicts involved in denying one's identity—national, ethnic, racial, or otherwise—will be familiar. Apropos of today's concerns over multiple forms of English, Edgeworth emphasizes how the Irish speak and think in ways recognizably different from their English contemporaries, and so highlights the role of language in identity formation.

Quick Read

- Form: Prose story, quasi-folktale.
- Key Characters: Phelim O'Mooney (aka Sir John Bull); his brother; Miss Sharperson (Scottish heiress); Terence McDermod (devoted countryman).
- Plot Summary: Phelim O'Mooney sets out for England to marry a rich British bride under the assumed character of an English baronet; his brother bets him a hundred guineas that he will reveal his native character at least eight times in four days. Phelim slips

seven times. To avoid losing the bet, he hides himself away and refuses to speak even though accused of forgery. The time elapses; he
wins the bet and returns to Ireland, happy to give up adventures and
to work for an income.

- Seven Irish slips: (1) patriotic pride at custom house; (2) bull—ship
  upon the face of the earth; (3) bull—more like than the original;
  (4) bull—see with the eye that's knocked out; (5) practical bull—
  coach going in the wrong direction; (6) bull—dog-tax upon cats;
  (7) bull—illuminate with dark lanterns (joke).
- Moral: An Irishman cannot deny his identity, nor should he.

Teaching Suggestions

On the surface, the story is an amusing tale of an Irish adventurer who
learns that he must stay at home and work for a living. However, Edgeworth dances around potentially explosive cultural conflicts by dramatizing the ways in which a poor but elegant Irishman can adopt the ways of
the English and "pass" sufficiently to marry into English (or Scottish)
money. On the one hand, the story plays upon cultural prejudices against
the Irish by making the main figure an Irish adventurer and setting him
up to expose his native identity through verbal blunders. On the other, the
story suggests how permeable national identities are, in particular the
vaunted English character, by demonstrating how easy it is for Phelim to
become John Bull and how gullible the English are when he behaves according to their expectations about Englishness. One way to teach the
story is to examine those points where he exposes his Irishness and consider what they indicate about the clash of cultures. Pay particular attention to the way that Edgeworth conveys the moment of discovery because
it varies depending on the identity of the person who discovers it. In the
end, students may debate what the story concludes about Irish-English
relations.

Teaching Clusters

As a representative work of Irish culture, the story may be taught in the
cluster **Who Is a Poet, Writing for Whom?** Within the theme, the question of national identity arises, as poetry shifts to accommodate commonplace subjects and marginal voices. In this way, "The Irish Incognito"
could be taught with the work of Scottish writers such as Sir Walter Scott
and Joanna Baillie. The former's "Wandering Willie's Tale" would make an
interesting complement as another prose story. Edgeworth's own *Castle
Rackrent* would make an excellent novel to teach with this story.

Discussion Questions

1. What is an Irish Adventurer, and why is the figure so disreputable?
2. What characteristics of Irish identity is Phelim quick to conceal?
   Why?

3. At what point does Phelim begin to rely on his own cultural knowledge as an Irishman to form judgments about Miss Sharperson?
4. What are the implications of Edgeworth's use of the "bull"—or contradiction contained within a verbal blunder unperceived by the speaker—to indicate Irishness?
5. By what ways are the Irish known in English society? Are any of these positive qualities?
6. What sacrifices is Phelim willing to make to win his bet?
7. What is the "moral" of the story?
8. In what ways does the story represent language and thought as national characteristics? Can you think of any contemporary examples of such national characteristics?
9. In what sense is this a parable about "passing" in society? What does it say about "passing"?
10. As an Anglo-Irish writer, Edgeworth was herself a cultural hybrid. What evidence of this hybridity can you find in the story?

William Wordsworth

In an 1818 letter, Keats writes that "A Poet . . . has no Identity—he is continually in for—and filling some other Body." When Keats criticizes the self-aggrandizing tendencies of the Romantic lyricist, he singles out Wordsworth as the most offensive "Egotist," although a few months later he expresses his admiration for Wordsworth in another letter, praising him as a compassionate and insightful thinker. In still another letter, he coins the memorable phrase "the wordsworthian or egotistical sublime" to describe a poetic sensibility overly enamored of itself. William Hazlitt satirizes the tendency of mere mortals to worship at the shrine of the egotistical sublime, as much as poets' willingness to accept such worship, when he writes that "ever after" hearing Wordsworth praise a sunset, "when I saw the sunset stream upon the objects facing it, [I] conceived I had made a discovery, or thanked Mr. Wordsworth for having made one for me!" ("My First Acquaintance with Poets"). Byron skewers Wordsworth and his poetry as impossibly dull in Don Juan: "Wordsworth sometimes wakes, / To show with what complacency he creeps" (Canto 3, lines 874–75). No matter how one feels about Wordsworth the man, his writings occupy the central place in the Romantic period. Because most survey courses and period courses will include Wordsworth, the guide will highlight three different teaching strategies. Many other poems will be mentioned as companion pieces in the teaching clusters or in the discussion questions.

Preface to Lyrical Ballads and a selection of Lyrical Ballads

The Preface is important to teach as a text that displays "the spirit of the age" by advocating the incorporation of democratic principles into poetic practice. It is useful to teach in tandem with the Lyrical Ballads themselves, especially because students beginning or continuing a survey may expect their poetry to be more "poetic" and find the *Ballads* something like prose. Alternatively, you might teach the poems themselves in a class prior to teaching the Preface so as to re-create the sense of originality that Wordsworth's first readers may have experienced, to be followed by an explanation of Wordsworth's practice and theory.

Quick Read

- Preface: First version published in the second edition of *Lyrical Ballads* (1800) and expanded for the third edition in 1802. The 1802 version is included in *NAEL*.
- Major Concepts for the New Poetry: Scenes to be taken from common life with a coloring of imagination thrown over them; language of "men"—no different than language of prose; spontaneous overflow of powerful feeling, recollected in tranquillity; poetry brings pleasure in acknowledgment of the beauty of the universe.
- New Definition of a Poet: A poet is a "man speaking to men" but with heightened sensibility; not different in kind but in degree.
- *Lyrical Ballads*: A variety of forms, not necessarily ballads; "an experiment."
- Teaching Aids: *Norton Topics Online* "Tintern Abbey, Tourism, and the Romantic Landscape" contains related texts, background information on the land that inspired Wordsworth, and numerous illustrations.

Teaching Suggestions

Depending upon where you are in your course when you teach the Preface, it may be useful to inform students of the dominant characteristics of the poetic tradition that preceded it. A convenient discussion of Augustan poetic principles is presented in a lighthearted way by Johnson's Imlac in chapter 10 of *Rasselas*. Discuss with the students what Wordsworth means by "scenes taken from common life," perhaps by alluding to the epic literature of the past and the hierarchy of poetic genres wherein the lyric occupied a lowly status. Refer to the subjects—the characters—of *The Thorn*, "We Are Seven," and *Michael* as well as the occasion for poetry in "Expostulation and Reply" and "Nutting."

When discussing the arguments regarding the appropriate language of poetry, you might ask your students to look carefully at Gray's "Sonnet on the Death of Richard West" and Wordsworth's analysis of it: go line by line to try to determine why Wordsworth argues that the italicized passages "in no respect differ from good prose" and are moreover the only passages in the sonnet "of any value." Then ask them to make a similar analysis of some of the *Lyrical Ballads* to see if Wordsworth himself has succeeded in eradicating the "difference between the language of prose and metrical composition" by using plain diction and conversational syntax, incorporating dialogue, and so on. Wordsworth's attempt to use the "language used by real men" can be seen in the conversations that take place in some of the poems, such as "Expostulation and Reply" or "We Are Seven." Ask your students to speculate about why Wordsworth does indulge in a limited amount of figurative language despite his own injunctions against it: for instance, the homely simile in "Simon Lee" ("the centre of his cheek / Is red as a ripe cherry," lines 7–8), the adjoined metaphor and simile that make up the second stanza of "She dwelt among the untrodden ways," and the personification of Nature in "Three years she grew." Additionally, you might want to include Coleridge's later criticism of Wordsworth's claims for the language of poetry in *Biographia Literaria*; he disagrees that the language of rustics is the best language and that there is no difference between the language of poetry and prose.

The most memorable aspect of Wordsworth's theory is the idea of "the spontaneous overflow of emotion" and its reimagined and refined expression "recollected in tranquility." Several of the poems dramatize this poetic experience, most notably "Lines Composed a Few Miles above Tintern Abbey," but this will be discussed in detail below. Other poems that emphasize this include "I wandered lonely as a cloud" and "My heart leaps up."

Teaching Clusters

The Preface can be among the central documents in the cluster **Revolution, Freedom, Rights**, in as much as it calls for a literary revolution based in democratic principles. However, it is also the foundational text for the cluster on **Who Is a Poet, Writing for Whom?** "The Ruined Cottage" and "Resolution and Independence" also contribute to that cluster and can be taught as exempla of Wordsworth's theory.

Much of the Romantic-era writing included in *NAEL* has ties of one form or another to Wordsworth. In addition to teaching Coleridge's *Biographia Literaria* in dialogue with the Preface, you obviously could include one of the poems that Coleridge contributed to the *Lyrical Ballads*, *Rime of the Ancient Mariner*, and one intended for the volume but unfinished, *Christabel*. Similarly, Dorothy Wordsworth's journals provide interesting biographical details about the inspiration of the poems as well as original insights on the subject matter. See the entry on Dorothy Wordsworth for more ideas on teaching the two together. You may also wish to compare Wordsworth's poetry about laboring-class people—for example, *The Ruined Cottage*, *Michael*, and *The Thorn*—to poetry written by the farm laborer John Clare. With an emphasis on the perspective of children, "Lucy Gray" and "We Are Seven" could be taught in the cluster on **Education, the New Child, New Beginnings**, with Blake's *Songs of Innocence and of Experience* as companion pieces.

Discussion Questions

1. "Simon Lee": What expectations does the poet assume the reader has? Why? What does the poet mourn in the final lines?

2. "We Are Seven": How does the poem represent the consciousness or subjectivity of a child? How does this differ from the adult speaker's perspective? Which predominates in the end?

3. "Expostulation and Reply": In what sense is Nature a teacher? How does the form of a dialogue affect the point of the poem?

4. *The Thorn*: Why is the poem called *The Thorn*? To what extent is this a poem about landscape? What is Martha Ray's relationship to the natural world she inhabits? To what extent can you say that Martha Ray is insane? Does the speaker convey sympathy for the woman? Why or why not? What effect does the rhyme scheme have on the poem?

5. "Lucy Gray": What evidence does the poem provide to support Wordsworth's claim for the imaginative coloring of this scene from common life? How does it compare with Crabbe's representation of common life in *The Village*?

6. "Nutting": What is the significance of the feminine gender for nature in this poem? What prompts the speaker's pain or guilt?

7. *Michael*: In what sense is this a "pastoral" poem? Why does Wordsworth draw attention to that tradition? How does the poet account for Luke's fall from grace? What does the unfinished sheepfold represent? How does this poem about a father and son compare with Coleridge's "Frost at Midnight"?

Lines Composed a Few Miles above Tintern Abbey

As the final poem in the original collection of *Lyrical Ballads*, "Tintern Abbey" is part of Wordsworth's experiment. In many ways this poem embodies the principles he explains in the Preface—it is a meditative poem on the power of nature to bring amelioration of the soul through the spontaneous overflow of emotion recollected in tranquillity. It is written in purposefully plain, proselike language, an effect enhanced by the rhymeless lines of blank verse. And yet it is nonetheless sublime poetry. With *The Prelude*, it exemplifies Keats's notion of the "egotistical sublime" as the poet recounts his mind's ability to transform the images of nature into something akin to faith or religion. The pleasure of the poem extends from the poet's own spiritual satisfaction in contemplating the beauty of the universe and the hope for similar regeneration in the figure of his sister Dorothy. In many ways, "Tintern Abbey" is a paradigmatic Romantic poem.

Quick Read

- Form: Blank verse, meditative poem.
- Tone: Dignified, somber, and sublime.
- Key Passages: Stanza 1, description of the River Wye in the present, laden with emotion; stanza 2, reflection on the five years between his visits to the area, reaching to the sublime, 35–49; stanza 3, brief doubt and the comfort he derived from the memory; stanza 4, difference between nature of his youth and now; "abundant recompense"

or recognition of the sublime beauty of the universe; stanza 5, turns to Dorothy and projects her experience to be like his own.

- Key Theme: Nature becomes "the anchor of my purest thoughts, the nurse, / The guide, the guardian of my heart, and soul / Of all my moral being" (109–11).
- Teaching Aid: *Norton Topics Online* "Tintern Abbey, Tourism, and the Romantic Landscape" contains related texts, background information on the land that inspired Wordsworth, and numerous illustrations.

Teaching Suggestions

There are many entry points into this magnificent poem, and so an instructor need not feel bound to a single, orthodox approach. I will suggest four possible teaching foci: time and consciousness; the poet as a worshipper of nature; the transformation of the landscape (comparing the poem with documents about Tintern Abbey and tourism); and Dorothy— gender analysis and comparison with her writings.

Time and Consciousness. Basil Wiley said that Wordsworth was a poet "living on capital"; that is, his poetry centered on the memories of emotions spurred by an event or image—the spontaneous overflow of powerful emotions recollected in tranquillity. "Tintern Abbey" exemplifies this precisely, and it highlights the poet's process of recollection by staging the poem in different periods of the poet's consciousness. It begins in the present but immediately hearkens back five years. The second stanza focuses on the pleasure of memory and the production of "unremembered pleasures." Ask the students to analyze what the poet means by "unremembered" here and in line 34. Challenge the students to decipher the many different subjectivities the poem invokes: the present poet, the poet of five years past, the solitary, urban dweller of the years in between, the poet in his youthful exuberance, the poet in his sober maturity with "abundant recompense," the declining powers of the future poet and the hope he locates in seeing himself in Dorothy in the future. Ask the students to consider what role nature or the beauty of the landscape plays for each of these consciousnesses. What does the poem ultimately suggest about nature and the poet's growth through time? You might conclude by examining the way that Wordsworth figures memory as both an important resource and a dwindling power, and finally why he wants Dorothy to become his storehouse of memories.

Worshipper of Nature. Wordsworth infuses the language of the poem with sacred terms, even labeling himself in line 152 a "worshipper of Nature." His poetry becomes a service to nature, a prayer, a hymn of praise. You could structure a class around the religious elements of the poem and the ways in which nature comes to serve as the "soul / of all my moral being." The passages on the sublime power of recalling the beauty of nature are key. See the second stanza, lines 35–49, in which he describes how the pleasure of recalling the "beauteous forms" of the river Wye leads him to "that blessed mood, / In which the burthen of the mystery, / In which the heavy and weary weight / Of all this unintelligible world / is lightened." Here and in the passage that follows Wordsworth attributes tremendous spiritual power to the perception of nature's beauty. He retreats somewhat in the next stanza and reserves only the power of personal solace. In the third stanza, he contrasts his thoughtless engagement in nature as a youth with the sober joys of his present, adult consciousness, and in lines 88–111 he identifies the spiritual core of his current appreciation of nature. In this view, where Wordsworth becomes the high priest of nature, Dorothy in the final stanza is his acolyte. Examine the way the poem attempts to figure the religious power of nature as a respite from the inevitable pains and ills of human experience.

The Landscape Transformed. In *Norton Topics Online* "Tintern Abbey, Tourism, and the Romantic Landscape," students will find documents and illustrations that set Wordsworth's poem in the context of tourism. Because Tintern Abbey was a favorite tourist spot, this may prove to be a profitable way to approach the poem and the poet's artful transformation of the popular landscape vista. You can compare the visual representations in the paintings, as well as the verbal descriptions by Gray and Gilpin, with Wordsworth's notably minimal descriptions. Pay particular attention to Gilpin's description of the poor people who inhabit the area and their unpoetic begging. When you return to the poem, you can discuss how, and perhaps why, these people are overlooked by Wordsworth. Instead he imagines "vagrant dwellers in the houseless woods" akin to the "hermits" of pastoral tradition. Relevant here may be Wordsworth's claim in the Preface that the poet must be committed to truth as well as the principle of selection: "on this he will depend for removing what would otherwise be painful or disgusting in the passion." You could direct discussion toward what passions Wordsworth intends to raise in his particular transformation of the landscape and why certain elements are selected while others are passed by.

Dorothy Wordsworth. Dorothy has a conspicuous presence in the poem as the poet's companion in the landscape, as a means of mirroring his emotional satisfaction in the worship of nature, as his hope for future regeneration, as his memory when memory will fail him. She represents both his supplement and his lack, and Wordsworth's description of her is notably ambivalent. Ask the students to examine Wordsworth's representation of his "dearest Friend," especially in the emotionally complex final stanza. What role does he create for Dorothy? In what ways is this role informed by gender? (What characteristics does she share, for instance, with the nurse, the guide of his heart, nature?) For this approach, it may be helpful to assign passages from Dorothy's journal to provide more context for the poem. Ask the students to contrast Dorothy's representation of the landscape with Wordsworth's. You might also discuss the way she represents her relationship to her brother and the role that his poetry plays in her life.

Teaching Clusters

Science, Exploration, and Observation of the Natural World. Although commentators may disagree about the degree to which "Tintern Abbey" is actually a landscape poem, it certainly belongs in this cluster on the observation of the natural world. The focus may lie more on the mental processes involved in observation, but it nonetheless participates in the aesthetic appreciation of nature. It could be taught with many sections of the *Prelude*, in particular the description of crossing the Alps, as well as Coleridge's "This Lime Tree Bower" and Shelley's "Mont Blanc." It makes for an interesting contrast on the one hand to Charlotte Smith's *Beachy Head* because it eschews the scientific precision she employs, and on the other to Keats's "To Autumn" because it so intensely focuses on the poet's ego.

Discussion Questions

1. How does the form of "Tintern Abbey" differ from that of other works in the collection *Lyrical Ballads*? What is the significance of its poetic form?
2. How does the memory of scenes from the Wye aid the poet when he is "mid the din / Of towns and cities"?
3. What does Wordsworth mean by the gift of nature—an aspect more sublime (36–37 and following)? For information on the sublime, see excerpts from Burke's *Philosophical Enquiry* in *Norton Topics Online*.
4. What does Wordsworth value in his youthful experience of nature? How has it changed through maturity? What is his "abundant recompense"?
5. How do you understand the sense of joy he describes as "something far more deeply interfused"?
6. What does the poet hope for Dorothy in his final stanza? What role does memory play in this projected future?
7. In what ways does this poem exemplify the poetic principles explained in Wordsworth's Preface?
8. How does Wordsworth's representation of the Tintern Abbey landscape compare with the landscape portraits of the time? What aspects of the landscape are featured in both? What role do the emotions play in both? For examples, see the *Norton Topics Online* "Tintern Abbey, Tourism, and the Romantic Landscape."

Ode: Intimations of Immortality

Like "Tintern Abbey," this poem considers the loss of poetic vision that accompanies growth and maturity, but the theme receives added significance through the form of the ode. The ode became a favorite lyric form for Romantic-era poets because it maintained the short and musical lines of ballads but allowed for greater expansion through elaborately rhymed stanzas; it thus became a more suitable vehicle for profound meditation. The Immortality ode is sometimes a dirge or a farewell to poetic powers and sometimes a celebration of the child-seer that remains within. In this way, Wordsworth captures the dynamic between loss and faith, expressed in high tones that contrast with many of his earlier works.

Quick Read

- Form: Formal ode.
- Themes: Growth and maturity are accompanied by a loss of poetic vision; the child remembers the soul's immortality; loss of vision is compensated by philosophic wisdom.
- Key Passages: "The things which I have seen I now can see no more," 9; "That there hath past away a glory from the earth," 18; "Wither is fled the visionary gleam? / Where is it now, the glory and the dream?" 56–57; "Our birth is but a sleep and a forgetting," 58; "Thou, over whom thy Immortality / Broods like the Day, a Master o'er the Slave," 118–19; "Moving about in worlds not realized," 145; "In soothing thoughts that spring / Out of human suffering; / In the faith that looks through death, / In years that bring the philosophic mind," 183–86; "To me the meanest flower that blows can give / Thoughts that do often lie too deep for tears," 202–03.

Teaching Suggestions

This challenging ode may best be taught by beginning with the short poem that Wordsworth quotes in the epigraph: "My heart leaps up." Consider the paradoxical relationship proposed in the line "The Child is father of the Man" and use this to frame the ode's meditation on maturity and the losses and gains that accompany growth. Although it may seem obvious, it may be helpful to stress the orthodox understanding of the soul as the immortal part of the human being that survives death. Wordsworth's treatment of the theme of poetic vision is deeply bound to notions of the immortal soul in this poem and the "celestial light" through which the child's fresh soul perceives the world. Working stanza by stanza, you can develop the poem's dynamic theme of loss and faith by attention to the mood and connecting imagery.

The poet states the problem in the opening stanza: he has lost the ability to see "every common sight" "apparelled in celestial light," 2, 4. The poet continues to recognize the beauty of nature around him in the second stanza, but he is saddened by the knowledge "that there hath past away a glory from the earth," 18. Note the solipsism of the poet's vision; the earth's glory is directly related to what he can and cannot see. In the third stanza, the poet recollects a prior sense of grief from which he is released by a "timely utterance." If you have taught "Resolution and Independence," you might remind the students of poem at this point. Note that lines 19–21 will be echoed directly in the tenth stanza in an affirmation of the poet's vision of the earth's beauty, even though he is removed from its power. The stanza closes with an embrace of the rejuvenating spirit of the natural world figured most sympathetically in the "happy Shepherd-boy," 36. The fourth stanza begins with a continued celebration of the shepherd children in a May Day festival but ends with the poet's haunting return to melancholy: "Wither is fled the visionary gleam? Where is it now, the glory and the dream?" 56–57. Stanza 5 introduces the idea of the preexistent soul—"But trailing in clouds of glory do we come / From God, who is our home," 64–65. After birth, the heaven about us begins to fade, and lines 67–76 describe the decline in terms of light. The short sixth stanza presents Earth as the stepmother of man who does all in her power to make him forget his preexistent glory; this image raises the idea that nature is somewhat duplicitous toward man and envious of heaven. Stanza 7 recounts the active imagination of youth in images that appear increasingly frivolous. In stanza 8, the poet addresses the soulful child who is unaware of his gift and loads him with the praises of poetic greatness: best philosopher, mighty prophet, seer blest. Wordsworth invokes a common theme of childhood poems when he asks, "Why with such earnest pains dost thou provoke / the years to bring the inevitable yoke?" 123–24. In the ninth stanza, the poet reflects with gratitude on the adult perceptions of immortality that remain and the joy that comes as a result of remembering the childhood visions. You might ask the students to interpret the image of "Blank misgivings of a Creature / Moving about in worlds not realized," 144–45. The poet returns to the imagery of joyous nature from stanza 3 in the tenth stanza and embraces the memory of his former closeness to immortality as a harbinger of future immortality. Ask the students to consider the meaning of the lines "In the soothing thoughts that spring / Out of human suffering; / In the faith that looks through death, / In years that bring the philosophic mind," 183–86. The final stanza describes the poet's newly defined relationship to nature; he still loves nature but no longer feels under its "habitual sway." The line hearkens back to the image of the master and slave from the eighth stanza. Like the mature poet of "Tintern Abbey," Wordsworth proclaims a devotion that is not frivolous, but instead sees nature with an awareness of his own mortality.

Teaching Clusters

Education, the New Child, New Beginnings. The poem's focus on children as blessed with a heavenly vision makes this an appropriate poem to teach in this cluster. Like Barbauld in "Washing-Day" but in a far more developed and philosophical way, Wordsworth associates the play of childhood with poetic power and vision. The Romantic preoccupation with the loss of poetic powers appears as the dominant theme in a number of other odes, including Coleridge's "Dejection: An Ode," Shelley's "Ode to the

West Wind," and Keats's "Ode to a Nightingale" and "Ode to Melancholy."
For an earlier treatment of the theme of childhood innocence, see also
Gray's "Ode on a Distant Prospect of Eton College."

Discussion Questions

1. How do the language, tone, and style of this poem differ from those
   of the *Lyrical Ballads?* (For example, note the use of abstractions.)
2. In what ways are the language, tone, and style appropriate for the
   theme?
3. In what ways might the "timely utterance" of line 23 give relief, especially if it is another poem?
4. What is the significance of the Shepherd-boy in this poem? How
   does this compare with other poems about shepherd children, such
   as *Michael?*
5. What are the implications of the stepmother Earth helping man to
   forget his divine origins?
6. What is the relationship between the immortal soul and vision? What
   is the significance of the light imagery, particularly in stanza 5?
7. How is a child a "best Philosopher," a mighty prophet, a seer blest?
8. Compare the image of adulthood as "the inevitable yoke" (124) with
   the poet's freedom from the "habitual sway" of nature (191).
9. What does the poet gain by reflecting on "human suffering"? What is
   "the faith that looks through death"? How does this ending compare
   with the ambivalence in "Tintern Abbey"?

Further Resources

NORTON ONLINE ARCHIVE

A Poet!—He Hath Put His Heart to School
To My Sister
The Green Linnet
Composed in a Valley Near Dover, on the Day of Landing
Composed by the Side of Grasmere Lake
Afterthought
Yew Trees
The Two April Mornings

Dorothy Wordsworth

Excerpts from the Journals

On the one hand, Dorothy Wordsworth's journals offer today's readers a
detailed, intelligent description of nature and simple living in rural England; on the other hand, they narrate a story of intense, although repressed, emotion and passionate love. One could read the journals as a
supplement to the writings of Wordsworth and Coleridge, in that they of-

fer narrative context and biographical information about scenes and inter-actions that also inspired the poets. However, it is important to listen attentively to the voice that tells the history and to hear the distinct notes of originality. Then one finds in her journals the mixed pleasure and pain of a life dependent upon her famous brother and the strivings of an imagination that developed under his tutelage and in his shadow. Furthermore, one sees the ways in which Dorothy's friendship and writings helped to make possible her brother's success.

Quick Read

- Form: Prose journal entries; detailed descriptions in terse, frequently truncated sentences.
- Key Passages: Resolution to write a journal (14 May 1800); leech gatherer (3 Oct. 1800); another sad departure from William (4 Mar. 1802); trip to France (July 1802); William's marriage (24 Sept. 1802).
- Passages That Connect to Poems: *Christabel* (31 Jan. 1798 and 7 Mar. 1798); *Ruined Cottage* (4 Feb. 1798); *Rime of the Ancient Mariner* (8 Feb. 1798); "This Lime Tree Bower" (10 Feb. 1798); "Resolution and Independence" (3 Oct. 1800, 4 and 7 May 1802); *Michael* (11 Oct. 1800); "I Wandered Lonely as a Cloud" (15 Apr. 1802); "Composed upon Westminster Bridge" (July 1802); "It is a beauteous evening" (July 1802).
- Common Subjects: Flowers, trees, and seasonal change; the cottagers, laborers, beggars she meets; reading.

Teaching Suggestions

An obvious way to approach Dorothy Wordsworth's journals is to read them as an accompaniment to the poetry of Coleridge and Wordsworth. As mentioned in the headnote, both poets acknowledged their debt to Dorothy and gave her high praise for her unique view of the world around them. Literary history has been less forthright, and so one corrective measure might be to compare the entries from her journal with the corresponding features of the poets' later work. One could discuss the differences by focusing on issues such as mode (prose versus poetry); gender (masculine versus feminine perspectives or language); genre (autobiography versus lyric poem); audience (known and intimate acquaintance versus unknown public).

You might also choose to teach the journal entries as examples of Romantic women's writing. In this context, Dorothy Wordsworth's journals highlight some of the intense ambivalence inherent in the Romantic woman writer's project—for example, the positioning of the female self as an observer of nature when nature is predominantly figured as female or feminine. (See Wordsworth's "Nutting.") In this case, Dorothy Wordsworth's elision of the egotistical "I" is noteworthy. Frequently, her journal entries catalogue the natural surroundings with loving accuracy and detail, but she is rarely present in the description. Her most intense passionate responses are to human conflicts (for example, William's departures and, most notably, his marriage). In these cases, her observations of nature help to minimize or repress her emotions rather than mirror them (see the entry when she and Mary, now William's bride, return to their home for the first time). This is quite a different relationship to nature than that posed by poets such as William Wordsworth and Coleridge. Furthermore, her writings record biographical information and personal history of the rural folk she meets; while these characters still form a part of her landscape, she creates a greater sense of individuality and social awareness than is present in the poetry. Perhaps the greatest ambivalence surrounds the act of writing itself: Dorothy figures herself as writing for the pleasure of her brother rather than for herself, and frequently she records her activities in service of her brother's poetry. These issues relate to the woman writer's dependence and subordinate place in society and the literary hierarchy, as well as to a particular construction of femininity as passive, gentle, chaste, maternal, and good. Her writings in this context intersect with some of the ideas expressed in Wollstonecraft's *Vindication of the Rights of Woman*, although they greatly differ in tone, language, and purpose. An interesting unit on the Romantic woman writer might include the prose works of Wollstonecraft, Wordsworth, and Austen, to demonstrate the range and differences among the women and yet also show how the social constraints faced by women affect them all.

Teaching Clusters

Who Is a Poet, Writing for Whom? Given the collaborative nature of writing suggested by Dorothy's journals, these would make a good contribution to the cluster, especially if paired with the poems such as "Resolution and Independence" and "I Wandered Lonely as a Cloud," for which they provide detailed sources. With a focus on the female writer, these would teach well with Robinson's "The Poor Singing Dame," Felicia Hemans's "Corrine at the Capitol," and Mary Shelley's Introduction to *The Last Man*.

Because of the detailed descriptions of nature, particularly the abundance of flowers and vegetation, her journals could be taught in the cluster on **Science, Exploration, and Observation of the Natural World**. In addition to the obvious pairings with her brother's writings, these might be taught with Charlotte Smith's poems, particularly *Beachy Head*, Keats's "To Autumn," Coleridge's "This Lime Tree Bower," Percy Shelley's *Alastor* and "Mont Blanc," and Clare's "Nightingale's Nest."

Discussion Questions

1. Compare Dorothy Wordsworth's description of the leech gatherer with his representation in William Wordsworth's "Resolution and Independence." What differences do you observe? How can you account for them? What does Dorothy focus on and why? The same

questions could apply to a comparison of the field of daffodils as described in the journal and "I Wandered Lonely as a Cloud."

2. What do you learn about Dorothy from her journal entries? What are her interests? How would you describe her personality? In what sense are these journals an autobiography?

3. How does Dorothy represent the poor in her journal entries? See in particular 4 May 1801 and the woman abandoned by her husband. What motivates Dorothy's generosity?

4. How does Dorothy represent her relationship with her brother William in the journal entries?

5. How does Dorothy react to the wedding of her brother, and how does she recount this in the journal?

6. What is the tone of the final NAEL excerpt, 24 December 1802?

7. How does Dorothy's writing on nature compare with that of other Romantics, such as Charlotte Smith, William Wordsworth, Coleridge, Clare, or Keats? To what extent is nature engendered female in Romantic-era writings? In what ways does Dorothy Wordsworth avoid or elide such conventions?

8. Compare Dorothy's detailed descriptions of her walks through the countryside with the landscape paintings in *Norton Topics Online* "Tintern Abbey, Tourism, and the Romantic Landscape." How would you describe the aesthetic sensibilities of each?

9. Although Dorothy initially says that she will write the journal because it will please William, what other purposes might her journal serve?

Sir Walter Scott

Wandering Willie's Tale

Scott's tale provides an excellent example of marginal voices in Romantic literature and the increased attention given to the commonplace. Because it is written in the Scottish dialect, it emphasizes national or ethnic marginality, and because it is narrated by a peasant about a peasant, it concerns the life and subjectivity of the common people. Scott draws on Scottish history—the trauma of the "killing years" following the Restoration of the Stuart monarchy and the "prelatists"—and combines it with the culture's folklore to create a classic story about the devil with patriotic and democratic themes.

Quick Read

- Form: Prose narrative, ghost tale in Scottish dialect (excerpted from novel, *Redgauntlet*).
- Plot Summary: Steenie is a peasant-poet (piper) for the violent Scottish laird and royalist Sir Robert Redgauntlet; he falls behind in his rent and borrows to make his payment. Sir Robert immediately dies after receiving the bag of "siller." His heir, Sir John, calls Steenie for

the silver, and angrily Steenie says it is in hell with his father, according to legend, and he curses Redgauntlet. Steenie is invited by the devil to set things straight with Redgauntlet, and when he arrives he is warned by Dougal not to take anything. He passes his test, receives a receipt, and presents it to Sir John, who is outraged. Together they find the bag of silver from the clue Redgauntlet gave him, and Sir John grants Steenie credit and hushes up the affair.

- Characters: Wandering Willie, the storyteller; his grandfather Steenie (or Stephen); Sir Robert Redgauntlet; Dougal MacCullum, Sir Robert's butler; Major Wier, Sir Robert's monkey; Sir John Redgauntlet; the devil himself.
- Themes: The peasant-poet triumphs over rich laird; criminals will be held accountable; supernatural events create a powerful kind of logic that rational people fear.
- Online Resource: The readings of Burns's "Tam O' Shanter," which will let you and your students hear the Scottish dialect.

Teaching Suggestions

To maximize your students' pleasure and interest in the tale, you might want to deal with two obstacles at the start: history and dialect. Both are essential to understanding the significance of Scott's work, and both can be helped with a little preparation. For the dialect, have the students listen to the reading of Burns's "Tam O'Shanter" in *Norton Literature Online*. This will give them an auditory sense of the words they are reading, and it will demonstrate the musicality and charm of the Scottish dialect. It will also refresh their memory of the poem, which makes a nice pairing with Scott's tale. For the history, pay careful attention to the notes, but also refresh your memory of the events being described by reading the introduction to the Early Seventeenth Century and the "Religion and Politics" section of the introduction to the Restoration and Eighteenth Century. The important point to stress is the political and religious differences between Sir Robert Redgauntlet and those who populate his mansion in hell—the royalist/prelatists—and other characters such as Laurie Lapraik, the minister, and the narrator—the Whig/Presbyterians. Steenie's equivocal identity in politics and religion, because of his dependence on the laird, creates problems for him. After he has been accused of theft by both sides, he has to prove his honor by dealing with the devil.

The narrator's tact in representing his grandfather's potential guilt in the "killing times" is a significant narrative strategy. By suggesting that Steenie "saw muckle mischief, and maybe did some, that he couldna avoid" the narrator puts into question the independent morality of the peasant class in Scotland's complex history. Scott makes this a personal family history as well and so creates a parallel between public and private narratives of history. In this way, the story gives the marginal peasant figure a more central, vital, and sympathetic presence in Scotland's national history. On the other hand, the story primarily pits the clever, honest virtue of the poet-piper against the vice and crime of the evil laird and even Satan himself. In this archetypal battle between good and evil, though, Scott adds another twist that lends credibility to a supernatural tale. By making the new laird, a lawyer no less, suppress the real story of Steenie's battle to prove his honor, Scott suggests the power of the peasant-class superstitions and the ruling class's fear of that power. That the narrator tells the tale as he learned it speaks to the irrepressible spirit of the peasant class, and so suggests another victory over lordly oppression.

Teaching Clusters

Because it showcases the national identity of the Scottish poet/novelist, this work can be taught in the cluster **Who Is a Poet, Writing for Whom?** In this context it would teach quite well with the poetry of Burns and Baillie. As a counterpart in marginal British identities, Edgeworth's tale of the "Irish Incognito" would make for good discussion. Scott's poem "The Lay of the Last Minstrel" can also be taught in this group.

The story's supernatural episode and the predominant interest in superstition and gossip place this in the cluster on **Gothic Times, Gothic Enchantments, the Revival of Romance.** The particular interest in retelling Scottish history makes this an interesting partner for Walpole's *Castle of Otranto.* The focus on the power of the supernatural makes this appropriate for pairing with Coleridge's *Rime of the Ancient Mariner.*

Discussion Questions

1. How does Scott (or the narrator) represent the far past of Scotland's history (i.e., 1660–90)? Why is this important to the story?
2. What is the narrator's attitude toward his ancestor, Steenie?
3. What is the significance of the fact that Scott puts all the violent royalists in hell?
4. Would you consider Scott's version of the trip to the underworld in any way archetypal? What is this underworld like? What is the significance of these details?
5. What role does Major Wier play in the tale? Do you consider him a supernatural agent?
6. Compare Scott's depiction of supernatural events with Coleridge's in *Rime of the Ancient Mariner.* How do they differ in effect? How do they differ in purpose?
7. Compare the character of Tam O'Shanter with Steenie. What do they have in common? How is their interaction with the devil similar? Based on these two stories, what is the importance of the figure of the devil in Scottish folklore?
8. How does Steenie's real story get disclosed and why?
9. In what sense is this a story about the triumph of the peasant? How does Steenie triumph?
10. What is the significance of Steenie's profession as a piper?

Further Resources

NORTON ONLINE ARCHIVE

Coronach
The Heart of Midlothian
    Chapter I. Being Introductory
Lochinvar
Jock of Hazeldean
The Two Drovers
The Dreary Change
Lucy Ashton's Song

Samuel Taylor Coleridge

The Rime of the Ancient Mariner

In the *Lyrical Ballads*, Coleridge was primarily responsible for representations of the supernatural, a poetic objective he described—now famously—in chapter 14 of the *Biographia Literaria*: "a semblance of truth sufficient to procure for these shadows of imagination that willing suspension of disbelief for the moment, which constitutes poetic faith." His major poem in the collection, *The Rime of the Ancient Mariner*, employs several means to achieve that suspension of disbelief, including a strong but simple narrative, haunting images, and hypnotic rhythms and sounds. A perennial crowd-pleaser, the poem also invites serious reflections on life and death as well as the purpose and power of storytelling.

Quick Read

- Form: Narrative poem in seven parts, primarily in variations of the ballad stanza (*ababa* in alternating tetrameter/trimeter).
- Double Narrative: Present—the Ancient Mariner stops a wedding guest from attending a wedding to hear his tale; past—the Ancient Mariner sails to the south pole, killing an albatross; he is punished; his fellow sailors die; his redemption; spirits intervene; he returns and is forced to tell this tale as a punishment.
- Key Passages: Stopping the wedding guest, part 1; killing the albatross, 81–82; death of the sailors, 216–21; blessing the sea snakes (redemption), 283–91; confession and forgiveness with the hermit, 574–81; his punishment, 583–90; the moral, 612–17.
- Themes: Humans must learn to live in harmony with all of God's creatures; storytelling is a necessary, moral act.
- Supernatural Elements: Mesmerizing power of the Mariner, parts 1, 7; ghost ship and Life-in-Death, part 3; Mary's intervention and good spirits bring the ship home, part 5 and 6.

Teaching Suggestions

Teaching the *Ancient Mariner* should always begin with an oral reading so as to capture the hypnotic power of the lines. You can supplement this with comments on Coleridge's own famous incantatory readings; see Hazlitt ("On My First Acquaintance with Poets"). On one level, the poem can be taught as a clear story of sin and redemption based in the tenets of what became Romanticism. The Mariner's apparently unmotivated act of killing the albatross leads to disharmony in the natural world and death to the sailors. The Mariner is forced to live a deathly existence (Life-in-Death) until he learns to appreciate the beauty of the world (the sea-snakes), at which point he is refreshed with rain from heaven and the good spirits bring his ship home. He is "shrieved" by the Hermit, the figure closest to nature, and condemned to tell his tale intermittently throughout his life. Anna Barbauld criticized the poem as lacking a moral, but Coleridge insisted it was all too clear: "He prayeth well, who loveth well / Both man and bird and beast. / He prayeth best, who loveth best / All things both great and small; / For the dear God who loveth us, / He made and loveth all" (612–17). The Mariner's power over the wedding guest and the mysterious reaction the guest has to the story can lead to a discussion of the purpose of poetry, storytelling, and art in human cultures.

Teaching the *Ancient Mariner* takes on added dimensions when you combine it with a reading of passages from *Biographia Literaria* and compare it with "Kubla Khan." In addition to the parts of chapter 14 that describe the composition of the poem and the objectives of supernaturalism, relevant passages include Coleridge's discussion of the "esemplastic" qualities of the imagination, its ability to shape disparate elements into a new unity (see n. 6). The imagination's "synthetic and magical power . . . reveals itself in the balance or reconciliation of opposite or discordant qualities." Such a "reconciliation" occurs throughout "Kubla Khan," wherein Coleridge describes, for example, "a miracle of rare device, / A sunny pleasure-dome with caves of ice!" (lines 35–36). Likewise, throughout the *Ancient Mariner*, students can locate oppositions that come to be reconciled in new ways, for example, the allegorical figures of Death and Life-in-Death. This focus on reconciling discordant qualities can be used to discuss the tensions between the poetic narrative and the prose commentary that runs in the margins. There are places where the prose explains the poetry and places where it contradicts or exceeds the poetry. Coleridge creates a tension between the types of thinking represented by the two modes; you can draw attention to these oppositions to discuss the tension between rational thought and the imagination. A comparison between "Kubla Khan" and the *Ancient Mariner* can also focus on the representation of the power of music/poetry and the role of the supernatural in "explaining" mysterious experiences, such as sexual attraction or redemption.

Teaching Clusters

Outlaws, Outsiders, and Exiles. This cluster seems ideally suited for the Ancient Mariner, who is forced to wander as a result of his crime, but who is also redeemed and brought back home. The poem would pair well with Gothic works such as Walpole's *Castle of Otranto*, Lewis's *The Monk*, and more particularly Robert Maturin's *Melmoth the Wanderer*. The cluster might include Byron's *Manfred* as well as Shelley's *Prometheus Unbound*, Mary Shelley's "Mortal Immortal," and Wordsworth's *The Thorn*.

Gothic Times, Gothic Enchantments, the Revival of Romance. In this cluster, Coleridge's supernatural poetry could be taught well with Mary Robinson's poems, both "The Haunted Beach" and "To the Poet Coleridge." The in-text topic "The Gothic and the Development of a Mass Readership" is a natural fit, as is Coleridge's unfinished narrative poem *Christabel* and Hemans's "A Spirit's Return." Works that contain more playful representation of Gothic elements, such as Burns's "Tam O'Shanter" and Scott's "Wandering Willie's Tale," would also make good complements.

For additional teaching suggestions for Coleridge's works, see entries on William and Dorothy Wordsworth and Hazlitt.

Discussion Questions

1. Why did the Mariner shoot the albatross? What, if any, symbolic value does the action take on in the poem?
2. What is the significance of the Mariner's blessing of the sea snakes? What happens as a result?
3. Why is the pilot afraid of the Mariner? What is significant about the Hermit's reaction to him?
4. Explain the relationship between the present narrative and the past narrative in the poem. Why is it important for the Mariner to tell his story? Who or what forces him to do so?
5. Why does the wedding guest rise "a sadder and a wiser man" in the morn? What knowledge does he gain, and why does it make him sad?
6. Discuss the moral of the poem. To what extent do you agree with Coleridge's criticism of the "obtrusion of the moral sentiment"? If these lines were not here, what moral might you assign to the poem?
7. To what extent does the supernatural agency in the poem add or detract from the poem? Why?
8. What does the poem gain from the ballad tradition that it emulates? How does it differ?
9. How does the marginal commentary relate to the poem? In what ways might this opposition between prose and poetry represent the opposition between reason and imagination? To what extent does the poem reconcile this opposition?
10. Does the poem convey a sense of justice? Why or why not?

Further Resources

NORTON ONLINE ARCHIVE

What Is Life?
Limbo
Phantom or Fact
Sonnet to the River Otter
On Donne's Poetry
Work Without Hope
Recollections of Love
Constancy to an Ideal Object
Epitaph
Biographia Literaria
    Chapter I: The discipline of his taste at school
      Bowles's sonnets
      Comparison between the poets before and since Mr. Pope

Charles Lamb

Detached Thoughts on Books and Reading

This brief essay will appeal to all the readers and book lovers that survive among our undergraduates, and it may help convert those who have yet to see the light. Lamb's graceful and loosely structured meditation on books and reading offers an excellent opportunity to discuss the history of the book, reading practices, and changing literary values as well as developments in the periodical-essay form. The semi-autobiographical stance of the author engages even the contemporary reader with the self-deferential, playful tone, and it raises interesting points of comparison with the dominant autobiographical impulse in the poetry of the era—for instance, the egotistical sublime of Wordsworth. Lamb's success in the periodical-essay format renovated the popular eighteenth-century form and made it a vehicle for personal reflection and cultural criticism.

Quick Read

- Form: Short prose essay, written for a periodical.
- Style: First-person narration, polite, informal, well-read.
- Authors Briefly Valued: Shaftesbury, Fielding (several times), Steele, Farquhar, Thomson, Goldsmith (*Vicar of Wakefield*), Smollett, Sterne, Margaret Cavendish, Sidney, Jeremy Taylor, Thomas Fuller, Beaumont and Fletcher, Robert Burton, Marlowe, Drayton, Drummond, Cowley, Spenser, Voltaire, Richardson (several times).
- Authors Given Greater Attention: Milton and Shakespeare.
- Key Passages: Folios versus octavos, 507; appropriate atmosphere for reading Milton or Shakespeare, 508; reading aloud, 508; reading outdoors, 509; reading in bookstalls, 509.

Teaching Suggestions

After Lamb reviews the titles and authors that he deems worthy, he offers a rare description of the appreciation of books as artifacts, followed by an equally valuable description of preferred reading behaviors. In order to enhance your students' appreciation of the essay, you might consider introducing some concepts of book format, in particular the distinctions between folio—usually the larger, more expensive, and distinguished books—and octavo—generally smaller, less-stylized books, a "reader's book," according to Lamb. You can refresh your knowledge of format issues with Philip Gaskell's *A New Introduction to Bibliography* (Oxford UP, 1972) or William Proctor Williams and Craig S. Abbott's *An Introduction to Bibliographical and Textual Studies*, 3rd edition (MLA, 1999). Ideally, you could teach this essay in a reading room at your library, where you could show books in different formats and different bindings. Lamb's attention to the Russian leather evokes the tactile and aromatic experience of bibliophilia that beckons to be shared!

Lamb's descriptions of reading Milton after a prelude of solemn church music or of Shakespeare shut up against a cold winter's night suggest the choices of an engaged reader and can prompt a discussion of how best to read our favorite authors. His review of reading aloud, reading outside, and reading in book stalls offers us valuable insight into this early modern culture of readers and their habits. And while these scenarios are clearly situated in a nineteenth-century context, they suggest modern-day comparisons, most notably a contrast between the poor child who cannot afford to buy the books he wants to read and the contemporary phenomenon of voluntary illiteracy, where people are able to read but elect not to do so. The closing poem may stimulate interesting discussion about our cultural values. You might challenge your students to think of contemporary examples of personal essays that review reading tastes—perhaps a local newspaper column or book-review section. For a related writing exercise, you might ask your students to describe their personal "libraries," reading habits, and preferences in a way similar to Lamb's.

Lamb's essay also illustrates a new practice of informal literary criticism and in this way can be useful in a longer survey that traces the changes in literary values. It would be interesting to pair this with an essay by Addison from the early eighteenth century (the *Spectator* papers on the imagination or reading *Paradise Lost*, for example) to show the difference in the objectives of the periodical essays. While Addison sets out to educate a newly literate mass of readers in a mannerly and public forum of literary criticism, Lamb strikes an idiosyncratic pose of a dilettante reading for pleasure far more than moral or intellectual utility.

Teaching Clusters

Who Is a Poet, Writing for Whom? Lamb's blunt dismissal of certain writers—such as Hume, Gibbon, Beattie, Malthus—and his loving description of favorite works make this essay appropriate for this cluster. His descriptions of books as artifacts represent a tradition of specifically English literature as printed, and this contrasts with the oral culture of the Scottish and Irish writers of the era. It would teach well with his essay "On the Tragedies of Shakespeare," and it offers interesting parallels with Hazlitt's "My First Acquaintance with Poets," although it differs in tone and objective.

The semi-autobiographical stance of Lamb's essay makes this a good piece to include in the **Outlaws, Outsiders, and Exiles** cluster, if it includes a focus on the subjective point of view in Romantic-era writings. In this vein, the essay might be taught with other biographically inspired works, such as the *Prelude*, Dorothy Wordsworth's journals, *Biographia Literaria*, and *Confessions of an English Opium-Eater*.

Discussion Questions

1. What makes the works of Hume, Gibbon, Robertson, Beattie, Adam Smith, Malthus, etc., not "books" according to Lamb? What are the implications of this gesture?
2. Why is the Duchess of Cavendish's biography of her husband so valued by Lamb?
3. What are the differences between folio and octavo works? What values does Lamb associate with each?
4. Why is Milton's poetry best read after a prelude of solemn church music? Shakespeare's on a cold winter night? What do you see as the best environment in which to read Wordsworth's poetry? Coleridge's? The works of your favorite author?
5. What makes a work good for reading aloud? What does it tell us about a community that it shares texts through oral readings?
6. Examine the figure of the poor boy who is refused access to the books at the book stall. What is Lamb's attitude toward this reader? Does this representation contain elements of cultural criticism? What is your response? Would this happen today?

Further Resources

NORTON ONLINE ARCHIVE

A Letter to Wordsworth
New Year's Eve
An Artificial Comedy of the Last Century
Witches, and Other Night Fears
The Two Races of Men

Jane Austen

Love and Friendship

Austen's relationship to the dominant strands of Romanticism is clearly parodic, although some of her mature novels contain sympathetic representations, such as the emotional response to nature in *Sense and Sensibility* and *Persuasion* or the revolutionary individualism in *Pride and Prejudice*. At her best, Austen represents passionate ideals through multiple perspectives so as to avoid the pitfalls of unexamined, zealous belief. Highly satirical and less nuanced, *Love and Friendship* represents her youthful response to revolutionary impulses around 1789. In particular, the novella highlights the absurdity of rebellion against patriarchal authority based on motives of pure self-interest or, worse, reactionary feeling. The piece also anticipates the literary incorporation of such elements that would come to be hallmarks of Romanticism, including radical autonomy, aesthetic response to nature, and the immediacy of emotional bonds.

Quick Read

- Form: Short, epistolary novel; satire.
- Characters: Isabel, Laura (main correspondent), Marianne (Isabel's daughter), Edward (Laura's husband), Lady Dorothea, Sir Edward (the father-in-law), Philippa (Edward's aunt), Augusta (his sister), Sophia and Augustus (his married friends), Lord St. Clair (Laura's grandfather), Gustavus and Philander (other grandchildren of St. Clair), MacDonald (Sophia's cousin), Janetta (his daughter), Graham (her affianced), Capt. Mackenzie (Janetta's husband).
- Anti-themes: Beware the insipid vanities of London and the stinking fish of Southampton; run mad as often as you choose, but do not faint; immediate emotional ties supersede all familial or social obligations.
- Key Passages of Parody: Opening pedagogical framework, letters 1 and 2; mysterious knock at the door, letter 5; melancholy landscape, letter 13; madness, letter 13; fortuitous family reunion, letter 14; touring the picturesque Highlands, letter 14.
- *Norton Topics Online*: "Tintern Abbey, Tourism, and the Romantic Landscape" includes excerpts from Gilpin, mentioned in the story, and illustrations of appropriately picturesque landscapes.

Teaching Suggestions

The most difficult thing about teaching this madcap, farcical story is finding a way to contain it. You might begin by privileging the pedagogical framework offered by the epistolary structure. Austen parodies the obvious moralizing strategies of the bad fiction of her youth by staging a need for the heroine to tell her story for the benefit of an unexperienced relation of a friend, and then filling the story with endless anti-exemplars and anti-themes. Like many things in this fiction, the epistolary staging gives way, and after the first several letters straight narration more or less takes over. Austen maintains the letter format, however, with a commitment that reflects her protagonist's own commitment to empty forms and signs. Amid the flurry of anti-lessons—such as the need to avoid the lure of urban vice and the stinking fish of Southampton—Austen makes the sanctity of patriarchal authority conspicuous by the characters' flagrant neglect of their fathers' desires. If one can locate any genuine lesson in the story, it might lie in its ironic celebration of rebellion, most notably represented in Edward's determined disobedience of his father. The mock-pedagogy of the narrative is enhanced by Laura's continued belief in the propriety of her selfish, destructive, immoral, and anti-social behavior. Austen occasionally introduces a reasonable character, such as Augusta or MacDonald, whose interactions with the absurd characters involve genuine (if sarcastic) judgment. These characters represent the only stable moral vision in the story.

One may also teach this work as a parody of Romantic motifs, including Gothic mystery, aesthetic appreciation of the landscape, and concern with the subjectivity of madness or alienation. In this way, the work might be taught as a light alternative to a number of works that present the "egotistical sublime" or an infatuation with nature. Laura's adventures frequently feature a reliance on immediate emotional bonds over traditional familial or social ties, and the frantically paced plot operates as a formal analogue. The details of the plot transform with each letter just as Laura's relationships mutate with each meeting: mansions become cottages, the names of characters morph, relations appear and disappear, and people die without cause as all rational consistency gives way to the immediacy of the moment. More intriguingly, this work can be seen as an "anti-confessional" in that the heroine recounts her life story and her many sufferings without once recognizing the error of her ways. The narrative highlights the problems of autobiography and the self-construction of one's own subjectivity.

Teaching Clusters

Revolution, Freedom, and Rights. Austen's story is a send up of the revolutionary ideals represented in this cluster, and it would be an excellent complement to Burke's *Reflections on the Revolution in France*. Unintentionally, of course, Austen's juvenilia anticipates some of the prominent literary manifestations of Romanticism and so can be taught as a lighter side to works such as the Preface to *Lyrical Ballads*, the Lucy poems, *The Thorn*, and others.

Outlaws, Outsiders, and Exiles. Austen's story raises questions about the reliability of the speaking "I," and so might be interesting to teach with other narratives that feature this, such as De Quincey's *Confessions*, Lamb's essays, or Byron's *Don Juan*.

Science, Exploration, and the Natural World. Austen's inclusion of the family tour of the Highlands based on Gilpin's writing on the picturesque makes this a good work to include in this cluster. It would be amusing to teach with works that feature walking tours, such as Dorothy Wordsworth's journals, and Hazlitt's "My First Acquaintance with Poets."

Education, the New Child, New Beginnings. The pedagogical framework of the novella suggests its inclusion in this group. It would be a delightful contrast to the serious pedagogical epistolary framework of *Frankenstein*. It would also make for an interesting contrast to the representation of children's subjectivity in Blake's *Songs of Innocence and of Experience* as well as many of the *Lyrical Ballads*. Of course, as a juvenilia, the story itself is the product of a child's pen and could possibly be taught as the perspective of a child.

Discussion Questions

1. What is the effect of having Laura recount her own perfections (letter 3)?
2. What role does the letter form play in Austen's story? At what point does the letter function seem to become merely parody? Why?
3. Note the many inconsistencies or transformations that take place in Laura's narrative (her mansion in letter 3 becomes a cottage by letter 5, her husband begins as Lindsay and Talbot but inexplicably becomes Edward). What is the purpose of these inconsistencies?
4. What are the benefits of madness over fainting? Explore the implications of Sophia's dying wish.
5. What role does Augusta play in the narrative? How is she different from most of the other characters?
6. What is the significance of Edward's determined disobedience to his father? How is this related to the cultural anxiety over patriarchal authority at the time?
7. What effect does the natural landscape have on Laura and Sophia? Compare this with the excerpt from Gilpin in *Norton Topics Online*. In what ways is Austen parodying the picturesque?
8. Describe the pace of the action of the story. What effect does this have?
9. What are the implications of Laura's primary grief over Sophia's death? How does the story represent immediate bonds of emotional sympathy? How does it represent familial bonds? What are the implications of this contrast?

William Hazlitt

My First Acquaintance with Poets

Hazlitt's autobiographical essay provides a voyeuristic glimpse of Coleridge in his early years and an account of the authors' first meetings. It is a curiously rich and emotionally ambivalent piece of writing with surprisingly acerbic judgments on his one-time friend. This significant essay is at once a testimony to the power of the "new poetry" of Wordsworth and Coleridge, a hodgepodge collection of observations on reading and authors, and a painful recollection of lost opportunity. At the heart of this essay lies a poignant expression of loneliness, a motif shared by Romantic works from "I wandered lonely as a cloud" to *Frankenstein*.

Quick Read

- Form: Personal essay in prose.
- Style: First-person, disorderly, interruptive, with plentiful allusions and partial quotations.
- Key Passages: Youthful ignorance and loneliness, 541; description of Coleridge, preaching, 542; his father's history as minister, 543–44; Hazlitt's first conversation with Coleridge, Coleridge gets his annuity, Hazlitt invited to visit Coleridge, 545–46; on declining powers of imagination, 549; reading the new poetry, 549; description of Wordsworth, 550; reading styles of Wordsworth and Coleridge compared, 551; Coleridge comments on *Lyrical Ballads*, 553; Coleridge's reading tastes, 553; Hazlitt's friendship with Lamb, 564.

Teaching Suggestions

Like Dorothy Wordsworth's journals, this essay can be taught as a complement to the writings of Coleridge and Wordsworth, and it would balance well the case between the two poets because it treats Coleridge far more centrally. Hazlitt begins in an elegiac tone, and his early memories of Coleridge are suffused with a regretted sense of star-worship. Psychologically he seems to need to counter these youthful adorations with withering adult criticism, for example, when he says that Coleridge's nose, "the index of the will, was small, feeble, nothing—like what he has done" (543). He expresses gratitude toward Coleridge for first showing him the possibilities of combining philosophical and poetical thinking, but he implies that Coleridge failed him as a friend. He paints a picture of the preacher Coleridge publicly espousing the revolutionary beliefs of dissenting faith, but the remainder of the essay suggests that Coleridge betrayed his cause and his creed. Hazlitt says of Coleridge's odd way of walking: "I did not at that time connect it with any instability of purpose or involuntary change of principle, as I have done since. He seemed unable to keep a straight line" (546).

Hazlitt's essay has historical and literary importance, though, in its description of the power of the "new poetry" of Romanticism. His recollection of Coleridge and Wordsworth reading their poetry and devising their experimental *Lyrical Ballads* without regard to popular opinion is an important record. Despite his ambivalence, Hazlitt's essay repeatedly bears the marks of being influenced by this revolutionary style of poetry, both in the quotations that he strews throughout his prose and in his preoccupations with the declining power of the imagination and the need for a heartfelt connection with another mortal being. See Wordsworth's "Ode: Intimations of Immortality" and Coleridge's "Dejection" for poetic parallels. The essay makes for a complicated study of the emergence and reception of Romantic literature.

Taken on its own, the personal essay represents a change in the genre, and could be taught along these lines with Lamb's essays. See the entry on Lamb for suggestions. Hazlitt's affectionate remembrance of Lamb at the conclusion of this essay makes the comparison even more interesting. One can chart the ways in which the styles of the two essays reflect the characters of the two writers.

Teaching Clusters

Because of its account of the power of the "new poetry," this essay could be taught in either the cluster on **Revolution, Freedom, and Rights** or in **Who Is a Poet, Writing for Whom?** Apropos of the first, Hazlitt's commitment to revolutionary ideals persists well after most of his friends have abandoned the cause, and so the essay, along with Shelley's "To Wordsworth," could function as a sort of coda to the movement in the literature. It would teach well after the Preface to *Lyrical Ballads*, and it might make for an interesting comparison with Coleridge's own reflections on the literary experiment in *Biographia Literaria*.

In the cluster on **Who Is a Poet**, Hazlitt's essay would make for a nice pairing with Keats's letters, especially the ones that analyze Wordsworth. As mentioned, it would also teach well with Dorothy Wordsworth's journals in this cluster.

Outsiders, Outlaws, and Exiles. The theme of loneliness in this autobiographical essay connects it to other works in this cluster. In particular, it would teach well with De Quincey's *Confessions of an English Opium-Eater* and Lamb's essays.

Discussion Questions

1. What is the youthful Hazlitt's attitude toward Coleridge in this memoir-essay? How does it compare with the adult Hazlitt's attitude?
2. At what points does Hazlitt publicly criticize Coleridge? What does he find fault with? Why?
3. What does Hazlitt mean when he says, "My soul has indeed remained in its original bondage, dark, obscure, with longings infinite and unsatisfied; my heart, shut up in the prison house of this rude

clay, has never found, nor will it ever find, a heart to speak to"
(541–42)? Why does he say this?
4. What does Coleridge look like? What does Wordsworth look like?
   What type of person does each appear to be based on Hazlitt's descriptions?
5. Evaluate Hazlitt's comparison of Coleridge's and Wordsworth's reading styles.
6. Hazlitt claims that Coleridge said Wordsworth's "genius was not a
   spirit that descended to him through the air; it sprung out of the
   ground like a flower, or unfolded itself from a green spray on which
   the goldfinch sang" (550). How might this operate as a metaphorical
   description of their respective styles of poetry?
7. What do Coleridge's reading tastes suggest about him?
8. What role does dissenting religion play in this memoir? In what sense
   is this the source of Hazlitt's alienation?
9. How does Hazlitt's memoir of Coleridge differ from Lamb's semi-
   autobiographical depiction of Coleridge in the essay "Christ's Hospital"?

Further Resources

NORTON ONLINE ARCHIVE

On Shakespeare and Milton
The Fight
On Going a Journey
From Mr. Wordsworth

Thomas De Quincey

Confessions of an English Opium-Eater

De Quincey's autobiographical prose illuminates the dark side of Romanticism and the downside of addiction. With its frank depiction of the
hallucinatory dreams brought on by his reliance on opium, De Quincey's writing may appeal to the curious and experimental minds of the
eighteen- to twenty-year-old set. You can turn this to advantage to discuss
the representation of Romantic themes—alternative subjectivities (the
child, insanity, dream-visions), Orientalism, the dissolution of self. There
are biographical and thematic connections to Coleridge, De Quincey's
friend and fellow opium user, especially in their shared speculations on
supernaturalism. De Quincey's dream-state realities mimic the supernatural but have a more physiological basis in memory.

Quick Read

- Form: Autobiographical prose narrative, confession.
- Key Events or Personages Described: Memory of Ann, sixteen-year-

old prostitute who aided him on the streets in London, 557–58; visit from a Malaysian man, 559–60; four characteristics of his night-mares, 561–62; dreams of civil-war ladies, 563; Piranesi's dream of staircases, 563–64; architecture dreams, lake dreams, 564–65; the "tyranny of the human face" in dreams, 565; reasons for his fear of Asia, 565–66; nightmares of crocodiles, 566; contemplating death in summer, 567; dream of Ann, 568.

- *Norton Topics Online* "Romantic Orientalism" provides background, supplemental texts, and illustrations to help contextualize the inter-est in eastern parts of the world.

Teaching Suggestions

De Quincey's writings share with other autobiographical works of the Romantic era an interest in representing personal subjectivity, and for this reason you might want to highlight the author's strategies of self-repre-sentation. This would teach well with other works in the spectrum, in-cluding Wordsworth's egotistical sublime, Lamb's clever amalgamation of identities in his essays, Dorothy Wordsworth's virtual erasure of self from the landscape, and Byron's alternately coy and shameless self-representa-tion in *Don Juan*. In this vein, De Quincey's frequent speculations on the role of memory in the conjuring of dreams or other altered states speak to the fragility of the self. De Quincey's opium-induced visions are phantas-mic manifestations of this instability, dissolving not only self but also all logic and narrative sense: space and time are amplified or collapsed or dis-torted surreally in his dreams of the court of Charles I being overrun by Roman legions; of Piranesi's labyrinthine interiors; of oceans swelled with human faces; of landscapes that terrorize and honor him as victim or god.

Another fruitful line of inquiry arises from the representation of Asia and the Malaysian man who visits De Quincey. The *Norton Topic Online* "Romantic Orientalism" provides a good introduction to the issues related to the subject, as well as other "Oriental" narratives and illustrations. Building on some of the exploration questions from that site, you might consider the ways in which De Quincey's representation of the Asiatic other is founded on anxieties produced by England's increased presence as an imperial power and the settling of colonies in Asia. To what extent do the representations of the Asiatic characters and the phantasms of vio-lence and domination by the land and animals of Asia express nationalis-tic fears of colonialism? De Quincey's claim that "Man is a weed in those regions" certainly expresses an ambivalence toward the English cultural supremacy in those lands. The fact that opium itself derives from that re-gion enhances the author's ambivalence toward the empire and trade that Britons were building in that part of the world.

Teaching Clusters

Outlaws, Outsiders, and Exiles. De Quincey writes in the genre of the confession, and he positions himself as an outlaw. However, the sympathy he extends to other outsiders and his philosophy of catholic acceptance suggests a more complex understanding of the theme. Certainly, his respect and admiration for the prostitute Ann are unique among Romantic-era texts. In this way, his work might teach well with Blake's *Albion's Daughters* or Charlotte Smith's "On Being Cautioned . . ." Alternatively, one could teach this with less sanguine representations of criminal subjectivities, such as Wordsworth's *The Thorn* or Coleridge's *Rime of the Ancient Mariner*, "Kubla Khan," and *Christabel*.

Discussion Questions

1. What is important about the character Ann? Why is De Quincey so vehement in his defense of her memory? Why is Ann's act of giving De Quincey a drink significant?
2. What are the characteristics of his nightmares? Why does he catalogue their qualities?
3. How does De Quincey explain the workings of his dreams or how they come about?
4. To what extent do his dreams represent common psychological fears?
5. In what sense is De Quincey's narrative a study in the dissolution of self? How stable is the self? In what sense does his experience belie the fiction of an autonomous, discrete selfhood?
6. Why is De Quincey initially interested in the Malay? Why does the exotic other appeal to his aesthetic sense?
7. Why does De Quincey give the Malay opium? What happens as a result?
8. How might you explain the role the Malay plays in De Quincey's later nightmares?
9. What evidence of ambivalent imperial attitudes can you find in De Quincey's representation of Asia? How might we understand De Quincey's fear of Asia?
10. What do De Quincey's representations of his nightmares have in common with Coleridge's representation of the supernatural in his poetry?

Further Resources

NORTON ONLINE ARCHIVE

On Murder Considered as One of the Fine Arts. Second Paper
The English Mail Coach
    II. The Vision of Sudden Death
    III. Dream-Fugue Founded on the Preceding Theme of Sudden Death

The Gothic and the Development of a Mass Readership

There is no denying the pleasures of reading stories that produce terror. Although commentators have variously theorized the "why" and "how" of this phenomenon and although moralists have urged the baleful effects of indulging such tendencies, the craze for Gothic or Gothic-inspired media persists to this day. Any reader of Harry Potter will recognize immediately the time-tested conventions of talking portraits, winding staircases, flickering lights, supernatural figures, and magic talismans, not to mention the overweening power of evil. The excerpts in this In-text Topic are organized to introduce readers to some of the more successful Gothic plot conventions as well as to demonstrate the cultural resistance to the enormous popularity of this form of writing. Although excerpts from novels generally pose pedagogical difficulties for instructors, the formulaic nature of these fictions actually lends itself readily to excerpting. A student can get a fairly good feel for the genre from the anthologized passages. The critical essays prompt important questions on aesthetic standards in the popular novel and the effects of reading on youthful minds, two issues that are highly relevant in our culture today.

Quick Read

- Walpole's *Otranto*: The prototype of the genre; passage depicts villain's incestuous proposal to heroine; ghost moving out of portrait; heroine escaping through subterranean passage toward convent; candle extinguished in mysterious wind.
- The Aikins's essay and "Sir Bertrand": Critical defense of terror novels; novels should exercise the pleasures of the imagination (as well as moral edification); the imagination encountering new and unexpected things produces elevation and pleasure; "Sir Bertrand" includes haunted castle, winding staircase, hidden room, cold hand, and lady rising from coffin.
- Beckford's *Vathek*: Oriental tale of cruelty, terror, and eroticism; excerpt includes trip to the underworld, violent and sensual; seeking treasure with aid of evil magician, protagonists find eternal torment.
- Radcliffe's *Romance of the Forest*: Adeline alone at night, moving tapestry reveals secret passage to deserted room, moonlight, old dagger, and discovery of a scroll of paper.
- Radcliffe's *Mysteries of Udolfo*: Sublime forest scene, mountain gloom, decaying castle, imprisoned heroine.
- Lewis's *The Monk*: Novel of devilry, sadism, mob violence; first passage on Ambrosio's pride in virtue; second passage on his use of magic talisman to gain access to Antonia; rape averted by mother, whom Ambrosio murders.
- Terrorist Novel Writing: Satiric catalogue of Gothic conventions followed by genuine anxiety over effects of such books on young readers. Ends with recipe for writing such a novel.
- Coleridge's Review of *The Monk*: Praised for fine crafting and writing; condemned for gross violence, unmotivated evil, irreligion, and danger to youths.

- Coleridge's Note from *Biographia Literaria*: Mockery of the readers of circulating libraries.

Teaching Suggestions

Although the section as a whole can provide a good introduction to the Gothic genre and some of the cultural problems associated with mass readership, I recommend that you include a full Gothic novel in your syllabus if you choose to teach this section. The following suggestions develop two different strategies that incorporate outside novels. Each follows a theme derived from the anthologized excerpts: (1) a genuine contribution to the development of serious novels, such as *Frankenstein* or *Jane Eyre*, and (2) a source of satire and humor for literature of "high" taste, such as Austen's *Northanger Abbey*.

Theme 1: Despite its notable reliance on formula, the Gothic writing of the late eighteenth century exerted positive influences on literature that ultimately proved to be of higher intellectual and aesthetic interest. This includes some of the poetry of the Romantic period, such as Coleridge's *Rime of the Ancient Mariner* and *Christabel*, as well as Keats's *Eve of Saint Agnes*. You could also supplement this section with Mary Shelley's *Frankenstein* or, in a longer survey, Charlotte Brontë's *Jane Eyre*, both of which develop themes and plot devices borrowed directly from the Gothic. In the former, the excerpts that focus on the compulsive drive of curiosity and its fatal consequences, especially *Vathek*, would be appropriate. Frankenstein's morbid interest in death is at least prepared for by such encounters with corpses as seen in "Sir Bertrand," and Elizabeth's violent death at the hands of the monster is not unlike Ambrosio's murder of Elvira. For *Jane Eyre*, relevant thematic precursors can be found in the imprisoned women of "Sir Bertrand" and *Mysteries of Udolfo*, while Jane's wandering around the Gothic architecture of Thornfield is reminiscent of Adeline's inquisitive explorations in *Romance of the Forest*.

Theme 2: Adeline also features prominently in the second direction this section can take: the mock-Gothic. Jane Austen's humorous take on Gothic conventions, *Northanger Abbey*, directly adopts the excerpted scene from Radcliffe when she has her naïve heroine Catherine explore the room the Tilneys provide upon her arrival at the eponymous structure. The motif of murderous villains and elaborate plots to hurry the innocent, fainting female into a vile marriage all operate in Austen's sendup. Significantly, Austen also includes the theme of the pleasures of reading such novels, as all the important characters in the novel are avid readers of those "horrid novels," and in this way, the critical essays would make for excellent commentary on the plot. Austen is even-handed in her moral ending, leaving it open as to whether her story recommends the rebellion of children or the tyranny of parents.

Teaching Clusters

This section forms the foundation of the cluster on **Gothic Times, Gothic Enchantments, the Revival of Romance**. For more information on works included under that rubric, see the beginning of this chapter. Less obviously, this section also contributes to the cluster on **Who Is a Poet, Writing for Whom?**, especially as it relates to Wordsworth's Preface to *Lyrical Ballads*, in which he condemns the pernicious effects of reading "frenetic novels." Just as the authors of the new poetry were unconcerned with popular approval (see Hazlitt's "My First Acquaintance with Poets"), so Wordsworth describes his poetry as an intellectual and aesthetic experiment to oppose the tendencies he had witnessed among the mass readership that was developing around him. His revolution in poetic form and subject stopped short of democratic readership, as his condemnation of popular reading suggests. The excerpts from this section can serve as a representative of the type of "frenetic novels" about which he worried. This anxiety is given eloquent expression in Coleridge's review of *The Monk*, which suggests that a distinction can be drawn between the supernatural Gothicism of Coleridge's writing and the immoral and irreligious violence and licentiousness of some of the Gothic works.

Discussion Questions

1. How do the architectural environments of the Gothic stories, especially in *Castle of Otranto*, "Sir Bertrand," *Romance of the Forest*, and *Mysteries of Udolfo*, convey emotion? In what sense are the buildings characters in the plot?

2. Most of the excerpts involve dramatic movement of the protagonists. What is the symbolic or psychological significance of their movements through space? How do they navigate these passages?

3. The role of light and darkness in Gothic settings is pronounced. Examine any passage where light flickers or changes, and explore the significance in terms of "illumination." What does the dramatic use of lighting suggest about the endeavors undertaken by such light?

4. What is the significance of the object of a key in any given passage?

5. After reading the Aikins essay, discuss the reasons for taking pleasure in reading Gothic fiction. What produces the pleasure? Does the art (or lack thereof) have any role in the production of pleasure?

6. Taking the excerpt of *Vathek* for an example, discuss the role of curiosity in the Gothic. What are the implications for indulging one's curiosity? How might this serve as an analogue for the act of reading Gothic fiction?

7. What reasons do the critics offer for resisting Gothic fiction? What is dangerous about it? Are there similar arguments in our culture about certain forms of entertainment?

8. How do the critics (and Coleridge in the excerpt from *Biographia Literaria*) describe the readers of Gothic fiction? In what sense can we

discern a division between high and low art developing here? What are the attributes of each?

George Gordon, Lord Byron

Don Juan

Byron's deft parody of the lofty epic form, his wide-ranging satire on most things Romantic, and his hilarious irreverence for morals, religion, and authority of all types make Don Juan an incredibly appealing text for students and instructors alike. Perhaps the only subject upon which Byron lavishes genuine respect is sexual love, and in this way the poem conforms to what non-literary readers expect from the term "romantic." But nothing in this romping "epic survey of modern folly" escapes censure, not even Byron himself, as he playfully conceals and reveals his biographical details and personal opinions in the voice of the charming, garrulous, and worldly narrator. This great comic narrator traces its origins to the intrusive narrators of Fielding and Sterne and looks forward to the self-conscious narrations of modern and postmodern literature, as he digresses, cajoles, flirts, and conspires with, winks at, and teases the reader. As the octava rima stanzas and the comic rhymes flow on with an air of effortless improvisation, Byron's spirit seems effervescent and mobile, and his attitudes range from sardonic irony to high gaiety.

Quick Read

- Form: Epic narrative in octava rima; begun in December 1818; incomplete in sixteen cantos; narration interspersed with commentary, description, satire.
- Style: Intrusive narrator; improvisational, conversational language; numerous digressions; multilingual, wild, unconventional rhyming.
- Summary of Excerpts: Canto 1: Juan's parents, youth, and education, affair with the married Donna Julia; her husband catches them; he is sent away; she writes an Ovidian style letter; Canto 2: Juan travels to Cadiz; his ship sinks and he and sailors are cast away; they cannibalize his instructor; he swims to shore; saved by Haidee; their love affair; Canto 3: Digression on love and marriage; digression on taste in poetry; tragic erotic love of Haidee and Juan; Canto 4: Digression on morality of his tale; Haidee and Juan's love; Lambro (her pirate father) returns; Juan wounded and imprisoned; Haidee dies with unborn child; elegy.
- Notices of other writers: Stanzas mocking Wordsworth, Coleridge, or Southey, 1.90–91, 1.205, 1.222, 3.98–99; praise for Pope, Dryden, 1.205, 3.100; Milton and Dante, 1.205; 3.10–11.
- Pedagogical Aids: Norton Topics Online—"The Satanic and Byronic Hero" in the "Literary Gothicism" Texts and Contexts; Byron's orien-

tal tale "The Giaour" in "Romantic Orientalism"; poems in process show revisions of a couple of stanzas from *Don Juan*.

Teaching Suggestions

As with all long poems, there are several ways to teach *Don Juan*. Included here are three separate strategies: a focus on the anti-romantic Romantic; focus on self-conscious literary craft; and a focus on a biographical reading.

Anti-romantic Romantic. Like his contemporary Jane Austen, Byron's attitude toward Wordsworthian Romanticism was largely parodic, and this poem delights in raising the elder poet as an image of conventional—and authoritative—poetic stodginess. Characterized by its skepticism and irony, and often a late-Romantic malaise, Byron's work neither idealizes an imaginary past nor manifests an Enlightenment belief in human perfectibility and progress nor hopes for a new golden age in the present. One way to teach the poem, then, would be as a reply to the high seriousness of Wordsworth's meditative poems or his earnest statement of poetic principles in the Preface to *Lyrical Ballads*. One measure of Byron's play can be seen in his use of the language of common life, and many, many other languages! Byron's rebellion—which is quintessentially Romantic—takes many avenues in the poem, however, from satiric jibes at the poetry and character of Wordsworth, Coleridge, and Southey and an endorsement of the literary tradition established by Dryden and Pope, to the blatantly immoral representations of sexuality and irreligious belief: "Pleasure's a sin and sometimes sin's a Pleasure" (1.1060). Byron does not neglect the key Romantic motifs and themes, such as revolutionary, democratic impulses, the observation of the divine in nature (twilight especially), and metaphysical questions on mortality and the individual's place in the universe, but he treats them in a markedly irreverent manner, generally designed for erotic or humorous purposes. The guiding questions for this strategy involve the implications of Byron's argument with early Romantics.

Self-conscious Literary Craft. In this strategy, primary attention is paid to Byron's narrator and the frequent commentary he makes on his own craft: for example, "But this last simile is trite and stupid" (1.440). In part, his intrusive comments appear to accommodate the demanding rhyming pattern of the *octava rima*, but they are so frequent and playful (and often quite accurate) that the readers sense Byron is teasing us. In addition to the contrasts he draws with Wordsworth and Southey, the narrator also suggests how he adopts the epic form, for example in stanzas 1.200–202. The opening of canto 3 begins with a conscious parody of Milton's epic style, complete with epanalepsis ("Or know who rested there, a foe to rest / Had soil'd the current of her sinless years, / And turn'd her pure heart's purest blood to tears" (3.6–8). Associated with this adaptation of the epic, the poem is replete with digressions—on eroticism in the classics (stanzas 1.42–44), adultery (stanzas 1.62–64), getting drunk (stanzas 2.179–80), inconstancy (2.208–13), and love vs. marriage (stanzas 3.2–11). A study of Byron's craft ought to include discussion of his virtuoso rhyming, his commentary on his own poetic practice, and his incorporation of forms like the Heroidian epistle (Julia's love letter, canto 1), pastoral poetry (Haidee and Juan in love, cantos 2–3), elegy (Haidee's death, canto 4). The guiding questions for this strategy involve the effects of his poetic techniques.

The Biographical. Part of what made *Don Juan* appealing (and notorious) was Byron's conscious play between self and narrator. Throughout the work he courts the reading that the speaking "I" in the narrative is Byron, but throughout he also proves himself to be an untrustworthy narrator. In this light, the most interesting section among the excerpts comes when the narrator/author speaks of himself at the end of canto 1, stanzas 213–22. You might consider to what extent the appeal to the audience is genuine. In this strategy, you also might highlight places in the text where Byron shades into the narrator, in particular in the narrator's response to antagonists from Byron's life (his wife, moral critics) and places where the character of Juan reflects Byron's own (his education, his swimming ability). This strategy would work well if you are focusing on representations of the self and the Romantic use of the first person. As with most effects in this poem, Byron's use of the "I" is frequently playful and contradictory. He both reveals and conceals himself, particularly when he refers to morality, as in stanzas 103 and 104 of canto 3 and the opening seven stanzas of canto 4. The guiding questions for this strategy involve what we can interpolate about the famous poet Byron from his self-representation.

Teaching Clusters

Who Is a Poet, Writing for Whom? Byron's contribution in this cluster is mostly literary revolution; one could read his ten commandments of criticism against Wordsworth's Preface to *Lyrical Ballads*. His pervasive ironic vision would pair well with Austen's *Love and Friendship*. His rebellious rhyming is really unique for the age, but his playful use of the first-person could be compared with Lamb. He also rebels against constraints of conventional morality in his representation of erotic love and religious skepticism, and in this he might read well with some of Coleridge's more erotic poetry, "Kubla Khan" and *Christabel*.

Outlaws, Outsiders, and Exiles. With a focus on self-representation, this text could be taught with other works that experiment with techniques of self-representation, such as Lamb's essays and De Quincey's *Confessions*.

Discussion Questions

1. Byron opens his "epic" with the statement: "I want a hero." What does this opening suggest about heroic poetry in the Romantic period? Why does he opt for Don Juan? What kind of hero is he?

2. Throughout the poem, the narrator introduces critical precepts and judgments, such as "The regularity of my design / Forbids all wandering as the worst of sinning." How seriously are we to take this narrator's judgments? What do you make of his contradictions?

3. Donna Julia writes to Don Juan, "Man's love is of man's life a thing apart, / 'Tis woman's whole existence." How does Byron represent this theme in the various love affairs he narrates? To what extent is the poem sympathetic to women's limited existence? How does this compare with other discussions of women's place, for example, in Wollstonecraft or Landon's "Proud Ladye"?

4. How is Julia's good-bye letter similar to an Ovidian epistle from the *Heroides*? Compare it with Pope's *Eloisa to Abelard* or Landon's "Love's Last Lesson."

5. What do you learn from Byron's representation of Wordsworth, Coleridge, and Southey? Is there any valuable criticism in his satire?

6. Byron claims: "If I have a fault, it is digression" (3.858). In what sense are his digressions flaws? What role do they play? What topics does he digress upon and what relationship do they have to the narrative?

7. What is the narrator's attitude toward the scene of cannibalism? How do you know?

8. Evaluate the elegiac stanzas honoring Haidee and her unborn child. How do these compare with other elegies (e.g., "Lycidas" or *Adonais* or even "Lucy Gray")?

9. In what sense can you call this poem "Romantic"? What does the poem owe to the tradition of Milton, Dryden, and Pope?

10. How does this poem compare with Byron's works that feature the famous Byronic hero (e.g., *Childe Harold* or *Manfred*)? See the *Norton Topics Online* treatment of this topic in "Literary Gothicism."

11. The difficulty Byron experienced in publishing this work suggests the controversial reception it had. To what extent do you find the poem immoral? To what extent does it achieve Byron's ostensible purpose: "to be a moment merry" (4.39)?

Percy Bysshe Shelley

A Defence of Poetry *and Selected Shorter Poems*

"A Poet is a nightingale, who sits in darkness and sings to cheer its own solitude with sweet sounds; his auditors are as men entranced by the melody of an unseen musician, who feel that they are moved and softened, yet know not whence or why." Shelley's image of the poet as an isolated nightingale can be understood as a reflection of his own experience, as he wrote most of his major works in exile without an audience, but the description of the enchanted auditors and the mysterious power of poetry is an expression of his idealized belief in the power of poetry to regenerate the individual and thus to improve society itself. Shelley's incisive criticism of his society's political and moral ills in many of his poems is balanced by his fervent belief in the capacity for poetry to renew a vision of the permanent forms of beauty and truth. *A Defence* expresses that ardent idealism, and it offers a set of philosophical premises that help to explain the symbols and patterns of his lyrics (which demonstrate a great range and variety of forms and metrics). Moreover, the essay situates Shelley's poetry in relation to other Romantic-era poets, such as Barbauld, Smith, Wordsworth, Coleridge, Blake, Byron, and even Keats; because of this, the suggested class(es) on Shelley can serve as a capstone for key achievements in Romanticism.

Quick Read

- *A Defence of Poetry*: Prose essay written in reply to Peacock's *Four Ages of Poetry* (available in the Norton Online Archive); purpose is to explain the utility of poetry as (1) an imaginative force bringing new knowledge, pleasure, and power, and (2) the stimulation of the mind toward the apprehension of beauty and truth in the social world.
- "Mutability": Four quatrains in *abab* iambic pentameter; a series of symbols (clouds, wind harps) describe the permanence in impermanence of human experience; ends with paradoxical "Nought may endure but Mutability" (cf. Wordsworth's "Mutability," Keats's "Ode on a Grecian Urn" and "Ode to a Nightingale."
- "Hymn to Intellectual Beauty": Similar to the Horatian ode but with seven repeated stanzas of twelve lines and a regular rhyme scheme (*abbaaccbddee*); this is Shelley's reflection on the ineffable but omnipotent power of the imagination in apprehending the eternal forms of beauty and truth (cf. Wordsworth's "Lines Composed a Few Miles above Tintern Abbey" and "Intimations" ode, and Coleridge's "Dejection: An Ode").
- "London 1819": Sonnet (*abababcdcdccdd*), an overt political satire calling for revolution; opens with famous line on George III: "An old, mad, blind, despised, and dying King" (cf. Paine's *Rights of Man*, Barbauld's "1811," Blake's *Marriage of Heaven and Hell*, Byron's *Vision of Judgment*).
- "Ode to the West Wind": Five fourteen-line stanzas in *terza rima* (*aba bcb cdc ded ee*); the rising wind operates as an external stimulus for the revivification of the natural world and the poet's spirit (cf. Smith's "Written at the Close of Spring," Keats's "To Autumn").

Teaching Suggestions

A Defence of Poetry identifies the moral utility of poetry in an age inundated with unfiltered information and technological invention. When

Shelley describes his society as having "more scientific and economical knowledge than can be accommodated" and "having eaten more than we can digest," twenty-first-century readers will certainly feel his pain. Shelley's antidote to this demoralizing condition is poetry, which becomes an abstract category of "the best and happiest moments of the happiest and best minds." It stimulates the reader toward love or "the going out of our own nature, and an identification of ourselves with the beautiful which exists in thought, action or person, not our own." Poetry brings order to chaos by identifying the eternal forms of beauty and truth in human experience, and not, he pointedly says to his contemporary critics, by adhering to the self or the restrictions of the cultural present.

The source of poetry is within the poet; the poet is acted upon by nature: "Man is an instrument over which a series of external and internal impressions are driven." However, the poet is not entirely passive because a special element in human nature produces harmony by making intuitive internal adjustments to external conditions. His imagery in "Mutability" and "Ode to the West Wind" is suggestive of this process of external and internal collaboration. His descriptions of the poetic process as a combination of the external influences and internal imagination of the poet echo those of Wordsworth and Coleridge respectively in the Preface and *Biographia Literaria*.

For Shelley, the poet becomes transcendent in his ability to tell the truth and to produce pleasure through the productions of his imagination: "A Poet, as he is the author to others of the highest wisdom, pleasure, virtue and glory, so he ought personally to be the happiest, the best, the wisest and the most illustrious of men." On poetry and pleasure, see Byron's *Don Juan* for a playful contrast. Yet Shelley recognizes that the moments of poetic inspiration are transient and unpredictable; on this see his combined sorrow and joy in "Hymn to Intellectual Beauty." This theme is similar to, but more hopeful than, the Romantic preoccupation with the loss of poetic powers, seen in Wordsworth's "Tintern Abbey," "Immortality" ode, *Prelude*, Coleridge's "Dejection: An Ode," and Hazlitt's "My First Acquaintance with Poets."

Poetry, finally, has a powerful effect on society. The generalized notion of poetry as "the record of the best and happiest moments of the happiest and best minds" begets admiration and stimulates the reanimation of powerful emotions and thoughts of the good: "Poetry redeems from decay the visitations of the divinity of man" (cf. Wordsworth's "Intimations" ode). Through this process, poetry instigates the moral regeneration of society, one individual at a time. For this theme, see "Ode to the West Wind." (Note the way the *terza rima* creates sonic links that reinforce the idea of the fluidity and cyclic nature of change.) Hence, Shelley can claim that "Poets are the unacknowledged legislators of the World." The purity of the poet's vision is contrasted sharply with the moral stagnancy of the ruling classes represented in "London 1819."

Teaching Clusters

Science, Exploration, and Observation of the Natural World. Shelley's attack on the superfluity of ideas and inventions in society and his call for poetry to create and stimulate the mind toward the beautiful and the good make this an appropriate piece to include in this cluster. Shelley, in fact, makes science a subset of poetry. In this way, *A Defence* contrasts with Wordsworth's Preface and is more in line with Coleridge's *Biographia Literaria*.

Who Is a Poet, Writing for Whom? Shelley's reconception of poetry as "the best and happiest moments of the happiest and best minds" and of poets as the "unacknowledged legislators of the world" suggests the propriety of this cluster. Like many Romantic-era poets, Shelley is concerned about the nature and purpose of poetry in the changing society, and he shows great appreciation for the "new" style of poetry of the present day. This could be taught with the Preface to *Lyrical Ballads*, as well as Hazlitt's "My First Acquaintance with Poets" and Keats's letters.

Outlaws, Outsiders, and Exiles. As the figure of the poet as an isolated nightingale suggests, much of Shelley's writing might contribute to this cluster. Certainly, *A Defence of Poetry* and *Prometheus Unbound* would make a strong component and could be taught with Byron's *Manfred* and Keats's *Fall of Hyperion* as well as Keats's letters.

Discussion Questions

1. What does it mean when Shelley calls Bacon and Plato poets? How does Shelley's essay contribute to the disagreement between Wordsworth and Coleridge over the suitability of the language of prose in poetry?
2. What are the implications of Shelley's comparison between a poet and an isolated nightingale? How does this compare with Keats's "To a Nightingale"?
3. In what sense is poetry a moral exercise for its readers?
4. What is the source of Shelley's hope and idealism in the essay and in the poems? Does his hope have a practical basis?
5. Evaluate the paradox of the following line: "Nought may endure but mutability."
6. Consider the meaning of "hymn." What would you expect from a hymn? In what ways does Shelley's poem fulfill this expectation? Compare this, for instance, to "A Song: 'Men of England.'"
7. Shelley's description of the beautiful in this hymn is elusive. What images does he use to convey the idea of the beautiful, and what are the implications of such images?
8. What is the object of Shelley's criticism in "London 1819"? In what sense are these objects the graves of a revolutionary "phantom"?
9. How does the structure of "Ode to the West Wind" reflect its theme of cyclic regeneration?

10. Evaluate the poet's self-representation in parts 4 and 5 of "Ode to the West Wind." How might Shelley's description of the poet in "A Defence of Poetry" complicate this representation? In what sense might the "I" stand in for a symbol of the "poet"?

John Clare

The Nightingale's Nest

Pastoral Poesy

I Am

As a self-educated farm laborer, the son of an illiterate mother and near-illiterate father, John Clare is an authentic peasant poet whose naturalistic and introspective poems engage Romantic motifs with originality and immediacy. Clare's observant lines in search of the nightingale's nest resonate with the self-conscious and autobiographical "Nutting" by Wordsworth and the highly allusive and intricate "Ode to a Nightingale" by Keats. His joyous "Pastoral Poesy" upholds an unmediated natural environment in ironic contrast to the pastoral traditions of learned poets. The enigmatic lyric "I Am" describes the dissolution of subjectivity so frequently invoked by Romantic-era authors.

Quick Read

- "The Nightingale's Nest": 93 lines of rough iambic pentameter in a variety of end-rhyme patterns; detailed natural description of the nightingale's haunts, in search of her nest; after finding the nest, he ("we") leaves it unmolested.
- "Pastoral Poesy": 112 lines primarily in ballad stanzas (*abab* tetrameter/trimeter); identifies poetry in the images and language of nature, like the boy tending cows who finds joy in digging in the dirt; defines poesy as the power of self-creating joy; the poet ranges the still forest as a storm approaches, finds music and beauty in the land and sky, nature brings poetry to the simple shepherds; the old couple find happiness in the music of their cottage; closes with the poet's hope for that continued joy in harmless song.
- "I Am": 18 lines in three stanzas of alternating rhymes in rough iambic pentameter; stanza 1, speaker is forsaken, "I am"; and yet he is tossed . . . stanza 2, "into nothingness" and laments the "shipwreck of his esteems" and alienation from all who were dear; stanza 3, desire for utter solitude, to be with God, to sleep like a child in nature.

Teaching Suggestions

It would not be unwarranted to read each of these poems as self-expression and to find in the dominant images a representation for the poet (in this way, the poems could also be taught with the happy, biographical poem in third-person, "Peasant Poet"). You might teach the poems as a contrast in poetic voice, examining how Clare figures the poetic voice in each and the implications for his choice.

The rustic, unpretentious environment of the nightingale sets off her melodious and valued song, but she is timid of an audience. Compare this to Clare's reflections on his own fears of exposure in his autobiographical fragments. The poem's shift from past to present tense (at line 42) is accompanied by a shift from first-person to second-person, and this change raises questions about who is represented by the speaking voice. Who is the "we" who will leave the nightingale's eggs protected in their hiding place so as to preserve the "old woodland's legacy of song"? Whose legacy of song does the poet want to protect? You might teach this poem with William Wordsworth's "Nutting," about the poet's plundering and even ravishment of the natural world. Clare, by contrast, looks and listens intently, but is careful not to disrupt; he does not rob the nightingale's nest when he finds it unexpectedly, only pauses to learn how the nightingale weaves her nest and to note the precise color of her "curious eggs . . . / Of deadened green, or rather olive brown" (lines 89–90). This poem not only practices but also emphasizes the importance of careful and respectful observation of nature. Of all the Romantic lyrics describing nightingales and other rhapsodic birds, this is the only one that describes what a nightingale looks like when she sings, what materials she uses to make her nest, the number and color of her eggs. This makes it particularly interesting to teach with Keats's "Ode to a Nightingale" in light of Clare's disparaging comments about Keats (whom he in many ways admired) as a nature poet. Keats's writing, according to Clare, was overwrought and overstuffed with literary allusion, and "the frequency of such classical accompaniment makes it wearisome to the reader where behind every rose bush he looks for a Venus & under every laurel a thrumming Appollo."

"Pastoral Poesy" is more closely aligned with the peasant poet's voice, when he declares poetry to be the immediate effect of natural images, an effect that is joy. Unlike the elaborate and learned descriptions of the "new" poetry by Wordsworth, Coleridge, and Shelley, Clare's ebullient ballad stanzas state simply and with ease that nature imbues the rustic's heart with poesy: "Who inly fancy while they view / How grand must heaven be" (75–76). Clare's title challenges us to consider the pastoral tradition, and in this way one might compare Wordsworth's *Michael: A Pastoral Poem*, focused on the tragic pathos of a shepherd father and son, with Clare's representation of simple, rural folk and land.

The poetic voice of "I Am" presents a dramatically different tone and subject. "I am," the speaker-poet begins in what seems a simple and forceful assertion—but he qualifies that assertion steadily throughout the long sentence that takes up two-thirds of the poem. "None cares or knows" what he is; he has been "forsake[n] . . . like a memory lost" (lines 1–2); his unhappy thoughts are "like vapours tossed / Into the nothingness of scorn and noise" (lines 6–7). In the final stanza, he fantasizes about death, the final dissolution of self, much as Charlotte Smith longs for oblivion in "Written in the Church-Yard at Middleton in Sussex." It is possible to understand "I Am" within the context of Clare's long struggle with mental illness, but it's also useful to read it as one of many Romantic texts exploring the instability of the self, whether in a melancholic or an ecstatic or a Gothic register.

Teaching Clusters

Who Is a Poet, Writing for Whom? Clare's status as a peasant poet contributes meaningfully to a cluster that examines the way Romantic-era poetry revolutionized the concept of the poet and upended traditional hierarchies of literary genres and subject matter. In this way, his nature poems teach well with the *Lyrical Ballads* and offer distinct contrasts to the more learned and allusive nature poetry of Keats. More interestingly, his poems push the traditional Romantic motifs to new limits, and he posits an even more radical understanding of poetry as the expression of nature in "Pastoral Poetry." The poems should be taught in conjunction with Clare's brief autobiographical excerpts in *NAEL*, and they would pair well with other isolated poetic voices, such as Blake, Burns, and even Baillie.

Discussion Questions

1. Why does the poet exert such energy in quest of the nightingale's nest? What does he desire?
2. What is the significance of the contrast between the bird's magnificent song and her "russet brown" dress?
3. Evaluate Clare's detailed description of the bird, her environment, the makings of her nest, and the color of her eggs. How does this compare with other poetic representations of the nightingale in this era? (See Keats's "Ode to a Nightingale" for an important example.)
4. Why is the poet concerned with the bird's fears (in lines 60–68)? How does this empathy contrast with Wordsworth's violation of nature in "Nutting"? Why does the speaker in Clare's poem leave the curious nest unmolested?
5. The poet in "Pastoral Poesy" begins by saying "True Poesy is not in words, / But images that thoughts express." How does the poem, which relies on words, convey this sense of "true poesy"? Where is true poesy found?
6. The poet expresses a more fundamental sense of democratic access to poetry in this poem than even Wordsworth does in his Preface. Who are the subjects of his poem? How do they experience poesy?
7. In what sense is this poem "pastoral"? How does Clare's use of the term compare with Wordsworth's in *Michael*?
8. What connection does the poem make between poesy and joy? What is the source of joy?
9. How do the fragmented lines of "I Am" reflect the subjectivity of the poem?

10. What is the source of alienation in "I Am"? What solution does the poem offer for the alienated self?

Felicia Dorothea Hemans

Casabianca

How close is the ideology of patriotism to that of domesticity? The linchpin, of course, is the figure of the mother's son who goes forth to protect king and country in war. Hemans's poetry embraces themes of patriotic celebration and domestic duty, but the figure of the boy—and in particular the young victim in "Casabianca"—is the focus of competing emotions that ultimately allow for subversive readings of her poetry. At what point does the maternal pride in heroic sons give way to tears for the wasted lives of English soldiers? In our postcolonial era marked by continued war, Hemans's poetry of celebration easily deconstructs into more ambivalent, even cautionary, themes.

Quick Read

- Form: Forty-line poem in ballad stanza (*abab* tetrameter/trimeter).
- Summary: A thirteen-year-old boy maintains his place on the deck of the burning ship unless he hears his father, who lies near death below deck, tell him he is free to abandon ship; the son is killed in the conflagration when the fire reaches the ship's powder kegs; based on the death of the ten-year-old son of the French admiral Casabianca, whose ship, *The Orient*, exploded in the Battle of the Nile, Nelson's victory.
- Key Images: "The boy stood on the burning deck," 1; "'My Father! Must I stay?' / While o'er him fast, through sail and shroud, / The wreathing fires made way," 26–28; "The boy—oh! where was he? / Ask of the winds that far around / With fragments strew'd the sea!" 34–36; "But the noblest thing which perish'd there / Was that young faithful heart!" 39–40.

Teaching Suggestions

After the dramatic pathos of the heroic child's death, what stands out in Hemans's "Casabianca" is the pointed contradictions and tensions. The poem honors the son of the enemy, and this crucial identity is obscured in the poem, which idealizes and dramatizes the boy's loyalty to his father. When Hemans proclaims that the "noblest thing which perish'd there / Was that young faithful heart," the poem raises the dignity of the dead child above nation and wars of policy and government. The closing lines of this poem implicitly raise the values of family or domesticity above that of country. Discussion might focus on the implications of the victory of Nelson—a national hero—over a thirteen-year-old child. The tone of the poem is tragic, and her use of the ballad stanza helps to create a sense of

time that is ancient and universal. But the name of the poem and the author's annotation precisely date the poem to a recent historical event. You
might ask the students to explore the implications of these tensions between timeless poetry and historical specificity.

A class on "Casabianca" can also draw on other patriotic and domestic
poems by Hemans that are included in *NAEL*: for example, "England's
Dead" and "The Homes of England." If "Casabianca" draws up pathos for
the heroic child of the defeated enemy, in what direction does the emotional energy of "England's Dead" flow? That poem offers a morbid map
of British power marked by the apparently unmarked and perhaps unre-
garded graves of her dead soldiers and sailors. The poem reminds its readers that the sun does not set on those who have sacrificed their lives for
the cause of England. Lest one read the poem content to know that the
loss of life established England's wide and enduring dominion, one has
only to consider that America was lost to England well before the poem
was written. While her repeated image of the slumbering dead suggests a
certain peacefulness, her references to "sons" in the opening line and the
vast expanse of territory over which these dead sons are scattered counter
such complacency. The line "The boy—oh! where was he?" from "Casabianca" is answered with geographical exactitude in "England's Dead."

The combination of patriotic and domestic themes receives its most direct treatment in "The Homes of England," a poem that reviews the
homes of England's families from the stateliest to the most humble. The
closing stanza makes clear the need for England's children to be incul-
cated with a love of "Its country and its God!" (40) in order to be willing
to "guard each hallow'd wall!" (36). This poem ostensibly focuses on the
domestic, with "woman's voice" flowing "forth in song" in the heart of
the home, and the tradition of English freedom and safety, but it relies on
the image of the child as the future security against unnamed foes. Taken
with the other poems, the poem suggests a national nursery for soldiers.

It may be interesting to note that Hemans's "Casabianca," also sometimes known as "The boy stood on the burning deck," was an immensely
popular poem for recitation in children's education. Elizabeth Bishop's
poem of the same name recalls and rewrites Hemans's poem:

> Love's the boy stood on the burning deck
> trying to recite 'The boy stood on
> the burning deck.' Love's the son
>   stood stammering elocution
>   while the poor ship in flames went down.
>
> Love's the obstinate boy, the ship,
> even the swimming sailors, who
> would like a schoolroom platform, too
>   or an excuse to stay
>   on deck. And love's the burning boy.

Bishop's poem draws attention to the popularity of Hemans's lines, in America and elsewhere, and at the same time it suggests the multivalent passion of the poem. One could teach both poems together to assess the meaning and purpose of the boy's devotion and ultimately the role of poetry and passion/pathos.

Suggested Writing Exercise: Ask your students to find out why a thirteen-year-old child would be onboard a war vessel. Their research will teach them something about the history of the navy as well as get them thinking about what childhood is.

Teaching Clusters

Education, the New Child, New Beginnings. With its focus on the child, "Casabianca" ought to be included in this cluster, and it might make an interesting contribution to a study of the many elegies on children in NAEL such as those by Ben Jonson and Katherine Philips from the seventeenth century, Shelley's "To William Shelley," and even Wordsworth's "Surprised by Joy." In contrast, it might be taught with other poems that feature the relationship between father and son, such as Wordsworth's *Michael* or Coleridge's "Frost at Midnight." Hemans's close perspective on the victim of war might be contrasted with Charlotte Smith's distant view in "Sea View," as well as the domestic suffering of the people displaced by war in *The Emigrants*.

Discussion Questions

1. What is Hemans's tone in this ballad? What is the purpose of the poem?
2. What is the effect of quoting the boy's calls to his father?
3. What keeps the boy on the "burning deck"?
4. In the closing stanza, Hemans compares the mast, helm, and pennon to the boy's "faithful heart." What is the point of the comparison? In what sense did they all bear "their part"? Why is the boy's heart "the noblest" of all?
5. Is the boy a hero? If so, what does it mean to celebrate the boy of an enemy as a hero?
6. What does the poem suggest about filial duty? Patriotic duty? Are they the same?
7. What would be the point (or effect) of having children learn to recite this poem?
8. What might account for the immense popularity of the poem?
9. Given the precise historical reference of the poem, does the poem offer any social criticism? If so, what?
10. How would the poem differ if the child was a girl? What does the poem suggest about gender roles?

John Keats

Ode to a Nightingale and Ode on a Grecian Urn

"Beauty is truth, truth beauty." Keats's two great odes represent the sensual symbols of beauty that prompt the mind toward higher truths of eternity but revolve around the poignant limits of mortality. In rich, evocative language and luscious sounds, the poems join—if not reconcile—the frankly human experience of touch, taste, hearing, and sight with the moral and philosophical aspirations of timeless art. Keats focuses on the images of the nightingale and the urn in the unified, exalted strains of the higher ode to create what some critics read as a symbolic debate between the sensual pleasures and pains of mortal existence and the ecstatic dissolution of self in art. Others read the elaborate sympathetic identification between the speaker and the symbol (nightingale or urn) as a stage in the sequential process of the speaker's inevitable knowledge of its (the nightingale's or the urn's) limitations, which becomes an emblem for the tragedy of human experience. More so than other Romantic-era poets, Keats strives for an aesthetic objectivity in his poems, what he called "negative capability," where the personality of the poet never intrudes on the poem. Thus even while Keats engages some of the same Romantic preoccupations as Wordsworth, Coleridge, and Shelley, such as the failure of the imagination, heightened observation of nature, and innovation of lyrical forms, his works stand apart as finished, well-wrought objects brimming with plenitude.

Quick Read

- Form: Invented the ten-line stanza of his ode, combining heroic quatrain (*abab*) with Italian sonnet's sestet (*cdecde*) in iambic pentameter.
- Themes: Beauty is the inspiration of the human spirit; it is the inevitable nature of things to destroy beauty; art is the permanent expression of transient beauty.
- Symbols: The nightingale's song becomes the vehicle for the poet's imagination, expression, ecstasy; the urn is the timeless historian of human passion, the preserver of idealized song, love, and faith.
- Process: In "Nightingale," the poet becomes numb to the world and escapes to the dark realm of the nightingale's song, hopes he can die at that moment of joy; he considers the consequences of death, the eternal life of the nightingale—poetry; he is called back to his self and the fleeting experience of aesthetic pleasure.
- Process: In "Ode on a Grecian Urn," the poet praises the urn and considers its features with inquisitive joy; he imagines the idealized and permanent state of each unconsummated passion represented there; ecstatic sympathetic identification with the passion; considers the sacrifice, the mysterious motives of the pagan ritual; he contem-

plates the urn with objective coldness as an eternal mentor speaking to the mortal clay.

Teaching Suggestions

Keats's odes are a joy to hear and to say aloud. Encourage your students to do so, and to enhance their appreciation of your reading the odes in class, train them to listen for the sounds Keats contrived. According to Walter Jackson Bate, Keats strived for a lyric stanza "more interwoven and complete" (Keats's term from his letters) than the short sonnet forms that came so easily to him. He tired of the "pouncing rhymes" produced by the "a bb aa bb a" of the Petrarchan octave, and he found the monotonous Shakespearean quatrains (*abab cdcd efef*) too elegiac. The stanza form he ultimately produced was a ten-line combination of a single heroic quatrain (*abab*) with a Petrarchan sestet (*cdecde*), and with some variation this is the stanza form that he uses in the major odes of 1819. The musicality of the lines is "more interwoven" by internal rhymes and heavy use of alliteration and assonance. "To Autumn" uses a different stanza but maintains a euphonic density in the lines.

Like the odes of Wordsworth, Coleridge, and Shelley, Keats's odes are devoted to a single theme. However, unlike Coleridge's lament for his fading powers of imagination in "Dejection" or Shelley's dedication of himself to intellectual beauty, Keats's odes address concrete objects, and these objects serve as both image and metaphor. The symbolic meanings of each—the nightingale, the urn—multiply with each description. The suggested class on these odes focuses on the use of the dominant symbol in each, and so it would be useful to do an explication of the poem that aims to unpack the concentration of meaning in each symbol.

The nightingale ode begins with the bird singing to the poet in the darkness. One can remind the students of Shelley's image of the poet as the nightingale singing in isolation and the mythological associations of the nightingale with poetic song. The poet's happiness in listening to the song produces a languor and numbness—the poet's detachment. Note also how Keats sets up the lines to suggest the opposite effect from happiness: "My heart aches, and a drowsy numbness pains" (1). This is only the first of many oppositions that the poem seeks to reconcile in its representation of paradoxical human experience—the poem's truth. The nightingale in the first stanza is literal; she "Singest of summer in full-throated ease" (10). Stanzas 2 and 3 focus on the poet's desire to remove himself from the world "where men sit and hear each other groan" (24), and he imagines this dissolution or fading away first as an effect of drinking wine (stanza 2) and finally by the vehicle of "Poesy" (33). He figuratively joins the nightingale in the land of romance: "the Queen-Moon is on her throne, / Cluster'd around by all her starry Fays" (36–37). Stanza 5 describes the pastoral landscape among the flowering trees at night, through the images of scent and sound. In stanza 6, the poet listens to the bird who has come to personify poetry; here Keats expresses a desire we find frequently in his poems, to die at that very moment of sensual bliss: "Now more than ever seems it rich to die / To cease upon the midnight with no pain" (55–56). These reflections, however, bring him to realize that being granted his wish would deprive him of the reason for desiring it; that is, he will not be able to hear the bird when he is dead. Keats carries over the idea of death into the seventh stanza, where the nightingale most clearly becomes a symbol of the immortal power of song, of poetry. Examine the implications of his descriptions of the bird singing in "ancient days" for "Ruth" and to charm "magic casements." The latter is a trace of Keats's infatuation with medieval romance. The word "Forlorn" repeated as the last word of stanza 7 to the first of stanza 8 plays upon the dual meanings of "long ago" (line 70) and "sad" (71). Stanza 8 returns the nightingale to a bird who flies away and leaves the poet to his reflections. He bids adieu three times as the sounds become mute. He ends by questioning the entire experience. "Fled is that music:—Do I wake or sleep?"

The "Ode on a Grecian Urn" similarly attempts to capture the moment of intense aesthetic experience, and here the image upon which the poem dwells is the antique vase with three separate scenes wrought into its marble sides. The first four stanzas describe in sensual detail the people caught in an eternal state of unrealized potential. Begin your discussion with the three metaphors Keats uses to describe the urn: "still unravished bride of quietness," "foster-child of silence and slow time," "Sylvan historian." These human images for the vase contrast sharply with the "Attic Shape," "Fair Attitude," and "Cold pastoral" of the final stanza, and they serve as a measure of the poet's change in empathy for the artwork. The poet's voice in the following stanzas becomes increasingly frenzied as he becomes absorbed by the details of the artwork and the reflections it inspires in comparison with human experience. He idealizes the experience of art: "Heard melodies are sweet, but those unheard / are sweeter." Likewise, the poet imagines the perfection of the lovers: "Bold lover, never, never canst thou kiss" but "Forever wilt thou love, and she be fair" (20). The ideal is represented as superior to the flawed and transient reality of human experience. As the poet expands on the pleasure of these permanent ideals in the third stanza, he reaches a frenzied pitch of joy, "Ah Happy, happy boughs!" (21); "Happy melodist, unwearied" (23); "More happy love! More happy, happy love!" (25). Just as the poet compares this blissful state of permanent desire, he considers the heated, unpoetic effects of consummation: "a heart high-sorrowful and cloy'd / A burning forehead, and a parching tongue." This leads to the consideration of the ritual sacrifice displayed in the final scene on the urn in stanza 4. As he considers the depopulated village—the pious villagers have all gone to the sacrifice—he raises the idea of permanent loss or permanent emptiness. He reaches the limitation of the urn as he considers the question why the people left the village for the sacrifice. The notes of the piper and the passion of the lover represent timeless ideals to the poet, but the rituals of bygone pagan belief present a mystery locked in time. The final stanza presents the urn as an object that "doth tease us out of thought / As doth eternity" (44–45). The sympathetic connection with the urn is broken, and the poem resolves itself in enigma: "Beauty is truth, truth beauty, that is all / Ye know on earth, and all ye need to know." Much time can be spent discussing who is speaking and what the lines mean in light of the poem's interest in art and human passion.

Teaching Clusters

Gothic Times, Gothic Enchantments, the Revival of Romance. The traces of medievalism and romance imagery in "Ode to a Nightingale" suggest this cluster. In this light, it could be read with other works by Keats that develop romance elements: *Endymion, Eve of St. Agnes,* or in contrast one could teach his *Lamia* and the *Fall of Hyperion,* which stress epic values in contrast to romance.

Science, Exploration, and Observation of the Natural World. Keats's imagery in "Ode to a Nightingale" in particular suggests inclusion in this cluster. His observations are sensual and highly literary. In this way, they could be contrasted with the nature poetry of Clare and Smith's *Beachy Head,* which include imagery of nearly scientific specificity. Keats's poetry, and especially his exquisite "To Autumn" might be compared to Wordsworth's nature poems and the process poems of Coleridge ("Frost at Midnight," "This Lime Tree Bower") with attention paid to the difference in the role of the poet in nature.

Who Is a Poet, Writing for Whom?. Keats was the son of a London stableman, though his class origins would probably not be visible to a modern reader impressed by the intense and passionate erudition of such sonnets as "On First Looking into Chapman's Homer" and "On Seeing the Elgin Marbles." John Clare, perhaps, saw Keats's ecstatic displays of classicism as a betrayal of his lower-class origins, but many critics ridiculed them as the pretensions of a vulgar *arriviste* attempting to rise above his station. In an 1818 essay, the critic John Gibson Lockhart called *Endymion* a work of "drivelling idiocy" and Keats an "uneducated and flimsy stripling" who lacked the learning "to distinguish between the written language of Englishmen and the spoken jargon of Cockneys." A vital peasant-poet who composed verse in the fields was a pleasing novelty, but a "Cockney" apothecary-turned-professional poet who wrote about mortals in love with goddesses was apparently not to be borne. In any case, a comparison of Clare and Keats shows the danger of generalizing about the language and literary ambitions of lower-class writers.

Discussion Questions

1. How would you explain the poet's relationship to the nightingale in the ode? How does it change from the beginning to the end?
2. What does the Bacchanalian imagery of the second stanza suggest?

How does this affect the mood of the poem? What is the significance of the imagery (the scents and sounds) in stanza 7? What condition does the poet describe here? What are the implications for the symbolic debate or process in the poem?

3. What is it that the poet seeks to escape when he fades "far away" in the third stanza? What is the implication that Beauty will not keep her "lustrous eyes, / Or new Love pine at them beyond tomorrow"? Compare this to the poet's enthusiastic sympathy for the lovers on the Grecian urn.

4. Why does the poet desire death in stanza 6? Are we to understand this metaphorically? If so, what are the implications?

5. Evaluate the ending of "Ode to a Nightingale." What is the difference between a vision and a dream? What are the implications for the ambiguity?

6. In what sense are unheard songs sweeter than heard melodies? How might this signify the theme of the poem? What is the point of the poet's repetition of the word "happy" in stanza 3? Can happiness ever attain the idealized permanence represented here?

7. How do the scenes of the deserted town and the sacrifice affect the poet and change the tone of the poem? Why?

8. What is the difference between the poet's descriptions of the urn in stanzas 1 and 4? How does the poet's relationship to the urn change through the course of the poem? What are the implications of this change?

9. What are the limitations of the nightingale or the urn that initiate the poet's misgivings and questions?

10. In his letters, Keats writes that "poetry should surprise by fine excess and not by Singularity . . . Its touches of Beauty should never be half way thereby making the reader breathless instead of content." In another place he writes, "We hate poetry that has a palpable design upon us. . . . Poetry should be great and unobtrusive, a thing which enters into one's soul, and does not startle it or amaze it with itself but with its subject." To what extent does Keats achieve these goals in his two odes? How?

Further Resources

NORTON ONLINE ARCHIVE

Endymion
  Book IV: O Sorrow
In Drear-Nighted December
On the Sonnet

Mary Wollstonecraft Shelley

The Mortal Immortal

Like her famous novel, *Frankenstein*, Shelley's story qualifies as an early example of science fiction. Here she sets the scientific events and most of the narrative in the sixteenth century, but she creates a narrator of contemporary Europe who has lived with the consequences of his transgression for more than three hundred years. Shelley alludes to the questing motifs of Romanticism in this story, but unlike the more Promethean *Frankenstein*, her protagonist in "The Mortal Immortal" is motivated by heterosexual passion. Her narrator, who responds rather un-heroically to the name "Winzy," appears concerned primarily with satis-factory human relationships, namely with the love of his heart, Bertha. Although the ending leaves open the possibility of achieving individual greatness and therefore reprising the themes of personal ambition in *Frankenstein*, *Prometheus Unbound*, *Manfred*, and other representations of the Byronic hero, the story ultimately suggests a more conservative af-firmation of social bonds. Her treatment of the contrast between human mortality and eternal life resonates with other Romantic considerations of the brevity of life and longevity of art, such as Keats's sonnets and odes, but it is a far less attractive presentation of immortality.

Quick Read

- Form: Prose narrative in first-person; set in contemporary Europe but relating events of the sixteenth century; science fiction.
- Summary: Narrator "Winzy" is Agrippa's student who, in a pet about his longtime girlfriend, Bertha, impulsively drinks the elixir of im-mortality because he has been warned that it will "cure love"; in-spired by the draught, he wins her from her "protectress" and they marry. On his deathbed, Agrippa lets Winzy know the true nature of the potion he drank. He doubts that he is *really* immortal, but he continues to be youthful as Bertha ages. The rumors of dark magic surround them, isolate them, and force them to seek a new life else-where. Bertha becomes increasingly jealous of his youth; she dies. He is weary of life without human connection, considers suicide but decides to go on a dangerous adventure of discovery instead.
- Key Themes: Immortality of the body enslaves the soul; desire for immortality chiefly occurs in youth; existence is unendurable with-out social connection.
- Key Passages: Opening statement of narrator's ambiguous status: mortal or immortal? (961); his love for Bertha (962–63); Bertha spurs him toward ambition and to accept Agrippa's money (963); narrator drinks the elixir in fit of jealousy (964); narrator learns he is immortal, rationalizes the limits of science (966); differences be-tween Bertha and Winzy as she ages (967); his grief over her loss of

beauty (968); he wanders without direction after her death (969); he plans to court danger to end his life (969–70).

Teaching Suggestions

As a tale of science fiction, "The Mortal Immortal" is short on scientific details and more generous in the philosophical and moral implications of scientific invention. The mystery that impels the story is not how but why the narrator is in this baffling state of probable immortality. Shelley's treatment of science here is closely aligned with satanic arts, and in this way the story might teach well with Scott's "Wandering Willie's Tale" and the excerpts from *Vathek* and *The Monk*. Shelley's tale presents the narrator's entire employment in Agrippa's service as a function of his desire for Bertha, who says pointedly: "You pretend to love, and you fear to face the Devil for my sake!" His drinking of the elixir is an impulsive mistake not a calculated desire for immortality. Ironically, its effects bring him happiness for a time by way of securing him in marriage to his beloved. When he realizes that the elixir is meant to make him immortal rather than to cure his love, he rationalizes the limitations of science: "human science . . . could never conquer nature's laws so far as to imprison the soul for ever within its carnal habitation." The story would have us believe what the narrator cannot accept; he appears to be immortal. In this way, Shelley's tale opens up a way to explore the advancements of science that may have horrible consequences to which we as a society are blind.

The story also might be taught with a focus on the unreasonable desires for immortality and its symbolic correlative in Romantic poetry—fame. The story never presents the idea of immortality as attractive: the narrator begins his story because he is weary of his longevity. He creates rationalizations to prevent himself from believing that he is indeed immortal, because to believe it is to despair. Even the deathbed scene of Cornelius Agrippa, where the aged scientist holds out one final hope for obtaining the elixir, seems more desperate than exciting. The narrator's grief at his beloved's departing beauty certainly raises interesting points for discussion in class. Does love survive beauty? A study of the elaborate accommodations each spouse makes to their extraordinary conditions suggests that it is unlikely. The passages describing the narrator's wandering and his consideration of suicide further enforce the theme that one must have social connection to make life endurable. With its attention to the effects of aging on relationships, this story would serve well in a cluster on "Aging in Literature." Its consideration of the implications of longevity and immortality resonates with Swift's treatment of this topic in the Struldbuggs section of *Gulliver's Travels*, book 3.

Teaching Clusters

Outlaws, Outsiders, and Exiles. The narrator's severe isolation and desperation make him a candidate for this crew. His story would read well with Byron's *Manfred* and Hemans's "A Spirit's Return" because of the treatment of love that spans the mortal and immortal realms.

The story also might feature in a cluster on **Science, Exploration, and Observation of the Natural World.** In addition to the scientific elements highlighted above, the story ends with the narrator's courting death by engaging in a dangerous exploration. The story might be taught with works that represent world exploration, such as Coleridge's *Rime of the Ancient Mariner* and Wollstonecraft's *Letters Written in Norway, Sweden, and Denmark.* Because of its assertion of the limitations of science, it might also spark discussion with Joanna Baillie's "Address to a Steam Vessel" and William Wordsworth's "Steamboats, Viaducts, and Railways," which represent in ambivalent ways the effects of changing technology in England.

Discussion Questions

1. In what sense is the elixir of immortality a cure for love?
2. Why do the villagers abandon the narrator and Bertha when Winzy fails to age appropriately? What do they suspect?
3. The story suggests that scientific discovery and satanic arts share the same goals. What are the implications of this connection? Is there an ethical or moral limit to the advancements of science?
4. In what sense is the soul imprisoned by an immortal body? What metaphysical assumptions does the story make? Do we share these, and if not, what ethical codes guide our scientific explorations?
5. Why can't Winzy accept that he is immortal?
6. Why doesn't Winzy commit suicide? Why does Shelley include this consideration in her tale?
7. What is the narrator's final plan? He says, "I yield this body, too tenacious a cage for a soul which thirsts for freedom, to the destructive elements of air and water—or, if I survive, my name shall be recorded as one of the most famous among the sons of men." Why are fame and knowledge so difficult to come at that one must be willing to die?
8. Why does immortality become wearisome to the narrator? What, if anything, might this indicate about the author's attitude toward immortal fame or eternal art?
9. Examine the passage on Bertha's fading beauty. Why does Winzy lament this? To what extent is fading beauty an inevitable byproduct of age? To what extent is love dependent upon beauty?
10. What are the implications for Shelley's publishing this story in *The Keepsake*, a gift book published annually between 1828 and 1857?

Letitia Elizabeth Landon

The Proud Ladye

Born last of the Romantic-era writers included here, Landon certainly anticipates many aspects of Victorian literature, but her ballad of the "Proud Ladye" participates in the revival of romance characteristic of Coleridge, Byron, and especially Keats. As an immensely popular female poet whose reputation skirted the edge of scandal, Landon is herself an unconventional figure. Her revision of traditional romance motifs in "The Proud Ladye" is likewise innovative. Reading this next to Keats's "La Belle Dame Sans Merci," whose mysterious lady appears remarkably unmotivated, one senses the importance of granting the female figure agency, language, and suffering. Landon's poems consistently construct a feminine character that is directed principally by her passions, but Landon avoids overt didacticism. Sentimental to be sure, Landon's poems nonetheless raise questions about the implications of a culture that insists on female beauty, passivity, and erotic value in ways that recall Wollstonecraft's critique in *Vindication of the Rights of Woman*.

Quick Read

- Form: Ballad in eighteen four-line stanzas (*abcb*).
- Summary: A much-sought-after aristocratic lady resists marriage by making her would-be suitors perform a feat of skill that is frequently deadly. A "stranger Knight" captivates her heart and she prays he will not attempt to "ride the wall." He succeeds and she joyously extends her hand, which he refuses in triumph over her pride. She pines away in love and enters a convent.
- Key Details: Would-be suitors motivated by her land, gold, and name but mostly her beauty; the successful knight is motivated by revenge (his brother lost his life in pursuit of her); her unrequited love destroys or causes her to hide her beauty.

Teaching Suggestions

Ask students to consider the opening lines of Landon's poem: "Oh, what could the ladye's beauty match / An it were not the ladye's pride?" The rhetorical question—as opposed to a statement—allows for the possibility of alternative readings of the poem's main theme. On the one hand, the poem might be read as a moral lesson against female pride. On the other hand, the details of the poem and the fact that Landon does not punish her heroine with death (only with cutting her hair and joining a female community) suggest a more positive reading of the poem's significance. To facilitate this lesson, you might have the students revisit Mary Wollstonecraft's excerpts from *Vindication of the Rights of Woman*, especially the selection from chapter 4, which includes her criticism of female love of pleasure, vanity, and frivolity. The narrative of Landon's ballad offers an example of the type of contempt an overly refined woman earns from a worthy man. However, Wollstonecraft's criticism of a society that expects women to perform the role of erotic object also applies to Landon's poem. Landon particularly details the motivations for the would-be suitors as worldly and impersonal, and their deaths suggest that these are inadequate reasons for gaining the proud lady's hand. The "strange Knight," however, is motivated by revenge. Landon places his fraternal love far above heterosexual love and his commitment to "the honour that guides the soldier's lance" above marriage. In this way, the poem suggests the illusions of romance for women in a patriarchal world where male relationships take priority over domestic or heterosexual romantic love. Finally, you can evaluate the lady's voluntary actions to shield or destroy her erotic power by veiling and cutting her hair and removing herself to a convent. Are these the acts of humbled pride or self-preservation?

Teaching this poem also involves interpreting the stylistic conventions of romance and traditional ballads (see the entry on "Popular Ballads" in the chapter on the Restoration and the Eighteenth Century). In particular, you can emphasize the places in the story where the reader needs to supply information. Why, for instance, does the "stranger Knight" inspire her love? How does he succeed on the wall where all others fail? Also encourage your students to interpret the narrative on a symbolic register as well as one of story and image. It might be helpful to teach Keats's "La Belle Dame Sans Merci" and Tennyson's "Lady of Shalott" as companion pieces. All feature narratives of mysterious desire, doomed love, and fatal women in a medieval setting. Unlike Keats's ballad, which tells the story from the perspective of the suffering male lover, Landon focuses on the actions of the female. As is typical of the genre, she does not supply explanations for the behavior, and you can encourage your students to read the poem attentively for clues that suggest motivation. A comparison between the gendered dynamic in Keats's poem, where the lady punishes the knight, and in Landon's, where the Knight punishes the Lady, would be productive.

Teaching Clusters

Gothic Times, Gothic Enchantments, the Revival of Romance. Although the poem offers more pragmatic details than Gothic enchantments to explain its action, it nonetheless participates in the revival of romance and can be taught in this cluster. Companion pieces, as suggested above, include Keats's "La Belle Dame Sans Merci" and Tennyson's "Lady of Shalott."

Discussion Questions

1. What other reasons, besides pride, might cause the lady to resist getting married? See the headnote to Mary Wollstonecraft for information on the conditions of marriage for women in the era.
2. What connection can you find between the motivation of the would-

be suitors and their ultimate failure? What is the symbolic meaning of their dying?

3. How does the lady treat the "stranger Knight"? Why does she treat him in this way?

4. Evaluate the knight's response to the lady's hand (lines 45–60). What is the significance of his commitment to "the honour that guides the soldier's lance"? Why does he place a higher value on his dead brother's love "Than woman's love"?

5. How does the Knight punish the lady in Landon's poem? Compare this to the punishment that the knight endures in Keats's "La Belle Dame Sans Merci." Can you read Landon's poem as a response to Keats? If so, how does it respond?

6. What happens to the lady's beauty after the Knight leaves? What is the symbolic meaning of cutting her hair and putting on a veil?

7. Evaluate the opening lines of the poem: "Oh, what could the ladye's beauty match, / An it were not the ladye's pride?" Do these lines suggest a moral for the ballad? Why or why not?

The Romantic Period: Texts in the Norton Online Archive by Authors Not in *NAEL* (also Textual Clusters)

George Darley
    Over Hills and Uplands High
    The Phoenix
    It is not Beauty I demand
    The Mermaidens' Vesper Hymn
William Lisle Bowles,
    Languid, and Sad, and Slow
    To the River Itchin, Near Winton
Robert Southey
    My Days Among the Dead are Past
Leigh Hunt
    The Fish, the Man, and the Spirit
Thomas Love Peacock
    The War Song of Dinas Vawr
    The Four Ages of Poetry
Walter Savage Landor
    On Seeing a Hair of Lucretia Borgia
    On His Seventy-Fifth Birthday
    Mother, I Cannot Mind My Wheel
    Rose Aylmer
    Past Ruined Ilion
    Twenty Years Hence
    The Three Roses
    Dirce

CHAPTER 10

The Victorian Age
1830–1901

INTRODUCING THE PERIOD

The Victorian era is a rich, diverse period full of contradictory ideologies and cultural changes grouped together almost arbitrarily by virtue of the longevity of Queen Victoria. Despite its tremendous variability, however, it is arguably the period of British literature about which first-time students (American students, at least) have formed the most stereotypes. Ask your students to begin the class or this section of the survey by listing what they think are typical Victorian characteristics and they will likely say that the Victorians were stodgy, repressed, prudish, class-conscious, formal, earnest, and so on. Yet, as the selections in *The Norton Anthology of English Literature* make clear, it is misleading to make sweeping statements about "all" Victorians. Students will soon see that for every literary instance that confirms a stereotype of "the Victorian," one can find another that explodes it.

The heterogeneity of the period was due, in part, to the drastic changes that occurred in Britain between 1830 and the turn of the century. The Industrial Revolution had begun in the late eighteenth century with James Watt's steam engine and the improvement of machines for processing textiles, and by the 1850s Britain's transformation from an agrarian-based to an industrial economy was complete. National prosperity was fueled by large-scale manufacturing and commerce—coal mining and processing, steelworks, and textile mills; railways and steamships—rather than agriculture. Power shifted from the land-holding and land-inheriting aristocracy to those in manufacturing and trade—the middle classes, whose values, beliefs, and social customs were increasingly identified as those of the Victorian mainstream. Landless laborers and small peasant farmers migrated to the newly important industrial centers, and thus was created a new class, the urban proletariat, earning a wage within a capitalist and laissez-faire economic system rather than subsisting on the products of their labor. With industrial capitalism there came an increasing separation of public and private spheres and an increasing identification of each sex with a particular sphere. Middle-class women were more and more often identified with the home and the raising of children, while men were associated with the world of manufacturing and commerce. Further shifts in social organization took place with the progressive institution of universal manhood suffrage and the gradual extension of other basic rights to the working classes and to women. Increased literacy rates, moreover, and new educational opportunities for all groups disrupted traditional social patterns. In the latter decades of the century, opportunities for middle-class women to work outside the home expanded, while class divisions became less rigid. At the same time, Britain's overseas empire grew to encompass nearly one-fourth of the earth's terrain, bringing a sharper consciousness of national identity to the British people. These changes in social relations and British identity were accompanied by new modes of producing and distributing commodities and new technologies like electric telegraphy and the steam press (both of which allowed for immediate coverage of news events), photography, railway and steamship travel, phonographic recording, and the typewriter, which transformed the texture of daily life. A concomitant to the consolidation of secular culture was the rise of not only evolutionary biology and other materialist sciences but also the human sciences: ethnography, psychology (especially alienism, the study of mental aberrations), sexology, criminology, and sociology.

Such rapid, unprecedented changes evoked wildly differing responses—enthusiasm, despair, optimism, anxiety, exhaustion, or some combination thereof. "What is all this but a mad Fermentation; wherefrom, the fiercer it is, the clearer product will one day evolve itself?" asks the narrator of Thomas Carlyle's *Sartor Resartus*—"Such transitions are ever full of pain." Many Victorians lamented the loss of an older, more stable social order (whether real or imagined) and regarded the new age, unfolding beneath their feet, with both anticipation and terror. In *Characteristics* (1831), Carlyle complains that "the doom of the Old has long been pronounced, and irrevocable; the Old has passed away: but, alas, the New appears not in its stead; the Time is still in pangs of travail with the New." Similarly, in Tennyson's *Idylls of the King*, the dying King Arthur says to Sir Bedivere, "The old order changeth, yielding place to new"; "Comfort thyself: what comfort is in me?" (lines 408, 411). And in "Stanzas from the Grand Chartreuse," Matthew Arnold writes of being caught "between two worlds, one dead, / The other powerless to be born, / With nowhere yet to rest my head" (lines 85–87). Yet despite the overwhelming amount of Victorian writing that spoke to despair and confusion, there were many expressions of confidence envisioning economic growth, imperial expansion, and an evolving human species. This view is most often associated with mid-Victorian complacency or with late-Victorian patriotic assertions of imperial prowess, but can be also discerned in unexpected quarters. Charles Darwin's *The Origin of Species*, for instance, while upsetting traditional religious views of self and society, carried with it a belief in the perfectibility of humankind. "[A]s natural selection works solely by and for the good of each being," writes Darwin, "all corporeal and mental endowments will tend to progress towards perfection." Even Tennyson sounds a cautious note of hope for a new social order, whose outlines are as yet unknown, when the barge bearing the dead King Arthur passes on "Down that long water opening on the deep / Somewhere far off" and vanishes, not into darkness, but "into light," while "the new sun [rises], bringing the new year."

Instructors have many options in teaching Victorian literature. You may organize the syllabus according to genre (poetry, prose, and fiction, for instance), follow a linear timeline, or proceed thematically. Poems that describe Victorian crises of faith, like Tennyson's *In Memoriam*, can be taught with prose works detailing spiritual and emotional turmoil and its resolutions, such as Mill's *Autobiography* and Carlyle's *Sartor Resartus*. Robert Browning's *Caliban upon Setebos: Or Natural Theology in the Island* and verses 54, 55, 56, 118, and 120 of *In Memoriam*, which deal with nineteenth-century evolutionary science ironically in the one case and despairingly in the other, can be folded into the "Victorian Issues" special section on "Evolution." For insight into the lives of Victorian women, Elizabeth Gaskell's "The Old Nurse's Story" is well matched with Christina Rossetti's *Goblin Market*. Moreover, the section of Norton Topics Online entitled "The Painterly Image in Poetry" gives a number of suggestions for teaching works by Browning, Tennyson, and the Rossettis, among others. To help guide you in making your own groupings, the teaching clusters below present several large thematic categories within which to arrange your selections.

TEACHING CLUSTERS

Gender and Sexuality

The doctrine of separate spheres is revealing for what it tells us about the Victorian middle classes and their own vision of themselves. According to this belief, women were naturally suited to the private sphere of the home and identified with qualities of docility, goodness, and maternal compassion; in contrast, men were suited to the public sphere of business and politics, demonstrating attributes of courage, strength, and leadership. Consequently, the home was a place of harmony and spiritual sustenance, far removed from the callous self-interest of the marketplace. Texts in this category take up issues relating to prescribed gender roles for men and women and the division between private and public spheres.

Concerns about prostitution and female sexual transgression, women's intellectual and vocational pursuits, and Victorian manhood all fall within this cluster. Also under this rubric are texts that question or display anxiety about gendered boundaries.

Poverty, Unrest, and Social Criticism

The flip side of domestic ideology's comforting fantasy of secure middle-class existence was the reality of widespread urban poverty among the least fortunate members of society. In London, the poor were hidden from sight in slum neighborhoods so tortuous and inaccessible, so dangerous, even, that investigative parties would not venture in without a policeman for a guide. Sanitary conditions were unimaginable and ill health was rampant. For those fortunate enough to have a job, the hours were long and the compensation barely enough to sustain life. Reformers hoped to bring this misery to light. Many railed against the alienating effects of industrial capitalism and took refuge in nostalgic visions of the feudal past. Others hoped to eliminate child labor and prostitution through government regulations. Still others imagined an entirely new economic system based on the principles of socialism. This category includes texts relating to industrialization, poor working conditions, child labor, prostitution, crime, poverty, Victorian paternalism, social reform, social unrest, and apprehensions about the specter of revolution.

Doubt, Self-Reflection, and Romanticism

Concerns about the implications of evolutionary science for spiritual belief and worries about the excesses of industrial capitalism or the possibility of revolution set the tone for introspective, anguished explorations of self and society. The middle decades of the century, in particular, gave rise to poetry and prose infused with a sense of melancholy. Spiritual misgivings, self-doubt, and questions about humankind's place in the universe are all matters given thoughtful consideration here. There is a sense in this literature that the present is seriously flawed and that the future may hold only uncertainty. In some cases, responses to these problems take the form of intimate reflections on personal emotional crises or the loss of religious faith. In other cases, nostalgia gives shape to idealized images of the remote past. The quest motif, Arthurian romance, and medieval themes make frequent appearances in this category. Texts under this rubric may also explore individual psychology or social identity in varying ways—through the use of dramatic monologue or gothic renditions of the fragmented psyche.

Aesthetics, Aestheticism, and the Critique of Victorian Values

Victorian aesthetics followed several trajectories. John Ruskin, for example, fused social critique with a laudatory view of medieval art and architecture. Medievalism in this context was more than an imaginative space of utopian social relations; it was a self-conscious appeal to aesthetic considerations. This line of thought rejected the perfection and symmetry of classical forms in favor of rough, energetic creations that were willing to risk a certain crudeness of expression in pursuit of inspired brilliance. An appreciation of medieval aesthetics, however, could be communicated in very different ways. Ruskin argued that a work of art should enlighten the viewer in some manner, through its moral or intellectual content. In contrast, artists such as D. G. Rossetti and other Pre-Raphaelites moved further and further toward a purely sensual appreciation of their subject matter, both medieval and otherwise. This movement away from a didactic art toward one that existed in and for itself was most clearly expressed in the aesthetic movement, which believed above all else in the value of "art for art's sake." The conscious rejection of moral content in art that developed in the aesthetic movement can also be seen in other trends, particularly of the late nineteenth century. During this period there was a general questioning of Victorian social conventions and gender roles, appearing across a broad spectrum of genres and modes. The texts in this cluster address issues relating to art and the rejection of bourgeois social values.

Progress, Science, and Colonial Expansion

Although scientific findings in the nineteenth century were the cause of many tormented speculations on religion and faith, they also offered a rationale for a forward-thinking view of British society and of humankind. In *The Origin of Species*, for instance, Darwin expressed the belief that through the process of natural selection, species were evolving toward perfection. This concept of a biological network, full of competing interests that ultimately yielded to a stronger organic whole, provided a way of envisioning social and cultural systems that worked, presumably, toward the betterment of society. Laissez-faire economics, in particular, extended this logic by viewing the misery of the poor as a "natural" process of checks and balances that resulted in a healthier economy overall. British imperialism and colonial domination provided yet another outlet for this narrative of progress. Under the banner of advancement, the drive to discover new sources of commodities and natural resources was reinvented as a civilizing mission, an altruistic move on Britain's part to bring light to all corners of the world. These texts speak to the spirit of progress in the context of scientific inquiry, imperial expansion, and the formulation of a specifically British national identity.

AUTHORS AND WORKS

Thomas Carlyle

Sartor Resartus

Sartor Resartus is not an easy read; the inverted syntax, exaggerated style of writing, and rambling narration can be challenging to students. Yet for these very reasons it can be extremely rewarding in the classroom, as readers untangle the various conceits and begin to grasp the basic concepts. In so doing, they will come much closer to understanding the internal struggle that haunts much Victorian writing. Moreover, *Sartor Resartus* speaks to a kind of despair and confusion many readers have encountered at one time or another in their lives. To this end, Carlyle's message is one of hope, suggesting that the independent thinker can move beyond conventional beliefs and come to a clearer, more profound understanding of life.

Quick Read

- Form: Combination novel, fictional autobiography, and essay. A fictional editor narrates the main part of the essay, putting Professor Teufelsdröckh's statements in quotation marks.
- Summary: An imaginary German philosopher, Professor Diogenes Teufelsdröckh, undergoes a spiritual crisis and rebirth ("The Everlasting No"), surveys history (the "Centre of Indifference"), and arrives at a new understanding of the world and the divine ("The Everlasting Yea").
- Style: Use of hyperbole, vivid allusion, word play, and inverted syntax.
- Controlling Metaphor: In the larger work from which the NAEL selection is extracted, traditional Christian beliefs are termed "Old Clothes," which Professor Teufelsdröckh discards for a newly fashioned set of clothes (his new spiritual beliefs).
- Key Passages: "[W]hat is all this but a mad Fermentation; wherefrom, the fiercer it is, the clearer product will one day evolve itself?" (1006); the narrator criticizes the "Profit-and-loss Philosophy," of Bentham and the utilitarians, claiming that "Soul is *not* synonymous with Stomach" (1007); the emptiness of the universe compared to the industrial age: "To me, the Universe was all void of Life, of Purpose, of Volition, even of Hostility: it was one huge, dead, immeasurable Steam-engine" (1009); the effect of spiritual doubt: "I lived in a continual, indefinite, pining fear; tremulous, pusillanimous, apprehensive of I knew not what" (1010); the "Everlasting No": "*I* am not thine [the Devil's], but Free" (1011); Romantic self-absorption disparaged: "the old inward Satanic School" (1011); great men: "Great Men are the inspired . . . Texts of the divine BOOK OF REVELA-

TION" (1015); happiness and renunciation: "there is in man a HIGHER than Love of Happiness: he can do without Happiness, and instead thereof find Blessedness!" (1022); the "Everlasting Yea": "Love not Pleasure; love God. This is the EVERLASTING YEA wherein all contradiction is solved" (1022); the remedy: "Be no longer a Chaos, but a World, or even Worldkin. Produce! Produce!" (1024).

Teaching Suggestions

You would be wise to give students a solid context for understanding Carlyle's thought before they plunge into the reading. Discuss Carlyle's personal experience with religion: his background of Scottish Calvinism, later abandonment of beliefs, and eventual development of a philosophy that rejects organized religion but embraces an unorthodox spirituality. Students need to understand that Carlyle spoke to one of the great issues of the time; his sense of confusion and desolation following his loss of faith were shared by many of his contemporaries. At the same time, however, you can encourage students to enjoy the humor and playfulness of Carlyle's prose. A good way to start the session, then, would be to invite students to analyze the rhetorical modes used and discuss their effectiveness. This can be done in small groups or a large classroom, depending on the situation. After this exercise, students should be more comfortable with Carlyle and able to look more closely at the content. At this point, a close reading of several passages is recommended, taking the work one section at a time and starting with some of the suggestions listed above. Given the circuitous style of the piece, significant issues, images, allusions, and metaphors recur throughout, in seemingly digressive passages that return to previous ideas in new and different ways. Thus, it's a good idea to ask students to underline and share the portions they thought were the most intriguing or confusing; these discussions will most likely bring you back to the main issues.

Past and Present

Quick Read

- Form: Book.
- Summary: Carlyle exhorts the "Captains of Industry"—the new industrial leaders—to govern forcefully and responsibly, with concern for the larger interests of society.
- Themes: England is facing a social and economic crisis involving the laboring poor, who endure wretched lives; this crisis can only be averted by the appearance of strong leaders with foresight and a sense of obligation to the masses; these strong leaders should be modeled on the feudal leaders of the past, who governed harshly but cultivated stable societies; laissez-faire economics ("Every man for himself") will not help the situation; serfs of the feudal age were

far better off than today's industrial workers because the serfs had their basic needs covered; today's freedom is merely the freedom to starve.

- Key Passages: "Gurth to me seems happy, in comparison with many a Lancashire and Buckinghamshire man . . . Gurth's brass collar did not gall him" (1026); "Liberty requires new definitions" (1027); William the Conqueror as a "true God-made King" (1027); "A child, in this William's reign, might have carried a purse of gold from end to end of England" (1028); when the descendants of feudal lords "cease entirely to *be* the Best, Nature's poor world will very soon rush down again to Baseness . . . Hence French Revolutions, Five-point Charters, Democracies, and a mournful list of *Etceteras*, in these our afflicted times" (1028); "Mock-Superiors" versus "Real-Superiors" (1029); the real work of governing must be done by those who "stand practically in the middle of it" (1029); "You cannot lead a Fighting World without having it regimented, chivalried . . . And can you any more continue to lead a Working World unregimented, anarchic?" (1031); "the Feudal Baron had a Man's Soul in him; to which anarchy, mutiny, and the other fruits of temporary mercenaries, were intolerable" (1032); "Awake, ye noble Workers, warriors in the one true war" (1032).

Teaching Suggestions

Past and Present goes to the heart of the problems of the industrial age: extensive poverty, an unregulated economy based on personal profit rather than social welfare, and disenfranchised masses on the verge of revolt. While this work contains some of the flamboyant rhetorical devices used in *Sartor Resartus*, it is generally more coherent and accessible. If you do not have time to assign a full-length novel on the "condition of England" issue, this will be an invaluable introduction to Victorian paternalism. The main idea that students need to explore here is how and why paternalism was such an attractive option for members of the middle class concerned with social reform (such as Charles Dickens, for example). Ask them why, according to Carlyle, Gurth was so much better off working under Cedric, his master; what do nineteenth-century industrial workers lack that Gurth had? You may want to point out that while many middle-class reformers were sincerely concerned about the mass poverty they saw, they were also afraid of revolt and wanted the social hierarchy to remain in place. This kind of conflict shows up in Carlyle's writing. Carlyle, himself born into poverty, in many ways sympathizes with and champions the working classes: "It is not to die, or even to die of hunger, that makes a man wretched. . . . But it is to live miserable we know not why; to work sore and yet gain nothing; to be heartworn, weary, yet isolated, unrelated, girt-in with a cold universal Laissez-faire: it is to die slowly all our life long, imprisoned in a deaf, dead, Infinite Injustice." In passages like this the laboring classes are not a "they" but a "we," as if Carlyle were one of them: like other reformers, he proposes to speak for those who have no voice. Yet epithets like the "Dumb Class" or the "dumb millions" seem condescending in light of Carlyle's argument that the working classes do not require reform bills, or suffrage, or the other liberties prized by Romantic revolutionaries but rather secretly crave the sort of kindly, beneficent leadership that prevailed in feudal times. "Liberty? The true liberty of a man," in the days of feudalism, "consisted in his finding out, or being forced to find out, the right path, and to walk thereon." The working-class individual who tries to forge out "the right path" toward freedom on his own is like a "madman" who must be restrained for his own good, lest he do himself some irreparable harm.

Teaching Clusters

The theme of spiritual crisis places *Sartor Resartus* firmly in the category of **Doubt, Self-Reflection, and Romanticism.** A good companion piece would be J. S. Mill's *Autobiography*, which covers similar territory in a very different rhetorical mode. In addition to the trauma of spiritual doubt, however, this selection also addresses anxieties about the new social order, so in this sense could be included in the cluster on **Poverty, Unrest, and Social Criticism**, along with *Past and Present*. Literary works that would fit nicely in this cluster include Tennyson's "Locksley Hall" and *Idylls of the King*. Students also need to have more context for understanding the urgency of the issues that Carlyle addresses, so nonliterary pieces such as Engels's "The Great Towns," Ruskin's "The Stones of Venice," Morris's "How I Became a Socialist," and Ada Nield Chew's "A Living Wage for Factory Girls at Crewe" are all good choices for study in this grouping.

If time permits, longer readings that capture the spirit of Carlyle's paternalistic message include novels such as Elizabeth Gaskell's *Mary Barton* (1848) and *North and South* (1855), Benjamin Disraeli's *Sybil* (1845), and Dickens's *Hard Times* (1854). In a Victorian-only survey you may wish to supplement *NAEL* with one of these; *Mary Barton* in particular (see the *Preface* in Norton Topics Online) works well with the readings both on industrialism and on the "woman question."

Discussion Questions

1. Carlyle meant his prose to affect and involve the reader. What rhetorical methods does he employ for these purposes? Think about his sentence structure and the metaphors, allusions, and unique terms he creates. Do his methods ultimately succeed or fail at engaging the reader?

2. The central message in Carlyle's essay is that we must go through a form of spiritual evolution to develop as full human beings. How does Professor Teufelsdröckh evolve? What are the issues that prompt his spiritual musings and transformation?

3. What is the "Everlasting No"? What does Professor Teufelsdröckh repudiate and why?
4. Why is Carlyle's essay critical of contemporary Utilitarian thought: "Profit-and-loss Philosophy"? How does this philosophy conflict with the essay's larger themes?
5. Explain Teufelsdröckh's theory of "great men."
6. What is the "Everlasting Yea"?
7. What does Carlyle mean when he suggests that the nineteenth-century Gurth has "the 'Liberty to die by starvation'"? How does Carlyle play on the word "liberty"?
8. Why does Carlyle think William the Conqueror is a "true God-made King"?
9. Who are the "Mock-Superiors" and who are the "Real-Superiors"?
10. According to Carlyle, in what way can the feudal lords of the past provide a model for the "Captains of Industry"?

Further Resources

NORTON ONLINE ARCHIVE

American Visitors
    Daniel Webster at Fifty-seven
    Ralph Waldo Emerson at Thirty
    Emerson at Forty-four
    Bronson Alcott at Forty-two
Carlyle's Portraits of His Contemporaries
    Queen Victoria at Eighteen
    Samuel Taylor Coleridge at Fifty-three
    William Wordsworth in His Seventies
    Alfred Tennyson at Thirty-four
    Charles Lamb at Fifty-six
    William Makepeace Thackeray at Forty-two
    King William IV at Sixty-nine
From Characteristics
Sartor Resartus
    Natural Supernaturalism
The French Revolution
    September in Paris
    Place de la Revolution
    Cause and Effect

John Henry Cardinal Newman

The Idea of a University

Newman's views on the proper function of a university education will be of interest to students, who are very likely thinking about their own future goals and education. The argument he raises here—that a university should train students in the pursuit of knowledge for its own ends rather than for professional or practical purposes—is just as relevant today as it was in the nineteenth century.

Quick Read

- Form: Published lectures.
- Summary: The goal of a university should be to prepare individuals to pursue knowledge in a broad sense, not to train them for a specific trade or profession.
- Themes: Knowledge is an "acquired illumination," not to be confused with "instruction"; the aim of a liberal education is to pursue knowledge for its own sake, not for vocational or practical purposes; knowledge should not be measured primarily by utility; Locke and his followers have misguided notions about education; a liberal education provides an excellent foundation for responsible citizenship and enlightened social exchange; the "true gentleman" is polite, kind, gentle, and respects differing religious views.
- Key Passages: Definition of knowledge, Discourse 5.6; definition of a liberal education, Discourse 7.1; usefulness versus utility, Discourse 7.5; Locke's ideas about education do not further the ultimate ends of society, Discourse 7.9; correct university training "rais[es] the intellectual tone of society, . . . purif[ies] the national taste, . . . and facilitat[es] the exercise of political power," Discourse 7.10; definition of a gentleman in relation to knowledge and religion, Discourse 8.10.

Teaching Suggestions

Guide students' reading through the major passages, engaging discussion on the larger issue Newman addresses: the meaning of knowledge and the proper aim of a university education. Ask students about Newman's rationale for a specifically "liberal" education. Besides being, in general, an admirable goal, how can a liberal university education help individuals to be better social beings and citizens? This is a good place to open up questions about education today, a topic of some urgency for students. Finally, allot a fair amount of time to the final section, which has much to say about masculinity and "proper" middle-class behavior. Invite students to explore what Newman means by "a true gentleman." Note in particular Newman's view that a gentleman should cultivate "gentleness and effeminacy [tenderness] of feeling." You might want to ask students if this idea of masculinity seems in accordance with some of the poetry they've read—by Tennyson, Arnold, and Robert Browning, for example.

Teaching Clusters

This selection would fit nicely within the **Gender and Sexuality** cluster because it defines a particular type of masculine conduct. A thought-provoking companion piece would be George Eliot's review of Margaret Fuller and Mary Wollstonecraft, or any reading that addresses issues of female education, such as Barrett Browning's *Aurora Leigh* or Tennyson's *The Princess*. An equally successful placement would be in the **Doubt, Self-Reflection, and Romanticism** cluster, insofar as the work addresses issues of social identity in a thoughtful manner. The moral earnestness of the piece captures the introspective, self-searching approach of other items in the grouping. Moreover, Newman's concept of the gentleman defines a larger view of "proper" middle-class behavior with regard not only to manners and morals, but also to social and national responsibility. In this sense, the selection could be included in the **Progress, Science, and Colonial Expansion** section, read alongside other pieces that speak to the formation of national identity (Matthew Arnold on Celtic literature, for example).

Discussion Questions

1. According to Newman, what is knowledge? How does it differ from mere instruction?
2. How does one acquire knowledge? Why is the acquisition of true knowledge different from "mere acquirement"?
3. What does Newman mean by "useful"? How is usefulness different from mere "Utility"? In what way can usefulness lead to the "*instrument* of good"?
4. Why does Newman object to the way in which "Locke and his disciples" view education?
5. According to Newman, how is the cultivation of the intellect related to the "formation of the citizen"?
6. What does Newman mean when he says that "a University is not a birthplace of poets . . . or conquerors of nations"?
7. What is Newman's definition of a "true gentleman"? How does Newman envision masculinity? Why does Newman believe a gentleman should cultivate "gentleness and effeminacy [tenderness] of feeling"?
8. Should universities today train students for the job market or for a more broadly conceived role in society?

Further Resources

NORTON ONLINE ARCHIVE

Apologia Pro Vita Sua
From Chapter 3. History of My Religious Opinions from 1839 to 1841
From Chapter 5. Position of My Mind Since 1845

John Stuart Mill

Having fought against the tyranny of his father's utilitarian education, Mill continued to struggle against other types of tyranny throughout his life. In the selections in *NAEL*, he compares marriage to slavery, worries about the loss of individual freedoms in a democratic society, and reveals his own inner struggle against a meaningless existence. Students will be drawn especially to the *Autobiography*, with its description of mental collapse and self-renewal through the study of poetry. Most importantly, the *Autobiography* introduces, in a straightforward manner, the themes that recur repeatedly throughout all of Mill's work. Among the "prime necessities of human well-being," Mill asserts, is attention to "the internal culture of the individual." As he explains, "The cultivation of the feelings became one of the cardinal points in my ethical and philosophical creed." The importance of individual self-expression and the development of non-quantifiable human qualities are similarly emphasized in. "Human nature is not a machine to be built after a model, and set to do exactly the work prescribed for it, but a tree, which requires to grow and develop itself on all sides, according to the tendency of the inward forces which make it a living thing," Mill states in an observation that would have been equally fitting in the *Autobiography* (*On Liberty*). Mill's views on individuality and freedom for all human beings influenced many writers of the century and remain essential reading today.

What Is Poetry?

Quick Read

- Form: Essay.
- Themes: Mill describes poetry as distinct from other cultural forms such as fiction; in so doing, he accords poetry a special place in the development of a healthy individualism.
- Key Passages: "The truth of poetry is to paint the human soul truly: the truth of fiction is to give a true picture of life" (1046); "The persons and the nations who commonly excel in poetry are those whose character and tastes render them least dependent upon the applause or sympathy or concurrence of the world in general" (1049).

On Liberty

Quick Read

- Form: Book.
- Themes: The cultivation of individuality is important to society and to the strength of a government; geniuses arise out of free societies that allow great latitude for self-expression; democracy is not conducive to genius and free thinking; geniuses are lacking in Victorian England, but they are needed to prevent England's decline.
- Key Passages: "[T]o conform to custom, merely *as* custom, does not educate or develop in [a person] any of the qualities which are the distinctive endowment of a human being" (1052); "[S]ociety has now fairly got the better of individuality" (1054); the development of individuality advances society: "[E]ach person becomes . . . more valu-

able to others" (1055); "[W]hatever crushes individuality is despotism" (1055–56); Society needs to recognize the "importance of genius" and the "necessity of allowing it to unfold itself freely" (1057); "The greatness of England is now all collective. . . . But it was men of another stamp than this that made England what it has been; and men of another stamp will be needed to prevent its decline" (1059); progress is not the same as individuality (1059–60).

Teaching Suggestions

This is a rich essay that should provide much material for a spirited classroom discussion. Mill's ideas on individuality and nonconformity offer a good entryway into the piece. Although his initial comments on these points will be fairly clear, students may not immediately understand that ultimately Mill is criticizing democracy (or "collectivity") because, in his view, it smothers individual self-expression. Moreover, to Mill's way of thinking, genius is lacking in the England of his day because society does not foster the individuality in mind and spirit that is necessary for its development. In an ominous prediction, he warns that "The greatness of England is now all collective. . . . But it was men of another stamp than this that made England what it has been; and men of another stamp will be needed to prevent its decline." To encourage a more thoughtful discussion on Mill's concept of the genius in society, have students compare his view to Carlyle's description of "great men" in *Sartor Resartus*.

The Subjection of Women

Quick Read

- Form: Book.
- Theme: The subordination of women to men is a barbaric, outmoded practice.
- Key Passages: "[T]he principle which regulates the existing social relations between the two sexes—the legal subordination of one sex to another—is wrong in itself" (1061); Most men want "not a forced slave but a willing one. . . . They have therefore put everything in practice to enslave [women's] minds" (1063); "The social subordination of women thus stands out an isolated fact in modern social institutions; . . . a single relic of an old world of thought and practice" (1064); "What is now called the nature of women is an eminently artificial thing—the result of forced repression" (1065); Men "are afraid, not lest women should be unwilling to marry, . . . but lest they should insist that marriage should be on equal conditions" (1070).

Teaching Suggestions

Mill, like Romantic-era philosophers before him, compares marriage to slavery. Women are "compelled" into marriage, their "alleged natural vocation," because they have internalized cultural admonitions about woman's duty and because "all other doors" are closed against them. The "clue to the feelings of those men, who have a real antipathy to the equal freedom of women," says Mill, is their fear that if given the opportunity to support themselves, "all women of spirit and capacity should prefer doing almost anything else" than "degrading" themselves through marriage. Students should find Mill's argument fairly straightforward, but it will help to give them some understanding of the radical nature of his pronouncements, especially in comparing marriage to slavery. This piece thus needs to be taught alongside others in the "Woman Question" section, such as Ruskin's "Of Queens' Gardens," Mona Caird's "Marriage," and Sarah Ellis's *The Women of England*. Additionally, George Eliot's essay on Margaret Fuller and Mary Wollstonecraft will shed light on the role that female education plays in the debate.

Autobiography

Quick Read

- Form: Book.
- Summary: Mill looks back to his youth and talks about a mental breakdown that occurred as a result of his father's utilitarian teachings; by reading poetry and developing a new philosophy in life that made room for human emotions, he was able to recover.
- Key Passages: Initial description of Mill's mental breakdown (1071–72); attitude toward his father's utilitarian teachings (1072–73); the "habit of analysis" tends to "wear away the feelings" (1072); the turning point in his depression comes when reading Marmontel's *Mémoires* (1074); Mill's new "philosophy of life" (1075); "What made Wordsworth's poems a medicine for my state of mind, was that they expressed . . . states of feeling" (1077); "I . . . value Wordsworth less according to his intrinsic merits than by the measure of what he had done for me" (1077).

Teaching Suggestions

Writing in 1873, Mill remembers the crisis of his youth, when he lost all pleasure in his usual occupations, all confidence in the Utilitarian social philosophy promoted by his father, and all belief in his life's ambition, "to be a reformer of the world." With this reading, it is important for students to understand that, for Mill, the cultivation of feeling is related to the concept of individuality—and thus this selection sheds light on Mill's other work. Mill was able to overcome his intense depression with the help of Romantic poetry, which taught him to balance his too-ingrained "habit of analysis" with the "cultivation of the feelings." William Wordsworth's poems in particular, he comments, "expressed, not mere outward beauty, but states of feeling, and of thought colored by feeling, under the excitement of beauty. . . . In them I seemed to draw from a source of inward joy, of sympathetic and imaginative pleasure, which could be shared in by all human beings." Students may benefit from reading Wordsworth alongside this piece; "Tintern Abbey," for instance, explores the access of emotion through beauty that Mill admires. Mill's encounter with Wordsworth is central, but it is useful to note that his praise for the poet is always tempered; other poets are greater. As Mill explains, "I . . . value Wordsworth less according to his intrinsic merits than by the measure of what he had done for me." One feels the old Utilitarian "habit of analysis" always pulling at Mill, devaluing "*mere* . . . feeling."

Teaching Clusters

While a piece such as *The Subjection of Women* is an obvious fit in the **Gender and Sexuality** cluster, it works equally well with *On Liberty*, since both are concerned with individual freedoms. You might want to point out that when Mill equates the idea of the "unnatural" with what is "uncustomary" in *The Subjection of Women*, he questions the value of majority opinion, as he does in *On Liberty* and elsewhere. In this context, both *On Liberty* and *The Subjection of Women* could be taught within the **Poverty, Unrest, and Social Criticism** section. While the *Autobiography*, on the other hand, makes sense in the **Doubt, Self-Reflection, and Romanticism** cluster because of its intensely introspective quality, it would also be illuminatingly paired with "What Is Poetry?" and other works that address aesthetic issues in the teaching cluster on **Aesthetics, Aestheticism, and the Critique of Victorian Values**.

Discussion Questions

1. In "What Is Poetry" how does Mill distinguish poetry from other literary forms such as fiction?
2. According to Mill in *On Liberty*, how is the cultivation of individual genius advantageous for society?
3. What does Mill mean when he says, in *On Liberty*, that "The spirit of improvement is not always a spirit of liberty"?
4. In *On Liberty* Mill states that "[p]rogress is not the same as individuality"; how are the two different?
5. Mill claims in *The Subjection of Women* that most men want "not a forced slave but a willing one. . . . They have therefore put everything in practice to enslave [women's] minds." In Mill's view, how are women's minds enslaved?
6. How does Wordsworth help in Mill's recovery from mental and emotional collapse?

Elizabeth Barrett Browning

Aurora Leigh

Elizabeth Barrett Browning's *Aurora Leigh* is significant both because it charts the development of a woman writer and because it treats present-day events as fitting material for an epic poem. Students will enjoy Aurora's irreverent description of her pious aunt, whose "virtuous life . . . was not life at all" (Book 1, lines 288–89) and her spirited refusal of her cousin Romney's offer of marriage because "[w]hat [he] love[s] / Is not a woman . . . but a cause" (Book 2, lines 400–401). Aurora's voice is bold and her observations razor-sharp, countering popular Victorian stereotypes of female docility.

Quick Read

- Form: Verse novel; some have called this a female bildungsroman.
- Main Theme: The development of a female poet from childhood to adulthood.
- Key Passages: Aurora's description of her aunt's "quiet life," Book 1, lines 287–309; books on womanhood, Book 1, lines 427–38; the works of women, Book 1, lines 455–65; headaches versus heartaches, Book 2, lines 92–115; Aurora's rejection of Romney, Book 2, lines 400–412; a woman's soul, Book 2, lines 485–97; poets and the present age, Book 5, lines 183–213.

Teaching Suggestions

Aurora's scathing description of her aunt's quiet life makes an excellent starting point: "She had lived, we'll say, / A harmless life, she called a virtuous life, / A quiet life, which was not life at all" (Book 1, lines 287–89). Begin by looking at the larger passage (Book 1, lines 287–309) and ask students what this tells us about the narrator and her views. Why does Aurora look down on her aunt? What does the tone tell us? What do Aurora's comments about her aunt's "virtuous life" (Book 1, line 288) and her "Christian gifts" (Book 1, line 297) of petticoats and stockings tell us about Aurora's attitude toward religion? Move from here through the other key passages, paying particular attention to Aurora's scornful appraisal of "books on womanhood" (Book 1, line 427); why does she reject these books? What do they tell us about Victorian views of women? How do these passages correspond to the earlier ones about living a virtuous life? Is there a connection? Aurora's attitudes toward feminine stereotypes lay the groundwork for the succeeding passages on her relationship with Romney. Have students read Romney's discussion with Aurora about poets (Book 2, lines 80–115); what is his view of women poets? What does he mean when he says, "even dreaming of the stone and bronze / Brings headaches, pretty cousin, and defiles / The clean white morning dresses" (Book 2, lines 94–96)? Aurora counters with a discussion of "ease and whiteness" (Book 2, line 99); what does whiteness represent here? What does it mean in the next line, when Aurora talks about "walk[ing] in white" (Book 2, line 102) and "soil[ing] [her] gown" (Book 2, line 105). In the next passage, Aurora returns to Romney's topic of "headaches"; why does she "choose headaches" (Book 2, line 108) rather than "heartache[s]" (Book 2, line 112)? What does each represent? How are these terms gendered? By the time you have addressed all of these issues, students will have gained some insight into the difficulties facing women of this period.

Finally, after a close reading of the narrator's comments about poets and contemporary events (Book 5, lines 183–213), ask students to imagine what an epic poem about events in their own lives might be like. If you have time for an individual or group project, invite students to write a brief outline—or a few lines—of a novel-length poem based on events similar to those in Aurora's life: childhood influences, experiences with gender stereotypes, personal aspirations, and encounters with social strictures. What elements make a life worthy of poetry? What is the proper subject of poetry? These are the issues that Aurora Leigh asks us to contemplate.

Sonnets from the Portuguese

Begin with some biographical information about Barrett Browning and her marriage to Robert Browning to engage students' interest in these selections. The first line of Sonnet 43 will be familiar to many readers: "How do I love thee? Let me count the ways." Students may think of these words as flowery or sweet, but ask them also to look closely at other lines, such as "I love thee with the passion put to use / In my old griefs, and with my childhood's faith" (lines 9–10). (Sonnet 43 has been set to music; you can find a recording in the online archive.) Encourage students to move beyond a surface reading of the sonnets by directing their attention to unusual line breaks, enjambments, and vivid imagery or diction so that they get a sense of the energy of some of the writing. In Sonnet 22, for example, the narrator exclaims, "Let us stay / Rather on earth, Belovèd, —where the unfit / Contrarious moods of men recoil away . . ." (9–11); the break after "unfit" disrupts normal expectations and focuses attention on "Contrarious moods." Ask students to compare words and phrases such as "unfit," "Contrarious," "erect and strong" (line 1), and "bitter wrong" (line 4) with "two souls" (line 1), "pure spirits" (line 12), and "our deep, dear silence" (line 9). What kind of speaker is this? A close reading will illuminate some of the complexity of the sequence.

The Runaway Slave at Pilgrim's Point

The sobering subject matter of this poem—the murder of a half-white baby by its black slave mother—demonstrates Barrett Browning's concern with social issues. Begin by asking students to discuss the central problem addressed: the narrator's murder of her child (lines 112–54). The interesting point here for students to focus on is the fact that the woman has committed a terrible crime—yet the poem asks us to pity her. Invite students to consider why and to what extent the reader is asked to empathize with the narrator. Note the first-person address by a black female slave; how does this affect the impact of the story? How does the refrain ("I am black, I am black") function? Pair this with "The Cry of the Children," which describes underage factory workers ground down by the "mailed heel" of industry (line 155). You may want to open up a discussion about art and politics: What can imaginative literature do that nonliterary accounts of political and social injustice cannot?

Teaching Clusters

Given Aurora Leigh's focus on the struggles of an independently minded woman, this poem would be most usefully placed within the **Gender and Sexuality** category. John Ruskin's "Of Queens' Gardens" is essential reading here. Compare Aurora's comments about "books that boldly assert / Their right of comprehending husband's talk / When not too deep, and even of answering / With pretty 'may it please you,' or 'so it is' " (Book 1, lines 430–33) with Ruskin's directive that "[a wife] must be enduringly, incorruptibly good; instinctively, infallibly wise—wise, not for self-development, but for self-renunciation: wise, not that she may set herself above her husband, but that she may never fail from his side." In the same vein, read Coventry Patmore's The Angel in the House for Aurora's absolute poetic antithesis. Also essential is the excerpt from Harriet Martineau's Autobiography, which describes the stultifying restrictiveness of her early life, attitudes toward women intellectuals, and her own early experiences as a writer. Another interesting choice here would be Virginia Woolf's A Room of One's Own, a much later work, but one that directly addresses the problems of female authorship.

A few poems by women poets would round out the grouping. Barrett Browning's own poems to George Sand ("To George Sand: A Desire" and "To George Sand: A Recognition") address matters of gender and female intellect. Other works that do not specifically focus on female writers but which will give students a feeling for mid-Victorian women's issues include Goblin Market and "In an Artist's Studio," by Christina Rossetti; and "Stars" and "Remembrance," by Emily Brontë. Barrett Browning's Sonnets from the Portuguese also could be placed in this cluster. "The Runaway Slave at Pilgrim's Point," on the other hand, could be placed in the **Gender and Sexuality** category, discussed in connection with motherhood, or it could be taught under the rubric of **Poverty, Unrest, and Social Criticism**, alongside "The Cry of the Children" and works from the "Victorian Issues" section on "Industrialism." "The Cry of the Children," in particular, could be paired with the excerpts from the Royal Commission describing the horrible conditions under which child mine workers labored.

Discussion Questions

1. What do Aurora's views about her aunt tell us about Aurora herself?
2. How does Aurora feel about the typical education of a Victorian woman?
3. How do Victorian expectations of correct feminine behavior conflict with Aurora's desires to be a poet?
4. Why does Aurora reject her cousin Romney's offer of marriage?
5. Why does Aurora think that epic poetry should be about the here-and-now rather than past events?
6. Examine the tone, imagery, diction, and line breaks in Barrett Browning's *Sonnets from the Portuguese* and explain their effects.
7. What is the attitude of "The Runaway Slave at Pilgrim's Point" toward the mother who has killed her child? In what ways does this poem appeal to the emotions of the reader?
8. Compare "The Runaway Slave at Pilgrim's Point" with "The Cry of the Children." How does each poem demonstrate its concern for the welfare of children? Where does each poem put the ultimate blame for that welfare?
9. Why does the epigraph to "The Cry of the Children" relate Medea's words to her children before she kills them: "Alas, my children, why do you look at me?"

Further Resources

NORTON ONLINE ARCHIVE

To George Sand: A Desire
To George Sand: A Recognition
A Year's Spinning
A Musical Instrument

Audio:
Sonnet 43, from *Sonnets from the Portuguese* (music by Elizabeth Everest Freer; performed by Susan Bender and Carol Feather Martin)

NORTON TOPICS ONLINE

Industrialism: Progress or Decline?

Alfred, Lord Tennyson

Arthur Hallam, Tennyson's closest friend and the subject of the elegiac *In Memoriam*, described Tennyson as a poet of "sensation" rather than of ideas. Although it would be misleading to think of Tennyson's poetry as lacking in ideas, the ability to capture emotion in differing guises— through the thoughts of an abandoned woman or a Greek king, through the description of landscape or Arthurian legend—is one of Tennyson's strengths. Often his characters seem suspended between desire and action: Mariana can only wait in frustrated isolation for her lover, while Ulysses asserts a forcefulness undermined by a pervasive sense of decline. Yet at the same time Tennyson wants to believe in human progress and the promise of the future. *In Memoriam* offers possibilities for a meaningful existence in the face of emotional and spiritual despair, while "Locksley Hall" attempts to exorcise the demons of social unrest. Feelings of loss and melancholy, ever present in Tennyson, find full expression in imaginative renderings of the Arthurian tales. Tennyson's medieval protagonists are plagued by failed aspirations and unfulfilled yearnings, struggling against death or decay, like the dying King Arthur and the Lady of Shalott. In Tennyson, students will encounter a range of moods and inner conflicts that make him an engrossing object of study.

Mariana

In this poem the protagonist languishes "without hope of change" (line 29). Like many of her nineteenth-century female counterparts, Mariana suffers from the enforced confinement dictated by the separation between public and private spheres for men and women. As a woman of the affluent classes, she has little latitude in sexual relationships and so exists in a state of stagnation underscored by the repetition of the nearly identical quatrain: "She only said, 'My life is dreary, / He cometh not,' she said; / She said, 'I am aweary, aweary, / I would that I were dead!' " Invite students to think about the way in which the natural landscape connects to Mariana's emotional state. Nature affords no relief to Mariana: pent up within her own misery, she cannot "look on the sweet heaven" with pleasure, and birdsong and wind and sunshine irritate and "confound" rather than soothe her senses (lines 15, 76). In large part, the natural world seems to reflect Mariana's own gloom. The moat that surrounds the grange is a "sluice with blackened waters"; the flower beds are "thickly crusted" with "blackest moss"; from her window she sees only the "level waste" of a dead, "gray" country (lines 38, 2, 1, 44, 31). The reader suffers from the same sense of claustrophobia as Mariana, as each verse describes her surroundings in almost oppressive detail.

The Lotos-Eaters

Tennyson chooses a relatively obscure episode from the *Odyssey* that illustrates neither the valor of Greek heroes nor the wiliness of Odysseus, giving you an excellent opportunity to discuss Victorian attitudes toward masculinity and the work ethic. The lotos-eaters wish only to withdraw from the world and lose themselves in "drowsy numbness," like the speaker of Keats's "Ode to a Nightingale," who has "been half in love with easeful Death" (lines 1, 52). "We have had enough of action" (line 150), Tennyson's mariners proclaim; they prefer the stasis of "A land where all things always seemed the same" (line 24), where they might "dream and dream" (line 102) with "half-shut eyes, . . . [e]ating the Lotos day by day" (lines 100–105). In Keats's ode, and in the Romantic tradition generally, one might deliberately seek out a narcotized state to enable flights of imaginative fancy, but in Tennyson the drugged mind that turns inward on itself is lethargic, torpid, even paralyzed. Carlyle's Professor Teufels-dröckh exhorts the Victorian reader to "Produce! Produce! Were it but the pitifullest infinitesimal fraction of a Product, produce it, in God's name! . . . Work while it is called Today; for the Night cometh, wherein no man can work" (*Sartor Resartus*). But poems like "The Lotos-Eaters" reveal a certain ambivalence about those supposed Victorian desiderata—activity, labor, and struggle—and thus, by extension, a discontent with the frenetic pace and clamor of modern times.

The Princess

The selection from *The Princess*, however much it upholds the ideal of the complementarity of the sexes, insists that men and women, "Distinct in individualities," are at the core radically unlike. Students should understand that *The Princess* advocates woman's rights in a very guarded way, arguing against a woman-centered or separatist version of feminism. Instead, man must make woman's battles his own, for their fates are intertwined: "The woman's cause is man's: they rise or sink / Together, dwarfed or godlike, bond or free" (lines 243–44). A limited version of the "woman's cause" in fact serves male interests, for, as the speaker points out, uneducated, narrow-minded women make poor wives: "If she be small, slight-natured, miserable, / How shall men grow?" (lines 249–50). Man should foster woman's growth and self-improvement; however, she should not be encouraged to grow *outside* of her basic nature: let her "live and learn and be / All that not harms distinctive womanhood" (lines 257–58). Thus, female education should not make women more like men, but should develop their "distinctive womanhood." In the ideal future, perhaps, men and women will grow to be more alike—but not too much; necessary distinctions between the sexes must remain intact. While the man will "gain in sweetness and in moral height" (line 265), he will retain the strength that enables him to contend with the duties of the world ("Nor lose the wrestling thews that throw the world" [line 266]); the woman, on the other hand, will gain "mental breadth" (line 267) from the man, but will retain the "childlike" innocence that suits her for domestic duties ("nor fail in childward care, / Nor lose the childlike in the larger mind" [lines 267–68]). Invite your students to think about the larger discussion on female education taking place in the nineteenth century by having them read these selections alongside other works that address similar issues, such as Barrett Browning's *Aurora Leigh*.

In Memoriam A. H. H.

This elegy to Arthur Hallam established Tennyson as a major writer and captured the mood of the moment. Intensely personal, *In Memoriam* mourns not only the loss of a close friend, but also the loss of religious certainty. It may act as an important centerpiece for many types of courses on Victorian literature, not only because it provides a way for students to understand how new findings in science and evolution touched so many aspects of nineteenth-century thought, but also because its sense of multivalent suffering speaks to a host of anxieties about the self, society, and the universe.

Quick Read

- Form: Elegy; long lyric poem; a series of four-line stanzas, rhyming *abba*, which became known as the *In Memoriam* stanza.
- Themes: Loss; bereavement; spiritual doubt; the implications of evolutionary science; homoerotic desire; masculine identity.
- Key Passages: Verses 2 and 39, the yew tree as a symbol of longevity; verse 6, loss of Hallam imagined as paternal, maternal, and romantic grief; verse 7, city street as metaphor for desolation; reconceptualized in verse 119; verse 8, loss of Hallam figured as male lover's grief; verse 13, loss of Hallam figured as widower's bereavement; verse 27, "Tis better to have loved and lost / Than never to have loved at all," lines 15–16; verse 54, expresses spiritual doubt: "Behold, we know not anything," line 13; verse 55, questions the divine plan; the individual seems expendable to nature; verse 56, not only the individual, but also the entire species is expendable to nature, seen as ruthless: "Nature red in tooth and claw," line 15; verse 95, describes a metaphysical experience, possibly signaling a turning point in Tennyson's grief; verses 118 and 120, attempts to come to terms with evolution; verse 124, cannot find God in the works of nature; verse 130, attempts to come to terms with bereavement.

Teaching Suggestions

Before addressing specific verses, it would be helpful to give students a general understanding of the structure of the poem and the circumstances under which it was composed. *In Memoriam* is notable for its quatrain form, used throughout, and the *abba* rhyme scheme. As the *NAEL* headnote to the poem observes, this form helps to give the entire sequence a sense of unity. Moreover, as some critics have suggested, the rhyme scheme establishes a sense of progression in the middle two lines by moving away from the initial rhyme, yet returns to this rhyme in the fourth line, mirroring the poem's larger movement of loss, exploration, and return to the past.

Written over a period of seventeen years, *In Memoriam* mourns the death of Tennyson's close friend, Hallam, while meditating on larger issues of the self, God, and nature. Its structure is unusual for an elegy. Each lyric is separate, but taken as a whole the verses follow the narrator's stages of grief over a period of about three years, punctuated by descriptions of three very different Christmas seasons. At the same time, however, the poem does not present an unbroken narrative, but examines a range of moods, presented as discrete experiences. Verses 54, 55, and

56, in particular, constitute a crisis point, wherein the narrator's personal doubts and anxieties lead him to question the existence of a divine plan and to contemplate the implications of recent scientific findings. The final verses attempt to come to terms with loss and with evolutionary thinking, affirming the value of life. Whether and to what extent the narrator succeeds in these attempts is something for your students to determine.

Some of the early selections provide a good starting point for discussion. Verses 1, 2, and 7, for example, all provide useful ways to introduce the theme of grief and the various modes of emotion. Ask your students to think about the different approaches to loss that Tennyson employs. What does Tennyson mean by "clasp[ing] Grief" in verse 1 (line 9)? Similarly, verse 7 presents the city street as a metaphor for desolation: "On the bald street breaks the blank day" (line 12). Such private expressions of loss and grief move into a larger public arena that explores issues of spiritual crisis. Verses 54, 55, and 56 form a crucial grouping that questions the existence of a divine plan and establishes a conflict between science and religious belief. Ask students how the concept of nature changes in the three verses and how the notion of the individual figures within the larger spiritual scheme. In verse 55, the narrator wonders whether God and nature are in conflict, suggesting that there may be no ultimate purpose in life; the narrator can only "faintly trust the larger hope" (line 20), for example. The questions about religion and science that verses 54, 55, and 56 bring up could be fruitfully compared with later observations about evolution in verses 118 and 120.

Another important theme to address is that of masculine identity and forms of male love. Although not all critics agree that there is a current of homoeroticism in the poem, certain passages imagine male friendship in terms of romantic love, in addition to other forms of love. Verses 6, 8, 13, and 27 make a good grouping in this regard. Verse 6, for example, equates the "perpetual maidenhood" of a young woman who has lost her lover with the speaker's avowal that he will have "no second friend" (lines 43–44). Students should also note that these scenarios allow the narrator to inhabit different forms of grief, demonstrating the breadth and nuanced cadences of his sorrow.

Idylls of the King

Medieval romance, especially Malory's *Morte Darthur*, projected against a background of social disorder and decay, captured the imagination of some Victorian writers and artists. They felt their time was out of joint and turned to Arthurian subjects as an escape from the tawdry England of the Industrial Revolution. In many instances, Arthurian characters, especially the women, are pictured rebelling against the social and moral restrictions of the nineteenth century. Tennyson's Lady of Shalott, for example, trying to escape her web and the shadows in her mirror, dies floating down the river. In Morris's *Defense of Guenevere*, the queen, on trial for adultery, passionately denies the evidence against her, yet at the same time justifies her love as natural and good, something higher than her wedding vow to the cold king. You will want to draw students' attention to Tennyson's very different portrayal of the medieval era in *Idylls of the King*, which has a moralizing strain more commonly associated with Victorian beliefs. The portion entitled "The Coming of Arthur," for instance, completely revises Malory. It is centered on Arthur's marriage to Guinevere and the efforts of King Leodogran, her father, to make sure that Arthur is King Uther's legitimate son. The Middle Ages portion of *Norton Topics Online* has a range of materials on the origins and development of the Arthurian tradition that will be instructive to your students.

Teaching Clusters

In Memoriam fits most clearly in the **Doubt, Self-Reflection, and Romanticism** cluster. The poem works especially well with other readings that detail spiritual and emotional turmoil and its resolutions, such as Mill's *Autobiography*, Newman's *Apologia Pro Vita Sua* (available in the archive), and Carlyle's *Sartor Resartus*. Additionally, verses 54, 55, 56, 118, and 120, which deal with nineteenth-century evolutionary science, could be taught in the cluster on **Progress, Science, and Colonial Expansion**, along with the readings from Darwin and other selections in the "Victorian Issues" section on "Evolution." Robert Browning's "Caliban upon Setebos: Or Natural Theology in the Island" would make an excellent comparison here. Additionally, *In Memoriam* and works such as "The Lotos-Eaters" and "Ulysses" could be taught in the cluster on **Gender and Sexuality**, paired with other writings that address aspects of Victorian masculinity, such as Newman's *Idea of a University*. Tennyson's masculine protagonists, for example, often seem conflicted about their role and purpose in society. On the other hand, the selections from *The Princess* would be an obvious fit in the same category, read alongside works that speak to women's issues—by John Ruskin, George Eliot, and Barrett Browning, for instance.

Discussion Questions

1. In "Mariana," how does the natural world reflect the central character's despondency?
2. Compare the languor of "The Lotos-Eaters" to the "drowsy numbness" described in Keats's "Ode to a Nightingale."
3. Discuss the concept of Victorian masculinity as depicted in "The Lotos-Eaters" and "Ulysses." Compare Ulysses' avowal that he "cannot rest from travel" to the enervation depicted in "The Lotos-Eaters." Yet note also that Ulysses keeps referring to his advanced age and to approaching death.
4. According to Tennyson's *Princess* ("The woman's cause is man's"), how should men's and women's separate characters be shaped?
5. What is the significance of the yew tree in verse 2 of *In Memoriam*?
6. Verse 6 of *In Memoriam* compares the loss of male friendship to a fa-

ther's loss of his son, a mother's loss of her son, and a young woman's loss of her lover. How do these comparisons affect your understanding of the narrator's grief?

7. Compare the relationship between God and nature in verses 54, 55, and 56 of *In Memoriam*.

8. What do the lines "An infant crying in the night; / An infant crying for the light" refer to in verse 54 of *In Memoriam*?

9. In verses 118 and 120 of *In Memoriam*, the speaker attempts to come to terms with the theory of evolution. Does he succeed?

10. Compare the section of *Idylls of the King* entitled "The Passing of Arthur" with its source in Malory's *Morte Darthur*.

Further Resources

NORTON ONLINE ARCHIVE

Rizpah
In Love, If Love Be Love
To E. FitzGerald
Locksley Hall Sixty Years After
By an Evolutionist
June Bracken and Heather
Idylls of the King: Dedication
A Dedication
I Stood on a Tower
The Silent Voices
St. Agnes Eve
You Ask Me Why, Though Ill at Ease
Lines ("Here often, when a child I lay reclined")
Sonnet ("How thought you that this thing could captivate?")
Move Eastward, Happy Earth
The Revenge
The Kraken
The Eagle: A Fragment
Sweet and Low
The Splendor Falls
Ask Me No More
Come Down, O Maid
Flower in the Crannied Wall
Sonnet ("She took the dappled partridge flecked with blood")
Maud
    Part 1
        6.5 ("Ah, what shall I be at fifty")]
        6.8 ("Perhaps the smile and tender tone")
        6.10 ("I have played with her when a child")
        8 ("She came to the village church")
        11 ("O let the solid ground")
        12 ("Birds in the high Hall-garden")

Edward FitzGerald

The Rubáiyát of Omar Khayyám

Discontent with both Victorian sobriety and Victorian anguish could take the time-honored hedonistic turn of *carpe diem*, as in Edward FitzGerald's translation of *The Rubáiyát of Omar Khayyám*, which urges the reader to "fill the Cup:—what boots it to repeat / How Time is slipping underneath our Feet" (lines 145–46). Rather than urging seekers of spiritual fulfillment to "Produce! Produce! . . . in God's name!" as Carlyle does in *Sartor Resartus*, FitzGerald's *Rubáiyát* proclaims that it is better to be "merry with the fruitful Grape" (line 155) than to engage in "infinite Pursuit / Of This and That endeavor and dispute" (lines 153–54). For these reasons, the poem was admired by early disciples of the aesthetic movement, such as D. G. Rossetti and Swinburne, who enjoyed its breezy endorsement of epicurean pleasures. By the same token, however, there was nothing seriously shocking here that would offend the sensibilities of the average Victorian—unlike Swinburne's poetry, for example—and the speaker's frequent exhortations to enjoy the moment are interspersed with brief meditations on one's place in the universe. Moreover, the *Rubáiyát* appealed to the many English readers who saw the East as a fantasy space where sensual delights could be indulged and the conventions of middle-class society tossed aside. In this sense, FitzGerald's translation is an important example of nineteenth-century Orientalism and the British construction of an Eastern Other.

Quick Read

- Form: A *rubáiyát*, the Persian term for a collection of quatrains (four-line stanzas).
- Source: Nineteenth-century English translation of twelfth-century Persian poem by Omar Khayyám.
- Themes: The transience of life; the need to seize the moment; the unknowability of larger questions about God and the universe; the conflict between spiritual doubt and earthly pleasures.
- Key Passages: "Come, fill the Cup, and in the Fire of Spring / The Winter Garment of Repentance fling," lines 25–26; "Here with a Loaf of Bread beneath the Bough, / A Flask of Wine, a Book of Verse—and Thou / Beside me singing in the Wilderness— / And Wilderness is Paradise enow," lines 41–44; "Into this Universe, and *why* not knowing, / Nor *whence*, like Water willy-nilly flowing: / And out of it, as Wind along the Waste, / I know not *whither*, willy-nilly blowing," lines 113–16; "For in and out, above, about, below, / 'Tis nothing but a Magic Shadow-Show, / Play'd in a Box whose Candle is the Sun, / Round which we Phantom Figures come and go," lines 181–84; "Who *is* the Potter, pray, and who the Pot?" line 240.

Teaching Suggestions

It's important for students to understand that they are reading a translation and that the original Persian text may be quite different from FitzGerald's version. His translation caught the public eye because it appealed to the zeitgeist of mid-Victorian England; part of that zeitgeist was a fascination with all things Eastern. Before you begin your discussion of the *Rubáiyát*, give your students a brief introduction to Edward Said's concept of Orientalism. Said's point was that when Western scholars take "the Orient" as an object of study, they not only flatten out significant differences among diverse peoples and cultures, but also project a vision of their own rejected attributes onto the cultural Other. A scholarly, literary, or artistic study of a supposed "exotic" culture is anything but objective; it is, rather, mired in political and social assumptions and serves the interests of those who conduct the study. The Other becomes, then, whatever the self-appointed authority wants it to be. To FitzGerald's audience, the "Orient" was everything Britain was not: languorous, violent, seductive, barbaric, irrational, and heathen. Thus, one way of reading the *Rubáiyát* is as a text that constructs British national identity and middle-class values. The poem's frequent entreaties to "fill the Cup" (line 25) or to abandon all "endeavor and dispute" (line 154) are in direct contrast to those qualities of temperance and hard work that the English valued, at least in theory. For those who saw this as a subversive text, advocating the discarding of bourgeois constraints, the East became a place where that emancipation could be realized: "Here with a Loaf of Bread beneath the Bough, / A Flask of Wine, a Book of Verse—and Thou / Beside me singing in the Wilderness— / And Wilderness is Paradise enow" (lines 41–44).

The substitution of wine, women, and poetry for spiritual paradise was not something that accorded with middle-class Britain's view of itself.

You may also want to set aside some time to think about this text in relation to aesthetic principles that valued "art for art's sake" rather than for moral or intellectual enlightenment. Although the aesthetic movement is usually associated with the late nineteenth century, it had its roots in French literature of the early nineteenth century and in the mid-century writings of Walter Pater, D. G. Rossetti, and Swinburne. Pater's conclusion to *The Renaissance*, although published several years after FitzGerald's *Rubáiyát*, discusses ideas about the transience of artistic pleasure that are relevant to the poem's themes. Moreover, a comparison with Dowson's "Cynara" and "They Are Not Long," although much later publications, would help students understand that there are many ways of talking about ephemerality. Dowson's work contains themes of plenitude, loss, and the relationship of the present to the past that will enhance your discussion of the *Rubáiyát*.

Teaching Clusters

FitzGerald's *Rubáiyát* could be taught in several categories. If you placed it in the cluster on **Aesthetics, Aestheticism, and the Critique of Victorian Values**, the poem could be studied alongside selections from Pater, D. G. Rossetti, Swinburne, and Dowson. Yet it would also make an interesting contrast to Carlyle's *Sartor Resartus* in the **Doubt, Self-Reflection, and Romanticism** cluster. Additionally, you might want to teach the poem in this cluster along with readings that express nostalgia for the medieval past or escape from the present, such as Ruskin's *Stones of Venice* or medieval-themed works by Morris and Tennyson. Finally, by placing it in the cluster on **Progress, Science, and Colonial Expansion**, you could emphasize the poem's connections to colonizing views of exotic Others. If you decide to take this route, selections that focus on national identity would be especially instructive, such as Arnold's lecture on Celtic literature.

Discussion Questions

1. How does your understanding of Orientalism affect your reading of FitzGerald's *Rubáiyát*?
2. Compare the idea of sensual pleasure and the transient moment in the *Rubáiyát* and Ernest Dowson's "They Are Not Long."
3. Compare ideas about faith, spiritual doubt, and work in Carlyle's *Sartor Resartus* and the *Rubáiyát*.
4. The *Rubáiyát*'s vivid endorsements of the pleasures of "the Cup" are interwoven with more thoughtful meditations on one's place in the universe. The speaker consults "Doctor and Saint" (line 106), for example, but to his disappointment "[comes] out by the same Door as in [he] went" (line 108). In a manner reminiscent of Tennyson's "An

infant crying in the night; / An infant crying for the light" (*In Memoriam*, verse 54, lines 18–19), the *Rubáiyát* speaker declares: "Into this Universe, and *why* not knowing, / Nor *whence*, like Water willy-nilly flowing: / And out of it, as Wind along the Waste, / I know not *whither*, willy-nilly blowing" (lines 113–16). Discuss the idea of spiritual reflection in the *Rubáiyát*.

Elizabeth Gaskell

The Old Nurse's Story

Windswept moors, spooky organ music, and a desolate manor house provide the backdrop to this gothic tale of ghosts, sin, and retribution. At least as far back as *Hamlet*, specters have appeared in countless stories to expose a concealed past of crime or wrongdoing. But Gaskell's tale offers a twist on the classic formula and invites the reader to pity the agonized child-spirit and her outcast mother. Joining Victorian social issues with the familiar machinery of the supernatural plot, "The Old Nurse's Story" questions patriarchal law and class divisions even as it supports conventional beliefs about women, motherhood, and madness.

Quick Read

- Form: Supernatural story with first-person narrator.
- Summary: An elderly nursemaid (Hester) recounts the story of her young charge's encounter with a ghostly mother and child. The mother is deserted by her husband, renounced by her cruel father, and driven out into the freezing night to die, along with her little girl.
- Themes: Female sexual/social transgression; female madness; motherhood; class differences.

Teaching Suggestions

Students will be immediately interested in the story's central conflict: the expulsion of Maude and her child from the father's home. Instructors can engage students' attention by asking about the text's attitude toward the father (the "old" Lord Furnivall) and his two daughters, Maude and Grace. The supernatural formula suggests that Grace—the living sister—is being punished for past indiscretions. But what is she being punished for? It is Maude, her elder sister, who secretly marries a "foreign musician" and bears a child without her father's knowledge. Moreover, Maude has married someone far beneath her in social status—a man who plays both sisters off against each other and later leaves because "they led him such a life with their jealousy and their passions." This is a telling statement because respectable Victorian women were not supposed to be ruled by violent emotions. However, it's worth noting that Maude's deep love for her young daughter offsets some of her faults and complicates her character. A central question, then, is: Are both sisters punished for their very unladylike passions? Why do Maude and the "Spectre-child" haunt the manor house each winter? Why is the elderly Grace "hard [and] sad"? And lastly, there is the question of Grace's final words, spoken when the ghosts of her long-dead father, sister, and niece appear: "Oh, father! father! spare the little innocent child!" These words will remind students of the "sound of a blow" heard during Maude's final confrontation with her father and the "terrible mark" that is left visible on the child's shoulder. Grace, who stood silent during the initial fracas, now relives that terrible moment— and relives her guilt, too, for not having spoken in defense of her sister when she should have.

Another theme worth discussion is the recurring focus on class differences. The story makes a strong distinction between the warmth and generosity of upper servants James and Dorothy and the cold and harsh presence of Grace and her paid companion, Mrs. Stark. Miss Rosamond, the child who is endangered by her encounter with the phantoms, shows a marked preference for the company of the servants. Added to this are minor animosities between upper and lower servants and the disgrace of Maude's marriage to the music teacher. Questions directed toward these issues will help illuminate a theme that will not be initially obvious.

It's also useful to note that the story is told in the first person by Hester, the nursemaid of Miss Rosamond. Students may be interested to learn that gothic stories often use this form as a way to undermine narrative certainty and enhance psychological interiority.

Teaching Clusters

"The Old Nurse's Story" fits nicely within the **Gender and Sexuality** teaching cluster. Some discussion of gender conventions is necessary here, so teaching this story along with mid-Victorian social commentaries on proper feminine behavior is highly recommended. Coventry Patmore's *The Angel in the House*, John Ruskin's "Of Queens' Gardens," and Sarah Stickney Ellis's *The Women of England* are especially recommended to give students an understanding of the disapproval with which many Victorian readers would have viewed Maude's secret marriage. Additionally, Christina Rossetti's *Goblin Market* would make a perfect pairing with this selection; both works focus on the relationship between two sisters and address issues of female social and sexual transgression. If time permits, Charlotte Brontë's *Jane Eyre* would round out the cluster and give students a chance to think about the gothic genre in relation to gender issues.

A few comments about the connection between madness and maternity will be of interest in the context of this cluster. Maude's evident insanity in response to her child's death supports conventional beliefs about female mental frailty and the importance of motherhood. Students will gain a greater understanding of these beliefs by reading Wordsworth's *The Thorn* alongside Gaskell's story. Both narratives describe the misfortunes of a woman who is deserted by her lover, bears a child who later dies, and becomes mentally unhinged as a result of her experiences. Closely related in theme is John Everett Millais's *Ophelia*, included in the illustrations to *NAEL*. Although not concerned with motherhood in any way, Millais's painting (which corresponds directly to the time frame of "The Old Nurse's Story") illustrates the Victorian fascination with the triple theme of women, madness, and sexuality.

Discussion Questions

1. How does this text judge Maude and her sister, Grace? Has Maude committed a disgraceful act by entering into a secret marriage with a "foreign musician"? Or have both Maude and Grace been destroyed by their jealousies and their passions? Why is Grace "hard [and] sad"?
2. What is the significance of Grace's last words before her death: "Oh, father! father! spare the little innocent child!"?
3. Is the text's portrayal of the ghostly Maude and her little daughter sympathetic or unsympathetic? How so?
4. What kinds of masculine behaviors are illustrated here, and what do they suggest? Think about the "old lord" who plays on the spectral organ; the younger Lord Furnivall, who brings Miss Rosamond to live in his home; the "foreign musician" who deserts Maude; and James, an upper servant.
5. How does "The Old Nurse's Story" portray differences between the upper class and the servant class? What are the qualities and faults of each class?
6. Compare "The Old Nurse's Story" to Wordsworth's *The Thorn*.

Further Resources

NORTON TOPICS ONLINE

Industrialism: Progress or Decline?
  Preface to *Mary Barton*

Charles Dickens

A Visit to Newgate

This early journalistic piece by Dickens contains many of the themes that would later appear in the author's novels: the hardships of poverty, the consequences of crime, and the sufferings of the condemned criminal. The Newgate Prison of Dickens's London was a central fixture, a reminder to all of what lay in store for the petty criminal or the hopeless debtor. In imaginative prose, Dickens describes the environment of the prison and the behavior of those incarcerated behind its walls. Although somewhat mixed in its appraisal, this work demonstrates sympathy for some of the more wretched inmates and a fascinated horror of the doomed prisoner's suffering. In a larger cultural context, it is significant as an illustration of the increasing public attention given to social issues, such as those having to do with prisoners, the insane, prostitutes, and children.

Quick Read

- Form: Essay/sketch.
- Summary: Dickens visits Newgate Prison and describes the behavior and surroundings of the prisoners.
- Themes: The suffering of condemned prisoners; prison conditions; the psychology, morals, and behavior of various inmates.
- Key Scenes: Mothers and daughters visiting in the women's ward; young boys in the schoolyard; the prison chapel; the condemned ward; the imagined thoughts of the condemned prisoner.

Teaching Suggestions

Perhaps the best place to start would be at the end, with Dickens's fictionalized account of a condemned prisoner's final hours. Ask students what Dickens's attitude toward the convict is and what his purpose in writing this scene might be. Imagining the prisoner's state of mind, Dickens writes, "He paces the narrow limits of his cell with rapid strides, cold drops of terror starting on his forehead, and every muscle of his frame quivering with agony." Given the extreme pathos of the portrait, students might assume that Dickens wanted the reader to feel sympathy for the inmate and is perhaps criticizing the use of capital punishment. Yet note the references to the Bible and repentance immediately following. Is this a cautionary tale against a life of sin? A journalist's morbid fascination with gruesome scenes? A plea for leniency toward the condemned?

When students have decided on the overall scope of these final pages, ask them to consider some very different earlier passages. Dickens's depiction of the young boys in the schoolyard section, for example, is less sympathetic. "There was not one redeeming feature among them," he comments. Compare this description with the portrayal of mothers and daughters visiting in the women's ward. One incarcerated woman, "Hardened beyond all hope of redemption," listens impassively to her ragged and desperate mother, for example. Draw students' attention also to Dickens's delineation of the physical surroundings; the female ward is "light and airy" and the women sit in front of a fire doing needlework. They are "all cleanly—many of them decently—attired." The room for condemned male prisoners is similarly "large, airy, and clean." Ask students to analyze and compare the varying tones and emotional tenor of different scenes, which are sometimes highly wrought, sometimes neutral, sometimes critical or approving. This is a good time to jot down ideas and make lists on the blackboard as everyone shares their insights. Invite students to reflect on the piece as a whole and return to the question of what the purpose of the sketch might be.

Teaching Clusters

Dickens's essay on Newgate Prison can be usefully included in **Poverty, Unrest, and Social Criticism.** While issues of crime and prisons are not exclusively related to those of poverty and class struggle—there is a section of the prison reserved for "respectable" prisoners, for example—Dickens shows much sympathy for the poor and the neglected as he chronicles the realities of prison life. To expand students' understanding of the difficulties that drove many of the poor to a life of crime, Dickens's sketch may be read alongside Friedrich Engels's *The Condition of the Working Class*, which describes the slums of London. Engels's documentary account can be paired with Dickens's fictional description of Coketown, an excerpt from *Hard Times*. Additionally, both Henry Mayhew's *London Labour and the London Poor* and Ada Nield Chew's "A Living Wage for Factory Girls at Crewe" offer firsthand nonfictional accounts of working conditions among the impoverished. Also of particular concern to Victorians at the time were the conditions under which the children of the poorest classes labored. The two short excerpts from *The Children's Employment Commission*, depicting the situation of young mine-workers, may be read along with Elizabeth Barrett Browning's "The Cry of the Children." These works give students a framework for reading Dickens's description of a young female visitor to the prison, "born and bred in neglect and vice, who [has] never known what childhood is."

If time permits, this piece would make an excellent supplement to one of Dickens's novels, such as *Great Expectations* or *Oliver Twist*. In the former, students could compare the ideas in the essay to the portrayal of Magwitch as he lies dying in the prison infirmary; in the latter, the view of Fagin in the condemned cell can be discussed. Both novels explore themes related to prisons and the psychology of the criminal.

Discussion Questions

1. What is Dickens's attitude toward the prisoners? In what way is he sympathetic and in what way is he critical?
2. How does he describe the living conditions in the prison? Does he think the prisoners are treated unfairly?
3. Compare Dickens's portrayal of male and female inmates.
4. How does Dickens's tone change in each of the passages? Does the tone or technique give you a clue to the writer's feelings on the topic?
5. What is Dickens's view of children in this essay? Compare his comments about the lack of redeeming features among the school-age boys ("There was not one redeeming feature among them") with his observations about the young daughter of an inmate: "Barely past her childhood, it required but a glance to discover that she was one of those children, born and bred in neglect and vice, who have never known what childhood is."
6. What is the purpose or point of this essay? Does Dickens want just to entertain people? Or is he making a social—or moral—criticism?

Further Resources

NORTON ONLINE ARCHIVE

Martin Chuzzlewit
    Mrs. Gamp and Mr. Mould
David Copperfield
    The Journey to Salem House School
    The Journey from London to Dover
Bleak House
    In Chancery
Hard Times
    The One Thing Needful
    Murdering the Innocents
    Coketown
Our Mutual Friend
    Podsnappery

Robert Browning

Robert Browning is well known for his vibrant use of dramatic monologue; his characters leap off the page, inviting readers to contemplate the darker aspects of the human psyche. While the dramatic monologue was a familiar form to Victorians, Browning brought to it a brashness that was startling and fresh. Natural speech rhythms, interruptions, and random associations bring the speakers to life and help sustain the illusion of an overheard conversation. More jarring, however, was his use of inverted syntax and unlovely diction, qualities not always appreciated by his earliest readers but much admired by later followers, including many poets of the twentieth century. Students will enjoy Browning's vivid portrayals of highly flawed human beings. Murderers, egotists, and self-described failures all find full expression here, speaking both to the uncertainties of the nineteenth century and to the discordances of the twentieth.

My Last Duchess

Quick Read

- Form: Dramatic monologue.
- Summary: A wealthy aristocrat in Renaissance Italy, commenting on a portrait of his deceased wife (whom he has had murdered), reveals his vicious jealousy of her. He addresses his observations to the agent of a potential future wife.
- Themes: Jealousy; women as aesthetic objects; the psychology of the art collector.
- Key Passages: "That's my last Duchess painted on the wall, / Looking as if she were alive," lines 1–2; "Sir, 'twas not / Her husband's presence only, called that spot / Of joy into the Duchess' cheek," lines

13–15; "She had / A heart—how shall I say?—too soon made glad," lines 21–22; "Notice Neptune, . . . / Taming a sea horse . . . cast in bronze for me!" lines 54–56.

Teaching Suggestions

Viewing a painting of his deceased wife, the speaker of "My Last Duchess" reveals, in chilling detail, an excessive jealousy and callous aestheticism. Invite students to analyze the speaker's character and values. How does he describe his former wife? How does the speaker reveal himself in this poem? It's important for students to see that, in describing the "last Duchess," the narrator tells us more about himself than he does about her. Note also that there is a difference between what the speaker knows and what the reader knows. The Duke exposes himself without realizing that he does so. "Sir, 'twas not / Her husband's presence only, called that spot / Of joy into the Duchess' cheek," he complains (lines 13–15). It irks him especially that "she ranked / [His] gift of a nine-hundred-years-old name / With anybody's gift" (lines 32–34). Not only does he feel that she was not sufficiently impressed with his status, but he seems to have been jealous of her every pleasure. We get the sense of a spirited, joyful woman whose smallest moves were watched and judged to be deficient: "She had a heart—how shall I say?—too soon made glad; . . . she liked whate'er / She looked on, and her looks went everywhere" (lines 21–24). Students may wonder if the speaker has cause to be jealous, but ask them to note the way that he is equally jealous of "The bough of cherries some officious fool" (line 27) brings to his wife and "the white mule / She rode with round the terrace" (lines 28–29). The Duke's complaints mount until he says, ominously, "I gave commands; / Then all smiles stopped together" (lines 45–46). It is also important to draw students' awareness to the way that the poem conflates the actual woman with her portrait: "That's my last Duchess painted on the wall" (line 1). This vision of woman-as-aesthetic-object is further emphasized in the poem's concluding lines, when we see that for the speaker, the "last Duchess" is just another piece of art: "Notice Neptune . . . Taming a sea horse, . . . cast in bronze for me" (lines 54–56). Throughout your discussion of the poem, invite students to reflect on how Browning's syntax, diction, awkward phrasing ("My gift of a nine-hundred-years-old name" [line33]), and unexpected line breaks ("that spot / Of joy" [lines 14–15]) affect their reading of the poem. There's an energy in the language and formal techniques that matches the speaker's aggression.

"Childe Roland to the Dark Tower Came"

Quick Read

- Form: Dramatic monologue.
- Summary: A young knight travels through a bleak landscape to find the Dark Tower; after years of travel, he sees the Tower in the dis-

tance, is haunted by a vision of his dead predecessors, and announces his intent to forge ahead to the Tower.

- Themes: The quest as an analogy for a psychological journey; loss of faith; inability to find one's way in the world; uncertainty in the future; confrontation with one's worst fears; courage in the face of despair.
- Key Passages: "My first thought was, he lied in every word, / That hoary cripple," lines 1–2; "Seldom went such grotesqueness with such woe; / I never saw a brute I hated so; / He must be wicked to deserve such pain," line 82; "Who were the strugglers, what war did they wage," line 129; "Then came some palsied oak, . . . Like a distorted mouth . . . Gaping at death," lines 154–56; "noise was everywhere! . . . Names in my ears / Of all the lost adventurers my peers," lines 194–95; "I saw them and I knew them all. And yet / Dauntless the slug-horn to my lips I set, / And blew . . . ," lines 202–04.

Teaching Suggestions

Readers may be perplexed by this poem; it does not yield easily to interpretation. You may help students to get a sense of the nature of Roland's journey by having them look closely at the images of devastation that pervade the landscape. Discuss the concept of the quest motif and its relation to inner psychological states. The protagonist of "Childe Roland" has outlived his time: not only have Roland's fellow knights died, but they have been humiliated and disgraced, and the age of chivalry has died out with them—the landscape and the appearance of Roland's ragged predecessors attest to this. Beaten down by failure and despair, the last of "all the lost adventurers my peers" (line 195), Roland no longer has any faith in his own capacity for heroism. As he comes to the end of his quest for the Dark Tower, he feels "neither pride / Nor hope . . . So much as gladness that some end might be" (lines 16–18). Invite students to compare the description of the desolate landscape with Roland's inner confusion and despair. Anthropomorphizing his surroundings, he sights "Drenched willows . . . in a fit / Of mute despair, a suicidal throng" (lines 117–18) and "some palsied oak . . . Like a distorted mouth . . . Gaping at death" (lines 154–55). To Roland, the natural world is like a mutilated or deformed human body: thistles are beheaded, leaves are "bruised," grass grows "scant as hair / In leprosy" on muddy ground that "underneath looked kneaded up with blood" (lines 70–75). This surreal landscape is reminiscent of the wasteland of the Fisher King in Arthurian legend or a blighted modern industrial landscape. Nature offers no consolation here, only nightmarish spectacles, like that of a "stupefied" and "stiff blind horse" with "every bone a-stare," or the "dank" plashed soil of a battlefield where long-forgotten men struggled savagely and died (lines 76–77, 130). Despite all this, "Childe Roland" ends on a note of very cautious optimism. As the hideous mountains crowd around him "like giants at a hunting" (line 190) and the ghosts of his dead predecessors assemble to watch, all signs point to the likelihood that Roland will die when he fights whatever is to come out of the Dark Tower. He is nonetheless "dauntless" as he sounds his challenge and the poem ends, abruptly and ambiguously. One does not know whether Roland successfully completes the quest and avenges his peers or dies alone, in pain and terror. But perhaps it does not matter: despite so many years of self-doubt and discouragement, at the end Roland displays both courage and a sense of duty, qualities necessary in the difficult nineteenth century no less than in the age of chivalry.

Caliban upon Setebos

Quick Read

- Form: Dramatic monologue.
- Summary: Caliban, the half-man, half-beast creature of Shakespeare's *Tempest*, muses on the nature of an unjust and unpredictable god (Setebos).
- Themes: In the absence of revelation, natural theology alone will not reveal the full scope of the divine; human understanding of the divine is limited by one's own consciousness and perceptions.
- Key Passages: "Thou thoughtest that I was altogether such a one as thyself," epigraph; "He would not make what he mislikes or slights . . . But did, in envy, listlessness, or sport, / Make . . . Things He admires and mocks too," lines 59–65; "Ask, for that, / What knows—the something over Setebos / That made Him, or He, may be, . . . Worsted, drove off . . . / There may be something quiet o'er His head," lines 128–32; "His dam held that the Quiet made all things / Which Setebos vexed only: 'holds not so . . . ,'" lines 170–71.

Teaching Suggestions

Students may have some trouble understanding the pronoun references, both missing and present, so it will help to explain the various allusions: to Caliban, the speaker; to Setebos, his god; and to Prospero. It doesn't help that Caliban is not always stable in his references; while he usually refers to himself in the third person, for instance, sometimes he refers to "I" or "me." The epigraph makes an excellent starting point for a discussion of one of the poem's major themes: that human understanding of the divine is circumscribed by one's own experiences and thoughts ("Thou thoughtest that I was altogether such a one as thyself"). You may want to explain how this theme relates to the concept of divine revelation. Natural theology alone, the poem suggests, will not yield full knowledge about a supernatural or supreme deity; Caliban's observations of nature do not lead him to greater spiritual understanding. Direct students' attention to Caliban's view of the universe: it is one inhabited by a fickle god who "would not make what he mislikes or slights, . . . But did, in envy, listlessness, or sport, / Make . . . Things He admires and mocks too" (lines 59–65). All of Caliban's reasoning is based on his experience of his own feelings. Thus, Caliban surmises that just as he is made bitter by Prospero's ill treatment, so too does Setebos take out his frustrations on his inferiors: "A bitter heart that bides its time and bites. / 'Plays thus at being Prosper in a way, / Taketh his mirth with make-believes: so He" (lines 167–69). While Caliban's reflections about Setebos may be somewhat evident to students, his thoughts about another deity—"the Quiet" (lines 137, 170, 246, 281)—will be less apparent. Caliban has heard from his mother that "There may be something quiet o'er [Setebos's] head, / Out of his reach, that feels nor joy nor grief, / Since both [Setebos and the Quiet] derive from weakness in some way" (lines 132–34). Attempting to visualize a sphere beyond Setebos, Caliban wonders which deity is responsible for creating living beings and why so many of these beings were made vulnerable to attack. Although Caliban's mother believed that "the Quiet made all things / Which Setebos vexed only" (lines170–71), Caliban thinks that this is "not so": Setebos meant to create "weakness He might vex" (lines 171–72). In this manner, Caliban struggles to make sense of the cosmos, but only becomes more confused and frightened.

Another approach to analyzing Caliban's character would be to discuss his relationship to language. Why does he usually omit the personal pronoun in his speech? Can this be seen as his way of hiding from Setebos, whom he greatly fears? "If He caught me here, / O'erheard this speech, and asked 'What chucklest at?'" Caliban says, "[I] 'Would, to appease Him, cut a finger off" (lines 269–71). On the one hand, Caliban worries that Setebos may discover him enjoying himself, but on the other hand, Caliban grants language a certain power in validating identity. You might want to ask students to connect this statement to Caliban's earlier comment about cheating Prospero and Miranda by his speech: "it is good to cheat the pair, and gibe, / Letting the rank tongue blossom into speech" (lines 22–23). What does speech mean to this blinded, frightened creature?

Teaching Clusters

Several of Browning's poems may be placed within the **Doubt, Self-Reflection, and Romanticism** cluster either because they evidence a certain amount of self-examination or they invite such examination from the reader. The dramatic monologues, in particular, open up questions about identity construction and self-perception that are appropriate to this category. Works such as "My Last Duchess," "Soliloquy of the Spanish Cloister," "The Bishop Orders His Tomb at Saint Praxed's Church," "Childe Roland to the Dark Tower Came," "Fra Lippo Lippi," "Andrea del Sarto," and "Caliban upon Setebos" can be usefully taught in this manner. In the same cluster, "Childe Roland" would make a good companion piece to some of the medieval poems, such as the selections from Tennyson's *Idylls* *of the King.* Many of Browning's works would also be well situated in the cluster on **Gender and Sexuality.** "My Last Duchess" is an obvious choice here, along with "Porphyria's Lover"; both poems describe women who are "killed into art" as a result of the tyranny or insane possessiveness of their men. These two selections would connect nicely with Christina Rossetti's "In an Artist's Studio," another poem about objectified, aestheticized women. Additionally, "Childe Roland" would make an excellent pairing with pieces that explore masculinity. Tennyson's "Ulysses" and "The Lotos-Eaters" come to mind here, although there are many other possibilities. In this connection, you may want to consider adding Keats's "La Belle Dame sans Merci"; like Roland, who is haunted by the specter of "the lost adventurers my peers" who "met / To view the last of me" (lines 195, 199–200), Keats's "knight at arms" is visited by "pale kings, and princes too, . . . [who are] death pale" (lines 1, 37–38). In both works, questions about masculinity and the abdication of the chivalric ideal are addressed.

Discussion Questions

1. Discuss the historical context of any one of Browning's dramatic monologues. What relationship does the poem have to problems and issues of the Victorian period? Why has Browning chosen to present them in a historical setting?
2. How does the speaker of "My Last Duchess" reveal himself in his description of his deceased wife's portrait?
3. How does "My Last Duchess" comment on the relationship between women and art?
4. How does the description of the bleak, surreal landscape in "Childe Roland to the Dark Tower Came" relate to the protagonist's inner turmoil?
5. Discuss the use of the quest motif in "Childe Roland." Can Roland's journey on an unmarked road toward an uncertain future be a metaphor for a spiritual or psychological journey?
6. Caliban's world is one of great pain and suffering. Prospero has enslaved Caliban, "Blinded [his] eyes," "split [his] toe-webs," and "now pens the drudge / In a hole o' the rock" (lines 164–66). Caliban inflicts similar cruelty upon weaker creatures: when he sees "two flies" who "Bask on the pompion-bell above," he "kills both" for no reason (lines 158–59). How does Caliban's understanding of cruelty limit or shape his vision of a supreme deity?
7. Compare Caliban's statement that "it is good to cheat [Prospero and Miranda], and gibe, / Letting the rank tongue blossom into speech" (lines 22–23) with his fear that Setebos may overhear him talking and take revenge: "It was fool's play this prattling! Ha! The wind / Shoulders the pillared dust . . . And fast invading fires begin!" (lines 287–89). What significance does language have to Caliban?

Further Resources

NORTON ONLINE ARCHIVE

Up at a Villa—Down in the City
In a Year
Respectability
Confessions
The Householder
The Laboratory
Home Thoughts, from Abroad
Home Thoughts, from the Sea
Meeting at Night
Parting at Morning
Memorabilia
The Last Ride Together
Two in the Campagna
Prospice
Women and Roses
A Toccata of Galuppi's
A Woman's Last Word
Youth and Art
Dîs Aliter Visum; or, Le Byron de Nos Jours
Apparent Failure
House
To Edward FitzGerald
Abt Vogler
Epilogue to *Asolando*

Emily Brontë

While Emily Brontë's intimations of immortality in nature do not convey the sense of crisis and loss one meets so often in the Romantics, her poems create a rich inner landscape where feminine desire can express itself. Both the Gondal writings and the personal lyrics show a yearning for release from the physical world into an infinite expanse of darkness and nonbeing. It is not a poetry of self-transcendence but rather one that hints at self-annihilation. In "Remembrance," for example, the too-insistent embrace of earthly vitality is overshadowed by the lure of "that divinest anguish" found in the contemplation of her lover's death (line 31), while in "Stars" the speaker "hide[s] . . . from the hostile light," longing for the "boundless regions" of the "Gentle Night" (lines 43, 14, 41). Only in this imagined space of nonexistence can the spirit find release.

Remembrance

Quick Read

- Form: Lyric.
- Summary: In this poem from the Gondal saga, the speaker fears that she is forgetting her long-dead lover, but asserts that she wishes to embrace life; this assertion, however, is contradicted by the poem's desire for the forbidden pleasure found in "Memory's rapturous pain," line 30.
- Key Passages: "Then did I learn how existence could be cherished / Strengthened and fed without the aid of joy," lines 23–24; "[I] [s]ternly denied [my young soul's] burning wish to hasten / Down to that tomb already more than mine," lines 27–28; "I . . . [d]are not indulge in Memory's rapturous pain; / Once drinking deep of that divinest anguish, / How could I seek the empty world again?" lines 29–32.

Stars

Quick Read

- Form: Lyric.
- Summary: The speaker rejects the appearance of the morning sun, characterizing it as "hostile" and appealing to the stars and the night, wherein she can find fullness and peace (line 43).
- Key Passages: "I was at peace, and drank your beams / As they were life to me," lines 9–10; "Why did the morning dawn to break / So great, so pure a spell," lines 17–18; "Blood-red he rose, and arrow-straight / His fierce beams struck my brow," lines 21–22; "Oh Stars and Dreams and Gentle Night . . . Let me sleep through this blinding reign, / And only wake with you!" lines 41–48.

Teaching Suggestions

"Stars" and "Remembrance" make an excellent pairing; both find plenitude in darkness or death while conveying different kinds of struggle. In "Remembrance," the struggle is to avoid the pull of "Memory's rapturous pain" (line 30), while in "Stars," the speaker "turn[s] . . . to the pillow . . . To call back Night," trying to avoid the "hostile light" (lines 29–30, 43). Focus the discussion on the nature of the conflict in each, paying particular attention to the vivid and sometimes unexpected imagery. Rather than conveying warmth and a fresh beginning, as one might expect, the "morning dawn" of "Stars" is "Blood-red," with "fierce beams" (lines 17, 21, 22). Ask students what kind of qualities the speaker finds in the night. Darkness contains not only the somberness of "worlds of solemn light" but also the joy of "life" and "boundless regions" (lines 31, 10, 14). In contrast, the most passionate expressions of feeling in "Remembrance" lie in the description of pain and mourning. These selections also work well with other Brontë poems, such as "The Night-Wind," in which the speaker resists but is attracted by the promise of the "dark . . . woods" and the gentle "breathing" of the night wind (lines 12, 9). You may want to draw students' attention to the combination of attraction and repulsion to darkness and death in "Night-Wind," which is less apparent than in "Remembrance."

Teaching Clusters

The yearning, melancholic quality of Brontë's poems makes them a good fit in the **Doubt, Self-Reflection, and Romanticism** cluster. Yet these works also would be very well placed within the **Gender and Sexuality** cluster, read alongside poems by other women writers such as Barrett Browning and Rossetti. Although their approaches differ, these writers all address issues of female agency and identity in some manner. Moreover, the strain of sorrow, so familiar in Tennyson and other Victorian writers, in Brontë's writing brings up questions about social pressures on feminine behavior. These questions may not be immediately obvious, but can be brought into relief by comparison to other similar works.

Discussion Questions

1. In "Remembrance," how convincing is the speaker's decision to move beyond her grieving state and "check the tears of useless passion" (line 25)?
2. Discuss the role of memory in "Remembrance." Is memory a source of pleasure, pain, or guilt?
3. Why does the speaker in "Stars" find the night a source of "life" (line 10)?
4. How does Brontë's use of diction and imagery in "Stars" convey the hostility of the "dazzling sun"?
5. Compare the portrayal of conflict in "Remembrance" and "Stars" or "The Night-Wind."
6. In "The Night-Wind," how does the description of the natural landscape reflect the speaker's emotions?

John Ruskin

John Ruskin's writings combine a powerful critique of Victorian industrial society along with a rejection of contemporary classical aesthetics. Instead of valuing the Greek ideal, as did most of his contemporaries, Ruskin saw in medieval culture a model for improved labor relations and artistic creativity. In *The Stones of Venice*, Ruskin looks back to feudalism for a solution to the "condition of England" problem. Workers engaged in "vain, incoherent, destructive struggling for a freedom of which they cannot explain the nature to themselves" require wise guidance more than liberty, like Carlyle's Gurth the swineherd. "I know not if a day is ever to come when the nature of right freedom will be understood, and when men will see that to obey another man, to labor for him, yield reverence to him or to his place, is not slavery. It is often the best kind of liberty—liberty from care," Ruskin asserts. However, Ruskin also proposes a certain leveling of class distinctions, a sort of meritocracy in the workplace, whereby one distinguishes operatives "only in experience and skill." Moreover, intellectual and manual labor should not be separate activities: "always in these days . . . we want one man to be always thinking, and another to be always working, and we call one a gentleman, and the other an operative; whereas the workman ought often to be thinking, and the thinker often to be working; and both should be gentlemen, in the best sense." A similar concern with social and moral issues can be found in the selections from *Modern Painters* and "Of the Pathetic Fallacy." Whereas *Modern Painters* claims that art should have a significant message to convey to the viewer, *Of the Pathetic Fallacy* demands absolute fidelity to truth in art. In both cases, truth lifts the aesthetic object out of the realm of mere pleasure and transforms it into something with intellectual, moral, and social value.

The Stones of Venice

Quick Read

- Form: Book.
- Summary: Redeems the aesthetic concept of "gothic" from its pejorative associations and praises medieval architecture on several grounds; advocates a medieval ethic for modern labor relations.
- Themes: "[R]ude and wild" medieval architecture has a scope of vision not found in classical architecture; workers who executed classical architecture (literally slaves) were allowed no room for imagination, while medieval architectural workers could express their creativity; imperfection has its virtues; the pursuit of perfection should not get in the way of the appreciation and pursuit of larger intellectual and cultural goals, even if those efforts result in imperfection; industrial "perfection" is a sign of slavery in England, recalling the inhuman and soul-depleting conditions of Greek slaves; Victorian workers should be allowed more intellectual and imaginative freedom, even if this results in imperfect products, because often the faulty creation aspires to and achieves brilliance.
- Key Passages: Gothic architecture, though "rude and wild," should not be condemned (1324); Victorian managers should look for the *"thoughtful"* part of the laborers and not "unhumanize" them, "the whole human being [is] lost at last—a heap of sawdust, so far as its intellectual work in this world is concerned" (1328); freedom of Victorian England contrasted with the feudal past ("more freedom in England") (1328); the division of labor and the degradation of men ("Divided into mere segments of men") (1330); "the architect . . .

must either make slaves of his workmen in the old Greek, and present English fashion . . . or . . . take his workmen as he finds them, and let them show their weaknesses together with their strength, . . . [which] will render the whole work as noble as the intellect of the age can make it" (1333).

Teaching Suggestions

Stones of Venice goes to the heart of some of Victorian England's most pressing social issues. Students may at first think Ruskin is simply training his readers in aesthetic valuation, inviting them to consider art and architecture from an organicist perspective, as he shows how forms of architecture should be in harmony with and suitable to their environment. Thus Greek and Italian standards of beauty are not timeless and universal standards, as Arnold would have it: one must learn to value seemingly ruder, more primitive forms of art, to "reverence" the "rough strength" of the Gothic builder of the north, who "smites an uncouth animation out of the rocks which he has torn from among the moss of the moorland." Making an argument rather like Robert Browning's in "Andrea del Sarto"—"a man's reach should exceed his grasp, / Or what's a heaven for?" (lines 97–98)—Ruskin sweeps the reader up in his eloquent aesthetic valuation, but then suddenly turns midparagraph to consider the more controversial topic of present-day labor relations. Direct students' attention to Ruskin's criticism of the demand for "smooth minuteness" and technical perfection in jewelry, housewares, and other commodities of the modern English consumer; by extension, the modern factory owner is not willing to accept errors and imperfections from his workers, but requires, like the Greek slave drivers, that they "work with the accuracy of tools" and "be precise and perfect in all their actions." To demand such accuracy, such precision, is to "unhumanize" the workers, says Ruskin the social conservative, in an argument that resonates startlingly with that of Marx, his contemporary, on dehumanized and alienated industrial labor.

Modern Painters

In *Modern Painters*, Ruskin sees painting as a means of communication: "a noble and expressive language, invaluable as the vehicle of thought." He asserts that great art is more than technique, although technique is not to be discounted. Ideas, however, are of the utmost importance; "the greatest picture is that which conveys to the mind of the spectator the greatest number of the greatest ideas," as Ruskin explains. Turner's painting, *The Slave Ship*, perfectly illustrates Ruskin's point because its evocation of fiery turbulence "condemn[s]" the "guilty ship" and so reveals the "purest truth." You will want to point out that Ruskin's convictions about moral or intellectual content in art were shared by many Victorians, but there was also a very strong reaction against this concept by followers of the aesthetic movement. Invite students to compare Ruskin's aesthetic principles to Walter Pater's, as expressed in *The Renaissance*: "[A]rt comes to you proposing frankly to give nothing but the highest quality to your moments as they pass, and simply for those moments' sake."

Of the Pathetic Fallacy

In "Of the Pathetic Fallacy," Ruskin tells us that our perception of "the ordinary, proper, and true appearances of things" can be distorted "when we are under the influence of emotion, or contemplative fancy." In an overwrought or daydreaming state, our minds can impute to the world around us qualities that are not actually there; our emotions color what we see. Ruskin terms this "[false] impression of external things" the "pathetic fallacy" and argues that art is good, useful, and pleasurable only when it is faithful to nature and the external verities. Ask students if they see a link between Ruskin's theories on intellectual or moral content in art, as expressed in *Modern Painters*, and his view here about truth in art. In particular, invite students to consider how Ruskin judges "truth." It seems to be a very different kind of truth than the artistic perception that Walter Pater encourages. While Ruskin acknowledges that pleasure can be received from fanciful similes and metaphors having a less than firm footing in reality and even admits that some of our favorite poetry might feature this "willful fancy," he nonetheless claims that we allow for such fancies in this case because we know that poetry is a special form that is created to emulate a passionate response. The finest poets, however, such as Dante, "do not often admit to this kind of falseness"; only the "second order of poets," like Coleridge, indulge immoderately in such practices. For Ruskin, unlike Pater, a strong emotional response to art gets in the way of true perception.

Teaching Clusters

The Stones of Venice can be taught in either of three clusters: **Poverty, Unrest, and Social Criticism**, to the extent that it addresses labor relations; **Doubt, Self-Reflection, and Romanticism**, because it yearns nostalgically for the medieval past; or **Aesthetics, Aestheticism, and the Critique of Victorian Values**, because of its concern with aesthetic valuation. Other works by Thomas Carlyle and William Morris make good companion pieces in the first two groupings. Morris, for example, in "How I Became a Socialist," shares Ruskin's concern for the worker, advocating a society where class divisions are eliminated. In the second category, any number of medieval-themed works by Tennyson or Morris would help contextualize Ruskin's theories. And in the third category, *Stones of Venice* could be fruitfully studied along with the selections from *Modern Painters* and "Of the Pathetic Fallacy," contrasted with works by Pater, D. G. Rossetti, and Swinburne.

Discussion Questions

1. What does Ruskin mean when he asserts, in *Stones of Venice*, "while
   . . . [we should] desire perfection, and strive for it, we are nevertheless not to set the meaner thing . . . above the nobler thing"? What is
   he saying about the pursuit of perfection?
2. Why does Ruskin believe that medieval architectural workers were
   better off than their classical counterparts?
3. According to Ruskin in *Stones of Venice*, in what way should Victorian labor relations follow the medieval model?
4. In his conclusion to *The Renaissance*, Walter Pater asserts that "art
   comes to you proposing frankly to give nothing but the highest quality to your moments as they pass, and simply for those moments'
   sake." Contrast this view of art with Ruskin's view as stated in *Modern Painters*.
5. Compare Ruskin's assessment of truth in art in the selections from
   Modern Painters and "Of the Pathetic Fallacy."

Further Resources

NORTON ONLINE ARCHIVE

The Storm-Cloud of the Nineteenth Century, Lecture 1
From Lectures on Art [Imperial Duty]

NORTON TOPICS ONLINE (TWENTIETH CENTURY)

Imperialism to Postcolonialism: Perspectives on the British Empire
   Ruskin, *from* Lectures on Art

George Eliot

Margaret Fuller and Mary Wollstonecraft

Under the auspices of reviewing past works by Margaret Fuller and
Mary Wollstonecraft, Eliot advances her own somewhat startling views
about contemporary women. Rather than praising her own sex, as an independent woman of the time might do, she claims that women are, indeed, inferior to men, both morally and intellectually. In fact, she asserts,
history is littered with stories about wily and wrong-minded women who
seduce powerful men into making grave mistakes. Audacious but serious,
Eliot makes a plea for true freedom of education and activity for women.

Quick Read

- Form: Review essay.
- Summary: Eliot reviews works by Fuller and Wollstonecraft, published years earlier, and finds that both writers make significant and
  similar points about women's position in the world; Eliot uses these
  readings to advance and explain her own ideas on the subject.

- Themes: Contrary to some contemporary thinking, women are not intellectually equal or morally superior to men; women have been restricted in education and experience, which has resulted in their inferiority; women should be allowed comprehensive, high-quality education so that they can exercise full reason and independent judgment; the unreasoning person is difficult to control, like an obstinate child; history is full of examples of vain and cunning women who have caused untold damage to others through their misguided influence on sensible men.
- Key Passages: "One point on which [Fuller and Wollstonecraft] write forcibly is the fact that, while men have a horror of such faculty or culture in the other sex as tends to place it on a level with their own, they are really in a state of subjection to ignorant and feeble-minded women" (1338); "Wherever weakness is not harshly controlled it must *govern*, as you may see when a strong man holds a little child by the hand, how he is pulled hither and thither" (1339); "Men pay a heavy price for their reluctance to encourage self-help and independent resources in women. The precious meridian years of many a man of genius have to be spent in the toil of routine, that an 'establishment' may be kept up for a woman . . . who is fit for nothing but to sit in her drawing-room like a doll-Madonna in her shrine" (1341); "many overzealous champions of women assert their actual equality with men— nay even their moral superiority to men—as a ground for their release from oppressive laws and restriction. They lose strength immensely by this false position. . . . [W]e want freedom and culture for woman, because subjection and ignorance have debased her" (1341).

Teaching Suggestions

At the center of this essay are Eliot's strong views about what she sees as the superficiality and immaturity of women. Students may be surprised at first that Eliot is so critical of her feminine counterparts, since she herself is a woman writing under a male pseudonym. Begin by asking about Eliot's disparagement of women. What precisely does Eliot think of women? Women, Eliot asserts, are too often trivial-minded, and this is a problem—but why? Agreeing with Fuller and Wollstonecraft, Eliot states that "while men have a horror of such faculty or culture in the other sex as tends to place it on a level with their own, they are really in a state of subjection to ignorant and feeble-minded women." There are two parts to this sentence; ask students what each part means, then put the whole together. This will lead into a discussion about covert forms of female power and influence. The final segment of the discussion should focus on what Eliot is actually suggesting for women in terms of education and experience. After students have a clearer idea of what Eliot is getting at, ask them why she objects so vehemently to the claim that women are men's moral and mental equals or superiors. The answer to this question will go a long way toward explaining Eliot's critical tone.

Silly Novels by Lady Novelists

Quick Read

- Form: Review essay.
- Summary: Eliot satirizes several novels by contemporary women writers, lambasting them for their triviality.
- Themes: Many contemporary women's novels are frivolous; these novels are superficial because the writers themselves have had little experience and education.
- Key Passages: "To judge from their writings there are certain ladies who think that an amazing ignorance, both of science and of life, is the best possible qualification for forming an opinion on the knottiest moral and speculative questions" (1345); "it must be plain to every one who looks impartially and extensively into feminine literature, that its greatest deficiencies are due hardly more to the want of intellectual power than to the want of those moral qualities that contribute to literary excellence—patient diligence, a sense of the responsibility involved in publication, and an appreciation of the sacredness of the writer's art" (1348); "we believe that the average intellect of women is unfairly represented by the mass of feminine literature, and that while the few women who write well are very far above the ordinary intellectual level of their sex, the many women who write ill are very far below it" (1349).

Teaching Suggestions

Students will enjoy the first paragraph of Eliot's essay, with its satirical description of popular women's novels. Questions about why Eliot denigrates these novels, however, take students into the second paragraph, which asserts that the writers of these novels create improbable scenes because they themselves have had little experience of the world. After discussing these opening paragraphs, direct students' attention to Eliot's description of the first category of "silly novel," the "*oracular* species," which contains some of her most pointed remarks on the topic of female education and female vanity. The "oracular" approach is ultimately very damaging to the cause of female education because it parades half-digested information as lofty truths, suggesting to male readers that education is wasted on women. Your questions at this point may focus on Eliot's views about female education, which will be clearer now. The last part of the discussion should pay close attention to the final three paragraphs; direct your questions toward the passages listed above. A good way to wrap up the session would be to ask students what Eliot meant by this statement about the critical response to women's writing: "By a peculiar thermometric adjustment, when a woman's talent is at zero, journalistic approbation is at the boiling pitch; when she attains mediocrity, it is already at no more than summer heat; and if ever she reaches excellence, critical enthusiasm drops to the freezing point. Harriet Martineau, Currer Bell, and Mrs. Gaskell have been treated as cavalierly as if they had been men."

Teaching Clusters

Both of Eliot's essays specifically address issues of female authorship and so fit squarely into the **Gender and Sexuality** teaching cluster. If time permits, they should be taught together; the second essay follows the logic of the first, blaming the superficiality of "silly" novels on the limited scope of women's lives. If there is time only for one, the Fuller/Wollstonecraft piece is more complex. Several other works make excellent pairings within the gender and sexuality grouping. Barrett Browning's *Aurora Leigh* would be especially fruitful here, along with Tennyson's *The Princess*. Good prose and documentary works include Sarah Stickney Ellis's "Women of England," John Ruskin's "Of Queens' Gardens," Harriet Martineau's *Autobiography*, and Florence Nightingale's *Cassandra*. A more unusual but interesting pairing would include Cardinal Newman's lectures on "The Idea of a University." Newman believes that a comprehensive liberal education is necessary to be a fully rounded human being. Ask students to compare his ideas about the usefulness of a liberal education to Eliot's ideas on female education.

Discussion Questions

1. Why is Eliot critical of women in her review of Margaret Fuller and Mary Wollstonecraft?
2. In the Fuller/Wollstonecraft essay, why does Eliot object to the "overzealous champions of women [who] assert their actual equality with men . . . [and] even their moral superiority to men"?
3. Why does Eliot label certain popular women's novels as "silly"?
4. In "Silly Novels," what specific objections does Eliot have to what she terms the "oracular" type of novels?
5. Why does Eliot say that "the most mischievous form of feminine silliness is the literary form, because it tends to confirm the popular prejudice against the more solid education of women"?
6. Compare Eliot's views on female education in the two essays. Also compare them to Aurora's observations on the same topic in *Aurora Leigh*.
7. Is Eliot being unduly harsh on women in either of these pieces? Is she more critical of women in one or the other?

Further Resources

NORTON ONLINE ARCHIVE

The Mill on the Floss
  Book First. Boy and Girl, Chapters 1–5

Matthew Arnold

Arnold's poetry and prose look for meaning in a modern world that has become increasingly discordant. Alluding to the pessimism that deformed (in his own opinion) his poetry, in the Preface to *Poems* Arnold explains why he has excluded his long work *Empedocles on Etna* from the collection. In wishing to "delineate the feelings of one of the last of the Greek religious philosophers, . . . having survived his fellows, living on into a time when the habits of Greek thought and feeling had begun fast to change," Arnold had taken on a "poetically faulty" scenario—the situation of a man of an older era entrapped within a new and inimical one, and convulsed with longing for what he has lost—and found himself unable to describe timeless emotions, only "doubt" and "discouragement," those "exclusively modern" sentiments. In "Dover Beach," as well, the speaker suffers from a sense of displacement. Nostalgic for a more meaningful time ("The Sea of Faith / Was once, too, at the full" [lines 21–22]), he offers a bleak view of the modern age. In a similar fashion, the poet in "The Scholar Gypsy" inhabits an era infused with "sick fatigue" and "languid doubt," the symptoms of "this strange disease of modern life" (lines 164, 203). In Arnold, students will find the doubt and melancholy that infused so much of Victorian writing.

Dover Beach

Quick Read

- Form: Lyric; some critics have characterized this as a type of sonnet, although it does not adhere strictly to this form. The first stanza has fourteen lines, while the second and third stanzas together make up another fourteen lines. The final stanza is shorter, but the last three lines contain a turn in the logic, so that the effect is that of a sonnet. Scattered end rhymes evoke a sense of order overall, but there is no coherent rhyme scheme throughout.
- Themes: The modern world is without faith and stability; the illusion that all is well is false; human relationships may or may not be a defense against the uncertainty of modern life; the present can only be understood in relation to the past.
- Key Passages: "But now I only hear / [the Sea of Faith's] melancholy, long, withdrawing roar, / Retreating," lines 24–26; "And we are here as on a darkling plain / Swept with confused alarms of struggle and flight, / Where ignorant armies clash by night," lines 35–37.
- Key Image: The sea.

Teaching Suggestions

The image of the sea in "Dover Beach" will provide a good entryway into the poem for your students and a link to several of its themes. The first stanza contrasts two ways to apprehend the sea: Visually, it is deceptively calm ("The sea is calm tonight" [line 1]), while aurally, it is disturbingly noisy ("Listen! you hear the grating roar / of pebbles which . . . bring / The eternal note of sadness in" [lines 9–14]). Already we have several contrasts here: between what is seen and what is heard; between tranquility and turbulence, between illusion and reality; and between the present moment and eternity. In the second stanza, the sea is the link to the historical past and to a generalized feeling of discontent, to "the turbid ebb and flow / Of human misery" (lines 17–18). Ask students what happens to this image of the sea in the third stanza, when "The Sea of Faith . . . Retreat[s]" (lines 21–26). Note the difference between present and past here: "The Sea of Faith / Was once . . . like . . . a bright girdle furled. / But now I only hear / Its melancholy, long, withdrawing roar / Retreating . . . down the vast edges drear / And naked shingles of the world" (lines 21–28). In the past, the "Sea of Faith" encircled the world, as if to secure it, whereas in the present, the sea has abandoned the world and left it unclothed, exposed. The enjambment of the "withdrawing roar, / Retreating" emphasizes this backward movement and the sense of desertion. Invite students also to think about what kind of faith the narrator is talking about. Critics have surmised that Arnold had in mind the religious certainty of the medieval era when he wrote that the "Sea of Faith" was like "a bright girdle furled" (lines 21, 23). Yet "Faith," as used here, seems to include more than just religious faith; the complete vulnerability of the "naked shingles" (line 28) suggests a world devoid of stability or certainty. The final stanza at first appears to offer a remedy to this uncertainty ("Ah, love, let us be true / To one another!" [line 29–30]), yet the hope offered here is placed in doubt: "[T]he world," the narrator tells us, "Hath really neither joy, nor love, nor light, / Nor certitude, nor peace, nor help for pain" (lines 30, 33–34). Does this mean that love and faith cannot exist in this world? Or, if fidelity in human relationships is meant to substitute for all the world lacks, then why does the poem end as it does, with the narrator—and all of humanity—"on a darkling plain / Swept with confused alarms of struggle and flight, / Where ignorant armies clash by night" (lines 35–37)? This is a grim vision of modernity. Can human alliances overcome the obstacles presented here?

Preface to Poems

Poetry, Arnold wrote in the Preface to Poems, should not only gratify the reader's "natural interest in knowledge of all kinds" but also "inspirit and rejoice the reader; . . . convey a charm, and infuse delight." But whereas Mill believed that such delight stemmed from "the delineation of the deeper and more secret workings of human emotion" by poets such as the Romantics, who were carefully attentive to the nuances of their own inner lives ("What Is Poetry?"), Arnold argued that the poet should strive for self-effacement, rejecting the Romantic aesthetic that "a true allegory of the state of one's own mind" is "the highest thing that one can attempt in the way of poetry." Modern poetry, he believed, suffered from too much emphasis on the poet's subjective states, too much "interruption from the intrusion of his personal peculiarities." Romantic poetry's pre-occupation with imaginative apperception, Arnold feared, might lead to disabling self-consciousness and self-absorption. Such overattentiveness to one's own subjectivity, he believed, was an especial danger in the present, an "age wanting in moral grandeur" that offered no "sufficiently grand, detached, and self-subsistent object[s]" for poetic contemplation.

The Function of Criticism at the Present Time

Arnold spoke out against middle-class cultural insularity and anti-intellectualism, advocating a type of criticism that concerned itself not only with English literature, but also with *"the best that is known and thought in the world."* For Arnold, "the best" meant the Western tradition of European thought and classical culture, and in this sense he meant to broaden the scope of contemporary British criticism. Moreover, Arnold felt strongly that literary criticism should inhabit what he termed a "pure intellectual sphere," free of political or practical influences. In his view, the English were far too concerned with "material progress" ("our railways, our business, and our fortune-making") and cared nothing for the cultivation of the intellect for its own sake (the "free play of the mind"), as he stated in "The Function of Criticism at the Present Time." This hindered the British, keeping them from achieving the objectivity that Arnold demanded. The ultimate goal of good criticism, as Arnold explains, is to follow the European model and attempt to "see the object as in itself it really is."

Quick Read

- Form: Essay.
- Central Theme: Good literary criticism encourages the creation of superior literature and enriches society.
- Key Passages: "[T]he main effort . . . [of intellectual enterprise in Europe] has been a critical effort; the endeavor, in all branches of knowledge, theology, philosophy, history, art, science, to see the object as in itself it really is" (1384); "critical power" as contrasted with "creative power" (1385–86); "The Englishman has been called a political animal, and he values what is political and practical so much that ideas easily become objects of dislike in his eyes, and thinkers, 'miscreants'" (1390–91); the business of criticism should be to "keep aloof from what is called 'the practical view of things'" (1392); "It is because criticism has so little kept in the pure intellectual sphere, has so little detached itself from practice, has been so directly polemical and controversial, that it has so ill accomplished, in this country, its best spiritual work" (1393); "Wragg is in custody": An example of "grossness" in the "Anglo-Saxon breed" (1394); "I am bound by my own definition of criticism: *a disinterested endeavour to learn and propagate the best that is known and thought in the world*" (1396).

Teaching Suggestions

Probably the most familiar passage in this essay—and a good starting place for your discussion—is the one in which Arnold rails against a newspaper story describing a young woman, Wragg, who had been arrested for strangling her illegitimate child. The article ends with the brief statement, "Wragg is in custody," causing Arnold to let loose with a stream of sardonic invective:

> [H]ow eloquent, how suggestive are those few lines! . . . If we are to talk of ideal perfection, of "the best in the whole world," has anyone reflected what a touch of grossness in our race, what an original shortcoming in the more delicate spiritual perceptions, is shown by the natural growth amongst us of such hideous names—Higginbottom, Stiggins, Bugg! In Ionia and Attica they were luckier in this respect than "the best race in the world"; by the Ilissus there was no Wragg, poor thing! . . . And the final touch—short, bleak and inhuman: Wragg is in custody. The sex lost in the confusion of our unrivaled happiness; . . . the superfluous Christian name lopped off by the straightforward vigor of our old-Anglo-Saxon breed!

Unfortunately for Wragg, she has an aesthetically displeasing name and has committed an aesthetically displeasing crime. Arnold's contrasting of Wragg's miserable situation with the graciousness of Greek culture is strikingly inappropriate. The passage reveals the prickly underside to Arnold's lofty pursuit of cultural progress and can lead you into questions about his basic ideas: Can criticism be kept "aloof from what is called 'the practical view of things,'" as Arnold proposes? Is the distinction between aesthetic and practical spheres one that can—or should—be maintained? According to Arnold, what is "good" literary criticism and how can society benefit by it? What is the difference between "critical power" and "creative power"?

Culture and Anarchy

Arnold's essay combines an aesthetic critique of modernity with social analysis. On the one hand indicting the Puritanism, pragmatism, crass aesthetic sensibilities, and materialism of the middle classes, and on the other, the coarse hooliganism of the laboring classes, Arnold condemns his era for its "vulgarity, hideousness, ignorance, violence." The working classes, he says satirically, are "beginning to assert and put in practice an Englishman's right to do what he likes; his right to march where he likes, meet where he likes, enter where he likes, hoot as he likes, threaten as he likes, smash as he likes." The Second Reform Bill, as far as Arnold is concerned, was the last straw, placing political power in the hands of the brutes as well as the philistines, so that England now was "in danger of drifting towards anarchy" as well as ugliness. Arnold's solution to the "vulgarity" of modern life is to return to what he defines as "Hellenic" values: to pursue the timeless ideals of beauty and truth, to cultivate "spontaneity of consciousness," and to reverence "sweetness and light," in his perhaps most famous phrase.

Literature and Science

In a lecture delivered at the opening of a scientific college, Thomas Henry Huxley had quoted Arnold as a kind of high priest of the cult of classical education. Arnold's rejoinder may be read in "Literature and Science," written for an American lecture tour; the talk is tailored to an audience Arnold suspects of being predisposed to "abasing what is called 'mere literary instruction and education,' and exalting what is called 'sound, extensive, and practical scientific knowledge,' . . . in this intensely modern world of the United States." For Arnold, "practical" means "interested"; it is not "liberal" or free from some ulterior motive. Arnold tries to dispel the notion that "classical education" means little more than an ornamental smattering of ancient language and culture. Rather it involves a thorough absorption of Greek and Roman civilization with the aim of developing a "sense for conduct" and "a sense for beauty," phrases used repeatedly throughout the essay. These, Arnold argues, cannot be provided by an exclusive study of science; moreover, no other literature and art can so powerfully serve the instinct for beauty as the Greek.

Teaching Clusters

Arnold's prose can be taught within several different clusters. "The Function of Criticism at the Present Time," for example, in its treatment of English intellectual and social progress and its concern with Anglo-Saxon racial identity, could be usefully placed in the **Progress, Science, and Colonial Expansion** grouping. Arnold's "On the Study of Celtic Literature," located in the "Empire and National Identity" section of NAEL, would make an excellent companion piece here. *Culture and Anarchy* could be included either in this grouping, because of its concern with progress and English identity, or in the **Poverty, Unrest, and Social Criticism** category, because of its concerns about the working classes. Moreover, the prose selections that speak directly to questions of aesthetics, such as *Culture and Anarchy*, the Preface to *Poems*, and "The Function of Criticism at the Present Time," could be taught within the cluster on **Aesthetics, Aestheticism, and the Critique of Victorian Values**. Arnold's poetry, with its melancholy, reflective approach, demands a different context, however, and would be better placed within the **Doubt, Self-Reflection, and Romanticism** grouping. "Dover Beach," for example, belongs in this cluster, as does "The Scholar Gypsy."

Discussion Questions

1. Explore the image of the sea in "Dover Beach."
2. How does the narrator of "Dover Beach" view the modern world? What role can human relationships play in this world?

3. Compare the view of poetry in Arnold's Preface to *Poems* with that in Mill's "What Is Poetry?"
4. According to Arnold in "The Function of Criticism at the Present Time," how can good criticism advance English society?
5. How are "critical power" and "creative power" related in Arnold's "The Function of Criticism at the Present Time"?
6. In Arnold's "The Function of Criticism at the Present Time," why is the journalistic statement "Wragg is in custody" an example of "grossness" in the "Anglo-Saxon breed"?
7. Is Arnold being elitist in his description of a "pure intellectual sphere" that disregards the Wraggs of the world?
8. According to Arnold, what are "Hellenic" values (*Culture and Anarchy*)?
9. In Arnold's view, what are the merits of a classical education and the limitations of an education that focuses solely on science?

Further Resources

NORTON ONLINE ARCHIVE

The Function of a Professor
Stanzas in Memory of the Author of *Obermann*
Longing
Requiescat
Palladium
The Better Part
Shakespeare
In Harmony with Nature
Philomela
The Forsaken Merman
Thyrsis
To a Friend
Isolation. To Marguerite
Memorial Verses
Growing Old
From Maurice de Guérin ["A Definition of Poetry"]
From Wordsworth

Thomas Henry Huxley

Huxley is an interesting figure in that he joins the moral earnestness of the Victorians to a modern vision of science. For Huxley, science is valuable not merely because it gives us the truth, but more precisely because it does so in an ethical and socially conscious manner. In defending the study of science as a solid basis for a liberal education, he appeals to the reform-minded public in his lecture "Science and Culture," by pointing out that humanism had begun as a movement of reform in education and that the task of reformation was not complete. As he asserts, "The representatives of the Humanists, in the nineteenth century, take their stand upon classical education as the sole avenue to culture as firmly as if we were still in the age of the Renaissance." Yet this traditional view of education is no longer adequate to the modern age, an age in which "The notions of the beginning and the end of the world entertained by [society's] forefathers are no longer credible." Thus it is scientific inquiry, and not a classical education, that will prepare students most fully to understand Western culture and its relation to the world.

Science and Culture

Quick Read

- Form: Essay (originally an address for the opening of a scientific college).
- Central Theme: Huxley argues that a classical education is not a necessary foundation to understanding and appreciating culture; a strictly scientific education, he asserts, will prepare students for this task as fully as will a classical training.
- Key Passages: "[T]he diffusion of thorough scientific education is an absolutely essential condition of industrial progress" (1430); "neither the discipline nor the subject matter of classical education is of . . . direct value to the student of physical science; and . . . for the purpose of attaining real culture, an exclusively scientific education is at least as effectual as an exclusively literary education" (1431); Huxley agrees with Arnold that "a criticism of life is the essence of culture" but not that "literature contains the materials which suffice for the construction of such criticism" (1431); science has changed everyone's view of the world: "The notions of the beginning and the end of the world entertained by our forefathers are no longer credible . . . " (1434); scientific inquiry prepares students to seek for truth through the study of nature: "this scientific criticism of life . . . bids the learner seek for truth not among words but among things" (1434).

Agnosticism and Christianity

Quick Read

- Form: Essay.
- Main Idea: "Agnosticism," a term that Huxley coined, is an intellectual position that holds that you cannot find truth in unprovable absolutes; only knowledge derived from observable evidence should be believed. Huxley defends this belief on moral grounds.
- Key Passages: Theists cannot take the moral high ground by claiming that only their creed can judge what is "morally wrong" for agnosticism is a position that has an ethical component: "[agnosticism] ex-

presses absolute faith in the validity of a principle, which is as much ethical as intellectual" (1436); theists do not believe in seeking the truth. For the theist "the attainment of faith, not the ascertainment of truth, is the highest aim of mental life" (1437); maintaining civilized "bonds of human society" (1438) does not depend on Christianity because "Greek science, Greek art, the ethics of old Israel, [and] the social organization of Rome" (1438) preceded the Christian era; the modern world has grown out of the gifts of these pre-Christian cultures (1438); morality is in accordance with a belief in Darwinian evolution because the "notion that morality is more the child of speculation than of practical necessity and inherited instinct" (1439) is absurd.

Teaching Suggestions

Your students will need to understand, first of all, what Huxley means by a "classical education" and why it was important to Victorian society. In Huxley's time, such an education meant a thorough training in Greek and Latin language and literature, which prepared students for entrance into university. A central issue, then, in deciding whether the classics would continue to define liberal education, was one of class—whether such an education would be available only to a privileged minority in the future, as in the past. When Huxley disputes the views of "the great majority of educated Englishmen . . . [who believe that] culture is obtainable only by . . . [instruction in the literature of] Greek and Roman antiquity," he is arguing against firmly entrenched class and cultural attitudes. Another point that will need some clarification is that Huxley defends the study of science on the grounds that it can help open up a larger view of culture. Thus, the aims of scientific inquiry are not narrow or self-serving, but encompass nonmaterial values usually ascribed to the humanists. In this respect, Huxley joins together ideas that were usually thought of as disparate. The same kind of reasoning is apparent in "Agnosticism and Christianity," where Huxley argues that it is ethical to reject formal religious views that are based solely on faith. Following this line of thinking, morality is consistent with a belief in science, but for many Victorians, this was a shocking thought. You can bring the two articles together by comparing the issue of morality in "Agnosticism and Christianity" with cultural appreciation in "Science and Culture." Finally, the pursuit of truth is central to both works; discussions on this topic will shed light on Huxley's reasoning.

Teaching Clusters

Both "Science and Culture" and "Agnosticism and Christianity" can be usefully taught in the **Progress, Science, and Colonial Expansion** cluster because both works see scientific inquiry as conducive to progress—industrial, intellectual, and moral. Moreover, "Science and Culture" would make an excellent pairing with the excerpt from Newman's *The Idea of a University*, which directly addresses issues of education in relation to larger views of the world. Less obvious but more provocative companion pieces would be Mill's *Autobiography* and Carlyle's *Sartor Resartus*, for very different reasons. The selection from Mill critiques Utilitarian education for its overly analytical and narrowly quantitative view of life; only through the reading of poetry was Mill able to overcome his mental exhaustion and appreciate the importance of human emotion. For Mill, then, a full education has to speak to something other than what can be measured by scientific reasoning—a position that contradicts some of Huxley's claims. Carlyle's *Sartor Resartus*, on the other hand, while not directly discussing the same issues as Huxley, shares a similar kind of reasoning. While Carlyle believes that spirituality can be attained in a nonreligious context, Huxley, in "Agnosticism and Christianity," believes that morality can be attained in a post-Darwinian world. The two selections would make a fruitful comparison.

Discussion Questions

1. Why is the study of classics not necessary for a sound liberal education, according to Huxley? What does he see as the goal of a liberal education?
2. Compare Huxley's view of a liberal education to Newman's.
3. In "Science and Culture," Huxley asserts that scientific education is different from other forms of education. What is his reasoning? How does a scientific education prepare people to understand culture?
4. In what way is agnosticism a moral choice, according to Huxley?
5. Discuss the importance of truth in both "Science and Culture" and "Agnosticism and Christianity."

Further Resources

NORTON ONLINE ARCHIVE

A Liberal Education
A Game of Chess
An Address on University Education
The Function of a Professor

George Meredith

George Meredith's *Modern Love* was surprisingly frank for its time, offensive to many of its first readers in its candid portrayal of infidelity in marriage. It offers a rare glimpse into mid-Victorian social and sexual relationships, countering the abundance of literature and essays that promoted idealized images of men, women, and matrimony. A mere two years after the publication of *Modern Love*, for example, Ruskin declared that "the true nature of home [is] the place of Peace" ("Of Queens' Gardens"). The centerpiece of this haven was the "true wife," who must be "enduringly, incorruptibly good; instinctively, infallibly wise" ("Of Queens' Gardens"). Meredith's narrative of marital betrayal and bitter emotions demolishes such platitudes, showing not only that the state of marriage was deeply flawed, but also that, in matters of love and sex, human beings were less than paragons.

Modern Love

Quick Read

- Form: A sequence of fifty sonnets; verse novel.
- Summary: The entire sequence, from which the NAEL selections are excerpted, follows the experiences of a husband and wife in an unhappy marriage.
- Themes: Marital unhappiness; infidelity; silence; secrets; masks; shadows.
- Key Passages: "Like sculptured effigies they might be seen / Upon their marriage tomb, the sword between; / Each wishing for the sword that severs all," verse 1, lines 14–16; "But here's the greater wonder: in that we, / Enamored of an acting naught can tire, / Each other, like true hypocrites, admire," verse 17, lines 9–11; "That night he learned how silence best can speak / The awful things when Pity pleads for Sin," verse 49, lines 11–12.

Teaching Suggestions

After reading these selections, students may wonder why the couple would stay in such a miserable state with each other rather than seeking escape. It would be helpful to begin class with a few comments about Victorian marriage and the difficulty of divorce. Divorce had become easier to obtain in the previous decade, but was still costly and created a public scandal. You might also want to point out that these sonnets mock the Petrarchan love sonnet, which praised the female object of love. This mockery underscores the sense of bitterness that pervades the sequence. Some general questions about tone and characterization will get the discussion going. How is the man portrayed? Is he angry, despondent, self-pitying, or thoughtful—or all of these at different points? What is his attitude toward his wife? Is he misogynistic? How does he compare to her? Can we find the woman's voice at all here? Is one character more sympathetic than another? In the first verse, the wife is "strangled mute," evidencing "muffled pulses" (lines 5, 8), yet her suppressed sobs are like "little gaping snakes / Dreadfully venomous to him" (lines 5–6); note the conflict between empathy and anger or fear. Additionally, most of the verses are in the third person, but from the husband's perspective; verse 17 is in the first person, but the husband is the speaker. Ask students how this limited point of view affects their reading of the poem. In verse 2, we hear more about the man's pain: the wife's eyes are "guilty gates," while the husband "sickened" and "went mad, / And raged deep inward" (lines 2, 6, 8–9). Yet you can contrast this with the first verse, where we witness the woman's misery, although we know she has committed adultery. (The husband will commit adultery later in the sequence, but those passages are not included in NAEL.) Additionally, students may want to trace various themes and recurring images: the wife's "mute" suffering in verse 1 is a foreshadowing of her final "silence . . . [which] speak[s] / The awful things" in verse 49, when she kills herself by drinking poison (lines 11–12). Other useful themes include actors and masks (verses 2 and 17); and shadows and ghosts (verses 17 and 49). Moreover, several other sonnets from the Modern Love sequence are included in the online archive; students will get a much clearer sense of the overall narrative from reading these.

Teaching Clusters

Modern Love needs to be studied in relation to other works of the period, for it is especially valuable as a social document. John Ruskin's "Of Queens' Gardens" and Coventry Patmore's The Angel in the House are excellent sources for illustrating the ideal that was popular at the time and for giving students a sense of the poem's unorthodox treatment of its subject matter. Also helpful would be Mona Caird's article "Marriage," which supports free unions between sexual partners rather than legal ties. Caird's article, shocking for its time, was published more than twenty-five years after Modern Love, which will give students an idea of how much Meredith is pushing the envelope. These selections are especially pertinent, but many of the other works in the Gender and Sexuality teaching cluster would also be constructive. Finally, these sonnets, because of the sequence's rejection of mid-Victorian moral views, would be well placed in Aesthetics, Aestheticism, and the Critique of Victorian Values.

Discussion Questions

1. Compare the portrayal of husband and wife in Modern Love. Which character is more sympathetic? Which one is more fully delineated? Why?
2. Is the husband misogynistic? Does he show any sensitivity toward his wife or her suffering?
3. What does the title, Modern Love, tell you about the work's attitude toward love and marriage? Why are the problems depicted here specifically "modern"?
4. What is the poem's attitude toward the wife's infidelity? Is morality a factor here?
5. In verse 2 we are told that "each wore a mask" (line 4), while in verse 17 we hear that both are "[e]namored of an acting naught can tire" (line 10). Discuss the role that masks and acting play in these sonnets.

Further Resources

Norton Online Archive

Modern Love
  3 ("This was the woman; what now of the man?")
  15 ("I think she sleeps; it must be sleep, when low")
  16 ("In our old shipwrecked days there was an hour")
  23 ("'Tis Christmas weather, and a country house")
  35 ("It is no vulgar nature I have wived")
  42 ("I am to follow her. There is much grace")
  43 ("Mark where the pressing wind shoots javelinlike")
  48 ("Their sense is with their senses all mixed in")
Dirge in Woods

Dante Gabriel Rossetti

With their sensuous imagery, evocation of feminine mystery, and engagement with a symbolic vocabulary, Dante Gabriel Rossetti's writings offer a prime example of Pre-Raphaelite poetry. Like his paintings, Rossetti's poems linger on the female form, rendering in lush detail qualities that are at once spiritual and earthly. "Her eyes were deeper than the depth / Of waters stilled at even," says the speaker of "The Blessed Damozel" about his deceased lover (lines 3–4). Moreover, Rossetti's work anticipates the later aesthetic movement, which held that art should be pleasurable within its own terms rather than serve a didactic purpose. Even Rossetti's "Jenny," a poem that reflects on the sleeping form of a prostitute, is more concerned with the woman's symbolic value as an undecipherable code than with the morality of her profession. For the speaker, the young prostitute is "A cipher of man's changeless sum / . . . A riddle . . . from the scornful sphinx" (lines 278–81). Taken together with other Pre-Raphaelite poetry and painting, Rossetti's work will introduce students to a vibrant moment in Victorian aesthetics.

The Blessed Damozel

Quick Read

- Form: Lyric.
- Summary: A speaker describes his deceased lover (the "Blessed Damozel") as she gazes on him from heaven; she expresses sorrow at their separation and longs to be united with him once again.
- Main Theme: Relationship between physicality and spirituality.
- Key Passages: "Surely she leaned o'er me—her hair / Fell all about my face," lines 21–22; "her bosom must have made / The bar she leaned on warm," lines 45–46; "There I will ask of Christ the Lord . . . Only to live as once on earth / With Love . . . ," lines 127–30; "And then she cast her arms along / The golden barriers," lines 141–42.

Teaching Suggestions

The first stanza of "The Blessed Damozel" contains the themes and types of imagery that imbue the rest of the poem: the Damozel's physicality, the concreteness of heaven, and the symbols that invest the Damozel with a mystical and spiritual significance. You may want to point out that heaven is presented in material terms, suggesting a rigid, circumscribed space not unlike a prison. The woman leans over the "gold bar of heaven," for example (line 2), and "God's house" is a "rampart" (line 25) that, rather than protecting her, seems to keep her separated from the earthly pleasures she yearns for. This prison-like aspect is made clear at the poem's conclusion, when the Damozel "cast[s] her arms along / The golden barriers . . . And [weeps]" (lines 141–44). The Damozel herself, although invested with numerous symbols that connect her to the Virgin Mary (the "white rose of Mary's gift," for example [line 9]) and other symbols that are more vaguely multivalent (the "three lilies" [line 5]), is nonetheless endowed with a sensual physical presence. As she leans over the heavenly barrier, the speaker imagines that "her bosom must have made / The bar she leaned on warm" (lines 45–46). Similarly, he thinks, "Surely she leaned o'er me—her hair / Fell all about my face" (lines 21–22). This may only be wishful thinking on the part of the speaker, but the Damozel also longs to be united with her earthly lover, imagining a time when she will "lay [her] cheek / To his, and tell about [their] love" (166–17). The aspect of the poem that will be most confusing for students is the relationship of Christianity to corporeality, for rather than the body being a vehicle for experiencing spiritual plenitude, as one might expect, the spiritual is a vehicle for imagining physical union. The Damozel's desire for her lover is expressed in devotional language ("the dear Mother will approve / My pride" [lines 119–20]), for instance, and enacted within a spiritual context ("I'll take his hand and go with him / To the deep wells of light; . . . / And bathe there in God's sight" [lines 75–78]). Ultimately, the Damozel states that she will "ask of Christ the Lord . . . / Only to live as once on earth / With Love—only to be, / As then awhile, forever now, / Together, I and he" (lines 127–32). Questions about the depiction of the soul and the body will help direct students toward the poem's thematic center.

Jenny

Reflecting on the sleeping form of a young prostitute who lies beside him in bed, the speaker of "Jenny" muses silently, "Jenny, looking long at you, / The woman almost fades from view. / A cipher of man's changeless sum / . . . A riddle . . . from the scornful sphinx" (lines 276–81). For the male scholar who narrates the poem, the prostitute's body is a mystery that speaks more to his own qualities of mind than to any specific aspects of the woman herself: "Why, Jenny, as I watch you there,— / For all your wealth of loosened hair, / . . . You know not what a book you seem, / Half-read by lightning in a dream!" (lines 46–52). While Jenny sleeps, the scholar's thoughts move from the "stilled features" of a "living woman's simple face" that inspired the "highest painters" (lines 233, 232, 231) to "God" and "men's souls" (lines 240, 238), among other subjects. Direct your questions to the speaker's situation and character and the way in which the woman's body functions as an open book for the young intellectual. Where is Jenny in this poem?

Teaching Clusters

Rossetti's poetry can be taught in a number of different contexts. "The Blessed Damozel" is a good example of the Victorian idealization of medieval culture, so in this sense it can fit within the **Doubt, Self-Reflection, and Romanticism** grouping. All of the poems could be placed in the cluster on **Aesthetics, Aestheticism, and the Critique of Victorian Values** because of their concern with beauty and sensuality, but "The Blessed Damozel" and the selections from *The House of Life* make particularly good choices here. "Jenny" would be especially well situated in the **Gender and Sexuality** cluster, along with works that address issues of female sexual fallenness, such as Christina Rossetti's *Goblin Market* or William Morris's "The Defence of Guenevere." All of the poems should be studied alongside the Pre-Raphaelite paintings included in the color insert to *NAEL* and *Norton Topics Online*: "The Painterly Image in Poetry."

Discussion Questions

1. How are spiritual concepts portrayed in "The Blessed Damozel"? What kinds of imagery define heaven? How do God and the Virgin Mary figure in this poem?
2. Is the speaker of the poem more concerned with the Damozel's soul or her body? How are the two related?
3. What importance do the body and physicality have in "The Blessed Damozel"?
4. Compare the visual quality of one of Rossetti's paintings to "The Blessed Damozel." Do the painting and poem share a richness of imagery, for example, or concreteness of detail?
5. What does the description of the prostitute in "Jenny" tell us about the male speaker of the poem?
6. Compare the depiction of female sexual fallenness in D. G. Rossetti's "Jenny" to the same issue in Christina Rossetti's *Goblin Market* or William Morris's "The Defence of Guenevere."

Further Resources

NORTON ONLINE ARCHIVE

The House of Life
   4. "Lovesight"
   49. "Willowwood—1"
   50. "Willowwood—2"

Christina Rossetti

Christina Rossetti's poems focus to a great extent on themes of renunciation and self-denial that are set off against lush visions of plenitude and desire. "Sweeter than honey from the rock. / Stronger than man-rejoicing wine, / . . . She sucked and sucked and sucked the more / Fruits which that unknown orchard bore," says the narrator of *Goblin Market* in an image that merges religious references with bodily sensuality. Yet this surrender to longing will yield nothing in the end, as Laura admits: "I ate and ate my fill, / Yet my mouth waters still" (lines 165–66). Here, sisterly sacrifice will eventually heal the wounds Laura suffered in the male marketplace, yet elsewhere the suffering remains unalleviated. In Rossetti's poetry, feminine yearning is often the result of failed male-female relationships. Women are betrayed, silenced, or objectified by men, as is the "nameless girl" of "In an Artist's Studio," who is painted "Not as she is, but as she fills [the male artist's] dream" (line 14). Although Rossetti's women are often positioned outside of a fully realized social existence— they are dead or "all short of life" ("A Triad," line 14)—her lyrics give voice to the silenced and offer a critical appraisal of Victorian gender relations.

Goblin Market

Quick Read

- Form: Narrative poem.
- Themes: The mercantile aspects of male-female relationships; the power of sisterly devotion and healing; the dangers of yielding to desire.
- Key Passages: "We must not look at goblin men, / We must not buy their fruits," lines 42–43; "You have much gold upon your head. . . . Buy from us with a golden curl," lines 123–25; "I ate and ate my fill, / Yet my mouth waters still," lines 165–66; "Golden head by golden head, / Like two pigeons in one nest / Folded in each other's wings," lines 184–86; "They trod and hustled her, / Elbowed and jostled her, . . . Tore her gown and soiled her stocking, / Twitched her hair out by the roots," lines 399–404; "For there is no friend like a sister," line 562.

Teaching Suggestions

A good place to start for students new to Rossetti is with her treatment of gender relations in poems such as Goblin Market, "A Triad," "An Apple-Gathering," "In an Artist's Studio," and "Promises Like Pie-Crust." The first three works, in particular, form a resonant grouping that addresses both gender issues and self-denial.

Goblin Market is a significant work that can be studied alone or in connection with Rossetti's other writing. Students may at first find the poem's combination of fairytale motif and sensual imagery puzzling; thus, it is helpful to begin simply by asking what the goblin men represent. Students will very likely offer responses such as "sin," "evil," and "sexuality." From here you may talk about the poem as a cautionary tale against unruly female appetites or as a religious allegory of sin and redemption. It is useful to point out, for example, that while Lizzie "thrust[s] a dimpled finger / In each ear, shut[s] [her] eyes and [runs]" away from the goblin men (lines 67–68), Laura "suck[s] and suck[s] and suck[s] [the goblin fruit] . . . until her lips [are] sore" (lines 134–36). These passages highlight the struggle between temptation and desire, and a discussion of these motifs can lead in several directions; a consideration of the ideal Victorian "angel," female (hetero)sexuality, or homoerotic imagery (as suggested in the final passages, when Laura sucks the juices from Lizzie's body) are all possible avenues. In some cases, instructors may wish to extend discussions of female sexuality with questions about the role of Jeanie, the "fallen" woman who dies as a result of her submission to the goblin men. Some students may see in the fallen "Jeanie" a reference to D. G. Rossetti's "Jenny," a prostitute.

In all of these discussions, it is illuminating to explore the theory of separate spheres and traditional attitudes toward women in the nineteenth century. On the one hand, *Goblin Market* supports middle-class Victorian views of ideal women as self-sacrificing and nurturing through its portrayal of Lizzie. On the other hand, Lizzie's heroic actions blur traditional boundaries between private and public spheres; she moves freely between the spaces of home and marketplace, regenerating the one through her manipulation of the other. Along these lines, students may also want to examine the conflict between the goblin men and the two sisters; the violent action of the men (their "claw[ing]" [line 401] and "[s]tamp[ing]" [line 405] result in Lizzie's "bruises" [line 467]) and Lizzie's refusal to yield are portrayed in epic terms. It is striking, moreover, that the conflict between men and women takes place within an economic framework. Upper-division students may thus benefit from an examination of the poem's suggestive economic language, which equates female sexual exchange with mercantile exchange. The action revolves around buying and selling fruits in "goblin market," for example, while Laura's "golden lock" (line 126) is paralleled with "coin" (line 116). (In nineteenth-century slang, a "goblin" was a gold coin—see the footnote to "Jenny" [line 491]—so the goblin men are actually equated with money.) Invite students to consider to what extent and in what manner the poem is critical of conventional gender relations and of domestic ideology.

Goblin Market can be successfully studied alongside "An Apple-Gathering" and "A Triad," both of which envision female sexual desire in terms of spiritual desolation and social transgression. "An Apple-Gathering," in particular, equates the exchange of fruit with seduction and abandonment; after plucking her apple blossoms and being abandoned by her lover, the narrator "loiter[s]" (line 28) while "the night [grows] chill" (line 26), an activity that Victorian readers would associate with illicit sexual activity, if not prostitution. Similarly, the three women in "A Triad" give themselves over to sexual desire, with disastrous consequences. Echoes of *Goblin Market*'s vocabulary of female hunger can be found in the third woman, who "famished died for love" (line 11). By grouping these poems together, students gain greater insight into Rossetti's views on female desire and moral reckoning.

Other resonant works include "In an Artist's Studio," which reflects on the figure of Elizabeth Siddal, the model in the sonnet and later Dante Gabriel Rossetti's wife. The model remains "hidden just behind those screens" (line 3)—that is, behind the canvases, which "mirror" the desire of the painter and conceal the real woman's complex desires, disappointments, and aspirations. Clothing his model in all the conventional forms of femininity ("A saint, an angel"), the painter shows her "Not as she is, but as she fills his dream" (line 14). (Christina herself was painted as the Virgin Mary by her brother; see *Ecce Ancilla Domini* ["The Annunciation"] in *Norton Topics Online* "The Painterly Image in Poetry.") This poem speaks to the treatment of women as aesthetic objects and would make a good contrast to Robert Browning's "My Last Duchess."

In "Cobwebs," Rossetti describes "a land with neither night nor day, /

Nor heat nor cold, nor any wind, nor rain, / Nor hills nor valleys" (lines 1–3). It is a featureless landscape of "twilight grey" (line 5), even bleaker than the one Tennyson's Mariana sees from her window (line 5). This place of utter negation is perhaps the terrain of the mind, an inner wasteland of spiritual and emotional deadness: "No future hope no fear for evermore" (line 14). Despite joyous and lushly sensuous poems like "A Birthday," Rossetti's works often detail the plight of one who exists in a state of self-cancellation. Echoing the last line of "Cobwebs," the speaker of "Dead before Death" describes a living death that forecloses any possibility of fulfillment: "All lost the present and the future time . . . So cold and lost for ever evermore" (lines 10–14).

Teaching Clusters

Christina Rossetti's works can be successfully taught within the **Gender and Sexuality** cluster, alongside selections by other women poets such as Elizabeth Barrett Browning and Emily Brontë, whose writings explore issues of female identity. Also useful here would be nonfictional pieces that will give students some framework for understanding gender conventions of the nineteenth century. John Ruskin's "Of Queens' Gardens" is a central text in this regard, and selections by Sarah Stickney Ellis and Florence Nightingale would be illuminating here also. Additionally, Rossetti's writing could be usefully placed in the context of Pre-Raphaelite literature, in the **Doubt, Self-Reflection, and Romanticism** cluster. In this category, consider including the works of D. G. Rossetti, William Morris, and Robert Browning ("Fra Lippo Lippi").

Discussion Questions

1. What do the goblin men of Rossetti's *Goblin Market* represent?
2. Are conventional Victorian ideas about women contested or supported in *Goblin Market*? Can the poem be seen as demonstrating a power struggle between men and women?
3. Compare the portrayal of male and female spheres of existence in *Goblin Market*.
4. In what way is *Goblin Market* a moral fable of sin and redemption?
5. How does economic language function in *Goblin Market*?
6. Discuss the attitude toward sexuality—both heterosexual and homoerotic—as illustrated in *Goblin Market*, "A Triad," and "An Apple-Gathering." How is female desire portrayed in each?
7. Compare the portrayal of male-female gender relations in *Goblin Market*, "An Apple-Gathering," and "Promises Like Pie-Crust."
8. How is the concept of death connected to identity and self-realization in "Song," "After Death," and "Dead before Death"?
9. Compare the aestheticization of women as depicted in Rossetti's "In an Artist's Studio" and Robert Browning's "My Last Duchess."

Further Resources

NORTON ONLINE ARCHIVE

Winter: My Secret

NORTON TOPICS ONLINE

The Painterly Image in Poetry
The Illustrated Text
  Moxon's Illustrated Tennyson
  D. G. Rossetti's Illustrations for *Goblin Market*

William Morris

The Defence of Guenevere

William Morris's Arthurian poems illustrate the Victorian fascination
with the medieval era. Unlike Tennyson's *Idylls of the King*, however,
which has a distinct moral and social content, Morris's *The Defence of
Guenevere* condones the queen's adulterous sensuality and challenges the
chivalry of Arthur's knights. "[S]ee my breast rise, / Like waves of purple
sea, . . . And how my arms are moved in wonderful wise," she says to her
accusers (lines 226–28). "[W]ill you dare, / When you have looked a little
on my brow, / To say this thing is vile?" (lines 236–38). Guenevere defends herself not by denying her unfaithfulness, but by unashamedly as-
serting her sexuality and questioning the virtue of her interlocutors. With
the injunction, "Gauwaine, . . . Remember in what grave your mother
sleeps," she reminds the knight that his own mother, Morgan Le Fay, was
accused of adultery (lines 150–153). Similarly, she terms Mellyagraunce,
her would-be rapist, a "stripper of ladies" (line 192). This is no chastened
Guenevere, but a bold and shrewd woman, trying every possible argument
in a desperate attempt to avoid a ghastly end.

Quick Read

- Form: Dramatic monologue.
- Summary: Rewrites an episode from Thomas Malory's *Morte Darthur*
  in which Queen Guenevere is accused of committing adultery with
  Launcelot, King Arthur's knight. In Morris's version, Guenevere defends herself against her incriminators, who plan to burn her at the
  stake. At the conclusion, Launcelot arrives to free her.
- Key Passages: "[S]till she stood right up, and never shrunk, / But spoke
  on bravely, glorious lady fair!" lines 55–56; "She stood, and . . . /
  Spoke out at last with no more trace of shame, / With passionate twisting of
  her body there," lines 58–60; "Gauwaine, . . . Remember in what
  grave your mother sleeps," lines 150–153; about Mellyagraunce:
  "stripper of ladies," line 192; "will you dare, / When you have looked
  a little on my brow, / To say this thing is vile?" lines 236–38.

Teaching Suggestions

Students will need a little background on Victorian medievalism and on the Pre-Raphaelites before you begin your discussion of the poem. Have them view the paintings of Dante Gabriel Rossetti, William Holman Hunt, John Everett Millais, and other Pre-Raphaelite artists included in *NAEL's* color insert and Norton Topics Online (see "The Painterly Image in Poetry"). Rossetti's lush paintings of women, emphasizing their sensuality, will help provide some context for understanding Morris's portrayal of Guenevere.

Your students also will be interested to know that Morris decided to omit an introductory passage explaining the events leading up to the trial scene depicted here, thus throwing the reader into the middle of the action. Note that the poem begins with a conjunction—"But"—which indicates that we are actually in the middle of a sentence, not to mention the middle of a scene. Ask students how this sudden entry into the episode affects the tone and emotional impact of the poem. Following this, direct their attention to the description of Guenevere. By stating that she "stood right up, and never shrunk, / But spoke on bravely, glorious lady fair!" the poem leads us to visualize a courageous woman who stands up to her attackers (lines 55–56). Yet the narrator also lingers suggestively on her features and movements, observing that Guenevere "threw her wet hair backward from her brow, / Her hand close to her mouth touching her cheek" (lines 2–3). The main focus of your discussion can be centered on Guenevere's own stance and the arguments she adopts in her defense. Guenevere repeatedly refers to her beauty, accuses Gauwaine and Mellyagraunce of having less than pure motives toward her, and makes some confusing statements about "truth" and "lie[s]" that are never fully clarified: "you, O Sir Gauwaine, lie, / Whatever happened on through all those years, / God knows I speak truth, saying that you lie" (lines 142–44). At some points it seems as if Guenevere is saying anything and everything that comes into her head to distract the knights who are ready to put her to death. You may also want to discuss the lack of male chivalry here and the brawling, bleeding, lustful men who make up Arthur's court. Is Guenevere, with her overt displays of sexuality and suspected infidelity, responsible for social chaos and the breakdown of masculine codes of honor? Note, for example, Guenevere's description of Mellyagraunce's attempted rape (lines 168–221) and the "bawling, mad fit" (line 280) that erupts after a plot to catch Launcelot in the queen's room.

Teaching Clusters

The Defence of Guenevere can be taught in either the **Gender and Sexuality** cluster or the **Doubt, Self-Reflection, and Romanticism** cluster. In the first grouping, you may focus on gender issues in the poem: the dissolution of masculine chivalry and the sympathetic but highly sexualized portrait of Guenevere. The second grouping will lead you into the medieval context. Here, you will want to include other poems from the

Arthurian tradition, such as by Tennyson and D. G. Rossetti, and Ruskin's defense of medieval aesthetics in *The Stones of Venice*. Additionally, Carlyle's praise of feudal society in *Past and Present* will provide some insight on the medieval revival.

Discussion Questions

1. What is the narrator's attitude toward Guenevere? Does he admire her? Revile her?
2. What is Guenevere's attitude toward her judges?
3. What kind of argument does Guenevere use to defend herself?
4. According to Guenevere's description of events, what impression do you have of Arthur's knights? Do they seem to uphold the code of masculine chivalry? Is Guenevere to blame for dissension among the knights?

Further Resources

NORTON ONLINE ARCHIVE

I Know a Little Garden Close
Christ Keep the Hollow Land
For the Bed at Kelmscott
The Haystack in the Floods
The Earthly Paradise
An Apology
A Death Song

Algernon Charles Swinburne

In a defiant rejection of Christianity, the speaker of Algernon Charles Swinburne's "Hymn to Proserpine" declares, "Thou has conquered, O pale Galilean . . . [but] I kneel not" (lines 35, 46). This refusal to bow to social and religious norms is enacted time and time again in Swinburne's poetry. "Hermaphroditus," for example, contemplates gender duality while also suggesting homoerotic desire with the injunction to "Lift up thy lips, turn round, look back for love" (line 1). Similarly, "Ave atque Vale" elegizes the French poet Charles Baudelaire, whose celebration of sin and debauchery delighted the unconventional Swinburne. Although more explicit in its treatment of bodily pleasures than the poems of Dante Gabriel Rossetti, Swinburne's writing captures the frank appeal to sensuality apparent in much Pre-Raphaelite poetry. Moreover, its disregard of moral value anticipates the aims of the aesthetic writers in the later years of the century.

Hymn to Proserpine

Quick Read

- Form: Hymn; lyrical poem.
- Summary: Told from the viewpoint of a fourth-century Roman patrician and poet, the hymn laments the passing of paganism and the emergence of Christianity.
- Themes: The pagan gods are superior to the Christian gods; it's better to enjoy the extremes of pleasure and pain than live a life of meekness; Christianity is a mere moment in time; death is the ultimate seduction.
- Key Passages: "Nay for a little we live, and life hath mutable wings," line 30; "Thou has conquered, O pale Galilean; the world has grown gray from thy death," line 35; "Though all men abase them before you in spirit, and all knees bend, / I kneel not, neither adore you, but standing look to the end," lines 45–46; "All ye as a wind shall go by, as a fire shall ye pass and be past," line 67; "There is no god found stronger than death; and death is a sleep," line 109.

Teaching Suggestions

Students will most likely be intrigued with Swinburne's rejection of Victorian moral and religious conventions. In "Hymn to Proserpine," you may want to start with questions about the speaker's portrayal of Christianity as "barren," providing "days [that] are bare" (line 17). How does his reference to Christ as "O pale Galilean" compare with the more vivid description of the gold-haired Apollo, who is "A bitter god to follow, a beautiful god to behold" (line 8)? The pagan gods, whom the speaker reverences, are "cruel as love or life, and lovely as death" (line 12), while the "New gods" are "merciful, clothed with pity" (lines 15–16). Why does the speaker regret the demise of these seemingly more brutal gods? What is missing for him in the new order? You may also need to draw students' attention to the positioning of the fourth-century speaker in relation to the nineteenth century. In paying tribute to Proserpine and paganism, Swinburne is not merely reenacting a period of ancient history, but more specifically making a comment on the loss of religious faith in his own century. The speaker makes several references to a later time, when Christianity will vanish: "Yet thy kingdom shall pass, Galilean," he declares (line 74). Why does the speaker say this? This repudiation of Victorian norms is enacted in a very different manner in "Hermaphroditus," a poem that questions tidy middle-class assumptions about gender and sexuality. The poem's repeated references to nonreproductive sexuality ("the waste wedlock of a sterile kiss" [line 19] and "The double blossom of two fruitless flowers" [line 38]), for example, suggest not only gender duality, but also homoerotic desire. Taken together, these poems bring the full compass of Swinburne's moral refusal to light.

Teaching Clusters

All of Swinburne's poems may be usefully contextualized in the cluster **Aesthetics, Aestheticism, and the Critique of Victorian Values.** Works by D. G. Rossetti and William Morris would make excellent comparisons, especially in their different approaches to sensuality and the body. The selection from Walter Pater's *The Renaissance* would be an important companion piece because it articulates some of the aesthetic principles that Swinburne follows. "Hermaphroditus" would also be well placed in the **Gender and Sexuality** category, alongside works by D. G. Rossetti and others that address sexual issues.

Discussion Questions

1. In Swinburne's "Hymn to Proserpine," how are the "New gods" (line 15) different from the "dethroned gods" (line 13)? How do Swinburne's language and imagery highlight the distinction?
2. In what way is "Hymn to Proserpine" an indictment of Christianity?
3. Why does Swinburne situate the speaker in the fourth century, after Rome has condoned the practice of Christianity? Why does the speaker refer to a later time, when the Christian "gods . . . shall die" (line 68)?
4. How would you characterize the speaker of "Hymn to Proserpine"? What is the purpose of his hymn to the pagan goddess?
5. In Swinburne's "Hymn to Proserpine," the speaker declares, "Nay, for a little we live, and life hath mutable wings" (line 30), whereas in *The Renaissance*, Walter Pater states that "impressions of the individual mind . . . are in perpetual flight; . . . each of them is limited by time . . . ; all that is actual in it being a single moment, gone while we try to apprehend it." Compare Swinburne's sense of time with Pater's. How are the two contexts different or similar?

Further Resources

NORTON ONLINE ARCHIVE

Before the Beginning of Years
In Memory of Walter Savage Landor
An Interlude
In the Orchard
Choruses from Atalanta in Calydon
   When the Hounds of Spring
   Before the Beginning of Years
The Garden of Proserpine
The Triumph of Time
I Will Go Back to the Great Sweet Mother
The Lake of Gaube

Walter Pater

Pater's ideas were central to the aesthetic movement of the late nineteenth century. Although his followers may have viewed him as more subversive than he actually was, Pater's writings legitimized the sensuous aspects of art in place of didactic elements. Disregarding the twin Victorian virtues of hard work and moral earnestness, he argued in favor of an aesthetic that valued "the love of art for its own sake" (*The Renaissance*). In contrast to Ruskin, who declared that "the greatest picture is that which conveys to the mind of the spectator the greatest number of the greatest ideas," Pater believed that art had to be appreciated not for its content, but for its immediate effect upon the senses (*Modern Painters*). The aesthetic critic, Pater asserted, "regards . . . all works of art . . . as powers producing pleasurable sensations . . ." (*The Renaissance*). These pronouncements were embraced with enthusiasm by adherents such as Oscar Wilde, who took to heart Pater's declaration that "art comes to you proposing frankly to give nothing but the highest quality to your moments as they pass, and simply for those moments' sake" (*The Renaissance*).

Studies in the History of the Renaissance

Quick Read

- Form: Essay.
- Main Point: Aesthetic criticism should not concern itself with beauty, but with the sensations or effects of the art object and the means by which those sensations or effects are rendered.
- Themes: The aesthetic moment is transient; art should be valued for its own sake, for the immediate pleasure, not for any larger meaning.
- Key Passages: "Not the fruit of experience, but experience itself, is the end" (1512); "To burn always with this hard, gemlike flame, to maintain this ecstasy, is success in life" (1512); "Of such wisdom, the poetic passion, the desire of beauty, the love of art for its own sake, has most. For art comes to you proposing frankly to give nothing but the highest quality to your moments as they pass, and simply for those moments' sake" (1513).

Teaching Suggestions

It would be helpful for students to understand the conventional attitudes toward art that existed at the time in which Pater was writing. Ruskin's *Modern Painters* sets up this contrast nicely, illustrating the importance that prevailing aesthetic criticism gave to the notion of intellectual or moral content in art. William Holman Hunt's *The Awakening Conscience*, a popular painting that depicted the dawning moral awareness of a kept woman, demonstrates the kind of moral content that appealed to Victorians in the middle part of the century (available in Norton Topics Online and in the *NAEL* illustrations). This painting can be contrasted with Aubrey Beardsley's illustrations from the 1890s, which flout Victorian morality and embody the principles of the aesthetic movement in the extreme (available in the *NAEL* illustrations). With a basic grasp of some of these fundamental aesthetic concepts, students are ready to turn to Pater's central points: about aesthetic criticism, the purpose of art, and the significance of transient physical and emotional sensations in developing an aesthetic awareness. One aspect of the piece that might not be clear to students is Pater's interest in outward physical sensations and the "inward world of thought and feeling." Pater concentrates here on the idea that these sensations and feelings are in constant motion (a "whirlpool" of activity); in his view, this continual movement makes the aesthetic moment fleeting and elusive.

Teaching Clusters

Pater's *Studies in the History of the Renaissance*, so vital to an understanding of the aesthetic movement, belongs squarely in **Aesthetics, Aestheticism, and the Critique of Victorian Values**. It takes up precisely those concepts that so many followers of the aesthetic movement believed in, especially the need for art to be devoid of any moral, spiritual, or intellectual content. Although this is clearly the most logical placement, there's much to be said for teaching it alongside works that the piece argues against, such as Ruskin's *Modern Painters* or any writing that defines middle-class conventions and mid-Victorian views of art. The **Doubt, Self-Reflection, and Romanticism** cluster contains useful pieces for these purposes. Carlyle's vivid endorsement of work in *Sartor Resartus*, for example, would make a stimulating contrast. Additionally, John Stuart Mill's *Autobiography*, with its somewhat clinical endorsement of poetic emotion, would invite a thoughtful comparison.

Discussion Questions

1. How do Pater redefine the role of beauty for the aesthetic critic?
2. What do the "perpetual motion" of outward physical sensation and the "inward world of thought and feeling" have to do with the appreciation of art, according to Pater?
3. In Pater's view, what is the goal of aesthetic criticism?
4. What does Pater think art should do or accomplish? How does this compare with Ruskin's view that "the greatest picture is that which conveys to the mind of the spectator the greatest number of the greatest ideas" (*Modern Painters*)?
5. Do Pater's and Ruskin's aesthetic theories have any significance today? Do paintings or illustrations that have a direct political or social message fail as art?

Further Resources

NORTON ONLINE ARCHIVE

From Appreciations ["Style"]
From The Child in the House

Gerard Manley Hopkins

In his journal entry of February 1870, Gerard Manley Hopkins relates a moment when he, overcome by sorrow, "suddenly began to cry and sob and could not stop." Finding no "adequate cause" for such an outburst, he compares the experience of being swept up in emotion to being sliced with a sharp knife. The knife, Hopkins reasons, will not cut if merely pressed against the skin, but must be accompanied by something else: "one touch, something striking sideways and unlooked for, which in both cases undoes resistance and pierces." Hopkins's poetry attempts to capture this feeling of being pierced by the unexpected: it slices through the dull coating of familiarity that protects us from extremes of pleasure and pain, and brings us to a confrontation with that which, for Hopkins, reveals God's presence in the world. It is in this elevation of individual perception and sensation to something rare and beautiful that Hopkins most closely resembles his tutor, Walter Pater. Hopkins finds, for instance, in a falcon's perfect marshalling of energy as it hovers against the wind, a moment of sheer "ecstasy" before the "fire . . . breaks" ("The Windhover," lines 5, 10). This combination of force, control, and risk electrifies Hopkins, who sees God's power here. Such intense experiences characterize Hopkins's poetry and enact Pater's injunction: "To burn always with this hard, gemlike flame, to maintain this ecstasy, is success in life" (*The Renaissance*).

The Windhover

Quick Read

- Form: Sonnet.
- Themes: God's magnificence in the natural world; the intensity of the moment; beauty in violence.
- Key Words and Phrases: "I caught this morning morning's minion," line 1; "dapple-dawn-drawn Falcon," line 2; "Buckle!" line 10; "blue-bleak embers . . . Fall, gall themselves, and gash gold-vermilion," lines 13–14.

Teaching Suggestions

This is a challenging poem, but also intriguing to analyze. It's important for students to understand that Hopkins was deeply affected by his Roman Catholic faith and that his poetry both celebrates and interrogates that faith (see "Carrion Comfort," for example). For Hopkins, a falcon's balanced suspension against the force of the wind, depicted in "The Windhover," is evidence of God's presence. Thus, the bird's precision and power inspire awe and lead to thoughts about the magnificence in ordinary things. You will also want to discuss the techniques Hopkins developed in his poetry: the concepts of instress and inscape, and the method of sprung rhythm. The first octave offers several packed images. Ask students to discuss the effects of alliteration, repetition, and assonance in the first lines: "I caught this morning morning's minion, king- / dom of daylight's dauphin, dapple-dawn-drawn Falcon" (lines 1–2). Why the repetition of "morning morning's"? Why the line break between "king- / dom"? Note the several meanings of "dapple-dawn-drawn." Also direct students' attention to the changing sense of movement here. While these first lines are slow, deliberate, and ponderous, the third line begins to move more smoothly, sensuously, with "rolling" and "striding," which breaks into a joyous "ecstasy! then off, off forth on swing" (line 5), and finally "a skate's heel sweeps smooth on a bow-bend: the hurl and gliding / Rebuffed the big wind" (lines 6–7). This is all grace and rounded movement until "Rebuffed" abruptly enters the picture. You will also want to discuss the visual imagery: the upward, circular motion of the bird in flight and its skillful, controlled hovering as it pits itself against the wind's pressure. The final sestet offers more challenges and more options. "Buckle" (line 10) can take us in several directions, but in any case we have encountered something that is at once "dangerous" (line 11) and breathtaking; there is a force here ("the fire that breaks from thee" [line 10]) that causes the speaker to gasp, "O my chevalier!" (line 11). Ask students to consider how this flash of "fire" (line 10) compares to the image of flashing cinders in the last two lines: the "blue-bleak embers" that "Fall, gall themselves, and gash gold-vermilion" (lines 13–14). Why the violence of "Fall, gall"? Does this force have anything to do with the "ecstasy!" of line 5? Why is "the fire that breaks" "lovel[y] [and] dangerous" (lines 10–11)? Hopkins is describing a moment that is fleeting, hazardous, and beautiful. The last line leaves us with the sense of something thrilling yet also violent. As with all of Hopkins's poetry, this needs to be read out loud, so that listeners can get a sense not only of the poem's sound, but also of its drama.

Pied Beauty

Quick Read

- Form: Curtal sonnet (a shortened sonnet form of ten and a half lines, invented by Hopkins); also, a song of praise.
- Themes: The celebration of multiplicity and difference in God's plan; the relationship of distinctness to the larger whole; God's presence in all things.
- Key Words and Phrases: "Pied Beauty"; "couple-colour," line 2, "stip-

ple," line 3; "All things counter, original, spare, strange," line 7; "He fathers-forth whose beauty is past change," line 10.

Teaching Suggestions

In this poem, Hopkins celebrates multiplicity and difference, envisioned as part of a larger spiritual plan. For Hopkins, proof of God is everywhere, especially in the miraculous juxtapositions of color and form that make up, for him, a unified whole. The poem's title offers a useful starting point for discussion. "Pied" in itself means variegated color, yet the addition of "Beauty" requires the reader to see individual masses of color as a single entity. Thus, "Pied Beauty" suggests disparate colors that form a pleasing whole: singularity and unity at once. This concept informs the entire poem and can lead you into a discussion about Hopkins's concepts of instress and inscape. Invite students first to discuss the variable meanings of different words and phrases. "[C]ouple-colour" (line 2), for instance, suggests that two colors are joined together; yet note both the hyphenation of the word and its odd placement in the sentence. Is it a noun? An adjective? How does the meaning change in each situation? How does this compounding get at something unique? Moreover, the hyphenation enacts the very coupling the words describe. After looking closely at particular words, note also their placement in the sentence. What is the relationship between "skies," "couple-colour," and "brinded cow," for example? Moving beyond specific passages, what is the structure of the poem? Is there a shift from one image or idea to the next? The first four lines focus on animals; then the poem turns to "Landscape" in line 5, and then to "all trades" in line 6; thus, several types of natural entities are praised for their particular, distinctive qualities. The second stanza, however, is quite different in its approach. Rather than attending to the specific qualities that distinguish multicolored or multiuse objects, this stanza steps back a bit and describes things as a group, in broader terms, while still appreciating variation: "All things counter, original, spare, strange" (line 7); "swift, slow; sweet, sour; adazzle, dim" (line 9). Here we have opposites, oddities, and idiosyncrasies subsumed within a larger aggregate: "All things." Additionally, you will want to remind students that "stipple" (line 3) is a painting technique that uses dots and small splashes of color to produce an overall effect of vibrancy within a unified scheme. It would be instructive to have students view some of the paintings of the French Post-Impressionists who used this technique, especially Georges Seurat in the 1880s. The effect is dazzling, very much in line with the sensation of "Pied Beauty." In this context, Hopkins's God is an artist/creator who "fathers-forth" color and beauty in the natural world. The unusual juxtaposition of words and the unconventional syntax convey a sense of life and plenitude, which, for Hopkins, are proof of God's hand in the universe. Thus, the parenthetical question "who knows how?" (line 8) brings the reader back to the concept of a plan or unified vision encompassing such disparate beauty.

Teaching Clusters

Because of his unconventional syntax, meter, and language, and because his poetry was not published until 1918 (almost thirty years after his death), Hopkins was for years grouped with the twentieth-century poets. Now that he is with the Victorian writers, it is easier to get a sense of his relation to his own time. Pater's influence on Hopkins is apparent in works such as "The Windhover," "God's Grandeur," "As Kingfishers Catch Fire," and the journal entries, particularly in their celebration of intense feeling and perception. In this connection, Hopkins's work would be well situated in **Aesthetics, Aestheticism, and the Critique of Victorian Values.** The excerpt from *The Renaissance* would be instructive here, along with the lyrics of D. G. Rossetti and Swinburne. The meditative quality of the poems makes them also a good fit for **Doubt, Self-Reflection, and Romanticism.** Some of the later works, such as "Carrion Comfort" and "No worst, there is none"—the "terrible sonnets"—would be particularly appropriate. Among the earlier poems, "Pied Beauty" would make an excellent choice, especially when paired with Robert Browning's "Caliban upon Setebos"; both pieces speak to issues of divine revelation. Moreover, Browning's work, with its experimental approach to language and syntax, would provide a good contrast. You might also want to teach Hopkins with some of the Romantics, such as Wordsworth, Coleridge, Shelley, or Keats.

Discussion Questions

1. What does the falcon in "The Windhover" mean to the speaker of the poem?
2. How does the last image of "blue-bleak embers" that "gash gold-vermilion" (lines 13–14) in "The Windhover" relate to the "fire" (line 10) and "ecstasy" (line 5) of the earlier lines? Is the kestrel somehow connected to the flash of light revealed in dying embers?
3. Discuss the multiple meanings of the title "Pied Beauty" and its relation to the poem's themes.
4. "Pied Beauty" contains a number of compound words: "couple-colour" (line 2), "rose-moles" (line 3), "Fresh-firecoal" (line 4), "chestnut-falls" (line 4), and "fathers-forth" (line 10). What effect does this technique of hyphenation have on your reading of the poem? How do the hyphenated words relate to the poem as a whole?
5. In what way is color significant in "Pied Beauty"? How does color relate to Hopkins's vision of the world and to God?
6. What is the relationship between singularity and unity in "Pied Beauty"?

Further Resources

NORTON ONLINE ARCHIVE

Audio:
The Windhover *and* Spring and Fall (read by M. H. Abrams)

Light Verse

Humorous literature of the nineteenth century provided an antidote to the tone of moral seriousness apparent in so much writing of the period. Students used to the soul-searching works of Carlyle and Mill may be surprised to learn that nonsense lyrics and comical sketches—often meant for children—found a wide and approving audience in Victorian society. Yet humor often serves other functions in addition to acting as entertainment; it can help to relieve pressure or provide strategies for dealing with vexing cultural problems. In some cases, humor can be anarchic and disruptive: political and social orthodoxies are overturned, linguistic meaning is challenged, and problems of knowledge are examined. In other cases, it can be deeply conservative, attacking anything that threatens communal stability or individual certainty. All of these tendencies are at work in the selections below. The nonsense writings of Edward Lear and Lewis Carroll explore states of subjectivity or social cohesion, while the works of W. S. Gilbert speak to middle-class concerns. Light verse acts as Victorian culture's "other": it locates social boundaries, defining what can or cannot be said or thought. Above all, it demonstrates the importance of popular art forms in revealing the preoccupations of more legitimized cultural expressions.

Edward Lear

The Jumblies

Quick Read

- Form: Nonsense poem.
- Summary: The protagonists sail far away in a leaky boat, demonstrate chirpy courage and clever thinking in the face of disaster, and return twenty years later to general acclaim.
- Key Passages: "They went to sea in a sieve, they did," line 1; "For the sky is dark, and the voyage is long," line 22; "Far and few, far and few, / Are the lands where the Jumblies live. Their heads are green, and their hands are blue . . . ," lines 65–67.

Teaching Suggestions

Edward Lear's "The Jumblies" offers a prime example of how nonsense and humor can attempt to resolve profound personal and cultural anxieties. By parodying that which it deeply fears, the poem provides a way to diffuse concerns about life's uncertainties. The theme of the journey in Lear's jaunty tale is an evocative one, recalling medieval quest narratives and later works that employed the quest motif to explore psychological turmoil. Invite students to pursue this line of thought by comparing "The Jumblies" with Robert Browning's "Childe Roland to the Dark Tower Came." In Lear's poem, it is significant that the mode of conveyance is a leaky boat ("They went to sea in a sieve, they did" [line 1]); this is a precarious world and the protagonists are ill-equipped to navigate its murky waters. Yet the plucky sailors, determined to sail to far-away lands, announce their determination to continue: "we don't care a button; we don't care a fig— / In a sieve we'll go to sea!" (lines 9–10). In Browning's poem, Childe Roland makes a similar decision to continue on to the Dark Tower although he is surrounded by ominous signs of previous failures. Students may be reluctant to read any kind of anxiety into Lear's cheerful lyrics, but there are several signs that point to this. Not only is the sailors' boat described repeatedly as a "sieve" (the first stanza alone repeats this word five times), but the narrator tells us that "the sky is dark, and the voyage is long" (line 22; repeated in revised form in line 32) and that some spectators predict trouble ahead: "won't they soon be upset, you know . . . ; / And, happen what may, it's extremely wrong / In a sieve to sail so fast" (lines 21–24). In addition to addressing issues of anxiety, the poem has quite a bit to say about colonial exploration. The title, "The Jumblies," refers to a strange group of creatures in a distant land: "Far and few, far and few, / Are the lands where the Jumblies live. / Their heads are green, and their hands are blue" (lines 65–67). Moreover, the mariners sail far away "to the Western Sea . . . To a land all covered with trees" (lines 45–46) and purchase "a lovely monkey with lollipop paws" (line 51), along with other unusual items. In "The Jumblies," as in nineteenth-century England and other European countries, remote locales are often seen as exotic sources for raw materials and tales of heroic adventure.

Lewis Carroll

The White Knight's Song

Quick Read

- Form: Nonsense poem from Carroll's *Through the Looking-Glass*.
- Summary: The narrator meets an elderly man and asks him how he makes his living; he pays little attention to the man's answers, which are nonsensical. This piece parodies Wordsworth's "Resolution and Independence."
- Key Passages: "But I was thinking of a plan / To dye one's whiskers green," lines 17–18; "So, having no reply to give . . . [I] thumped him on the head," lines 21–24; "I hunt for haddocks' eyes / Among the heather bright," lines 41–42; "I thanked him much for telling me / The way he got his wealth, / But chiefly for his wish that he / Might drink my noble health," lines 61–64.

Like Edward Lear's "The Jumblies," "The White Knight's Song" attempts to contain and diminish anxieties through parody. Taking his cue from Wordsworth's "Resolution and Independence," Charles Dodgson (Lewis Carroll) tells the story of an elderly man who makes a meager living in the margins of society. Whereas in Wordsworth's poem the man is a tragic figure, dignified by his perseverance, in Carroll's version he is a whimsical, slightly crazy "aged, aged man" who "hunt[s] for haddocks' eyes / Among the heather bright, / And work[s] them into waistcoat-buttons / In the silent night" (lines 41–44). Invite students to compare Dodgson's poem with Wordsworth's, noting Dodgson's changes and emphases. Both poems, for instance, contain a framing device in which the narrator encounters an older man and asks how the man makes his living. Draw your students' attention to the different descriptions of the characters, paying particular attention to the relationship between the narrator of each poem and the elderly man. In Wordsworth's account, the narrator learns something from the "old Man" about dealing with adversity, but, of course, Dodgson's parody has no such serious conclusion. Moreover, while Wordsworth's "old Man" hunts in the receding tide for leeches, which he then sells, Dodgson's "aged man" looks for items out of context, where they are unlikely to be found: "I sometimes dig for buttered rolls, / Or set limed twigs for crabs; / I sometimes search the grassy knolls / For wheels of hansom-cabs" (lines 49–52). By turning the elderly man's hunt into something fruitless and bizarre, Dodgson eliminates the significance of the encounter between the two figures; the White Knight narrator has nothing to learn from the absurd character. There is no respect here for the "aged man," but neither is there any for the speaker, who daydreams while the other talks: "But I was thinking of a plan / To dye one's whiskers green" (lines 17–18). Both are equally foolish. Dodgson's parody makes light of very real social and economic problems that existed in Victorian society, yet it doesn't offer any comforting solutions. While the jaunty sailors in Lear's "The Jumblies" at least had companionship and a "crockery-jar" to protect them (line 30), Dodgson's fools exist in an alienated world where social bonds are nonexistent.

W. S. Gilbert

If You're Anxious for to Shine in the High Aesthetic Line

Quick Read

- Form: Lyric from light opera.
- Summary: Satirical portrayal of an aesthete.
- Key Passages: "I'm an aesthetic sham!" line 4; "Of course you will pooh-pooh whatever's fresh and new, and declare it's crude and mean," line 35; "If that's not good enough for him which is good enough for *me*, / Why, what a very cultivated kind of youth this kind of youth must be!" lines 39–40.

Teaching Suggestions

W. S. Gilbert's amusing spoof of the "High Aesthetic Line" will provide you with an opportunity to discuss the roots of aesthetic thought and its various manifestations, both as a self-conscious preoccupation of nineties writers such as Oscar Wilde, and as an earlier drive that sought to detach art from any moral or didactic purpose, typified in writings by D. G. Rossetti and Algernon Swinburne, and codified in Walter Pater's conclusion to *The Renaissance*. Moreover, Gilbert's satire comments on (and collapses) several other aesthetic trends: the medievalism of the mid-century, the repudiation of industrialism, and the elitism suggested by Matthew Arnold's art criticism. Artistic and literary movements, your students will learn, do not fall into neat, pre-ordained categories, but are constantly in dialogue with disparate ideas and constantly strive to find new modes of expression. John Ruskin, for example, argued for precisely the kind of socially and intellectually meaningful art that was denigrated in the art-for-art's-sake philosophy. Yet Ruskin's ringing endorsement of medieval art forms in *Stones of Venice* will remind students of Reginald Bunthorne's assertion, "my medievalism's affectation, / Born of a morbid love of admiration!" (lines 23–24). Ruskin's medievalism, moreover, carried with it an implicit critique of the industrial era, a critique lampooned in Bunthorne's avowal to "pooh-pooh whatever's fresh and new, and declare it's crude and mean" (line 35). Even more pertinent here is Morris's "How I Became a Socialist"; although written after the earliest production of *Patience*, this essay offers a clear account of the rejection of industrialization on aesthetic grounds. Additionally, students who have viewed the paintings of D. G. Rossetti and other Pre-Raphaelite artists will immediately recognize Bunthorne's allusions to "stained-glass attitudes" and "a languid love for lilies." Yet despite the numerous references your students are bound to detect, they may not notice the conflict between class perspectives that is enacted here. Bunthorne captures the essence of this conflict when he exclaims, "If that's not good enough for him which is good enough for *me*, / Why, what a very cultivated kind of youth this kind of youth must be!" (lines 39–40). The ideas promoted in aesthetic and artistic circles were, to many of the middle classes, impractical and condescending. Gilbert's opera openly mocks aesthetic principles, giving voice to those who felt belittled by the self-appointed pundits and revealing the aesthetes to be as crass as their philistine counterparts.

Teaching Clusters

The humorous pieces in this section can be taught in a number of different ways. If you would like to focus on colonial paradigms or racial otherness, for instance, Lear's "The Jumblies" could be included in the **Progress, Science, and Colonial Expansion** cluster. Yet it would be equally appropriate in the section on **Doubt, Self-Reflection, and Romanticism**, taught alongside Robert Browning's "Childe Roland to the Dark Tower Came" or other works that explore psychological turmoil. This piece could also fit nicely in the category on **Gender and Sexuality**, as a model for plucky masculine behavior or one that illustrates the fissures in such cultural stereotypes; why do the protagonists take refuge in a "crockery-jar," for example? Similarly, W. S. Gilbert's portrayal of dubious masculine behavior in the selection from *Trial by Jury*, "When I, Good Friends, Was Called to the Bar," could work with this cluster. His spoof of the aesthetic movement, on the other hand, in the excerpt from *Patience* seems most fitting in **Aesthetics, Aestheticism, and the Critique of Victorian Values**, paired with Wilde's *The Importance of Being Earnest* and readings from Pater, Rossetti, Ruskin, and Morris. Lewis Carroll's "Jabberwocky" and Humpty Dumpty's Explication of "Jabberwocky" present other questions, however, about language and problems of knowledge. Humpty Dumpty insists that words and things have a direct relationship to one another, yet the randomness of his approach introduces more problems than can be resolved; for these reasons, it might provide an interesting point of departure for selections in the **Doubt, Self-Reflection, and Romanticism** cluster. Carroll's "The White Knight's Song" could also work in this grouping as an exploration of solipsism or subjectivity.

Discussion Questions

1. How are the protagonists in Edward Lear's "The Jumblies" portrayed? Do they depend upon sheer luck to solve their problems, or do they draw upon their inner resources?

2. Compare the concept of the journey or quest in "The Jumblies" and in Robert Browning's "Childe Roland to the Dark Tower Came." What kind of world does Lear create in his poem? Is it safe and predictable or filled with disaster? What is the relationship between the self and the world here? Is this a comforting poem?

3. Compare Lewis Carroll's "The White Knight's Song" to Wordsworth's "Resolution and Independence." How is the relationship between the narrator and the elderly man different in each?

4. What kind of social world does Carroll create in "The White Knight's Song"? What do you make of the narrator's violence toward the "aged man": "So, having no reply to give . . . [I] thumped him on the head" (lines 21–24)? Why does the narrator ask a question of the other man but pay no attention to the answer? What does the poem tell you about the narrator? What does it tell you about the "aged man"?

5. Discuss the conflict between middle-class values and the theories of the aesthetic movement as depicted in W. S. Gilbert's "If You're Anxious for to Shine in the High Aesthetic Line."

Further Resources

NORTON ONLINE ARCHIVE

EDWARD LEAR
How Pleasant to Know Mr. Lear
Cold Are the Crabs

LEWIS CARROLL
Anagrammatic Sonnet
The Walrus and the Carpenter
The Hunting of the Snark
The Baker's Tale

W. S. GILBERT
When Britain Really Ruled the Waves

Audio:
"If You're Anxious for to Shine in the High Aesthetic Line" (recorded by
Walter Passmore)

Victorian Issues

Evolution

Charles Darwin

Charles Darwin's *The Origin of Species*, published in 1859, opened up
a contentious debate on the role of God in the creation of the universe.
Although Darwin deliberately excluded human beings as a primary focus
of *The Origin*, many of its first readers recognized the implications of his
claim that "all animals and plants are descended from some one prototype." When Darwin asserted that he viewed "all beings not as special creations, but as the lineal descendants of some few beings that lived long
before the first bed of the Cambrian system was deposited," he was up-
braided for calling into question the Genesis time scheme and the biblical
account of creation. In the aftermath of *The Origin*'s publication, many
people contested the book's theories, the most famous example being
Bishop Samuel Wilberforce's ill-informed attack on Darwin's supporter
Thomas Henry Huxley at the Oxford Meeting of 1860. While *The Origin*
was perhaps the most widely debated scientific treatise of its time, Darwin's later book, *The Descent of Man*, contained similarly disturbing
propositions. In this work, Darwin made explicit his earlier suggestions
about the connections between human beings and animals, stating outright that "man is the codescendant with other animals of a common pro-
genitor." This view not only disrupted assumptions about humankind's
special place in the world, but also blurred the boundaries between "civilized" and "uncivilized" peoples, unleashing profound cultural anxieties in
the process.

The Origin of Species

Quick Read

- Form: Book.
- Themes: Animals and plants are similarly engaged in a struggle for
  existence; groups of species are interdependent, inextricably con-

nected within a larger system; species are not immutable; all species, plant and animal, are descended from one species.

- Key Passages: "I should premise that I use this term ['struggle for existence'] in a large and metaphorical sense including dependence of one being on another, and including (which is more important) not only the life of the individual, but success in leaving progeny" (1539); "Why, it may be asked, until recently did nearly all the most eminent living naturalists and geologists disbelieve in the mutability of species?" (1542); "Analogy would lead me . . . to the belief that all animals and plants are descended from some one prototype" (1543); "as natural selection works solely by and for the good of each being, all corporeal and mental endowments will tend to progress towards perfection" (1545); "It is interesting to contemplate a tangled bank, . . . and to reflect that these elaborately constructed forms . . . have all been produced by laws acting around us" (1545).

Teaching Suggestions

The excerpts from *The Origin* in NAEL do not focus in an explicit manner on the concept of natural selection, but Darwin's speculations in this vein can be deduced from his discussion of two main themes: the interconnectedness of collective species and the mutability of all species. Ask students to pay close attention to Darwin's logic so they will understand how his various points work together. Why, for example, is he concerned with the mutability of species? Questions along this line will lead you toward the logic of natural selection and the ramifications of such a theory. Darwin was refuting the prevalent "immutability" theory of fellow scientists who held that, rather than evolving over eons from the same original genetic material, each species "has been independently created" and is "subject to no variation." This biological theory comported well with a belief in Old Testament creationism, allowing religiously faithful scientists such as Philip Henry Gosse to propose dubious alternate theories to "justify geology to godly readers of Genesis." Taking his cue not from writings with a theological cast but from social theorist Thomas Malthus's treatise on the natural checks to overpopulation and geologist Charles Lyell's gradualist theories on the earth's formation, Darwin offers a vision of a biological system in which flora and fauna struggle amid cycles of abundance and destruction as part of a perfecting process of "natural selection." Darwin felt that the struggle for existence within this system led to a positive outcome because the characteristics that ensured survival—strength, speed, skill, and the like—would be passed on to succeeding generations. "[A]s natural selection works solely by and for the good of each being," he states, "all corporeal and mental endowments will tend to progress towards perfection." Students need to understand, however, that the concept of conflict within this interconnected system—the "tangled bank"—was, for many people, just as disturbing as the theory of species mutability. Some writers, such as Thomas Hardy, saw human

uniqueness and agency overwhelmed by this larger biological network. In
this view, the individual was hopelessly pitted against the natural order in
a losing battle. Yet you might also want to point out that although Darwin
helped bring these views to wide public attention, these concepts were
certainly not new. Several years before *The Origin* appeared, for example,
Tennyson anguished over the insignificance of both the individual and the
species within a cruel natural world, where "A thousand types are gone,"
devoured by "Nature, red in tooth and claw" (*In Memoriam*, verse 56,
lines 3, 15). Here, not only is individual life meaningless, but there is not
even a guarantee that the species will survive. For other people, however,
the vision of an organic whole containing competing factions was a self-
serving logic that justified numerous economic and social occurrences.
The model of laissez-faire economics, for instance, so loathed by Carlyle
and applauded by Macaulay (in "A Review of Southey's *Colloquies*"), visualized an "organic" system in which some sectors failed and others flourished, to the betterment of the whole. Where earlier writers, such as
Adam Smith, spoke of self-regulating economic systems, Darwin spoke
of "checks" (*The Origin*) in the biological sphere. The assumption here
is that some individuals and species will die out, but will be replaced
by healthier organisms better suited to the environment. For Darwin
and others enamored of this concept, such "checks" were acceptable because they were the result of biological law. "It is interesting to contemplate a tangled bank," Darwin muses, "and to reflect that these
elaborately constructed forms . . . have all been produced by laws acting
around us."

The Descent of Man

Quick Read

- Form: Book.
- Themes: "Man" is descended from a lower form of life and is not the
  product of a separate act of creation; sexual selection has assisted in
  the development of certain physical and mental qualities in animals.
- Key Passages: "The main conclusion arrived at in this work . . . is
  that man is descended from some less highly organized form"
  (1546); "He who admits the principle of sexual selection will be led
  to the remarkable conclusion that the cerebral system . . . has indirectly influenced the progressive development of various bodily
  structures and of certain mental qualities" (1548); "there can hardly
  be a doubt that we are descended from barbarians" (1549); "For my
  own part I would as soon be descended from that heroic little monkey . . . as from a savage who delights to torture his enemies" (1549);
  "Man still bears in his bodily frame the indelible stamp of his lowly
  origin" (1549).

Teaching Suggestions

In *The Descent of Man*, Darwin clearly states what had been only implied in his earlier work, that "man is descended from some less highly organized form." *The Descent* upset accepted views of "man's" place in the natural hierarchy. For Darwin, however, more disturbing than being related in some distant manner to animal forms is his certainty that humankind was "descended from barbarians." He is especially troubled when he meets the native inhabitants of Tierra del Fuego, whom he identifies as a less highly evolved species of human being: "The astonishment which I felt on first seeing a party of Fuegians on a wild and broken shore will never be forgotten by me," he declares, "for the reflection at once rushed into my mind—such were our ancestors." Rather than seeing the Fuegians as culturally different from himself, Darwin describes the typical islander as "a savage who delights to torture his enemies, offers up bloody sacrifices, practices infanticide without remorse, treats his wives like slaves, knows no decency, and is haunted by the grossest superstitions." You can begin a discussion on the racism of Darwin's observations by asking students to think about the relationship between inherent biological characteristics and cultural differences suggested in the description. Moreover, you may note that Darwin's anxieties about being related to such "savages" found expression in fictional works. Robert Louis Stevenson's *Dr. Jekyll and Mr. Hyde*, for example, gave imaginative shape to the fear, generated by Darwin's thought, that underneath the veneer of Victorian respectability was a savage being.

The other aspect of *The Descent* that you might wish to explore is its claims about the central role of sexual selection in the processes of biological development. Darwin emphasizes that "vigorous females" in certain bird species have contributed to physical changes in the species by choosing to mate with "the more highly ornamented males." He concludes that "the principle of sexual selection . . . has indirectly influenced the progressive development of various bodily structures and . . . certain mental qualities." Invite your students to think about what the implications for human gender roles are here.

Leonard Huxley and Sir Edmund Gosse

While Darwin's writings are of primary importance in this section, the selections by Leonard Huxley and Sir Edmund Gosse will help students understand the public controversy and personal spiritual upheavals that his work prompted. It would be worthwhile to clarify that figures such as Bishop Wilberforce (who, according to Huxley, "assured us there was nothing in the idea of evolution; rock pigeons were what rock pigeons had always been") were not in the minority at the time. Moreover, the Gosse selection shows that many Victorian scientists as well as clergymen were not prepared to make the conceptual leaps that Darwin's theory demanded. Gosse's introductory statements about the "year of scientific crisis" illustrate the intellectual somersaults that leading figures of the day thought necessary to reconcile the new evolutionary perspective with the "turbid volume" of Victorian received opinion.

Teaching Clusters

The selections in this category belong most clearly to the **Progress, Science, and Colonial Expansion** cluster; they help define a line of thinking that held that the world was changing and that the British were at the forefront of modern advances. Yet Darwin's works, in particular, would help contextualize some of the readings in the cluster on **Doubt, Self-Reflection, and Romanticism**, such as portions of Tennyson's *In Memoriam* or Carlyle's *Sartor Resartus*. Even though *The Origin* didn't appear until some years after these works were published, it identified issues that had already caught the attention of the public. Additionally, any of the selections that speak to Victorian paternalism or laissez-faire economics—such as Carlyle's *Past and Present*, the excerpt from Engels's *The Condition of the Working Class*, or Macaulay's "A Review of Southey's Colloquies"—could be read alongside *The Origin*, bearing in mind its description of a rule-based organic system comprised of elaborate checks and balances that worked toward the betterment of the whole.

Discussion Questions

1. Why was Darwin concerned about the mutability of species? According to Darwin, how and why do species change? What are the religious implications of his thought?
2. How is the phrase "the struggle for existence" related to Darwin's views about the natural world and individual organisms within that world? How can this idea be compared to issues about a self-regulating economic system (the laissez-faire model) hated by Carlyle and endorsed by Macaulay?
3. Read verses 54, 55, and 56 of *In Memoriam* and compare Tennyson's view of nature and the individual to Darwin's.
4. Why were many Victorians disturbed by Darwin's view, stated in *The Descent of Man*, that "man is descended from some less highly organized form"?
5. What were Darwin's thoughts on humankind's relationship to animals and to "barbarians," as stated in *The Descent of Man*?
6. Darwin stated that "the principle of sexual selection . . . has indirectly influenced the progressive development of various bodily structures and . . . certain mental qualities." What are the ramifications of this idea for existing Victorian gender roles?
7. According to Leonard Huxley's account, why was the audience won over by Thomas Henry Huxley's speech?
8. Describe Edmund Gosse's attitude toward his father, Philip Henry Gosse, as demonstrated in the excerpt from *Father and Son*. In what way is he critical of or sympathetic to his father?

Industrialism: Progress or Decline?

The readings in this section chronicle, sometimes in appalling detail, the sufferings of the industrial poor. They provide an essential background for understanding not only the reforming efforts of writers such as John Ruskin and Thomas Carlyle, but also the romantic nostalgia for social, economic, and aesthetic forms of the medieval era. William Morris's desire to escape "hateful modern society," for example, because of its "eyeless vulgarity which has destroyed art, the one certain solace of labour" connects the ugliness of poverty detailed by writers such as Friedrich Engels to the knowledge that the consolations of art were unavailable to the poor ("How I Became a Socialist"). For Morris and those who shared in the aesthetic critique of industrialization, the modern age destroyed the "simple pleasures which everyone could enjoy but for its folly" ("How I Became a Socialist"). While Engels and Thomas Mayhew provide documentary accounts of human suffering, Charles Dickens and Charles Kingsley offer fictionalized versions that found a wide readership. Dickens is acutely aware that the "comforts of life . . . [enjoyed by the] fine lady" are produced at the expense of others who labor in "town[s] of machinery and tall chimneys" with rivers that "[run] purple with ill-smelling dye." Engels is similarly outraged at the "narrow, coal-black, stinking river full of filth and rubbish." Despite public concern over the condition of the poor, however, many believed that England was progressing and that any short-term problems were far outweighed by long-term gains. This attitude is forcefully expressed by Thomas Babington Macaulay, who asserts, "The present moment is one of great distress. But how small will that distress appear when we think over the history of the last forty years" ("Review of Southey's *Colloquies*"). For Macaulay and others like him, the future belonged to England, and any particular instances of human misery were merely minor setbacks on the way to the nation's grand destiny.

Thomas Babington Macaulay

A *Review of Southey's* Colloquies

Quick Read

- Form: Essay.
- Summary: Attacks the view set forth by Robert Southey that the manufacturing system degrades workers and puts an ugly blight on the nation. Supporting a laissez-faire approach to financial markets, Macaulay articulates the theory that over the long term, the nation is becoming more prosperous.
- Key Passages: "[P]eople live longer because they are better fed, better lodged, better clothed, and better attended in sickness, and that these improvements are owing to that increase of national wealth

which the manufacturing system has produced" (1558); "Here are
the principles on which nations are to be governed. Rosebushes and
poor rates, rather than steam engines and independence. Mortality
and cottages with weather stains, rather than health and long life
with edifices which time cannot mellow" (1559); "We . . . rely on . . .
those general laws which it has pleased [God] to establish in the
physical and in the moral world" (1560).

In "A Review of Southey's *Colloquies*," Thomas Babington Macaulay attacks Robert Southey's contention that "the manufacturing system" has
brought nothing but misery to the people of England. It is not the case
that industrialism "destroys the bodies and degrades the minds of those
who are engaged in it," Macaulay asserts; drawing on statistics about the
longevity and prosperity of the urban laborer, he concludes that "the people live longer because they are better fed, better lodged, better clothed,
and better attended in sickness, and that these improvements are owing
to that increase of national wealth which the manufacturing system has
produced." Southey saw the uniform and drab living quarters of the urban
working classes ("as offensive to the eyes as to the mind") as symptomatic
of the misery of working-class lives and contrasted them unfavorably to
the picturesque, homey cottages of poor rural laborers. Macaulay, however, jeers at a social critique that rests on the fact that "the dwellings of
cotton-spinners are naked and rectangular." "Here is wisdom," he writes
contemptuously. "Here are the principles on which nations are to be governed. Rosebushes and poor rates, rather than steam engines and independence. Mortality and cottages with weather stains, rather than health
and long life with edifices which time cannot mellow." To Macaulay's way
of thinking, Victorian progress would prevail throughout much of the
nineteenth century, economic improvement was natural and inevitable,
and the march toward greater and greater national wealth would be
steady and triumphant. British prosperity, in fact, was divinely sanctified,
a gift of "the supreme being" and of "those general laws"—such as the
laws governing a laissez-faire economic system—"which it has pleased
him to establish in the physical and in the moral world." While acknowledging that the "present moment is one of great distress" for certain
classes of people, he predicts an England that will grow "richer and
richer," so long as its government is careful not to overregulate its indus-
tries. Summing up his view on the economic "laws" that will produce
such riches, he states: "Our rulers will best promote the improvement of
the nation by strictly confining themselves to their own legitimate duties,
by leaving capital to find its most lucrative course, commodities their fair
prices, industry and intelligence their natural reward."

Friedrich Engels

The Great Towns

Quick Read

- Form: Book.
- Summary: Examines the material conditions of Manchester's slums, noting extreme problems with crowding and sanitation. Objects to the "selfish egotism" of modern society.
- Key Passages: "[T]his isolation of the individual—this narrow-minded egotism—is everywhere the fundamental principle of modern society. But nowhere is this selfish egotism so blatantly evident as in the frantic bustle of the great city" (1566); "Here men regard their fellows not as human beings, but as pawns in the struggle for existence" (1566); "In one of these courts . . . [the] privy is so dirty that the inhabitants of the court can only enter or leave the court if they are prepared to wade through puddles of stale urine and excrement" (1569).

Friedrich Engels's *The Condition of the Working Class* demonstrates that the prosperity applauded by Macaulay and others enriches only the few who achieve full self-realization through their exploitation of the poor. "The vast majority" of the working classes "have had to let so many of their potential creative faculties lie dormant, stunted and unused in order that a small closely-knit group of their fellow citizens could develop to the full the qualities with which nature has endowed them," he asserts. Like Carlyle, Engels attacks the laissez-faire political economy as a system based on "barbarous indifference and selfish egotism"; yet ultimately Engels would propose a more radical solution than paternalistic benevolence to the conflict between manufacturer and worker. This extract focuses on the abominable conditions of the Manchester slums: their overcrowded streets and their lack of sanitation. "In one of these courts," he writes, "just at the entrance where the covered passage ends, there is a privy without a door. This privy is so dirty that the inhabitants of the court can only enter or leave the court if they are prepared to wade through puddles of stale urine and excrement." Moreover, there is no hope of proper sanitation when, as Engels observes, "all that is available is the dirty water of the Irk," a "narrow, coal-black, stinking river full of filth and rubbish," whose banks are covered with "revolting blackish-green puddles of slime." And yet it was possible for such misery to remain invisible to those who did not choose, or did not know where, to look for it. Laborers needed to walk to their workplaces, so the slums were built up in belts around Manchester's inner industrial core; the middle classes, who conducted their business in the city core and had once lived there, had moved to the "suburban heights" connected by direct thoroughfares to the factories and shops at the city center. Thus "plutocrats" and their families could travel in and out of town, by omnibus or carriage, on streets that ran "entirely through working-class districts, without even realizing how close they [were] to the misery and filth which [lay] on both sides of the road." As Engels argues here, such conditions were the inevitable result of an economic system that pitted individual against individual, ignoring the needs of the social whole.

Teaching Suggestions

The Macaulay piece is an essential starting point in any discussion of industrialization. Students need to understand that many Victorians believed in the long-term viability of the laissez-faire economic rationale that Macaulay offers in response to Southey. Questions directed toward Macaulay's logic will help illuminate the ideas that formed the basis of this approach and which still inform economic policy today. Pay particular attention to Macaulay's emphasis on bottom-line "facts" that lead him to believe that "the manufacturer [factory worker] is both in a more comfortable and . . . less dependent situation than the agricultural laborer." He observes, for example, that "The mortality still is, as it always was, greater in towns than in the country. But the difference has diminished in an extraordinary degree." This assumes that only the length, not the quality, of life is important. Note that mortality rates are still higher in the towns than in the country and that the rates themselves could be caused by a number of factors. Macaulay's complete reliance on "bills of mortality and statistical tables" rather than the observable evidence of the slums may seem self-serving to some. Also, his belief in the "general laws" that will lead inevitably to "improvement" is significant. If you are so inclined, you may want to ask students to compare Macaulay's ideas about unregulated markets and bottom-line statistics with the current move to deregulate global markets. Rather than being bothered with labor conditions, Macaulay asks that "capital" be left alone to "find its most lucrative course." Both current and former approaches share a belief in the long-term efficacy of laissez-faire economics.

After reading and discussing Macaulay, students will be startled by Engels's depiction of slum conditions. Rather than going directly to the material details, however, draw attention to Engels's concern with the social relations of modern industrial society: "Here [in the industrial towns] men regard their fellows not as human beings, but as pawns in the struggle for existence." The signs of "barbarous indifference and selfish egotism" are everywhere. Engels's reasoning suggests that it is not enough that working conditions be improved, since the entire social system produced by industrial capitalism is debased; this system puts individuals at odds with each other in a "struggle for existence." It is clear that Engels is envisioning a social system that speaks to communal needs. When you turn to Engels's horrifying descriptions of the slums of Manchester and London, pair these with Charles Kingsley's *Alton Locke*. It is important that your students know that Engels and Kingsley are not exaggerating.

The rural poor had poured into London and the industrial centers in search of employment and found no decent housing ready to receive them. There was no public planning, and no regulation of slum development. Whole families, or a "group of families," might be crowded into a single room, as we see in *Alton Locke*. Landlords had no financial incentive to improve their ramshackle properties or hook up the tenements to the sewage and water systems, if these even existed. One filthy, overflowing privy might serve two hundred families; thus Engels's recurrent emphasis on the "heaps of dirt and filth" spread about the Manchester slum neighborhoods was not empty rhetoric.

It will be helpful to balance these accounts with Ada Nield Chew's first-person description of factory conditions for women. Note that Chew addresses not only the material needs of the workers, but also a desire for something beyond mere existence, such as "Cultivation of the mind" and "enjoy[ment] [of the] beauties of nature." As she states, "the seasons come and go, and we have barely time to notice whether it is spring or summer."

Teaching Clusters

These readings form the backbone to the **Poverty, Unrest, and Social Criticism** cluster. They are most usefully taught as a group, along with selections from reform-minded writers such as Ruskin, Carlyle, and Morris. Carlyle, Engels, and Annie Besant are particularly concerned with the plight of the working poor, as is Elizabeth Barrett Browning, whose "The Cry of the Children" describes underage factory workers ground down by the "mailed heel" of industry (line 155). The excerpts from the 1842–43 Royal Commission on Children's Employment will give added context to Barrett Browning's poem. Dickens's "A Visit to Newgate," on the other hand, focuses on "the guilt and misery" of the criminal classes, while Henry Mayhew's *London Labour and the London Poor* concerns the vagrants, beggars, and street-finders who exist on the margins of the wage economy, like the "boy inmate of the casual wards," a former child factory hand who has "begged [his] way from Manchester to London" (see also *Statement of a Vagrant* on NTO). Additionally, many of these readings would be usefully situated in the **Gender and Sexuality** cluster, paired with selections on women's working conditions. Annie Besant's "The 'White Slavery' of London Match Workers" is a reading that resonates with Ruskin's indictment of glass-cutting factory work, also likened to "the slave trade" in *The Stones of Venice*. Besant describes the inhumane, grueling working conditions of women in the match factory who perform tedious and repetitive tasks for hours on end and receive a pittance in return. Similarly, in "A Living Wage for Factory Girls at Crewe," Chew laments that "To take what may be considered a good week's wage the work has to be so close and unremitting that we cannot be said to 'live'— we merely exist. We eat, we sleep, we work, endlessly, ceaselessly work, from Monday morning till Saturday night, without remission." Chew

longs for some of the leisure hours that Florence Nightingale finds so oppressive: "Cultivation of the mind? How is it possible?" The factory girls
have no time to read, to enjoy nature, or to take recreation. All of these
selections would be usefully contextualized by the photographs and illustrations of factory workers and industrial conditions included in *Norton
Topics Online* "Industrialism: Progress or Decline?"

Discussion Questions

1. Why does Macaulay believe that the manufacturing system is not as
   "tyrannical" as Robert Southey believed it was? What is Macaulay's
   logic?
2. Explain Macaulay's views on historical progress.
3. Macaulay states that "Our rulers will best promote the improvement
   of the nation by strictly confining themselves to their own legitimate
   duties, by leaving capital to find its most lucrative course, commodities their fair prices, industry and intelligence their natural reward."
   These ideas are still current today in the global market, where there
   is a move to deregulate business and smooth the way for free trade.
   Do you agree with Macaulay that rulers should let businesses set
   their own labor standards rather than interfere with regulations about
   safety and quality of life?
4. Discuss Engels's view of "modern society." How are social relations in
   industrial society connected to economic conditions?
5. Compare Annie Besant's description of working conditions for the
   London match workers with Ada Nield Chew's account. How is each
   approach different?

Further Resources

NORTON TOPICS ONLINE

The Civilizing Mission
   Thomas Babington Macaulay, Minute on Indian Education
Industrialism: Progress or Decline?
   Elizabeth Barrett Browning, The Cry of the Children
   Elizabeth Gaskell, *Preface to* Mary Barton
   Henry Mayhew, *from* London Labour and the London Poor
   Annie Besant, *from* The 'White Slavery' of London Match Workers
   C. Duncan Lucas, *from* Scenes from Factory London
   Ada Nield Chew, A Living Wage for Factory Girls at Crewe
   Parliamentary Testimony

NORTON ONLINE ARCHIVE

The Communist Manifesto

The "Woman Question": The Victorian Debate about Gender

Even the most radical authors on the "woman question" seldom argued that men and women were essentially similar. They debated instead about the extent of their dissimilarity, what proper relations between the sexes ought to be, which "womanly" qualities were fixed and inherent and which culturally determined, and what sorts of activities women were best suited to or disabled from attempting. The notions that the sexes complement one another in their differences, that essential characteristics befit men and women for certain duties and activities and disqualify them for others, and that each sex is best suited for a particular social space underpin the Victorian ideology of separate spheres: men's work lies in the marketplace, women's in the home. A troublesome contradiction underlies arguments like these and Victorian gender ideology in general: woman is said to be intrinsically nobler than man, yet is at the same time an inferior who must be (in Ruskin's words) "protected from all danger and temptation" because she lacks the moral strength to stand on her own ("Of Queens' Gardens"). In Coventry Patmore's best-selling poem *The Angel in the House*, which celebrates woman's "worth as Maid and Wife" (line 38), the angel-woman is eulogized as "The best half of creation's best" (line 29), nature's "aim and its epitome" (line 32), almost as if in compensation for her delimitation within the domestic sphere. "I'll teach how noble man should be / To match with such a lovely mate" (lines 43–44). Yet many Victorian women showed little resemblance to Patmore's angel and objected to the limitations placed upon them by the domestic ideal. Florence Nightingale asks, for instance, "Why have women passion, intellect, moral activity—these three—and a place in society where no one of the three can be exercised?" (*Cassandra*). A few decades after Nightingale wrote these words, Mona Caird advocated for "the real independence of women, and thence of the readjustment of their position in relation to men and to society" by challenging the institution of marriage ("Marriage"). Caird's position on "free marriage" was radical for the time, but illustrates the increasing unhappiness middle-class women felt in their restricted roles. The 1890s would bring not resolution to the "woman question," but more questions and a full attack on the gender assumptions of mid-Victorian England.

Sarah Stickney Ellis

The Women of England: Their Social Duties and Domestic Habits

Quick Read

- Form: Book.
- Summary: Defines women's role as that of moral arbiter in relation to men.
- Key Passages: "To men belongs the potent—(I had almost said the *omnipotent*) consideration of worldly aggrandizement" (1584); man's

vision of "[woman's] character, clothed in moral beauty, has scattered the clouds before his mental vision, and sent him back to that beloved home, a wiser and a better man" (1584); "The women of England . . . have obtained a degree of importance in society far beyond what their unobtrusive virtues would appear to claim" (1584).

This excerpt argues for the "separate spheres" appropriate to men and women. Men pursue "worldly aggrandizement" and "close their ears against the voice of conscience" when they labor within "the mart, the exchange, or the public assembly." The "influence of women" is necessary to "counteract . . . the growing evils of society"; in fact, woman goes into the workplace herself in a certain sense, as man's "second conscience," a "secret influence" borne inwardly. Ellis values self-renunciation, or what she calls "disinterested kindness," in women. They should not aspire to philosophical knowledge or learnedness in general, but rather to "the majesty of moral greatness," and train themselves to begin and end each day "on the watch for every opportunity of doing good to others." Though Ellis argues adamantly for the constriction of women's roles, she aggrandizes women nonetheless and argues that they "have obtained a degree of importance in society far beyond what their unobtrusive virtues would appear to claim" because theirs is "the high and holy duty of cherishing and protecting the minor morals of life, from whence springs all that is elevated in purpose, and glorious in action." Ellis writes approvingly of the domestic woman's pervasive and invisible power: "female influence" guides the husbands, fathers, sons, and brothers who inhabit the public realm, and spreads even to the far reaches of the Empire—"as far as the noble daring of Britain has sent forth her adventurous sons, and that is to every point of danger on the habitable globe."

Coventry Patmore

The Angel in the House

"The nuptial contrasts are the poles / On which the heavenly spheres revolve," writes Coventry Patmore in The Angel in the House (lines 63–64). Patmore's sentimental depictions of marriage were popular at the time, highly praised by Ruskin and others who supported the tenets of domestic ideology. "How fortunate it is they're friends / And he will ne'er be wroth with her!" Patmore says brightly, describing an indulgent and loving husband; within the domestic circle, or so the official story goes, the wife is reverenced and pampered, and the husband is solicitous and appreciative. However, not all husbands were benign, and marriage could be a dangerous trap for a woman. Marriage was said to be woman's mission, but it was a perilous mission; by law, a husband had full rights over his wife's body and property. Novels like Anne Brontë's The Tenant of Wildfell Hall (1848), Wilkie Collins's The Woman in White (1860), and Anthony Trollope's He

Knew He Was Right (1869) depict the terrible circumstances of women trapped within unhappy marriages. In Elizabeth Gaskell's "The Old Nurse's Story," after proud Miss Maude disgraces her class standing and allies herself to a "dark foreigner," she and her child are abandoned by her husband and disowned by her father, who turns mother and child out into the winter storm where both die from exposure. Maude's ghost haunts the pages of the text, rather as the figure of the abused and miserable wife haunts Victorian society as the spectral double in Patmore's *Angel in the House*.

John Ruskin

Of Queens' Gardens

Quick Read

- Form: Lecture.
- Summary: Defines men's role as being in the public sphere, women's as being in the domestic sphere.
- Key Passages: "The man's power is active, progressive, defensive. . . . His intellect is for speculation and invention" (1587); "the woman's power is for rule, not for battle,—and her intellect is not for invention or creation, but for sweet ordering, arrangement, and decision" (1587); the "woman . . . must be enduringly, incorruptibly good; instinctively, infallibly wise—wise, not for self-development, but for self-renunciation" (1588).

One of the most thorough mid-Victorian explications of the ideology of "separate spheres" can be found in Ruskin's "Of Queens' Gardens" (1865), one of two lectures collected under the title *Sesame and Lilies*. "By her office, and place," the woman, safe at home, is "protected from all danger and temptation," asserts Ruskin. The man, meanwhile, is busy with "his rough work in the open world," where he is battered and bruised by his efforts in the public sphere: "often he must be wounded, or subdued, often misled, and *always* hardened." But then he returns at night to his household, which is a "sacred place, a vestal temple" watched over by the domestic angel. Here he is soothed and softened by the feminine influence (just as he guards his wife from the dangers of the marketplace), and can return to his "rough work" the next day with fresh vigor and a renewed moral sense. The ideal woman in "Of Queens' Gardens" is "enduringly, incorruptibly good; instinctively, infallibly wise—wise not for self-development, but for self-renunciation." And yet a great deal of training must be expended in making her realize her enduring goodness and instinctive wisdom, as such lectures as Ruskin's were designed to accomplish.

Florence Nightingale

Cassandra

Florence Nightingale takes aim at the useless pursuits engaged in by well-to-do women. For her, the home is no Ruskinian haven of feminine virtue, but a place where women are encouraged and even obligated to while away their hours with trivial activities ("sitting around a table in the drawing-room, looking at prints, doing worsted work, and reading little books"); they "find it impossible to follow up . . . systematically" any worthier occupation, because they must "allow themselves *willingly* to be interrupted at all hours" by the exigencies of social engagements. The self-abnegation that Ellis, Ruskin, and Patmore praise, Nightingale criticizes: women "have accustomed themselves to consider intellectual occupation as a merely selfish amusement, which it is their 'duty' to give up for every trifler more selfish than themselves." To their exalted view of the "separate spheres" of men and women, compare Nightingale's description of marriage among the privileged classes, in which partners chatter about dinner guests, social engagements, and other trivialities, and "never seem to have anything to say to one another . . . about any great religious, social, political questions or feelings."

Teaching Suggestions

Although the writings of Patmore, Ruskin, and Ellis will seem hopelessly outdated to students, they provide an essential context within which to read much nineteenth-century literature, from Dante Gabriel Rossetti's "The Blessed Damozel" to George Bernard Shaw's *Mrs Warren's Profession*. It might be helpful to organize these readings into three groups: those that elucidate the doctrine of separate spheres, those that depict working-class sexuality, and those that reject the principles of domestic ideology (supported by other readings as suggested below in the "Teaching Clusters" section). In the first group, direct your questions toward the particular qualities that define women as separate from men. Ask students to pay particular attention to the logic at work in Ruskin's "Of Queens' Gardens." Ruskin doesn't actually say that women are inherently good or pure, only that the "true wife . . . must be enduringly, incorruptibly good." The implication is that she must be educated to her position, and thus must also be guarded and "protected from all danger and temptation." In the second group of readings, it is important for students to know that the doctrine of separate spheres for men and women was largely a middle-class doctrine; working-class women, married and otherwise, could not afford to stay within the domestic sphere. By mid-century, one-quarter of England's female population worked, the majority as domestic ser-vants, seamstresses, factory operatives, and rural laborers. In addition to these lawful occupations, many women worked as prostitutes. The anonymous selection on "The Great Social Evil" offers an insight into the life of the prostitute, although whether this piece was written by a prostitute or by someone else is unclear. The writer's demand that society should "Teach [prostitutes] what is right and tutor [them] in good before you punish [them] for doing wrong" is not completely out of line with Ruskin's view of women as needing moral guidance before they can achieve their "true" nature. Questions about the authorship of the selection will lead students into a closer evaluation of the separate-spheres doctrine. The third grouping will provide students with some historical perspective. Mona Caird's piece against the institution of marriage dismantles Ruskin's view of the home as a haven from worldly cares. At one point, Caird suggests that marriage is one of society's "systems of legalized injustice." Although these are harsh words, even for the 1890s, they demonstrate the extensive social transformations taking place in the last decade of the century.

Teaching Cluster

The "Woman Question" readings can be taught as a self-contained unit or in tandem with literary works from the **Gender and Sexuality** cluster, such as Barrett Browning's *Aurora Leigh*, Gaskell's "The Old Nurse's Story," Christina Rossetti's *Goblin Market*, or Bernard Shaw's *Mrs Warren's Profession*. Instructive prose pieces in this category include George Eliot's "Margaret Fuller and Mary Wollstonecraft" and John Stuart Mill's *Subjection of Women*. These selections can also be usefully supplemented by those in *Norton Topics Online*, "The Woman Question." Moreover, this last category can be taught in conjunction with the extracts from Annie Besant's "The 'White Slavery' of London Match Workers" and Ada Nield Chew's "A Living Wage for Factory Girls at Crewe," both in the special section "Industrialism: Progress or Decline?" (See also the "Industrialism" section in *Norton Topics Online*.) From the "Evolution" section, Charles Darwin's extract on sexual selection is relevant. If you are teaching a Victorian-only survey and have time to include a novel that deals explicitly with the situation of women (Charlotte Brontë's *Jane Eyre* or Eliot's *Middlemarch*, for example), you may find it useful to break up your discussion midway through and use some or all of the woman-question selections to historically contextualize and deepen your readings of the novel.

Discussion Questions

1. Compare John Ruskin's and Sarah Stickney Ellis's ideas about women's roles in relation to men's. What kind of education are women suited for? Are women equal to men in importance? What are women's particular qualities?
2. Florence Nightingale states, "Husbands and wives . . . talk about who shall come to dinner, who is to live in this lodge and who in that . . . or when they shall go to London." Compare Nightingale's view of male-female relationships and domestic life with Ruskin's.
3. Do the ideas set forth in "The Great Social Evil" conflict with the views of womanhood set forth by Ruskin, Patmore, and Ellis? The anonymous writer states, for example, that "virtue . . . is . . . the prin-

ciple, the essence, which keeps watch and ward over the conduct. . . .
No such principle ever kept watch and ward over me." Compare this
with Ruskin's comments about the man who "guards the woman"
from the hardened public sphere.

4. Do you think that "The Great Social Evil" was written by a prostitute
   or by someone else? Think about the writer's request to "Teach us
   what is right and tutor us in good before you punish us for doing
   wrong"; compare this to the writer's bold assertion, "What have [pros-
   titutes] to be ashamed of?"

5. Compare the views of marriage in Mona Caird's essay, "Marriage,"
   and George Meredith's sonnet sequence, *Modern Love*.

Further Resources

NORTON TOPICS ONLINE

The Woman Question
   The Nature of Woman
      John Ruskin, *from* Of Queens' Gardens
      Charlotte Brontë, *from* Jane Eyre
   The New Woman
      Eliza Lynn Linton, *from* The Girl of the Period
      George Gissing, *from* The Odd Women
   Other Voices
      Henry Mayhew, The Life of a Coster Girl
      Henry Mayhew, Interview of a Trousers Hand
Industrialism: Progress or Decline?
   Elizabeth Gaskell, *Preface to* Mary Barton
   Henry Mayhew, *from* London Labour and the London Poor
   Annie Besant, *from* The 'White Slavery' of London Match Workers
   Ada Nield Chew, A Living Wage for Factory Girls at Crewe

Empire and National Identity

Any serious study of Victorian literature must take into account
Britain's history as an imperial power, for this history shapes the nation's
understanding of its own identity: its sense of itself as a superior culture
and civilizing presence in the world. Few writings dramatize this connection between culture and politics as vividly as does Thomas Babington
Macaulay's "Minute on Indian Education," written just two short years
before the beginning of Victoria's reign. In his memorandum, Macaulay
advocates the imposition of British literature and language in place of India's own rich literary tradition, which he dismisses as "of small intrinsic
value only." He argues that it is necessary to indoctrinate "the millions
whom we govern" with "English . . . taste[s] . . . opinions, . . . morals, and
. . . intellect" to achieve the "intellectual improvement of the [Indian]
people." The unspoken idea here is that education and political control

are synonymous. By "improving" the Indian masses with the "intrinsic superiority of . . . Western literature," Britain can remake its colony in its own image and achieve a control unattainable by any other means. Political dominance is thus figured as the benign face of cultural hegemony, enacted in the service of altruistic motives. This mollifying image of benign imperialism was similarly employed at home, imbuing the British public with an elevated conception of its culture and endowing its triumphalism with a higher, more idealistic justification than mere economic exploitation. To this end, the apparatus of imperial propaganda was expanded, manufacturing new ways to overlay economic desires with uplifting moral concepts. Such gestures can be found in the poetry of Tennyson and Eliza Cooke, for instance, or in the work of historian James Anthony Froude, who insists on the improved lot of the British-governed Trinidad peoples.

All of these myths were contested by anticolonial critics through a variety of means. In his rebuttal to Froude, Trinidad scholar John Jacob Thomas deduced from a dismantling of Froude's own writings that skin color rather than intellectual capacity was the basis for the colonial hierarchy Froude defended. The language that Macaulay wished to force on the colonial populations now becomes the subject of Thomas's linguistic examination as he explodes the myth of the "imperial whole" by showing how the rapacious intentions of the colonialists were revealed in their use of possessive pronouns. A similar turning of the tables is accomplished by the Indian commentator T. N. Mukherji, who co-opts the gaze of anthropological inquiry that has been directed toward his countrymen at the Indian and Colonial Exhibition of 1886 and directs it toward the British themselves. Mukherji's narrative suggests that, by constructing an arbitrary opposition to a cultural other, the British create their own national identity, "any deviation from which is seriously noticed." Other writings, moreover, alerted the public to the naked face of imperial aggression. The investigative works of William Howard Russell, for example, covering the aftermath of the Indian Mutiny, stressed the fact that imperialists were "only excited by considerations of revenue." Russell further underscored the ignoble motives of empire by exposing its use of violent force and coercion to gain its ends. "That force is the base of our rule I have no doubt," Russell wrote, "for I see nothing else but force employed in our relations with the governed." By the time Joseph Chamberlain made his speech on the "the true conception of empire," what he took to be the first phase of empire, the era of "pecuniary advantage [taken by] the grasping and absentee landlord," had become an embarrassment. The selections in this topic introduce students to a range of responses to British imperialism and provide a critical context within which to read literature that seems less obviously related to questions of empire. Concepts of British strength or superiority, images of masculine fortitude or wifely subjection, and fantasies of wise paternalism or preordained social divisions all find their cognates in the imperial enterprise.

Thomas Babington Macaulay

Minute on Indian Education

Quick Read

- Form: Official memorandum.
- Summary: Countering East India Company council members who desire the continuation of education in Sanskrit and Persian for Indian students, Macaulay advocates that imperial educational funds be directed to a curriculum of primarily European texts, taught exclusively in English.
- Key Passages: "I am quite ready to take the Oriental learning at the valuation of the Orientalists themselves. I have never found one among them who could deny that a single shelf of a good European library was worth the whole native literature of India and Arabia" (1610); "I certainly never met with any Orientalist who ventured to maintain that the Arabic and Sanscrit poetry could be compared to that of the great European nations. But, when we pass from works of imagination to works in which facts are recorded and general principles investigated, the superiority of the Europeans becomes absolutely immeasurable" (1610); "It is said that the Sanscrit and Arabic are the languages in which the sacred books of a hundred millions of people are written. . . . But to encourage the study of a literature admitted to be of small intrinsic value only because that literature inculcates the most serious errors on the most important subjects, is a course hardly reconcilable with reason, with morality, or even with that very neutrality which ought, as we all agree, to be sacredly observed" (1611); "it is impossible for us, with our limited means, to attempt to educate the body of the people. We must at present do our best to form a class who may be interpreters between us and the millions whom we govern; a class of persons, Indian in blood and colour, but English in taste, in opinions, in morals, and in intellect" (1611–12).

As Britain moved toward the second half of the nineteenth century, colonial rule was increasingly advanced as a mission of enlightenment and improvement. Under the guise of a pedagogical policy to educate the Indian masses, Macaulay advocates a program of social engineering in which a class of indigenous peoples is taught to be surrogates for their British overlords and spread Western learning to the wider population. In this way, the English texts that Macaulay decrees the Indians should be compelled to learn become the real counterparts to their colonial rulers. Macaulay considers the English works themselves to be "vehicles of ethical and political instruction." Essential in this project is the exclusion from the curriculum of indigenous literatures, which cannot be allowed to divert attention from a Western canon and which must be suppressed and devalued in order to reinforce the marginalized, subordinate position of the satellite culture. As always, national identity is forged by comparison with the cultural other. Discrediting Indian language, learning, and religion, Macaulay says that these are "barren of useful knowledge" and "hardly reconcilable with reason, morality, or even with that very neutrality which ought, as we all agree, to be sacredly preserved." His ultimate goal is to create "a class of persons, Indian in blood and colour, but English in taste, in opinions, in morals, and in intellect."

James Anthony Froude

The English in the West Indies

Quick Read

- Form: Book.
- Summary: Arguing against self-rule for Trinidad, Froude insists that the colonized population is content and that the British government, in the present period as well as during the years before the slaves were emancipated, has always been beneficial for the black inhabitants of the English West Indies.
- Key Passages: "One associates colonial life instinctively with what is new and modern" (1622); "the earth does not contain any peasantry so well off, so well cared for, so happy, so sleek and contented as the sons and daughters of the emancipated slaves in the English West Indian Islands" (1622); "theirs is a condition which admits of no improvement: were they independent, they might quarrel among themselves, and the weaker become the bondmen of the stronger; under the beneficent despotism of the English Government, which knows no difference of colour and permits no oppression, they can sleep, lounge, and laugh away their lives as they please, fearing no danger" (1623); "[the slave] had a bad time of it occasionally, and the plantation whip and the branding irons are not all dreams, yet his owner cared for him at least as much as he cared for his cows and his horses" (1623).

Froude tries to ensure the maintenance of the imperial status quo by demonstrating that the ruling hierarchy is in perfect balance, using language that suggests a "natural"—even divine—order. As Froude states in his first paragraph, the British influence in the West Indies has been present in the islands long enough to "take root and grow." The imperial expedient of overlaying an indigenous culture with a foreign one is presented as an organic process that has resulted in an environment where the local population is "perfectly contented." To bolster this view of a predetermined order that must not be upset, Froude brings a panoply of Christian images to bear on his subject. In the tones of an evangelist fulminating from the pulpit, Froude warns that the colonizers "will be sinning against

the light" if they sanction self-rule. According to Froude, even the enslaved ancestors of the current islanders had been rescued from a fallen
state, for the slaves who "were taken away out of Africa, as compared with
those who were left at home, were as the 'elect to salvation,' who after a
brief purgatory are secured an eternity of blessedness." If the colonial ad-
ministrators "force them to govern themselves," the present islanders will
"inevitably fall" from their present Edenic state. All of Froude's Christian
rhetoric, however, cannot disguise the economic principle underpinning
the imperial project. Nowhere is this made clearer than in the passage in
which Froude praises the bygone slave owner for caring for his slaves "at
least as much as he cared for his cows and his horses." "Kind usage to animals is more economical than barbarity," he concludes.

John Jacob Thomas

Froudacity

Quick Read

- Form: Book-length essay.
- Summary: Thomas exposes the racist basis of Froude's *The English
  in the West Indies* and dismantles his argument against island self-
  rule.
- Key Passages: "Mr. Froude is speaking dogmatically here of *his*, or
  rather *our*, West Indies" (1624); "Why, Mr. Froude, who speaks of us
  as dogs and horses, suggests that the same kindliness of treatment
  that secures the attachment of those noble brutes would have the
  same result in our case" (1625); "What are *we* Negroes of the present day to be grateful for to the US, personified by Mr. Froude and
  the Colonial Office exportations?" (1625); "does Mr. Froude, in the
  fatuity of his skin-pride, believe that educated men, worthy of the
  name, would be otherwise than resentful, if not disgusted, at being
  shunted out of bread in their own native land, which their parents'
  labours and taxes have made desirable, in order to afford room to
  blockheads, vulgarians, or worse, imported from beyond the seas?"
  (1625).

This excerpt is an illustration of a sophisticated anticolonial critique that
was beginning to develop among the indigenous intellectual classes of
the colonies in the last quarter of the nineteenth century. Thomas's essay
pierces the filters of self-justification and rationalization in Froude's writings and clarifies that author's racist stance, calling attention to "Mr.
Froude's scorn of the Negroes' skin," and the "fatuity of his skin-pride"
while bringing our attention to the peculiarities of imperialist language, a
medium through which the British Empire maintained its power as tenaciously as it did through the threat of armed violence. Thomas throws into
question the principal message of Froude's essay—that the central colo-

nial administration should continue to preside over the population of the British West Indies. Moreover, he illuminates the central discrepancy in Froude's polemic—that although Froude maintains that no difference exists between the capabilities of whites and blacks, he nonetheless argues that some alleged natural order of things has ordained that whites dominate blacks. Thomas implicitly asks: if blacks do not fail to measure up "for any intellectual or moral disqualification," and if Froude himself states that "there is no original or congenital difference between the capacity of the White and Negro races," what then is left to support Froude's call for the maintenance of the imperial status quo? Through a process of elimination, Thomas isolates skin color as the basis of Froude's convictions about the difference between the West Indians and their rulers.

T. N. Mukherji

A Visit to Europe

Quick Read

- Form: From a collection of newspaper articles.
- Summary: Mukherji, an Indian Brahman and government administrator attending the 1886 Indian and Colonial Exhibition in England as part of an official delegation, observes how he and his Indian compatriots are perceived by the British and, in turn, appraises the customs and attitudes of the Britons themselves.
- Key Passages: "They were as much astonished to see the Indians produce works of art with the aid of rude apparatus they themselves had discarded long ago, as a Hindu would be to see a chimpanzee officiating as a priest in a funeral ceremony and reading out Sanskrit texts from a palm leaf book spread before him" (1627); "Of course, every nation in the world considers other nations as savages or at least much inferior to itself. . . . We did not therefore wonder that the common people should take us for barbarians, awkward as we were in every respect" (1628); "She was delighted with everything I said . . . and complimented me for the performance of the band brought from *my country, viz.,* the West Indian band composed of Negroes and Mulattos, which compliment made me wince a little, but nevertheless I went on chattering for a quarter of an hour and furnishing her with sufficient means to annihilate her friend Minnie, Jane or Lizzy or whoever she might be, and to brag among her less fortunate relations for six months to come of her having actually seen and talked to a genuine 'Blackie'" (1630).

In this journalistic piece, Mukherji uses the occasion of the Indian and Colonial Exhibition of 1886, whose ostensible object was to provide an educational survey of colonial cultures, to supplant the Empire's sweeping, inexact representations of India's people by representing himself as an individual, an astute social commentator, and a proud Brahman who by no means takes the British way of life as the apex of civilization. Mukherji attempts to show what it is like to be a member of a colonized race in Victoria's Empire, one who must endure being not only an object of economic exploitation but also an object of a curious gaze that is forever trying to categorize his every trait in the service of a "scientific" system of classification. As he surveys the exhibition, a paradigmatic site of the nexus of knowledge and power in the colonial enterprise, and where the conquest of the Indian self and culture is staged in the exhibits created by English Orientalist "authorities," Mukherji debunks this power by demonstrating how it seems always to be on the brink of degenerating into a hunt for sensational, "interesting" novelty. Mukherji first shows the parochial, circumscribed nature of the British viewpoint as the British visitors gaze and comment on the human "exhibits" at the Indian and Colonial Exhibition. Having been inspired by his European experience "to philosophise on the material difference that exists between our own estimate of ourselves and the estimate which others form of us," Mukherji then tries to reclaim his non-European subjectivity by directing, toward the Britons themselves, the anthropological gaze encouraged by the exhibition. Succeeding sections of his essay present reversals of perspective between colonizer and colonized that call into question the unwritten imperial rule that colonized peoples cannot define or represent themselves but must be defined and represented through "objective," scientific Western interpretation.

Teaching Suggestions

Macaulay's "Minute on Indian Education" provides an excellent vantage point from which to introduce students to the tenets of high-imperial ideology. His insistence upon the "intrinsic superiority of . . . Western literature" in the service of "the intellectual improvement of the [Indian] people" exposes an underlying rationale discernable throughout many of the readings in this section. Direct students' attention in particular to Macaulay's dismissive attitude toward Indian learning and religion, which he defines as "false history, false astronomy, false medicine . . . [and] false religion." From here you can move into an examination of the self-legitimating rhetorical devices of pro-imperial writings, ranging from Chamberlain's influential political speeches redefining empire-building as a civilizing mission to the patriotic writings, of Tennyson and Eliza Cook. Cook's poetry, for example, disguises a system where the "Briton may . . . boldly claim his right" to a "vast domain" on which "the sun never sets" by representing Britons as international custodians protecting the "wronged and the weak" (lines 31–34, 22). Ask students to take particular note of the manner in which imperialism is justified in the pro-imperialism selections. For example, in a poem on the Indian and Colonial Exhibition of

1886, Tennyson capitalizes on the myth of there being "one imperial whole" or imperial "family" and constructs a union among peoples that are in actuality radically divided in terms of power. Like Tennyson, Froude takes up the idea of the happy imperial family, self-contentedly claiming that "these poor brothers-in-law of ours [the former slaves of Trinidad under British domination] are the most perfectly contented specimens of the human race to be found upon the planet." Froude perpetuates the idea of a neutral, disinterested paternalism as he celebrates the "beneficent despotism of the English Government, which knows no difference of colour and permits no oppression." Invite students to examine Froude's rationale, comparing it with Macaulay's. While Macaulay's point is that Western culture is "intrinsically" better than Indian culture (an idea that is taken for granted) and therefore more beneficial to the indigenous population as a learning tool than its own intellectual traditions, Froude argues that the British presence benefits the West Indian people because they would be unable to govern themselves as wisely as their benevolent overseers. The "West Indian negro," Froude maintains, "has been a lucky mortal. He was taken away from Dahomey and Ashantee—to be a slave indeed, but a slave to a less cruel master than he would have found at home."

Such avowals did not go unchallenged, of course, and it is important for students to read and understand the range of responses to colonial dominance. Thomas's rebuttal to Froude is lively and witty, worthy of a good close read. Remind your students that Thomas was a linguist who pays careful attention to the language of the imperialist apologist. Note, for example, Thomas's use of italics and capital letters, his scathing use of irony, and his appropriation of Froude's language. In addition to Thomas's piece, Mukherji's rich, entertaining essay provides another important response to the colonial situation. This selection makes a good contrast to Macaulay's condescending assertions about Indian language and learning, reversing the perspective of the colonial gaze. Students may be invited here to examine how national identity is formed through comparison with a cultural other. The complex exchanges in this narrative bring up questions of class, gender, race, and nationality. Mukherji makes several references to the "common people" and the "simple villagers," for example, and at one point notes that the "good old lady" who wants Mukherji to carry news back to her nephew in India does "not speak the English [he] ordinarily hear[s]." Along with Mukherji's essay, Russell's news dispatches on the Cawnpore massacre provide an excellent rejoinder to Macaulay. Russell is very explicit in his criticism of the British, asking "whether India is the better for [British] rule, so far as regards the social condition of the great mass of the people." In the wake of the massacre, he also questions "if there is not some lesson and some warning given to [the British] race in reference to India by the tremendous catastrophe of Cawnpore." While Russell's ideas may not have been shared by the majority of his fellows, these excerpts from the London *Times* demonstrate that the news was not comprised solely of jingoistic rhetoric.

Teaching Clusters

The works in this section generally fall into the category of **Progress, Science, and Colonial Expansion**; however, they can also be usefully included in the **Gender and Sexuality** cluster to give context to writings on Victorian masculinity. William Ernest Henley and Rudyard Kipling are the obvious companion pieces here; Kipling's "The Man Who Would Be King," along with "The White Man's Burden," for example, would be appropriate in either grouping. Additionally, earlier works by Newman and Tennyson (the passive masculinity depicted in "The Lotos-Eaters," for instance, or the conflicted musings of the "Ulysses" narrator) would provide an instructive contrast in the **Gender and Sexuality** cluster, especially placed alongside Arnold's comments about the "feminized" Celts. If you would like to focus particularly on British national identity, then this piece by Arnold is a must, in addition to his "The Function of Criticism at the Present Time," which is included in the individual author section. Macaulay's "Minute on Indian Education" is also essential here, as is Eliza Cook's "The Englishman." Students will be thus reminded that women (including non-elite women) helped to sustain images of patriotic masculinity. It's also worth noting that the readings in the "Empire and National Identity" section can be taught in pairs, especially if you do not have time to address several selections together. Thus, the Macaulay and Russell pieces speak to each other, as do the Cook and Mackay pieces, and so on.

Discussion Questions

1. What is Macaulay's attitude toward Indian learning, language, and religion? How does that attitude influence his ideas about the proper way to educate the Indian people?
2. Can education, as envisioned by Macaulay, be a form of political domination? Why or why not?
3. What do you think of Macaulay's mission to "form a class of persons, Indian in blood and colour, but English in taste, in opinions, in morals, and in intellect"?
4. How does the poetry of Tennyson and Eliza Cook legitimize the imperial project?
5. How is the idea of the happy "imperial family" depicted in works by Froude and Tennyson?
6. According to Froude, why are the Trinidad people of his time better off under British rule than under their own self-rule?
7. In his rebuttal to Froude's essay, Thomas quotes liberally from Froude. Locate and discuss examples of how Thomas uses Froude's statements against Froude himself.
8. Discuss how Thomas's rhetorical style differs from Froude's. How does Thomas use irony?
9. Discuss the phenomenon of the Indian and Colonial Exhibition and the ways in which Indians participated in it. What is the relationship

between the collector of knowledge and the subject of that knowledge, between the collection's exhibitor and his exhibits? Explore how being an authority on a subject implies having authority over that subject. In other words, examine what Mukherji's narrative suggests about the alliance between knowledge and power.

10. Discuss Arnold's views of the English national character. What do you make of his statement that "Celtic nature, [in] its nervous exaltation, [has] something feminine in [it]," for example? How does this compare with the "Anglo-Saxon temperament"?

Further Resources

NORTON TOPICS ONLINE

Victorian Imperialism
  Race and Victorian Science
    Edward Tylor, Primitive Culture
    Benjamin Kidd, The Control of the Tropics
    John Jacob Thomas, Froudacity
  Colonialism and Gender
    Charlotte Brontë, *from* Jane Eyre
    Anna Leonowens, The English Governess at the Siamese Court
    Josephine Butler, Our Indian Fellow Subjects
  The Civilizing Mission
    Thomas Babington Macaulay, Minute on Indian Education
    Rudyard Kipling, The White Man's Burden
    Joseph Chamberlain, The True Conception of Empire

Late Victorians

Michael Field (Katherine Bradley and Edith Cooper)

Using the pseudonym of Michael Field, Katherine Bradley and Edith Cooper wrote lyrics that celebrated lesbian desire and harmonious relationships between women. Much of their early poetry draws from Greek mythology and the Sapphic tradition, creating a pagan world of exuberant sensuality. In "It was deep April and the morn," for example, the speaker proclaims, "My Love and I took hands and swore, / Against the world, to be / Poets and lovers evermore, / To laugh and dream on Lethe's shore, / ... Indifferent to heaven and hell" (lines 4–16). Like Swinburne, the Field poets found in classical antiquity a way of exploring nonheteronormative sexuality and bodily pleasures. Unlike Swinburne's verse, however, Field's lyrics articulate a joyful, life-affirming, and salubrious vision of erotic love. "When injuries my spirit bruise, / Allaying virtue ye infuse," notes the speaker of "Maids, not to you my mind doth change" (lines 15–16). Here same-sex desire and the contemplation of the female body offer ways of experiencing one's full being, intellectually, emotionally, and physically.

Maids, not to you my mind doth change

Quick Read

- Form: Sapphic lyric.
- Themes: Lesbian desire; intuitive sympathy between women; the healing capacity of female same-sex relationships.
- Key Passages: "Men I defy, allure, estrange," line 2; "ye to manifold desire / Can yield response," lines 9–10; "When injuries my spirit bruise, / Allaying virtue ye infuse," lines 15–16.

Teaching Suggestions

Field's Sapphic lyric "Maids, not to you my mind doth change" imagines a feminine world of mutual sympathy between like spirits. Invite students to compare the different spheres of male and female love presented here. "Men I defy, allure, estrange, / Prostrate, make bond or free" (lines 2–3), asserts the speaker. Sexual desire between men and women is marked by alienation and debasement. Moreover, in the heterosexual world of male-female relationships, "Soon doth a lover's patience tire" (line 8). The homosocial, homoerotic world of feminine companionship, in contrast, offers "no thought of pain, / Peril, satiety" (lines 6–7). Ask students to think about the invocation: "But ye to manifold desire / Can yield response" (lines 9–10). Here, "manifold desire" is connected to an intuitive understanding of the lover's state of mind: "ye know / When for long, museful days I pine, / The presage of my heart divine" (lines 10–12). Inherent in lesbian desire is an empathic understanding of the lover's thoughts and feelings; there is no division between self and other, no conflict between lover and beloved, much like the sexual, literary, and intellectual union enacted by the designation "Michael Field." Draw students' attention, in particular, to the restorative qualities of female companionship: "When injuries my spirit bruise, / Allaying virtue [a healing agent] ye infuse / With unobtrusive skill" (lines 15–17). Here we have woman as healer, yet this healing is also intrinsically related to the female same-sex bond. This poem would make an excellent companion piece with C. Rossetti's *Goblin Market*, which focuses on the healing power of sisterly love.

Teaching Clusters

Field's work can be taught either in the cluster on **Gender and Sexuality** or in the one on **Aesthetics, Aestheticism, and the Critique of Victorian Values**. In the first category, Swinburne's poetry would provide a useful contrast ("Hermaphroditus," for example), along with Christina Rossetti's *Goblin Market*, mentioned above. In the second category, any number of works would provide an instructive context, such as the selections from Walter Pater's *The Renaissance*, several of Swinburne's poems, or Mary Coleridge's lyrics. "It was deep April, and the morn," in particular, would be well matched with Swinburne's "Hymn to Proserpine." Both

pieces forcefully reject Christianity and turn to paganism to express vitality, yet Swinburne's approach to his material is very different from Field's
jubilant, wholesome sensuality.

Discussion Questions

1. In Field's "Maids, not to you my mind doth change," how does the
   speaker differentiate between male and female spheres of desire?
2. Compare the idea of healing through female love in "Maids, not to
   you my mind doth change" and Christina Rossetti's *Goblin Market*.
3. In "It was deep April, and the morn," the speaker says, "My Love and
   I took hands and swore, / Against the world, to be / Poets and lovers
   evermore" (lines 4–6), while in "A girl," the speaker "leave[s] a page
   half-writ" after being visited by her seductive female muse. Compare
   the connection between writing and desire in each selection.
4. Both Field's "It was deep April and the morn" and Swinburne's "Hymn
   to Proserpine" reject the world of Christian values in favor of a vital,
   dynamic paganism. Compare the concept of paganism in each.

William Ernest Henley

Henley today is perhaps most immediately associated with the plucky
invocation of manly courage expressed in the final lines of "Invictus": "I
am the master of my fate; / I am the captain of my soul" (lines 15–16).
Here, Henley's writing exemplifies quintessential Victorian concepts of
masculinity and imperial fortitude. Like his friend Rudyard Kipling, Henley's brand of manliness was inextricably connected to a patriotic zeal that
has come under sharp criticism since the early twentieth century. Yet students may be surprised to know that Henley was also appreciated by some
of the decadents, such as Arthur Symons, who saw in Henley's writing a
stark vision of a godless world and a unique attention to the suffering
body. "In Hospital," for example, details the actions of a hospital aide who
"has a probe [that] feels to [the speaker] a crowbar" (line 9). Moreover,
Henley's unflinching, spare descriptions and everyday diction brought a
new kind of poetic realism to the genre. "Plasters astray in unnatural-
looking tinware; / Scissors and lint and apothecary's jars," Henley writes,
conveying the bleakness of his surroundings in economical language ("In
Hospital," lines 3–4). Henley's work reminds us that the nineties contained not only aesthetes and New Women, but a multiplicity of voices
and attitudes.

In Hospital

Quick Read

- Form: Blank verse; this piece is the opening section of a twenty-
  eight-part poem.
- Themes: The suffering body; empathy with others; life's unfairness.

- Key Images and Passages: "A square, squat room," line 1; "Scissors and lint and apothecary's jars," line 4; "One has a probe—it feels to me a crowbar," line 9.

Teaching Suggestions

"A square, squat room . . . Drab to the soul, drab to the very daylight": in this manner, the speaker defines the hospital where he waits to be admitted (lines 1–2). Ask students to think about Henley's diction and the general style of writing: spare, plain, ordinary. "Scissors and lint and apothecary's jars," Henley writes. What do these words tell us? What mood do they establish? Clinical? Detached? Cold? Dismal? There are no adjectives here, but the context of the first two lines emphasizes their grim connotations. How does the first stanza set the scene for our understanding of the rest of the poem? The speaker does not make his appearance until the second stanza, in which we learn that he's waiting on "a bench a skeleton would writhe from" (line 5). He is keenly aware that his reality is different from the reality of those around him: "I wait . . . till my heart is lead upon my stomach, / While at their ease two dressers do their chores" (lines 6–8). He experiences pain while others do not: we are drawn into his suffering. Note, however, that his feelings are contained; these lines do not have the detachment of the first stanza, but there is a reserve here that suggests stoicism. The final stanza moves beyond the narrator's agony to the suffering of others: "One [of the dressers] has a probe—it feels to me a crowbar" (line 9). Although the reference is unclear, the implication is that the speaker feels this pain as if it were his own. This line frames the rest of the stanza, which emphasizes the discomfort of others: "A small boy" and "A poor old tramp" (lines 10–11). And finally, in the last line, the speaker concludes: "Life is (I think) a blunder and a shame" (line 12). Ask students what kind of person the speaker is—and how do they arrive at their conclusions? Is he resigned? Self-pitying? Courageous? How do his observations of others lead him to his final conclusion?

Invictus

Quick Read

- Form: Lyric.
- Themes: Courage in the face of danger; the world as overwhelmingly threatening.
- Key Passages: "Out of the night that covers me, / Black as the Pit from pole to pole, / I thank whatever gods may be / For my unconquerable soul" (lines 1–4); "I am the master of my fate; / I am the captain of my soul" (lines 15–16).

Teaching Suggestions

"Out of the night that covers me, / Black as the Pit from pole to pole, / I thank whatever gods may be / For my unconquerable soul," proclaims Henley in the first stanza of "Invictus" (lines 1–4). Although "Invictus" is usually remembered for advocating an extreme form of masculine self-reliance, it also suggests that the world is a very threatening place, without benefit of spiritual solace or any alleviating comfort. It would be instructive to contrast this poem with Kipling's "Recessional," which envisions imperial strength within the context of a divine order. Henley's paean to manly courage, in contrast, admits only the faint possibility of "whatever gods [there] may be" (line 3) and insists instead on the assertion of an isolated self. Moreover, where Henley finds triumph in the solitary, "unconquerable soul," Kipling cautions against "frantic boast" ("Recessional," line 29). Ask students to pay particular attention to the description of the self and its relation to the world in Henley's "Invictus."

Teaching Clusters

As a delineation of late-Victorian masculinity, Henley's poetry can be read alongside other similar works in the **Gender and Sexuality** cluster. Poems such as Kipling's "The White Man's Burden" and "If," as well as Eliza Cook's "The Englishman," will help contextualize "Invictus" and "In Hospital." These same selections would make a useful grouping in the category of **Progress, Science, and Colonial Expansion.** References to an "unconquerable soul" (line 4) and a head that is "bloody, but unbowed" (line 8) in "Invictus" suggest a colonizer's view of the globe, wherein savage races contest but ultimately submit to the civilizing influence of the British. Moreover, although it has a very dark view of the world, "Invictus" conveys a gung-ho attitude conducive to progress in general. This poem would make an interesting contrast with Kipling's "Recessional," which envisions imperial strength in relation to divine wisdom.

Discussion Questions

1. What do we learn about the narrator of "In Hospital" from the description of his surroundings and of other people? How would you characterize him?
2. How does the first stanza of Henley's "In Hospital" affect your reading of the remainder of the poem?
3. How do Henley's diction and style affect your reading of "In Hospital" or "Invictus"?
4. Compare Henley's "Invictus" with Kipling's "Recessional."

Further Resources

NORTON ONLINE ARCHIVE

Waiting
Madam Life's a Piece in Bloom
Barmaid

Robert Louis Stevenson

After more than a century, Robert Louis Stevenson's *Dr. Jekyll and Mr. Hyde* is still an exciting read. It is a resonant work, one that captures the anxieties and contradictions of *fin-de-siècle* Britain. Jekyll's torment in the latter stages of his "strange case" speaks to anyone who has ever possessed a dark secret or felt the yearnings of an unruly id. Freudian analogies spring easily to mind here, but there are also numerous social and cultural implications. *Dr. Jekyll and Mr. Hyde* depicts an enclosed universe, claustrophobic, but very real in its evocation of discreet male friendships, mysterious late-night meanderings, and a legal system that is impotent to protect its citizens against thugs and maniacs. The London of *Jekyll and Hyde* is uncertain and unstable, a place where nothing is as it seems and where its inhabitants are hurled into a post-Darwinian nightmare of frightening proportions. Traditional borders between humans and animals are dissolved, while individuals are hopelessly attached to one another in a horrifying parody of biological relatedness: Utterson's cane is found to be the instrument of Carew's grisly murder, Lanyon supplies his former friend with the repugnant drug, and Enfield is inadvertently responsible for putting Utterson on the trail of Jekyll's secret. Both students and instructors alike will find much to mull over here. Stevenson's tale makes a fitting addition to any survey course on Victorian literature, revealing the hysterical underside of an insecure era.

The Strange Case of Dr. Jekyll and Mr. Hyde

Quick Read

- Form: Novella; gothic genre.
- Summary: Dr. Jekyll, a respected London doctor, develops a drug that enables him to separate his evil, pleasure-loving self from his upright, respectable self. He lives a double life until his evil side starts to overpower him, then commits suicide.
- Themes: The duality of human nature; the instability of the self; the effects of repression; the breakdown of society; the primitive nature of human beings; the code of secrecy among professional men; the double life; the desire to destroy the father.
- Key Passages: "No, sir, I make it a rule of mine: the more it looks like Queer Street, the less I ask" (1648); "man is not truly one, but truly two" (1676); "man will ultimately be known for a mere polity of mul-

tifarious, incongruous and independent denizens" (1676); "Jekyll had more than a father's interest; Hyde had more than a son's indifference" (1680).

Teaching Suggestions

While many students will think of Stevenson's themes as "universal," there is also a cultural and historical context that makes the story very much of its time. It would be instructive to start by discussing some tangents that are relevant to the story's overall feeling of anxiety. From a broad perspective, it was a time of increased class mobility and changing gender roles. Moreover, shifts in power on the European continent after 1871 and economic depressions on the British home front led to a feeling of national insecurity and a move to expand colonial territories. And scientific theories about evolution, degeneration, and criminal anthropology gave many people cause for alarm. It is significant, for example, that Jekyll breaks from his longtime friend, Lanyon, over his own "scientific heresies." Jekyll's heresies are not only of the Frankenstein mold, suggesting a desire to deploy scientific knowledge toward unethical ends, but more especially related to evolutionary thought. Hyde is described as "hardly human," reminding readers of his uncomfortable proximity to animal origins (the selections from Darwin's *Descent of Man* would provide an interesting reference point) and relating possibly to new theories about criminal degeneration. And despite Utterson's portrayal as a man who likes to read tracts of "dry divinity" in the evening, this is very much a godless universe, devoid of spiritual certitude or guidance.

Students will also benefit from a discussion of the book's structure. The story begins somewhat conventionally, using the technique of third-person narration to follow the activities and thoughts of a single character, Mr. Utterson, Dr. Jekyll's lawyer. At this point the reader is in familiar territory: a presumably "objective," all-knowing narrator relates the ordinary pursuits of an ordinary man who is drawn further and further into a strange mystery. This pattern is broken, however, when Utterson discovers the existence of three letters, two of which make up the latter part of the book. The switch from third- to first-person narration signals a descent into uncertainty and complete subjectivity as the more fantastic elements of the text make their appearance, first, through Dr. Lanyon's narrative, and finally, through Henry Jekyll's "Full Statement of the Case." The reader is thus drawn into Jekyll's mind and experiences his pain firsthand.

You will certainly want to ask students to think about what kind of society this is. As many critics have noted, women are curiously absent from this text (except for brief appearances); instead, there is a very tight circle of middle-class professional men whose loyalty toward each other far exceeds any juridical or moral laws. Utterson, a lawyer and agent of the legal system, does not attempt to bring Hyde's whereabouts to light after Carew's murder. In fact, he is relieved when Jekyll swears that he "will never set eyes on [Hyde] again" and assures him that Hyde is "quite safe" and out of the way of discovery. "I hope you may be right," the lawyer says; "If it came to a trial, your name might appear." Utterson's views demonstrate the code of silence that binds the men together. Lanyon goes to his death without exposing Jekyll's secret (he leaves Utterson a letter to be opened after Jekyll's death, knowing that Utterson will also keep the faith), and Enfield determinedly avoids any knowledge of others' secrets. Enfield's musings on this topic are revealing:

> I feel very strongly about putting questions; it partakes too much of the style of the day of judgment. You start a question, and it's like starting a stone. You sit quietly on the top of a hill; and away the stone goes, starting others; and presently some bland old bird (the last you would have thought of) is knocked on the head in his own back garden and the family have to change their name. No, sir, I make it a rule of mine: the more it looks like Queer Street, the less I ask. (1647–48)

This is an excellent passage for discussion; it outlines the trajectory of the narrative, with any number of characters (Utterson, Lanyon, or Enfield himself) standing in as the "bland old bird." Your discussion of male secrecy can lead you to questions about the double life depicted here. Some critics have seen this as a story about the dangers of Victorian repression, and certainly this is an avenue you will want to explore. Yet it can also be seen as a cautionary tale about the dangers of unrestricted pleasure. Jekyll is not evil to begin with; he is merely someone whose "pleasures" do not accord with his "grave countenance before the public." However, by indulging his "appetites," he unleashes a seemingly infinite desire for viciousness. In this sense, the story addresses problems of not only good and evil but also the duality of human nature.

Additionally, you will want to spend a fair amount of time on the issue of identity and the self. What does it mean to be a "self" in the post-Darwinian world? The story brings up questions not only about the duality of the self, but also about whether it's possible to ever know the self. Identity here is shifting, unstable, and multiple. Jekyll muses, for instance, that in the future, "man will ultimately be known for a mere polity of multifarious, incongruous and independent denizens." In approaching the topic of identity, you may take a cultural approach, connecting psychic fragmentation to social, economic, and historical issues, or you may take a psychoanalytic approach. Does the Jekyll/Hyde example offer a good model for understanding Freud's id, ego, and superego? The story also provides much suggestive material for thinking about the Oedipal drama. Why does Hyde burn the letters and destroy the portrait of Jekyll's father? In what way does Jekyll function as Hyde's father? In his "Full Statement of the Case," Jekyll says, for instance: "Jekyll had more than a father's interest; Hyde had more than a son's indifference." Is this a case of unresolved Oedipal rage? Clearly, this is a text that is as "multifarious" as its divided protagonist. No single approach will lead you to its center.

Teaching Clusters

Nighttime encounters between men, avowals of "professional honour and faith" sealing male comradeship, and deep bonds of affection forged at cozy, all-male dinner parties offer numerous reasons to place this in the **Gender and Sexuality** cluster. *Jekyll and Hyde* would make an interesting contrast with other late-Victorian portraits of masculine behavior by writers such as Rudyard Kipling and W. E. Henley. The inclusion of Wilde's *The Importance of Being Earnest*, although the play is in an entirely different register, would help highlight issues of the double life and social constructions of Victorian manhood. This latter piece could also work nicely in the category of **Aesthetics, Aestheticism, and the Critique of Victorian Values** and could give you a way to talk about the socially subversive qualities of *Jekyll and Hyde*. There is also a good case to be made for placing this text in the **Doubt, Self-Reflection, and Romanticism** cluster, paired with readings that address questions of fragmented or split identity. This would make an excellent companion piece to Mary Shelley's *Frankenstein*, for example, if you wanted to talk about the Frankenstein creature as a psychological projection or double of its creator. Mary Coleridge's poems of fragmented identity would also provide some interesting comparisons.

Discussion Questions

1. What does Jekyll/Hyde's split identity suggest about selfhood in the late-Victorian era? How does this model connect to ideas about evolution and human beings' descent from animal forms?
2. Is *Dr. Jekyll and Mr. Hyde* a story about the dangers of repression? What does it tell us about Victorian convention and the double life?
3. What does *Dr. Jekyll and Mr. Hyde* tell us about evil? Where does pleasure fit in here? Does the indulgence of pleasures automatically lead to evil, or is evil inherent in all human beings?
4. How does *Dr. Jekyll and Mr. Hyde* define male society? What role do secrets play? Is there a male code of honor here? Why does Utterson say that he "incline[s] to Cain's heresy"?
5. Is this a stable society? Is it a patriarchal society? How effective are the police? How effective are fathers?
6. Using Freud's model of the id, ego, and superego, discuss the character of Jekyll/Hyde.
7. In his "Full Statement of the Case," Jekyll states that "Jekyll had more than a father's interest; Hyde had more than a son's indifference." Is *Dr. Jekyll and Mr. Hyde* a story of unresolved Oedipal rage?
8. Compare *Dr. Jekyll and Mr. Hyde* with Mary Shelley's *Frankenstein*. In what way are both stories about psychological doubles? How are the stories different?

Oscar Wilde

Oscar Wilde, in costume, manner, conversation, and writings, played the perfect aesthete, delightfully satirized by W. S. Gilbert in the character of Reginald Bunthorne, the poet whose "high aesthetic line" is really "affectation, / Born from a morbid love of admiration." It suited Wilde's purpose to shock and amuse with declarations such as "No artist has ethical sympathies" and "All art is quite useless" (Preface to *The Picture of Dorian Gray*). Yet Wilde is serious in claiming for art an independence from and superiority to life. Thus his spokesperson in the dialogue *The Critic as Artist* argues that the artist's depiction of an action is greatly superior to the action itself; that criticism is a higher art than painting or poetry because the critic's subjective opinion is less bound to reality and may be far more original and interesting than the object he is talking about; and that abstraction in art is better than realism. "The highest criticism . . . really is . . . the record of one's own soul. It is more fascinating than history, as it is concerned simply with oneself." In statements like these, Wilde is implicitly criticizing the realism and moralism of much nineteenth-century fiction.

The Importance of Being Earnest

Quick Read
- Form: Play; farce.
- Summary: Two young dandies seek marriages with two young women. Identity, character, personality, and ideals are tenuous and ephemeral.
- Themes: Appearance is more important than substance; lies are more real than truth; Victorian society is based on false appearances; ideals such as honesty, morality, and sincerity are meaningless.
- Key Passages:"To be born, or at any rate, bred in a handbag, whether it had handles or not, seems to me to display a contempt for the ordinary decencies of family life that reminds one of the worst excesses of the French Revolution. And I presume you know what that unfortunate movement led to?" (1710); "I hope you have not been leading a double life, pretending to be wicked and being really good all the time. That would be hypocrisy" (1716); "The home seems to me to be the proper sphere for the man. And certainly once a man begins to neglect his domestic duties he becomes painfully effeminate, does he not?" (1725); "We live, I regret to say, in an age of surfaces" (1734); "He has nothing, but he looks everything. What more can one desire?" (1735); "It is a terrible thing for a man to find out suddenly that all his life he has been speaking nothing but the truth" (1740).

Teaching Suggestions

Discussion of the play's title provides a fertile starting point for study. Multiple meanings concerning identity and concepts such as sincerity can be wrung out of Earnest/Ernest while social truths such as the "importance of a name" in high society can be inferred from the title as a whole. The Victorian middle class was known for its earnestness and for its elevation of qualities such as duty, honesty, and hard work. Wilde's play dismantles these revered concepts by creating a topsy-turvy universe in which lies have a fundamental truth to them and the truth has no value at all; characters are perfectly happy to reside in a realm of false appearances. Ask students to think about how humor undermines Victorian social convention in characters such as Lady Bracknell, the play's strongest representative of upper-class sham propriety. "Algernon is an extremely, I may almost say an ostentatiously, eligible man. He has nothing, but he looks everything. What more can one desire?" Lady Bracknell's comments here parody Victorian society by their overt concern with style over substance. Gwendolyn's speech to Jack similarly lampoons the idealism of the age: "We live, as I hope you know, Mr. Worthing, in an age of ideals . . . and my ideal has always been to love someone of the name of Ernest." In order to emphasize the arbitrariness of social values, Wilde gives us characters whose values are always relative, changeable, and self-serving, especially those connected with the central Victorian institutions of marriage and the family. Invite students to explore how the young protagonists, Jack and Algernon, find ways to escape from identities imposed on them by a rule-bound society through anarchic self-invention and through their facility with a liberating, epigrammatic language that seems to spontaneously create a world of its own (albeit one based just as much on appearances as the one it overturns).

Teaching Clusters

The Importance of Being Earnest belongs most clearly to the cluster on **Aesthetics, Aestheticism, and the Critique of Victorian Values** because it embodies principles that were central to the aesthetic movement. In this piece, surface appearance takes precedence over didactic content and morality is presented as an illusory surface effect. Walter Pater's extract from *The Renaissance* would be an important addition to the reading, along with the Preface to Wilde's *The Picture of Dorian Gray*, both primary readings for aestheticism. In addition, poems by Dante Gabriel Rossetti and Algernon Charles Swinburne would provide some insight into the earlier work that inspired the aesthetic writers of the 1890s. Don't miss the recording of Gilbert and Sullivan's musical lampoon of the aesthetic movement, "If You're Anxious for to Shine in the High Aesthetic Line," included in the online archive. In the *NAEL* color insert you'll find an illustration by Aubrey Beardsley, an artist whose drawings exemplify aesthetic concepts. Finally, George Bernard Shaw's *Mrs Warren's Profes-*

sion, which also satirizes Victorian social convention, would be a perfect companion piece to *The Importance of Being Earnest.*

Discussion Questions

1. In *The Importance of Being Earnest,* many of the presumed lies turn out to have a grain of truth in them. Jack, who is pretending to be Ernest, really does turn out to be named Ernest. And while Jack has pretended to have a brother, he does, in fact, turn out to have a real brother. What role does lying play here?
2. What significance does the title of *The Importance of Being Earnest* have to the play's themes?
3. In the first act, Lady Bracknell cross-examines Jack about his habits and background to determine if he is a suitable match for her daughter, Gwendolen. She comes to the conclusion that "To be born, or at any rate, bred in a handbag, whether it had handles or not, seems to me to display a contempt for the ordinary decencies of family life that reminds one of the worst excesses of the French Revolution." What does this exchange tell you about the values of the upper classes?
4. How does the play undermine Victorian social conventions? Pay close attention to the use of wordplay, paradox, and satire.
5. What is the play's attitude toward the working classes, as exemplified by Algernon's servant, Lane? Is Lane ridiculed as much as Lady Bracknell? Are the servants butts of humor or just as verbally adept as those who employ them?
6. In the Preface to *The Picture of Dorian Gray,* Wilde asserts that "It is the spectator, and not life, that art really mirrors." Evaluate this statement in relation to *The Importance of Being Earnest.*

Further Resources

NORTON ONLINE ARCHIVE

On the Sale of Keats's Love Letters
Symphony in Yellow
Hélas
E Tenebris

Bernard Shaw

Mrs Warren's Profession

Written in the 1890s, as the self-assurance of the Victorian age was beginning to wane, *Mrs Warren's Profession* conveys an ambiguous sense of suspended judgment in its portrayal of human relationships while directing a steadier spotlight on the grim realities that constitute the foundations of modern industrial capitalism. At first sight, Shaw's drama appears to be a problem play with the ostensible purpose of exposing the socioeconomic causes of prostitution, and was taken as such by the play's scandalized first audiences, critics, and official censors. Through the figure of Mrs. Warren, the play suggests that society imposes prostitution on impoverished working-class women who have few other ways of escaping the workhouse or the factory. Middle-aged, "formerly pretty," and "on the whole, a genial and fairly presentable old blackguard of a woman," Mrs. Warren is also an antidote to stereotypes of pleasure-loving courtesans, tragic fallen women, and scheming *femmes fatales*. "It's not work that any woman would do for pleasure, goodness knows," Mrs. Warren admits, "though to hear the pious people talk you would suppose it was a bed of roses." As the play progresses, however, prostitution becomes a metaphor for the way society actually carries out all of its transactions, commercial and social. Human intercourse of all kinds is contaminated by the profit motive, a fact that cannot be disguised by the attempts of Mrs. Warren and Praed to offer, respectively, an ideal of bourgeois familial devotion and the escapism of aesthetic pursuits, above and beyond exploitative economics. A more forceful attempt to find a way out of this impasse is offered by Mrs. Warren's daughter, Vivie, a characteristic New Woman of the 1890s. Her endeavor to find her way through society's illusions to self-determination is at the center of the drama in the play. Vivie does not object to the choices her mother has had to make, but ultimately forsakes her because her mother hypocritically continues to hide her occupation behind a facade of "affectations of maternal authority and conventional manners." Vivie especially condemns her mother for being "conventional," illustrating her belief that Mrs. Warren's continuing unapologetic endorsement of and participation in the system make her a typical capitalist exploiter. But, finally, there is something problematic about the representation of Vivie Warren, not least because of her belief that salvation lies exclusively in a white-collar career in which, as she says, "I . . . must make more money than I spend." Although Vivie seems, on the one hand, to be the moral center of the play, on the other, her remarks are superficial; her mother has clearly subjected her own choices to deeper reflection and gained wisdom from difficult experience.

Quick Read

- Form: Social satire.
- Summary: The play depicts the relationship between a woman who has made her fortune from prostitution and her daughter, an independent-minded example of the New Woman. The mother explains the socioeconomic roots of her career choice to her daughter, who later learns that capitalist society has everything in common with prostitution.
- Themes: Prostitution was one of the few options open to disadvantaged women who wished to escape their economic limitations in a patriarchal society; middle-class social relations and capitalist economic exchange in Victorian England are forms of prostitution; inde-

pendent-minded women of the late nineteenth century who sought
more autonomy had to make personal trade-offs in their lives.

- Key Passages/Scenes: Vivie: "I like work and getting paid for it. When
  I'm tired of working, I like a comfortable chair, a cigar, a little
  whiskey, and a novel with a good detective story in it" (1749); Mrs.
  Warren's speech, briefly interrupted at intervals by Vivie, explaining
  the poverty-stricken circumstances that led her into prostitution
  (1766–69); Mrs. Warren: "What is any respectable girl brought up to
  do but catch some rich man's fancy and get the benefit of his money
  by marrying him?—as if a marriage ceremony could make any difference in the right or wrong of the thing! Oh! the hypocrisy of the world
  makes me sick!" (1768); Crofts: "Come! you wouldn't refuse the acquaintance of my mother's cousin the Duke of Belgravia because
  some of the rents he gets are earned in queer ways. . . . If you're going to pick and choose your acquaintances on moral principles, you'd
  better clear out of this country, unless you want to cut yourself out of
  all decent society" (1777); Vivie: "If I had been you, mother, I might
  have done as you did; but I should not have lived one life and believed
  in another. You are a conventional woman at heart. That is why I am
  bidding you goodbye now. I am right, am I not?" (1790).

Teaching Suggestions

In *Mrs Warren's Profession*, as the anthology headnote points out, Shaw
has "created a drama of ideas, in which his characters strenuously argue
points of view that justify their social positions." Some of the characters,
certainly Vivie and Mrs. Warren, and even less sympathetic characters
such as Crofts, argue their positions with great facility. Ask students to
identify the main points of view as portrayed by the different characters
and their situations. Which views are more convincing and why? The play
is primarily concerned with the issue of prostitution and its relation to accepted social and economic practices. How does *Mrs Warren's Profession*
comment on the traditional Victorian view of prostitution as "the great social evil"? Draw students' attention to the important passage in which
Mrs. Warren explains the reasons that she decided to go into her profession. Note especially the way that marriage is equated with prostitution.
As Mrs. Warren exclaims, "What is any respectable girl brought up to do
but catch some rich man's fancy and get the benefit of his money by marrying him? . . . Oh! the hypocrisy of the world makes me sick!" Crofts is
also an important character to focus on because his economic theories
connect lawful business practices to the concept of prostitution. Advocating the exploitation of impoverished female factory workers, he states,
"Do you expect me to turn my back on 35 per cent when all the rest are
pocketing what they can, like sensible men? No such fool!" Crofts is ready
to engage in immoral or unethical practices if they turn a profit. This
questionable system of ethics is not limited to Crofts alone, however, but
extends to the rest of respectable society. "If you're going to pick and

choose your acquaintances on moral principles, you'd better clear out of this country, unless you want to cut yourself out of all decent society," he explains in a telling statement that connects a lack of "moral principles" to "decent society." Questions of moral decency and personal integrity are further explored through the character of Vivie, who objects not so much to her mother's profession as to her mother's hypocrisy. At the play's conclusion, Vivie says to her mother, "If I had been you, mother, I might have done as you did; but I should not have lived one life and believed in another. You are a conventional woman at heart. That is why I am bidding you goodbye now." How are we to judge Vivie here? Is she simply the spokesperson for the play's primary message, or is a more nuanced reading possible? Is Vivie perhaps too harsh a judge of others? How does her depiction as a stereotypical New Woman—independent and educated, yet unromantic and businesslike—affect the way that we understand her character? What are these two types of women—prostitute and New Woman—doing in the same play? Questions such as these may help students see that Shaw may be moving beyond the certainties of earlier Victorian writers, into an age when art allowed for life's ambiguities.

Teaching Clusters

Mrs Warren's Profession can be included in at least three teaching clusters. The humor of the piece may be brought out by teaching it within the grouping of **Aesthetics, Aestheticism, and the Critique of Victorian Values** along with Oscar Wilde's The Importance of Being Earnest. Both pieces lampoon the conventions of respectable Victorian society, exposing social hypocrisies through witty dialogue. The brilliance of the conversation in both plays calls attention to language at the expense of believable plot and characterization. Unlike Wilde's play, however, Mrs Warren's Profession has a serious undercurrent and can be taught in clusters that speak to serious social questions. The theme of prostitution can be best addressed in the **Gender and Sexuality** grouping, alongside some of the selections in the "Woman Question" section of the in-text topic "Victorian Issues." "The Great Social Evil," a letter purporting to be from a prostitute, would be especially instructive here. Another good companion piece would be Dante Gabriel Rossetti's "Jenny," a poem in which a young man reflects on the life of the prostitute with whom he has spent the night. Shaw's play could also be included in the cluster on **Poverty, Unrest, and Social Criticism**; many of the selections in this grouping focus on mid-Victorian social critiques and would give students an understanding of the changing attitudes toward female sexual transgression.

Discussion Questions

1. How does Mrs Warren's Profession depict prostitution? What does the play have to say about respectable Victorian society in relation to prostitution?

2. In the first act, Praed tells Vivie that he is glad that her upbringing has not made her too "conventional." In the final scene, Vivie calls her mother "a conventional woman at heart." Explore the use of the word "conventional." Are there other examples of the word's use in the play?

3. Is *Mrs Warren's Profession* concerned with morality? Who or what constitutes a moral standard here? What does the play see as immoral?

4. At one point Vivie says, "I don't believe in circumstances." Is the play critical or supportive of Vivie on this point? Can everyone rise above their circumstances?

5. At the end of *Mrs Warren's Profession*, Vivie leaves her mother, whom she accuses of hypocrisy. Is the play as critical of Mrs. Warren as Vivie is? Is Mrs. Warren's hypocrisy on the same order as other hypocrisies in the play?

6. Vivie is portrayed as a typical New Woman: she is independent, uncompromising, educated, and practical. How does this characterization affect your understanding of the play?

7. *Mrs Warren's Profession* illustrates three different possibilities for Victorian women: prostitution, marriage, or living as a New Woman. What do these three possibilities say about each other? What do they say about Victorian society?

Mary Elizabeth Coleridge

Mary Coleridge's haunting lyrics address questions of female identity and the unstable self. Her wild women and roaming witches hover on the margins of society, hoping to be let in. Yet to allow them access is to destabilize the female subject and to banish her from the realm of language and culture. "Her lips were open—not a sound / Came through the parted lines of red. / Whate'er it was, the hideous wound / In silence and in secret bled," cries the speaker in "The Other Side of a Mirror" (lines 13–16). Coleridge's female narrators have a tenuous hold on existence; they seem to be of neither one world nor the next, and they continually collapse the division between self and other. This psychic fragmentation gives them more in common with the tradition of gothic literature than with the poetry of the 1890s. Like female Dr. Jekylls and Mr. Hydes, they engage in strange encounters, hiding their "hideous wound[s]" from public view.

The Other Side of a Mirror

Quick Read

- Form: Lyric.
- Themes: The splitting of the self; unstable female identity; the suppressed female voice.
- Key Passages: "The vision of a woman, wild / With more than womanly despair," lines 5–6; "No sigh relieved her speechless woe, / She had no voice to speak her dread," lines 17–18; "I am she!" line 30.

The Witch

Quick Read

- Form: Lyric.
- Themes: The splitting of the self; unstable female identity; the female voice; the transgression of boundaries.
- Key Passages: "I have walked a great while over the snow," line 1; "Oh, lift me over the threshold, and let me in at the door!" lines 7, 14; "Her voice was the voice that women have, / Who plead for their heart's desire," lines 15–16; "She came—she came—and the quivering flame / Sank and died in the fire," lines 17–18.

Teaching Suggestions

"The Other Side of a Mirror" and "The Witch" make an excellent pairing because both address the problem of unstable female identity. In "The Other Side of a Mirror," the speaker is disturbed by "The vision of a woman, wild" (line 5) whom she identifies with herself ("I am she!" [line 30]). Students may not immediately understand why the speaker's despair is "more than womanly despair" (line 6), but it would be instructive to talk about the restrictions placed on feminine behavior in the nineteenth century. Emotions such as "despair" (line 6), "jealousy" (line 23), and the desire for "fierce revenge" (line 23) were considered unladylike at the very least and possibly indicative of illness or even insanity in some cases. The speaker's suppressed rage is embodied by this other woman, who has "no voice to speak her dread" (line 18). Coleridge's vision of the suppressed female voice is startlingly brutal: the "wild" woman's mouth is a "hideous wound" (line 15) that bleeds "In silence" (line 16). Invite students to discuss the meaning of the "wild" woman's "speechless woe" (lines 5, 17). Why is she speechless? Why does she despair? The answer is partially suggested in the speaker's description of the "lurid eyes . . . Made mad because its hope was gone" (lines 19–21), but this does not explain why the "wild" woman's hope has left her.

The splitting of the self enacted visually in "The Other Side of a Mirror" is demonstrated through shifts in pronoun usage in "The Witch." In the first two stanzas, the speaker is the "Witch" of the title, yet in the final stanza, the speaker's voice splits: the "I" becomes separate from the witch, who is suddenly referred to in the third person as "Her voice." This is a good place to ask students to compare this female voice with the voice of the "wild" woman in the first poem. In "The Witch," the voice is "the voice that women have, / Who plead for their heart's desire" (lines 15–16). Is this similar to the suppressed voice of the "wild" woman? Or is it a "social" voice like that of the speaker in "The Other Side of a Mirror"? Why does the witch speak in her own voice in the first two stanzas, then lose that voice to another speaker in the final stanza? And what is the relationship between these two speakers? You might also want to open up a discussion about the meaning of the word "Witch": What are the various historical, cultural, and social connotations of this designation? And what does it have to do with the woman who "wander[s] over the fruitful earth" (line 5)? Coleridge assigns her the status of an outsider, but what is she outside of and what does she want to be allowed into? Additionally, you will want to draw students' attention to the concept of the threshold. What kind of threshold is this—sexual, spiritual, social? By crossing the boundary, the witch—and the second narrator—seems to enact a transgression of some kind. Although the second narrator invites the witch inside, her doing so makes the "quivering flame" (line 17) die and it "never [is] lit again" (line 19). By comparing the two poems, students will be better able to make the connection between the "I" and "her" of the final stanza of "The Witch."

Teaching Clusters

Coleridge's poetry could be taught in either the **Gender and Sexuality** cluster or the **Doubt, Self-Reflection, and Romanticism** cluster. In the first category, it would be helpful to include documentary readings about Victorian women and their social roles by writers such as Sarah Stickney Ellis, John Ruskin, and Florence Nightingale. Additionally, both Robert Louis Stevenson's *Dr. Jekyll and Mr. Hyde* and any of Emily Brontë's poems would make excellent literary companion pieces in either of the above clusters. Stevenson's novella considers the splitting of the male subject, while Brontë's poetry addresses issues of female identity and nonbeing. "The Witch," moreover, begs to be compared with Samuel Taylor Coleridge's *Christabel*—again, in either of the clusters mentioned.

Discussion Questions

1. What does the "vision of a woman, wild" (line 5) represent for the narrator of "The Other Side of a Mirror"? How is she connected to this vision of another woman?
2. Why is the "wild" woman's unhappiness "more than womanly despair" (line 6)?
3. Why is the female voice in "The Other Side of a Mirror" unable to "speak her dread" (line 18)?
4. What does it mean to be a "Witch"—historically, culturally, or socially? In what way is the woman in the poem a witch?

5. Describe the speaker as presented in the first two stanzas of "The Witch." Why is she "not tall [or] strong" (line 2)? Why does she wander? Why does she want to be let in the door?

6. When the speaker of "The Witch" says, "Oh, lift me over the threshold, and let me in at the door," what kind of "threshold" is she referring to? Is there a symbolic meaning to it?

7. Why does the speaker's identity change in the last stanza of "The Witch"? Is the "I" of the first two stanzas connected to the "I" of the last stanza? How is the witch connected to the speaker of the last stanza?

Rudyard Kipling

Kipling's writings about the British Empire are characterized by pride and patriotism, yet these elements are tempered by a sense of duty and moral obligation that is quintessentially Victorian. "Recessional," written for Victoria's Jubilee, is a prayer for humility and remembrance that the wealth and power of empire are held under the dispensation of the "Lord God of Hosts," the "Judge of the Nations" who laid low the Assyrian and Phoenician empires (lines 5, 17). Moreover, Kipling's patriotism does not preclude sympathy for the enlisted men who shoulder the burdens of the nation. Many of Kipling's most popular poems are written in Cockney dialect from the point of view of the common soldiers, "poor beggars in red" who fight in the "barbarious wars" for the "the Widow at Windsor" and who most likely will "never see 'ome" (lines 5, 10, 11, 45). Kipling's interest in the lot of the common man finds another kind of expression in "The Man Who Would Be King," a story in which two working-class conmen attempt to launch their own imperial project. The Loafers' original aim is exploitation, as if the land they seek to conquer is a mine to be drained of its minerals ("the country isn't half worked out"). Their shallow motives and insensitive methods bring up questions not only about the right way to rule, but also about the ethics of empire.

The Man Who Would Be King

Quick Read

- Form: Short story.
- Summary: A story that charts the rise and fall of two ex-military conmen who set out to create their own kingdom on the Afghan frontier; narrated by a journalist who has met with the two men before their adventure and later hears the tale from the sole survivor.
- Themes: Loyalty toward one's group; duty to one's country; the right and wrong way to govern; the ethics of empire.
- Key Passages: "Englishmen are not usually softened by appeals to the memory of their mothers . . . " (1796); "[The colonized rulers of the Native States] do not understand that nobody cares a straw for the internal administration of Native States so long as oppression and

crime are kept within decent limits, and the ruler is not drugged, drunk, or diseased from one end of the year to the other. Native states were created by Providence in order to supply picturesque scenery, tigers, and tall-writing" (1797); Description of the "Contrack" (1801–02); "Then the Chiefs come round to shake hands, they was so hairy and white and fair it was just shaking hands with old friends" (1809); "A Queen out of the strongest tribe, that'll make them your blood-brothers, and that'll lie by your side and tell you all the people thinks about you and their own affairs" (1812); "We're done for. . . . They are Englishmen, these people,—and it's my blasted nonsense that has brought you to this," spoken by Dan (1816).

Teaching Suggestions

The task in teaching Kipling will be to help students see the ambivalence about colonial conquest and rule in his writing. "The Man Who Would Be King," in particular, can be interpreted in a number of different ways. A close reading of a few of the poems will help define some of the issues before tackling the story. "Recessional," for example, counsels "An humble and a contrite heart" and avoidance of "frantic boast" as the poet's Jubilee audience celebrates its "Dominion over palm and pine" (lines 10, 29, 4). On the other hand, the imperial fate of the Dominion has been ordained by the "Lord of our far-flung battle-line" (line 1), suggesting a grander view of British rule. "The White Man's Burden" returns to the issue of proper disposition in governing, advising the best-bred sons of empire to adopt a stoic, responsible attitude to their imperial duty. "If" further suggests that the conscientious stance needed in the imperial field begins at home with a code of masculine conduct: integrity, endurance, and sound judgment in all matters prepare the way for being custodian of "the Earth and everything that's in it" (line 31). When you turn from the poetry to "The Man Who Would Be King," ask students to evaluate the motives behind the Loafers' grandiose plans. How do these plans measure up to Kipling's view of imperial governance, as depicted in the poems? Invite students to evaluate statements made by the Loafers, such as Daniel's declaration that "a man who knows how to drill men can always be a King. We shall go to those parts and say to any King we find—'D'you want to vanquish your foes?' and we will show him how to drill men; for that we know better than anything else. Then we will subvert that King and seize his Throne and establish a Dynasty." Depending only on martial skill, creating conflict in lieu of diplomacy, and acting toward client states disloyally—all are the wrong ways to govern. When Dan is hit by a bullet fired by the tribesmen he trained and calls Englishmen (rulers) because of their skill with a rifle, he still equates being a ruler with martial skill only: "We're done for," he cries; "They are Englishmen, these people." At the same time, Dan's and Peachey's blundering tactics and cultural insensitivity (violating tribal customs, as, for example, when Dan—considered a god—attempts to marry one of the tribe's women) allow for a broader critique of empire. Ask students to think about whether and to what extent this text is critical of the larger project of colonial conquest. Are these two hapless tricksters simply unfit to govern, or in exposing their methods does the story bring the less savory aspects of imperial dominance in general to light?

Teaching Clusters

Issues of colonial rule and observations about race and national identity situate Kipling's poetry and fiction in the category of **Progress, Science, and Colonial Expansion.** Kipling's work is most usefully taught alongside other accounts of empire, such as William Howard Russell's "My Indian Mutiny Diary," which addresses the situation of the British in India. Eliza Cook's poem, "The Englishman," would make an excellent pairing with "Danny Deever" and "The Widow at Windsor." These pieces could also be taught with some of the selections from the **Gender and Sexuality** cluster that address issues of Victorian masculinity, such as William Ernest Henley's poetry. If time allows, consider teaching Kipling's work with Joseph Conrad's *Heart of Darkness*, a far less humorous account of imperialist hubris.

Discussion Questions

1. Describe some of the aspects of the Anglo-Indian hierarchy in "The Man Who Would Be King." Where do the story's characters fit into this hierarchy?
2. Does the narrator of "The Man Who Would Be King" have any particular function, or is he merely a neutral conveyor of events?
3. Explore the theme of loyalty in "The Man Who Would Be King," particularly in connection with characters such as Dan, Peachey, and Billy Fish. Are there examples of disloyalty? Does the narrator display disloyalty in any way?
4. How important is the concept of duty in "The Man Who Would Be King"? What are some examples of characters that do or do not fulfill their duty?
5. Does "The Man Who Would Be King" present Daniel and Peachey's bid for power as similar to the British colonial quest, or does it distinguish their project from a more enlightened kind of colonialism? In what way is this text concerned with the appropriate manner of governing an empire? Does it allow for a critique of imperial conquest in general?
6. What role do women play in "The Man Who Would Be King"? In what way do they help or hinder the task of governing?
7. Compare the concept of masculinity in "The Man Who Would Be King" and "If."
8. Compare the depiction of working-class soldiers in "The Widow at Windsor" and "Danny Deever."

Further Resources

NORTON ONLINE ARCHIVE

Edgehill Fight
The Runes on Weland's Sword
Harp Song of the Dane Women
The Ladies
The Hyenas

NORTON TOPICS ONLINE

Victorian Imperialism
  The Civilizing Mission
    Kipling, The White Man's Burden

Ernest Dowson

Dowson's work offers a poetry of renunciation; loss and insufficiency are aestheticized, the past is idealized, and the present offers no prospect of fulfillment. "They are not long, the days of wine and roses," the speaker of "They Are Not Long" tells us (line 5), but the poem finds no consolation in the moment. Similarly, in "Cynara" the speaker mourns an irretrievable past while lamenting the inadequacy of a present filled with wine, music, and women—none of which offers any solace. It is this lack of satisfaction that makes up what the speaker describes as a kind of "faithful[ness]" to his past love (lines 6, 12, 18, 24). In contrast to Walter Pater, who advised readers "To burn always with this hard, gemlike flame" (*The Renaissance*), Dowson creates narrators who are unable to move; they are cut off from the fullness of experience, always situating that fullness beyond reach. For students interested in the decadent movement, Dowson's writing offers an excellent introduction to some of its major themes.

Cynara

Quick Read

- Form: Lyric.
- Themes: The inadequacy of the present; sorrow over the loss of the past; inability to experience the pleasure of the moment.
- Key Passages: "I have been faithful to thee, Cynara! in my fashion," lines 6, 12, 18, 24; "betwixt her lips and mine / There fell thy shadow, Cynara!" lines 1–2; "when the feast is finished and the lamps expire, / Then falls thy shadow," lines 20–21.

They Are Not Long

Quick Read

- Form: Lyric.
- Themes: The transience of life; the finality of death.

- Key Passages: "Love and desire and hate: / I think they have no portion in us after / We pass the gate," lines 2–4; "They are not long, the days of wine and roses," line 5.

Teaching Suggestions

Dowson's poems are concerned with the relationship of the present to the past, with narrators trapped in passive resignation. To bring out these themes, you might want to begin with questions about the speaker of "Cynara." Why is the speaker "desolate" (lines 4, 5, 10, 16, 22)? Why does he say he has been "faithful" to Cynara (lines 6, 12, 18, 24)? These considerations can lead you into a discussion about the figure of Cynara and her significance to the poem. Cynara embodies a past that is completely foreclosed to the narrator: "betwixt her lips and mine / There fell thy shadow, Cynara!" (lines 1–2). The image of Cynara as shadow is repeated in the last stanza: "when the feast is finished and the lamps expire, / Then falls thy shadow" (lines 20–21). It is this foreclosure, enacted by Cynara's shadow, that prevents the speaker from enjoying anything in the moment and seems to make him incapable of action. He is caught up in events that, although of his own making (he "crie[s] for madder music and for stronger wine" [line 19] and sleeps with the prostitute, for example), seem not to proceed from any explicit desire on his part; rather, they are ways to avoid the pain of daily existence. Cynara functions as an idealized concept that, by its identification with the past, forecloses fulfillment in the present. This theme is addressed in a less-evident manner in "They Are Not Long," but is easier to grasp after reading "Cynara." Ostensibly, "They Are Not Long" is about the transience of time: "They are not long, the weeping and the laughter, / Love and desire and hate: / I think they have no portion in us after / We pass the gate" (lines 1–4). Yet this is not an injunction to seize the day, as in FitzGerald's *Rubáiyát of Omar Khayyám* ("Come, fill the Cup, and in the Fire of Spring / The Winter Garment of Repentance fling" [lines 25–26]) or Pater's *The Renaissance* ("Not the fruit of experience, but experience itself, is the end"). It is, rather, a determined conviction that the moment can never be enough; we are caught up in perpetual longing and perpetual dissatisfaction, with no possibility of action. In "They Are Not Long," experience—so dear to Pater—is diminished because it is not palpable. There is no body, no sensate being, and no present: "Out of a misty dream / Our path emerges for a while, then closes / Within a dream" (lines 6–8). As in "Cynara," we are cut off from experience by the "shadow" (line 2) of an indistinct past.

Teaching Clusters

As representative of the decadent movement, Dowson's poetry can be studied in **Aesthetics, Aestheticism, and the Critique of Victorian Values.** Decadent writing is not equivalent to aesthetic writing, though the two are similar in significant ways and do share some sources. Good companion pieces include Pater's conclusion to *The Renaissance* and the poetry of D. G. Rossetti and Swinburne. Other works that question the status quo in terms of morality or sexuality would also be useful here, such as Michael Field's lyrics.

Discussion Questions

1. What does Cynara represent to the speaker of Dowson's poem?
2. What does the speaker mean when he says he has been "faithful" to Cynara ("I have been faithful to thee, Cynara! in my fashion" [lines 6, 12, 18, 24])?
3. How does the speaker of "Cynara" view the past? How does this view compare to the representation of the past in "They Are Not Long"?
4. Compare the examination of past and present in "Cynara" and Edward FitzGerald's *Rubáiyát of Omar Khayyám*.
5. How does the technique of repetition affect your reading of "Cynara" and "They Are Not Long"?
6. Do "Cynara" and "They Are Not Long" offer the possibility of agency?
7. Compare the concept of death in Dowson's "They Are Not Long" and Michael Field's "Nests in Elms."

Further Resources

NORTON ONLINE ARCHIVE

To One in Bedlam
A Last Word
Spleen
Flos Lunae
Dregs
Exchanges
Carthusians

The Victorian Age: Texts in the Norton Online Archive
by Authors Not in NAEL

Arthur Hugh Clough
  Dipsychus
  I Dreamt a Dream
  "There Is No God," the Wicked Saith

CHAPTER 11

The Twentieth Century and After

INTRODUCING THE PERIOD

"Modernity is the transient, the fleeting, the contingent," Charles Baudelaire wrote in 1863 ("The Painter of Modern Life"). Clearly modernity was not new to the twentieth century, but in the twentieth century, even more so than in the fast-paced nineteenth, the rate and intensity of sociocultural and technological change came to seem almost unbearable. In an extended moment that the philosopher Jacques Derrida refers to as a "rupture" in intellectual history ("Structure, Sign, and Play in the Discourse of the Human Sciences," 1966), Nietzsche and other antimetaphysical thinkers argued that there was no such thing as absolute truth, only knowledge obtained perspectivally; the rising science of ethnology showed that human cultural practices and beliefs were variant and situational rather than universal; Freud and other theorists of the unconscious challenged the Cartesian view of human beings as rational, integral, self-aware, and self-present; and Darwin's theory of natural selection described an imperfect, half-animal human species, whose continued mutability was governed by chance rather than providential design. Twentieth-century authors such as James Joyce, Virginia Woolf, Joseph Conrad, and D. H. Lawrence "wrote in the wake of the shattering of confidence in the great old certainties about the deity and the Christian faith, about the person, knowledge, materialism, history, the old Grand Narratives." As David Harvey argues, the twentieth century also struggled to come to terms with the failure of the Enlightenment project, which had proposed the scientific domination of nature to protect humans from calamity and need, and promoted rational, just forms of social organization rather than a state founded on superstition, oppression, and the arbitrary practice of power (*The Condition of Postmodernity: An Enquiry into the Origins of Cultural Change*, 1989). The Enlightenment promise of universal democracy, justice, and liberty, however, seemed shattered by the events of twentieth-century history. Science had provided human beings with the means for warfare and genocide; the domination of nature meant widespread environmental destruction; and democracy threatened to yield to fascism and other forms of totalitarian government, or seemed inseparable from the brutal exploitation of workers under capitalism.

Literary responses to the new century's social and cultural changes varied dramatically. Thomas Hardy's "On the Western Circuit" describes a world in which neither religion nor any other traditional belief system lends shape or meaningfulness to human existence. Rejecting earlier fictions of heroic identity, the story moves remorselessly toward its apotheosis of disillusionment as its characters confront the certainty of life-long unhappiness with "dreary resignation." William Butler Yeats's "The Second Coming" offers an even more cataclysmic view of the future, one in which the old order disintegrates into a whirling chaos ("Things fall apart; the centre cannot hold; / Mere anarchy is loosed upon the world" [lines 3–4]) and the new human subject that emerges from the wreckage is an admixed monstrosity (a "rough beast" with "lion body and the head of a man, / A gaze blank and pitiless as the sun" [lines 21, 14–15]), abominable and yet compelling. In contrast to these dark views, Virginia Woolf saw in the chaos of the modern era connections among individual consciousnesses. Even though she claims "emphatically there is no God," she nonetheless visualizes a vibrant world where "all human beings" are joined together in one vast "work of art" ("A Sketch of the Past"). One sees throughout her work a delight in sensory impressions and contemporary existence. "Why, if one wants to compare life to anything, one must liken it to being blown through the Tube at fifty miles an hour—landing at the other end without a single hairpin in one's hair! . . . Yes, that seems to express the rapidity of life, the perpetual waste and repair, all so casual, all so haphazard," she writes in "The Mark on the Wall." From James Joyce, we get a similar sense of readiness to embrace modern existence, as Leopold Bloom wanders through the Dublin streets, alive to every sight and perception: "Grafton street gay with housed awnings lured his senses. Muslin prints silk, dames and dowagers, jingle of harnesses, hoofthuds lowringing in the baking causeway."

Modernity, however, was not just trains and crowded streets or even the sure sense of impending war; for the inhabitants of Britain's former and existing colonies, the experience of modernity was complicated by the effects and processes of colonization and decolonization. The so-called postcolonial authors (a term that must be understood to encompass writers from countries with a wide variety of political and cultural ties to Britain) document the strategies—economic, military, ideological, rhetorical—whereby one nation gains control over, subjugates, and maintains power over another, and analyzes the stories the dominant culture tells itself about why imperialism is justified and necessary. Many of these writers, moreover, explore the typical postcolonial dilemma of hybridity. Postcolonial subjects find themselves asked to choose between incompatible cultures or are dispersed among multiple cultures; they cannot lay claim to a singular, an unambiguous, a racially or culturally unmixed identity. The speaker of Walcott's "The Schooner *Flight*" has red hair, dark skin, and "sea-green eyes": "I have Dutch, nigger, and English in me, / and either I'm nobody, or I'm a nation" (lines 36, 42–43). This quintessentially postcolonial and postmodern subject may experience transnationality as a state of dispossession, melancholy, and exile. But it is also possible to embrace deliberately the hybridized identity that is perhaps the inevitable product of postcolonialism. As Salman Rushdie writes of the novel that made him, arguably, the most famous exile of postcolonial times: "*The Satanic Verses* celebrates hybridity, impurity, intermingling, the transformation that comes of new and unexpected combinations of human beings, cultures, ideas, politics, movies, songs. It rejoices in mongrelization and fears the Pure. . . . It is a love-song to our mongrel selves." Your students will want to consider how their understanding of literary modernity and history alters when imperialism is identified as an integral part of modernism and postmodernism. The richness, diversity, and multiplicity that mark twentieth-century literature and subsequent works stem from their engagement with the complicated history and politics of the era.

TEACHING CLUSTERS

Transition, Modernity, and Modernism

The decades before and after the turn of the twentieth century saw a rejection of Victorian optimism and a move toward skepticism and resignation. The new century brought with it a sense of flux and indeterminacy—a perception that truth and certainty no longer existed and that identities, social relations, and meaning structures could be made and unmade according to need, opportunity, and inclination. Some writers responded to these changes with dark pessimism, stoicism, or outright despair, while others cheerfully embraced the chance to experiment with new forms. After World War II, the dynamism and innovation that had inspired many literary and artistic trends in earlier decades manifested themselves in ever more diversified techniques. Some writers questioned the simple division between popular and elite art, while others drew attention to the self-referentiality of language and texts. Works in this cluster include those that evidence an awareness of changing social and cultural paradigms; those that revise or discard traditional approaches to literature; and those that self-consciously experiment with form or content, be they modernist, postmodernist, avant-garde, or otherwise in the forefront of artistic creation.

Gender, Desire, and Sexuality

In the late nineteenth century, a transformation in gender relations began that continued in earnest throughout the twentieth century. More women were getting university educations and entering the workforce, sometimes choosing to live independently rather than marry. Marriage was no longer seen as the *raison d'être* for women or as an idealized sphere of domestic harmony. Many writers were openly pessimistic about long-term relationships between men and women, while others felt that the institution of marriage itself was faulty. At the same time, there was a new openness about sexuality evident in fiction, cultural essays, and medical literature. James Joyce's *Ulysses*, for example, was originally banned in Britain and the United States on grounds of obscenity. Moreover, despite the arrest and sentencing of Oscar Wilde in 1895 for homosexuality and the prosecution of Radclyffe Hall's explicitly lesbian *Well of Loneliness* in 1928, an increasing number of authors wrote candidly about same-sex desire. The second half of the century witnessed political and cultural movements dedicated to freer sexual expression, gay rights, and feminism. Texts in this grouping address issues having to do with changing sexual and marital relationships, heterosexual or homosexual desire, gay and lesbian concerns, women's independence, and feminist politics.

History, Memory, and Politics

This category is concerned with the way that we understand the past—individual, collective, political, cultural—and how the past becomes a narrative for public consumption. Two world wars, numerous genocides, social change, postcolonial struggles for independence, and a sense that history is moving at an ever-increasing pace prompted twentieth-century writers to respond in myriad ways. Some chose to reflect directly on specific historical or political occurrences in an attempt to process the past and put it into some kind of comprehensible framework. Others seemed less concerned with large-scale upheavals and more concerned with recovering a personal history, mythologizing the communal past, examining the way in which memory functions, or mediating between private and public attitudes toward social and cultural transformation. In this grouping, there is a drive to make the past legible, to revise accepted historical narratives, and to understand disruptive cultural occurrences. Works placed in this cluster cover a range of themes having to do with war, politics, imperialism, collective history, national mythologies, rethinking the past, memory, the passage of time, and the individual experience in relation to the broader historical sweep.

Culture, Language, and Identity

In the middle and later years of the twentieth century, Britain's hold on its overseas territories diminished as decolonization took place first in one region and then another. As the British empire dissolved, a wealth of writing poured out of the former colonies, reinvigorating Britain's literary scene and introducing new themes and concerns. Many postcolonial authors found themselves suspended between two or more cultures, sharing allegiance to multiple geographic sites and multiple social customs. Such hybrid or "transnational" subjects might be most at home in the language of their former colonizers or they might embrace the language of their native culture. Some, emigrating to Britain, experienced marked feelings of dislocation, alienation, or cultural displacement, while others suffered from a fragmented sense of identity within indigenous communities economically and psychologically devastated by years of colonization. At the same time, Britons' view of their place in the world changed, leading to new types of cultural identifications. The newly multi-ethnic society spawned revised views of Englishness, British culture, and British national identity. Texts collected under this rubric address issues of cultural displacement and alienation, hybridity, exile, fragmented identity, Englishness, British culture, language identification, and power relations between social or cultural groups.

AUTHORS AND WORKS

Thomas Hardy

Looking out across the landscape of the dying nineteenth century on December 31, 1900, the speaker of Thomas Hardy's "The Darkling Thrush" perceives the "death-lament" (line 12) of Victorianism in the wind ("The Century's corpse outleant, / . . . The wind his death-lament" [lines 10–12]). Against the "growing gloom" he hears "An aged thrush" in "full-hearted evensong / Of joy illimited" and wonders at the decrepit bird's happiness in such a bleak world (lines 24, 21, 19–20). Hardy's fiction and poetry capture this sense of decline and almost none of the optimism of the thrush's song (an optimism not shared by the speaker). In stories such as "On the Western Circuit," the dawning modern age is a cruel burden foisted upon unprepared individuals who struggle vainly against forces they are unable to control or understand. The characters in Hardy's fiction face uncompromisingly harsh conditions, and many students find his work depressing, lacking the pleasing melancholy of the Romantics or the mid-Victorians. At the same time, however, his startlingly modern view of sexual alliances and his rejection of bourgeois attitudes appeal to students, who respond to the anti-Victorian elements of his work. Changing sexual mores, shifting relationships between individuals and society, and clashes between urban and rural modes of life are themes that Hardy returns to again and again. His writing offers readers an insightful glimpse into the cultural and psychological conflicts of the period, setting the tone for the massive upheavals of the twentieth century.

On the Western Circuit

Quick Read

- Form: Short story.
- Summary: A London lawyer seduces a young servant woman and enters into an extended correspondence with her. Impressed with her quality of mind as revealed through her letters, he marries the young woman, only to discover that the letters were written by her married female employer.
- Themes: Modern individuals are trapped by cultural and cosmic circumstances that work against them; they are driven to action like objects in a mechanical universe; marriage is a legal straitjacket that can only bring misery to those involved; sexual desire is an impediment to full self-realization; modernity and urban trends are destroying rural modes of existence.
- Key Passages: "Their motions were so rhythmical that they seemed to be moved by machinery" (1853); "they gazed at each other with smiles, and with that unmistakable expression which means so little at the moment, yet so often leads up to passion, heart-ache, union, disunion, devotion, overpopulation, drudgery, content, resignation, despair" (1855); Charles is described as "the end-of-the-age young man" (1858); Edith was "[i]nfluenced by the belief of the British parent that a bad marriage with its aversions is better than free womanhood with its interests, dignity, and leisure" (1861).

Teaching Suggestions

"On the Western Circuit" is an excellent choice for introducing students to Hardy's major themes, especially those that he pursued in his fiction. Both "Hap" and "The Darkling Thrush" (discussed below) are perfect companion pieces that will help bring some of these themes to light. You will first want to address Hardy's vision of individuals as being in conflict with society and with larger metaphysical and biological forces. In Hardy's landscape, insignificant human beings are pushed and pulled around by the machinations of fate. The image of the carousel in the first scene makes a good talking point in this regard; the characters in the story think they are on a pleasant "ride," whereas in reality they are caught up in a mechanical universe that propels them along while they struggle helplessly to pursue their goals. "Their motions were so rhythmical that they seemed to be moved by machinery," the narrator tells us. Thoughtful students will find other ways to expand the metaphor: the carousel suggests the circular relationship between the three major characters and perhaps also Charles's repeated movements between London and Melchester.

Other important topics to discuss include the story's attitude toward both marriage (as a constricting legal contract) and sexual desire (as something that always exacts a social cost). In many ways, "On the Western Circuit" takes up themes that Hardy addressed more explicitly a few years later in *Jude the Obscure*. In each, the male protagonist's social ambitions are thwarted when he yields to his own sexual desires and are further destroyed when he enters into marriage (under misleading circumstances, in both cases). By marrying Anna, Charles slips down a notch on the social scale; although he hopes to raise her up to a higher standard, he nonetheless realizes that he must leave his London position and move to the country. Embedded in this seemingly simple movement is another Hardy theme: the conflict between urban and rural forms of life. As Anna's seducer, Charles can be seen to represent the destruction of rural existence by urban and modern encroachments (and the carousel is another indicator of this). Yet at the same time, Charles is not a winner in this scenario: urban pressures create modern individuals who are too vulnerable to withstand the onslaught of the age. This theme is probably better suited to upper-division courses, as it is not obvious to first-time readers of Hardy. The description of Charles as a "gentlemanly young fellow, one of the species found in large towns only, and London particularly, built on delicate lines . . . [with] nothing square or practical about his look" will help you to pursue this line of thought. The "square or practical" look that Charles lacks is identified with rural modes of behavior more suited to the earlier part of the century, when "sordid ambition [was] the master-passion." Charles, in contrast, is an "end-of-the-age young man." You might also want to mention that although Charles doesn't have the best of motives, he nonetheless demonstrates some sensitivity in his response to the letters that Edith has written. This refinement of feelings marks both Edith and Charles as "modern"—and hence fragile.

Charles, of course, is not the only character whose life is ruined; Anna has been robbed of her innocence, and it is unlikely that either will be happy in their marriage. Students will want to talk about who comes out losing the most here, among the three protagonists. Charles, after all, is "no great man, in any sense," so he is not completely sympathetic. And Edith's position is especially tragic. She is pressured into an unhappy marriage because of the "belief of the British parent that a bad marriage with its aversions is better than free womanhood with its interests, dignity, and leisure." In Hardy's world, rigid social conventions deform and delimit human lives no less than the cruelty of blind chance. All human aspirations are doomed; all emotions are futile. In the first flush of their attraction, Anna and Charles smile at one another "with that unmistakable expression which means so little at the moment, yet so often leads up to passion, heart-ache, union, disunion, devotion, overpopulation, drudgery, content, resignation, despair." Sexual desire in Hardy's fiction is especially problematic, destroying any chance at self-fulfillment.

Hap

Quick Read

- Form: Sonnet.
- Themes: The universe is indifferent, random, and cruel; there is no rhyme or reason to human suffering; misery could be more readily borne if one knew there was a supreme being who had some kind of motive—albeit a cruel one—to cause people pain.
- Key Passages: "[I would be] Half-eased in that a Powerfuller than I / Had willed and meted me the tears I shed," lines 7–8; "And why unblooms the best hope ever sown?" line 10; "These purblind Doomsters had as readily strown / Blisses about my pilgrimage as pain," lines 13–14.

Teaching Suggestions

"Hap" is quintessential Hardy; it rails at a cruel, indifferent universe that destroys lives for no reason. Begin by inviting students to examine the change in point of view between the first two quatrains and the turn in the final sestet. If some "vengeful god" were oppressing him with demonic glee, says the speaker of "Hap," then he could bear the "suffering," knowing at least that one "Powerfuller" than the speaker shaped his life to some purpose, however malevolent (lines 1–2, 7). This train of thought is completely rejected in the first sentence of the final sestet, however: "But not so" (line 9). Ask students why the speaker would prefer a vengeful god to a capricious one. Life unfolds according to chance, and it is this randomness that the speaker finds particularly galling: "These purblind Doomsters had as readily strown / Blisses about my pilgrimage as pain" (lines 13–14). Closely read these lines, looking at the meaning of "pilgrimage" (equating life with a pilgrimage) and at the arbitrary actions of the "purblind Doomsters." Also, ask students to think about the effects of Hardy's awkward language, apparent in words such as "Powerfuller" (line 7) and "unblooms" (line 10). There is a raw kind of anger that takes this poem out of the realm of pretty melancholy and into something more jarring and immediate. Readers will see how the themes in "Hap," taught alongside "On the Western Circuit," play out in the relationship between Anna, Charles, and Edith.

The Darkling Thrush

Quick Read

- Form: Lyric; a type of elegy.
- Themes: The desolation of the nineteenth century and uncertainty of the twentieth; the lack of regenerative capacity in the vanishing way of life; the exhaustion of poetic inspiration.
- Key Passages: "The Century's corpse outleant," line 10; "An aged

thrush, frail, gaunt, and small, / In blast-beruffled plume," lines 21–22; "I could think there trembled through . . . / Some blessed Hope, whereof he knew / And I was unaware," lines 31–32.

Teaching Suggestions

"The Darkling Thrush" takes up issues of modernity and older, spent forms of existence. The speaker begins by surveying a bleak landscape in the middle of winter. In the second stanza, we realize that he is concerned with the passing of the nineteenth century, which he imagines as a human corpse ("The Century's corpse outleant" [line 10]). Note that the speaker is concerned not only that the past century is dead and gone, but also that it lacks the biological powers of regeneration, as represented in nature: "The ancient pulse of germ and birth / Was shrunken hard and dry" (lines 13–14). This is key to understanding Hardy and the themes of his fiction, which are often concerned with the inability of the modern age to reproduce healthy, vigorous forms of life. It is significant also that the reproductive metaphor is centered on the countryside ("The land's sharp features" [line 9]), because the modern age has destroyed a specifically rural past, one rooted in the land. This concept can also be traced in "On the Western Circuit"; just as Anna, the naïve country girl, comes in contact with a modern world that strips her innocence and takes the vitality out of her life, so too does the nineteenth century of "The Darkling Thrush" find itself desolate, with an uncertain future ahead.

In the third stanza, you will want to focus your attention on the dilapidated condition of the "aged thrush, frail, gaunt, and small, / In blast-beruffled plume" (lines 21–22). Invite students to compare this bird with the nightingale of Keats's ode. This is a good place to discuss the literary tradition invoked in words such as "Darkling" (which has a rich poetic legacy, used in Keats's "Ode to a Nightingale" and in Milton's *Paradise Lost*, for example, both in reference to birds). The lyre, too, traditionally associated with poetry and music, is here "broken" (line 6), suggesting that poetic inspiration is lacking. Whereas Keats's nightingale is a source of delight, capable of sparking poetic regeneration, Hardy's thrush, although singing joyfully, is not going to last much longer in the next century, and the final stanza rather cruelly eliminates any faint hope for rebirth suggested by the bird's "full-hearted evensong" (line 19). Ask students to pay close attention to the last two lines: "I could think there trembled through . . . / Some blessed Hope, whereof he knew / And I was unaware" (lines 31–32). Does the reference to "Hope" posit an optimistic future, or does the speaker's unawareness foreclose such hope?

Teaching Clusters

Hardy's work falls generally into the categories of **Transition, Modernity, and Modernism** and **Gender, Desire, and Sexuality**. "On the Western Circuit" may be taught in either category, since it addresses both sexual issues and the difficulties of living in a modern world in which individuals are helpless against larger cosmic influences. "Hap" and "The Darkling Thrush" belong in this latter category, as do poems that may not directly address modernity or human helplessness but convey attitudes of pessimism, skepticism, and resignation in relation to history, time, or political, social, or metaphysical circumstances; "I Look into My Glass," "Drummer Hodge," "Channel Firing," "The Convergence of the Twain," "Ah, Are You Digging on My Grave?," and numerous other selections may be taught in this cluster. Several of Hardy's works may also be included in the **History, Memory, and Politics** grouping, such as "The Darkling Thrush" and "Drummer Hodge," among others. "The Ruined Maid," on the other hand—a parody of the fallen woman theme—may be studied in the **Gender, Desire, and Sexuality** cluster, alongside D. G. Rossetti's "Jenny" and Christina Rossetti's *Goblin Market*. Alternatively, since class position in this poem is demonstrated through linguistic indicators, "The Ruined Maid" could be placed in the cluster on **Culture, Language, and Identity**.

Discussion Questions

1. Explore the image of the carousel as a governing metaphor in "On the Western Circuit."
2. What is Hardy's attitude toward marriage in "On the Western Circuit"? Compare Edith's marriage to Anna and Charles's; in what way are people trapped or restricted by their marriages? What in particular is problematic about marriage as depicted here?
3. How does sexual desire complicate the characters' lives? How is the fulfillment of this desire in conflict with other aspects of their lives?
4. Of the three protagonists of "On the Western Circuit"—Anna, Charles, and Edith—who is the most tragic? Do these characters have any control over their own lives? What causes their suffering?
5. Is Charles a sympathetic character? To what extent does his seduction of Anna affect the way you judge him and the way you understand the story? Is he unfairly tricked by Anna into marrying her?
6. How are concepts of modernity and urban life treated in "On the Western Circuit"? Why is Charles described as "the end-of-the-age young man"? Compare Anna's rusticity to Edith's more cosmopolitan ways. In what way are Charles and Edith "modern"?
7. What does the title "Hap" mean? How is it related to the poem's themes?
8. Why does Hardy use the word "Powerfuller" (line 7) in "Hap" rather than some other more lyrical word or phrase?
9. What does "The Darkling Thrush" have to say about the fading of the nineteenth century and the dawning of the twentieth? How does this poem comment on rural devastation?
10. Compare "The Darkling Thrush" to Keats's "Ode to a Nightingale." How are birds in each poem related to poetic inspiration and emotional sustenance?

Joseph Conrad

Heart of Darkness

Joseph Conrad's *Heart of Darkness* is an essential text for any course on twentieth-century literature; it may act as a centerpiece for introductory discussions on both imperialism and modernism—two major lines of inquiry that are central for a critical understanding of the period. As a modernist text, *Heart of Darkness* destabilizes meaning, dissolves the boundary between self and other, and bars the reader from epistemological certainty. It describes a modern world in which the self is unknowable and experience is ineffable. The atrocities committed in the Congo in the "cause of progress," for instance, defy Marlow's powers of description. "Do you see him? Do you see the story? Do you see anything?" he cries. "It seems to me I am trying to tell you a dream—making a vain attempt." Moreover, as a text that critiques the imperialist project, *Heart of Darkness* exposes the horrors of colonial exploration and trade. As Marlow declares, "The conquest of the earth, which mostly means the taking it away from those who have a different complexion or slightly flatter noses than ourselves, is not a pretty thing when you look into it too much." At the same time, however, the African people exist not as complex human beings, but as a reflection of Marlow's inner agitation and presumed latent savagery. Steaming down the river, he hears the beating of drums and sees "a whirl of black limbs, a mass of hands clapping, of feet stamping, of bodies swaying, of eyes rolling." Marlow does not see individuals, only a "black and incomprehensible frenzy," a spectacle of undifferentiated African-ness that speaks to him of his own ongoing concerns: the terrifying affinity between "prehistoric man" and himself, the tenuousness of the European's civilized identity, and the ephemerality of Western culture. It is this reduction of unique, thinking beings to mindless bodies and baffling ciphers that caused Chinua Achebe—and others after him—to see Conrad's novella as racist. Because this text has elicited so many differing responses, and because of its very conflicted treatment of imperialism, race, and the modern condition, *Heart of Darkness* offers students an exceptional opportunity to explore some of the most important issues addressed by twentieth-century writers.

Quick Read

- Form: Novella.
- Summary: *Heart of Darkness* tells the story of one man's journey into the African interior, where he discovers that brutality and greed underlie the imperialist enterprise.
- Themes: The imperialist endeavor is sullied by inhumanity and rapaciousness; the depths of human savagery are unfathomable; barbarity and cruelty lie under the surface of "civilized" humankind; epistemological certainty is impossible; the world and the self are incompre-

hensible: distinctions between savagery and civilization, self and other, truth and lies, ideals and corruption, are unstable.

- Key Passages: "The conquest of the earth, which mostly means the taking it away from those who have a different complexion or slightly flatter noses than ourselves, is not a pretty thing when you look into it too much. What redeems it is the idea only" (1894); "Black shapes crouched, lay, sat between the trees, . . . in all attitudes of pain, abandonment, and despair. . . . The work was going on. The work! And this was the place where some of the helpers had withdrawn to die" (1901); "But suddenly, as we struggled round a bend, there would be a glimpse of rush walls, of peaked glass-roofs, a burst of yells, a whirl of black limbs, a mass of hands clapping, of feet stamping, of bodies swaying, of eyes rolling, under the droop of heavy and motionless foliage. The steamer toiled along slowly on the edge of a black and incomprehensible frenzy" (1916); "what thrilled you was just the thought of their humanity—like yours—the thought of your remote kinship with this wild and passionate uproar. Ugly" (1916); "The last word [Kurtz] pronounced was—your name" (1947).

Teaching Suggestions

One of the concepts that students need to grasp about this text is that its modernist tendencies go hand-in-hand with the historical and political realities it addresses. Like later, more self-consciously modernist—and modern—literary experiments, *Heart of Darkness* employs new forms of language and expression to convey the unfathomability of wide-scale social alienation, cultural dislocation, and institutionalized brutality. The other concept students need to understand is that the charge of racism does not relegate this text to some remote historical dustbin, but speaks to controversies relevant both to much twentieth-century literature and to today's political realities. Some readers will see parallels between the "civilizing mission" of imperialism's first wave, for example, and current trends to spread Western-style global capitalism around the world.

A good way to begin the session is by talking about some of the historical circumstances related to the story, such as Leopold II's exploitation of the Congo, the abuse of Africans, and connections between the ivory trade and the slave trade. Certainly an extended discussion on imperialism is necessary here, and in particular its claims to being a noble mission to spread Western moral and cultural values. From this point you might want to look at some of the passages that address both the wrongs of imperialism and the civilizing "idea" behind it. A key section that requires a careful close reading is the one in which Marlow talks about the differences between the Roman conquerors and the modern European colonizers. "[The Romans] were not much account, really. They were no colonists. . . . They were conquerors, and for that you want only brute force. . . . It was just robbery with violence," Marlow states. "The conquest of the earth," he continues, "is not a pretty thing when you look into it too much. What redeems it is the idea only . . . an unselfish belief in the idea." Elsewhere, complaining about the European traders, Marlow asserts, "To tear treasure out of the bowels of the land was their desire, with no more moral purpose at the back of it than there is in burglars breaking into a safe." Ask students to focus on Marlow's concept of the "idea"; how is it related to a "moral purpose"? What differentiates the Roman "conquerors" from the European "colonists"—at least in theory? And what is *Heart of Darkness* saying about the "idea"? Is the concept of high moral purpose in the imperialist endeavor a tarnished notion in itself, or are human beings themselves flawed in some way? For Marlow, the imperial "idea" has something noble in it, although human beings lack the integrity to follow through in the correct spirit.

This line of thought will lead you into one of the story's major themes—that nothing separates the modern "civilized" European from the African "savage"—and directly into questions of racism. Describing the Africans, Marlow states: "It was unearthly, and the men were—No, they were not inhuman. . . . They howled and leaped, and spun, and made horrid faces; but what thrilled you was just the thought of their humanity—like yours—the thought of your remote kinship with this wild and passionate uproar. Ugly." Disparaging comments such as these prompted Achebe to write a trenchant response accusing Conrad of racism (see "An Image of Africa: Racism in Conrad's *Heart of Darkness*"). Achebe's essay provides a valuable tool for exploring this and other condescending images of Africans in Conrad's text. In an even more insulting passage, Marlow ridicules "the savage who was fireman," describing him as "a dog in a parody of breeches and a feather hat, walking on his hind legs." Yet students also need to see the other aspects of the narrative that demonstrate how deeply divided Marlow is on the matter. While Kurtz is the text's quintessential "savage," for example—vividly illustrated by the shrunken human heads that surround his mud hut—Marlow's African cannibal companions onboard the steamer prove themselves to be men of principle, unexpectedly capable of "restraint" despite their month-long fast. Kurtz, in contrast—the exemplary European—utterly lacks "restraint in the gratification of his various lusts." Moreover, Marlow demonstrates sincere compassion for the emaciated, chained Africans ("these men could by no stretch of the imagination be called enemies") and for the dying African workers who "crouched, lay, sat between the trees, . . . in all attitudes of pain, abandonment, and despair." Although confusing to readers, these contradictions are important in exploring the anatomy of the colonialist frame of mind—and of those who attempt to break out of that frame. Marlow's genuine abhorrence at the treatment of the African workers is tempered by his construction as an imperialist subject; his language is the language of the colonizer. This is not to excuse any racism in the text or to locate it as an historical anomaly, but rather to scrutinize the complex relations between culture and identity that are just as operative today as they were in Conrad's time. Marlow participates in the mythologizing of Western civilization and perpetuates some of its imperialist assumptions because he has no self-conception or language outside of that construct. In fact, Marlow recognizes his own complicity in the imperialist enterprise when, after being disgusted at the sight of the shackled workers and meeting with an African guard who concedes to Marlow's authority, he dryly comments, "After all, I also was a part of the great cause of these high and just proceedings." This collusion with the imperialist mythos is made complete at the end of the narrative, when Marlow meets with Kurtz's "Intended" and utters the famous lie: "The last word [Kurtz] pronounced was—your name." Invite students to think about why Marlow lies here, and what that means for everything that has gone before. To what extent can we trust him as a narrator? Marlow continually oscillates between compassion for the African people and revulsion at their cultural difference; between the "idea" of European civilization and the reality of crude self-interest; and between belief in the possibility of real knowledge and a complete disavowal of such. He is profoundly conflicted, and this state of confusion speaks not only to the trauma of witnessing horrific events, but also to being unable to keep oneself separate from those events. Marlow is both surrounded by an unintelligible "darkness" and finds that he is unintelligible to himself.

After you have explored the topics of imperialism and race, students are in a much better position to discuss the modernist elements of the text. There are many approaches you can take here, but you will want to draw parallels between the "incomprehensible" (an oft-repeated word) aspects of the text itself (many students will have trouble following the basic plot line) and the disturbing occurrences it describes; in other words, the narrative mode reflects the traumatic and disorienting content. Modernist texts tend to destabilize meaning and dislocate the reader: meaning is not transparent, knowledge is not a simple given, and the boundary between subject and object (or self and other) is not always clear. Time, moreover, is often disrupted rather than linear and coherent. All of these elements are applicable to *Heart of Darkness*, thus making this an excellent introduction to the concept of modernism.

Moreover, you may, if you wish, approach the topic of incomprehensibility through the motif of the quest. Marlow's journey up the river is also a metaphorical journey into the inner recesses of the psyche. As in Robert Browning's "Childe Roland to the Dark Tower Came" and other quest narratives, the landscape and people in *Heart of Darkness* reflect the protagonist's mental turmoil. The "whirl of black limbs . . . [and] bodies swaying" that alarms Marlow as they float along the river cuts him off from "the comprehension of [his] surroundings." This "black and incomprehensible frenzy" mirrors the speaker's mental disorder in the same way that the desolate landscape and ghostly figures in "Childe Roland" mirror Roland's state of mind." Yet the historical specificity of Marlow's African landscape and shadowy figures put this story in an entirely different register. We learn a great deal about Marlow and about turn-of-the-century European anxieties from this incident, but nothing about the people he describes with such apprehension. The Africans are objectified and made into aesthetic props devoid of any individuality. It is interesting to compare this scene (one of the scenes Achebe singles out for criticism in "An Image of Africa") with chapters 5 and 6 of *Things Fall Apart*, wherein another village celebration accompanied by pounding drumbeats is used to explore social relations among the people of Umuofia and further to develop the troubling, intricate character of Okonkwo. In Achebe, an African festival is presented as not irrationally frenzied but exuberant, not "incomprehensible" but deeply meaningful, carefully planned by the community rather than the result of some obscure savage impulse.

Teaching Clusters

Heart of Darkness is an important transitional piece that would make a valuable addition to the cluster on **Transition, Modernity, and Modernism**. It would be an equally essential component of the **History, Memory, and Politics** grouping, studied alongside Achebe's *Things Fall Apart* and "An Image of Africa: Racism in Conrad's *Heart of Darkness*." Achebe's trenchant comments on Conrad's novella are helpful in focusing discussion on the text's view of Africans, which Achebe sees as condescending. Comparison with Kipling's "The Man Who Would Be King," on the other hand, would help clarify the ways in which *Heart of Darkness* is critical of the colonial project. Additionally, it would make a good deal of sense to pair the 1899 *Heart of Darkness* with J. M. Coetzee's 1960 *Waiting for the Barbarians*, because both works show the arbitrariness and hollowness of such concepts as "barbarian" and "civilized," satirize the rationalizations that the imperialist employs, and portray empire building as a nightmarish and brutal activity founded on self-delusion. *Heart of Darkness* could also be profitably studied in the **Culture, Language, and Identity** category, with particular emphasis placed on issues of British national identity, psychic fragmentation, and cultural disjunction.

Discussion Questions

1. Early on in *Heart of Darkness*, Marlow says, "The conquest of the earth . . . is not a pretty thing when you look into it too much. What redeems it is the idea only . . . an unselfish belief in the idea." What does Marlow mean by the "idea"? Why does this tell you about his attitude toward European imperialism? Is the "idea" itself suspect in this text, or are human beings incapable of such lofty goals?

2. What does *Heart of Darkness* have to say about imperialism? How does your knowledge of historical context—the Belgian Congo, the ivory trade, the treatment of Africans—affect your understanding of the story?

3. Discuss Marlow's conflicted attitude toward the Africans. In what way is he condescending? In what way is he respectful? How can you reconcile this polarization?

4. Explore *Heart of Darkness* in relation to Chinua Achebe's "An Image of Africa: Racism in Conrad's *Heart of Darkness*."

5. What does Kurtz represent to Marlow? Why does Marlow want to meet Kurtz? What does Marlow learn from his meeting with Kurtz?
6. Why does Marlow lie to Kurtz's "Intended" and tell her that "The last word [Kurtz] pronounced was—your name"? What are the implications of this lie for Marlow's attitudes about imperialism, about the treatment of Africans, and about Western civilization?
7. Explore the concept of "savagery" in this text. Who and what constitutes savagery? What does it mean to be civilized?
8. Compare the description of Kurtz's "Intended" with the description of his African mistress. What role does each woman serve in the narrative?
9. In what way is this a modernist text? What techniques does it use to disrupt conventional assumptions about time, history, identity, knowledge, and communication? Why are there two narrators here? In what way are the reader's expectations thwarted? What kinds of problems did you encounter in reading and understanding this text?
10. Discuss *Heart of Darkness* as a quest narrative. In what way is this a journey into the self? What is the end result of that journey and self-scrutiny? What does it mean to encounter the "heart of darkness"? How do the African people and landscape reflect Marlow's state of mind?

A. E. Housman

Housman is often overlooked in surveys of twentieth-century poetry, but there is much here for students to think about. Although he does not break new ground in terms of form, his use of irony and the tone of resignation and pessimism give his poems a modern sensibility. In Housman's writing, the future is regarded with mistrust and sadness must be borne with cool detachment. In "The Chestnut Casts His Flambeaux," for instance, the speaker comments, "Our only portion is the estate of man: / We want the moon, but we shall get no more" (lines 19–20). And while the past is irretrievable ("Now, of my threescore years and ten, / Twenty will not come again" ["Loveliest of Trees," lines 5–6]), there is no cloying sense of nostalgia. Moreover, there is humor here: Housman is wryly self-mocking when the speaker of "Terence, This Is Stupid Stuff" asserts, "malt does more than Milton can / To justify God's ways to man" (lines 21–22). Themes of loss, death, and hopelessness in Housman's poetry are approached with spare language and an unsentimental eye.

To an Athlete Dying Young

Quick Read

- Form: Elegy.
- Themes: It's better to die young, while one is in the first flush of success, than to live a long life and see one's reputation fade; for those who live, the future is bleak.
- Key Passages: "And home we brought you shoulder-high. / . . .

Shoulder-high we bring you home," lines 4–6; "Smart lad, to slip be-
times away / From fields where glory does not stay / And early though
the laurel grows / It withers quicker than the rose," lines 9–12.

Teaching Suggestions

Sharp irony underlies Housman's treatment of death in "To an Athlete
Dying Young." Ask students to compare the first two stanzas, focusing in
particular on the repeated phrase "shoulder-high" and the ironic connotations of the very different contexts in which each appears (lines 4 and 6).
How does this juxtaposition of situations affect the tone and meaning of
the poem? Note also the discrepancy between the jaunty meter and the
sober content. Such pairings increase the sense of pessimism and point to
a bleak view of life. In the third stanza, the images of the "laurel" (line 11)
and the "rose" (line 12) offer possible ways to pursue the poem's themes.
While the laurel denotes accomplishment, the rose—usually an image of
youth and beauty—here refers to impermanence and decline. This yoking
of concepts occurs throughout the poem; success is always attenuated because it is set against the failure of success. Thus, the fourth stanza describes victory as something that can never be realized again by the
athlete, who is dead, while the fifth stanza tells us that even the living
cannot hope to see their triumph endure. While the elegiac lyric usually
consoles the reader and affirms the value of life, "To an Athlete Dying
Young" tells us that life leads only to diminishment.

"Terence, This Is Stupid Stuff"

Teaching Suggestions

"To an Athlete Dying Young" can be usefully compared to "Terence,
This Is Stupid Stuff." In both poems, life is oppressive and the future is
cheerless. The "Terence" speaker yearns to escape the reality of the present by "Look[ing] into the pewter pot / To see the world as the world's
not" (lines 25–26). After a bout of drunkenness, he wakes to find that the
world, which had seemed "none so bad" when he was intoxicated, now
seems a dismal place (line 33). Significantly, however, "Terence" is a poet,
like Housman, although an unprepossessing one. To his friends who disparage his poetry, he says "malt does more than Milton can / To justify
God's ways to man" (lines 21–22). After describing the world as containing "Much good, but much less good than ill," the speaker ends with an
anecdote about an Eastern king who inoculated himself against poison by
ingesting small amounts of the substance over time. Ask students to consider what the poem says about the role of poetry and the poet. Can we
take Terence at his word when he says that beer can do more good than
poetry? Or can poetry help human beings endure their dreary lives? Why
does Housman create a character that shares his vocation as a poet but
who is boorish and ridiculous? Both "To an Athlete Dying Young" and
"Terence, This Is Stupid Stuff" contain ironic contrasts worth pursuing.

Teaching Clusters

The sense of dissatisfaction with the present and mistrust of the future in Housman's poetry, along with his sardonic tone and use of irony, illustrate some of the transitional aspects of modern writing, so in this sense could be placed in the **Transition, Modernity, and Modernism** cluster. His poems are well matched with those of Hardy, in particular. Additionally, because of their preoccupation with the loss of the past, they would make an interesting comparison with Ernest Dowson's work; such a comparison would emphasize the pessimism of Housman's poetry and the way that it avoids nostalgia. In this latter context, Housman's work could be studied in the cluster on **History, Memory, and Politics.**

Discussion Questions

1. How does "To an Athlete Dying Young" describe death? Does this poem console the reader? What does it say or imply about grief?
2. How do the images of the laurel and the rose relate to the larger themes of "To an Athlete Dying Young"?
3. Why does the speaker of "To an Athlete Dying Young" say that the athlete is a "Smart lad" (line 9)?
4. In what way is "To an Athlete Dying Young" ironic?
5. Compare the view of life in "To an Athlete Dying Young" with that in "Terence, This Is Stupid Stuff."
6. Why is the story about the king who inoculated himself against poison by taking small amounts of poison significant in "Terence, This Is Stupid Stuff"? What does this anecdote have to do with poetry? Why would Housman, a poet, create such a foolish alter ego as Terence?

Voices from World War I

To read the work of the writers of the First World War is to observe creative minds searching for new modes of expression in the midst of an unprecedented crisis. That this event was unique in British history is undoubted: Britain, which in the previous century had fought substantially smaller wars with a compact professional volunteer army, found this force drastically depleted within the first years of World War I, necessitating the instatement of a draft that contributed to the eventual loss of nearly a generation of young men. Modes of expression pioneered in the atmosphere of doubt, anxiety, and instability of the late Victorian era—Thomas Hardy's stripped-down poetic rhetoric and the patriarchy-challenging models found in Samuel Butler's *The Way of All Flesh* and Edmund Gosse's *Father and Son*, for example—provided some signposts for the World War I writers. However, as this generation of writers began to comprehend the unparalleled scope of the conflict, urgency forced them to create their own innovations in form and perspective. A new graphic realism sprang from the need to bring home vividly to an uninformed public that this was a different kind of war, one without room for traditional heroism or blind patriotism. Biting irony grew from the sundering of ennobling military ideals from reality; new poetic formal means evolved from the need to echo the asynchronous rhythms of a long and complicated conflict; and a fresh, intensely empathetic but anti-heroic way of looking at the warrior's lot came out of the contrast between what the conscript was led to expect while on native soil and his actual, everworsening plight on the stalemated European front line. During the war, the work of the poets served as a wake-up call and a warning to the civilian population back home, while in the great conflict's immediate aftermath, the writings of the memoirists joined with the poetry in carrying on the antiwar mission to forestall such an event from ever happening again.

Siegfried Sassoon

Glory of Women

Quick Read

- Form: Sonnet.
- Themes: The unheroic nature of a soldier's life; the perpetuation of romantic notions of war by women and other noncombatants; the disgrace of war.
- Key Passages: "You love us when we're . . . wounded in a mentionable place," lines 1–2; "you believe / That chivalry redeems the war's disgrace," lines 3–4; "You can't believe that British troops 'retire' / When hell's last horror breaks them, and they run," lines 9–10; "O German mother dreaming by the fire, / While you are knitting socks to send your son / His face is trodden deeper in the mud," lines 12–14.

Teaching Suggestions

The poetry of Sassoon and other prominent World War I writers evinces a belief that war on the frontline is an experience so alien to other human activity that anyone who has not suffered the same ordeal cannot truly understand or empathize with the combatant. It's worth noting, therefore, that "Glory of Women" does not necessarily deride women because they are women, but because they are a significant part of a larger group of civilians in general. Besides civilian women, all people not in the trenches, such as the Bishop in "They" and the General behind the frontline in "The General," are deemed by the poet to experience a separate reality and thus are seen as incapable of sharing his perspective. Students might initially mistake this attitude as a celebration of militaristic life, but a closer look at the majority of poems in this section will help illustrate that the war poets are speaking of estrangement and regret over lack of real sensitivity to the soldiers' plight in a senseless, mismanaged war rather than of any sort of heroic exceptionalism. Indeed, anti-heroism distinguishes the endeavors of the common soldiers who figure in the work of these poets. The highlighting of the euphemistic nature of the word "retire," for instance, in "Glory of Women" evokes a scene of soldiers fleeing, displaying justifiable timidity in the face of an intolerable barrage. The fallen warriors in Sassoon's poetry are not glorious figures, but "terrible corpses" trampled "in the mud" (lines 11, 14).

A good place to begin here would be with a discussion of the sonnet structure and the turn that occurs in the final tercet of this poem. The phrase "mentionable place" (line 2) establishes the direction of the first eleven lines and offers a useful talking point. The poem is concerned with what can and can't be said about war: how euphemisms and romantic notions of military bravery conceal a grisly reality. "[T]ales of dirt and danger"—appropriately expurgated—"delight" the listeners (lines 6, 5), but a candid explanation as to why British troops "retire" is not welcome. Invite students to think about why the speaker objects to these social niceties. Why does he want to expose the reality of war? Note also that this poem rejects another convention of military talk when, rather than urging hatred for the enemy, it demonstrates a compassion for and identification with the foreign adversary. The final three lines, then, go a step further in the poem's critique of military idealism and ask for a sympathetic response from the reader for the German son whose "face is trodden deeper in the mud" (line 14). In choice of idiom and image, the World War I poet is always a champion of the common man, no matter what side he is on. The poems show that the deepest anger of Sassoon and others like him is reserved for generals, clergymen, and other figures of authority whom the poets see as totally discredited by their misdirection and support of a hopeless, enormously wasteful war.

Isaac Rosenberg

Break of Day in the Trenches

Quick Read

- Form: Lyric.
- Themes: War reduces civilization to a subhuman level, soldiers from opposing sides share common experience, war is the enemy.
- Key Passages: "Only a live thing leaps my hand, / A queer sardonic rat," lines 3–4; "Now you have touched this English hand / You will do the same to a German," lines 9–10; "Poppies whose roots are in man's veins / Drop, and are ever dropping," lines 23–24.

Teaching Suggestions

A variety of images are introduced in rapid staccato bursts at the beginning of the poem: dissolving darkness, the universe's endless time, a "queer sardonic rat," and a yanked poppy. Ask students to focus first on the image of the rat; what effect does this unexpected form produce? As in Sassoon's "Glory of Women," British and German soldiers are not mortal enemies, but men who share the indignities and dangers of war. Physically connected by this lowly creature, the soldiers are confined to their respective holes, ignominiously "[s]prawled in the bowels of the earth" while the rat runs free (line 17). Rather than displaying manly heroism, the men endure the passive victimhood implicit in the trench soldiers' lot. Exhausted and paralyzed by fear as the "shrieking iron and flame" of shells sail over their heads (line 20), the men "quaver," each with a "heart aghast" (line 22), presenting a vivid contrast to the idealized picture of war. The words applied to the rat, moreover—"sardonic," "droll," "cosmopolitan"—besides signaling the attitude of the poem as a whole, suggest something else. Just as his plague-carrying ancestors came to be seen as malevolent symbols of pestilence and death, the sardonic, disinterested rat too may signify the presence of death. Imagining the rat's eye view, with its knowing "[inward] grin," the poet goes beyond the exposition of a single event and seems to capture a general, comprehensive view of the essence of the Great War— not a view of glorious martial tableaux but of all participants being eyed and taken note of by Death (line 13). In the company of beings, flesh and vegetable, doomed to "Drop, and . . . ever dropping," the rat is truly the only "a live thing" on the scene (lines 24, 33).

Students will find the poppy image a rich source of discussion as well. It would be worthwhile to bring students' attention to the fact that, in choosing the poppy image, Rosenberg is making a reference to one of World War I's most famous propaganda poems, the patriotic "Flanders Fields" by John McCrae. In that poem, poppies that grow between the crosses in soldiers' cemeteries at first suggest a peaceful rest, but McCrae ends the poem by urging that the war must continue, because if it is not avenged, the dead "shall not sleep, though poppies grow / In Flanders fields." The opiate peace that is promised by McCrae's poppies, provided his countrymen are avenged, is countered by the implication in Rosenberg's poem that the poppies flourish on the fertilizer of ever larger mounds of corpses supplied by an unending war effort. First plucked, presumably at some risk of death, from the parapet of a trench, the poppy in "Break of Day" is initially a whimsical decoration to momentarily brighten drab wartime existence. However, the reader is soon reminded that the area before these parapets is an extensive "no man's land" where corpses lie rotting for days or years, thus feeding the "[p]oppies whose roots are men's veins" (line 23). Rosenberg may also be inviting us to liken the poppies to the bodies of soldiers destined soon to drop or to drops of blood whose origins are in men's veins and "are ever dropping" because of this war (line 24). Ironically, in its plucked state, the poppy is far from "safe" (line 25); it is no longer its original crimson self, but "a little white with the dust" (line 26), a reminder of the journey of all living things—and the fate of many World War I soldiers—to dust. In a world in which man and nature have been leveled to the same low plane of existence, the fate of the speaker seems linked with that of the poppy. A sense of transience and precariousness haunt a poem that begins with crumbling and ends with dust.

Wilfred Owen

Strange Meeting

Quick Read

- Form: Elegy; lyric.
- Themes: War's savage ironies; the pity of war; the poet's role in society; war is killing the poets; the soldier's real enemy is not his counterpart on the other side of no man's land, but war itself.
- Key Passages: "I mean the truth untold, / The pity of war, the pity war distilled," lines 24–25; "Courage was mine, and I had mystery, / Wisdom was mine, and I had mastery," lines 30–31; "I am the enemy you killed, my friend," line 40.

Teaching Suggestions

While perfecting the blend of realistic imagery and savage irony introduced into war poetry by his friend Siegfried Sassoon, Owen also declares the importance of a theme that will mark all war poetry after him—the unheroic, unglamorous "pity of War." Ask students to read Owen's unfinished "Preface" alongside his poetry and reflect on what he might have meant when he says, "Above all I am not concerned with poetry. My subject is War, and the pity of War." To Sassoon's black satire Owen adds something more: an attempt at a new kind of war poetry in which compassion mingles with tragedy. "Strange Meeting" alludes to this approach when the ghostly enemy—a poet, like Owen—laments his own death because he will not be able to impart his message, but will instead leave "the truth untold, / The pity of war, the pity war distilled" (lines 24–25). Note that Owen's view of the common soldier stresses his victimhood rather than the heroic attributes that earlier writers often stressed in military-themed poetry. There is no place in Owen's world for Victorian ideals such as the glory of individual sacrifice or the nobility of war.

You may want to direct students' attention to Owen's declaration, "I am not concerned with Poetry" ("Preface"). As with many comments made by authors about their work, this last statement need not be taken at face value; allusions to precursors such as Dante, Shelley, Keats, Wordsworth and the "graveyard poets" of the Romantic era, among others, are dispersed throughout Owen's writing. The title of "Strange Meeting" comes from Shelley's "The Revolt of Islam," while the inspiration for the scene that Owen sets at the beginning of the poem has been attributed to the first canto of Keats's *The Fall of Hyperion: A Dream*. In Keats's work, a poet dreams of his descent into a wasteland where, in a state approaching death, he meets the last survivor of a race of old gods who sounds a note of warning and questions the usefulness to humanity of the poet or his poetry. The speaker of Owen's poem makes a similar descent into a devastated landscape, where he meets a figure whose kind has been annihilated and who speaks words of warning about the loss of poets from the world.

The inhabitants of such a place, the specter cautions, "will go content with what we spoiled, / Or, discontent, boil bloody, and be spilled" (lines 26–27). Students may not at first understand that this imaginary figure is a combination of poet, enemy, and alter ego of the speaker. You can ask them to focus on phrases such as "what we spoiled"; who is the "we" here? What is being spoiled and how? Note that although the poet says his experience can help him illuminate war's mysteries and "truth untold," adding that "Wisdom was mine, and I had mastery," the survival of poets under the threat of modern warfare is threatened. "I am the enemy you killed, my friend," says the speaker's counterpart (line 40). Still underground, slipping toward inviting and permanent sleep, both of Owen's poets seem severed from their edifying mission while a complacent and blind world will never benefit from their hard-won wisdom.

It is in Owen's language itself that the break from Keats and other Romantic models is best appreciated. In the dissonant language of his mature poetry, Owen also diverges from his mentor Sassoon's reliance on imagery as the foremost mode of anti-war critique by adding specific techniques of form and sound to express the unique horror of World War I. Owen uses rhyme schemes that introduce a note of discord to frustrate the pleasures gained from the harmonious lyricism of traditional romantic elegy forms. Direct students' attention to Owen's use of pararhyme, a form of consonance in which identical consonant sounds precede and follow different vowels of which the second usually has a deeper tone. (See the *NAEL* headnote to Owen.) Examples such as hall-Hell, groined-groaned, grained-ground, and moan-mourn add to the poem's sense of discordance and incongruity. By supplanting the familiar affinities of sound and meaning with this technique, Owen creates a formal analogy to his theme of a world out of order whose once-dependable relationships have been disrupted by war. Modern without being modernist, Owen was an inspiration to later twentieth-century poets who sought new methods to express the turbulence of the period.

Teaching Clusters

The works of the World War I writers may be studied in the clusters on **Transition, Modernity, and Modernism** or **History, Memory, and Politics**. In the first category, you will want to focus attention on the new forms and attitudes demonstrated in these selections. The dissonant pararhymes of Wilfred Owen, for example, evidence a need to develop techniques that parallel the grim experience of modern trench warfare. Additionally, the startling break with heroic imagery and themes apparent in these works signals a desire to reject conventions of poetic diction and romantic notions of war. In the second category, you may concentrate on the thematics of war or pay particular attention to poems that look retrospectively at wartime experiences, such as Edward Thomas's "Tears" or "Adlestrop."

Discussion Questions

1. In Siegfried Sassoon's "Glory of Women," the speaker states, "You love us when we're . . . wounded in a mentionable place" (lines 1–2). How does the word "mentionable" relate to the rest of the poem? For the speaker, what is "unmentionable" about the war? What does he want to "mention"?
2. Why does the speaker of "Glory of Women" talk about the son of the German mother at the poem's conclusion? How is this different than talking about the son of a British mother?
3. In what way is the image of the rat in "Break of Day in the Trenches" significant? How does it affect the meaning of the poem? Why is the rat "sardonic" (line 4)?
4. What kind of landscape does the speaker of "Break of Day in the Trenches" describe? Why is no man's land a "sleeping green" (line 12)? What is the effect of juxtaposing "Strong eyes, fine limbs" (line 14) with "the bowels of the earth" or the "torn fields of France" (lines 17, 18)?
5. Who and what is the "Strange friend" that the speaker of "Strange Meeting" encounters (line 14)? How is he connected to the speaker—and to Owen himself?
6. What does the specter of "Strange Meeting" mean when he says "I am the enemy you killed, my friend" (line 40)? Who is the "enemy" here? How does this use of the word reverse the usual meaning of the word?
7. Compare the attitude toward the common soldier in any two World War I poems and in Rudyard Kipling's "Danny Deever" and "The Widow at Windsor."

Further Resources

Norton Online Archive

Audio:
To Juan at the Winter Solstice (read by Robert Graves)

Norton Topics Online

Representing the Great War

Modernist Manifestos

For twentieth-century modernist writers, traditional poetic and fictional forms were no longer adequate to encompass, or even adequately represent, chaotic modernity and the inchoate human subject newly theorized by evolutionism and psychoanalysis. Rejecting the conventions of their mainstream Victorian predecessors, the modernists employed techniques such as "formal experiment, dislocation of conventional syntax, radical breaches of decorum, disturbance of chronology and spatial order, ambiguity, polysemy, obscurity, mythopoeic allusion, primitivism, irrationalism, structuring by symbol and motif rather than by narrative or argumentative logic," as David Lodge observes (*Modernism, Antimodernism, and Postmodernism*, 1981). Such a variety of approaches attests to the fact, illustrated by the works in this section, that modernism was not a single movement or set of ideas, but a disparate assortment of modes, preoccupations, and theoretical positions. The *Blast* manifesto, signed by Ezra Pound, Wyndham Lewis, and others, for instance, has neither the restraint nor the precision advocated by T. E. Hulme, who urged a "dry and hard" poetry. The manifesto authors, moreover, were careful to distance themselves from other avant-garde artists, such as the Italian Futurists. And while Mina Loy's "Feminist Manifesto" employs the iconoclasm and typographical experimentalism of the *Blast* manifesto, her aim is quite different. Denouncing the current feminist movement, she exhorts women: "Cease to place your confidence in economic legislation, vice-crusades & uniform education"; rather than looking to be the equal of men, Loy advises women to look within themselves for a model of the feminine. Yet despite vast differences among the modernists, all demanded a radical break from established practices and possessed a passionate belief in the importance of art. The selections here are not only worthwhile in their own right, but provide valuable insights into the writings of modernist authors such as Virginia Woolf, James Joyce, and T. S. Eliot.

T. E. Hulme

Romanticism and Classicism

Quick Read

- Form: Lecture.
- Summary: Hulme condemns a vagueness and expansiveness in poetry that he identifies with romanticism and argues instead for a poetry that is precise, accurate, and concrete—in his view, a classic approach to poetry.
- Key Passages: "Here is the root of all romanticism: that man, the individual, is an infinite reservoir of possibilities; and if you can so rearrange society by the destruction of oppressive order then these possibilities will have a chance" (1999); "Man is an extraordinarily fixed and limited animal whose nature is absolutely constant. It is only by tradition and organisation that anything decent can be got out of him" (1999–2000); "In the classic, . . . man is always man and never a god" (2002); "It is essential to prove that beauty may be in small, dry things" (2002).

Teaching Suggestions

Many of your students may not be familiar with the conventional opposition between "romantic" and "classical" that Hulme is drawing upon, so you will want to give them some guidance on these very slippery terms. If you are willing to spend a little time with this topic, it would be worthwhile to assign some readings from the Romantic and Neoclassical writers along with this piece. Keats's "Ode to a Nightingale" or Wordsworth's Immortality ode, for example, would give you a way to begin a discussion on Romantic views of the limitlessness of human nature and the self's relation to the infinite—issues which Hulme repeatedly addresses. Excerpts from Pope's "An Essay on Man" ("Epistle 1. Of the Nature and State of Man, With Respect to the Universe") or John Locke's "An Essay Concerning Human Understanding" would offer useful Neoclassical perspectives. Hulme denounces what he sees as imprecision and a lack of restraint in Romantic writing—a tendency to get carried away with the imagination and to yearn to transcend the limits of the concrete. "Here is the root of all romanticism," Hulme complains, "that man, the individual, is an infinite reservoir of possibilities; and if you can so rearrange society by the destruction of oppressive order then these possibilities will have a chance." It is this reaching for the infinite, Hulme believes, that causes Romantic authors to be always "moaning or whining about something or other"; "there is always the bitter contrast between what you think you ought to be able to do and what man actually can." Instead of the Romantic vision of humankind as unlimited, Hulme advocates the classical approach, which he describes as an attention to order and accuracy. "Man is an extraordinarily fixed and limited animal whose nature is absolutely constant. It is only by tradition and organisation that anything decent can be got out of him," he explains. The poet who recognizes human limitations, he reasons, will produce writing that is spare and precise—and this is the only way that poetry can become fresh and immediate. Going against conventional wisdom, Hulme declares: "It is essential to prove that beauty may be in small, dry things."

Ezra Pound

In a Station of the Metro

Quick Read

- Form: Free verse; haiku-like.
- Summary: In two short lines of verse, Pound describes a moment in a busy Paris Metro station when he is moved by the loveliness of several passing faces.
- Themes: Beauty discovered in unlikely places; the quality of startling and moving sensations; the freshness of the natural world; the unexpected possibilities of the urban landscape.

Teaching Suggestions

"In a Station of the Metro" exemplifies the principles of imagist poetry espoused by Pound. Students will be able to get much more out of this poem if they also read Pound's essay on imagist principles, "A Few Don'ts by an Imagiste." You will want to first draw their attention to Pound's own explanation of the circumstances of the poem's composition and his description of it as "*hokku*-like" (see the footnote to "In a Station of the Metro"). Although not strictly a haiku poem, it contains the brevity, spareness of description, intensity of perception, grounding in nature, and focus on a single effect associated with the Japanese form. This single effect is centered on a brief moment in a crowded Paris train station when Pound was struck by the beauty of several passing faces. Invite students to think about the effect that is achieved by placing the image of the faces next to that of "Petals on a wet, black bough." It is a fresh, surprising vision, one that is very much in opposition to the city scene described in the first line, but that captures the unexpectedness of the urban "apparition." The use of the term "apparition," moreover, gives the reader a sense of how very unlovely the average scene at the station is and how pleasantly startling—and dreamlike—the seeming mirage is. After examining this particular word, you can discuss the allusiveness of each word in the poem—all carefully chosen for maximum effect.

You will also want to discuss Pound's definition of an image in relation to this poem. As he explains in "A Few Don'ts by an Imagiste," "[a]n 'Image' is that which presents an intellectual and emotional complex in an instant of time." The fleeting quality of the image, its immediate impression, is central to Pound's definition. There is no context, no narrative—nothing to detract from the impact of that momentary experience of feeling and perception. To Pound's way of thinking, this instantaneous effect "gives that sense of sudden liberation; that sense of freedom from time limits and space limits; that sense of sudden growth, which we experience in the presence of the greatest works of art" ("A Few Don'ts"). Note that the lack of any verbs adds to the quality of this moment being suspended in time. This static aspect of the imagist poem, moreover, is the very element that Pound later rejected in favor of vorticism.

Wyndham Lewis et al.

Blast

Teaching Suggestions

Students should be able to have some fun with the *Blast* manifesto and enjoy it for its energetic denouncement of convention and its celebration of art and individuality. They will immediately recognize the revolutionary fervor ("To make the rich of the community shed their education skin, to destroy politeness, standardization and academic, that is civilized vision, is the task we have set for ourselves") and the irreverent humor ("A VORTICIST KING! WHY NOT!"). You may need to draw their attention, however, to its rejection not only of traditional art forms, but also of other non-English types of avant-garde art—particularly Futurism, the Italian movement that embraced technology and the machine. To emphasize their disgust with Futurism and to insult it in the greatest way possible, they align Futurism with Impressionism, a form of painting that was revolutionary in its time but was already passé, eclipsed by Post-Impressionistic experiments such as Cubism. "[W]e are not Naturalists, Impressionists or Futurists (the latest form of Impressionism)," they declare. In fact, even love of the future and of the machine is out of date: "Wilde gushed twenty years ago about the beauty of machinery. Gissing, in his romantic delight with modern lodging houses was futurist in this sense." (To remind students of how loaded the term "romantic" is for modernists, refer them to Hulme's lecture, "Romanticism and Classicism.") In order to drive home the point that English artists are the only true radicals, they assert, "It may be said that great artists in England are always revolutionary."

Teaching Clusters

The most fitting placement for all of the works in this section is the cluster on **Transition, Modernity, and Modernism**. Ideally, these selections should be read alongside other modernist or transitional writings by authors such as Joseph Conrad, William Butler Yeats, Virginia Woolf, James Joyce, D. H. Lawrence, and T. S. Eliot. The Hulme piece in particular can be usefully paired with T. S. Eliot's poems. In general, it would be best to have a range of both the fiction or poetry and the theoretical essays; Woolf's "Modern Fiction," for example, would make a good counterpoint to Hulme's "Romanticism and Classicism." Loy's "Feminist Manifesto," on the other hand, can be studied either in the **Modernity** cluster or the **Gender, Desire, and Sexuality** grouping.

Discussion Questions

1. In "Romanticism and Classicism," Hulme states, "Here is the root of all romanticism: that man, the individual, is an infinite reservoir of possibilities; and if you can so rearrange society by the destruction of oppressive order then these possibilities will have a chance." In Hulme's view, why does a belief in humankind's limitless abilities lead to sloppiness and vagueness in writing?
2. Discuss what Hulme means when he says, "It is essential to prove that beauty may be in small, dry things."
3. In "A Few Don'ts by an Imagiste," Pound describes the "Image" as "that which presents an intellectual and emotional complex in an instant of time." Apply this principle to his short poem, "In a Station of the Metro."
4. What ideas, sensations, or associations does the phrase "Petals on a wet, black bough" convey ("Metro," line 2)? Why does Pound connect the natural world with the crowded city? What might he be saying about his response to this appearance of beauty in an unlikely spot?
5. In his essay on imagist poetry, Pound recommends familiarity with the uses of assonance and alliteration ("Let the neophyte know asso-

nance and alliteration . . . as a musician would expect to know harmony and counterpoint" ["A Few Don'ts"]). How does Pound employ
these techniques in "In a Station of the Metro"?
6. What does the *Blast* manifesto say about the Futurists? How do the
Blast manifesto authors differentiate themselves from the Futurists?
7. In the *Blast* manifesto, what is the relationship between art and the
individual? What does it have to say about artists?

Further Resources

NORTON TOPICS ONLINE

Modernist Experiment

William Butler Yeats

Yeats is well known for the many masks he adopted and approaches he
has used; his work is varied, contradictory, and rich, offering decades of
critics and readers much to mull over. In recent years, literary scholars
have turned their attention more fully to Yeats's role as a postcolonial
writer, and it is this context that may prove most fruitful in introducing
students to his verse. Although the term "postcolonial" is as variable as
Yeats's political leanings, it serves as a useful category within which to
group issues relating to the effects of colonization on literary production.
Nationalism, antinationalism, the creation of a national identity, resistance to colonization, vacillating attitudes toward the colonizer, and hybridity are all concepts relevant to aspects of Yeats's poetry. Most
intriguing to students may be the connection between art and politics that
his writing brings to mind—and that Yeats himself proposed. In "Man and
the Echo," for example, Yeats asks, "Did that play of mine send out / Certain men the English shot?" (lines 11–12). The play, *Cathleen ni Houli-
han*, co-authored by Yeats with Lady Gregory, may have helped mobilize
the revolutionaries who participated in the Easter Rising of 1916. Certainly Yeats—not accidentally—draws attention to the political power of
his own writing through this rhetorical move, while also bringing up questions about the effect of art on politics in general. Literature in this sense
is not merely decorative or confined to rarefied academic circles, but
something with the potential to touch and influence events in the real
world. At the same time as Yeats's poetry helped to shape attitudes, however, it also tells us much about existing attitudes, and thus offers significant insights into Irish culture and history. Moreover, Yeats's conflicted
literary responses to this history can shed light on tensions in the work of
other postcolonial authors and on the broad range of approaches to their
material. An exploration of some of these issues will help students understand the profound impact Yeats has had on generations of writers and
provide a rewarding basis for study.

The Lake Isle of Innisfree

Quick Read

- Form: Lyric.
- Themes: Longing for an idealized pastoral Ireland; imagining rural self-reliance and escape from urban desolation; mythologizing and constructing an independent, non-British Ireland.
- Key Passages/Words: "Innisfree," line 1; "And live alone in the bee-loud glade," line 4; "While I stand on the roadway, or on the pavements grey," line 11; "the deep heart's core," line 12.

Teaching Suggestions

This much-anthologized poem will offer students some sense of the early Yeats as traditionalist and romantic. At the same time, however, it also reveals Yeats as Irish nation-builder and myth-maker. Begin by discussing the idea of art having an effect on politics, a concept that Yeats is keenly aware of. How does he imagine a free Ireland here? You may want to discuss the parallels between the speaker's intention to "live alone" (line 4) and plant his "Nine bean-rows" (line 3), and a self-sufficient Ireland. The island's name provides an excellent basis for introducing students to notions of hybridity and nationalism, and to the contradictions that such terms imply. Innisfree is literally "heather island" in Gaelic; yet it is also a hybrid word, punning on "island free" in English, and so demonstrating the way that the two cultures are intertwined. Although this is a real location in the west of Ireland, Yeats made a conscious decision not to use the Gaelic spelling. From this point, it's easier for students to understand the poem not only as mythologizing an idyllic Ireland, but also as constructing a national identity separate from British identity. You can then discuss the differences between the pastoral view of Ireland that is presented here, where the "cricket sings" (line 6), and the forlorn urban landscape of London, with "the pavements grey" (line 11). Note in particular the description of this utopian Ireland as "the deep heart's core" (line 12); this is the "real" Ireland, not the streets of Dublin or elsewhere. Innisfree is thus not just a lovely spot meaningful to the speaker alone, but one that represents the life (the heart), the center, of Ireland, and as such becomes a national symbol.

Easter, 1916

Quick Read

- Form: Elegy.
- Themes: The Irish revolutionaries are no longer targets of humor, but are worthy of respect; the men and women of the Easter Rising, although admirable, may have been confused in their tactics and judgment; intense political commitment can make one impervious to life's richness.

- Key Passages: "[I was] certain that they and I / But lived where motley is worn," lines 13–14; "Hearts with one purpose alone / Through summer and winter seem / Enchanted to a stone / To trouble the living stream," lines 41–44; "Too long a sacrifice / Can make a stone of the heart," lines 57–58; all "changed, changed utterly: / A terrible beauty is born," lines 15–16; 79–80.

Teaching Suggestions

This is a deeply ambivalent poem—one that did not please Maude Gonne—and it is this ambivalence that will provide the spark for an initial discussion. Going stanza by stanza, ask students to examine Yeats's fluctuating view of the Irish revolutionaries who carried out the rebellion. The first stanza creates a distance between the "I" and "them" of the first line, which is very different from the "they and I" (line 13) of Yeats and his companions. Why were the men and women involved in the uprising figures of ridicule (the source of "a mocking tale or a gibe" [line 10]) to Yeats and his circle of friends? Note that these individuals come from "counter or desk" (line 3), whereas Yeats meets his friends at a club; these are clear class markers. Yet we find that Yeats is questioning his original view when he states that "All [is] changed, changed utterly: / A terrible beauty is born" (lines 15–16). When you move to the second stanza, invite students to think about the revised view of the revolutionaries outlined here and about Yeats's self-criticism. How far does Yeats's changed vision extend? There is sincere respect, but there are also some disparaging remarks that cannot be entirely erased by recognition of the rebels' martyrdom: the "shrill" voice (line 20) of Constance Gore-Booth, for example, or the "drunken, vainglorious" description of John MacBride, Maude Gonne's estranged husband. The third stanza is more ambiguous and has been interpreted in various ways by critics. You might want to focus your questions here on the contrast between the "stone" (lines 43 and 56 [stone's], and line 58 in the final stanza) and the "living stream" (line 44); the "stone" implies immutability, while the stream implies mutability—and life. In the final stanza Yeats clearly states "Too long a sacrifice / Can make a stone of the heart" (lines 57–58) and he asks "O when may it suffice?" (line 59). Yeats admires the commitment of the revolutionaries but he questions their tactics and their judgment. Believing that the English government may eventually grant the Irish their independence, he asks: "Was it needless death after all? For England may keep faith" (lines 67–68). Moreover, he wonders: "what if excess of love / Bewildered [the slain nationalists] till they died?" (lines 72–73). By the final lines, the refrain (all "changed, changed utterly: / A terrible beauty is born" (lines 79–80) has been complicated. What is "born" here? What does Yeats think of Ireland's future and why? (For reference materials on the Easter Rising, see *Norton Topics Online*, "Imagining Ireland.")

The Second Coming

Quick Read

- Form: Lyric.
- Themes: One historical epoch is ending—in chaos—while another epoch—unknown and potentially frightening—is being born.
- Key Passages: "The falcon cannot hear the falconer; / Things fall apart; the centre cannot hold," lines 2–3; "A shape with lion body and the head of a man, / A gaze blank and pitiless as the sun, / Is moving its slow thighs," lines 14–16; "And what rough beast, its hour come round at last, / Slouches towards Bethlehem to be born?" lines 21–22.

Teaching Suggestions

Written during a time mired in war and revolution, "The Second Coming" presents an explosive vision of the coming era. While "Easter, 1916" describes violent events that lead to the birth of a new and unsettling time ("A terrible beauty is born" [lines 16, 40, 80]), the voice is controlled and calm. The historical birth prophesized in "The Second Coming," on the other hand, is of such catastrophic proportions that the speaker yields to his own fevered imaginings: "a vast image . . . [t]roubles my sight: . . . A shape with lion body and the head of a man, / A gaze blank and pitiless as the sun, / Is moving its slow thighs" (lines 12–16). You might want to begin with the concept of the "rough beast" (21) that alarms the speaker so much. What is this beast? Why does it appear after "twenty centuries of stony sleep" (line 19)? Why is the new era imagined as half man, half beast? You will want to provide students with some historical context about World War I, the Russian Revolution, and the impending Anglo-Irish War, so that they will understand the poem's sense of complete upheaval. Also, although students can understand the poem without knowledge of Yeats's symbol of the gyre, some discussion of his theory will help shed light on the way that this poem imagines the two historical trajectories (see the NAEL headnote on Yeats for some insight into this).

There are many ways to approach this poem, but you will want to discuss the manner in which Yeats turns Christian rhetoric against itself in the concept of the "Second Coming" and throughout the poem. In Christian terms, the Second Coming is the end of the world when all are judged and sent to their respective fates. In Yeats's scenario, the Christian era is not the entire or most significant aspect of history; it is dismissed as merely "twenty centuries of stony sleep" (line 19) that are about to be replaced by another historical epoch—one that is disturbing, coarse, and fragmented, but perhaps just as long-lived as the former. Here, the righteous will not ascend to heaven, but life will go on in some crude manner. In images such as the "rough beast . . . [that] / Slouches towards Bethlehem" (lines 21–22), Yeats invokes Christian language, yet completely reverses Christian views of history, time, and the universe.

Another useful focus for discussion is the concept of the falcon and the falconer and their relationship to the disintegrating center ("The falcon cannot hear the falconer; / Things fall apart; the centre cannot hold" [lines 2–3]). Ask students what these terms ("falcon" and "falconer") might represent: Christ and the modern era? A more generalized concept of a strong leader and his public? Or something more abstract? If you are teaching an upper-division course, you might want to discuss Yeats's ambivalent politics at this point—his anti-democratic tendencies, especially in his later years. The question of Yeats and fascism, though, is complicated and needs to be treated in some detail. Even without this discussion, however, students can see that the speaker of "The Second Coming" is worried about the loss of order in the world—a disorder growing out of the disturbances of war and revolution that were occurring when Yeats wrote this piece. It would also be useful to compare the image of the falcon and falconer to a similar image in Gerard Manley Hopkins's "The Windhover." In "The Windhover," a kestrel (a small falcon) spirals into the air and hovers against the wind, demonstrating, for Hopkins, proof of Christ's presence and magnificence. Although completely different in their treatment of religious belief, both poems contain images of circling falcons that connect to larger views about spirituality and the universe.

Teaching Clusters

Because Yeats's work is so varied, it encompasses several categories. Most of his poetry can be studied in the cluster on **Transition, Modernity, and Modernism,** allowing you to focus on the breadth of his technique and style; the early work that is considered Romantic or Pre-Raphaelite in sensibility, however, may be more usefully placed in appropriate thematic categories. Poems such as "The Lake Isle of Innisfree" or "Who Goes with Fergus?," for instance, that draw upon Irish myth or history, or those that reflect on political and historical events, such as "Easter, 1916," "September 1913," or "Man and the Echo," may be placed in the **History, Memory, and Politics** cluster. The Maude Gonne poems and those that address the topics of love or desire, or that take women as symbols of abstract concepts, are well suited to the cluster on **Gender, Desire, and Sexuality.** Poems such as "Adam's Curse," "No Second Troy," and "The Sorrow of Love" fall under this rubric. Works that focus on issues of Irish nationalism or cultural conflict, such as "Easter, 1916" and "The Second Coming," would be especially well situated in the **Culture, Language, and Identity** grouping.

Discussion Questions

1. How does "The Lake Isle of Innisfree" imagine independence and self-reliance for both individuals and the Irish nation? In what way does the spelling of "Innisfree" comment on the latter?
2. What does it mean for Innisfree to be described as "the deep heart's core" (line 12)? How does this relate to Irish national identity?

3. Discuss the contrast between urban and rural spheres depicted in "The Lake Isle of Innisfree."

4. What is Yeats's attitude toward the men and women involved in the "Easter, 1916" rebellion as depicted in the first stanza? How does his view of the revolutionaries change in the rest of the poem? To what extent does Yeats support them and to what extent does he qualify his endorsement of them?

5. The *NAEL* headnote to Yeats's work states that "Yeats's nationalism and antinationalism, his divided loyalties to Ireland and to England, find powerfully ambivalent expression in 'Easter, 1916.'" In what way does Yeats demonstrate his divided loyalties to the two nations in "Easter, 1916"? To what extent is Yeats both a nationalist and an antinationalist in this poem?

6. The final refrain to "Easter, 1916" states that the revolutionaries "Are changed, changed utterly: / A terrible beauty is born" (lines 79–80). What does this change mean for Ireland? Does Yeats have faith in the future? What is "born" here?

7. In "The Second Coming," what does Yeats mean when he writes "The falcon cannot hear the falconer" (line 2)? How does this relate to "the centre cannot hold" (line 3)?

8. Why is the new era described in "The Second Coming" connected to the image of a body that is half man and half lion? Why is this body not either one thing or another?

9. How does Yeats use Christian terminology to disorient and shock the reader? How does Yeats's vision of the "Second Coming" gain meaning when contrasted with the Christian concept? Why does the "rough beast" (line 21) "[slouch] towards Bethlehem" (line 22)?

10. Compare the concept of birth in "Easter, 1916" with that in "The Second Coming."

Further Resources

NORTON ONLINE ARCHIVE

Audio:
Down by the Salley Gardens (set to Benjamin Britten's
    arrangement of a traditional Irish tune)
The Lake Isle of Innisfree (read by W. B. Yeats)

NORTON TOPICS ONLINE

Imagining Ireland

E. M. Forster

In Forster's work, imperialism corrupts the conquering as well as subject peoples, fostering cruelty, egotism, and mistrust. *A Passage to India*, for example, which explores the fraught relations between Englishman and Indian after the British conquest and colonization of India has become a long-established fact, leaves one with the sense that friendly relations be-tween colonizer and colonized are inevitably, terribly, tragically impossible. Similar themes are examined in "The Other Boat," a sexually frank story setting homoerotic desire against the social and cultural attitudes incul-cated by imperialism. Events here take place in a liminal geographical space between East and West, as the passengers on a British ship sail from England to India. Playing off the word "other," this narrative stages a colli-sion between culture and illicit sexuality, exposing the social hypocrisies and psychological delusions that make up the myth of British national identity. "The Other Boat" gives instructors an excellent opportunity to dis-cuss the concept of otherness as a free-floating, circulating term connect-ing issues of sexuality, race, national identity, and class.

The Other Boat

Quick Read

- Form: Short story.
- Summary: While onboard a ship headed toward India, a young British officer engages in a homosexual relationship with a young man of mixed ethnicity. After unsuccessfully attempting to suppress his desires and adapt to bourgeois codes of conduct, the officer kills his lover and commits suicide.
- Themes: Racial, sexual, class, and geographical otherness; the con-sequences of suppressed homoerotic desire; the East as a place of unrestrained passions; the mother as enforcer of social convention; duplicity and doubleness; cultural conflict and disjunction.
- Key Passages: "[Lionel's] colour-prejudices were tribal rather than personal, and only worked when an observer was present" (2065); "Cocoanut possessed two passports, not one like most people, and they confirmed a growing suspicion that he might not be altogether straight" (2070); "How decent and reliable they looked, the folk to whom he belonged! . . . If he forfeited their companionship he would become nobody and nothing" (2077).

Teaching Suggestions

To highlight the importance of cultural conflict in "The Other Boat," it will be helpful to begin by discussing the spatial and geographical frame-work of the story. Lionel's adherence to social convention and heteronor-mative sexuality breaks down as the ship enters the Mediterranean, leaving England—and its codes of conduct—firmly behind. Here, Forster draws upon what Edward Said identified as Orientalist thinking, a fre-quent companion to imperialism. Orientalist thought works in terms of oppositions: the Occident is civilized, but the Orient is barbaric; the Westerner is rational, democratic, law abiding, Christian, and self-restrained, while the Easterner is superstitious, undisciplined, sensual, heathen, and primitive. For the Westerner, the East may function as a place where restraints can be tossed aside and sensual fantasies indulged or where lawless violence is unleashed. At the same time, however, Forster is critical of British imperial hubris, ironically terming Britons the "Ruling Race." Note also that while cultural differences are represented by geographical oppositions, the ship itself is divided into similarly contrasting regions; Lionel and Cocoanut's taboo sexual trysts occur "below deck," while a large portion of the upper deck is appropriated by the British elites. Near the story's conclusion, when Lionel is attempting to suppress his homosexual longings, he is invited to sleep on deck "like the rest of the gang." As Colonel Arbuthnot tells Lionel, "We've managed to cordon off this section of the deck, and woe betide anything black that walks this way, if it's only a beetle." This arrangement is replicated in Lionel and Cocoanut's cabin, where Lionel takes the upper berth and Cocoanut the lower. Cocoa's transgression of this unspoken law causes Lionel's reserve to break, leading to his violent outburst.

The theme of cultural opposition is rendered not only spatially, but also through a motif of duality and duplicity. Cocoanut owns two passports, reflecting both his construction as ethnically mixed (he "belonged to no race") and as a conniving manipulator. When Cocoa suggests that Lionel also acquire two passports so that he can escape the shame of his father's disgrace (Major Corrie March abandoned his family and was dishonorably discharged), Lionel is affronted. "So as I can cheat like you? No thank you," he responds. "My name is Lionel March and that's my name." Unlike Cocoanut, Lionel's father's family can "trace itself back nearly two hundred years" and his mother's "goes back to the War of the Roses." Yet as we know, despite his "pure" ancestry, Lionel lives a double life, hiding his homosexual activities from public view and invoking racial slurs for the benefit of his mother and British acquaintances while being less concerned about "colour-prejudices" in private. Lionel's duplicity, moreover, is mirrored in the secret sexual liaisons of his British counterparts: Lady Manning has been spotted "in the cabin of the Second Engineer," while the reader wonders about the relationship between Lionel's mother ("the very soul of purity") and Captain Armstrong (the "valued family adviser"). Although the British take pains to keep the boundary between themselves and their cultural others distinct, in reality their behavior is not much different from those whom they look down upon.

Teaching Clusters

"The Other Boat" falls most obviously in the clusters on **Gender, Desire, and Sexuality** and **Culture, Language, and Identity**. In the first category, you would focus on sexuality, while in the second category, you would focus on issues of hybridity and postcoloniality in relation to identity. An equally useful placement would be in the **Transition, Modernity, and Modernism** cluster. Here, you would emphasize the instability of identities and social relations in the story—these are not what they appear to be on the surface—and the critical view of human relationships and social structures. Moreover, this placement would allow you to extend your discussion of literary modernism to include matters of imperialism and nonheteronormative sexuality. Modernist literature is sometimes taught within a very narrow context, as if it were sealed off from colonial and postcolonial influences. Forster's story would add a much-needed component to your repertoire.

Discussion Questions

1. Trace the use of the word "other" in this story ("The Other Boat"; "'I hope I never shed blood,' the other said"; "The other roused himself from the twilight"). Who is the "other"? Is it a stable or a fluid concept? Can the "other" be within the self? Who and what defines the "other"? What kinds of social and cultural beliefs does "otherness" support?
2. In what way is space—geographical and onboard the ship—significant in "The Other Boat"?
3. Discuss the notion of duplicity and hypocrisy in "The Other Boat."
4. In what way is Lionel's mother important in Forster's story? What does she represent to Lionel? Think about her views on Cocoanut during the first journey from India to England and Lionel's letter to her.
5. How is Britishness defined here? Is it dependent on exclusion and hierarchy? Who or what represents the British way of thinking? How do issues of ethnicity enter into the equation?

Virginia Woolf

"Examine for a moment an ordinary mind on an ordinary day. The mind receives a myriad impressions—trivial, fantastic, evanescent, or engraved with the sharpness of steel. . . . Let us record the atoms as they fall upon the mind in the order in which they fall, let us trace the pattern, however disconnected and incoherent in appearance, which each sight or incident scores upon the consciousness," writes Virginia Woolf in "Modern Fiction." For Woolf, the break-up of traditional meaning structures and formal unity in early twentieth-century writing was a welcome opportunity to depict life as actually experienced. Conventional narrative form could not do justice to the tumultuous randomness of modern existence, so Woolf experimented with methods that would convey momentary sensations and the discontinuities of human consciousness. The self was not something circumscribed by objects and linear narratives, but perceived only in flashes. By allowing the boundaries of the self to crumble, by leaving oneself open to "exceptional moments" or "sudden shocks" of insight, one may experience "a peculiar horror and a physical collapse" as the self dissolves, but also "ecstasy" and "rapture" ("A Sketch of the Past). Woolf's writing attempts to capture the fragmented, spontaneous richness of life as perceived through the human mind. Along with James Joyce and T. S. Eliot, Woolf is essential reading for any study of literary modernism.

The Mark on the Wall

Quick Read

- Form: Short story.
- Summary: The narrator notices a mark on the wall, which leads to thoughts about life, literature, knowledge, and reality.
- Themes: Life is more than a material description of reality; reflections, perceptions, and sensations—transitory impressions that cannot be pinned down with any precision—are the real stuff of life and the deserving subjects of modern fiction.
- Key Passages: "And the novelists in future will realise more and more the importance of these reflections . . . leaving the description of reality more and more out of their stories" (2084); "What now takes the place of . . . those real standard things? . . . Whitaker's Table of Precedency . . . I suppose" (2084); "No, no, nothing is proved, nothing is known" (2085).

Teaching Suggestions

This story, although brief, demonstrates some of the techniques and themes that appear in Woolf's novels: stream-of-consciousness narration, interior monologue, and meditations on reality, life, history, and thought itself. Before attempting to answer what may perhaps be the question that students will be most curious about—what does the mark on the wall *mean?*—discuss some of the key passages noted above. What does Woolf think that "the novelists [of the] future" will write about? Why does she think that they will leave "the description of reality more and more out of their stories"? The novel that commences cleanly, unfolds a sequence of events logically and evenly, and concludes unambiguously is too much like "Whitaker's Almanack" with its "Table of Precedency" that explains how the various ranks of society must comport themselves in public life. Fiction should instead convey the fluidity and disjunction of relations and experiences: life is much like looking out the window of a fast-moving train and being "torn asunder . . . from the old lady about to pour out tea and the young man about to hit the tennis ball in the back garden of a suburban villa." One glimpses a series of brief impressions, unfinished vignettes, unfolding in random order, unrelated to one another, and of no particular consequence.

"The Mark on the Wall" enacts Woolf's theories about fiction (described in "Modern Fiction," discussed below) by having the narrator's thoughts meander back and forth in time, reflecting on the meaning of knowledge and reality. "No, no, nothing is proved, nothing is known," the narrator muses"; "And if I were to get up at this very moment and ascertain that the mark on the wall is really—what shall we say?—the head of a gigantic old nail, driven in two hundred years ago . . . what should I gain?—Knowledge? . . . And what is knowledge?" The narrator dismisses such material details as trivial. When the reader—and the narrator—discovers at the story's conclusion that the mark on the wall is actually a snail, both "knowledge" and "reality" seem to be as transitory and insignificant as the discovery itself.

Modern Fiction

Quick Read

- Form: Essay.
- Themes: Fiction cannot capture life by concerning itself mainly with materiality or with formulaic ideas about subject matter and narrative order; our perception of life comes from the elusive, random, and discontinuous movement of thoughts in our minds—these are the qualities that modern fiction should attempt to convey.
- Key Passages: "If we fasten, then, one label on all these books, on which is one word, materialists, we mean by it that they write of unimportant things" (2088); "Examine for a moment an ordinary mind on an ordinary day. The mind receives a myriad impressions—trivial, fantastic, evanescent, or engraved with the sharpness of steel" (2089); "'The proper stuff of fiction' does not exist; everything is the proper stuff of fiction" (2092).

Teaching Suggestions

In this well-known essay, Woolf criticizes realist novelists John Galsworthy, Arnold Bennett, and H. G. Wells (the "materialists") because they are too intent on representing the details of the physical world; while attending too closely to inconsequential matters, they fail to capture "life or spirit, truth or reality . . . the essential thing." Novelists such as Conrad and Joyce, in contrast, are "spiritual"—by which Woolf does not mean they are transcendentalists, but rather that their writing conveys the mercurial qualities of the mind." Joyce "is concerned at all costs to reveal the flickerings of that innermost flame which flashes its messages through the brain," and when necessary to disregard "probability" and "coherence" in his plotting in order better to represent the erratic motion of subjectivity. (For the editors' discussion of Joyce's stream-of-consciousness narrative, see the headnote to the Joyce selections.) Woolf thus advocates a type of fiction that attempts to capture life as it is perceived through the mind.

Students new to modernist literature will need to read this theoretical piece alongside some of Woolf's fiction, such as "The Mark on the Wall." The stumbling point for most first-time readers of Woolf (and Joyce) will be figuring out the relationship of literary technique to "reality." It is thus especially helpful to focus discussion on Woolf's thoughts about life and human consciousness: the former is only accessible through the latter. As she states, "Life is not a series of gig-lamps symmetrically arranged; life is a luminous halo, a semi-transparent envelope surrounding us from the beginning of consciousness to the end." Ask your students to reflect on the way that their own thought patterns and feelings intersect with their daily activities in the physical world. Can human experience best be conveyed through objective description or through an attempt to follow the mind's twists and turns? Why does Woolf think that the "materialist" writers fail in capturing life's essence?

A Room of One's Own

Quick Read

- Form: Extended essay (developed from two lectures).
- Summary: Woolf reflects on the situation of women writers over the centuries, exploring the effect of material conditions and patriarchal attitudes on their intellectual and imaginative work.
- Themes: Women writers and intellectuals have not had the money, independence, or material comforts necessary to create their best work; women have served as supportive props to the male ego rather than developing their own abilities; anger toward men and oppressive social conditions have tarnished the writing of some women; an androgynous mind is necessary to the creation of great literature.
- Key Passages: "It is strange what a difference a tail makes" (2098); "Why was one sex so prosperous and the other so poor? What effect has poverty on fiction?" (2104); if Shakespeare had had an "extraordinarily gifted sister," she would not have been able to realize her potential (2116); "Anger had snatched my pencil while I dreamt. But what was anger doing there?" (2108); "What is meant by 'reality'?" (2149); "Some collaboration has to take place in the mind between the woman and the man before the act of creation can be accomplished" (2146).

Teaching Suggestions

A Room of One's Own has become a feminist classic. Although it has generated debate among both feminist and nonfeminist scholars and critics, it is still influential today because it addresses fundamental issues relating to women writers and the material and social conditions under which they produced (and perhaps still produce) their work. This essay contains many memorable observations, but Woolf's thoughts on what would have happened if Shakespeare had had an "extraordinarily gifted sister" make an especially worthwhile starting place for discussion. "Judith" Shakespeare, Woolf speculates, would never have been able to realize her potential, but instead would have "found herself with child . . . and . . . killed herself one winter's night." From this point it would be helpful to focus on the central issue of women's writing and female poverty. "Why was one sex so prosperous and the other so poor? . . . What conditions are necessary for the creation of works of art?" Woolf asks. Draw students' attention to the way that Woolf develops this theme through various examples, such as the very different meals men and women are served in their respective colleges. After a skimpy meal at a woman's college, the narrator comments, "Indeed, conversation for a moment flagged. The human frame being what it is, heart, body and brain all mixed together . . . a good dinner is of great importance to good talk. One cannot think well, love well, sleep well if one has not dined well." You may also want to discuss to what extent Woolf's theories hold true not only for women, but also for both men and women of the working classes. At one point Woolf muses, "Yet genius of a sort must have existed among women as it must have existed among the working classes." Woolf has sometimes been criticized for being elitist; ask your students how Woolf's class position affects her views. Are her theories about writing and poverty—for both men and women—valid today?

One of the more controversial sections of the essay focuses on Charlotte Brontë, whom Woolf describes as possessing a type of "genius" that will never be "expressed whole and entire" because of the writer's anger over women's position in the world. "Her books will be deformed and twisted. She will write in a rage where she should write calmly," Woolf asserts. While this passage appears in chapter 4, the question of the relationship of anger to the creation of art is developed at length in chapter 2. Adopting the persona of a formerly poor woman who comes into some money, she explains, "by degrees fear and bitterness modified themselves into pity and toleration; and then in a year or two pity and toleration went, and the greatest release of all came, which is freedom to think of things in themselves." In Woolf's view, the ability "to think of things in themselves" requires a sufficient extent of economic security—something that Brontë did not have. Yet many critics do not agree that indignation and rage marred Brontë's work or that these topics are not suitable for literary contemplation. It would be interesting to contrast Woolf's comments about Brontë's rage against Woolf's own statement that "'The proper stuff of fiction' does not exist; everything is the proper stuff of fiction" ("Modern Fiction").

Teaching Clusters

Woolf's writing falls generally into two teaching clusters: **Transition, Modernity, and Modernism** and **Gender, Desire, and Sexuality**. Both "The Mark on the Wall" and "Modern Fiction" fall neatly within the first cluster, since each either portrays or addresses what has come to be known as literary modernism. Students will get much more out of "The Mark on the Wall," moreover, if they read it alongside "Modern Fiction," which explains the theory behind the technique used in the short story. A Room of One's Own and "Professions for Women," on the other hand, belong clearly to the second category. Additionally, "A Sketch of the Past" (which contains a disturbing account of the sexual abuse Woolf suffered as a child) can be read in the cluster on **Gender** or on **History, Memory, and Politics**.

Discussion Questions

1. In "The Mark on the Wall," what does the narrator think about reality? How does this view relate to fiction?
2. What significance does "Whitaker's Table of Precedency" have in "The Mark on the Wall"? How does it function as a metaphor here?
3. In her essay, "Modern Fiction," why does Woolf criticize the work of writers such as John Galsworthy, Arnold Bennett, and H. G. Wells, whom she characterizes as "materialists"?
4. In "Modern Fiction," what does Woolf say about life? How can writers best capture the essence of human experience?
5. In *A Room of One's Own*, what does Woolf mean when she asserts, "Intellectual freedom depends upon material things"? What is her rationale? How does this idea relate to women writers?
6. Why does Woolf invent a sister for Shakespeare in *A Room of One's Own*? What relationship does this illustration have to women's writing throughout history? Does Woolf's fictional anecdote have any relevance to women writing today?
7. In Woolf's view, why does anger spoil the quality of writing? How is women's anger related to material circumstances and patriarchal social attitudes?
8. Why does Woolf say "It is fatal to be a man or woman pure and simple"? In what way does androgyny affect writing?
9. In *A Room of One's Own*, Woolf asks, "What is meant by 'reality'? It would seem to be something very erratic, very undependable—now to be found in a dusty road, now in a scrap of paper in the street, now in a daffodil in the sun. . . . It overwhelms one walking home beneath the stars . . . and then there it is again in an omnibus in the uproar of Piccadilly." Discuss Woolf's views on reality and fiction as elaborated in "The Mark on the Wall," "Modern Fiction," and *A Room of One's Own*.

James Joyce

Joyce's name is synonymous with modernist literature. His fiction disrupted conventional expectations about narrative certainty, heroism, and religious faith that had been declining since the late nineteenth century, offering instead a look at human consciousness in a world where grand cultural myths and systems of belief were breaking down. In place of spiritual conviction and epistemological certitude, Joyce substituted the "epiphany": a momentary flash of awareness, a heightened personal experience, that revealed the ordinary in an extraordinary light. Adapted from Christian doctrine, Joyce's epiphany became the secular equivalent of a spiritual experience. Gabriel Conroy's realization of his own insignificance in "The Dead" and Stephen Dedalus's sudden insights in *A Portrait of the Artist as a Young Man*; both illustrate the fleeting intensity of such moments. More challenging to students than the epiphany, the stream of consciousness method in *Ulysses* and the linguistic virtuosity of *Finnegans*

Wake will enrich any discussion of Joyce, modernism, or literary technique.

Araby

Quick Read

- Form: Short story; the third of the *Dubliners* collection.
- Summary: A young boy falls in love with a neighboring girl and attends an Eastern-themed bazaar, hoping to find "enchantment" and a gift for the girl. The bazaar is a disappointment and the boy leaves dejected and empty-handed.
- Themes: The futility of the quest (for beauty, love, fulfillment); the hopelessness of desire; the limitations of life; the insufficiency of religion.
- Key Passages: "I imagined that I bore my chalice safely through a throng of foes" (2169); "Nearly all the stalls were closed and the greater part of the hall was in darkness" (2171); "Gazing up into the darkness I saw myself as a creature driven and derided by vanity; and my eyes burned with anguish and anger" (2172).

Teaching Suggestions

Although each of the stories in *Dubliners* is a separate narrative in itself, it will help students to understand that taken together, they form a comprehensive view of Dublin life. "Araby" is an uncomplicated tale, but stands up to a thorough close reading. Invite students to think about the boy's experience as a quest. He imagines, for example, that he carries a "chalice safely through a throng of foes." But what exactly does he seek? What are his visions, desires, and dreams? Contrast these against the prosaic nature of life on North Richmond Street, where people live "decent lives" and "[gaze] at one another with brown imperturbable faces." The color brown seems to cast its shadow across this part of Dublin, from the "dark muddy lanes" to the "sombre" houses dim in the bleak winter days. Moreover, the object of the boy's love is nothing extraordinary, but a "brown figure," which he invests with a simple poetry: "The light from the lamp opposite our door caught the white curve of her neck, lit up her hair that rested there and, falling, lit up the hand upon the railing." The drabness of time and place are exacerbated as the boy travels on an empty train and arrives to find the bazaar almost deserted: "Nearly all the stalls were closed and the greater part of the hall was in darkness," he explains. Ask students how the exchange between the two English gentlemen and the young woman at the stall add to the sense of desolation ("O, I never said such a thing!"). The reader is not surprised to find that the only available gifts are far too expensive for the young protagonist. By this time we suspect that the situation described here relates to more than just this brief moment, but somehow encompasses the boy's entire life and the lives of those around him: "Gazing up into the darkness I saw myself as a creature driven and derided by vanity; and my eyes burned with anguish and anger." Why vanity? What does that have to do with a larger sense of hopelessness? You may also want to discuss the references to Catholicism here; the description of the "charitable priest" who inhabited the house before the boy's family did, the religious retreat that the girl must attend, and the aunt's suspicion that the bazaar might be a "Freemason affair" and hence anti-Catholic suggest that religion is inadequate to alleviate the narrator's isolation and despair.

The Dead

Quick Read

- Form: Short story, the last in the *Dubliners* collection.
- Summary: At an annual celebration given by friends, Gabriel Conroy, the protagonist, vacillates between egotism and insecurity; later in the evening, he discovers that while he has been thinking of how much he desires his wife, she has been thinking of a passionate love from her youth.
- Themes: Class and social differences; Irish nationalism; Irish hospitality; the blinding effects of self-conceit and self-preoccupation; women as aesthetic objects.
- Key Passages: "The men that is now is only all palaver and what they can get out of you. Gabriel coloured as if he felt he had made a mistake" (2173); "I didn't think that you were a West Briton" (2179); "And haven't you your own language to keep in touch with—Irish? asked Miss Ivors" (2180); "While he had been full of memories of their secret life together, . . . she had been comparing him in her mind with another" (2197); "His own identity was fading out into a grey impalpable world. . . . His soul swooned slowly as he heard the snow falling faintly through the universe and faintly falling, like the descent of their last end, upon all the living and the dead" (2199).

Teaching Suggestions

You may want to begin your session on "The Dead" with questions about Gabriel's character and his interactions with other people. Starting with Lily, the servant girl who opens the door for Gabriel, "The Dead" is filled with women characters who make Gabriel feel ill at ease and inadequate. Well-meaning and well-educated, Gabriel in his mind patronizes his aunts, the Misses Morkan, and their other guests at their annual dance party: "their grade of culture differed from his," he thinks. In fact, he is out of tune with the festivities, the music, and the talk about old times, all of which evoke the fading romantic and chivalric traditions of Ireland, which his aunts, relics of another era, personify, and to which Gabriel, not altogether sincerely, pays tribute in his speech toasting them. At the end of the evening, a sense of impotence overwhelms him after his desire to make love to Gretta, his wife, is defeated by her tears over the memory of her first love, a young man she believes died for her. It is clear in this final scene that Gabriel has no insight into his wife's thoughts or feelings and that he has been projecting his own fantasies onto her.

Students may not immediately recognize the significance of Gabriel's encounter with Miss Ivors, the Irish nationalist. When she accuses him of being a "West Briton," she means that she believes he does not support an independent Ireland because he writes for what she thinks of as a pro-British newspaper. Her accusation throws Gabriel into confusion: "He did not know how to meet her charge. He wanted to say that literature was above politics. But they were friends of many years' standing and . . . he could not risk a grandiose phrase with her." Later she nettles him with questions about why he vacations in Europe rather than Ireland. Miss Ivors's comments clearly get under his skin. Ask students to reflect on what Gabriel thinks of Ireland and the Irish. Does he look down on the Irish? Is intellectual superiority to be found elsewhere in the world? Does Gabriel really think literature is or can be "above politics"? Can "The Dead" be thought of as a political story in its evocation of Ireland and the Irish—or is it "above politics"?

The end of this story is perhaps the most commonly given illustration of Joyce's notion of the epiphany. Startled out of his complacency by Gretta's story of her youthful romance, exhausted by the rapid play of emotions that have shifted from amorous tenderness to humiliation to "dull anger" to "vague terror," Gabriel, at least briefly, is released from the burden of self. "His own identity was fading out into a grey impalpable world: the solid world itself which these dead had one time reared and lived in was dissolving and dwindling. . . . His soul swooned slowly as he heard the snow falling faintly through the universe and faintly falling, like the descent of their last end, upon all the living and the dead." As the NAEL headnote explains, this moment in the story relates to Joyce's own views on artistic objectivity. Released from his crippling egotism, Gabriel may now finally be able to view the world and others in a clearer light.

Ulysses

The "Proteus" and "Lestrygonians" episodes of Ulysses take us into the minds of the two protagonists, Stephen Dedalus and Leopold Bloom, respectively. You will want to review the material in the NAEL headnote on Ulysses so that students have a general grasp of the book's structure, themes, and techniques. Students will probably need some assurance that they will not be expected to master the selections from Ulysses in detail, although the footnotes and introductory material will be of great help. It is worth focusing on one or two passages to illustrate not just the difficulty of the novel or its revolutionary treatment of time and consciousness, but also Joyce's love of wordplay, his humor, and his humanity. For instance, in the "Lestrygonians" chapter, Bloom catches sight of the brother of the late Irish leader Parnell, who is a pathetic reflection of the great man; characteristically, Bloom feels sorry for him: "There he is:

the brother. Image of him. Haunting face. . . . Look at the woebegone walk of him. Eaten a bad egg. Poached eyes on ghost." Parnell, "brother," and "haunting" trigger one of the allusions to the ghost of Hamlet's father, who is on Bloom's mind because of adultery, which he fears will take place when his wife meets Blazes Boylan later that afternoon. As Bloom knows, Parnell fell from power because he had an adulterous affair, and Hamlet's uncle seduced Hamlet's mother. But everything in this chapter puts Bloom in mind of food, because it is lunchtime and he is hungry; thus pity and fear and hunger combine to produce "Poached eyes on ghost."

Stephen's mind works very differently from Bloom's; Bloom is compassionate, while Stephen is erudite, and the differences are evident in the type of associations that filter through their thoughts. The "Proteus" episode opens with Stephen walking along the beach, musing on perception, reality, and truth. Contemplating ideas about transparency and the physical world, he thinks, "Diaphane, adiaphane. If you can put your five fingers through it, it is a gate, if not a door. Shut your eyes and see." These thoughts are mixed with reflections on his own life and actions. He wonders, "Am I going to Aunt Sara's or not?" and instead of actually visiting, he imagines the scene as if it might have happened: "Malt for Richie and Stephen, tell mother." Later, he thinks, "Houses of decay, mine, his and all," which is prompted by thoughts of friction among his relatives and the steady decline of his family's social standing. Although seemingly without structure, his meditations and conviction about what would take place during such a visit capture the circumscribed, airless quality of his aunt and uncle's existence.

In both chapters (and the whole of *Ulysses*), Homer's *Odyssey* provides an allusive framework upon which to structure plot and meaning. Clearly these parallels are meant, in one sense, to be ironic, but Bloom cannot simply be described as a modern antihero. According to Aristotle, epic demands an elevated style. What seems to be happening in *Ulysses* is that the conception of what constitutes an epic subject matter and style has changed radically. The moment-by-moment sensations of sight, sound, smell, taste, and touch that Bloom and Stephen experience as they wander through Dublin often seem trivial in themselves. But as they register in the character's consciousness, they undergo a momentous expansion in time and space through multiple allusions to literature, art, music, and history. To raise these large questions in a short time, even a small sampling of the text should suffice to demonstrate the complexities of modernist fiction.

Teaching Clusters

All of Joyce's work can be studied in the cluster on **Transition, Modernity, and Modernism**. Although the selections from *Ulysses* are technically more experimental than the earlier pieces, these prior works are also modernist in that they contain no unnecessary details and resist explaining all of the characters' motives and feelings. The *Dubliners* stories, moreover, depict uncertainty and instability in their characters and situations; epiphanies are revealed, but the world is confusing and disillusioning. Alternatively, both "Araby" and "The Dead" can be placed in the **Gender, Desire, and Sexuality** cluster; under this rubric you may examine the function of female characters in relation to male protagonists or study the sexual or marital relationships in the stories. "The Dead" would also be well placed in the cluster on **Culture, Language, and Identity,** studied alongside readings that highlight issues of hybridity, conflicted identity, and national identity in the aftermath of colonialism.

Discussion Questions

1. Why does the narrator of "Araby" imagine himself carrying a "chalice safely through a throng of foes"? What does he desire out of life? How does the largeness of his dreams contrast with the reality of his circumstances?

2. How does "Araby" convey a sense of desolation and gloom? What words, symbols, and motifs contribute to this atmosphere? Is the narrator's despair at the end confined to his frustration with the bazaar itself or does it extend to larger issues?

3. What do Gabriel's thoughts about and interactions with other people tell us about his character? What words would you use to describe him? How comfortable is he with himself and with the world?

4. What does Gabriel think about Ireland, the Irish people, and Irish nationalism? Why do Miss Ivors's comments irritate him so much?

5. Discuss Joyce's depiction of female characters in "Araby" and "The Dead." For example, how do Gretta and the "brown-clad" girl (in "Araby") function in reference to the male protagonists?

6. What does the phrase "Ineluctable modality of the visible" mean in relation to Stephen's thoughts about appearance and knowledge?

7. At one point in the "Proteus" chapter, Stephen Dedalus imagines what might have happened had he visited his aunt and uncle. What do his reflections tell us about Stephen's mind, character, and feelings?

8. How does hunger inform the "Lestrygonians" episode? What does food mean to Bloom? What is Bloom's relationship to the body?

9. What do we learn about Bloom during his exchange with Mrs. Breen?

10. Compare and contrast the characters of Leopold Bloom and Stephen Dedalus. What is important to each? How does each approach life? How do their relationships with people differ?

Further Resources

NORTON TOPICS ONLINE

Twentieth-Century Irish Writers

D. H. Lawrence

Lawrence's fiction often concerns a relentless struggle for possession and dominance between men and women. Viewing the dead body of her husband, killed in a mining accident, Elizabeth Bates in "Odour of Chrysanthemums" reflects on their marriage: "she knew she had never seen him, he had never seen her, they had met in the dark and had fought in the dark, not knowing whom they met or whom they fought." She feels the blame to be hers because she had tried to control his manhood, to force him into an alien mold of domesticity and respectability: "She had denied him what he was. . . . She had refused him as himself." Similarly, "The Horse-Dealer's Daughter" depicts the beginning of just such another marriage. Having rescued a girl from an attempted suicide, a young doctor is drawn, in spite of himself, into a sexual encounter that is like a surrender of his own will, a parallel to her wading into "the dead cold pond" from which he rescued her. He both desires her and is repelled by her, his declarations of love and offer of marriage forced from him by her desperate need. Students will be intrigued with Lawrence's stories of passion and self-discovery; more so than the other modernist writers, he explores elemental emotions and the human imperfections that keep people from understanding one another.

Odour of Chrysanthemums

Quick Read

- Form: Short story.
- Summary: Elizabeth Bates, the wife of a mine worker, grows more and more angry when her husband does not return home from work; later, viewing his dead body, she reflects on a marriage in which neither knew the other.
- Themes: The self-centered and alienating nature of many human relationships; the otherness of people: seeing others as they are and letting them be who they are; the reaffirmation of life.
- Key Passages: "[S]he, suddenly pitiful, broke off a twig with three or four wan flowers and held them against her face" (2246); "she knew what a stranger he was to her. . . . [S]he knew she had never seen him, he had never seen her, they had met in the dark and had fought in the dark, not knowing whom they met or whom they fought" (2257); "She had denied him what he was—she saw it now. She had refused him as himself" (2257); "She was grateful to death, which restored the truth. And she knew she was not dead" (2257).

Teaching Suggestions

Begin your session on "Odour of Chrysanthemums" by asking students to describe Elizabeth Bates—first, in general, then in relationship to her children and others in the story. Very early on we are told that "Her face was calm and set, her mouth was closed with disillusionment"; in fact, many of her expressions are bitter ("she laughed bitterly"). Note that she jumps to the (wrong) conclusion that her young son, John, is up to no good, and that the boy is "sulky" and "taciturn" with her. Elizabeth's encounter with her father is no less encouraging: he approaches in a "cheery, hearty fashion," but is met with a "brief censure"; Elizabeth is disturbed—perhaps rightfully so—that he is marrying so soon after the death of her mother. Does this knowledge make Elizabeth any more sympathetic? Why or why not? Direct students' attention to the moment when Elizabeth breaks off a few of the chrysanthemums and holds them "against her face." What does this gesture tell us? And why does she later disparage the flowers when her daughter delightedly sights them in her apron pocket ("the first time they ever brought him home drunk, he'd got brown chrysanthemums in his buttonhole")?

Once you have examined Elizabeth's character and her relationship with others, turn to the scene in which she confronts her husband's dead body and ask students to notice the different emotions and responses she displays: she attempts to "get some connection," then later "shudders"; she experiences "fear and shame" and at the same time "grief and pity." All the time that Elizabeth is being pulled apart by various feelings, she has little to say, while her mother-in-law utters platitudes: "He went peaceful, Lizzie—peaceful as sleep. . . . Ay—he must ha' made his peace." Worried that she is not acting in the proper way, Elizabeth "strove to weep and behave as her mother-in-law expected. But she could not, she was silenced." On the surface, Elizabeth seems more harsh and uncaring than her mother-in-law, who cries for her son and talks about how much she loved him. Yet Elizabeth is being honest with herself and sees her husband for perhaps the first time in her life: "[S]he knew what a stranger he was to her. . . . [S]he knew she had never seen him, he had never seen her, they had met in the dark and had fought in the dark, not knowing whom they met or whom they fought." What is Lawrence saying here about marriage, honesty, and respect for differences? How can people best show love for others? And to what extent is Elizabeth to blame for the rift between herself and her husband?

Teaching Clusters

Because of its frank treatment of sexuality and its sense that traditional approaches to social and sexual relationships must be rethought, most of Lawrence's fiction, poetry, and prose can be studied either in the cluster on **Transition, Modernity, and Modernism** or on **Gender, Desire, and Sexuality**. Works that focus specifically on sexual and marital relationships, such as "Odour of Chrysanthemums," are especially well suited to the **Gender** grouping. This story, moreover, would make an excellent pairing with Joyce's "The Dead"; like "Odour of Chrysanthemums," the central protagonist of "The Dead" comes to realize that he did not know his spouse as well as he thought. "Why the Novel Matters," on the other hand, needs to be studied with comparable selections on modern writing in the **Modernism** cluster (Woolf's "Modern Fiction" would make a good companion piece here).

Discussion Questions

1. Describe Elizabeth's character. What do we learn about her from her encounters with her children, her father, her neighbors, and her mother-in-law? Is she unrelentingly harsh, or is she sympathetic in any way? What circumstances have made her what she is?
2. Why did Lawrence title his story "Odour of Chrysanthemums"? What symbolic value do chrysanthemums have here? Although Elizabeth is portrayed as stern and bitter, she nonetheless breaks off a few of the flowers, holds them to her face, and puts a few in her pocket. How can we reconcile these contrasting descriptions?
3. Discuss the difference between the way that Elizabeth reacts to the presence of her husband's dead body and the way that her mother-in-law reacts. What does this scene tell you about honesty, love, or human relationships?
4. Describing Elizabeth, the narrator of "Odour of Chrysanthemums" says, "She was grateful to death, which restored the truth. And she knew she was not dead." What "truth" does Elizabeth discover?
5. Compare this story with Joyce's "The Dead." In both narratives, the protagonist realizes that even after many years of marriage, he or she did not really know the spouse. How does this lack of understanding shape the way the protagonists think and feel? How does the realization that they have been mistaken change them?

T. S. Eliot

In his 1921 essay "The Metaphysical Poets," T. S. Eliot argues that modern poetry "must be *difficult*" to match the intricacy of modern experience. "Our civilization comprehends great variety and complexity," he asserts, "and this variety and complexity, playing upon a refined sensibility, must produce various and complex results. The poet must become more and more comprehensive, more allusive, more indirect, in order to force, to dislocate if necessary, language into his meaning." Eliot's theories about modern poetry are enacted in his work; his writing exemplifies not only modernity, but also the modernist mode, in that it seeks to put the reader off balance so as to capture the incoherence and dislocations of a bewildering age. For Eliot, "the ordinary man's experience is chaotic, irregular, fragmentary" ("The Metaphysical Poets"). Like the speaker in Eliot's "Journey of the Magi," the modern individual is "no longer at ease here"; he has witnessed the birth of something new and unprecedented, and finds the change to be a "[h]ard and bitter agony" (lines 41, 39). Yet at the same time as Eliot seeks to convey the difficulties of the modern era, he also attempts to counteract its disorderliness by synthesizing disparate elements into a conceptual unity. Thus, he claims, "The poet's mind is in fact a receptacle for seizing and storing up numberless feelings, phrases, images, which remain there until all the particles which can unite to form a new compound are present together" ("Tradition and the Individual Talent"). This attempt at consolidation can be seen in *The Waste Land*, which uses myth as a unifying idea. Loosely based on an anthropological study of the medieval grail romances and primitive fertility rites, the poem presents the reader with dissimilar textual fragments woven together in a kind of mantra to restore some sort of order and life to a civilization left spiritually empty and sterile by World War I. In Eliot's view, it is not only the unprecedented slaughter but the eradication of all faith in God, in nature, and even in literature that has rendered the soil—and modern culture—barren. As a modernist text, *The Waste Land* resists narrative closure and easy resolutions; yet Eliot's personal brand of religious faith and his belief in the unifying elements of myth offer possibilities for spiritual and aesthetic consolation, albeit in a very abstract sense. Eliot's poetry is crucial for any study of modernist literature. Along with readings by James Joyce, Virginia Woolf, and Ezra Pound, it demonstrates the very different types of approaches that literary modernisms may take.

The Waste Land

Quick Read

- Form: Dramatic lyric.
- Themes: The impotence and sterility of the modern world; the (disrupted) cycle of death and regeneration or decay and growth; cultural fragmentation and the possibility of spiritual and aesthetic unity through religious belief and mythic structure; disaffected sexual relationships in the modern, faithless world.
- Key Passages: "April is the cruelest month, breeding / Lilacs out of the dead land," lines 1–2; "That corpse you planted last year in your garden, / Has it begun to sprout? Will it bloom this year?" lines 71–72; the pub scene, lines 139–72; the description of the typist and the clerk, lines 222–56; "Who is the third who walks always beside you?" line 360; "These fragments I have shored against my ruins," line 431.

Teaching Suggestions

One of your first tasks in teaching *The Waste Land* will be to encourage students not to be put off by the extensive range of references and arcane knowledge exhibited in the poem. If you are teaching an upper-division elective course, you may wish to supplement this selection with other readings from sources such as the Bible, Dante, Shakespeare (*The Tempest*, in particular), or Jessie Weston. Many instructors prefer not to follow this route, however, and instead provide contextual information through lectures and handouts. This approach has the benefit of enabling students to put aside their fears and plunge into the reading. Rather than assigning supplemental sources, you may want to have students read some of Eliot's critical essays, especially "The Metaphysical Poets," and his other poems, such as "Prufrock," both of which would make an excellent preparation for *The Waste Land*.

Before students begin their reading of this poem, it would be a good idea to say a few words about the historical and cultural circumstances of the early twentieth century, especially regarding World War I and the decline of religious faith. The war was an immensely disorienting experience that led to disillusionment in the idea of progress and a sense of widespread disorder that spiritual belief seemed inadequate to manage. Eliot attempts to impose an order on the chaos through the use of the Fisher King myth, which describes the eventual regeneration of a desolate land after long drought and hopelessness (see the *NAEL* headnote). Spend some time discussing this myth with your students: its concerns with barrenness and fertility, with the concept of death and regeneration, and with Christianity. After students understand the feelings of disorder and fragmentation felt by Europeans in the aftermath of the war and have given some thought to the possibilities of myth, they will be better prepared to reflect on the disconnected structure of the poem as it relates to a disconnected culture and on the way that the various sections might speak to each other thematically. This is a good place, moreover, to talk about both the structure of the poem and modernist aesthetics. Rather than the linear form of narrative students are familiar with, modernist writing uses narrative techniques that disorient the reader but which approximate the inconsistent way that emotions, sensations, and thoughts come to us. Eliot's comments on structure in "The Metaphysical Poets" are interesting in this regard. Referring to George Herbert's verse, Eliot states that "The *structure* of the sentences . . . is sometimes far from simple, but this is not a vice; it is a fidelity to thought and feeling" (emphasis in original). From this passage, students will see that *The Waste Land* also has a complicated structure that relates to "thought and feeling." You may wrap up your session with a few pointers on ways to read this kind of material—not with the expectations that we bring to narrative, but with more focus on images, motifs, themes, juxtapositions, analogous relationships, and disruptions in conventional patterns of diction, rhyme, rhythm, and structure. Encourage students to keep all of these things in mind as they read *The Waste Land*.

After students have read the poem, you could open your discussion by asking what a wasteland is and how certain images convey the sense of utter ruin that it conjures up. "What are the roots that clutch, what branches grow / Out of this stony rubbish?" (lines 19–20), asks the speaker. Clearly, this wasteland is one that does not support growth, as the references to "roots" and "branches" attest. From here you can begin talking about the themes of sterility/fertility, death/regeneration, and decay/growth that the poem considers. Invite students to list some of the themes they see emerging in the first stanza. They will no doubt notice the juxtaposition between spring ("breeding / Lilacs" [lines 1–2]) and winter ("Dull roots" [line 4]), for example. Note also the use of "breeding" in the first line, emphasized by enjambment. Additionally, direct students' attention to the reversal of expectations here: Why is April the "cruelest month" (line 1)? What concepts do we usually associate with spring (new growth, flowers, warmth, life, planting seeds, and, in Christian belief, the resurrection of Christ celebrated at Easter)? What kinds of things do we associate with winter (death, coldness, sterility, bare trees, a lack of growth)? And why are "memory and desire" (line 3) painful? After this point, you may trace the elaboration of these concepts throughout the poem in several ways. In *The Waste Land*, the thought that a fertile and joyous new world might spring from the site of mass slaughter ("so many, / I had not thought death had undone so many" [lines 62–63]) is grotesque and unreal. The death and destruction of war is a major presence here: "That corpse you planted last year in your garden, / Has it begun to sprout? Will it bloom this year?" (lines 71–72). No rebirth is possible in this barren landscape. Not surprisingly, arid human relations provide no more consolation than nature. Sex is not life-affirming but sordid, and brings no pleasure. The "bored and tired" typist yields with indifference to her clumsy lover, a "young man carbuncular" (lines 256, 231), for example, while Lil's friend advises her to smarten herself up a bit so that her husband, returning from his stint in the army, won't look elsewhere for "a good time" (line 148). Invite students to think about sexual relations in this wasteland and about the inability of these disaffected couplings to sustain growth in a spiritual and emotional sense. Note also the sudden, sometimes jarring changes in tone, diction, and rhyming patterns, which add to the sense of disjunction. The bartender's repeated interruption into Lil's conversation with her friend, for example—"HURRY UP PLEASE ITS TIME" (lines 141, 152, 165, 168, 169)—disrupts the continuity of the exchange while emphasizing its crass nature. Another kind of formal shift occurs in the scene between the typist and the clerk, which is written partially in iambic pentameter with alternating end-rhymes, followed by a stanza with slower cadences and no distinct rhyming pattern. In each case, a change in form signals a change in mood and tone.

You will want to spend some time discussing the enigmatic concluding section, "What the Thunder Said." Eliot's note will alert students that this section addresses themes about Christ, the Grail myth, and conflict in Eastern Europe. Questions about the way that these themes relate to the earlier themes, discussed above, will be helpful. Do these final passages offer any sort of resolution to the problems of skewed personal relationships and decaying societies alluded to in earlier sections? Or do they envision continued sterility, ongoing fragmentation and death, futile mourning and impersonation and ventriloquism? There are many different ways to read this section, but the convergence of Eliot's three themes might suggest that both the Grail legend and faith in Christ have something to offer all desperate souls, although that offering does not take place within the poem itself. If myth, as Eliot believed, can impose order on chaos, do the allusions to the Chapel Perilous (lines 386–95) imply (by following the logic of the Fisher King legend) that if the questing knight continues his journey and participates correctly in the ritual, vitality will return to the land? Does the Chapel Perilous passage illuminate the previous references to Christ's journey to Emmaus, implying that if one can have faith in the resurrected Christ, figuratively seeing "the third who walks always beside you" (line 360), then spiritual sustenance will be forthcoming? Can religious faith in some way alleviate the misery caused by political turmoil and cultural dislocation? Or does the poem's invocation of the Upanishads ("Datta. Dayadhvam. Damyata. / Shantih shantih shantih" [lines 433–34]) suggest the insufficiency of a Christian framework for addressing the crisis the poem describes? Does the poem concede the failure of poetry or religion to rejuvenate the wasteland, to "set" these "lands in order" (line 426)?

Teaching Clusters

Eliot's work is most clearly associated with the cluster on **Transition, Modernity, and Modernism**; along with Joyce and Woolf, he is a key figure in the modernist movement. Any of Eliot's writings could be placed in this category, paired with other modernist writings, both theoretical and expressive. Additionally, the selection by T. E. Hulme ("Romanticism and Classicism") would be of interest in this context, grouped with Eliot's "The Metaphysical Poets" or "Tradition and the Individual Talent" and some of the poems. *The Waste Land* and *Little Gidding*, part 2, also could be situated in the **History, Memory, and Politics** cluster with other readings that comment on World War I or II. Alternatively, you could focus on sex and gender relations in *The Waste Land* by studying it in the category on **Gender, Desire, and Sexuality**. The exchanges between the typist and her lover or between Lil and her friend would be of particular relevance here.

Discussion Questions

1. What is a wasteland? What images and words in the poem describe or suggest a "Waste Land"? Can these images or words be grouped according to themes?
2. What references to death and rebirth can you find here?
3. Discuss the image of the "hyacinth girl" (line 35). How does this image relate to themes of death and rebirth?
4. Describe the attitude toward sexuality and love as depicted in the passage about Lil and her husband, Albert (lines 139–72). How does the repeated interruption of the bartender, "HURRY UP PLEASE ITS TIME" (lines 141, 152, 165, 168, 169), affect your reading of this section? Compare this passage to the one describing the relationship between the typist and "the young man carbuncular" (line 231).
5. In a footnote, Eliot states that the character of Tiresias "is yet the

most important personage in the poem, uniting all the rest." What does Eliot's comment suggest to you? How does Tiresias—who spent seven years as a woman and can see into the future—bring together the poem's themes?

6. Explore concepts of fragmentation and unity as depicted in the poem's imagery, themes, and structure.

7. How is water significant in *The Waste Land*?

8. Why is the reference to "the third who walks always beside you" (line 360) significant in this passage, which describes the resurrected Christ on his journey to Emmaus? Can this journey be seen as a metaphorical spiritual journey relating to other themes in the poem? Why is the speaker unsure of whether there is a third person? How can the speaker's uncertainty be seen in relation to spiritual or emotional confusion?

9. In section V of *The Waste Land*, the speaker describes a forlorn scene involving "tumbled graves," "the empty chapel," and "Dry bones" (lines 388, 389, 391), all of which allude to the myth of the Holy Grail and the journey to the Chapel Perilous. How does this scene relate to the poem's larger themes?

10. What does the speaker mean by the statement "These fragments I have shored against my ruins" (line 431)? How does the concept of "fragments" relate to the poem's larger structure and themes?

Katherine Mansfield

Mansfield's stories are notable for their nuanced observations of gender, class, and family alliances, especially in the aftermath of World War I. "The Daughters of the Late Colonel" describes women who are remnants of an earlier era, unable to break free of the limitations that Victorian patriarchy placed upon their sex even after their tyrannical father has passed away. Helpless and provincial, Constantia and Josephine have never been allowed any scope for intellectual development, a situation that is comically highlighted when their young nephew comes to visit. Similarly, the young female protagonist of "The Garden Party" is circumscribed by another kind of cultural limitation, one that she is only just beginning to wake up to. As Laura's family readies itself for an elaborate outdoor party, complete with band, they learn that a neighboring working-class man has died in an accident not far from their home, leaving an impoverished wife and several children on their own. Although Laura assumes that the festivities will be cancelled, she discovers that others feel differently. The conflict between her dawning awareness of the injustice of class disparities and her family's stubborn refusal to let the misfortunes of the poor disturb the tranquility of their privileged existence form the drama of this piece. Mansfield's touch is subtle and restrained, encouraging careful reading. Students will learn much from these thoughtful stories about the personal and cultural dilemmas of the inter-war period.

The Garden Party

Quick Read

- Form: Short story.
- Summary: When her affluent family demonstrates a lack of concern about a destitute neighbor's accident, a young woman discovers that her own feelings differ markedly from theirs.
- Themes: The painful separation of the adolescent self from the family; the complacency of the affluent classes; the disparity between the working classes and the middle classes.
- Key Passages: The scene with Laura and the workmen who have come to set up the marquee (2347); the exchange between Laura and her mother after Laura learns of the accident (2352–53); the scene in which Laura visits the Scott family (2355); the final exchange between Laura and her brother (2356).

Teaching Suggestions

Many students will be able to identify with Laura's feelings of separation from her family, so questions along these lines will likely elicit a lively response. The scene in which Laura talks to the workmen who have come to set up the marquee will provide a good focus for this initial discussion, which can segue into a consideration of class relations. Laura is clearly unsure of herself and as she copies her mother's tone, she is aware that she sounds "fearfully affected." Just as she will later discover that her mother's values do not match her own, so now she finds that her mother's voice is not right for her. As the scene progresses, Laura tries to negotiate her feelings. She's not sure if the workman is being "respectful" when he talks to her about "bangs slap in the eye," yet she's eager to dispense with "these absurd class distinctions" and decides that "She [feels] just like a work-girl." You can then trace Laura's developing consciousness about class relations and her emergent awareness that she feels differently about the working class than some of her family members. When Laura implores her mother to put a stop to the party preparations in light of the accident, for example, she is distraught that her mother is as unconcerned as her sister, Jose, had been. At the same time, however, she is pleased with a new hat. As she looks at the "charming" reflection of herself in the mirror, she wonders, "Is mother right? . . . And now she hoped her mother was right." Questions about Laura's conflicting feelings in this scene will help draw out some of the contradictions that the story pursues. On the one hand Laura is shocked at her mother's response and feels that "it [is] all wrong," yet on the other she wants to enjoy herself at the party, as her mother has encouraged her to do. It's also significant that up to now, Laura's relationship with her mother has been close, so Laura may not be eager either to disagree with or think ill of her mother. The same can be said about Laura's relationship with her brother, Laurie. The similarity of the names alerts us to the closeness between the two, as does the affectionate "quick squeeze" Laura gives her brother as she looks forward to the party. Of all the family members, it is Laurie to whom she looks for guidance. As she worries about her mother's and Jose's wish not to cancel the party, Laura reflects that "If Laurie agreed with the others, then it was bound to be all right." However, when Laurie admires her hat, Laura decides not to ask him about his view. All of Laura's confused feelings come to the fore at the end of the story, when she visits the deceased man's family and witnesses their poverty. Scott's corpse looks "wonderful, beautiful," yet the widow's sister has an "oily smile" and is somewhat sinister. When Laurie appears to escort Laura home, she sobs and is unable to fully articulate her feelings; her brother seems to understand Laura when he finishes her half-formed comment about "life": "*Isn't* it, darling?" he responds. But what has Laurie "understood"? And what is on Laura's mind? The ending is ambiguous, asking us to think about whether and to what extent Laura has shed her family's beliefs.

Teaching Clusters

Mansfield's interest in social and cultural change—on outmoded class and gender distinctions and relationships, for instance—situates her work in the cluster on **Transition, Modernity, and Modernism.** "The Daughters of the Late Colonel," moreover, would make an excellent addition to the **Gender, Desire, and Sexuality** grouping, as an example of the kind of behavior twentieth-century women were striving to escape. Woolf's *A Room of One's Own* would add some context here, as another perspective on the problems of women's enforced dependency. "The Garden Party" would also be useful in this grouping, as an illustration of a young woman's developing independence of thought.

Discussion Questions

1. How does Laura feel when she discovers that her mother and sister don't agree with her about the accident? When Laura tries on the new hat, why does she want her mother to be right about continuing with the party? How are Laura's thoughts conflicted?
2. Describe Laura's relationship with and attitude toward her mother both before and after Laura finds out about the accident.
3. What do we learn about Laura when she talks to the workmen about the placement of the marquee? How sure of herself is she? How does she compare herself to her mother? How does she demonstrate confused feelings toward the workmen?
4. How important is Laura's brother, Laurie, in this story? How close is Laura to him? Why does she decide not to tell him about the accident after he compliments her new hat?
5. Describe Laura's thoughts and feelings when she visits the Scott family and views the corpse. Why are Mrs. Scott and her sister described in unflattering terms (Mrs. Scott's face is "puffed up, red, with

swollen eyes and swollen lips," while her sister has "an oily smile")?
Why does Laura think Scott's dead body is "wonderful, beautiful"?
6. What has Laura learned by the end of the story? Has she completely
rejected her family's values? Does Laurie really understand his sister?
7. What does "The Garden Party" tell us about class relations?

Jean Rhys

In Jean Rhys's "Let Them Call It Jazz," Selina Davis, the female narrator, states, "I don't belong nowhere really, and I haven't money to buy my
way to belonging." Like Selina, the characters in Rhys's fiction often suffer from a sense of displacement or internal conflict; caught between two
cultures, they bear the marks of colonialism's destructive influence on the
psyche. Some are economically disadvantaged, yet others, such as the
young female narrator of "The Day They Burned the Books," are from
comfortable backgrounds. Despite the fact that the speaker in this story is
white, she finds herself rejected by the "few 'real' English boys and girls"
she meets." To them, she is merely a "horrid colonial," the object of
ridicule. Here and elsewhere, Rhys deftly explores the complexities of human beings trying to survive oppressive and disorienting social and cultural circumstances. Intensely personal, her writing is sensitive to the
thoughts and feelings of the disenfranchised.

The Day They Burned the Books

Quick Read

- Form: Short story; first-person narrator.
- Summary: A young white girl is friends with a boy whose mulatto
mother is mistreated by his white English father; when the father
dies, the mother destroys his collection of British books, while the
boy attempts to thwart her.
- Themes: Racial prejudice; British imperial oppression; books as instruments of cultural identification and construction; the painful effects of cultural hybridity; metacommentary on Rhys's own mixed
feelings about her British inheritance.
- Key Passages: "I don't like daffodils" (2359); "You're not English;
you're a horrid colonial" (2359); "My room . . . my books" (2359);
"Now I've got to hate you too. Now I hate you too" (2360).

Teaching Suggestions

Students will probably first notice the cruel treatment of Mr. Sawyer toward his wife, a woman of mixed ethnicity, and the symbolic meaning of
his collection of British books. These are important aspects of the story
and a good place to start, but you will need to also draw their attention to
the conflicted thoughts and feelings of the boy, Eddie, and to the narrator's similar sense of cultural confusion. When Eddie asserts, "I don't like

strawberries" and "I don't like daffodils either," he is making a bold declaration against British cultural domination, represented by his father,
whom he resembles (he is "the living image of his father"). You will want
to explain that both Eddie and the girl, because they live in a country colonized by the British, are given a classic English education; daffodils figure prominently in English poetry, yet these West Indian children have
never seen such a flower. The young female narrator is at first "shocked"
at Eddie's rejection of British values, but also "admire[s]" him, since she
too has similar resentments. As she explains, the "few 'real' English boys
and girls" she meets insult her. "You're not English," they say, "you're a
horrid colonial." Not surprisingly, like Eddie, she is "tired of learning and
reciting poems in praise of daffodils." Despite their avowed dismissal of
these symbols of British oppression, however, both children covet the volumes in Mr. Sawyer's extensive library. One of the first things that we
learn about the young narrator is that she visits Eddie's home to borrow a
copy of *The Arabian Nights*, an interesting choice given the British
propensity to imagine the East and their colonial dominions as "other" to
their native land. In Eddie's case, moreover, although he does not show
any sorrow when his father dies, he immediately identifies with and becomes possessive of his father's textual legacy: "My room . . . my books,"
Eddie calls them." No wonder, then, when his mother decides to burn or
sell the books, Eddie erupts in anger against her, crying, "Now I've got to
hate you too." Note that he doesn't *want* to hate her, but he feels he *must*,
because she has targeted the source of his identity. The tears that the
children shed at the story's conclusion indicate more than frustration over
the loss of treasured objects, but for Eddie, especially, it illustrates a very
deep psychological fissure produced by the colonial situation. Not only
has his mulatto mother been the object of his white father's racism, but
Eddie's British education has stamped him with some of the desires and
beliefs of his despised oppressors. Like the author of this story, both children are products of cultural hybridity and as a result will suffer the identity confusion and perhaps the self-hatred that can sometimes arise from
such an upbringing.

Teaching Clusters

Both of the Rhys selections fall under the rubric of **Culture, Language, and Identity**. "The Day They Burned the Books" addresses issues
of cultural hybridity and the psychological damage inflicted by the colonial legacy that are specific to this cluster. The excerpts from James Anthony Froude's very biased *The English in the West Indies* and John Jacob
Thomas's trenchant response, *Froudacity* (both in NAEL's "Victorian Issues" section), would make excellent contextual readings; Froude's book
is one of several that are explicitly named as belonging to Mr. Sawyer's
collection. "Let Them Call It Jazz" illustrates another type of cultural disjunction also relevant to this category—that of the immigrant experience.
In this context, V. S. Naipaul's "One Out of Many" would make a perfect

companion piece. Alternatively, "Let Them Call It Jazz" could be placed in the **Gender, Desire, and Sexuality** cluster; as a woman, the speaker is doubly powerless in the new, inhospitable country.

Discussion Questions

1. Why does Eddie say that he doesn't like daffodils? What do these flowers mean to both Eddie and the young narrator of "The Day They Burned the Books"? How do they both feel about the English—and why?
2. What do Mr. Sawyer's books represent to Mrs. Sawyer? Why does she want to destroy them?
3. When Eddie's mother decides to destroy or sell Mr. Sawyer's books, why does Eddie say, "Now I've got to hate you too"? Why are the books important to him? Does his attachment to the books conflict with his feelings toward his father or toward Englishness?
4. Explore the concept of hybridity in "The Day They Burned the Books." How does being the child of a white Englishman and a mulatto mother affect Eddie? Why—and how—is Eddie's relationship to Englishness different from his mother's?
5. How does the age of the protagonists affect your understanding of "The Day They Burned the Books"? What does the story gain by locating events in childhood?
6. Discuss the effect of first-person narration on "The Day They Burned the Books." We do not know how old the speaker actually is at the time she tells the story, but the point of view is that of a young girl; how would her viewpoint be different from that of an older person's?

Stevie Smith

In poetry that combines the cadences of light verse, the whimsicality of nonsense poems and nursery rhymes, and pessimistic philosophical probings to rival the most stark and tragic conceptions of more celebrated poetic surveyors of postwar Western civilization, Stevie Smith creates a vision that has often been called eccentric because it falls into no single camp. Through personae ranging from innocent schoolgirl to desolate spinster to doubting metaphysician, Smith opens views upon a world that exhibits enchantment but also harbors treacherous territory where the blackest quagmires of despair lurk. In a quintessential Smith poem such as "Not Waving but Drowning," Smith exhibits a talent for intermixing light and dark moods, showing her to be among the best practitioners of black humor yet also demonstrating her ability to transcend the simple grotesqueries of that genre with empathetic, compressed portraits of lives (and deaths) of quiet desperation. Always, an unpredictable element of play pervades her work, both in her choice of subjects and in her formal technique; yet whenever she seems to playfully bumble into self-contradiction ("There I go again, Smile, smile" ["Person from Porlock," line 52]), what we are really seeing in action are the methods of a rigorous searcher for the truth trying out different propositions.

Thoughts About the Person from Porlock

Quick Read

- Form: Light verse.
- Summary: Humorously addresses a famous episode in literary history in which Coleridge claimed that he was unable to finish "Kubla Khan" after being interrupted by a visitor (identified as "a person on business from Porlock" in Coleridge's note to "Kubla Khan").
- Themes: Questions literary myths about poetic inspiration; reflects on the need to be liberated from thought, from work, and from life itself.
- Key Passages: "I long for the Person from Porlock / To bring my thoughts to an end," lines 26–27; "I am hungry to be interrupted / Forever and ever amen," lines 34–35; "Why do they grumble so much? / He comes like a benison," lines 42–43.

Teaching Suggestions

No useful exchange on "Thoughts About the Person from Porlock" can be held without some discussion of Samuel Taylor Coleridge and the circumstances under which he composed and left unfinished "Kubla Khan." You may direct students' attention to Coleridge's poem and his note on its composition, contained in the NAEL section on the Romantic Period. Coleridge's claim to have had his poetic vision abruptly aborted by "a person on business from Porlock" has become one of English literary history's most enduring legends. This story of Coleridge's abandonment by his muses, moreover, has come to be seen as a dramatic embodiment of the fleeting nature and fragility of poetic inspiration, an archetypal illustration of the difficulties great poets must undergo for their art. This background will bring out in bolder relief the iconoclastic spirit with which Smith addresses her subject matter. As with her agnostic poems, such as "Our Bog is Dood," Smith brings her skepticism and puckish humor to bear on a historical account whose authenticity is widely taken for granted. From this point you may ask students to identify some of the ways in which Smith debunks her subject. The fifth and sixth stanzas, for instance, incorporating Smith's bogus biography of Coleridge's visitor, mock the idea that a special status has ever been attached to this particular legend. As with her poem "Pretty," Smith seems to be interested in spotlighting for our consideration the "underrated" and the peripheral in life ("Pretty," line 1). While the ignominious water rat is given sympathy and a prominent role in "Pretty" ("The water rat is pretty," line 9), the anonymous Person from Porlock is similarly singled out for attention. As Smith tells us, the visitor "wasn't much in the social sense" (line 19) and hails from Rutlandshire, traditionally considered to be England's smallest county.

In the later stanzas, the poem moves away from a focus on the Coleridge incident to a more personal sphere. When Smith writes, "I long for the Person from Porlock / To bring my thoughts to an end," we are clearly in a different register; as some critics have noted, the Person from Porlock might be a symbol of distraction from the exhausting burden of creative thought, an escape from loneliness, or a symbol of death itself—the ultimate answer to a yearning for release from the rigors of consciousness. It's worth noting that Smith always had an avid attraction to the subject of death and once attempted, unsuccessfully, to commit suicide. The final stanzas move into darker territory that evidence both a desire for oblivion and greater spiritual knowledge.

Lastly, turn to an exploration of Smith's language and tone. Ask students to identify the devices Smith uses to establish a deceptively light air. Alliteration is often used for comic effect, as in the repeated phrase, "Person from Porlock," and a poem's rhythm often disguises a serious content, as does the jaunty trimeter in lines such as "I long for the Person from Porlock / To bring my thoughts to an end" (lines 26–27). It's also useful to note that beginning with the seventh stanza, the impetus to mock seems to dwindle. A last gasp of the satirical tone is attempted with reference to the "cat named Flo" but seems to fail with another repetition that sounds like the refrain to a schoolyard nursery rhyme, creating a general feeling of regression and diminishment. The repetition of the name "Flo," Stevie Smith's original given name, may be a form of emphasis that jogs the poem into the more personal tone of the final stanzas.

Teaching Clusters

Smith's poetry is difficult to pin down, but its quirky combination of the grim and the lighthearted, along with its innovative approach to form and content, make it a fitting selection for the **Transition, Modernity, and Modernism** grouping. This placement would be an especially effective means by which to focus on the originality of Smith's style and its break with more traditional modes. Its dark view of life and metaphysical reflections, moreover, may be usefully compared to similar themes in poems by writers such as Hardy ("Ah, Are You Digging on My Grave" comes to mind). Additionally, "Thoughts About the Person from Porlock" and "Not Waving but Drowning" would make a good pairing within this category, grouped alongside works that address the topic of death. **Gender, Desire, and Sexuality** is another fertile cluster in which to highlight Smith's brilliant use of mock naïveté as a means of deflecting and subverting masculinist norms.

Discussion Questions

1. In "Thoughts About the Person from Porlock," how does Smith use satire and humor to diminish the importance of the story about Coleridge's composition of "Kubla Khan"?
2. Discuss how the comic and the serious interact in "Thoughts About the Person from Porlock." How do such seemingly contradictory elements complement one another and make the poem's messages more powerful?

3. How does Smith use the concept of the "Person from Porlock" to address personal issues not directly related to Coleridge? Why does the narrator of this poem say, "I long for the Person from Porlock / To bring my thoughts to an end" (lines 26–27)?
4. Discuss the theme of death or oblivion in "Thoughts About the Person from Porlock" and "Not Waving but Drowning."
5. Stevie Smith's poetry often assumes a childlike tone, prompting some critics to suggest that the poet and the child, in their imaginative ways of viewing the world, share a similar outlook. How might this observation be applied to the naïveté evidenced in "Our Bog Is Dood"? What is the function of the child's persona in this poem?

George Orwell

Owing to the accuracy with which he foresaw and identified many political and cultural developments in the twentieth century, especially the variety of guises assumed by authoritarian forces compromising personal freedom in both socialist and democratic societies, George Orwell has often been given the label of "prophet." Yet such an identification would not have sat well with the author of *Animal Farm* and *Nineteen Eighty-Four*, who prized above all else intellectual independence and who was opposed to appropriation by the official representatives of any ideological camp. Orwell's unique vision was forged through personal experience. As a colonial administrator's son sent from India to Eton at an early age for his formal education, he gained insights into the prejudices of England's ruling elite; as a policeman he observed firsthand the failures of imperialism in colonial Burma; and as a witness to the duplicity of his Stalinist-Communist affiliates during his fight for the antifascist cause in the Spanish Civil War he developed a disillusioned view of organizations that professed to represent the interests of the proletariat. In a tight, concise writing style combining a journalist's eye for concrete detail with an allegorist's eye for the emblematic moment, Orwell passed on to readers the moral vision he gained from his background and travels. His concern with language demonstrates his belief that, in the hands of accurate, honest writers, words can have a substantial positive effect on people's thoughts and actions while, in the hands of those who are muddleheaded or exploitative, they can be instruments of self-deception or oppression. Students will find Orwell's ethical and political reflections still relevant, fresh, and provocative today.

Shooting an Elephant

Quick Read

- Form: Essay.
- Summary: As a police officer in Lower Burma, Orwell had to decide what to do when an elephant was reported to have gone on a ram-

page. Against his better judgment, he decides to kill the elephant because he feels pressured by the crowd and by his role as a colonial representative.

- Themes: Imperialism creates a situation in which the maintenance of the mask of power takes precedence over doing the right thing; colonialism affects both colonizer and colonized adversely; the individual's internal needs are always at odds with institutional demands.
- Key Passages: "All I knew was that I was stuck between my hatred of the empire I served and my rage against the evil-spirited little beasts who tried to make my job impossible. . . . Feelings like these are the normal by-products of imperialism" (2379); "it is the condition of [the colonial administrator's] rule that he shall spend his life in trying to impress the 'natives' and so in every crisis he has got to do what the 'natives' expect of him. He wears a mask, and his face grows to fit it" (2382).

Teaching Suggestions

In this 1937 autobiographical essay, Orwell reflects on "the dirty work of Empire at close quarters." Invite students first to think about Orwell's attitude toward imperialism. Why is he critical of the British presence in Burma? From this point, you may turn to his conflicted thoughts as he tries to decide whether to shoot the elephant. Ask students to focus especially on the difference between what Orwell thinks is the right thing to do and the action that he decides he must take. How does his personal experience before the elephant become a motivation for his condemnation of empire? Despite his internal desire not to shoot and his belief that it is the wrong thing to do, why does he feel compelled to take the action that he does? Draw students' attention to Orwell's discomfort with any entities that stifle individualism, from the colonial apparatus to the street mob, and to his ability to put abstract social observations into dramatic, personal terms. You will also want to have students look at Orwell's own treatment of the colonial subjects. Although he is candid and self-aware with regard to the petty hatreds that his position inspires in him, he refers to the indigenous Burmese as a mass of "sneering yellow faces." What is the effect of Orwell's choice to represent the Burmese not as individuals, but as an undifferentiated throng? What are we to make of his difference in attitude toward the elephant (for whom he has much empathy) and the faceless, predatory crowd? Aside from Orwell's ethical disillusionment, is there a sign here that he was not yet able to imagine an independent Burmese society that would be able to govern itself? At this point, students might be asked why, in spite of these limitations in Orwell's point of view, the essay still continues to be effective and have an air of relevance today.

Politics and the English Language

Quick Read

- Form: Essay.
- Summary: Orwell asserts that the use of precise, honest, cliché-free language is necessary to think clearly and to enact political change.
- Themes: The uncritical acceptance of bad English in one's own prose and in the writing of others can lead to thought erosion; good prose is intelligible, honest, and accurate; good writers must stop to think through what they are saying and how they are saying it; language can be a tool of political oppression.
- Key Passages: "If one gets rid of these [bad] habits [in modern English usage] one can think more clearly, and to think clearly is a necessary first step towards political regeneration: so that the fight against bad English is not frivolous and is not the exclusive concern of professional writers" (2384); "A scrupulous writer, in every sentence that he writes, will ask himself at least four questions: What am I trying to say? What words will express it? What image or idiom will make it clearer? Is this image fresh enough to have an effect?" (2389); "if thought corrupts language, language can also corrupt thought" (2391).

Teaching Suggestions

Written during the period in which he was conceiving the outlines of his novel, *Nineteen Eighty-Four*, "Politics and the English Language" exhibits Orwell's growing absorption in the social ramifications of language, especially language that "is designed to make lies sound truthful and murder respectable, and to give an appearance of solidity to pure wind"—in other words, political language. Students may at first tend to dismiss this essay as simply another writing and vocabulary primer or as a call for linguistic purity, but you can direct their attention toward those passages that address the connections among language, thought, and action. "If one gets rid of these [bad] habits [in modern English usage]," Orwell explains, "one can think more clearly, and to think clearly is a necessary first step towards political regeneration: so that the fight against bad English is not frivolous and is not the exclusive concern of professional writers." You may want to ask students to bring in examples of language misuse from current newspapers, magazines, or the Internet to encourage greater understanding of Orwell's ideas. Metaphors that are no longer "fresh enough to have an effect," mixed metaphors that cause misunderstanding, cumbersome phrases used in place of simple verbs, pretentious words, foreign expressions, and words used to give "an air of scientific impartiality to biassed judgements" are just some of the linguistic habits he condemns. Lastly, focus discussion on the central contention of Orwell's essay that human thought is eroded by using and being subjected to bad writing. Explore how "ready-made phrases . . . will construct your sentences for you—even think your thoughts for you." How can you end up "partially concealing your meaning even from yourself" by using such phrases?

Teaching Clusters

The two Orwell selections address very different concerns. "Politics and the English Language" is especially well suited to the **Culture, Language, and Identity** cluster, studied alongside works that draw attention to the way in which language shapes social and political relationships. Both Samuel Beckett's *Endgame* and Brian Friel's *Translations* would make provocative companion pieces here, in addition to many of the readings in the "Nation and Language" section of *NAEL*. "Shooting an Elephant," on the other hand, could be studied either in the grouping on **History, Memory, and Politics** or in **Culture, Language, and Identity**. In the first category, your focus will be on Orwell's attitude toward the politics of imperialism and his attempt to make sense out of the past. In the second category, you may explore the cultural conflict Orwell experiences and the essay's comments on British national identity.

Discussion Questions

1. Why does Orwell have "an intolerable sense of guilt" about British imperialism ("Shooting an Elephant")?
2. In "Shooting an Elephant," Orwell states that the colonial administrator "wears a mask, and his face grows to fit it." What does Orwell mean by this?
3. What do Orwell's descriptions of his thoughts during his mission to kill the elephant say about the nature of power and authority? What intricacies in the power relationship between colonizer and colonized are illuminated in "Shooting an Elephant"?
4. What does Orwell think about the relationship of individuals to larger institutions and groups of people? Are these two entities always at odds? Why or why not?
5. In "Politics and the English Language," Orwell states that his defense of English "has nothing to do with . . . the setting-up of a 'standard English' which must never be departed from." If Orwell's aim is not simply to list some composition rules, what is his aim?
6. How does ridding oneself of bad writing habits cause one to think more clearly? Why is letting "the meaning choose the word" preferable to "the other way about"?
7. How can the unthinking acceptance of lazy language habits bring about concession to indefensible political action? How might the use of bad writing by writers and its acceptance by readers be used to assist in the development of totalitarianism?
8. Toward the end of "Politics and the English Language," Orwell says: "Look back through this essay, and for certain you will find that I have again and again committed the very faults I am protesting against." Find one of these faults (a phrase such as "sheer cloudy vagueness," for example) and explain why it breaks one of Orwell's own rules.

Samuel Beckett

"Finished, it's finished, nearly finished, it must be nearly finished," says Clov "tonelessly" in *Endgame*'s very first line of dialogue. Throughout the play, Samuel Beckett's characters hope for some resolution, some event that will bestow meaningfulness on their empty lives, some emotional apotheosis that will bring release—or perhaps they just wait for a death they can never experience. But no closure is achieved, or ever can be achieved. There are only four people confined together in a shabby room, performing the same repetitive activities, indulging in the same petty bickering, thinking the same fruitless thoughts, again and again. Beckett shows himself to be one of theater's great innovators by sweeping away the conventions of traditional drama and developing a minimalist, stylized form that draws attention to social structures, rituals, and language itself. By distancing the audience with an exhausting surplus of symbolism and little psychological depth, Beckett invites us to break the theater's fourth wall, as Clov twice does with his telescope, and not take the words and action of the play as a representation of reality, but rather as a text to be interpreted. This being said, *Endgame* is not just an abstract intertextual transaction between writer and audience, but a project that examines the ways in which people relate to one another and the fictionality of the constructs that sustain them. In his observations of a species that obsessively exhausts its energies in endless conflict on all levels, Beckett demonstrates an interest in process, not in events themselves—in the rules of the game, not a particular chess tournament. Although we are not required by Beckett (as we are by more conventional playwrights) to suspend our disbelief so as to briefly accept the reality of what is happening to the characters on stage, we are required to entertain the idea that the seemingly senseless motions his characters drag themselves through may accurately reflect and lay bare the processes of power relations, of familial codependency, of the making of meaning, and of a living that is dying.

Endgame

Quick Read

- Form: Drama; Theater of the Absurd.
- Summary: Hamm, elderly, blind, and confined to a chair, is attended to by Clov, his servant. Clov attempts to leave Hamm throughout the play, but it is not clear at the end whether he will succeed.
- Themes: Life is similar to a chess game played by two inept players who cannot finish the game; we have a limited number of possible moves that we repeat over and over again in different combinations; life is meaningless and random, yet human beings try to invest it with meaning and order by relying on fictional constructs and empty rituals; language is self-referential; if we are not dead, we are dying; human beings are caught up within relationships of power: parent

and child, master and slave; power resides in those who control language and historical narrative.

- Key Passages: Clov: "Finished, it's finished, nearly finished, it must be nearly finished" (2395); Hamm: "It was I was a father to you" (2406); Clov: "I use the words you taught me. If they don't mean anything any more, teach me others. Or let me be silent" (2408); Hamm: "Ah, you mean my chronicle?" (2413); Hamm: "The end is in the beginning and yet you go on" (2416); Clov: "I say to myself—sometimes, Clov, you must learn to suffer better than that if you want them to weary of punishing you—one day" (2419).

Teaching Suggestions

The initial reaction of students to Beckett's plays will most likely be one of frustration and annoyance. After reading *Endgame*, they may feel that its action is too narrowly circumscribed, that the characters are impossible to identify with, or that the story doesn't have anything to do with "reality." Yet all these objections may provide good openings for your discussion. As to the last charge, for example, you may explain that Beckett's work is principally concerned with the reality of the human condition and with ways to perceive some processes of that reality. The predetermined nature of the "old questions" and "old answers" that make up the play's dialogue, moreover, demonstrates how the relationships of power that govern most human interactions are sustained. With the aid of imagery derived from chess, the oldest game of power strategies, Beckett has structured his play to expose the mechanics underlying such relationships. Hamm's reference to Clov's having "inspected [Hamm's] paupers," for example, suggests that Hamm might be a king figure, and the action of the play, highlighting this king's limited moves, may suggest a king pinned down in the corner of a chessboard in the "endgame" of an ineptly played chess game. Students might be reminded at this point that realistic underpinnings can be seen in this seemingly fanciful play. Historical readings equate *Endgame*'s devastated setting ("[w]here there's no more nature") with a ruined post-World War II Europe, for instance, while the activities of Hamm can be compared to the dangerously inept leadership that led to the war. Hamm's counterpart in the central master/servant relationship, Clov, is a character with a greater range of physical movement (in fact he cannot sit down), like a pawn or a knight in a chess game, suggesting that power relationships are not as simple as they seem—for, after all, the servant is one whose service, strength, and allegiance necessarily make the king's position possible. "Gone from me you'd be dead," Hamm says, but Clov can reply, "And vice versa." It's also worth noting that the constraints on Clov's behavior may be seen as psychological rather than material and so may be harder to revolt against, a fact that has led some contemporary critics to suggest that Beckett's play is a symbolic reenactment of relationships in a postcolonial environment. In this reading, Clov is a postcolonial subject who struggles with language displacement, appropriation of native custom and history, and other legacies of colonial rule. You might point out that although Hamm's actual power is demonstrably on the wane, Clov's view of the world for most of the play is determined by Hamm's language and attitudes. Hamm corrects Clov's grammar, for example, while Clov admits that he uses the words Hamm taught him: "If they don't mean anything any more, teach me others," he tells Hamm. Yet while Clov is a slave to his master's language, Hamm also is bound by a language he is not entirely master of. Faultily recalled quotations such as "My kingdom for a nightman!" indicate that Hamm's thoughts and actions depend to a great extent on words and narratives that may be completely fictional or that have no real connection to his life." Despite the meaninglessness of his words, however, Hamm insists that his version of events is true and that his language is the legitimate one. Thus, he not only corrects Clov's grammar, but he narrates (or invents) a personal history that casts himself in the role of caring father and Clov as the adopted son. "It was I was a father to you," Hamm says to Clov, to which Clov dutifully responds, "Yes. . . . You were that to me." Since Hamm seems to be more of a cranky autocrat than a loving father, we suspect his version of the past, just as we suspect everything he says. When he tells Clov, "Outside of here it's death," or that Clov cannot survive without him, we are similarly suspicious. Clov too, we might infer, is getting suspicious, and by the end of the play may be willing to take the risk to venture outside the house. In the meantime, Hamm struggles to keep hold of his authority over language and history, because herein lies power. When Hamm tells Clov that he is "[getting] on with [his] story," Clov mimics Hamm's language and responds, "Oh, . . . your story? . . . The one you've been telling yourself all your days." In his contrary way, Hamm resists Clov's use of the word "story" and replies, "Ah you mean my chronicle." Perhaps for Hamm, "chronicle" has more of an air of authority and veracity than "story"; in any case, his fictions only have meaning if they can convince Clov to remain in thrall to him. In the end, we find that the only way for Clov to break free of Hamm is by looking beyond the official myth Hamm has established, perhaps signaled by Clov and Hamm's disagreement over the boy Clov spies through the telescope. Is Clov finally seeing through the fictionality of words and of Hamm's aura of power when he says, "I ask the words that remain. . . . They have nothing to say"? Invite students to speculate as to whether Clov has performed an act that moves beyond acceptance of Hamm's interpretation of the order of things. Clov's telescope is turned toward the audience a second time at the play's close, and an ultimate resolution is left up in the air by the final curtain, all suggesting that the next move on the chessboard is up to the audience. Will *Endgame*'s "final," unexpected changes in course truly precipitate a "final" departure? Or is all this dialogue just another activity to help us simply to "keep going"?

Teaching Clusters

Endgame's minimalist approach, disregard of conventional dramatic form, and postmodernist foreshadowings make it especially well suited to the cluster on **Transition, Modernity, and Modernism.** The perfect companion piece to this play would be Pinter's *The Dumb Waiter*, which also features two characters trapped together in a confined space. A less obvious grouping would include some of Thomas Hardy's writings, which would give students a broader context within which to understand Beckett's play. Although much earlier than Beckett, Hardy explores similar thematic territory: the random meaninglessness of existence and the hollowness of human relations. *Endgame* would also be a good choice for the **Culture, Language, and Identity** section, studied with other texts that focus on power structures and the relationship of language to political and social dominance. In this context, George Orwell's "Politics and the English Language" would offer an interesting gloss on the play. Additionally, placement in the **History, Memory, and Politics** category would help bring out the specifically political implications of *Endgame*.

Discussion Questions

1. How powerful is Hamm in this play? Is he just an authority figure whose power seems to be slipping? To what extent does he control Clov (or not)?

2. At one point Clov says, "I love order. It's my dream." Why is order important to Clov or to any of the other characters? What kind of activities impose a sense of order on the lives depicted here?

3. What role does the setting perform in *Endgame*? The details of its layout seem to be specific, yet is the room suggestive of other kinds of spaces? Are the room's two windows, which apparently look out upon the world, of any special significance? Can any reliable conclusions be drawn from the descriptions of the "outside" made in the play?

4. Explore the theme of time in *Endgame*. Does the play present a world that is ending, has ended, or is endless? Is the duration of time enacted here winding down, cyclical, or some reconciliation between the two?

5. Discuss some of the props in the play, starting perhaps with the telescope. What might the telescope and its uses symbolize? Discuss how the telescope might symbolically function in the two scenes in which the device is pointed toward the audience. Choose another prop—say, the handkerchief, the clock, or the gaff—and think about its possible functions in the play.

6. Examine the theme of parents and children or son and father. Nagg and Nell are apparently Hamm's parents and Hamm claims to be Clov's adopted father. What do these parental figures suggest about power structures within families? Why are Nagg and Nell shown as confined to trash bins?

7. Discuss the role of codependence in the power relationships that make up the play. If *Endgame* is moving toward freedom for Clov, what will Clov and his life be like when he is no longer joined to Hamm? Why does Clov want to leave Hamm? What makes him stay?

8. What significance does the boy whom Clov sights through the telescope have?

9. Explore the theme of death in the play. Why does Nell die? What do the other characters think or feel about death?

10. Why did Beckett entitle this play *Endgame*?

Further Resources

NORTON TOPICS ONLINE

Imagining Ireland

W. H. Auden

Auden is most closely identified with the 1930s and the leftwing politics espoused by writers and intellectuals concerned about the spread of fascism during this period. As the *NAEL* selections and headnote demonstrate, however, in his later life Auden rejected many of his earlier political views and, moreover, came to see poetry as an ineffective means of political reformation. "Poetry is no better and no worse than human nature," he writes in his introduction to *The Poet's Tongue*; "it is profound and shallow, sophisticated and naïve, dull and witty, bawdy and chaste in turn" ("Poetry as Memorable Speech"). For this reason, his later work concentrates increasingly on the commonplace and the personal, such as the limestone landscape in which he perceives a "faultless love" ("In Praise of Limestone," line 91). His technical style is remarkably diverse, mixing popular and lofty expressions and adopting numerous poetic forms to establish different moods. Although Auden's poetry does not have the self-conscious sense of importance identified with modernist writing, it is modern in its concern with political issues of the day and in its experimental use of form and technique.

In Memory of W. B. Yeats

Quick Read

- **Form:** Elegy. Three-part structure, each containing different verse forms.
- **Summary:** Reflects on the death of Yeats and the role of the poet in society.
- **Themes:** The inability of poetry to effect political change; the healing power of poetry; the separation of the poet from the poet's works; the problems of Yeats's politics.
- **Key Passages:** "The death of the poet was kept from his poems," line 11; "A few thousand will think of this day / As one thinks of a day

when one did something slightly unusual," lines 28–29; "For poetry makes nothing happen: it survives / In the valley of its saying," lines 36–37; "Let the healing fountain start, / . . . Teach the free man how to praise," lines 75–77.

Teaching Suggestions

This well-known poem illustrates Auden's desire to move away from the legacy of Yeats and from the idea that poetry can have a political force. You will want to draw students' attention first to the three-part structure of the poem, each with a very different metrical organization and mood. The first section focuses on the day of Yeats's death (from the point of view of the speaker) and on the separation between the poet and his work. The shifting line lengths and alternating rhythms add to the feeling of discordance here. The second section, with its loose iambic pentameter, has a stronger sense of internal coherence. Reflecting on the value of poetry, this section is complex but central to the poem's concerns. The last section is the most formal, with its quatrains, trochaic lines, and pairs of rhyming couplets. As the NAEL footnote observes, this movement follows a pattern similar to that in Yeats's "Under Ben Bulben."

When you are ready to discuss the first section, ask students to think about the setting and Yeats's placement in it. The first stanza describes the coldness and isolation of the scene: "The brooks were frozen, the air-ports almost deserted" (line 2). As the poem develops, the scene becomes larger; Yeats "is scattered among a hundred cities" (line 18). What kind of world is this, where "the brokers are roaring like beasts on the floor of the Bourse, / And the poor have the sufferings to which they are fairly accustomed, / And each in the cell of himself is almost convinced of his freedom" (lines 25–27)? What is Yeats's relationship to this cold, dreary, and very modern world? Although this is an elegy, Yeats's death is seen as insignificant when measured against all of life, its turmoil and its suffering: "A few thousand will think of this day / As one thinks of a day when one did something slightly unusual" (lines 28–29).

In the second section, Auden questions the value of poetry, stating flatly, "For poetry makes nothing happen" (line 36). Auden denies that poetry can effect significant change in a world that is so large, complex, and bleak. Note, however, that the sentence does not end there, but continues: "it [poetry] survives / In the valley of its saying where executives / Would never want to tamper" (lines 36–38). Students may have a number of responses to these lines, yet they will probably notice that Auden accords poetry some kind of positive status here, however attenuated. Moreover, "it survives" is repeated in the last two lines of this section ("it survives, / A way of happening, a mouth" [lines 40–41]), implying that despite the existence of "ranches of isolation" and "busy griefs," poetry remains as a constructive force (line 39). These constructive aspects of poetry are more specifically described in the final section, when Auden urges the poet: "With your unconstraining voice / Still persuade us to rejoice" (lines 68–69). Here, poetry is a "healing fountain" that can "Teach the free man how to praise" (lines 75, 77)—a mild antidote to "the night-mare" of prewar Europe (line 58).

To help students place Yeats in this poem, it will be helpful to discuss briefly his identification with right-wing politics. Critics are divided on whether or to what extent Yeats actually supported fascism or was anti-democratic, yet the point to remember is that Auden disapproved of what he believed to be Yeats's politics. It is significant, moreover, that Auden later excised the three stanzas referring to the politics of Kipling and Claudel (the second, third, and fourth stanzas of the third section, ac-cording to the *NAEL* footnote). The result is a less specifically political indictment of Yeats (or other suspected conservative writers), although the poem still questions whether the poetry of Yeats or anyone else can have a real political impact. You will want to encourage students to decide where Auden is drawing the line here; how can poetry make "nothing hap-pen," yet at the same time possess "healing" power (lines 36, 75)?

Teaching Clusters

If your goal is to highlight Auden's technical skills, his contributions to poetic innovation, or his interest in modern life, then you may teach any of his works in the cluster on **Transition, Modernity, and Modernism.** Poems with direct political or historical content, such as "Spain" or "Sep-tember 1, 1939," are especially well suited to the **History, Memory, and Politics** cluster, studied alongside Yeats's "Easter, 1916" or "September 1913," in particular. Additionally, the selections that reflect on the rela-tionship between past and present or that mediate between public and private consciousness, such as "Musée des Beaux Arts" or "In Memory of W. B. Yeats," are also good choices for this category. "In Memory of W. B. Yeats," moreover, would make an excellent companion piece to Wilfred Owen's "Strange Meeting," another poem that reflects on the role of the poet in society.

Discussion Questions

1. Compare the three sections of "In Memory of W. B. Yeats." How is the tone, purpose, and setting different in each? What words, sounds, and rhythms contribute to each section's effects?
2. What is Auden's attitude toward Yeats in "In Memory of W. B. Yeats"? How does Auden negotiate the differences between his and Yeats's poetics and politics?
3. In "In Memory of W. B. Yeats," Auden writes, "For poetry makes noth-ing happen: it survives / In the valley of its saying where executives / Would never want to tamper" (lines 36–38); what role for poetry does Auden imagine here? How does this passage relate to the ideas in the final stanza, where he urges the poet to "Let the healing fountain start, / . . .[and] Teach the free man how to praise" (lines 75–77)?
4. In a later version of "In Memory of W. B. Yeats," Auden removed the

second, third, and fourth stanzas from the third section. How does this removal affect the overall meaning of the poem?

5. Compare the role of the poet in Wilfred Owen's "Strange Meeting" and "In Memory of W. B. Yeats."

6. Discuss the social and political views contained in "September 1, 1939" or "Spain."

7. How does Auden use landscape in "In Praise of Limestone" or "In Memory of W. B. Yeats"?

Further Resources

NORTON ONLINE ARCHIVE

Audio:
Musée des Beaux Arts
The Shield of Achilles
In Memory of W. B. Yeats
—read by W. H. Auden

Louis MacNeice

MacNeice's poetry is full of contrasts, at once embracing the vitality of modern life and recognizing its stasis and discordances. Embedded within the cheerful rhythms of "Bagpipe Music," for example, is a critique of contemporary culture. "All we want is a bank balance and a bit of skirt in the taxi," asserts the speaker (line 10). Yet the sheer energy of the ballad form and the sweeping spectacle of (quickly declining) cultural practices, from the "merrygoround" to the "picture palace," offset the poem's grim references to the stagnancy of life in the 1930s: "Sit on your arse for fifty years and hang your hat on a pension" (line 30). This is a society that has replaced spiritual belief with senseless activity. "It's no go the Herring Board, it's no go the Bible, / All we want is a packet of fags when our hands are idle," as MacNeice writes (lines 25–26). Similarly, "Sunday Morning" contrasts the frantic movement of a speeding car taking "corners on two wheels" with the somber peal of church bells that seem out of place in this secular setting. Studied in conjunction with Auden's work, MacNeice's writing gives students a sense of the issues and concerns that occupied poets during the interwar years.

Sunday Morning

Quick Read

- Form: Sonnet with rhyming couplets.
- Themes: In the modern era, Sunday mornings are no longer spent in religious devotion; seize the moment, but be aware that death waits for us all; time keeps moving at the same pace, no matter what day of the week it is and regardless of our attempts to slow it down.

- Key Passages: "[You may] Take corners on two wheels until you go so fast / . . . That you can abstract this day and make it to the week of time / A small eternity," lines 7–10; "the church spire / Opens its eight bells out, . . . there is no music or movement which secures / Escape from the weekday time," lines 11–14.

Teaching Suggestions

"Sunday Morning" reflects on time, death, and the enjoyment of the moment. It begins jauntily enough, seemingly endorsing the transitory pleasures of the modern age, yet the final quatrain sounds a cautionary note and reminds us that death comes to us all eventually. Ask students first to think about the imagery in the opening octave; the musical notes that "vanish with a wink of tails" and the suggestion that "you may . . . / Take corners on two wheels" establish a breezy, lighthearted mood (lines 2, 7). Students probably will not realize that MacNeice's use of the informal personal pronoun "you" in place of the (more typically British) indefinite pronoun "one" also contributes to the casual tone. Moreover, the speaker advises the reader to "Regard these means as ends, concentrate on this Now," even proposing that by entering into the fast and spirited pace of contemporary life, it might be possible to "clutch a fringe or two of the windy past, / . . . [or] abstract this day and make it to the week of time / A small eternity" (lines 5, 8–10). The playful tone of the first section gives this recommendation a not-too-sincere air, further emphasized by the winking self-reference to "a sonnet self-contained in rhyme"—this sonnet perhaps being MacNeice's attempt to make his own Sunday morning last a little longer.

The carefree tone of the first stanza is reversed in the last four lines, a reversal clearly signaled by "But listen" (line 11). You will want to explain that such a change in thought is usual in the last part of a sonnet. Note also that this phrase both marks a turn in the poem's thinking and continues with the motif of sound established earlier. In the first octave, the speaker listens to someone "practising scales" and further states that if you "concentrate on this Now, / . . . you may grow to music" (lines 1, 5–6). Yet rather than cheerful music associated with fanciful images, this last section brings us a melancholy sound: the "eight bells" of the "church spire," equated with "skulls' mouths which will not tire / To tell how there is no music or movement which secures / Escape from the weekday time. Which deadens and endures" (lines 12, 11, 12–14). The "eight bells" remind us not only of time (the eight bells of a four-hour watch on a ship), but also of death. As John Donne writes in a familiar passage from *Devotions Upon Emergent Occasions*, "never send to know for whom the bell tolls; it tolls for thee." The introduction of the church, the bells, and the specter of death calls to mind that Sunday morning in this area was at one time most likely spent in religious contemplation. You may want to point out, moreover, that the thematic contrasts in this poem are echoed in its meter and rhyme scheme: the sprightly pace hinted at in the rhyming couplets is offset by the slower cadences of lengthy lines in iambic heptameter and in the formal patterning of the sonnet structure.

Teaching Clusters

The focus on time, death, and remembered vignettes in MacNeice's poetry make it a fitting candidate for the **History, Memory, and Politics** cluster. By adding Auden's poetry to this grouping, you will be able to give students a coherent sense of 1930s concerns about culture and politics. All of the MacNeice selections included in *NAEL* are to some extent about the passage of time, while "Star-Gazer" also addresses the theme of memory. "Bagpipe Music," moreover, would be well placed in the category on **Culture, Language, and Identity.** In this ballad, traditional culture is not only fading into the past, but the new culture is jarring, empty, and static.

Discussion Questions

1. What role does sound play in "Sunday Morning"? How does the music of the first octave contrast with the "eight bells" of the final quatrain (line 12)?
2. In *Devotions Upon Emergent Occasions*, John Donne cautions: "never send to know for whom the bell tolls; it tolls for thee." Discuss this passage in connection with "Sunday Morning."
3. What is the speaker of "Sunday Morning" saying about time? How is the portrayal of time different in the two stanzas?
4. What is "Fate's great bazaar" ("Sunday Morning," line 4)? Does the mention of "Fate" have anything to do with time or death?
5. Compare the depiction of modern life in "Sunday Morning" and "Bagpipe Music."

Further Resources

NORTON TOPICS ONLINE

Imagining Ireland

Dylan Thomas

Students will find Thomas's work immediately accessible; it is personal and evocative, while also addressing larger themes of life, death, and the passing of time. "Poem in October" and "Fern Hill," for instance, recall the joys of childhood. Yet his poetry also can combine poignancy with a surprising intensity. "Old age should burn and rave at close of day; / Rage, rage against the dying of the light," Thomas writes, thinking of his dying father ("Do Not Go Gentle into That Good Night," lines 2–3). "The Hunchback in the Park," on the other hand, examines the cruelty of young boys and the imaginative life of a man afflicted with a physical deformity. Thomas's language is both ironic and disturbing here, as he describes "the wild boys innocent as strawberries / [who follow] the hunchback / To his kennel in the dark" (lines 40–42). At the same time, Thomas is a skillful poet at home in a strict form such as the villanelle, used in "Do Not Go Gentle into That Good Night." The combination of Thomas's technical skills and his thoughtful reflections on life's complexities make his work a useful focus of study in general courses on poetry or specific courses on twentieth-century literature.

Fern Hill

Quick Read

- Form: Lyric.
- Summary: Thomas remembers childhood days spent at his aunt's farmhouse and meditates on death and the passing of time.
- Themes: The freedom of childhood; the passing of time; the poignancy of youthful memories recollected in adulthood; the loss of innocence and unfettered joy from adult life; the presence of death in life.
- Key Passages: "As I rode to sleep the owls were bearing the farm away," line 24; "Nothing I cared, in the lamb white days, that time would take me / Up to the swallow thronged loft by the shadow of my hand," lines 46–47; "Time held me green and dying / Though I sang in my chains like the sea," lines 53–54.

Teaching Suggestions

In "Fern Hill," Thomas draws upon his youthful experiences at his aunt's home in the Welsh countryside while he contemplates the passage of time. Invite students first to think about the way that Thomas envisions childhood. What kind of mood does Thomas establish? How does the repetition of certain colors (green, gold, and white) add to the overall effect of the poem? Take some time to discuss the myriad techniques the author uses to create a pleasing sense of harmony (alliteration, assonance, consonance, near-rhymes, scattered or irregular rhymes). Although the language is naïve and seemingly simple—the speaker is "carefree . . . / About the happy yard," for example (lines 10–11)—at the same time the images are compact, fresh, and evocative—the speaker remembers "rivers of the windfall light" (line 9) and "spellbound horses walking warm" (line 34). Note also the way in which the landscape, sounds, colors, and animals mingle and merge with the speaker's entire being. When students have become somewhat familiar with these images and techniques, turn more specifically to some of the poem's major themes, such as time. In the early stanzas, time (a personified entity) allows the speaker, as a child, to be "Golden in the heydays of his eyes" (line 5): alive, radiant, fortunate. Time is, moreover, connected to the rhythms of the natural world: "All the sun long [time] was running . . . / All the moon long I heard . . . the nightjars" (lines 19–25). There is a feeling of enchantment and freedom in the first four stanzas.

A different tone and perspective appears in the fifth stanza when the speaker states, "And nothing I cared, at my sky blue trades, that time allows . . . so few and such morning songs / Before the children green and golden / Follow him out of grace" (lines 42–45). The language, sound, and rhythm of these lines are repeated in the last stanza: "Nothing I cared, in the lamb white days, that time would take me / Up to the swallow thronged loft by the shadow of my hand, / In the moon that is always rising" (lines 45–48). Both passages take the reader forward in time to a point when the speaker is no longer merely recollecting his boyhood days, but noticing the difference between his adult and his youthful awareness. As an adult, time takes the "shadow" of the child—now just a memory—back to those recollected scenes, yet the perspective has changed. Whereas in the earlier stanzas the speaker was "green and carefree" and time "let [him] play and be / Golden in the mercy of his means, / And green and golden," now he thinks of his youthful self as "green and dying" (lines 10, 13–15, 53). Seen through the lens of his adult consciousness, green takes on bittersweet connotations, with the suggestion of loss or death—perhaps the recognition that even in life we are always nearing death or that the loss of childish pleasures is unavoidable. Similarly, whereas in the third stanza the boy "[rides] to sleep" as the "owls [bear] the farm away," in the final stanza when the speaker is "riding to sleep," the context has changed. Here, the farm is not momentarily borne away, but will never return. "Nothing I cared," the speaker tells us, that "I should . . . wake to the farm forever fled from the childless land" (lines 46–51). The adult speaker imagines himself as "wak[ing]" to a world without childhood memories—waking to an absence or void equal to death or emotional emptiness. When, in the last lines, he says, "Oh as I was young and easy in the mercy of his means, / Time held me green and dying / Though I sang in my chains like the sea," we see the speaker's childhood retrospectively, not from the earlier perspective (lines 52–54). Even as a child, he seems to be saying, he was dying, as we all are, because we are bound by time.

Teaching Clusters

Poems such as "Fern Hill," "Poem in October," and "Do Not Go Gentle into That Good Night" are best studied in the cluster on **History, Memory, and Politics**. The themes of time passing and of memories recollected in adulthood can be understood more fully when these poems are read with other similar selections. Works by both Auden and MacNeice, for example, would make illuminating companion readings here. Additionally, D. H. Lawrence's poetry, with its sense of life and connection to the elemental, would make a useful comparison to Thomas's work. Lawrence's "Piano" and Thomas's "Fern Hill," in particular, would make a good pairing.

Discussion Questions

1. How does the speaker of "Fern Hill" imagine his childhood days? What kinds of images does he use and what do these images convey? What does the phrase "spellbound horses" suggest, for example (line 34)?

2. In "Fern Hill" Thomas uses color to evoke a certain feeling; metaphors such as "lamb white days," "green and carefree," and "Golden in the heydays of his eyes" are sprinkled throughout (lines 46, 10, 5). Discuss the way in which color is used in this poem.

3. How is the theme of time developed in "Fern Hill"? Does the quality and attitude toward time change as the poem progresses?

4. What does the speaker mean when he says, "As I rode to sleep the owls were bearing the farm away" (line 24)? How does this statement take on different connotations in the final stanza, when he says, "Nothing I cared . . . [that I should] wake to the farm forever fled from the childless land" (lines 46–51)?

5. Locate examples of Thomas's use of alliteration ("wanderer white," line 28), assonance ("walking warm," line 34), consonance ("farm was home," line 11), and scattered or near rhymes ("Flying . . . Flashing," lines 26–27; "spinning . . . whinnying," lines 34–35) in "Fern Hill." What is the overall effect of these techniques?

6. Compare and contrast the themes of life or death in any two of Thomas's poems.

Further Resources

NORTON ONLINE ARCHIVE

Audio:
Poem in October (read by Dylan Thomas)

Voices from World War II

The writers of World War II do not have quite the same reputation as those of World War I, yet like their predecessors, they write about the horror, waste, and futility of war with eloquence. Rejecting the simple heroism of Tennyson's "The Charge of the Light Brigade," these poets attempt to make sense out of the unimaginable. Henry Reed's "Naming of Parts" conveys the incongruity of war by juxtaposing the prosaic dismantling and identification of rifle components to the beauty of the natural world: "Japonica / Glistens like coral in all of the neighboring gardens, / And today we have the naming of parts" (lines 4–6). The disparity between the mechanistic world of the military and the vibrancy of the garden emphasizes the ugliness of war and the way its emotional devastation has infected all areas of life. Edith Sitwell talks about another kind of disparity—between war and spiritual faith, imagined in terms of darkness and light; the world is "dark-smirched with pain," but redemption is possible through the "innocent light" of Christ (lines 29, 33). In contrast to

Sitwell's passionate rhetoric, Keith Douglas's tone is restrained; seeing both "stupidity and chivalry" in the fallen soldiers, he asks, "How can I live among this gentle / obsolescent breed of heroes and not weep?" ("Aristocrats," lines 13, 9–10).

Edith Sitwell

Still Falls the Rain

Quick Read

- Form: Lyric.
- Themes: War reduces all human beings to a base existence; redemption is possible through faith in God.
- Key Passages: "Still falls the Rain," line 1; "Under the Rain the sore and the gold are as one," line 15; "He bears in His Heart all wounds,—those of the light that died, / The last faint spark / In the self-murdered heart, the wounds of the sad uncomprehending dark," lines 18–20; "Still do I love, still shed my innocent light, my Blood, for thee," line 33.

Teaching Suggestions

Unlike many other poems critical of war, "Still Falls the Rain" was written in the middle of the conflict rather than afterwards, giving it a somewhat controversial edge. Students may not immediately realize that the poem indicts all of humankind, not just the Axis powers, for engaging in war. You will need to say a few words about World War II, its difference from the First World War, and the terrifying experience of the London blitz. You may begin your discussion simply by asking students about the title, noting the double meaning of "Still" and "Rain"/reign. The most apparent image that comes to mind is the raining of bombs, with the added implication of being caught in a storm that will not end, although other readings are possible. The insistent repetition of the phrase "Still falls the Rain" takes on an incantatory effect, somewhat like a religious ritual. In fact, some critics consider this poem a canticle, similar to a liturgical song. This may be a way for you to draw students' attention to the religious theme. The subtitle, "The Raids, 1940. Night and Dawn," alerts the reader to the motif of light and dark that runs through the poem, and to the association of Christ with light ("He bears in His Heart all wounds,— those of the light that died, / The last faint spark" [lines 18–19]; and "Still do I love, still shed my innocent light, my Blood, for thee" [line 33]). For Sitwell, the struggle is between light and dark, good and evil, and all parties are diminished by their involvement in war: "Under the Rain the sore and the gold are as one" (line 15). The quotation from Marlowe's *Doctor Faustus* is also worth noting: "O Ile leape up to my God: who pulles me doune— / See, see where Christ's blood streames in the firmament" (lines 25–26). There is a faint echo here of Christ's words on the cross: "My

God, my God, why hast thou forsaken me?" (Matthew 27.46). Like Faustus, the world is in spiritual darkness, under the reign/rain of horror. Unlike Christ on the cross, however, Faustus is responsible for his own fall from grace, just as the twentieth-century world is responsible for the war. Finally, it is possible to discern a few connections with metaphysical poetry here. As some critics have noted, Sitwell was an admirer of the metaphysical poets, especially Andrew Marvell. The religious subject matter, the powerful emotion, and the unlikely analogies (Christ's wounds equated with "The wounds of the baited bear," for instance [line 21]) contain some resemblance to techniques used by Marvell and others.

Keith Douglas

Aristocrats

Quick Read

- Form: Lyric; elegy.
- Themes: The upper-class military heroes of the past are outdated and slightly ridiculous in the more pragmatic era of World War II, yet they are fondly remembered by some; during wartime, a nonchalance towards self-preservation produces both bravery and innocent foolishness.
- Key Passages: "The noble horse . . . puts the pipe back in his mouth," lines 1–4; "It's most unfair, they've shot my foot off," line 8; "How can I live among this gentle / obsolescent breed of heroes and not weep?" lines 9–10; "The plains were their cricket pitch," line 15.

Teaching Suggestions

Douglas's "Aristocrats" balances gentle irony with admiration and respect for a vanished breed. A brief explanation of the English class system and its demise will help students situate the tensions in this poem. The aristocratic classes of the mid-twentieth century were greatly diminished in power; for many, they were the object of ridicule or loathing, while for others, their airs and graces had something enviable about them. In this poem, Douglas locates aristocratic cool in a type of military composure and stoicism. When "[t]he noble horse . . . puts the pipe back in his mouth," this is a gesture of extreme nonchalance in the face of gunfire (lines 1–4). It is a humorous image, moreover, because it is a horse (and a "noble" one at that) rather than a man making this familiar movement. The humor is extended in the second stanza with the story of "Peter," who says, with complete tranquility, "It's most unfair, they've shot my foot off" (line 8). In this passage, Douglas echoes a well-known story about another "aristocrat," the Earl of Uxbridge, who had a similar exchange with the Duke of Wellington during the Battle of Waterloo. According to legend, the Earl's calm statement, "By God, I have lost my leg" was met with a casual glance directed to where the cannon ball had just hit and accompanied by the equally casual response, "By God sir, so you have." It might be worth mentioning that the *NAEL* headnote observes that Douglas's interest in the heroic aspects of warfare span back to his early youth, at which time he wrote a poem about this same battle. Having been so immersed in military history, Douglas is well aware of the mythic aura around the older soldier heroes, yet he is also aware that both the ruling class and the elevated rhetoric that described pre-World War I soldiers and wars are outdated. "How can I live among this gentle / obsolescent breed of heroes, and not weep?" he asks; "Unicorns, almost" (lines 9–11). Like the mythologized unicorn, these former warriors are fading into legend—and disregard. In the final stanza, Douglas abandons his faintly mocking tone and takes up the attitude of the most traditionally patriotic and romantic of the World War I poets, Rupert Brooke, whose "corner of a foreign field / That is forever England" ("The Soldier," lines 2–3) can be discerned in the "stones and earth" (line 18) of the Tunisian desert that Douglas's imagination has converted to the "cricket pitch[es]" and "drop fences" (lines 15, 16) of the English shires. Like Brooke, Douglas finds that something positive and redeemable can be wrested from the midst of modern warfare.

Teaching Clusters

The subject matter of the poems in this section places them squarely in the cluster on **History, Memory, and Politics**. Any of the World War I poems would make good companion readings for these selections. Sitwell's "Still Falls the Rain," moreover, could be read alongside the second section of T. S. Eliot's *Little Gidding*, which also reflects on the London blitz. Additionally, both Sitwell and Douglas would be well paired with Wilfred Owen, in particular. Douglas's "Aristocrats" would also work well in the **Culture, Language, and Identity** grouping, as a commentary on Englishness.

Discussion Questions

1. Discuss the various meanings of the title "Still Falls the Rain." What effect does Sitwell achieve with the repetition of this phrase?
2. Explore the themes of light and dark in "Still Falls the Rain." How are these themes related to war? What connection is there to religious faith?
3. What is the poem's attitude toward war? Who or what is at fault? What are the consequences of war?
4. Why does Sitwell quote Faustus's words to Mephistopheles: "O Ile leape up to my God: who pulles me doune— / See, see where Christ's blood streames in the firmament" (lines 25–26)? What does the Faust story or this passage have to do with the poem's concerns?
5. Why does Douglas use the word "Aristocrats" to describe the military

heroes of the poem? How can this word be both complimentary and critical?

6. What does Douglas mean when he talks about "stupidity and chivalry" (line 13)? How is any of this connected to the pipe-smoking, unconcerned English gentleman?
7. What is the speaker's attitude toward the "aristocrats" of the poem?
8. Trace the use of humor and irony in "Aristocrats."

Further Resources

NORTON ONLINE ARCHIVE

Audio:
Still Falls the Rain (read by Edith Sitwell)

Nation and Language

The use of the English language in former British colonies is a topic much in dispute today. Many believe that, as a legacy of colonial rule, Standard English perpetuates the forms of thought and cultural values of the imperial center. Anglophone writers may themselves be haunted by a sense of dispossession when they use the "native tongue" that is not "native." The Kenyan writer Ngũgĩ wa Thiong'o describes how, under the British educational system, the imposition of English on students disrupted traditional standards of loyalty among community members and replaced the cultural narratives of his youth with alien narratives that had no bearing on the social fabric of his life. "Language carries culture, and culture carries, particularly through orature and literature, the entire body of values by which we come to perceive ourselves and our place in the world," Ngũgĩ explains. His views on the destructive effects of the colonizer's language on Kenyan culture have led him to reject English as a means of literary expression and return to his native Gĩkũyũ. Kamau Brathwaite describes a similar educational experience in the West Indies, where children learned to write about snow, which they had never seen, and poets struggled to work within the unsuitable rhythms of the British pentameter. Only by rejecting these imposed forms and embracing the sounds and cadences of "nation language"—a creolized, spontaneous adaptation of English—could Caribbean writers capture the lived experience of the West Indies. Rather than rejecting English completely, as Ngũgĩ does, Brathwaite sees Afro-Caribbean variations of Standard English as vitally expressive of West Indian culture. Like Brathwaite, Salman Rushdie sees local renditions of English as flexible tools fully capable of expressing the unique qualities of individual cultures. Rushdie is far less concerned with the colonial past than most of the other authors in this section, however, seeing in English a useful medium in the globalized world and a practical solution to India's internal conflicts over the adoption of Hindi as a national language. Taken as a whole, the views expressed in this section cover a wide range of positions. Given the significance of postcolonial writing within English literary studies today, it is essential for students to have a nuanced understanding of the debates on language use and cultural identity.

Louise Bennett

Jamaica Language

Quick Read

- Form: Radio monologue.
- Summary: Humorous monologue written in Jamaican English that argues that Jamaican language is not a corruption of English, but a vital and creative expression drawn from multiple sources.
- Key Passages: "For if dat be de case [that Jamaican dialect is a corruption of the English language], den dem shoulda call English Language corruption of Norman French an Latin an all dem tarra language what dem seh dat English is derived from" (2469); "English is a derivation but Jamaica Dialec is a corruption! What a unfairity!" (2469); "For Jamaican Dialec did start when we English forefahders did start musan-bound we African ancestors fi stop talk fi-dem African Language altogedder an learn fi talk so-so English" (2470).

Teaching Suggestions

Louise Bennett's delightful monologue wittily argues that Jamaican language is no more a "corruption" of English than English is a corruption of languages such as Norman French and Latin. "English is a derivation but Jamaica Dialec is a corruption! What a unfairity!" she exclaims, making her point while illustrating the creativity of Jamaican speech. Ask students to read through the passage at least twice, once to pick up the gist of the piece and the meaning of unfamiliar words, and another time to get a sense of the humor, vitality, and inventiveness of the language. Direct their attention, in particular, to Bennett's discussion of the development of Jamaican language: "For Jamaican Dialec did start when we English forefahders did start musan-bound we African ancestors fi stop talk fi-dem African Language altogedder an learn fi talk so-so English." Bennett emphasizes both the trickery and strategic intelligence of African slaves who were ordered to speak English rather than their native languages so that their British overseers could follow what they were saying. Seeming on the one hand to be speaking "English," on the other hand the captives could talk among themselves without being understood. "But we African ancestors-dem . . . [p]op dem an disguise up de English Language fi projec fi-dem African Language in such a way dat we English forefahders-dem still couldn understan what we African ancestors-dem wasa talk bout when dem wasa talk to dem one annodder!"she explains. Employing

"Aunty Roachy" as the ultimate authority on such matters, Bennett makes the important observation that Jamaican language draws both from English and African speech: "Aunty Roachy seh dat if Jamaican Dialec is corruption of de English Language, den it is also a corruption of de African Twi Language to, a oh!" Lastly, note the way that Bennett contrasts the liveliness of Jamaican English with the listless formality of Standard English, turning "Mumma, Mumma, dem ketch Puppa" into the hilariously restrained "Mother, Mother, they apprehended Father." Some of Bennett's poems will help bring this last theme alive, moreover, while "Colonization in Reverse," like "Jamaica Language," turns what is usually thought of as capitulation (emigration to the imperial center) into empowerment (reverse colonization).

Brian Friel

Translations

Quick Read

- Form: Historical drama.
- Summary: Two British colonial representatives come to the Irish town of Baile Beag to remap and rename all geographical sites. At the same time, the local hedge schools are about to be replaced with British-run schools.
- Themes: The act of naming or renaming something is an assertion of authority and ownership; language is a repository of culture, history, and identity; no translation is an exact rendering of another language.
- Key Passages: Bridget: "It's easier to stamp out learning than to recall it" (2485); Owen: "We name a thing and—bang!—it leaps into existence!" (2505); Hugh: "We must learn those new names. . . . We must learn where we live. We must learn to make them our own" (2521); Hugh: "[I]t is not the literal past, the 'facts' of history, that shape us, but images of the past embodied in language" (2521).

Teaching Suggestions

Brian Friel's Translations dramatizes a determining moment in the history of Ireland in the early 1830s when the island's native Celtic culture was poised to be fatally undermined through the supplanting of indigenous hedge schools with a British system of education and the simultaneous remapping and renaming of townships by the British Royal Engineers. Before discussing this play, it would be instructive to have students read the selections by Brathwaite and Ngũgĩ to alert them to the discordances that an Anglocentric colonial education imposed upon its colonized subjects. When you turn to the play itself, invite students to trace the motif of renaming that occurs throughout and reflect on the psychological, cultural, and material effects of such renaming. It would be worthwhile to take the time to thoroughly review the passages in Act II in which Owen and Yolland go through the Irish place-names and assign new, anglicized versions. Note that in its original Gaelic form the name was not only a geographical designation but also a repository of the nation's history and legends. When Owen recounts to Yolland the origin of "Tobair Vree," for example, he explains that "Tobair" is Irish for "well" and that "Vree" comes from a story about a man who was found drowned in a well that he thought had magical powers. Ask students to compare this renaming with other forms of naming that occur. The play opens with the usually mute Sarah learning to name herself—a great victory that is sadly reversed at the play's end when she is unable to verbalize her name to Lancey, the British officer. Similarly, early in the drama we hear about the naming of Nellie Ruadh's baby, yet later find that the baby dies after only a few days. Clearly, naming is a form of empowerment that is slipping away from the Irish.

Just as the Irish are being disenfranchised through the renaming of their land, so too is their history and culture about to be destroyed when the Irish hedge schools are replaced with British national schools. Maier urges Manus to apply for a job in "the new national school" because she knows, as she explains, that "[w]hen it opens, this is finished: nobody's going to pay to go to a hedge-school." When the British schools open, as students will know from reading Brathwaite and Ngũgĩ, the English language will be imposed, the Irish language will be banned, and Irish history, lore, and folktales will be replaced with British versions. Hugh foresees all this and says, "We must learn those new names. . . . We must learn where we live. We must learn to make them our own." As history demonstrates, later generations will lose touch with the ancestral language, and although there is a strong movement to restore and recover Irish language, legends, and place-names, English has permanently altered the cultural landscape.

You will also want to ask students to think about the theme of "translation" that the play addresses. Renaming Irish topography is the most rudimentary form of translation in the play—one that results in definitions that are often quite arbitrary, "neither fish nor flesh," as Owen puts it—yet there are other instances worth exploring. Owen's euphemistic rendering of Lancey's first speech to the Baile Beag residents is a humorous example of the incommensurability of different languages, and the final encounter between Yolland and Maire, in a very different manner, demonstrates the difficulties inherent in any translation—even one based on profound sympathy. The lovers are able to express their desire for each other quite clearly, but that desire is based on a misunderstanding: Yolland dreams of settling in Baile Beag forever, while Maire envisions escape to a faraway place. The act of translation itself, Friel shows us, is always vulnerable to making "[t]he wrong gesture in the wrong language."

Kamau Brathwaite

Nation Language

Quick Read

- Form: Essay modified from lecture.
- Summary: Brathwaite advocates the use of "nation language," a mixture of Standard English and African words and cadences, as a way of recovering the African cultural legacy.
- Key Passages: "In other words, we haven't got the syllables, the syllabic intelligence, to describe the hurricane, which is our own experience; whereas we can describe the imported alien experience of the snowfall" (2525); "can English be a revolutionary language? . . . [I]t is not language, but people, who make revolutions" (2526–27); "nation language in the Caribbean . . . largely ignores the pentameter" (2526); "Nation language . . . is the submerged area of that dialect that is much more closely allied to the African aspect of experience in the Caribbean. It may be in English, but often it is in an English which is like a howl, or a shout, or a machine-gun, or the wind, or a wave" (2527).

Teaching Suggestions

Like Louise Bennett, Kamau Brathwaite advocates the use of a creolized English that is alive to the sound and sense of the African languages that are the inheritance of the West Indies. In a more formal manner than Bennett, Brathwaite describes the history of the European slave trade in the Caribbean, the imposition of the colonizers' languages upon African slaves, and the subsequent infusion of English language, history, and literary forms into British colonial schools and West Indian culture. One of Brathwaite's points is that the result of this forcing of British language and thought upon the slaves and their descendants was that the British model did not correspond to the actual experience of living in the Caribbean. Only "nation language"—a combination of African and Standard English speech patterns and words—could give voice to the perceptions of the colonized and enslaved peoples. In your discussion of this piece with students, you will want to emphasize several themes that emerge: the mutability of language; the incompatibility of the enforced language with the lived experience of West Indians; and the need to allow the local language to flourish by acknowledging and valuing its Afro-Caribbean heritage. It is also important to note that Brathwaite, himself a poet, is concerned with language not only as a political and social expression, but also as a literary mode. To bring this point home, you can ask students to trace Brathwaite's use of the hurricane as a symbol for the Caribbean and its indigenous literary formulations. He introduces this image somewhat humorously, to remind his audience (who might not know that the Caribbean exists, he implies) that at the time of his address a hurricane was raging through the islands ("You must know of the Caribbean at least from television, at least now with hurricane David"). As he develops his theme, he posits the English pentameter as the linguistic straightjacket by which generations of West Indian poets were bound. "[T]he pentameter . . . carries with it a certain kind of experience, which is not the experience of a hurricane," Brathwaite declares, which leads him to ask "how do you get a rhythm that approximates the natural experience, the environmental experience"? His answer, elaborated throughout the essay, is to ignore the restrictions of the pentameter and follow the rhythms of Afro-Caribbean speech, which is the only way truly to convey the texture of West Indian life.

Ngũgĩ wa Thiong'o

Decolonising the Mind

Quick Read

- Form: Book excerpt.
- Summary: Ngũgĩ describes the experience of having his native language, Gĩkũyũ, devalued and criminalized under the British colonial educational system. He explains the reasons why, after years of writing in English, he decided to return to the language of his culture.
- Key Passages: "We therefore learnt to value words for their meaning and nuances. Language was not a mere string of words" (2536); "English was the official vehicle and the magic formula to colonial elitedom" (2537); "The domination of a people's language by the languages of colonising nations was crucial to the domination of the mental universe of the colonised" (2538); "I believe that my writing in Gĩkũyũ language, a Kenyan language, an African language, is part and parcel of the anti-imperialist struggles of Kenyan and African peoples" (2539).

Teaching Suggestions

This excerpt from Ngũgĩ wa Thiong'o's *Decolonising the Mind* makes an eloquent and compelling argument against the acceptance of the colonizer's language, in whole or in part, by former colonized peoples. He explains precisely and clearly how language conveys cultural beliefs and how it can be used as a tool for domination even after decolonization has occurred. Invite students first to think about Ngũgĩ's experience with his native Kenyan language, Gĩkũyũ, and what values it imparted to its speakers. Ngũgĩ's description of boyhood evenings spent in storytelling is not only poignant, but it illustrates the way in which cultural narratives shape communal beliefs and social relations. In Ngũgĩ's case, these stories about how various animals struggled against, compromised with, and triumphed over adversaries taught valuable lessons in cooperation among community members. "Co-operation as the ultimate good in a community was a constant theme," Ngũgĩ explains. Generations of community-building and cultural rapport, however, were undone when the British instituted strict rules about language and educational advancement. With the proscription against his native language came the eradication of an entire cultural past: "Dickens and Stevenson" replaced "Hare, Leopard and Lion"; and along with the substitution of one set of defining cultural narratives for another came the substitution of a different set of values for the existing ones. Encouraged to betray other students who disregarded the colonizer's rules and spoke the forbidden language, children were taught to break faith with their fellows and unlearn the lessons of their upbringing. Added to this were the very material restrictions placed on students who did not succeed in English studies. Ngũgĩ's description of the boy who had high marks in all subjects except English, which he failed, and who was thus condemned to a low-level job, illustrates the cause-and-effect relationship between the imposition of a language and the shaping of a region's economic and social structure. Given this background of colonial subjugation and cultural destruction, Ngũgĩ's words have a particular force: "Economic and political control can never be complete or effective without mental control. To control a people's culture is to control their tools of self-definition in relationship to others." As Ngũgĩ demonstrates, the regulation of language is the key to cultural and psychological dominance.

Salman Rushdie

English Is an Indian Literary Language

Quick Read

- Form: Essay.
- Summary: Rushdie argues that English is not only a tool of the British; rather, it is a language that is greatly adaptable to individual cultures, with a life of its own in India and elsewhere.
- Key Passages: "English is an essential language in India, not only because of its technical vocabularies and the international communication which it makes possible, but also simply to permit two Indians to talk to each other in a tongue which neither party hates" (2540); "it is completely fallacious to suppose that there is such a thing as a pure, unalloyed tradition from which to draw" (2541); "The English language ceased to be the sole possession of the English some time ago" (2541).

Teaching Suggestions

Students may at first think Rushdie is making the same argument as Brathwaite and Bennett, but although there are some correspondences, there are also significant differences. While Brathwaite and Bennett look to affinities with African linguistic sources for a sense of a separate, pre-

or anticolonial identity, Rushdie has no interest in drawing from the past or in validating contemporary versions of English by their association with inherited traditions. As he asserts, "it is completely fallacious to suppose that there is such a thing as a pure, unalloyed tradition from which to draw." Brathwaite and Bennett are not claiming linguistic purity in any form—in fact, they both embrace multiplicity and creativity—but their work rewrites a painful history of slavery by giving dignity and recognition to Africa's rich legacy. Rather than taking a specifically anticolonial stance, as Brathwaite, Bennett, Ngũgĩ, and others in this section do, Rushdie is content to focus on the current life of the English language in India and the world and not its link to colonial oppression. "I don't think it is always necessary to take up the anti-colonial—or is it post-colonial?—cudgels against English. What seems to me to be happening is that those peoples who were once colonized by the language are now rapidly remaking it." Rushdie acknowledges the colonial past, but also that the younger generation of people raised in post-British India do not see the use of English in the same way as earlier generations. "The children of independent India seem not to think of English as being irredeemably tainted by its colonial provenance. They use it as an Indian language, as one of the tools they have to hand," he states. Moreover, you will want students to understand that Rushdie believes English has much practical value today. Referring to political and ideological conflicts between North and South regions of India, he observes, "English is an essential language in India, not only because of its technical vocabularies and the international communication which it makes possible, but also simply to permit two Indians to talk to each other in a tongue which neither party hates." Ultimately, Rushdie's take on the global use of English is very optimistic; he sees it as malleable and vibrant, very much open to indigenous expressions.

Teaching Clusters

All of the readings in the "Nation and Language" section are most profitably situated in the cluster on **Culture, Language, and Identity**. As noted above, Brathwaite and Bennett make an excellent pairing, and Friel's *Translations* will gain much from being read alongside Brathwaite and Ngũgĩ. There are also many works outside of this section that would greatly enhance students' understanding of the relationships among language, culture, identity, and power. Orwell's "Politics and the English Language," discusses connections between language and political control, for example; Jean Rhys's "The Day They Burned the Books" addresses the importance of cultural, linguistic, and textual inheritances; and Beckett's *Endgame* makes some thought-provoking connections between language and power.

Discussion Questions

1. According to Louise Bennett, how did the African slaves use the English language to their own advantage?
2. In "Jamaica Language" and "Colonization in Reverse," how does Bennett invert conventional views of the postcolonial relationship?
3. Why is the renaming of Irish place-names in Friel's *Translations* significant? What is gained or lost in a translation? Compare this renaming of Irish towns by British representatives with the two failed attempts by Sarah and the off-stage Nellie Ruadh to engage in different types of naming.
4. In *Translations*, what is at stake for the Irish when the British national schools replace the Irish hedge schools? Do Brathwaite's and Ngũgĩ's observations on the effects of a British education on colonized peoples give you any insights into Friel's play?
5. Brathwaite uses the pentameter and the hurricane as symbols (or synecdoches) for larger cultural modes of expression. Discuss his use of these words, their meaning, and the way that they relate to one another.
6. Brathwaite relays an anecdote about a young West Indian student who wrote, "The snow was falling on the cane fields"; "She was trying to have both cultures at the same time. But that is creolization," Brathwaite comments. Why is the student's statement an example of creolization? What are Brathwaite's thoughts on the persistence of British literary models in the Caribbean?
7. According to Ngũgĩ, why is the practice of storytelling important? What did it mean to him as a child? What kinds of ideas did he glean from these stories?
8. How did the imposition of the English language and restrictions on educational advancement under British rule affect Ngũgĩ and other students?
9. According to Rushdie, how important is the past—either colonial or precolonial—in viewing contemporary versions of English? How are his views different from or similar to those of Bennett and Brathwaite?
10. Why does Rushdie advocate the use of English in today's India? How is it possible for the younger generation to make English their own?

Further Resources

NORTON TOPICS ONLINE

Imperialism to Postcolonialism: Perspectives on the British Empire

Doris Lessing

By now some of the themes explored in Doris Lessing's feminist story "To Room Nineteen" may seem familiar, but the careful attention Lessing gives to the female protagonist's changing state of mind and the honesty with which she explores the disintegration of the Rawlings' marriage make this a rewarding focus of study in the classroom. The narrator tells us that after marriage, "the essential Susan [was] in abeyance"; more disturbingly, we find, Susan herself does not seem to know where or what the "essential Susan" is. Lessing's story demonstrates that the fictions society dispenses about the contentment that marriage and motherhood bring only serve to alienate women from themselves. Rather than trusting her instincts, Susan has learned to rely on a cultural narrative that does not allow space for an autonomous female identity apart from the domestic unit. Unable to find a domain of self-expression in the mainstream of social life, Susan searches in ever more marginalized spaces, until her search leads her to the final space of absolute nonbeing.

To Room Nineteen

Quick Read

- Form: Short story.
- Summary: A married woman with four children finds herself increasingly estranged from her husband and family. Seeking a private sanctuary, she rents a cheap London hotel room several days a week, but when her hiding place is discovered, commits suicide.
- Theme: Social expectations about marriage and motherhood become internalized and stifle self-expression.
- Key Passages: "This is a story, I suppose, about a failure in intelligence" (2544); "A high price has to be paid for the happy marriage with the four healthy children in the large white gardened house" (2548); "She was filled with emotions that were utterly ridiculous, that she despised" (2551); "She was no longer Susan Rawlings, mother of four, wife of Matthew. . . . She was Mrs Jones, and she was alone, and she had no past and no future" (2559); "Inside she was dissolving in horror at them both, at how far they had both sunk from honesty of emotion" (2563).

Teaching Suggestions

Students will likely have strong ideas about why Susan Rawlings becomes progressively more and more alienated from her role as wife and mother in Lessing's story. You can spark the initial discussion by asking whether Susan's unhappiness is related to her husband, Matthew, or if the causes are more diffuse. Some students may believe that Susan's problem lies primarily with her husband, whose infidelity causes Susan much inward anger that she struggles to suppress. Yet you will want to point out that both Susan and Matthew feel "flat" in their life with one another for some time before Matthew enters into his first extramarital sexual encounter. As the narrator explains before Matthew's infidelity occurs, two educated people "could scarcely be unprepared for the dry, controlled wistfulness which is the distinguishing mark of the intelligent marriage." The concept of the "intelligent marriage" can lead you into the next phase of your discussion. Lessing foregrounds the importance of "intelligence" from the opening sentence: "This is a story, I suppose, about a failure in intelligence." Throughout the narrative, Lessing further underscores this theme with references to "intelligent love," Susan's "intelligent husband," and Susan's own "intelligent" attitudes. What exactly does "intelligence" mean in the context of this story? How is "intelligence" at odds with a more fulfilling marriage, perhaps for both Susan and Matthew? After Matthew confesses to his indiscretion, "There was no need to use the dramatic words, unfaithful, forgive, and the rest: intelligence forbade them." Note that Susan is unable to express her own anger. By the end of the story, Susan is disturbed by the inability of either Matthew or herself to talk candidly with each other: "Inside she was dissolving in horror at them both, at how far they had both sunk from honesty of emotion." "Intelligence" seems to foreclose the possibility of real communication or of truthful self-expression and instead condones ultra-rational modes of thought advocated by a specific kind of cultural narrative. Susan and Matthew read all the right books—"psychological, anthropological, sociological"—but these books only serve to indoctrinate them both into social expectations about marriage and parenthood. In this sense, both Susan and Matthew are victims of societal and patriarchal myths. At the same time, however, this is a story about a very particular type of gendered oppression experienced by women. It is important for students to understand that the hotel room Susan rents is a metaphor for the personal and material space women are denied by the societal myth of women's emotional fulfillment through marriage and motherhood. Susan drifts through life following the existing script rather than making the difficult choices that would allow her to find out who she is.

Teaching Clusters

The most appropriate placement for Lessing's "To Room Nineteen" is undoubtedly the cluster on **Gender, Desire, and Sexuality**. Within this category, several other works would help bring out the themes and issues that Lessing pursues. One obvious companion piece in this grouping would be Virginia Woolf's *A Room of One's Own*. As the NAEL headnote observes, Lessing's story, like Woolf's feminist classic, addresses issues of "gender, space, and identity." Additionally, "The Daughters of the Late Colonel," Katherine Mansfield's humorous tale of two women emotionally and intellectually stunted in caring for their overbearing father, would make a useful comparison. For more focus on self-diminishment and the desire for self-annihilation, Stevie Smith's poetry ("Thoughts About the Person from Porlock" and "Not Waving but Drowning") would add an illuminating dimension. If you are planning on teaching this piece in a women's studies course not specifically limited to British literature, Kate Chopin's *The Awakening* would make a superb complement. Both stories feature women in conventional upper-middle-class marriages who drift further and further away from their role as wife and mother. Edna Pontellier, moreover, like Susan Rawlings, establishes a separate space for herself—a separate house, in fact—away from the family home. For both women, suicide arguably is not a defeat, but an escape into a realm where the self can be free.

Discussion Questions

1. Why is Susan Rawlings unhappy in her marriage? Is her husband, Matthew, to blame? Is motherhood to blame? Does it have to do with Susan quitting her job? Do social beliefs about marriage and parenthood stifle both men and women equally?
2. In what way is "To Room Nineteen" about "a failure in intelligence"? What does "intelligence" mean in this story? How does "intelligence" keep both Susan and Matthew from experiencing fuller lives?
3. The narrator of "To Room Nineteen" tells us that Susan "was filled with emotions that were utterly ridiculous, that she despised." Why does Susan "despise" her emotions?
4. Why is Susan still not happy even after she hires Sophie to manage the house and take care of the children? Why does she rent the dingy room in the London hotel? What does the room mean to her?
5. Why is Susan upset when Matthew discovers where she has been spending her weekdays? Why does Susan decide to commit suicide?
6. Compare the concepts of female identity and space in "To Room Nineteen" and Virginia Woolf's *A Room of One's Own*.

Philip Larkin

"They fuck you up, your mum and dad," writes Larkin in "This Be The Verse" (line 1). Not all of Larkin's writing is this bold, but much of it contains the same colloquial phrasing and the sense of discontent apparent here. Often, discontent with the world finds its analogue in alienation between fellow human beings, such as in "Talking in Bed." In this poem, two people lying together are "An emblem of . . . being honest," but the speaker reflects that "It becomes still more difficult to find / Words at once true and kind, / Or not untrue and not unkind" (lines 3, 10–12). The psychological distance between the two lovers is matched by the landscape, where "the wind's incomplete unrest / Builds and disperses clouds about the sky, / And dark towns heap up on the horizon" (lines 5–7). "None of this cares for us," the speaker adds, placing this scene of human estrangement within a forbidding universe. Larkin's poem seems a modern rewriting of Matthew Arnold's "Dover Beach," in which the speaker hopes for fidelity in love ("Ah, love, let us be true / To one another!" [line 29–30]), but concedes that "[T]he world . . . / Hath really neither joy, nor love, nor light, / Nor certitude, nor peace, nor help for pain" (lines 30–34). Like Arnold's "darkling plain . . . / Where ignorant armies clash by night" (lines 35–37), Larkin's "dark towns . . . on the horizon" (line 7) suggest a hopeless future. Yet Larkin brings to Arnold's themes a relaxed, aloof tone and conversational idiom that is the hallmark of his verse. Rejecting the romantic excesses of Dylan Thomas and the modernist experimentalism of T. S. Eliot, Larkin's poetry embraces the ordinary while still maintaining lyric complexity.

Church Going

Quick Read

- Form: Lyric.
- Summary: A casual visit to a church results in a reflection on the decline of spiritual faith and the tendency to search for meaning in the remnants of religious authority.
- Themes: The meaninglessness of religion in postwar Britain; the desire to invest churches with meaning despite a decline in spiritual belief; the search for spiritual purpose in a faithless world persists.
- Key Passages: "I . . . / Reflect the place was not worth stopping for. / Yet stop I did," lines 17–19; "Wondering . . . / When churches turn completely out of use / What we shall turn them into," lines 21–23; "And what remains when disbelief has gone?" line 35; "someone will forever be surprising / A hunger in himself to be more serious," lines 59–60.

Teaching Suggestions

To begin a class discussion on "Church Going," ask students to look closely at the first two stanzas, describing the speaker, tone, and setting. From the beginning, the conversational language establishes a casual attitude: "Once I am sure there's nothing going on / I step inside, letting the door thud shut" (lines 1–2). The relaxed mood turns into irreverence when the speaker notes "some brass and stuff / Up at the holy end" (lines 5–6) and then into outright mockery when he ascends the pulpit and, parodying a sermon, declares "Here endeth" (line 15). After adding a further insult by donating a worthless Irish coin, he thinks, "the place was not worth stopping for" (line 18). This cheeky posture is abruptly reversed at the beginning of the third stanza, clearly signaled by the words "Yet stop I did" (line 19). The self-conscious syntax of this phrase, moreover, marks a slight turn away from the colloquial rhythms of the earlier lines.

As you explore the remainder of the poem, invite students to think about what the church means to the speaker—and why, despite his insolence, he "often" stops to look at this or other churches (line 19). His ruminations on the possible uses of church buildings in a future faithless age draw attention to the disparity between the profound importance these places of worship used to have and their rapidly declining significance in postwar Britain. "When churches fall completely out of use / What [shall we] turn them into?" the speaker wonders (lines 22–23), imagining them filled with "rain and sheep" (line 26). Yet his seemingly indifferent attitude is tempered by his inability to let the question go;

clearly both the question and answer have some meaning to the speaker, who is drawn to these formerly significant structures again and again. Note that he envisions a time not only when "belief" has died (line 34), but—perhaps more disturbingly—"when disbelief has gone" (line 35), when faithlessness no longer has any meaning. The tone is cool and rational, but the speaker asserts his nonchalance perhaps a bit more forcefully than would a completely disinterested person. By the time we come to the final stanza, in fact, the tone has become more respectful, even ponderous; rather than an "accoutred frowsty barn" (line 53), the church has become "A serious house on serious earth . . . / In whose blent air all our compulsions meet" (lines 55–56). Students may notice that, although it seems as if the entire poem argues that churches are becoming obsolete, here the speaker declares that they "never can be obsolete / Since someone will forever be surprising / A hunger in himself to be more serious" (lines 58–60). Yet you will want to direct their attention to the possible distancing of the speaker from this "someone" who "gravitat[es]" to the church because "he once heard [that it] was proper to grow wise in, / If only that so many dead lie round" (lines 61, 62–63). Even so, how might this space resemble the contemplative space of poetry? Does the speaker mourn the loss of religious belief, despite his flippant remarks? Or is this a completely detached view of a major cultural institution in decline? What evidence can be found for reading the poem as religious and nostalgic, or as skeptical and irreverent?

Teaching Clusters

Because "Church Going" reflects on the decline of religion over time, it may be studied in the **History, Memory, and Politics** cluster. Larkin's "MCMXIV" would make a good companion piece here, since both poems contrast the present with the past, finding the present lacking in some manner. Both poems could, moreover, be placed in the cluster on **Culture, Language, and Identity** and explored in relation to British culture and identity. "Talking in Bed" would make another useful addition to the **History, Memory, and Politics** cluster, especially if paired with Matthew Arnold's "Dover Beach," with which it shares many similarities. In both "Dover Beach" and "Talking in Bed," the personal becomes the analogue to the collective experience of time, culture, and history. Additionally, despite Larkin's protests against literary modernism, his poetry could be studied in the **Transition, Modernity, and Modernism** cluster if you were to focus on the sense of alienation present in his writing. Poems such as "Talking in Bed" and "This Be the Verse" would work well here.

Discussion Questions

1. Describe the speaker of "Church Going." What is his attitude toward the church he visits?
2. Does the speaker in this poem care very much about the declining importance of churches?

3. Why does the speaker say that "the place was not worth stopping for" yet admit that it "pleases [him] to stand in silence [t]here" (lines 18, 54)? Do you see any ambivalence here or elsewhere in the poem? (One way to have your students dramatize the poem's conflicting impulses is to ask them to debate whether the poem seems to them more irreverent and skeptical or more nostalgic and even religious, scouring the poem for all the evidence on one or the other side.)

4. Larkin and other poets identified with "the Movement" are often described as evidencing a rational, detached attitude toward their subject matter. To what extent does Larkin succeed in maintaining an aloof attitude in "Church Going"? Carefully examine any changes in tone between the first two and the remaining stanzas.

Further Resources

NORTON ONLINE ARCHIVE

Audio:

MCMXIV *and* Aubade (read by Philip Larkin)

Nadine Gordimer

The literary eminence of Nadine Gordimer in her native South Africa and internationally owes much to the author's uncompromising response to the moral crisis brought about in her society by the system of institutionalized racism and segregation known by the Afrikaans word for "aparthood"—apartheid. In her novels and short stories, Gordimer's characters, both white and black, are very much subject to a determinism growing out of their repressive environment, and their stories effectively convey Gordimer's message that psychology, politics, and history are never separate realms. Such is the case in her story "The Moment before the Gun Went Off," which opens with a white South African farmer's vexed anticipation of condemnation from the international court of opinion for his accidental killing of a young black farmhand. In a twist ending, we learn that the farmer, "'a leading member' of the ruling Party," can neither dare to launch a defense against his detractors nor share the true depths of his grief with his community of Afrikaner grange owners because his past transgression—sexual intimacy with a black African employee that led to the dead laborer's conception—must remain unspoken. The lies and silence that were primary features of life under apartheid continue to exist even after the lifting of the South African government's prohibition against sexual relations between whites and other races. The iniquities that stretch back deep into the country's colonial past have created a habit of suppression that promises to extend into the country's future. Published in 1991, the year Gordimer won the Nobel Prize and the year the country's leading reformer Nelson Mandela was elected as president of the anti-apartheid African National Congress after his recent release from a prison term of nearly three decades, the story gives a taste of the atmosphere of a country in transition. Here, Gordimer captures a confused period during which the white South African government was in the process of dismantling its policy of apartheid, but had yet to make the final move toward constitutional racial equality that would not be voted into law until the following year. The ambitious, expansive scope, complex ironies, and vivid realism of her novels find a microcosmic counterpart in this story, which exhibits a remarkable amount of social contextualization within a very small compass.

The Moment before the Gun Went Off

Quick Read

- Form: Short story.
- Summary: A white South African farmer accidentally shoots and kills a black employee, who we later learn is his son.
- Themes: Individual identities are inextricably connected to their social, cultural, and historical contexts; psychological trauma and disjunction is the inheritance of a political system based on racial inequality; paternal legacies can be economic, psychological, and social at once.
- Key Passages: "[E]veryone in the district remembers Marais Van der Vyver as a little boy who would go away and hide himself if he caught you smiling at him" (2576); "this big, calm, clever son of Willem Van der Vyver . . . inherited the old man's best farm" (2576); "The rifle was one of his father's" (2576); "The dead man's mother and he stare at the grave in communication like that between the black man outside and the white man inside the cab the moment before the gun went off" (2578).

Teaching Suggestions

The narrative voice in "The Moment before the Gun Went Off" offers a convenient starting place for your discussion. Through this voice, the reader is asked to discriminate among various points of view: the narrator's, Marais Van der Vyver's, the community's, and the story itself. At first, students may believe that the narrating sensibility is that of what "Van der Vyver knows," but it can be shown that the chronicler's perspective is not convergent with the protagonist's. The narrative expression appears to share attributes with a chorus in a Greek tragedy, in that it articulates a communal consciousness representing the consensus of community opinion—in this case the conventional outlook of a society redolent with racial prejudice. There is potent irony here, almost in the tradition of Jonathan Swift's "Modest Proposal," in that we are supposed to be shocked by the narrator's views while recognizing that this is only a persona the author has assumed in the service of sharpening the effect of her social criticism. Ask students to distinguish between the racial attitudes of the narrator and those of Van der Vyver; both participate in the maintenance of racist hierarchies, but in very different ways. Gordimer does not ask us to excuse Van der Vyver, but to understand that racism takes many forms, and that numerous people are caught up in its self-perpetuating cycle. This effect underscores one of the story's central themes, that socio-historical influences are inextricably connected to the development of individual identities.

Another important theme is that of paternal inheritance. The story contains several references to Willem Van der Vyver, the late, great patriarchal figure whose presence seems to overshadow his son's life. Marais Van der Vyver's prominence in the community is directly related to his father's legacy; the son inherited the father's "best farm" and his employees are the children of those who worked for "old Van der Vyver." The mother of the dead farmworker, in fact, is the daughter of parents who worked for the elder Van der Vyver, suggesting that the son inherited an entire network of social, economic, and psychological relationships. Significantly, then, we learn that it is the gun of Marais Van der Vyver's father that kills Lucas, the farmworker who is Marais's son; this legacy of violence is passed on from grandfather, to son, and finally—tragically—to grandson. The fact that Marais Van der Vyver has had no volitional control over this pivotal event in his life emphasizes that responsibility for this misdeed does not reside exclusively with him and suggests that Marais may not be entirely responsible for his other inheritances. Marais Van der Vyver's own prehistory, then, in his father's generation—the generation that created the modern apartheid system in 1948—may be the historical "moment before" the story's fin-de-siècle epoch. By extending the guilt for this offense transgenerationally, Gordimer implicates a whole morally corrupt society in the fate of Lucas. In the end, we wonder whether, after the moment the gun goes off, Marais sees the inequities built into his unbalanced social system. Could his bewildered final silence be taken as symbolic of a whole society at an impasse? Marais himself may not see that his painful shyness ("as a little boy [he] would go away and hide himself if he caught you smiling at him"), his separation from all those around him, ensues from a society predicated on aparthood. The "high barbed security fence" that surrounds his home and land is the corollary to both the apartheid political system and the individual psyche produced by such a system.

Teaching Clusters

The best placement for "The Moment before the Gun Went Off" would be in the cluster on **Culture, Language, and Identity**, where you can focus attention on the connections between culture and individual behavior or consciousness. Good companion readings include Jean Rhys's "The Day They Burned the Books," which addresses the issue of paternal inheritance, and V. S. Naipaul's "One Out of Many," which explores racial prejudice and cultural identity. Gordimer's story may also be studied within the category of **History, Memory, and Politics,** with more emphasis placed on the political and historical aspects, not specifically in relation to identity. Coetzee's *Waiting for the Barbarians* would be a useful accompaniment in this section.

Discussion Questions

1. Whose point of view is represented by the narrative voice in "The Moment before the Gun Went Off"? How is the narrator's attitude different from Marais Van der Vyver's? Might this narrative voice also indirectly accent the silence of those who are given no voice of their own, such as black South Africans?
2. Describe the relationship between the father, Marais Van der Vyver, and son, Lucas. Does the disclosure of the father-son connection create more sympathy or disquiet in your view of Marais? Why does Gordimer reiterate the fact that communications take place between father and son in a setting that features the "black man outside and the white man inside"?
3. What do you make of the fact that Lucas's mother is the daughter of parents who worked for the elder Van der Vyver? Although the story does not give us the details of the intimate relationship between the mother and Marais Van der Vyver, how might she describe it?
4. To what extent is the theme of paternal inheritance important in this story? Is there any significance in the fact that it is the grandfather's gun (Willem Van der Vyver's) that kills the grandson, Lucas?

A. K. Ramanujan

Reading A. K. Ramanujan's philosophical meditations on identity, time, and life will be a pleasurable surprise for students, most of whom probably have not yet been introduced to the poet. Ramanujan's views on the paradoxes of the self and the formulation of identity are thought-provoking and allusive, open both to close readings and more contextual historical and cultural interpretations. As an author writing from multiple literary traditions, his reflections on the permutations of identity speak to the postcolonial condition of hybridity and displacement, yet these selections do not have the anguish or despair apparent in the work of other postcolonial writers such as Derek Walcott, Jean Rhys, and V. S. Naipaul. "Foundlings in the Yukon," for example, contains the promise of regeneration in the image of millennia-old seedlings accidentally preserved in ice: "they took root / within forty-eight hours / and sprouted / a candelabra of eight small leaves" (lines 12–15). The poem's very long view of history allows for such optimism, suggesting that, even after eons of dormancy, renewal is always possible. In a very different manner, "Elements of Composition" takes the long view, not only of history, but of the self. The speaker here is an accrual of bits and pieces—various cultures, religions, experiences—yet is at the same time always dissolving, coming apart, and coming together again in a different form. Rather than the torment of psychic fragmentation, however, we have a vision that is so broadly philosophical, so all-encompassing, that the feeling is not only of acceptance, but of a joyful expression of postmodern subjectivity. Ramanujan's poetry adds a very important voice to the fields of contemporary and postcolonial writing.

Elements of Composition

Quick Read

- Form: Lyric.
- Themes: Identity as fluid, fragmented, decentered, heterogeneous, omnivorous, transient, and unstable; the integration and disintegration of self.
- Key Passages: "[E]yes that can see, / only by moving constantly, / the constancy of things," lines 10–12; "I pass through them / as they pass through me, / taking and leaving," lines 36–38; "even as I add, / I lose, decompose / into my elements," lines 53–55.

Teaching Suggestions

"Elements of Composition" reflects on the permutations, erosions, and structures of identity. It turns on a paradox—or several paradoxes: that the self is continually coming together and falling apart, integrating and disintegrating, in flux and unchanging, timeless and transitory. Invite students first to think about the allusiveness of the title. "Elements" might mean components, features, chemical elements (minerals), fundamental principles, or any other number of things. "Composition" is equally resonant, suggesting at once a formation, an arrangement, a synthesis, or an essay. From here students can discuss the ways in which these various connotations appear throughout the poem. In the beginning stanzas, Ramanujan draws upon the suggestiveness of "elements," offering several recognized ways of envisioning the human body and psyche: biological ("father's seed and mother's egg" [line 3]), philosophical or religious ("gathering earth, air, fire" [line 4]), scientific ("mostly / water" lines 4–5), chemical ("moulding calcium, / carbon, even gold, magnesium and such" [lines 6–7]), and psychological ("a chattering self tangled / in love and work, / scary dreams" [lines 8–10]). He moves on to look at other "elements" of the self—family, friends, and the larger social whole—each one figured as an addition: "add uncle's eleven fingers / making shadow-plays of rajas / and cats, hissing"; "add the lepers of Madurai, / male, female, married, with children" (lines 14–16, 27–29). As Ramanujan moves further outside the family circle, he incorporates everything within the self, but reverses this gradual accumulation with the image of "the half-man searching / for an every-fleeing / other half" (lines 46–48). Rather than simple accretion, Ramanujan suggests something more complex: "I pass through them / as they pass through me / taking and leaving / affections, seeds, skeletons" (lines 36–39). There is give and take here, an inter-change, and continual flux; the "elements" are not merely accruing, gath-ering into a larger whole, but constantly shifting and changing, appearing and disappearing. "[E]ven as I add, / I lose, decompose / into my ele-ments," he muses, suggesting that the "Elements of Composition" include their seeming opposite, decomposition (lines 53–55). Other apparently antithetical concepts underscore this paradox of selfhood. "[E]yes that can see, / only by moving constantly, / the constancy of things" (lines 10–12) links movement with stability, while "millennia of fossil records / of insects that do not last / a day" joins the transitory with an ex-tended time scheme. Finally, when you have discussed a number of these images, ask students what they all add up to; what does the poem suggest about identity and the experience of the self?

Teaching Clusters

Both the **History, Memory, and Politics** and the **Culture, Language, and Identity** clusters would be fitting contexts within which to study Ra-manujan's writing. "Foundlings in the Yukon," in particular, makes some insightful observations about history and time. Seamus Heaney's "bog poems" on other kinds of historical excavations ("Punishment," for in-stance) would make provocative companion pieces in the first grouping. "Self-Portrait" and "Elements of Composition," on the other hand, be-cause of their focus on identity, would be more profitably situated in the second grouping. Derek Walcott's poetry would make an especially rele-vant contrast here, while Jean Rhys's "The Day They Burned the Books" and V. S. Naipaul's "One Out of Many" would offer students alternate views of postcolonial identity. The works of all three of these authors would help bring out the historical and cultural resonances of Ramanu-jan's poetry.

Discussion Questions

1. Explore the several meanings of the title, "Elements of Composition," as a whole and as a set of individual terms.
2. What are some of the "elements" that make up the self? Describe some of the ways that this poem thinks about the human body and psyche.
3. Ramanujan introduces a number of paradoxes in "Elements of Com-position"; discuss some of these.
4. How does this poem talk about composition and decomposition, wholeness and unwholeness, or integration and disintegration?
5. What is this poem saying about human identity?

Thom Gunn

Whether Thom Gunn is writing about young men in black leather jack-ets or the ravages of AIDS, he brings an honesty and immediacy to his subject matter that adds freshness to the traditional forms he uses. The poems reflecting on death and the losses that AIDS has brought will give students a chance to think about a very timely issue, one that has most likely touched some of them personally. Gunn's focus on the formation of identity in "The Missing," moreover—the way in which the self is related to a larger social whole—can open up discussions about how each of us is part of a larger entity: family, friends, culture, and nation. In contrast to what many students may think about identity, Gunn envisions it as something mutable and alive, not carved in stone. In this context, the death of others results not just in a loss of a separate being, but a loss or diminution of the self. If "The Missing" offers any form of consolation at all, it is in the recognition that to be human is to be connected to others.

The Missing

Quick Read

- Form: Elegy in iambic pentameter; *abab* rhyme scheme.
- Summary: The speaker mourns the passing of his friends from the AIDS virus.
- Themes: Grief over the loss of one's friends; the sense of incompleteness that results when so many die; the formation of identity through human connections.
- Motifs and Images: The incomplete, indistinct self; the "unlimited embrace," line 12; rigidity versus pliability and life; unwholeness versus the whole; the body as a metaphor for human connectedness.
- Key Passages: "The warmth investing me / Led outward . . . / In an involved increasing family," lines 6–8; "Supple entwinement through the living mass . . . / Image of an unlimited embrace," lines 10–12; "But death—Their deaths have left me less defined," line 17.

Teaching Suggestions

In "The Missing," Gunn takes as his subject the death of so many within the gay community from the AIDS virus. Before you begin discussing the specifics of this poem, it will be helpful to give students some background information on the impact of AIDS in the U.S. and on the gay population. It would also be helpful to discuss the elegy as a traditional genre and this poem's relationship to other earlier elegies. Note in particular that Gunn's poem addresses not one death (as in a traditional elegy), but many, and that these deaths have a larger cultural impact; it is both a personal poem and a public poem. Additionally, whereas a traditional elegy usually ends with some sort of resolution or comfort for the speaker, "The Missing" offers no such solace. This combination of convention and innovation is also found in the fusing of the structured form (iambic pentameter with an *abab* rhyme scheme) with modern content.

There are several themes and motifs here to pursue, but you may want to begin with the important issue of identity. Invite students to think about the way that the speaker sees his newly "incomplete" identity as opposed to the identity he had when connected to a larger group of friends (line 25). To get started, you can ask students to compile lists of words or phrases that define this new identity ("sculpted," "chill," "less defined," "unsupported," "incomplete," "unwholeness") and compare them against the former self ("warmth," "involved," "living," "the whole," "support"). The larger group of friends is seen both as a family ("an involved increasing family" [line 8]) and a living organism (a "living mass" [line 10]), with all the connectedness—physical, emotional, and biological—that this implies. With the loss of his friends, the speaker sees himself "Bared," without the framework that formerly gave shape to his being (line 3). Interestingly, Gunn conceives of this former identity as being in flux, yet whole, while the new identity is rigid, yet fragmented. This new self, with its "sculpted skin," may be "less vague" but has a "statue's chill contour" (lines 4, 3, 5). He imagines this self as being a partially formed sculpture, frozen in marble: "part-buried in the block, / Shins perfect and no calves, as if I froze / Between potential and a finished work" (lines 22–24). No longer connected to his extended family, he is an unfinished work of art, "Abandoned incomplete," and "Trapped in unwholeness" (lines 25, 27). In this new guise he is unable to return to his former intact and malleable identity, "Back to the play of constant give and change" (line 28). The main metaphor here is the body: "the living mass . . . / Image of an unlimited embrace" (lines 10–12). It is an image that is erotic, idealistic, and altruistic all at once—a "body" of friends alive, protean, and loving. Without this body, the speaker finds himself only an indistinct entity, lacking plenitude. "But death," he laments, "Their deaths have left me less defined" (line 17).

Teaching Clusters

Elegiac poems such as "The Missing" and "Still Life" may be studied in the cluster on **History, Memory, and Politics**. In this grouping, it would be instructive to include other elegies to give students a greater understanding of conventions and innovations within the genre. W. B. Yeats's "Easter, 1916" would make an especially illuminating companion piece to "The Missing," since both deal with a number of deaths that take on enormous political and cultural significance within the larger community. Yet both poets are also personally touched by these deaths and use the occasion to reflect on their own lives and thoughts. "Black Jackets," on the other hand, with its exploration of postwar youth culture, could be placed in the **Culture, Language, and Identity** grouping. Some of Philip Larkin's poems, such as "Sad Steps" and "High Windows," would make good companion readings here.

Discussion Questions

1. How does the speaker of "The Missing" define himself after the death of so many friends? How does he visualize his identity?

2. Why does the speaker see himself as being fashioned from "raw marble" (line 21)? How does this phrase relate to the "statute's chill contour" (line 5)?
3. Contrast images of wholeness with images of incompleteness throughout the poem. In what context does each image arise?
4. What relationship does the speaker's body have to the larger "body" of friends? (the "living mass" [line 10])? In what way is the body a metaphor for aliveness and human connectedness?
5. In what way is community important in this poem?
6. Both Gunn's "The Missing" and Yeats's "Easter, 1916" mourn the loss of a group of people whose deaths have meaning for the larger culture. Compare and contrast the two poems.

Further Resources

NORTON ONLINE ARCHIVE

Audio:
Considering the Snail *and* My Sad Captains (read by Thom Gunn)

Derek Walcott

Derek Walcott's poetry speaks to issues of colonial oppression and the psychological inheritances of slavery. Brought up on the former British colony of Saint Lucia, the descendant of slaves, the Caribbean-born Walcott is himself "a far cry from Africa," caught between two cultural traditions. Describing the conflicted position of the postcolonial hybrid, the speaker of "The Schooner *Flight*" defiantly asserts, "I had a sound colonial education, / I have Dutch, nigger, and English in me" (lines 41–42). Such an education produced ambivalent feelings about his multiple heritages. In "A Far Cry from Africa," Walcott expresses the feelings of many writers from former British colonies when he asks, "Where shall I turn, divided to the vein? . . . how choose / Between this Africa and the English tongue I love?" (lines 27–30). The psychic split referred to here is perhaps most hauntingly rendered in *Omeros*, where a central character must bear the symbolic wound of slavery and colonialism. Yet despite the torment apparent in so much of Walcott's poetry, there is room, too, for an image of hope or rest from despair; "The Season of Phantasmal Peace" depicts "all the nations of birds" flying above the earth, where "there was no longer dusk, or season, decline, or weather"; as they migrate further away, they take pity on the "wingless ones / below them who shared dark holes in windows and in houses" (lines 1, 9, 29). The "pause / . . . between fury and peace" is brief, but full of promise: "for such as our earth is now, it lasted long" (lines 32–33, 34). Students will find in this poetry a vivid and moving enactment of postcolonial subjectivity.

A Far Cry from Africa

Quick Read

- Form: Lyric.
- Theme: The trauma of cultural hybridity.
- Key Passages: "What is that to the white child hacked in bed? / To savages, expendable as Jews?" lines 9–10; "I who am poisoned with the blood of both, / Where shall I turn, divided to the vein? . . . how choose / Between this Africa and the English tongue I love?" lines 26–30; "How can I face such slaughter and be cool? / How can I turn from Africa and live?" lines 32–33.

Teaching Suggestions

Here Walcott confronts his own ambivalent, anguished responses to the Kikuyu insurrection in 1950s Kenya and the trauma of cultural hybridity. The poet hears the "far cry from Africa," a cry that emanates from those suffering in the rebellion and that recalls to him his ancestral roots. The poem cannot locate a place of ethical certainty from which to respond to the convulsive violence that often accompanies the break from colonial rule, which it condemns, while also condemning the history of British imperialism in Africa. On the one hand, the first stanza invites sympathy for the settlers, members of the oppressing class who may yet be innocent (like "the white child hacked in bed"), yet on the other, it notes bitterly that black "savages," as "expendable as Jews," have been subject to genocide (lines 9–10). Similarly, by observing in the second stanza that "upright man / Seeks his divinity by inflicting pain," the poem indicts both sides for their atrocities (lines 16–17). Note what happens in the third stanza, however, with the shift from third to first person: the reader is thrust directly into the body of the speaker, who has lost the nominally objective distance of the first two stanzas. "[P]oisoned with the blood of both," he asks, "Where shall I turn, divided to the vein?" (lines 26–27). He has despised "British rule," yet he loves the "English tongue," and does not want to choose between his beloved English language and Africa—especially "this Africa," "scattered" with corpses (lines 29–30, 4). To reject either is to betray himself: "How can I face such slaughter and be cool? / How can I turn from Africa and live?" (lines 32–33). "A Far Cry from Africa" illustrates the dilemma of the post-colonial hybrid subject, tormented by a conflicted identity and cultural disjunction.

Omeros

Quick Read

- Form: Book-length epic poem.
- Summary: Philoctete, a Caribbean fisherman, is wounded by a rusty

anchor; an obeah practitioner, Ma Kilman, heals him with magical herbs.

- Themes: Cultural and literary hybridity; suffering and redemption; the psychological wounds of slavery and colonialism are perpetuated in the bodies of their descendants.
- Key Passages: "He believed the swelling came from the chained ankles / of his grandfathers," Book One, lines 10–11; "What did it mean, / this name that felt like a fever?" Book One, lines 30–31; "She bathed him in the brew of the root," Book Six, line 1; "he stood like a boy in his bath with the first clay's / innocent prick! So she threw Adam a towel. / And the yard was Eden. And its light the first day's," Book Six, lines 58–60.

Teaching Suggestions

In *Omeros*, the classically trained Walcott deploys a hybrid literary form, infusing the Homeric epic with the dialect, syntax, and concerns of the West Indies. You will want first to give students a general overview of the poem's relationship to its literary forebears and a brief description of the plot line. As the *NAEL* footnotes observe, *Omeros* follows the terza rima stanza of Dante's *Divine Comedy* and adapts portions of Homer's *Iliad* and *Odyssey* and James Joyce's *Ulysses*. Philoctete is the name of a central character of *Omeros* and also of a character who, in the Greek tradition, is tormented by a snakebite wound that never heals, as dramatized in Sophocles' play *Philoctetes*. In Walcott's version, Philoctete is a Caribbean fisherman who is injured by a rusty anchor. After he has suffered from it a long time, Ma Kilman, a practitioner of obeah (West Indian magic with ties to African occultism), heals Philoctete in a ritual bath of magical herbs and medicines.

When you begin discussing the thematics of the poem, you will want to draw students' attention to the governing metaphor of the wound, a psychic trauma that the descendants of slavery and colonialism carry with them. Walcott makes this connection explicit, observing that Philoctete "believed the swelling came from the chained ankles / of his grandfathers" (Book One, lines 10–11). The wound haunts Philoctete; it is overwhelming and seemingly incurable, reminding him of "his race . . . a village black and poor / as the pigs that rooted in its burning garbage, / [and who] were hooked on the anchors of the abattoir" (Book One, lines 13–15). Like Philoctete, slavery's heirs are weighted down and wounded by the "anchor" of their history. Other important metaphors to follow include the name (Philoctete) and the magical bath. Philoctete's name "[feels] like a fever," the speaker tells us; "one good heft / of his garden-cutlass would slice the damned name clean / from its rotting yam" (Book One, lines 31–33). Technically, Philoctete's name reflects the Western literary inheritance of classical literature; historically, however, it recalls the naming of African slaves by their European captors, with the "rotting yam" being a traditional African food. Only after Ma Kilman cures the wound by bathing Philoctete in a special mixture of magical roots and leaves is "The yoke of the wrong name lifted from his shoulders" (Book Six, line 29). The name, then, recalls the kind of cultural hybridity suffered by the speaker of "A Far Cry from Africa" (and Walcott himself), rent in two by "this Africa and the English tongue I love" (line 30).

Additionally, both the wound and the bath reflect a similar hybridity. The wound that symbolizes the taking of Africans as slaves and the inherited injuries of European colonialism in the Caribbean also has Christian resonances. While his name and wound directly recall the Greek tradition, Philoctete thinks of his wound as "the cross he carried" and refers to his "corrupted blood" as the "sap of a wounded cedar" (Book One, lines 12, 29, 30). According to Christian symbolism, cedar represents the figure of Christ: "his countenance is as Lebanon, excellent as the cedars" (Song of Solomon 5.15). Philoctete's occupation, too, aligns him with Christ, who is traditionally associated with fishermen (some of the Apostles were fishermen) and fish, through the parables of the loaves and fishes (Matthew 15.32) and the draught of fishes (John 21; a similar miracle appears in Luke 5.1–11). The bath, moreover, is both an African and a Caribbean ritual and a kind of Christian baptism, cleansing and purifying Philoctete. The final section follows through with the water imagery of the bath, depicting first the sea that Philoctete emerges from and then returning to the image of the bath: "he stood like a boy in his bath with the first clay's / innocent prick! So she threw Adam a towel. / And the yard was Eden. And its light the first day's" (Book Six, lines 58–60). In this sense, Philoctete becomes not Christ, but Adam, awaking to a pre-fallen world. In addition, the wound recalls several medieval legends (the Fisher King, Parsifal, Erec and Enide) wherein the wounded king must be healed so the entire community can be regenerated. (See T. S. Eliot's use of the Fisher King in *The Waste Land*.) It is a particularly resonant metaphor.

Teaching Clusters

Much of Walcott's poetry may be placed in the cluster on **History, Memory, and Politics** ("A Far Cry from Africa," *Omeros*) because of its concern with historical events and the recalling or rethinking of those events ("The Season of Phantasmal Peace" could be studied here too, considered as cultural myth). The agonizing concern with cultural hybridity that appears in so much of the poet's work, however, is more fully appreciated within the context of the **Culture, Language, and Identity** category. Prose selections such as Ngũgĩ wa Thiong'o's *Decolonising the Mind* and fiction such as Jean Rhys's "The Day They Burned the Books" would make especially illuminating companion pieces to "A Far Cry from Africa" and *Omeros*. Achebe's *Things Fall Apart*, moreover, would provide *Omeros* with more historical context, demonstrating the devastating impact of European culture on precolonial African peoples.

Discussion Questions

1. In "A Far Cry from Africa," what is the speaker's attitude toward colonial and anticolonial violence? Does he condemn one side more than the other?
2. Why does the speaker of "A Far Cry from Africa" feel divided? Discuss the issues of identity, culture, and ethnicity that the poem addresses.
3. How does the shift from third to first person in "A Far Cry from Africa" affect the tone and intensity of the poem?
4. Explore the metaphor of the wound in *Omeros*. How is this wound related both to Philoctete's dual inheritance of slavery and to Western culture?
5. In what way is the magical bath that Philoctete receives from Ma Kilman a ritual cleansing or healing? Can his cure be thought of as a way to stop suffering in the world? How does the bath connect Philoctete both to the precolonial past and to his colonial legacy?
6. Why is Philoctete's name significant? If this Afro-Caribbean fisherman symbolizes the injuries of Western colonialism, then why does his name derive from European classical literature?
7. Explore the concept of postcolonial hybridity in *Omeros*—cultural, symbolic, and literary.

Further Resources

NORTON ONLINE ARCHIVE

Audio:
The Glory Trumpeter (read by Derek Walcott)

Ted Hughes

Ted Hughes's writing rejects the cool rationality of poets such as Philip Larkin, who sought for objectivity and detachment in their work. To Hughes's mind, objectivity will not get us to the essence of things; only through the recreation of subjective emotions can the poet hope to reveal the spirit or root of an experience or object. The Western world, in his view, was becoming ever more scientific in its approach to life, and the result was a sense of disconnectedness among people and an increasing tendency toward aggression. Hughes's poetry exposes this violence and uses it as a means of expression. In "Out," the trauma of the soldier "blasted to bits" in World War I is equated with a birth into a culture that clings tenaciously to memories of a devastating conflict. "And it's just another baby. . . . / The reassembled infantryman / Tentatively totters out, gazing around with the eyes / Of an exhausted clerk" (lines 32–36). Echoing Yeats's "rough beast . . . [who] / Slouches towards Bethlehem to be born," Hughes's soldier signals the decline of a civilization into brutality and stagnation ("Second Coming," lines 21–22).

Out

Quick Read

- Form: Lyric; elegy.
- Themes: The psychological inheritance of war; the stifling effect of the war, both cultural and personal; the need to put war's memories and the dead to rest; the son inherits the father's legacy; in a society that cannot let go of the violent past, every birth is a death; each new child dies into English culture.
- Key Passages: "I, small and four, . . . / His memory's buried immovable anchor, / Among jawbones and blown-off boots, tree-stumps, shell-cases and craters," lines 13–16; "The poppy is a wound, the poppy is the mouth / Of the grave, maybe of the womb searching," lines 37–38; "So goodbye to that bloody-minded flower," line 50; "You dead bury your dead," line 51.

Teaching Suggestions

"Out" describes Hughes's relationship with his father, one of the few survivors of the Gallipoli disaster in World War I, and Hughes's attempt to try to rid himself of the psychological burden of the war. It will be helpful for students if you begin by discussing the impact of World War I on England and the personal effects of the war on Hughes's father, who was a victim of shell shock. Massive numbers of soldiers died or came home physically or psychologically wounded. Not only was Hughes's family greatly affected, but many of Yorkshire's inhabitants were touched by the war in some way. The war—and its remembrance—became part of what defined England and Englishness. "Out" tries to exorcise the demons Hughes lived with and rejects the war as a defining cultural experience.

Explaining the structure of the poem before getting into specifics will help students get their bearings. Each of its three sections accesses the trauma of the war in a different manner, either as a memory, metaphor, or direct effect. The first part describes the depleted emotional state of Hughes's father when he returned from the war and its effect on Hughes as a child; the second part imagines Hughes (and perhaps, by extension, all children of war veterans or all children of England) being born or reborn into a predetermined cultural malaise; and the third section focuses on Remembrance Day, which commemorates the soldiers who died in battle. Students need to understand that Hughes is not describing events or images in a detached, intellectual manner as a poet such as Philip Larkin would. Instead, through violent imagery and jarring language, Hughes attempts to pull the reader directly into the feeling he is talking about. Hughes imagines himself as a child of four, his father's "luckless double, / His memory's buried, immovable anchor, / Among jawbones and blown-off boots, tree-stumps, shell-cases and craters" (lines 14–16). The hyphenated phrases, repetition of harsh consonants (jawbones/blown/ boots; cases/craters), and images of devastation convey a sense of the war's brutality, while "His memory's buried, immovable anchor" creates the feeling of being pinioned by the oppressive weight of war's memory. The second section conflates the concept of birth with war: the baby born into the violence of war is caught up in its destructive cycle. On the one hand, the baby could be Hughes himself, born into his father's legacy, yet on the other hand, the baby might be all English children born into the self-determining culture of war's memory. Ask students to focus on the associations and intersections of words such as "sweat," "melting . . . flesh," "baby-furnace," and "blood," many of which could refer equally to war or (a very grisly view of) childbirth (lines 20, 21, 23, 26). You might want to point out that the topic of birth in this section extends the idea of the son's inheritance from the father, described in the first section.

When you turn to the final section, you will want to explain the significance of the poppy, both in reference to John McCrae's poem "In Flanders Fields" and to its use as a decorative emblem to be purchased and worn on Remembrance Day. The poppy is made out of fabric ("canvas" here [line 39]) and attached to a wire ("puppet on a wire" [39]). Hughes loathes the practice of keeping the war's memory alive with this emblem: "A canvas-beauty puppet on a wire / Today whoring everywhere. It is years since I wore one" (lines 39–40). You may also need to explain the concept of the cenotaphs. These tombs were erected as World War I monuments and are specifically associated with that war; almost every sizable English town has a cenotaph honoring World War I soldiers. "So goodbye to that bloody-minded flower," Hughes writes; "You dead bury your dead. / Goodbye to the cenotaphs on my mother's breasts" (lines 51–52), thus rejecting not just the war but the clinging to the memory of that war. It is possible to see in these lines and in the closing line—"Let England close. Let the green sea-anemone close" (line 54)—a repudiation of both the father's legacy of war memories to the son and of England's saturation in the memory of that war. The mother here may be all mothers who lost their sons to the war, a symbolic mother of England, Hughes's own mother, or all three. You might want to follow up and ask students what role the mother—and the mother's womb—plays in this poem. Section 3 begins with the declaration: "The poppy is a wound, the poppy is the mouth / Of the grave, maybe of the womb searching" (lines 37–38). Both the grave and womb are connected here, as they are in the second section ("The dead man in his cave beginning to sweat; . . . / the mother in the baby-furnace" [line 20]). This is a grim view of birth into a culture that cannot let go of its memories of devastation and so is doomed to produce children oppressed by war's psychological legacies.

Teaching Clusters

Generally speaking, all of Hughes's poetry can be studied in the cluster on **History, Memory, and Politics.** Their concerns with myth, violence, and memories of the past all fall within this grouping. "Out," moreover, could be placed in either the **History, Memory, and Politics** or **Culture,**

Language, and Identity category. In this latter grouping, you could concentrate on Hughes's construction of Englishness in relation to its war memories. If you study this work in the former grouping, it would be instructive to have students read Eliot's *The Waste Land* (section I, "The Burial of the Dead"), Yeats's "The Second Coming," and Isaac Rosenberg's "Break of Day in the Trenches" as companion pieces. The first section of "Out," with its focus on buried memories and the detritus of war ("His memory's buried immovable anchor, / Among jawbones and blown-off boots, tree-stumps, shell-cases and craters, . . . / Its kingdom, which the sun has abandoned, and where nobody / Can ever again move from shelter" [lines 15–19]), shares some resonances with the first part of *The Waste Land* ("A heap of broken images, where the sun beats, / And the dead tree gives no shelter" [lines 22–23]). The second section, with its vision of a brutal birth and cultural collapse, brings to mind Yeats's well-known query: "And what rough beast, its hour come round at last, / Slouches towards Bethlehem to be born?" ("Second Coming," lines 21–22). Lastly, Rosenberg's "Break of Day" will give students a sense of the significance of the symbolic value of the poppy in the final section of "Out" ("Poppies whose roots are in man's veins / Drop, and are ever dropping" ["Break of Day," lines 23–24]).

Discussion Questions

1. In the first section of "Out," describe the son's relationship to the father. Why does Hughes see himself as his father's "luckless double" and "memory's buried immovable anchor" (lines 14, 15)? The "anchor" is again mentioned in the final section: "One anchor / Holding my juvenile neck bowed to the dunkings of the Atlantic" (lines 48–49). What does the anchor have to do with Hughes and his father?

2. Compare the concept of burial in section 1 of "Out" and the first two stanzas of Eliot's *The Waste Land*. How does each poem imagine World War I and its legacy?

3. Discuss the idea of birth as portrayed in the second section of "Out." Who or what might the baby represent? How might this topic relate to the father-son relationship in the first section? Why is this birth seen in such violent terms? Compare this birth to the one in Yeats's "Second Coming": "And what rough beast, its hour come round at last, / Slouches towards Bethlehem to be born?" (lines 21–22).

4. The first lines of section 3 assert: "The poppy is a wound, the poppy is the mouth / Of the grave, maybe of the womb searching" (lines 37–38). Why are the grave and womb connected here? The second section makes a similar connection between death and birth: "The dead man in his cave beginning to sweat; . . . / the mother in the baby-furnace" (line 20). Why is birth associated with death?

5. Why does Hughes write, "You dead bury your dead" (line 51)? What does Hughes want to bury here? How is this burial different from the one in the first section?

6. To what extent is memory important in this poem?
7. In the last line of "Out," Hughes writes: "Let England close. Let the green sea-anemone close" (line 54). What does this poem have to do with England as a whole?

Further Resources

NORTON ONLINE ARCHIVE

Audio:
Wind
Pike
Theology,
—read by Ted Hughes

Harold Pinter

As new dramatic forms were being developed in the two decades following World War II—including the absurdist theatrical tradition being established by Samuel Beckett, Eugene Ionesco, and others on the European continent and the "kitchen sink" social-realist manner being pioneered in Britain by John Osborne and Arnold Wesker—Harold Pinter added a distinctive voice and a few innovations of his own to these fresh, evolving dramatic vocabularies. In early plays such as *The Dumb Waiter*, Pinter combined the stylized minimalism, lack of exposition, black humor, and dreamlike structures of the theater of the absurd with the realistic settings and working-class milieu found in the uncompromisingly grim, naturalistic plays of British theater's Angry Young Men. In Pinter's plays, the enigmas of human psychology are purposefully left undecoded, but the habitual patterns underlying human transactions are foregrounded and illuminated for us so we can attempt to draw our own inferences. Yet Pinter's plays are never case studies with exclusive emphasis on psychological and social realism; realism seems always under threat by the emotional extremes, surreal comedy, and general theatricality that mark his work. In the amalgamation of comedy and terror as well as in the playwright's discovery of the compelling eloquence of silence, Pinter's contribution to drama can be seen most distinctly. The term "Pinteresque" has become part of our common language, and with good reason. His writing is central to any discussion of modern drama or late-twentieth-century literature.

The Dumb Waiter

Quick Read

- Form: Drama.
- Summary: Two hired killers await orders from an anonymous authority whose communications become increasingly bizarre. Eventually we learn that the intended victim is one of the killers himself.

- Themes: Power is often maintained through psychological means; power's victims must be kept ignorant; the exercise of absolute authority inevitably displays arbitrariness; everyone is expendable in modern corporate society; paranoia is the default human condition in the age of anxiety.
- Key Passages: Ben: "What do you mean, I mean the gas? . . . If I say go and light the kettle I mean go and light the kettle" (2609); Gus: "Why did he send us matches if he knew there was no gas?" (2620); Gus: "What's he doing all this for? What's the idea? What's he playing these games for?" (2620); closing stage directions, after final line of dialogue, regarding Gus's final reappearance (2622).

Teaching Suggestions

An effective way to initiate discussion of Harold Pinter's *The Dumb Waiter* is to ask students to examine the multiple meanings associated with the play's title. While a "dumbwaiter" is the term for a small elevator that carries food from a kitchen to another room, for example, the phrase "dumb waiter" plays on the double meanings of both words. Invite students to think about how the two characters enact various interpretations of this title. Ben, for instance, is the play's incarnation of a conformist company man who is unquestioning before the power of the anonymous authority controlling his life, while Gus's final lack of words denotes his impotence as he awaits execution by a power that he dared to question. The dumbwaiter itself, moreover, is the conduit to an offstage authority figure who serves as a perfect metaphor for the faceless societal, metaphysical, or internalized familial powers "from above" that we all strive to appease. This enigmatic figure is an absolute power unto itself in no need of proclaiming its authority, one whose increasingly arbitrary commands indicate its only purpose is the perpetuation of its own power.

To encourage a more profound understanding of the play's wider implications about the nuances of language and the oppressive ends to which language can be put, it would be instructive to ask two students to perform an exemplary exchange. Ben and Gus's conversation concerning the kettle, for example, is a good illustration of Pinter's techniques and concerns. You will want to guide students toward the staccato, sparring quality of the characters' dialogue, in which statements are used as weapons to set rules and determine dominance in their relationship. Small talk is a diversionary tactic to allay anxiety, pauses hold the quality of threat and seem to foreshadow the relationship's termination, questions have the potency of forbidden taboos, and emotion seems to be alternately masked in a tactical, paranoid manner or poised to degenerate into physical violence betraying unconscious or intentional motivations. Above all, it's important for students to get a sense of the most oft-noted aspect of Pinter's drama, its aura of menace. Pinter's work is meant to generate a feeling of free-floating anxiety in an audience. Magnifying this perception of anxiety is a very precise psychological realism that underlies Pinter's stylization, illustrated in the case of Gus who, by seeking an explanation for occurrences, acts out the self-destructive role of the paranoid, a person forever anxious about attacks from external threats but who can never pinpoint the source of his fears because the threat exists within himself. At the same time, however, Gus is in a real situation where events seem to defy logic and forbid analysis, yet which he feels compelled to question by his very nature as a rational human being, hardwired to seek meaning. As you discuss the techniques that contribute to the menacing atmosphere, don't forget to address another hallmark of Pinter's theater: the use of silence. The pauses and moments of ominous quiet in Ben and Gus's tempest-in-a-teapot argument provide disturbing gaps in which the characters' or the reader's imagination may fill any number of unnamable threats. Here the playwright taps into the feeling that what is not said is often more frightening than what is said. The unknown, anticipated danger creates an unbearable tension, a tension that Pinter's drama stretches to its utmost point.

Teaching Clusters

The experimental aspect of Pinter's drama and its dark view of the modern world make *The Dumb Waiter* a fitting selection for the **Transition, Modernity, and Modernism** cluster. Studying the play alongside works such as Conrad's *Heart of Darkness*, Eliot's *The Waste Land*, and Beckett's *Endgame* will highlight Pinter's innovations and give students greater insight into developments in twentieth-century literary responses to political, cultural, and social concerns. *The Dumb Waiter* may also be situated in **Culture, Language, and Identity**, where you may focus on the connections between language and power relationships. *Endgame* would make a profitable companion piece in this category.

Discussion Questions

1. Examine the multiple meanings of the play's title, *The Dumb Waiter*. In what way does each of the two characters, Ben and Gus, act as a dumb waiter or a dumbwaiter?
2. Why has Pinter chosen two hired killers as the subject of this play? What does *The Dumb Waiter* say about violence and fear?
3. Why has Pinter ended the play on an ambiguous note? Knowing what we know about the characters, is there any doubt about Gus's fate after the curtain falls? Is there significance in the silence that marks Ben's delay? What might Ben be thinking?
4. Does Gus develop as a character? Does his vision mature as the play progresses? Is his incessant questioning a sign of immaturity or maturity?
5. What do we learn from Ben and Gus's quarrel over whether it is correct to say "light the kettle"? What does this exchange tell us about their relationship? How is the control of language connected to maintaining power?

6. Why does the unknown person upstairs send down anonymous food orders to Ben and Gus via the dumbwaiter? Why do they send their own food back up? What does the incident tell us about Ben and Gus?

7. Cite and discuss any examples of foreshadowing in the play that you can locate. For example, when Ben and Gus reiterate their "liquidation" instructions, what does the omission that Gus notes in Ben's summary suggest? What do these hints in the dialogue of later actions suggest about the real-life consequences of words and the power of language?

Chinua Achebe

Chinua Achebe is a postcolonial hybrid subject, a Western-educated Nigerian born into a family with roots in both traditional Igbo society and the new Christian elite that supplanted it. *Things Fall Apart* is a product of this multiple identity. The title of his novel invokes the Western literary tradition by its reference to Yeats's "The Second Coming": "Things fall apart; the centre cannot hold" (line 3). At the same time, however, Achebe's story reverses the terms of Yeats's Christian reference point. In Yeats's poem, the Christian era is dying in a violent and chaotic fashion, only to be replaced by an unknown but troubling "rough beast" (line 21), while in Achebe's novel, African society comes to a cataclysmic end when Christianity intrudes. Responding to and revising British representations of Africa, including those contained in Conrad's *Heart of Darkness*, the novel shows that before colonialism Africa was not a "blank space" on the map (a place without history or culture, an undifferentiated site of primitivism), but a continent with numerous complex societies. As *Things Fall Apart* demonstrates, the Igbo had their own social traditions, civil order, and religious beliefs before the English came to "civilize" them. In "An Image of Africa: Racism in Conrad's *Heart of Darkness*," Achebe more directly responds to superficial and insulting views of Africans presented in Western literature. Accusing Conrad of racism, Achebe takes issue with what he describes as "the dehumanization of Africa and Africans" that is perpetuated in such writing. Achebe's work is essential in any course on postcolonial literature; it illustrates the centrality of texts, both historical and fictional, in defining cultural identity.

Things Fall Apart

Quick Read

- Form: Novel.
- Summary: Focusing on the central figure of Okonkwo, a brutal and inflexible man, this novel traces the fortunes and eventual European colonization of a small African village in the early twentieth century.
- Themes: The complexity and richness of African society; the decline and colonization of a village by European missionaries and officials;

the need for a revisionist history of African colonization; one's beliefs depend on one's perspective.

Teaching Suggestions

Achebe's novel was published in 1958, just after Ghana had become the first African nation to achieve independence, and just before Nigeria itself became an independent state (in 1960). The novel negotiates this cultural watershed not by looking forward to independence but by revisiting another cultural upheaval, the breakup of Igbo society under British imperialism. As students will learn from reading Achebe's essay on Conrad's *Heart of Darkness*, Achebe was outraged by Western literary stereotypes of "savage" natives; *Things Fall Apart* redresses some of the wrongs committed along these lines by giving the Igbo villagers dignity and complexity. One way to begin discussing this book, then, is by focusing on the description of Igbo society, both its similarities to and differences from Western culture. While *Things Fall Apart* describes precolonial Umuofia in careful and rich detail, and with a certain nostalgia for its lost culture, the novel does not romanticize or idealize it, presenting such traditional practices as the exposure of twins in the Evil Forest or the ritual sacrifice of Ikemefuna in an unvarnished manner. Yet we also see the Igbo people engage in elaborate preparations for the Feast of the New Yam, a harvest festival, in chapter 5, and the marriage of Obierika's daughter in chapter 12. Each ritual has its own rules and conventions that govern both the material preparations and social interactions, while the villagers look forward to these important events with anticipation. Achebe thus shows that, although different from Western culture, Igbo society has its own customs, laws, and codes of conduct.

In addition to portraying Igbo culture as rich and complex, Achebe presents Igbo individuals as unique and human. Each character has his or her own quirks and qualities and, while dignified, they are not idealized. You will want to take the time to explore Okonkwo's characterization in some detail, both in relation to his family and the other villagers. While Okonkwo is "a man of action and a man of war," he is motivated by "the fear of failure and weakness . . . the fear of himself, lest he should be found to resemble his father," Unoka, a "lazy and improvident" man who was only happy "when he was drinking or playing on his flute." His fear of being like his father causes him to be brutal and impulsive. In some ways, Okonkwo is a model member of the community—a physically powerful man who is a hard worker and prosperous farmer—but in other ways he is in conflict with it, making frequent trouble with his imprudent and violent actions. As a point of contrast, invite students to compare Okonkwo with his good friend, Obierika, a much more reasonable and thoughtful man. Obierika, for instance, advises Okonkwo against taking part in Ikemefuna's murder, yet is kind to Okonkwo when he ignores Obierika's advice and kills the boy he loved more than his own son. Okonkwo's suicide is in many ways the end result of an ever-increasing disjunction between himself and the rest of the world. The new colonial order has no room for the traditional warrior-hero, but it's important to note that Okonkwo could not live comfortably in traditional society either.

Lastly, you will want to look at the effects of the European incursion into Igbo society in parts II and III. The white men take over not only because of their superior firepower but because they also gradually convert the Igbo to their ways. The missionaries win over the outcast (the *efulefu*, or "worthless empty men") and the disaffected, like Okonkwo's oldest son Nwoye, alienated from his father and "haunted" by the memory of Ikemefuna's death. The English preach Western-style capitalism as well as Christianity: "The white man had indeed brought a lunatic religion, but he had also built a trading store and for the first time palm-oil and kernel became things of great price, and much money flowed into Umuofia." Moreover, when Igbo resisters are found guilty under British law, their punishment is administered by collaborators from Umuru. As Obierika says, "Our own men and our sons have joined the ranks of the stranger. They have joined his religion and they help to uphold his government. . . . How do you think we can fight when our own brothers have turned against us?" The dissolution of the community is not the result of only one cause, but a number of different influences, including the fragility of Igbo culture itself.

It is worth taking some time to look at the ironies of the final chapter. The District Commissioner is both a "resolute administrator" and an avid "student of primitive customs." Okonkwo's story, he thinks, will make "interesting reading. One could almost write a whole chapter on him. Perhaps not a whole chapter but a reasonable paragraph, at any rate." The complex and tragic history of Okonkwo, intertwined as it is with the equally complex and tragic history of British conquest of the lands that would become present-day Nigeria, will be reduced to a "reasonable paragraph" of a work titled, ominously, *The Pacification of the Primitive Tribes of the Lower Niger.* Though we are considering British representations of Africa and not the Orient, clearly Edward Said's work is very relevant here as well—Achebe shows the interrelation of scholarship and brute power (knowledge will be put to the service of "pacification"), and criticizes Western scholarship's tendency to reduce non-Western individuals, families, villages, and whole cultures to homogeneous types, or perhaps anthropological curiosities.

An Image of Africa: Racism in Conrad's Heart of Darkness

Quick Read

- Form: Essay.
- Summary: Achebe argues that Joseph Conrad's portrayal of Africans in *Heart of Darkness* is racist; Conrad denies the Africans the complexity, integrity, and depth that he gives to Europeans.
- Key Passages: "It is not the differentness that worries Conrad but the

lurking hint of kinship, of common ancestry" (2709); "But perhaps the most significant difference is the one implied in the author's bestowal of human expression to the one and the withholding of it from the other" (2711–12); "The point of my observations should be quite clear now, namely that Joseph Conrad was a thoroughgoing racist" (2713); "The real question is the dehumanization of Africa and Africans which this age-long attitude has fostered and continues to foster in the world. And the question is whether a novel which celebrates this dehumanization, which depersonalizes a portion of the human race, can be called a great work of art" (2714).

Teaching Suggestions

In "An Image of Africa: Racism in Conrad's *Heart of Darkness*," the Empire writes back, to borrow a famous phrase from Salman Rushdie. Achebe does not consider Conrad's novel a great anti-imperialist document by any means; in fact, he calls Conrad "a thoroughgoing racist" (a "bloody racist" in the original version), and argues that even though the novel criticizes nineteenth-century European beliefs, it uses the African continent merely as a "backdrop" against which to do so. Africa is thus evacuated of its actual history and becomes a "metaphysical battleground" wherein Europeans confront the possibility of their own barbarism. In a novel renowned for psychological complexity, Achebe argues, Africans are given neither motivation nor subjective depth, presented as fearsome enigmas or nonentities, scarcely allowed articulate speech. "This also . . . has been one of the dark places of the earth," says Marlow, noting that England, the center of the Empire, was once a site of "utter savagery" populated by "wild men" (*Heart of Darkness*); the novel will go on to show how European identity is fragile and unstable, because reversion to a "wild" state is always a possibility. Throughout the story, moreover, Africa remains inert, a mute symbol of the savagery of which humans are capable, or even of the essential meaninglessness of human existence.

Student reactions to Achebe's very direct assertion that *Heart of Darkness* should not "be called a great work of art" will be mixed. Some will empathize with his indignation, while others will be unnerved that he questions the value of a novel that may have given them pleasure or challenged them intellectually. One might say that the article is useful precisely because it provokes such controversy. Achebe reminds us of how much is at stake in the game of literary representation: texts and images have the power to shape the attitude of whole generations, and present a certain version of "reality" so convincingly that it becomes impossible to imagine alternatives. To help students grasp the bigger picture, it would be ideal to have them read both Conrad's *Heart of Darkness* and Achebe's *Things Fall Apart* before they read the essay. In so doing, they will be better able to recognize both *Heart of Darkness*'s quite scathing critique of imperialism and its insulting depiction of African people and culture. While it can be shown that Conrad's novel works consistently to break down the oppositions that underlie imperialist ideology—white/dark, civilized/barbaric, modern/prehistoric, human/animal, England/Africa—it displays no interest in African subjects and cultures in their own right, and offers the reader no "alternative frame of reference" to that of white Europe. Ultimately, Achebe is arguing for a literature that allows colonial and postcolonial subjects complexity, depth, and dignity.

Teaching Clusters

Things Fall Apart can be profitably studied either in the **History, Memory, and Politics** cluster or in the **Culture, Language, and Identity** cluster. In the first grouping, you would focus more on the novel's revisionist history, while in the second grouping, you would emphasize the cultural issues, especially in relation to the collision between European and African culture that occurs in the second half of the novel. In either category, Conrad's *Heart of Darkness* would make an invaluable companion reading, as would Achebe's essay on Conrad.

Discussion Questions

1. How is the community of Umuofia portrayed in *Things Fall Apart*? What do we learn about this culture from its festivals, rituals, and weddings? In what way is this society different from or similar to Western culture?
2. What is Okonkwo's attitude toward his father, Unoka? How do Okonkwo's thoughts about his father shape his character?
3. Discuss the relationship between Okonkwo and his oldest son, Nwoye. Compare this to Okonkwo's relationship with and feelings about Ikemefuna.
4. Describe the character of Ezinma, the daughter of Ekwefi and Okonkwo. What do we learn about Okonkwo from his attitude toward her? What does her characterization tell us about gender roles in Umuofia?
5. Compare and contrast Okonkwo with his close friend, Obierika.
6. How do the Europeans go about colonizing Umuofia and the surrounding villages?
7. What is the novel's attitude toward Christianity? Explore the portrayal of Mr. Brown and Reverend Smith, for example. Why does Nwoye convert to Christianity?
8. Compare the District Commissioner's scholarly treatise in *Things Fall Apart* with Kurtz's pamphlet for the International Society for the Suppression of Savage Customs (*Heart of Darkness*). Why is each man writing his document, and how does his document elucidate his other work as a colonizer? How does each understand or classify the native peoples? Would Kurtz approve of the District Commissioner's methods, and vice versa?
9. According to Achebe in his essay on *Heart of Darkness*, how does Conrad dehumanize the African people?

10. Why does Achebe object to Conrad's portrayal of Africa as "incomprehensible," a word that appears frequently in *Heart of Darkness*?

Alice Munro

"Walker Brothers Cowboy" is a fine introduction to Alice Munro's paradoxical vision, showing to good advantage the author's deft use of realistic description, subtle point-of-view orchestration, and poetically allusive image selection. Set against the backdrop of southern Ontario's "flat, scorched, empty" land and "stricken farmyards" marked by the poverty of the Great Depression, the story at first appears to be a simple reminiscence, told in essentially linear fashion, about humble, ordinary lives given significance through vivid, dense observations of the physical world. Autobiographical details from the author's life, such as the reference to her father's failed fox-breeding business, add to the air of straightforward personal anecdote. However, as seemingly meandering incidents accrue, the reader becomes aware that the story is opening out in unexpected ways to address cosmic themes of time and life's mutability. If the walk the youthful narrator takes with her father to the lake initially seems imbued with "shabby," "defeated," constrictive Depression-era hardship, later it conveys awe as the girl turns onto a "shifting, precarious" path that leads to vertiginous revelations about immense cycles of geological time and humankind's transient presence on earth. In scenes such as this, Munro's special gift for gleaning unique moments of consciousness from everyday existence is revealed. The ambiguities that Munro builds into her narrator's subjective angles of vision only serve as reminders that meaningful insights can never be captured conclusively, but only glimpsed passingly and indirectly.

Walker Brothers Cowboy

Quick Read

- Form: Short story, told by a first-person narrator.
- Summary: After accompanying her father on a visit to his female friend, a young girl reflects on the paradoxical nature of time and the mysteries of life.
- Themes: Change is life's one constant; growing up entails the loss of illusion, but also the acquisition of greater self-knowledge and communal feelings of empathy for fellow human beings; the adult forges many selves through a lifetime of experience.
- Key Passages: "The tiny share we have of time appalls me, though my father seems to regard it with tranquillity" (2716); "So my father drives . . . and I feel my father's life flowing back from our car in the last of the afternoon, darkening and turning strange, like a landscape that has an enchantment on it, making it kindly, ordinary and familiar while you are looking at it, but changing it, once your back is

turned, into something you will never know, with all kinds of weathers, and distances you cannot imagine" (2724).

Teaching Suggestions

Munro's stories often have a double movement in which vivid imagery and surprising analogies invest the "kindly, ordinary and familiar" moments of everyday life with a sense of the infinite. To start class discussion, a general question to pose might be: In the three journeys described in the story (the walk to the lake, the drive that ends at Nora's house, and the return home), how does Munro hint at dimensions beyond the quotidian events that are unfolding? Munro takes pains in describing with authenticity a time and a place, yet simple eyewitness verisimilitude seems not to be an end in itself; rather, she invests it with a fresh vision, like the vision of children, capable of perceiving the remarkable in things that adults have long ceased noticing. As the young narrator struggles with herself to comprehend the significance of her experiences, the reader shares her insights. Ask students to examine this narrative voice carefully. The speaker has a sensitive, almost poetic sensibility that is unusual in that she takes note of things imperceptible to her brother and other characters. However, the present tense of the story distracts attention from the fact that she sees significance in events because she is actually speaking from the removed standpoint of an adult recreating her childhood thoughts. Clues to this adult vantage point can be found in the narrator's description of the farmhouse that belongs "to that one decade in time" or her observation about the linguistic habits of country people. You might inquire as to how the temporal tension between youth and maturity in the narrator's viewpoint underscores the central themes of time and change in the story, invoking in the reader feelings similar to those felt by the girl when, at the end of the walk to the lake, her father awakens her awareness to some aspects of the enigma of time.

The story's final passages deserve particular attention, since these refine and focus the themes of time and change. When the narrator realizes that her father's life extends beyond her own brief glimpse of it, her understanding of her place in the world becomes broader. On the way home from Nora's house, she reflects: "So my father drives . . . and I feel my father's life flowing back from our car in the last of the afternoon, darkening and turning strange, like a landscape that has an enchantment on it, making it kindly, ordinary and familiar while you are looking at it, but changing it, once your back is turned, into something you will never know, with all kinds of weathers, and distances you cannot imagine." You might note that the darkening weather in the story's final sentence suggests the child's destroyed innocence; however, if pessimism is the story's closing keynote, why the use of the word "enchantment" in the narrator's epiphany statement? Although darkness, anxiety, and a feeling of curtailment of childhood's simplicity grip the narrator's younger self, positive signs of growth and hope are in evidence in the final scene as well, especially in the sense we get of an expansion of the young girl's boundaries. She seems to be becoming aware that, like her father, she has a self that exists apart from the self the family has defined. At the same time, however, her growing maturity and advancement into a community of adult thinking are signaled by her complicity with her father, their tacit understanding that "there are things not to be mentioned" about the visit to Nora's. Here, Munro's distinctive tendency to create double movements reflecting life's paradoxes becomes visible; thanks to the new, mature fellow-feeling she has for her father, she not only discovers her uniqueness but also her placement within a broader human and temporal landscape.

Teaching Clusters

The ruminations on time and personal history in Munro's story make it well suited to the cluster on **History, Memory, and Politics**. Moreover, the stories from James Joyce's *Dubliners* collection, both "Araby" and "The Dead," would make excellent companion readings here. Both stories focus on visions of the self in relation to the community, and "The Dead" shares some specific correspondences with "Walker Brothers Cowboy." Joyce's tale, for instance, features a protagonist who understands more about himself when he realizes that his spouse's life has extended far beyond his own time with her.

Discussion Questions

1. Describe the setting and atmosphere of "Walker Brothers Cowboy." What is the landscape like? What are people's lives like? Where do the narrator and her family fit in?
2. In the beginning of the story, the narrator takes a walk with her father and he tells her "how the Great Lakes came to be"; hearing her father, she thinks, "The tiny share we have of time appalls me, though my father seems to regard it with tranquility." Why is the theme of time important in this story? How does it relate to the narrator's visit with her father to Nora's house?
3. What is the narrator's attitude toward Nora? Compare her description of Nora with her description of her mother.
4. How does our view of the father change when he visits Nora? How does the narrator's view change? Does she feel estrangement or a greater sense of fellowship?
5. How does the first-person point of view affect your understanding of the story? What is the narrator's perspective?

Geoffrey Hill

Geoffrey Hill's poetry is challenging—allusive and complex—but students will find much here to engage them. Although his writing contains traces of various influences (modernism, metaphysical poetry), his voice is distinctive, deftly weaving history, politics, and ethical and philosophical concerns into a richly textured whole. Rather than bringing history into the present with the assertion of the subjective self, as Seamus Heaney does in "Punishment," for example, Hill avoids such self-positioning and plunges the reader into the historical moment with images of startling power. "Just so much Zyklon and leather, patented / terror, so many routine cries," he writes in "September Song," recalling the institutionalized brutality of the Holocaust (lines 6–7). Despite Hill's resolve not to privilege the personal element in his writing, his poetry is intense and gripping. In "Requiem for the Plantagenet Kings," the stone effigies of men slain in medieval battles are "well-dressed [in] alabaster and proved spurs / . . . secure in the decay / Of blood, blood-marks, crowns hacked and coveted" (lines 8–10). Hill is a poet of rare ability, one who can make the past visceral, tactile, and immediate.

September Song

Quick Read

- Form: Elegy.
- Themes: The institutionalized violence of the Holocaust; the uses or misuses of elegy; the location of the poet in his or her poetry.
- Key Passages: "Undesirable you may have been, untouchable / you were not. Not forgotten / or passed over at the proper time," lines 1–3; "Just so much Zyklon and leather, patented / terror, so many routine cries," lines 6–7; "(I have made / an elegy for myself it / is true)," lines 8–10.

Teaching Suggestions

This much-discussed poem concerns the extermination of Jews by Nazis during World War II. After touching upon some of the main points of the Holocaust, you might begin your analysis of the poem by asking students to think about the meaning of the title. Words in Hill's poetry often have multiple or ambiguous meanings, and "September Song" illustrates this tendency. "September" is associated with autumn, decline, and the prelude to winter, yet it is also on the cusp between summer and fall, at a moment that marks the end of the growing season but that contains the fullness of harvest; as such, it speaks of plenitude but also decay, suggested in the last four lines of the poem: "September fattens on the vines. Roses / flake from the wall. . . . / This is plenty. This is more than enough" (lines 11–14). The addition of "Song" adds another element. Technically, any poem may be a song, yet the word also recalls other terms such as "hymn" (perhaps in praise to the deceased child) or even a Greek "chorus." In this latter usage, the poem offers a commentary on the Holocaust from an ethical or empathetic vantage point.

As you discuss the remainder of the poem, you may focus on the allusiveness of particular words and phrases. The *NAEL* footnote offers a gloss on "untouchable" and "undesirable," for instance, two terms that set the tone of the poem. Several critics have noted that "passed over" brings to mind the Jewish Passover, an ironic association with a ritual that commemorates the Jews being protected from destruction, while also containing the sense of being "forgotten" that the passage argues against: "Not forgotten / or passed over at the proper time" (lines 2–3). The following stanza suggests the chilling technology of the Holocaust: "Just so much Zyklon and leather, patented / terror, so many routine cries" (lines 6–7). Here we have not only the accoutrements of genocide—the specific chemical used and the leather of official uniforms—but also the institutionalization of "patented / terror." It's worth noting that "patented" refers at once to a protected, legal right (like the patent on Zyklon-B) and scientific precision, with a hint of the alternate meaning of "patent" as something conspicuous (an obvious terror). The systematized, authorized violence suggested in the stanza overall is summed up in the "routine cries" of the victims (line 7).

The parenthetical third stanza is perhaps the most ambiguous: "(I have made / an elegy for myself it / is true)." Certainly the passage draws attention to the elegiac form of the poem, a metacommentary that places the reader outside of the action and brings up questions about the uses of elegy. This will give you an opportunity to discuss the elegy in general and other political elegies in particular. (See, for example, Heaney's "Casualty" and Yeats's "Easter, 1916.") You may want to ask students to think about the purposes of an elegy, its audience and intended effect. While a traditional elegy usually consoles the reader, Hill's poem does not—and, in fact, backs away from any kind of indulgence in emotion. There may be a suggestion here that the speaker is aware that an elegy tends to aestheticize its object, detracting from the horror of death and investing it with lyricism. Moreover, you will want to talk about the bracketed placement of the narrative "I" in this stanza. What is the poet's place in this poem?

Teaching Clusters

History is a major presence in Geoffrey Hill's poetry, and for this reason his work can best be studied in the cluster on **History, Memory, and Politics.** Seamus Heaney's poems would provide a good contrast and help spur discussion on Hill's distinctive approach. Heaney's "Punishment" and "Casualty" are good companion pieces to Hill's "September Song," as is Yeats's "Easter, 1916." To enhance students' understanding of the way that "September Song" fits within the genre of the elegy, works such as Auden's "In Memory of W. B. Yeats" or Gray's "Elegy Written in a Country Churchyard" would provide a useful context.

Discussion Questions

1. Explore the different meanings of the title "September Song."
2. How might this poem be thought of as performing the function of a Greek chorus?

3. How do the separate words and phrases in the second stanza contribute to its overall effect: "As estimated, you died. Things marched, / sufficient, to that end. / Just so much Zyklon and leather, patented / terror, so many routine cries" (lines 4–7)? How does a word such as "estimated" suggest coldness or scientific detachment? Why are the cries "routine"?

4. Why does the speaker refer to the "elegy" in the third stanza: "(I have made / an elegy for myself it / is true)"? Why might this be an elegy to the poet/speaker? Notice that the *NAEL* footnote points out that Hill was born one day before the date in the subtitle. Are there other ways of thinking about this stanza in relation to elegy? How is this poem different from or similar to other elegies you may have read?

5. Compare the use of history in Hill's "September Song" and in Heaney's "Punishment."

V. S. Naipaul

Raised in the East Indian community of Trinidad before leaving for Oxford in his teens, V. S. Naipaul writes from the experience of multiple racial and cultural displacements. Focusing on the strivings of immigrants and newly independent postcolonial states without romanticizing his protagonists, he often views with a skeptical or even jaundiced eye any hopes for the possibility of cultural adaptation for diasporic populations. For Naipaul, Western philosophical objectives such as the humanistic ideal of self-knowledge leading to freedom or the existentialist ideal of perpetual self-invention through a succession of personal choices all seem to come up short. Instead, historical and religio-cultural determinism holds the deracinated subject in a state of limbo that bars him or her from untroubled acculturation. In the quintessential Naipaul narrative of "One Out of Many," Santosh declares, "I had decided to be free, to act for myself," only to find that his choices result not simply in the alienation suffered by the isolated individual in Western culture but also in a further alienating separation from a native community that, though limited by caste and theological constraints, at least offered shared social relations and possibly a more meaningful context in which to live. In the end, the ordeal of identity fragmentation that Santosh has undergone leaves him suitable for crippled epiphanies at best, and ultimately only for the "free" choices of reclusiveness, self-limitation, and stasis.

One Out of Many

Quick Read

- Form: Short story; first-person narration.
- Themes: The painful difficulty of the immigrant's acculturation process; struggle and alienation experienced by immigrants to America; culture clash between alleged "freedoms" of a secular industrial-

ized democracy and the determinism of cultures defined by caste and religion; the impossibility of real freedom in modern society; imprisonment as an inescapable condition of modern life.

- Key Passages: "The discovery of my good looks brought its strains. I became obsessed with my appearance, with a wish to see myself. It was like an illness" (2738); "Now I found that, without wishing it, I was ceasing to see myself as part of my employer's presence, and beginning at the same time to see him as an outsider might see him, as perhaps the people who came to dinner in the apartment saw him" (2739–40); "When I adjusted to my imprisonment I had wanted only to get away from Washington and to return to Bombay. But then I had become confused. I had looked in the mirror and seen myself, and I knew it wasn't possible for me to return to Bombay to the sort of job I had had and the life I had lived" (2742); "I hadn't escaped; I had never been free" (2749).

Teaching Suggestions

In presenting the struggles of Santosh, "One Out of Many" illustrates the inner experience of a recently displaced immigrant from Bombay. Exile, Naipaul suggests, is a state of being that may lead to profound fragmentation of personality. You may start by taking students step-by-step through the incremental stages of recognition and renunciation that make up Santosh's story. Santosh's moment of self-recognition in front of the mirror, for example, may be a good starting point for discussion. As he says, "I was once part of the flow, never thinking of myself as a presence. Then I looked in the mirror and decided to be free." Santosh's discovery of his good looks and his separateness outside his native country's social scheme seem to promise the beginning of a passage toward merging with America, a culture that stresses individualism. Invite students to think about the significance of the mirror as a means by which Santosh constructs his American self. On the one hand, the story seems to suggest that this moment of self-recognition signals Santosh's release from his Indian caste conditioning, his native tradition in which a higher caste is considered a "presence" while his own lower caste is seen as "dirt." On the other hand, Santosh's dawning realization of selfhood may not lead to unqualified well-being. As he becomes more and more fascinated by his own image, he begins to feel that he is surrounded by a world of false appearances. He notices, for example, that the Mexican waiters are forced to wear turbans to add "authenticity" to Indian restaurants and that the hippies or (unnamed) Hare Krishna followers in Hindu clothing are not what they appear to be. "[H]ow nice [it would be]," Santosh muses, "if the people in Hindu costumes in the circle were real." Rather than a moment of self-knowledge, his self-recognition in the mirror seems to precipitate psychological fragmentation within himself and a growing alienation from those around him. This preoccupation with his outward appearance, he realizes, "was like an illness."

Instructors will also need to address the issue of racism in the text. San-tosh's denigration of African Americans and of the Mexican waiters in the restaurant will provoke many readers, as it has some critics. It may be useful to remind students that the story is written in the first person and that the views we see are a product of Santosh's own beliefs. What are we to make of Santosh, then? Is he a sympathetic character, exiled from his homeland and alienated from his adopted country? Is he a reprehensible creature, repro-ducing the prejudices of a rigid caste system? Do hierarchical social sys-tems automatically breed mistrust between different cultural groups? Or is such mistrust the result of cultural displacement in a globalized world?

Rather than concentrating on pivotal scenes, you may want to trace the repetition of certain resonant words such as "freedom," "prison," "real," "safe," "action," and "escape," which take on deeper and more varied meanings as the story progresses. For example, an examination of the word "escape" would track Santosh's usage from an idea embodied in the desire "only to get away from Washington and to return to Bombay" to the early despair that makes him desire that free choice be wrested from his hands ("I wanted escape to be impossible; I wanted the very idea of es-cape to become absurd"). As with many of Naipaul's repeated terms, the word "escape" takes on a darker inflection in the latter part of the story as Santosh admits, "I felt mocked when I remembered that in the early days of my escape I had thought I was in charge of myself"a feeling that leads to his conclusion that "I hadn't escaped; I had never been free."

Teaching Clusters

The focus on cultural dislocation and fragmented identity in "One Out of Many" places the story squarely within the cluster on **Culture, Lan-guage, and Identity.** Several other works would make excellent compan-ion readings, such as Jean Rhys's "The Day They Burned the Books" and the essays by Brathwaite and Ngũgĩ in the "Nation and Language" section of *NAEL*. As a first-person narrative about an Afro-Caribbean immigrant's difficulty assimilating into British society, Rhys's "Let Them Call It Jazz" would make for especially suitable comparisons. Additionally, poems by Ramanujan ("Elements of Composition") and Walcott ("A Far Cry from Africa") would help students extend their thinking on cultural identity.

Discussion Questions

1. Does "One Out of Many" hold out much hope for fusion and under-standing between different cultural groups in America?

2. Santosh often seems to misread his adopted culture. For example, looking at the hippies in a Washington D.C. park, he surmises, "Per-haps, as in some story, they had been brought here among the *hubshi* as captives a long time ago." At other times, Santosh seems to be able to see through the pretenses of American culture, as when he acutely observes the Americans' "television life." Describe the story's repre-sentation of America, as seen through Santosh's eyes.

3. What kinds of freedom and escape are possible in Santosh's world?
4. What is the significance of Santosh's preoccupation with his outward appearance? What does this preoccupation have to do with his changing feelings about who he is? In what way does it signal a changing view of himself in relation to the world and as a separate being?
5. Why and how does Santosh's relationship with his employer from Bombay develop throughout the course of the story?
6. In what way is Priya, the restaurant owner, connected to Santosh's changing view of himself and the world?
7. While thinking about his green suit, why does Santosh say, "When I considered all that cloth and all that tailoring I was proposing to adorn my simple body with . . . I felt I was asking to be destroyed." What is the meaning of the green suit? Why can't he put it on?

Tom Stoppard

Tom Stoppard's plays typically bring together a combination of seemingly disparate elements such as historical incidents and personages, literary parody, physical comedy from vaudeville and theater of the absurd traditions, linguistic puzzles, sophisticated Wildean wit, and abstract philosophical ideas that would not seem to lend themselves to dramatization. The artistic fusion of these ingredients results in work that is rich and complex in meaning and form. A wonderful example of Stoppard's art of finding order in chaos is *Arcadia*, a play that connects the sciences with the humanities and shows how both disciplines deepen our knowledge of the universe and humankind's place in it. In the impassioned intellectual exchanges between the professional and amateur scholars of the play, a series of images, metaphors, and relationships bring the hard sciences to life; Stoppard thus illustrates that science can be brought into dramatic forms that were once considered to be exclusively the province of the liberal arts and the humanities. In so doing, he reinvigorates the traditional staples of drama—the preeminent aspects of the human condition such as metaphysical philosophy, creativity, love, and death. In *Arcadia*, students will find humor, tragedy, and compassion in concert with thought-provoking scientific theories.

Arcadia

Quick Read

• Form: Drama (comedy).
• Summary: Alternating between the early nineteenth and the late twentieth centuries, the characters in two separate but intersecting stories pursue answers to questions about science, history, and intellectual creativity.

- Themes: Life's apparent randomness is marked by an underlying order; intuition-driven Romantic and logic-driven classical ways of thinking, although seemingly disparate, coexist in the human mind; the desire for knowledge is one of the fundamental things that makes us human; genius requires a combination of rational and intuitive approaches.
- Key Passages: Thomasina: "When you stir your rice pudding, Septimus, the spoonful of jam spreads itself round making red trails like the picture of a meteor in my astronomical atlas. But if you stir backward, the jam will not come together again," I.1; Valentine: "People were talking about the end of physics. . . . But they only explained the very big and the very small. The universe, the elementary particles. The ordinary-sized stuff which is our lives . . . these things are full of mystery. . . . It's the best possible time to be alive, when almost everything you thought you knew is wrong," I.4; Hannah: "It's *all* trivial—your grouse, my hermit, Bernard's Byron. . . . It's wanting to know that makes us matter," II.7; Valentine: "See? In an ocean of ashes, islands of order. Patterns making themselves out of nothing," II.7.

Teaching Suggestions

More than simply a farce that happens to feature scientists, mathematicians, historians, and landscape architects, *Arcadia* is a complex union of competing ideas. It will help students to grasp the significance of the play if you explain at the beginning that one of its central conceits is that complexity does not mean disarray and randomness does not suggest the complete absence of fundamental order. You will also need to say a few words about the transition from the age of Enlightenment to the age of Romanticism. Numerous speeches by characters in *Arcadia* are good sources for streamlined summaries of presumed differences between these two historical eras—although such differences are not as neat and clear as Hannah believes when she exclaims, "The whole Romantic sham, Bernard! It's what happened to the Enlightenment, isn't it? A century of intellectual rigour turned in on itself" (I.2). The scientific theories associated with each period may be confusing to students, but several characters offer insights into the premises under consideration here. For example, Valentine gives useful nutshell explanations, from Newtonian physics ("a pendulum, or a ball falling through the air—backwards, it looks the same" [II.7]), to the Second Law of Thermodynamics ("The heat goes into the mix . . . [a]nd everything is mixing the same way, all the time, irreversibly" [II.7]), to his own specialization, chaos theory.

Generally speaking, the play's central conflicts focus on the dichotomy between two approaches to viewing the universe: classical and Romantic. Although certain characters are connected to each philosophy, Stoppard demonstrates that these opposing ways of thinking never exist to the exclusion of the other in the human psyche. Hannah, the supreme rationalist, comes to her final theory about the identity of the hermit (actually, Septimus, as the reader knows) through intuition rather than empirical research ("I've got a good idea who he was, but I can't prove it" [II.7]); Bernard, the philandering academic, combines logical thinking with sloppy scholarship; Thomasina, the genius of the play, is just as concerned with learning to waltz as she is with solving her mathematical equations; and Septimus, the cynical realist, ends his days as a reclusive lunatic trying to prove the validity of Thomasina's scientific theory— driven, we assume, by obsessive love for his deceased pupil.

The classical perspective is introduced primarily through dialogue concerning Newtonian physics, which proposes a vision of a fully comprehensible mechanistic universe with repetitive functions that can be predicted and reduced to geometric calculations, a vision that is often considered "optimistic" as it presents a steady, consistent order where energy is constant. Septimus is initially the proponent of this deterministic view, expressing faith in Newton's symmetrical, reversible calculations that neatly classify processes such as the conservation of energy. "We shed as we pick up," Septimus declares, "like travellers who must carry everything in their arms, and what we let fall will be picked up by those behind. . . . Mathematical discoveries glimpsed and lost to view will have their time again" (I.3). Classicism is also manifested in the formal landscape architecture of Lady Croom's first garden at Sidley Park, where "trees are companionably grouped at intervals that show them to advantage" (I.1). In both science and landscape design, the classical view values fabricated human order, logic, and mind over untamed nature, intuition, and heart.

The Romantic approach, in contrast, expresses itself with a more fatalistic accent. Within post-Newtonian science, for example, the Second Law of Thermodynamics is the principle that stresses the irreversibility of time, the dissipation of energy, and the heat death of the universe. Thomasina, one of nature's mutations, intuits this advance on Newton's physics when she points out to her tutor, "When you stir your rice pudding, Septimus, the spoonful of jam spreads itself round making red trails like the picture of a meteor in my astronomical atlas. But if you stir backward, the jam will not come together again" (I.1). Thomasina's realization that the universe is disposed toward increasing entropic disorder is linked in Stoppard's play to the imagery of the Romantic movement of the early nineteenth century, one example of which is the then-fashionable Gothic– Romantic landscaping style that attempts to imitate nature's wildness (Noakes's "picturesque style" [I.1]) and hint at the finitude of the living universe (symbolized in architectural memento mori such as decaying ruins). While holding up the offstage figure of Byron as an exemplar of Romanticism, Stoppard also has some fun in presenting us with Bernard, a licentious academic who believes mainly in "a visceral belief in yourself" wherein "Gut [intuition] is no back-reference" and whose reckless, romantic impulses lead to the probable ruination of his career (I.4).

Arcadia's third scientific perspective is represented by chaos theory, a sort of reconciliation between the earlier dichotomies, which, like Romanticism, takes nature's wildness and unpredictability into account, but deemphasizes decay and death in favor of a cyclical paradigm. According to this new theory, nature is a volatile dynamic system whose multitude of variations is not perfectly predictable, but, through the use of iterated statistics taken from nature fed through a computer, universal patterns that govern this system can be discerned. This process is illustrated by Valentine's discovery that feeding Thomasina's "iterated algorithm" (I.4) into a computer produces an asymmetrical yet repeating pattern of fractals where "[e]ach picture is a detail of the previous one, blown up. And so on. For ever" (11.7). From this, he discovers "[i]n an ocean of ashes, islands of order. Patterns making themselves out of nothing" (II.7). Thus, Valentine has confirmation of Thomasina's "New Geometry of Irregular Forms," chaos theory's new geometry built not on the symmetries of purely conceptual classical Newtonian geometry but on the configuration of organic forms from nature itself (I.4). Invite students to consider the notion of ordered randomness suggested by this third theory in relation to characters and occurrences in the play. The final scene, for example, with its simultaneous display of two story lines and two historical eras, at first seems to splinter into chaos yet ends up conveying a sense of harmony. In the image of the two waltzing couples from two epochs, one duo containing a doomed genius and the other a prodigy filled with mysterious optimism, students may find that the world is "still doomed," as Valentine suggests, but they may agree with him that "if this is how it started, perhaps it's how the next one will come" (II.7).

Teaching Clusters

Arcadia's complex interweaving of past and present is best suited to the cluster on **History, Memory, and Politics.** The play's focus on knowledge, time, and the relationship between truth and intuition can be clarified by comparison with other selections that attempt to understand the present by recovering the past. Although *Arcadia* is unique in its perspective, studying works such as Yeats's Celtic poems alongside Stoppard's play might help students think about the similarities between acknowledged myths and historical distinctions (Romantic, classical), while Heaney's bog poems can open up a discussion about human identity and history. Additionally, T. E. Hulme's lecture denigrating Romanticism in favor of classicism (from "Romanticism and Classicism," in the "Modernist Manifestos" section), would give students a sharper sense of how these two movements are usually thought of in oppositional terms.

Discussion Questions

1. *Arcadia* explores the differences between classical and Romantic approaches to viewing the universe. Which characters are spokespersons for each view? In what ways do these characters correspond to the views they espouse and in what ways do they contradict themselves?

2. How do intuition and logic each play a role in the discovery of science and truth in this play?

3. What is the significance of the fact that Gus does not speak? What function does Gus play in *Arcadia*? How does Gus provide Hannah with the evidence that unlocks the mystery of the hermit in Sidley Park?

4. What are the greater thematic and plot ramifications arising from Septimus's lighting of Thomasina's candle in the last scene?

5. Aside from adding theatrical grace to the final scene, how does the waltz, with its similarly dressed dancers from two different epochs, underscore some of the themes of the play? Why is the modern couple dancing awkwardly while the couple from the earlier period is dancing gracefully? Is the final scene one of chaos and a decay of order or one of order and hope?

6. Compare the play's Romantic-era plot with the twentieth-century material. What connections, parallels, and differences can be found between them?

Les Murray

Les Murray's poetry combines a tough, rugged persona with a sophisticated technical sensibility, beautifully demonstrated in works such as "Morse." Reenacting a colorful incident from Australia's frontier days, "Morse" celebrates the independent spirit of men trying to survive in the continent's wild outback. According to the story, in 1917 a young man was injured and taken to Hall's Creek, where he was attended to by F. W. Tuckett, the town's postmaster and telegraph operator. Tuckett knew a little first aid, but not enough to help the man, who was seriously injured. Communicating by Morse Code, Tuckett located a medical doctor many miles away, and with only a small knife and the instructions of the surgeon, operated on the man's ruptured bladder. Murray ingeniously brings this incident to life by playing on the sounds of Morse Code, embedding its staccato rhythms in the clipped consonants and bunched stresses of his verse. The poem mourns the passing of a way of life, represented not only by Tuckett, but, interestingly, Morse Code itself. In Murray's rendition, this defunct telegraphic language is a metaphor for the hardy, rough, and adaptable outback pioneers of the past. Imaginative and playful, this poem will appeal to students' sense of fun yet also sensitize them to the sounds and rhythms of verse.

Morse

Quick Read

- Form: Narrative poem.
- Themes: The loss of a way of life is inextricably connected to a loss of language; Morse Code is a fitting metaphor for the Australian pioneers, who were a tough and resourceful breed.

- Key Passages: "Tuckett. Bill Tuckett," line 1; "morse keys have mostly gone silent / and only old men meet now to chit-chat in their electric / bygone dialect," lines 20–22; "The last letter many will forget / is dit-dit-dit-dah, V for Victory. The coders' hero had speed, / resource and a touch. So ditditdit daah for Bill Tuckett," lines 22–24.

Teaching Suggestions

Not all students may be familiar with Morse Code, so it will help to explain that it is a combination of dots, dashes ("dit" and "dah" are linguistic alternatives to "dot" and "dash"), and pauses or spaces. Also, you will need to explain that Morse Code is no longer commonly used; it has been eclipsed by newer forms of technology. When you begin your discussion of the poem, ask students to describe the sound and rhythm of this form of communication: harsh, abrupt, clipped, terse, rhythmic. Armed with these preliminary concepts, students can then take note of the way that the poem invests the sense of the code into its language and cadences. Obviously inspired by the clicking syllables of "Tuckett," which sounds like Morse Code, Murray begins and ends the poem with the postmaster's name. Students may notice that the sound of "Tuckett" is reflected in words and phrases such as "stuck it," "lack," "luck," "pluck," "epoch," "conducted," "bucket," and so on (lines 2, 3, 4, 5, 6, 13, 19). Passages such as "a man needing surgery right on the spot, a lot / would have done their dashes" (lines 8–9) and "you did it, you did it" (line 16) play on the rhythms and sounds of the code, while the ellipses that end the first full stanza (". . .") reflect the "(dot dot dot)" of line 8. The casually expressive "la-de-dah" and "chit-chat" similarly capture the mood (lines 17, 21). You will also want to point out the correspondences between the code and the people. The "convalescent" is "properly laconic," or succinct in his speech, and the people are tough and to the point—the living embodiment of Morse Code.

The final stanza strikes an elegiac note, and it is here that the poem's nostalgia is most present. "[M]orse keys have mostly gone silent / and only old men meet now to chit-chat in their electric / bygone dialect," laments the speaker (lines 20–22). Morse Code is a technological idiom that is adaptable to human ingenuity and the hardy men and women of the pioneer era; sadly, however, it is an outmoded language, a "vernacular" (the poem is part of a collection entitled "The Vernacular Republic") that represents a region and a people for whom Murray has great affection. He transforms these individuals into heroes, not only through his retelling of the tale, but also by linking them to the code operators of World War II, who prefaced their coded messages to underground operatives with the famous military slogan "dot-dot-dot-dash," representing both the first four notes of Beethoven's Fifth Symphony and "V" (in the Morse alphabet) for victory. "The last letter many will forget," the speaker explains, "is dit-dit-dit-dah, V for Victory. The coders' hero had speed, / resource and a touch. So ditditdit daah for Bill Tuckett" (lines 22–24). Students who are really paying attention may be able to crack the poem's visual code. The split structure of lines 6 and 15 divides the first stanza into three substanzas, which are followed by a full, unbroken second stanza, thus echoing the V for victory code sequence: "dit-dit-dit-dah" (line 23). It is a formal tour de force.

Teaching Clusters

Both "Morse" and "Corniche" may be studied in the **Culture, Language, and Identity** cluster. Although playful and amusing, "Morse" addresses thoughtful issues about language and culture. Other poems that comment on language, such as Louise Bennett's "Dry-Foot Bwoy" and John Agard's "Listen Mr Oxford Don," and even longer dramatic or fictional works such as Brian Friel's *Translations*, would make provocative accompaniments.

Discussion Questions

1. How does "Morse" echo the staccato rhythms of Morse Code? What kinds of sounds, rhythms, images, and words remind the reader of this telegraphic code language?
2. Why does "Morse" begin and end with the name "Tuckett"? How does the poem use this name for thematic and formal purposes?
3. If Morse Code were a person, what would he or she be like? Can you find any analogies between the Australian characters depicted here and the qualities of Morse Code?
4. What kind of sense does "Morse" convey of the people of Australia's pioneering era?
5. Why does the last stanza seem nostalgic about the loss of Morse Code as a usable language? How is this "bygone dialect" connected to a lost Australian culture (line 22)?

Seamus Heaney

In "Station Island," Seamus Heaney meets the ghost of James Joyce, who advises him, "Your obligation / is not discharged by any common rite. / What you must do must be done on your own" (lines 19–21). Here Heaney evidences a concern as to whether he is obliged, as a poet—and an Irish poet, in particular—to write for the public good and uphold a particular notion of political responsibility. Joyce lets him off the hook by telling him "You lose more of yourself than you redeem / doing the decent thing" (lines 46–47). Rather than being bound to a narrow vision of the Irish poet's role, Heaney finds his own way of defining his relationship to his country and his people, a process that is ongoing. Poems such as "Punishment" and "Casualty" show Heaney thinking through the individual's obligation to the community. While in "Punishment," Heaney acknowledges the influence of "tribal" thinking (line 44), in "Casualty," he affirms the freedom of the individual against the demands of the crowd, yet leaves unanswered the question, "How culpable was he / That last night when he broke / Our tribe's complicity?" (line 80). Heaney's thoughtful probing of one's ethical responsibilities in the face of political turmoil will stimulate class discussion and lead to a broader understanding of the dilemmas of cultural identity. His poetry will appeal to students and challenge them at the same time.

Punishment

Quick Read

- Form: Lyric.
- Themes: Tribal or cultural rituals; voyeurism; personal complicity in communal forms of public censure; the relationship of the past to the present.
- Key Passages: "I almost love you / but would have cast, I know, / the stones of silence," lines 29–31; "I am the artful voyeur / of your brain's exposed / and darkened combs," lines 32–34; "I who have stood dumb / when your betraying sisters, / . . . wept by the railings, / who would connive / in civilized outrage / yet understand the exact / and tribal, intimate revenge," lines 37–44.

Teaching Suggestions

This poem, which comments on the IRA's shaving, tarring, and feathering of young Catholic women accused of fraternizing with British soldiers, has provoked much discussion. The central question settles on whether and to what extent it exonerates sectarian violence in general and the IRA's actions in particular, yet this inquiry can also lead to wider explorations of history, culture, and communal practices. Preface your discussion with a few words about the two historical reference points that frame this poem: Northern Ireland during the violent sixties and seventies and the Iron Age of brutal pagan rites. In "Punishment," Heaney explicitly links these two cultural moments by comparing analogous acts of ritualized punishment for female sexual and social transgression. As surmised by the archaeologists who unearthed the ancient corpse, the girl was most likely condemned for committing adultery and purposefully drowned. The poem parallels this act of collective vengeance with the nationalist community's public castigation of the Catholic women in Belfast. To help students grasp the larger implications of such a comparison, it would be useful to discuss the cultural function of such ritualized forms of violence. In addition to punishing an individual breach of social conduct, for instance, such acts consolidate the social group, establish its rules of conduct, and construct a shared identity. It's important to note, however, that some critics are concerned that by placing the IRA's action in an anthropological framework, the poem condones communal violence by seeing it as a natural, inevitable, and ultimately comprehensible occurrence.

A good way to open up a discussion of the poem would be to ask students to focus on the speaker's point of view, paying particular attention to the shifts that occur near the conclusion. In the first stanza the speaker imagines the girl's own embodied feelings, yet in the second stanza he is scrutinizing her from the outside: "[The wind] blows her nipples / to amber beads, it shakes the frail rigging / of her ribs" (lines 5–8). Under the speaker's penetrating gaze, she becomes an erotic, fragile object. The next several stanzas continue this examination, evoking both empathy and pity. The speaker envisions "her drowned / body in the bog" and feels "the weighing stone" that drags the body down (lines 9–10, 11); caressingly, he calls her "My poor scapegoat" (line 28). Yet stanza eight introduces a surprise twist: "I almost love you / but would have cast, I know, / the stones of silence" (lines 29–31). Here, he alludes to the analogous public censure of the Catholic women. Recalling Christ's words to those who wished to stone the adulterous woman ("He that is without sin among you, let him first cast a stone at her" [John 8:7]), the speaker simultaneously invites compassion for the Belfast women and implicates himself in their metaphorical stoning. Returning to the trope of silence in the tenth stanza, he accuses himself more specifically: "I who have stood dumb / when your betraying sisters, cauled in tar, wept by the railings" (lines 37–40). Yet the final stanza pushes the envelope further, as the speaker continues: "[I] who would connive / in civilized outrage / yet understand the exact / and tribal, intimate revenge" (lines 41–44). The last two lines have provoked the most response. While the earlier lines suggest that the speaker feels guilty for condoning the brutality through silence or passivity while outwardly "conniv[ing] / in civilized outrage" (note that "connive" underscores the speaker's tacit approval), the final two lines suggest something more: a guiltless endorsement of the act, even a secret exultation in its cruelty. The question here is whether the concluding sentiment nullifies the compassion of the earlier stanzas, as some commentators have asserted, or whether Heaney pulls off an exquisite balancing act. Note that the speaker separates his intellectual from his emotional reaction. In so doing, does he absolve himself of blame? Or sanction the brutality? Or does he implicate himself in the violence?

Teaching Clusters

Most of Heaney's poetry can be usefully read within the category on **History, Memory, and Politics.** The political elegy "Casualty," for example, would fit nicely in this cluster, paired with Yeats's "Easter, 1916." "Station Island," which considers the poet's responsibility to the community, could be studied alongside Yeats's "Man and the Echo" in the same grouping. Both "Clearances" and "Digging" offer more personal views of memory and the past (about Heaney's father and mother), yet also fall under this rubric. Because of their grounding in the historical past, all of the "bog poems" can be studied in this cluster, although "Punishment" could also be placed in the **Culture, Language, and Identity** category, allowing for more emphasis on cultural (or "tribal") and national identity. "Casualty" could be placed here for the same reason and would make a good contrast to "Punishment."

Discussion Questions

1. Discuss the speaker's point of view toward the Iron Age girl in the first stanza. How does his view change throughout the poem? What kinds of feelings does he have toward the girl?
2. In what way is this poem concerned with tribal rites? How is the ancient paganism of the girl's background similar to its parallel in modern Northern Ireland? What is "tribal" about the treatment of the "betraying sisters" (lines 44, 38)? In what way is it ritualistic? Do all societies have "tribal" rituals? What communal needs do such rituals serve?
3. Why does the speaker say that he is an "artful voyeur" (line 32)? To what extent has he been a voyeur of the girl's body? What separates voyeurism from empathetic concern? Is all voyeurism necessarily erotic? Is the crowd that watches a spectacle of brutality voyeuristic? What is the difference between voyeurism and respectful witnessing?
4. What does the poem have to say about silence in the face of public brutality?
5. What is the difference between "conniv[ing] in civilized outrage" and "understand[ing] the exact / and tribal, intimate revenge" (lines 41–44)? How do these lines affect your understanding of the entire poem?
6. Does this poem render communal violence remote (and thus less tragic) through aestheticization or historicization, or more vividly immediate and intense? What is it saying about collective forms of public censure? Does the poem condone or repudiate violence?

Further Resources

NORTON ONLINE ARCHIVE

Audio:
The Skunk (read by Seamus Heaney)

NORTON TOPICS ONLINE

Twentieth-Century Irish Writers

J. M. Coetzee

J. M. Coetzee's novel *Waiting for the Barbarians* was written at a time when the apartheid government of South Africa, finding itself the last remaining postcolonial government administered by a white minority in Africa, felt itself to be in a particularly embattled position. Increasingly paranoid and desirous of self-perpetuation, the country's governing National Party turned to brutal police and military solutions to counter the threats it perceived. Violent incidents resulted from this policy, such as the 1976 Soweto massacre, in which hundreds of black South Africans demonstrating against the mandatory imposition of Afrikaans, the language of apartheid, upon black children of secondary school age were cut down by the indiscriminate fire of police squads. The following year, black activist Stephen Biko met his death at the hands of South African security forces while in prison. The ruling Afrikaners were also faced with growing local and international organized resistance to policies that ranged from micro-managed segregation of white, "colored" (Asian), and black populations in their everyday lives to wholesale geographic relocation and marginalization of the black majority. It is in the shadow of these events that *Waiting for the Barbarians* was published, and there is a strong likelihood that these historical circumstances may account for some of the novel's main preoccupations: the systematic use of torture and terror as instruments of state control; the appropriation of language for political purposes; the fabrication and legitimization of national identity through the definition of an opposing, scapegoated Other; and the perpetuation of an oppressive governmental regime through the complacency and timidity of the ruling populace. At the same time, Coetzee has insisted on the broader cultural connections of his narrative, saying of the novel's two principal characters—a man and a woman whose race is never identified—they "could as well be Russian and Kirghiz, or Han and Mongol, or Turk and Arab, or Arab and Berber." Brutally frank, this excerpt from *Waiting for the Barbarians* will give students insight into the psychology of political oppression.

Waiting for the Barbarians

Quick Read

- Form: Book.
- Summary: In this excerpt, describing the brutal tactics of an unnamed empire, the narrator is distraught as a crowd watches twelve men being cruelly beaten and abused; later the narrator is interrogated and beaten himself.
- Themes: We are the barbarians; silence or apathy in the face of human and civil rights abuses perpetuates oppressive regimes; language is unstable but the body speaks.
- Key Passages: "The circuit is made, everyone has a chance to see the twelve miserable captives, to prove to his children that the barbarians are real" (2840); "Does each [character] stand for a single thing, a circle for the sun, a triangle for a woman, . . . or does a circle merely stand for 'circle', a triangle for 'triangle' . . . ?" (2844); "On every face around me, even those that are smiling, I see the same expression: not hatred, not bloodlust, but a curiosity so intense that their bodies are drained by it and only their eyes live, organs of a new and ravening appetite" (2841).

Teaching Suggestions

One of the first points you will want to ask students about is Coetzee's use of the word "barbarians." Throughout the excerpt, this word is used in an ironic sense: "The circuit is made, everyone has a chance to see the twelve miserable captives, to prove to his children that the barbarians are real." But why is it necessary to "prove" that "barbarians" exist? Some discussion here of the construction of a political or social "Other" is helpful. The Other is not an objective or neutral descriptive category, but one that is in a direct oppositional relationship to the subject or self that defines the Other. The subject projects all undesirable attributes onto the Other, especially those traits that are in exact contrast to the qualities that the subject values most in his/her/its self-conception. Colonial regimes are well known for categorizing subject peoples in colonized territories as "barbarians," so the designation is one with a long history. The term not only suggests that the colonizer is "civilized," but also justifies the unequal treatment of the colonized or oppressed populace by the colonizers. In Coetzee's book, the political Other must be described as a "barbarian" so that the Empire can legitimize its power, privilege, and brutal tactics.

The label "barbarians" also brings up questions about the instability of language. Like the word "ENEMY," which is inscribed on the backs of the twelve prisoners, the term "barbarians" has no direct connection to any particular meaning; in poststructural terms, it is a signifier that takes its meaning from other signifiers, not a particular signified. In the political context of *Waiting for the Barbarians*, colonizers, ruling governments, or anyone with a big stick can impose meaning onto language, in the same manner as Colonel Joll can graft indictments onto the bodies of the oppressed. The Magistrate himself—a not entirely guiltless figure within the larger context of the novel—illustrates the arbitrariness of language when he invents a meaning for the inscribed wooden slips he has been collecting. "I have no idea what [the characters] stand for," he admits to the reader, then tells Colonel Joll, "This one reads as follows: . . . 'I am sorry I must send bad news.'" Privately, the Magistrate wonders, "Does each [character] stand for a single thing, a circle for the sun, a triangle for a woman . . . or does a circle merely stand for 'circle', a triangle for 'triangle' . . . ?" Words and meaning have no stable, fixed correspondence.

Although language may be a slippery thing, the body has substance. The novel's emphasis on grueling scenes of corporal punishment may seem excessive, but as with any history or exposé of human rights abuses, the body provides irrefutable, tangible evidence of wrongdoing: the tortured, mutilated human body has a validity that exceeds language and the polite codes of social interaction. In *Waiting for the Barbarians*, the body is mistreated and humiliated, not only through physical violation, but also through its exposure to the fascinated scrutiny of the crowd. The complicity of the crowd constitutes a major offense here because it illustrates one of the ways that oppressive regimes maintain their power—through the indifference of the general population. The little girl who watches the men being beaten with a "silent, terrified, curious" stare is a harbinger of things to come; her desensitization will help perpetuate the system in the next generation. As the Magistrate explains, it is "not hatred, not blood-lust, but a curiosity so intense that their bodies are drained by it and only their eyes live" that roots the crowd to the spot, the implication being that corrupt regimes are supported through the most banal means.

It is worth saying a few words about the similarity between this excerpt from Coetzee's novel and Franz Kafka's "In the Penal Colony," a story that concerns itself with the officer of a remote outpost of an unnamed Em-pire whose basic principle is that "[g]uilt is always beyond doubt" and whose torture apparatus executes by bloodily inscribing directives such as "honor thy superiors" on the bodies of its victims. Coetzee adapts Kafka's general method of merging allegory with deliberately meticulous and matter-of-fact detail, yet unlike "In the Penal Colony," *Waiting for the Barbarians* is sharply political and recognizably realistic.

Teaching Clusters

Coetzee's novel is especially well suited for study within the **History, Memory, and Politics** cluster. Its concern with public complicity in per-petuating corrupt regimes, its drive to analyze cultural and political sys-tems, and its reflections on the abuses of empire are issues that can be better grasped in connection with other works that focus on the psy-chology or analysis of imperialism. Conrad's *Heart of Darkness*, Achebe's *Things Fall Apart*, and Gordimer's "The Moment before the Gun Went Off" would all make good contextual readings in this category. You may highlight questions about language, moreover, by placing Coetzee's ex-cerpt in the **Culture, Language, and Identity** grouping; Friel's *Transla-tions*, which demonstrates the connections between political subjugation and renaming, would make a profitable comparison piece.

Discussion Questions

1. Watching the public abuse of the prisoners, the narrator of *Waiting for the Barbarians* comments, "The circuit is made, everyone has a chance to see the twelve miserable captives, to prove to his children that the barbarians are real." Who or what has to "prove" that the barbarians are real? Why are they called "barbarians"?
2. How is the narrator (the Magistrate) different from or similar to the rest of the people around him?
3. In what way is language important in Coetzee's novel? What do you make of the scene in which Colonel Joll writes the word "ENEMY" on the backs of the prisoners?
4. Why has Coetzee chosen an unspecified time and place for his story?
5. Why does Coetzee show us such brutal scenes of torture? What do they suggest about the coercive violence and moral corruption of colonialism?
6. How do stories like Coetzee's make us confront our own apathy, our

own inability to relate, our own lack of commitment, our own relation to the global operation of power and dominance, as enforced
through torture and physical degradation?

Eavan Boland

Eavan Boland's poetry reimagines Irish history and landscape in terms
of female experience. Rejecting the myths and tropes of her masculine
predecessors, she remaps the imaginative territory of the Irish poet, politi-
cizing the spheres of the domestic and the feminine. Whereas her literary
forebears envisioned women as mute emblems of Ireland's past, Boland
gives women voice and subjectivity as historical witnesses. In "The Dolls
Museum in Dublin," antique dolls are "hostages" who "cannot address /
the helplessness which has lingered in / the airless peace of each glass
case" (lines 41, 37–39). Similarly, "Fond Memory" invests the realm of
the homely with political significance: a child's memory of wearing
woolen clothing, learning English history at school, and listening to Irish
melodies at home leads to a painful awareness of cultural dislocation: "I
thought this is my country, was, will be again, / this upward-straining song
made to be / our safe inventory of pain. And I was wrong" (lines 16–18).
A pastoral interlude of youthful lovers becomes the occasion for a sudden
insight into the sufferings of Irish potato famine victims in "That the Science of Cartography Is Limited"; the sight of the truncated famine road
reminds the speaker of the curtailed lives that go unrecorded in scientifi-
cally precise renderings of the geographical terrain. Boland's luminous
meditations on culture, politics, and personal experience enliven and
make visible the correspondences between gender and history.

The Dolls Museum in Dublin

Quick Read

- Form: Lyric.
- Summary: The narrator visits the Dublin Dolls Museum and imagines the onset of the Easter Rising from the vantage point and context of the antique dolls.
- Themes: Women have been passive objects, not active subjects, of
  their own lives; they have been relegated a secondary role within history and culture; women's history deserves recognition.
- Key Passages: "The wounds are terrible. . . . / The cracks along the
  lips and on the cheeks / cannot be fixed," lines 1–2; "The eyes are
  wide. They cannot address / the helplessness which has lingered in /
  the airless peace of each glass case," lines 37–39; "To be the hostages ignorance / takes from time and ornament from destiny,"
  lines 41–42.

Teaching Suggestions

In "The Dolls Museum in Dublin," Boland refigures a masculinized historical idiom within a feminized sphere. Rather than viewing the Easter Rising of 1916 in terms of violence, bravery, and slain heroes, she sees it from the perspective of ordinary women. The heirloom dolls become an entryway into a densely textured history and a metaphor for a life of enforced feminine passivity. Some discussion of the Easter Rebellion and its place in Irish history will help students situate the poem. It might also be worthwhile to say a few words about the role of museums in creating a shared history or regional identity. Boland's choice to foreground this particular museum, as opposed to another museum housing major artworks or political artifacts, demonstrates her radical repositioning of cultural perspective. You will also want to explain that Boland objects to the way women have served as symbols in Irish mythology and literature—a literature dominated by men. This poem speaks to women's cultural and textual marginalization.

When you begin your reading of the poem, draw students' attention first to the general scene that is being depicted, then to the specific role of the museum dolls. The dolls provide a link to the past and locate that past in relation to women's lives. Details of ordinary feminine existence accrue: "the Quadrille" and "the waltz," and "children walking with governesses, / . . . cossetting their dolls" (lines 5, 29–30). Yet there is no doubt that this moment is historically specific; it is "Easter in Dublin" and the reader knows that this is a reference to the rebellion of the Irish Nationalists. Rather than the actual confrontation, however, we see a flurry of images—"Booted officers. Their mistresses"—as if we too were one of the bystanders relegated to a minor position in the drama (line 10). Children look up at a passing carriage, followed by "the shadow chilling them," a foreshadowing of the conflict that occurs offstage (line 32). The dolls, like Irish women, are "hostages ignorance / takes from time and ornament from destiny"—fixed in their roles, unable to be free agents (lines 41–42). Here, as elsewhere, the dolls stand in for the female vantage point: women consigned to the margins of history, enshrined as national symbols but passive and silent witnesses. At this point, you may return to the beginning and ask students to rethink the first stanza: "The wounds are terrible. . . . The cracks along the lips and on the cheeks / cannot be fixed" (lines 1–2). Whose wounds are these? Why can't they be remedied?

Teaching Clusters

All of the selections here may be studied within the cluster on **Gender, Desire, and Sexuality**; each in some way addresses issues of gender, women's history, or the domestic sphere. The **History, Memory, and Politics** section would be an equally fruitful context within which to discuss concerns about Irish history and politics. In this category, Yeats's "Easter, 1916" would make a thought-provoking contrast to Boland's "The Dolls

Museum in Dublin." Additionally, "Fond Memory" and "The Dolls Museum in Dublin" could be studied in the **Culture, Language, and Identity** cluster in connection with the formation of Irish national identity. Also, see the editorial commentary on Boland and "That the Science of Cartography Is Limited" in the *Norton Literature Online* link to *The Norton Anthology of Poetry*.

Discussion Questions

1. Describe the general scene depicted in stanzas two through eight. What does the onset of the Easter Rising look like from this perspective? Whose perspective is it?
2. What do the dolls represent? What kind of presence and context do they give to the poem? Why are the dolls "hostages ignorance / takes from time" (lines 41–42)? How does Boland draw a connection between the dolls and the lives of women? What are the similarities?
3. What is Boland saying here about women and history?
4. In the first line of the poem, the speaker states: "The wounds are terrible." What kinds of wounds are these? Do they refer to more than the condition of the dolls?
5. Why does Boland choose to write about the Dolls Museum rather than some other museum? In what way are museums important to culture and national identity?
6. Compare Boland's version of the Easter Rebellion to Yeats's in "Easter, 1916."

Further Resources

NORTON ONLINE ARCHIVE

Audio:
That the Science of Cartography Is Limited (read by Eavan Boland)

NORTON TOPICS ONLINE

Twentieth-Century Irish Writers

Salman Rushdie

Salman Rushdie is known for melding different cultures and traditions in his writing; he celebrates the heterogeneous postcolonial subject and questions conventional views on religion, politics, and social forms. "The Prophet's Hair" offers students an excellent introduction to Rushdie's approach; it combines elements of traditional realism, magical realism, satire, moral fable, and cinematic screwball comedy—admixing seemingly incompatible narrative styles, diction, and tone. The central protagonist, Hashim, and his children are dead by the end of the story and his wife has been driven mad: religious fundamentalism and the "old ways" have utterly destroyed this family. And yet "The Prophet's Hair" is as much comedy as tragedy. The grand denouement, with its mayhem and disaster, is unexpectedly hilarious. Taken together, the story's elements are excessive, parodic, flippant, horrifying, and humorous. All characters, all possible positions, all beliefs, are objects of satire; nothing is sacred. Set in the disputed state of Kashmir, the story takes on such thorny issues as religious intolerance, sexual stereotyping, domestic violence, crime, poverty, class disparity, and the erosion of "traditional" culture, yet combines its genuine social engagement with a principled refusal to identify a moral high ground. With its irreverent tone, and its casual mixing of realistic and nonrealistic narrative modes (for the relic is a truly magical artifact, effecting miraculous cures), "The Prophet's Hair" is typically postmodern fiction.

The Prophet's Hair

Quick Read

- Form: Short story.
- Summary: A wealthy Kashmiri businessman finds a religious relic and takes it home rather than returning it to the mosque; his ensuing fanaticism leads to the death of his children, his own suicide, and the mental breakdown of his wife.
- Themes: Explores clashes between tradition and modernity, Islam and secularism, wealth and poverty, social hypocrisies and solipsism.

Teaching Suggestions

In "The Prophet's Hair," the wealthy Hashim is a self-satisfied hypocrite with two spoiled, Westernized children; the "glassy contentment of that household, of that life of porcelain delicacy and alabaster sensibilities," marks the family out as the likely object of satire. Encourage students to explore the use of satire by first examining the portrayal of Hashim and his family. Breakfast conversation is "filled with those expressions of courtesy and solicitude on which the family prided itself," the narrator explains; yet after Hashim takes possession of the religious relic, he gushes forth "long streams of awful truths": he never loved his wife and is miserable in the marriage; he has a mistress; he visits prostitutes; he will disinherit his wife; his son is stupid; his daughter is shameless for going "barefaced"; and so on. We also learn that Hashim thinks of himself as "not a godly man" but that he "set[s] great store by 'living honourably in the world.'" But what kind of "honour" is there in a man who lends out money at the rate of "over seventy percent," making it impossible for his clients to ever be free of debt? He even deludes himself into thinking that by keeping the relic, he is not being selfish and acquisitive, but following the teachings of the Prophet Muhammad, who "abhorred the idea of being deified"; "by keeping this hair from its distracted devotees, I perform—do I not?—a finer service than I would by returning it." His comments are doubly hypocritical, since Hashim claims not to be a religious man.

The thief and his family form another point of satirical contrast. Sheikh Sín acts as Hashim's evil double: he supports a wife and children by cheating others of their money, values riches above all else, and believes he has done an excellent job of preparing his children to exist in the world. (Sheikh Sín has shown "a parent's absolutist love" by crippling his children so that they will be more effective beggars, while Hashim believes he has "inculcate[d] the virtues of thrift, plain dealing and a healthy independence of spirit" in Atta and Huma; neither parent shows any real concern for his offspring.) Hashim has a barely imperceptible ethical superiority over Sheikh Sín, but this dwindles to nothing when the money-lender commits ever escalating violent acts against his wife, his son, his daughter, and a debtor after the relic comes into his life. Yet in unmasking Hashim's hypocrisy and the complacency of the wealthy, the story does not offer a moral absolute; the poor are not virtuous in contrast to the rich and neither religious belief nor secular skepticism prove to have any particular virtue. We are left with a very postmodern kind of irreverence for pat conclusions and simple oppositions. Just as Hashim is shown to be an empty symbol of modern secular patriarchy, so too are all other possible ideological positions: tradition does not bring order or harmony, and the Qur'an does not offer any guidance. Finally, you will want to discuss possible meanings of the relic. Is it a sacred object, pure and simple, or does the story's satire extend to it also? Is it punishing Hashim for his avarice? If it is a sacred object, why does it punish Hashim by having his religious devotion lead to the destruction of the family?

Teaching Clusters

The postmodern mixture of social critique and moral ambivalence makes "The Prophet's Hair" a fitting candidate for the **Transition, Modernity, and Modernism** category. Beckett's *Endgame* would make a good companion piece, allowing students to focus on issues of meaning, narrative dislocations, and social and cultural relations. By placing the story within the cluster on **Culture, Language, and Identity**, on the other hand, you would be able to give more attention to postcolonial concerns about culture, identity, and heterogeneity.

Discussion Questions

1. Explore the depiction of Hashim in "The Prophet's Hair." In what way is he complacent or hypocritical? Hashim thinks of himself as "not a godly man" but he nevertheless "set[s] great store by 'living honourably in the world.'" What do we know about Hashim that suggests his code of "honour" is entirely self-serving?
2. Compare Hashim and his family with the thief, Sheikh Sín, and his family. One family is wealthy and full of airs, while the other is poor,

supporting themselves by stealing or begging. What are the beliefs and self-delusions of each family? How virtuous or ethical is Hashim and Sheikh Sín?

3. How does the use of satire in "The Prophet's Hair" affect your understanding of the story? Is there anything in it that is not satirical? Which characters and situations come under the harshest treatment?

4. What is the story's attitude toward the religious relic? Why does the relic cause such mayhem in Hashim's life? Why does it destroy Sheikh Sín and cure his wife and children of their afflictions?

5. Why does Hashim's religious zeal lead to such violence and destruction? What is the story saying about Islam and the modern secular family?

6. "The Prophet's Hair" contains elements of magic realism: the portrayal of supernatural or fantastic occurrences within a realistic framework. Locate some of these occurrences and discuss their effects on the story.

Anne Carson

Like much of her other work, Anne Carson's "The Glass Essay" freely mixes genres and modes. Here, Carson blends poetry and essay, academic writing and personal confession, philosophical speculation and fragments of literary or classical history, into an allusive, provocative whole. In its entirety, "The Glass Essay" is a thirty-eight-page narrative poem that meditates on aging parents, a failed love affair, and the life of Emily Brontë, with which the speaker identifies. Although Brontë appears only once as a distinct personage in the "Hero" section of the poem, excerpted in NAEL (when the speaker imagines her diminutive mother as "Emily Brontë's little merlin hawk Hero" [line 48]), aspects of her life and writings resonate with some of its motifs. Probably best remembered as the author of Wuthering Heights, Brontë spent most of her life at home, in a remote area of Yorkshire. Along with her sisters (Anne and Charlotte, also authors) and her brother (Patrick), she created a rich, fictional world in her youthful writings. The hermetic quality of Brontë's existence is repeated in the enclosed, triangulated relationship between the mother, father, and daughter of "Hero." Moreover, like Wuthering Heights, Carson's poem explores emotions, family dynamics, and the self in relation to others. The raw urgency of "Hero" will appeal to students while offering an excellent introduction to Carson's writing.

Hero

Quick Read

- Form: Long narrative poem.
- Summary: The speaker argues with her mother during breakfast, then both visit the speaker's father, who is suffering from Alzheimer's.

- Themes: The relationship of the past to the present; family dynamics; repetition and cyclical exchanges among intimates; suppressed emotions and overt conflict; unstable identity; the difficulty of communication.
- Key Passages: "I can tell by the way my mother chews her toast / whether she had a good night / and is about to say a happy thing / or not," lines 1–4; "It made me furious to hear him floundering," line 86; "Hello love, she says. He jerks his hand away. We sit," line 119; "He uses a language known only to himself, / made of snarls and syllables and sudden wild appeals," lines 124–25.

Teaching Suggestions

Students will benefit from a brief overview of "The Glass Essay" and a few words on Emily Brontë before you examine the "Hero" excerpt. The most immediately engaging aspect of the poem for students will probably be the relationship between the speaker and each of her parents, so you may direct your initial questions here, noting that the breakfast scene needs to be envisioned in connection with the final grim scene in the nursing home. All the conflict, the despair, and the fraught mode of communication in the earlier exchange prefaces and presages the lack of connection in the subsequent encounter among the three family members. The failed communication between father and daughter is especially agonizing. "He uses a language known only to himself," the speaker states, "made of snarls and syllables and sudden wild appeals" (lines 124–25). Adding to the quality of miscommunication are the small gestures that seem as if they have been constantly repeated but have no satisfactory result: "My mother lays her hand on his. / Hello love, she says. He jerks his hand away" (lines 118–19). A similar combination of repetition and futility occurs in the earlier disagreement between mother and daughter, which the speaker describes as "one of our oldest arguments" (line 8) and imagines as resulting in only three possible outcomes ("one of three channels" [line 18]); the familiarity of the argument, its endless and circular reiteration, conveys the sealed, airless quality of the family relationship.

Other significant issues to explore include the interweaving of past and present, enacted in the overt reference to Brontë and in the description of the father's World War II photograph. The speaker describes the details of the photograph that is "taped to [her] fridge at home" (line 149), yet seamlessly drifts into the present in the final stanza of the section: "He is still staring into my face. / Flaps down! I cry. / His black grin flares once and goes out like a match" (lines 163–65). For Carson, the past is not just a lineal precursor to the present, but something in dialogue with the here and now, affecting its texture and quality. The photograph will give you a timely opportunity to ask students about the title of this section, "Hero," and the speaker's anger toward her father. It would seem that the father, as the ace World War II pilot, is the hero; this context brings up questions about the speaker's identity, since the designation of "hero" implies a particular relationship to the narrator and a fixed (or fictional?) identity that the father, because of his dementia, has ruptured. This would explain the narrator's rage over her father's mental decline: "It made me furious to hear him floundering," she candidly admits (line 86). Yet "Hero" is also the name of Brontë's pet hawk, which reminds the speaker of her mother's "tiny sharp shoulders hunched in the blue bathrobe" (line 47). While sitting at the breakfast table with her mother, the narrator thinks of Brontë feeding "bits of bacon at the kitchen table" to the bird (line 48); in this context, the designation is ironic, diminishing the mother's importance.

Finally, ask students to think about the form of the poem, which has no specific rhyme scheme or meter, although there is a fluid cadence (and conversational rhythm) to many of the lines. Why has Carson chosen to insert line breaks where she does and organized particular lines into discrete stanzas? Note also her punctuation; in some cases she has a number of short sentences rather than a single longer sentence. Consider, for example, this description of the mother and father in the nursing home: "Hello love, she says. He jerks his hand away. We sit" (line 119). What happens when these brief sentences are juxtaposed? What is the effect of this economic manner of narration?

Teaching Clusters

"Hero" may be profitably studied within the category of **History, Memory, and Politics.** The poem's concern with time, repetition, and the interweaving of past and present could be highlighted more specifically in reference to other works that address memory and time. Alternatively, by placing it within the grouping on **Culture, Language, and Identity,** you could focus more precisely on issues of identity, which are less visible than other themes but equally significant. "Epitaph: Zion," which meditates on loss, the past, and the mythologies of place, may be studied in the **History, Memory, and Politics** cluster.

Discussion Questions

1. Why does the poem begin, "I can tell by the way my mother chews her toast / whether she had a good night / and is about to say a happy thing / or not" (lines 1–4)? What is the tone here? How does this stanza set the mood of what is to come?
2. What does the familiar argument that the speaker has with her mother at the breakfast table tell you about their relationship? Does it tell you anything about the dynamics of this family in general? How might this exchange be related to or foreshadow the scene in the nursing home with the three family members?
3. In what way is this poem about failed or difficult communication? Can you find instances of conflict, misunderstanding, or a lack of clear connection within the family?
4. Describing the onset of her father's dementia, the speaker says, "It

made me furious to hear him floundering" (line 86). Why does her father's failing mental faculties cause her to react with anger?

5. Who is the "Hero" of this section? The speaker's father, the brave World War II pilot? Or the mother, with her "tiny sharp shoulders hunched in the blue bathrobe" that remind the speaker of Emily Brontë's pet hawk (line 47)?

Paul Muldoon

Paul Muldoon's writing combines elements of satire, wordplay, and postmodern hybridity. A postcolonial poet, Muldoon avoids simple identifications with his Northern Irish literary brethren, opting instead for a complex, often irreverent exploration of heterogeneous, unstable subjectivities. He draws freely from history and literary traditions, yet resists the grand narratives that would make his writing pompous. "Meeting the British" re-creates a crucial historical moment when British officers during the French and Indian War purposefully infected Ottawa natives with smallpox; it indicts the British for their actions, yet at the same time explores questions of identity and language. The speaker here finds himself in the odd situation of "calling out in French," so that the reader shares his perplexed sense of displacement (line 8). "The Grand Conversation" explores issues of identity and culture in a very different manner, positing a dialogue between a Jewish woman and an Irish man who debate the terms of political oppression suffered by their separate ancestors. Rather than granting the topic the solemnity that many other writers would, Muldoon introduces a note of parodic extravagance and verbal playfulness in the penultimate stanza: "Between *fearsad* and *verst* / we may yet construct our future / as we've reconstructed our past / and cry out, my love, each to each / from his or her own quicken-queach" (lines 28–32). Muldoon's poetry will give students a broader understanding of the myriad ways that postcolonial writers approach their material and an insight into postmodern sensibility.

Meeting the British

Quick Read

- Form: Lyric.
- Themes: Heterogeneous or disjunct identity; convergences; barter as a trope for cultural exchange and political domination; linguistic multiplicity.
- Key Passages: "We met the British in the dead of winter," line 1; "no less strange, myself calling out in French," lines 7–8; "They gave us six fishhooks / and two blankets embroidered with smallpox," lines 17–18.

Teaching Suggestions

Students will be immediately concerned about the deliberate infection of the Ottawa tribes by the British depicted here; the final image of "two blankets embroidered with smallpox" is startling and affecting. The poem is more complex than it initially appears, however, and although this disturbing image offers a good starting point for discussion, you will want to lead students toward other more nuanced elements. You can generate a deeper involvement by asking them to locate points of convergence in the poem, signaled in the title and the first line with references to "meeting." Just as the speaker meets the British, so too are there meetings of other kinds occurring: the lavender of the sky and the "lavender-blue" of the snow (line 3); the "sound of two streams coming together" (line 5); the speaker "calling out in French" and Colonel Bouquet speaking French words (line 8); the scent of "willow-tobacco" and the scent of the Colonel's handkerchief (line 12); the speaker's description of the sky as lavender and the Colonel's merging of the sky with lavender in his description of the scented handkerchief; the fishhooks that, when in use, will enact another kind of convergence; and the blankets embedded with smallpox. Upon closer inspection, students will notice that most of these convergences are disparate or ironic couplings, such as the scent of the tobacco that the Colonel cannot "stomach" and which causes him to pull out his scented handkerchief, or the blankets infected with disease (line 12). Moreover, although two people here are speaking French, one will betray the other. What are we to make of these convergences, then? Rather than pinning down the poem to one privileged meaning, encourage students to enjoy the multiplicity and sense of displacement that such disjunct pairings suggest. Note that these off-kilter encounters mirror the speaker's disoriented identity: he hears himself "calling out in French" which is "strange" because it is not his language (lines 8, 7). Interestingly, the speaker separates himself from this voice ("myself calling out in French"), invoking an eerie disembodiment and a double displacement. "Meeting the British" invites a comparison between the Ottawa natives and the Irish people, both oppressed by the British; yet by showing the speaker's identity and the paired images to be disjunct, the poem complicates the notion of cultural identity and breaks down simple oppositions, thus giving it a postmodern edge.

Teaching Clusters

Muldoon's poetry may be studied in several categories. All of his work can be usefully situated in the cluster on **Transition, Modernity, and Modernism**, as an example of postmodern writing. "Meeting the British" and "The Grand Conversation," because of their explicit historical content, may be placed in the category on **History, Memory, and Politics**. Both "Gathering Mushrooms" and "Milkweed and Monarch" could be placed in this category, along with readings that focus on memory or the recovery of the past. Any of the poems that address issues of identity, hybridity, or cultural displacement—particularly "Meeting the British"—would be well situated in the **Culture, Language, and Identity** grouping. Poems that demonstrate an interest in language and wordplay, moreover (again, "Meeting the British"), may be placed here also.

Discussion Questions

1. What kinds of "meetings" or convergences can you locate in "Meeting the British"? Explore the qualities of each pairing that you can find. Are these pairings ironic or disparate in any way?
2. Discuss the theme of language in this poem. What role does the French language play here? Who speaks French and why?
3. Who is this speaker? What does he think about the British? How does he feel about using the French language?
4. Why does Muldoon divide the word "hand- / kerchief" in half (lines 14–15)?
5. What kind of effect does the word "embroidered" have in the last line: "two blankets embroidered with smallpox" (line 18)?

Further Resources

NORTON TOPICS ONLINE

Twentieth-Century Irish Writers

Carol Ann Duffy

Carol Ann Duffy's dramatic monologues give voice to marginalized female figures of myth and history. Neglected, misunderstood, unjustly maligned, these formerly silent women articulate their grief, rage, and desires, inviting the reader to share their radical alterity. In "Medusa," this virago of Greek legend attributes her monstrosity to a philandering mate: "A suspicion, a doubt, a jealousy / grew in my mind, / which turned the hairs on my head to filthy snakes" (lines 1–3). Embedded within Medusa's story are the experiences of other women, unfairly designated as witches and worse. "Mrs Lazarus" turns the idea of adultery around when the eponymous female protagonist finds her long-dead spouse to be returned from the grave; describing him as "my bridegroom in his rotting shroud, / . . . croaking in his cuckold name," the speaker is in the devastating position of having mourned her husband's loss, despaired, and come to life again, only to be required to relive the "stench" of his death and give up her newly found sexual happiness (lines 38–40). Erotic love is foregrounded in "Warming Her Pearls," but complicated by the inferior class position of the speaker, who silently lusts after her languorous mistress. The pearls the speaker wears around her neck during the daytime—to polish them before her employer dons them in the evening—become the link between the two women, suggesting an embodied sensuality of touch and scent along with the bondage of the servant. In "Warming Her

Pearls," as in the other poems, Duffy reminds us that both desire and repudiation are inherent in the experience of otherness.

Warming Her Pearls

Quick Read

- Form: Dramatic monologue.
- Summary: The speaker, a lady's maid, has erotic visions of her female employer as she wears her mistress's pearls during the day to
  give them luster.
- Themes: Class divisions; lesbian desire; the dislocations of otherness; the bondage of unrequited love and domestic servitude.
- Key Passages: "Next to my own skin, her pearls," line 1; "Slack on my
  neck, her rope," line 8; "I see / her every movement in my head . . .
  Undressing, / [. . .] slipping naked into bed," lines 17–20.

Teaching Suggestions

To begin your session on "Warming Her Pearls," explain a little bit
about the form of the dramatic monologue. More so than other forms, it
reveals the psychology of the speaker, a character who is not the poet.
Your initial questions should go to describing the scene, along with the
speaker's situation and attitude toward her employer. Words such as "carriage" tip us off that this is the nineteenth century or earlier (line 17); the
speaker is a lady's maid employed to help her mistress dress and groom
herself. Students will no doubt notice the elements of erotic longing in
phrases such as "All day I think of her" (line 4); the speaker lingers on the
other woman's features, imagining the "cool, white throat," the "soft
blush . . . [on] her skin," and her "naked" figure slipping into bed (lines 4,
14, 20). Yet the poem is also about class differences. The speaker sleeps
in an "attic bed" while her mistress rests in "the Yellow Room, contemplating silk / or taffeta, which gown tonight?" (lines 5–6). The mistress is
defined in terms of her idleness; she rests all day, "fans herself" while her
maid "work[s] willingly," sighs with "indolence" as her attendant "dust[s]
her shoulders with a rabbit's foot" (lines 6, 7, 15, 13). Thus, although the
speaker yearns for erotic fulfillment, she is doubly separated from her employer—by a class boundary and by a heteronormative standard (the mistress "danc[es] / with tall men"). We know that she "burn[s]" for her
mistress, yet we wonder: are there also other feelings, unarticulated, but
obliquely expressed by a recognition of the other's remote privilege
(line 24)? In light of this ambiguity, or absence of rancor, why does the
speaker describe the strand of pearls as "Slack on my neck, her rope"
(line 8)? This could be merely a rope of pearls, but the tension between
"*my* neck" and "*her* rope" implies that the speaker is fully aware she is imprisoned by her employer—an imprisonment that is both social and sexual. There is a suspicious contrast in this poem between the speaker's

calm tone and her obsessive preoccupation with the other woman's body, a contrast that suggests her unexpressed rage may be as fervent as her unsatisfied desire.

Teaching Clusters

Duffy's dramatic monologues are especially well suited to the cluster on **Gender, Desire, and Sexuality**, where you can focus on issues of female voice, erotic desire, and gendered social displacement. There's also much to be said about studying these poems in the **Culture, Language, and Identity** category, placing particular emphasis on unequal power relations between social classes or the way that the self is defined in relation to the cultural or social Other. Additionally, your students will have a richer understanding of the uses of dramatic monologue if you pair Duffy's poems with other works such as Yeats's "Crazy Jane Talks with the Bishop" or T. S. Eliot's "The Love Song of J. Alfred Prufrock," a well-known modern example of the form. Browning's "My Last Duchess" would make an excellent pairing with "Warming Her Pearls," giving students a glimpse into the nineteenth-century context and another perspective on obsessive love.

Discussion Questions

1. What kind of woman is the speaker of "Warming Her Pearls"? What is her tone? Her character?
2. What is the attitude of the speaker in "Warming Her Pearls" toward her female employer?
3. How is the speaker's life different from that of her mistress?
4. Why does the speaker describe the pearls as a "rope": "Slack on my neck, her rope" (line 8)?
5. Compare the use of mirrors in "Warming Her Pearls" and "Medusa." How do mirrors in each poem relate to issues of female identity and voice?
6. How does Duffy redeploy traditional resources of poetry toward nontraditional ends, such as the expression of lesbian and cross-class desire? You may wish to explore her use of such techniques as dramatic monologue (for the articulation of same-sex desire), enjambment (e.g., "mistress," "Undressing"), syntactic inversion (e.g., at the poem's beginning), ellipsis (for compactness, pacing, and interiority), imagistic contrast and development through repetition (e.g., warmth and coolness), and allusion (sexually inverting the Cinderella story).

CHAPTER 12

Examinations, Paper Topics, Study Questions

This chapter discusses ways of posing questions for students and setting topics for papers; it provides a variety of examples and offers some sample study questions to assist students in their reading. The examples are not designed to cover all the material in *NAEL*, nor do they include complete examinations. The purpose is merely to aid instructors in making up tests and paper topics suited to their own interests and class procedures.

We have arranged the sample questions in each part of the chapter in roughly chronological order, though many essay questions may range over two or more periods. Instructors will have no difficulty identifying the questions that apply to their course, and many questions asked about the selections in one period can easily be asked of the works in another period as well.

EXAMINATIONS

Though some instructors base the course grade entirely on papers, most use a combination of papers and examinations. In many courses that use *NAEL*, students are asked to write one or two hour-long exams and a two- or three-hour final. On any timed test, it is always difficult both to cover a lot of material and to ask questions that challenge students to write answers that show depth and understanding. Outside essays, of course, provide such an opportunity. But it is also possible to construct examinations, using a variety of questions, that test both the breadth and the depth of a student's knowledge.

Before the first test, students appreciate hearing what to expect on the exam and seeing examples of the kinds of questions they will be asked. Such sample questions might even be accompanied by good answers, saved from previous tests, with instructor comments pointing out the qualities that made them good. It is also useful to return a set of exams with a handout of superior answers, selected from several bluebooks and reproduced anonymously (with perhaps some minor editing). Although preparing such a handout takes time, ultimately it can lessen the amount of time instructors have to spend explaining to unhappy students why they did poorly and how to improve their performance. No comment on the deficiencies of a performance on an exam is likely to be as effective as the example of a good answer to the question. Students often cannot evaluate their own work because they have no standards by which to judge. They can, however, recognize good work when they see it, and the quality of their own work often improves dramatically as a result.

Identification Questions

This kind of question often comes first on a test and is meant to be brief (ten minutes at most), asking students to identify anywhere from five to ten items. A problem is to get students to observe the time limit, for a few will spill out everything they know about a single item. Therefore, it's a good idea to extend the instruction to "identify" with "in *no more* than a sentence or two" or to state even more specifically: "Say *briefly* who or what the following are, and cite the author and title of the work in which they appear; you need not write complete sentences."

Sample Identifications

The Middle Ages: Heorot, a "book of wikked wivys," Bertilak de Hautdesert, the Harrowing of Hell, a stolen sheep, Mordred

The Sixteenth Century: octave, Stella, Anne Askew, gold toilet bowls, "Venus' nun," Malvolio

The Early Seventeenth Century: carpe diem, "sweet swan of Avon," Bosola, Herod, *The Temple*, Pandemonium, Salomon's House

The Restoration and the Eighteenth Century: Jebusites, the Slough of Despond, Glumdalclitch, the Spectator's Club, Incognita, "These booksa are chiefly written to the young, the ignorant, and the idle, to whom they serve as lectures of conduct, and introductions into life," Atticus, Macheath, "Its form is that of a pastoral, easy, vulgar, and therefore disgusting"

The Romantic Period: "spontaneous overflow of powerful feelings," Mary Wollstonecraft Godwin, Madeline and Porphyro, an albatross, Adonais, Robert Southey, "the stinking fish of Southhampton," Captain Walton

The Victorian Age: Teufelsdröckh, Arthur Hallam, Andrea del Sarto, Philistines, a windhover, Bunbury

The Twentieth Century and After: "The horror! The horror!," Maude Gonne, Shakespeare's sister, Leopold Bloom, Little Gidding, Okonkwo

Short-Answer Questions

Instead of asking students to identify items from a list, one can write a variety of questions that elicit different kinds of information. Such questions require a little more thought—from both the instructor and the students—than straight identifications.

Sample Short-Answer Questions

THE MIDDLE AGES

1. Give one example each of a work in *NAEL* originally composed in (a) Latin, (b) a Germanic language, (c) a Celtic language, (d) a romance language.

2. Explain the differences between these three types of medieval religious life: (a) that of a monk or nun, (b) that of an anchorite or anchoress, (c) that of a mendicant friar.

3. What is a *pentangle*, who wore one, and what is one thing that it symbolized?

4. Identify Coll, Gib, Daw, and Good Deeds, and briefly explain how these characters illustrate one difference between a mystery and a morality play.

5. The following list contains pairs from three different works. Pick out the pairs, identify the works, and in a few words say how the pairs are related: the Virgin Mary, Lancelot, Pertelot, Gill, Chauntecleer, Guinevere.

THE SIXTEENTH CENTURY

6. Identify two of these characters and explain the significance of their names: Raphael Hythloday, Astrophil, Duessa.

7. Briefly define *pastoral* and *epithalamion*, and give the author and title of one work in each genre.

8. Through what Elizabethan stage device might the following stage direction have been carried out? [Exeunt DEVILS with FAUSTUS.]

THE EARLY SEVENTEENTH CENTURY

9. Identify the author and explain the double sense of the italicized words in the following quotations and title: (a) "When thou hast *done*, thou hast not *done*," (b) "Of man's first disobedience and the *fruit* / Of that forbidden tree," (c) "The Collar."

10. Name the authors of two of the following works and say what the title refers to: *The Temple*, "L'Allegro," *Novum Organum*, *Hydriotaphia*.

11. When Donne wrote that "new Philosophy calls all in doubt" what did he mean? Identify the poem in which this statement appears, and

briefly compare that poem's perspective on the new science with the perspective in works by Bacon or Sir Thomas Browne.

12. Poets often write poems about other poets—e.g., Jonson and Milton on Shakespeare, Jonson on Donne, Carew on Donne and Jonson, Herrick on Jonson. Take one of these cases, and discuss how the poet-author treats the poet-subject.

13. Identify the authors who held the following positions: Dean of St. Paul's Cathedral, Latin Secretary to Cromwell's Council of State, Lord Chancellor of England.

THE RESTORATION AND THE EIGHTEENTH CENTURY

14. Identify the author, the work, and the historical (not fictional) person represented by these figures: King David, Flimnap, Atticus.

15. What two passions motivate women, according to Pope, and how does Irwin criticize what he says?

16. What do Polly Peachum and Lucy Lockit have in common?

17. Who wrote that "the sound must seem an echo of the sense," and how do the following lines illustrate that principle?
    A Needless Alexandrine ends the song
    That, like a wounded snake, drags its slow length along.

18. In which two works do Clarissa and Imlac appear, and in what respects do they play similar roles?

19. What does Goldsmith identify as the primary cause for the decline of his village in *The Deserted Village*?

20. Name the author and/or work associated with the following:
    a. manumission
    b. Yarico
    c. "a woman that attempts the pen"
    d. "little victims play"
    e. "I have no children . . . my wife past childbearing"
    f. Coramantien
    g. Flecknoe's heir
    h. Ariel

THE ROMANTIC PERIOD

21. In what way is shooting an albatross like eating an apple?

22. Arrange in chronological order the following events: the Peterloo Massacre, the Battle of Waterloo, publication of *The Prelude*, Wordsworth's first visit to France, publication of *Lyrical Ballads*.

23. What is literary Gothicism in the Romantic period? Name three defining characteristics and two prominent authors.

24. With which Romantic writer do we associate each of the following?
    a. Negative Capability
    b. Major Wier
    c. Wedding Guest
    d. shaping spirit of Imagination
    e. Woo'd and married an 'a
    f. Montgolfier's "silken ball"
    g. Cold Pastoral
    h. Haydee
    i. "the road of excess"

25. Who wrote each of the following lines, and what is being addressed in each?
    a. "And all that mighty heart is lying still!"
    b. "Oh! Lift me as a wave, a leaf, a cloud!"
    c. "Thou still unravished bride of quietness"

THE VICTORIAN AGE

26. Identify the historical event or situation that motivated the following works: "The Cry of the Children," *Culture and Anarchy*, *De Profundis*.

27. Identify the works in which each of the following appear: a head in a bag, a manuscript in a handbag, a little girl in the snow.

28. Identify the author, speaker, and the person or persons addressed in two of these dramatic monologues: "Tithonus," "My Last Duchess," "The Bishop Orders His Tomb."

29. Name the author and title of each of the following: a sonnet sequence addressed to her husband; a translation from the Persian; an edition of the papers of August Teufelsdröckh with commentary.

THE TWENTIETH CENTURY

30. What are the main geographical settings of the following works? *Heart of Darkness*, *Ulysses*, *The Waste Land*, *Things Fall Apart*.

31. What does Virginia Woolf suggest that a woman must have if she is to write fiction?

32. What is outside the interior that contains Nag, Nall, Hamm, and Clov?

33. Who killed the Angel in the House? Why did she do it?

34. Who wrote the following? "Poetry is not a turning loose of emotion, but an escape from emotion; it is not the expression of personality, but an escape from personality. But, of course, only those who have personality and emotions know what it means to want to escape from these things."

35. Identify the following:
    a. Shakespeare's sister
    b. the Easter Rising
    c. theater of the absurd
    d. the Great War
    e. stream of consciousness
    f. fatwa
    g. the British Commonwealth
    h. moments of being
    i. the partition of India
    j. Martian School of Poetry

A series of short-answer questions can be combined into a 15- to 20-minute question that tests command of a particular author or work, as in the following example on Swift's *Gulliver's Travels:*

1. What are the main targets of satire in each of the four books of Swift's *Gulliver's Travels?*

2. How does the character of Gulliver contribute to the effect of the satire?

3. What aspect of human nature is chiefly criticized in the account of the *struldbruggs?*

4. In what ways does Part 4 sum up and conclude the major themes of *Gulliver's Travels?*

Spot Passages

One of the most useful kinds of identification question asks the students to identify and also to comment on significant passages. The spot-passage examination has the virtue of focusing attention on the text and of developing the students' analytical skills. It is also relatively easy to make up, though selecting passages that are sufficiently prominent and distinctive and covering the material of a course takes time. Disadvantages are that the exams tend to be long, and students, especially good students who have a lot to say, tend to get behind and feel considerable pressure.

There is almost always more to be said about a given passage than the allotted time permits. Therefore, one needs to decide how many passages the students can manage and to word the instructions so as to limit the parameters of the commentary. Only a minute or two are required to read a passage and to identify it by author, title, and speaker. Allowing six to seven minutes per passage, one might ask, in addition to identification: "In not more than a sentence or two, comment on whatever seems most significant or representative about the passage in context."

To prepare students for this type of question, one might advise them to avoid wasting time summarizing plot or simply paraphrasing the selected passage.

If an instructor wants detailed commentary, and is willing to reduce the number of passages so as to allow as much as eight to ten minutes each, he or she might direct the students to comment on the significance of specific details in the passage. The main reasons to ask students to elaborate on their comments is to train them to read closely and to give them a better chance to demonstrate imagination and originality.

Essay Exams Based on Passages

One can give a sharper focus to questions dealing with passage identification by arranging the passages in pairs and asking students to discuss the members of a pair with respect to a specific topic. The question could be worded as follows: "Relate the following passages on the topic suggested. Focus on the passages themselves and comment on the significance of specific details in them as they pertain to the topic. Avoid plot summary, paraphrase, and general interpretations except insofar as they bear directly on the passages. Make it clear in your answer that you recognize and understand both passages." Writing about two passages in a single answer is a bit more economical than discussing them separately, and it creates opportunities for making connections within a larger work and comparisons between two writers and their works or between two works by the same writer. Thus students are actually writing short essays, grounded in the text, which may deal with characterization, structure, theme, tone, style, and so on. The three examples that follow illustrate how this method works. Note that in this question, identification, though still important, matters less than understanding. Students should have little difficulty in identifying these passages (for which they should get credit, of course), but the key to a really good answer is seeing how the passages fit together and using detail to support that relationship.

1. *After the Fall*

    a.   Farewell, happy fields,
Where joy forever dwells! Hail, horrors! hail,
Infernal world! and thou, profoundest Hell,
Receive thy new possessor, one who brings
A mind not to be changed by place or time.
The mind is its own place and in itself
Can make a Heaven of Hell, a Hell of Heaven.

    b. Some natural tears they dropped, but wiped them soon;
The world was all before them, where to choose
Their place of rest, and Providence their guide.
They, hand in hand, with wandering steps and slow,
Through Eden took their solitary way.

2. *Epic and mock-epic style*

    a. Thus Eve with countenance blithe her story told;
But in her cheek distemper flushing glowed.

On th' other side, Adam, soon as he heard
The fatal trespass done by Eve, amazed,
Astonied stood and blank, while horror chill
Ran through his veins, and all his joints relaxed;
From his slack hand the garland wreathed for Eve
Down dropped, and all the faded roses shed.

b. The meeting points the sacred hair dissever
From the fair head, forever, and forever!
Then flashed the living lightning from her eyes,
And screams of horror rend the affrighted skies.
Not louder shrieks to pitying heaven are cast,
When husbands, or when lapdogs breathe their last;
Or when rich china vessels fallen from high,
In glittering dust and painted fragments lie!

3. Treatments of the class system

a. I confess I feel somewhat bewildered by what you have just told me. To be born, or at any rate, bred in a handbag, whether it had handles or not, seems to me to display a contempt for the ordinary decencies of family life that reminds one of the worst excesses of the French Revolution. And I presume you know what that unfortunate movement led to? As for the particular locality in which the handbag was found, a cloak room at a railway station might serve to conceal a social indiscretion—has probably, indeed, been used for that purpose before now—but it could hardly be regarded as an assured basis for a recognized position in good society.

b. I hope you don't think I dirty my own hands with the work. Come! you wouldn't refuse the acquaintance of my mother's cousin the Duke of Belgravia because some of the rents he gets are earned in queer ways. You wouldn't cut the Archbishop of Canterbury, I suppose, because the Ecclesiastical Commissioners have a few publicans and sinners among their tenants. Do you remember your Crofts scholarship at Newnham? Well, that was founded by my brother the M.P. He gets his 22 per cent out of a factory with 600 girls in it, and not one of them getting wages enough to live on. This kind of question can be made quite flexible by arranging the passages in pairs but placing the topics at the end and allowing students to write on the passages either individually or as pairs.

Exam Essays

In addition to brief-identification or short-answer questions, a test might include one or more short essays, or it might consist of a single essay to take up almost the whole period for an hour-long exam or a major part of a final. Some instructors like to word questions rather generally, letting students pick their own examples; others prefer to word questions specifically, limiting the choice to designated authors or texts. The possibilities are many. A few examples of both shorter and longer essays are given below.

Topics for 20- to 30-Minute Essays

Many of the sample short-answer questions listed above could easily be converted into brief-essay questions. Number 4, for instance, is getting at the distinction that characters in the mystery plays are "historical," in the sense that they exist in the Bible and that they are treated more or less realistically, while morality plays use allegorical figures. The same question could be expressed thus: "With reference to the mode of characterization in one of the mystery plays and in *Everyman*, explain the difference between the genres of the mystery and morality play." Writing on this topic, a good student could go further than in a short answer, pointing out that the difference between the genres is not altogether clear-cut: in the Nativity scene the shepherds become more symbolic; Everyman and his fairweather friends engage in some lively realistic dialogue.

On the other hand, longer essays that cover several writers can be scaled down to make a much shorter question. Many of the longer essay questions listed below can be broken up in the same way.

The advantage of short essays is that they allow time for other types of questions on the same test. They also tend to be fairly sharply focused, whereas long essays tend to elicit uneven writing and to become woollier as time runs out.

1. Compare the roles of women in one Old English or Old Irish epic or elegy (*Beowulf, The Wife's Lament, The Exile of the Sons of Uisliu*) and one medieval romance (*Lanval, Sir Gawain and the Green Knight, Morte Darthur*).

2. What does treasure signify in *Beowulf* and in *The Pardoner's Tale*, respectively? In what ways do the attitudes toward treasure reflect the value system of a Christian poet in Anglo-Saxon England and one in late-fourteenth-century London?

3. In what ways is the Redcrosse Knight's encounter with Despair different from his previous encounters with villains in Book 1 of *The Faerie Queene*?

4. Compare the Redcrosse Knight with *either* Beowulf *or* Sir Gawain. You might consider armor, speech, manners, and values. How does the hero, faced with seemingly insurmountable odds or in defeat, represent the ideals of the heroic held by the author and his culture?

5. How do Chaucer's treatment of the Pardoner and Spenser's of Archimago reflect pre- and post-Reformation attitudes toward the Roman Catholic church?

6. Discuss the function of comedy in *The Second Shepherds' Play* and in *Dr. Faustus*. How does comedy reinforce or problematize the larger themes of these works?

7. Define what is meant by a "metaphysical conceit," and give examples of two that work well and of one that fails.

8. Compare the title characters of Cary's *Tragedy of Mariam* and Webster's *Duchess of Malfi* as rulers, wives, and heroines of tragedy.

9. Compare and contrast the country estates described in Jonson's "To Penshurst," Lanyer's "A Description of Cookham," and Marvell's *Upon Appleton House*. Indicate how each of these estates relates to the resident community and to the society outside.

10. Briefly compare Dryden's treatment of bad poets in "Mac Flecknoe" with Pope's treatment of them in *The Dunciad*.

11. Compare Boswell's and Burney's accounts of Johnson's conversation. How does Johnson's character change (or seem to) when he talks to different people?

12. What role does the landscape play in the following poems: "Nocturnal Reverie," "Elegy Written in a Country Churchyard," "The Deserted Village," *The Village*?

13. Analyze Imlac's definition of poetry in Chapter 10 of *Rasselas* as a statement of Augustan poetic theory.

14. What would Johnson have said about the Preface to *Lyrical Ballads* if he had been around to write a *Life of Wordsworth*?

15. Discuss the influence of the French Revolution on *two* of the following authors: Blake, Wollstonecraft, Wordsworth, Shelley.

16. Compare the representations of memory in Wordsworth's "Tintern Abbey" and Coleridge's "Frost at Midnight."

17. How does Landon's "roud Ladye" respond to Keat's "La Belle Dame sans Merci"?

18. Explain the different concepts of nature in Wordsworth's "Tintern Abbey," Coleridge's "This Lime-Tree Bower My Prison," and Percy Shelley's "Mont Blanc."

19. What do *The Eve of St. Agnes* (a medieval romance narrative) and "Ode on a Grecian Urn" (a short meditation prompted by an antique artifact) have in common? Both were written by Keats. What else?

20. Briefly describe some differences between the Wordsworthian and the Keatsian odes, using the Immortality ode and "Ode to a Nightingale" as your principal examples.

21. Compare the representation of sensuality in the text and illustrations for "The Lady of Shalott" and *Goblin Market*.

22. Discuss the narrator's feelings about the objectification of women in Christina Rossetti's "In an Artist's Studio."

23. How do issues of race and motherhood converge in Elizabeth Barrett Browning's "The Runaway Slave at Pilgrim's Point"?

24. How does the structure of Stevenson's *Dr. Jekyll and Mr. Hyde* contribute to the sense of uncertainty and uneasiness in the novel? In what way does the shift from third to first person affect the reader's perception of events?

25. Compare the idea of comedy in *The Importance of Being Earnest* and *Mrs Warren's Profession*.

26. Why does T. S. Eliot compare the Victorian poets Robert Browning and Tennyson so unfavorably to Donne in his essay "The Metaphysical Poets"?

27. In Mansfield's "The Garden Party," the wealthy young protagonist Laura wants to do away with the class distinctions that separate her from her poverty-stricken neighbors. Has Laura broken out of her class insularity by the end of the story?

28. Compare the diction, tone, and style of MacDiarmid's Scots dialect poetry and of his poems written in standard English.

29. How do two of the following writers portray the psychology of European colonialism? Conrad, Orwell, Gordimer, Achebe

30. Who are the "barbarians" in Coetzee's *Waiting for the Barbarians* and Naipaul's "One Out of Many"?

31. Discuss the symbolic and narrative importance of the ritual sacrifice of Ikemefuna in Achebe's *Things Fall Apart*. How will the sacrifice affect Okonkwo's standing within the community and his relationship with Nwoye?

Topics for 45- to 60-Minute Essays

1. Trace the Arthurian legend from the twelfth century through to Malory's *Morte Darthur*. What specific changes are there in the role of Arthur and in his relationship with his knights?

2. "What desireth God of me?" Everyman asks Death, and Death replies, "A reckoning." Discuss how *three* of the following characters or poets face their reckoning, and comment in each instance on how the reckoning is conceived in terms appropriate to the genre or type of the work in question:
   a. Sir Gawain at the Green Chapel
   b. the Redcrosse Knight in the Cave of Despair
   c. John Donne on his deathbed or sickbed
   d. Herbert marveling at the Lord's "returns"
   e. Milton as the "uncouth swain" in "Lycidas"
   f. Everyman in *Everyman*

3. Identify and give an approximate date for three of the following quotations, and discuss how their conceptions of Jesus Christ are representative of the culture and the work from which each is taken:
   a. "Then the young hero stripped himself—that was God Almighty."
   b. "In the plate armor of Piers the Plowman, this jouster shall ride."
   c. "All our mothers bear us to pain and to dying. But our very [true] mother Jesu, he alone beareth us to joy and to endless living."
   d. "What is he, this lordling, that cometh from the fight / With blood-rede [garment] so grislich ydight [arrayed]?"

4. In the headnote to *Piers Plowman*, the editors write about Will the Dreamer that "mere knowledge is not enough for him: he must learn by experience and feel in his heart what he learns." Show how this statement applies to Will and to two other medieval or Renaissance figures (possibilities include Julian of Norwich, the Redcrosse Knight, Astrophil, Faustus, King Lear, Adam and Eve).

5. The hero is defined in a variety of ways in medieval and Renaissance literature. Write an essay that traces the changing conceptions of the hero in these periods. Be sure to focus on important attributes, physical descriptions, definitions of heroic action, and the forms the enemy takes. What different kinds of heroes have we seen? Why does the conception of the hero change over time?

6. Insofar as these can be inferred from *The Canterbury Tales*, compare Chaucer's notions about literature as an agent of moral education with those of Sidney and Spenser. What developments in the sixteenth century might explain differences in their literary theories?

7. Discuss the representation of other worlds and cultures in two or three texts (e.g., *Lanval*, *The Wife of Bath's Tale*, *Utopia*, *The Faerie Queene*, *Gulliver's Travels*, *Rasselas*). How do these "other worlds" sustain and/or subvert the dominant ideological agendas of the works themselves?

8. How does Faustus represent the attractions and dangers inherent of sixteenth-century humanism?

9. Johnson famously complained that Milton's "Lycidas" is "a pastoral, easy, vulgar, and therefore disgusting." But pastoral was an important and valued literary mode in the sixteenth and seventeenth centuries. Define that mode and indicate how it is used and to what purposes in any three of the following: Spenser's *Shepheardes Calender*, Marlowe's "The Passionate Shepherd," Marvell's Mower poems, Milton's "Lycidas," Herrick's "Corinna's Going A-Maying," Book 4 of Milton's *Paradise Lost*.

10. Discuss how and why female authors and characters present their own lives in three of the following texts: Chaucer's *The Wife of Bath's Prologue*; Speght's *Dream*; Moulsworth's *Memorandum*; Trap-

nel's *Report and Plea*; Milton's *Paradise Lost*, specifically Sin and Eve; Cavendish's *True Relation of My Birth and Breeding*. You may refer to comparable self-analyses by male writers and characters to strengthen your argument.

11. "Thus is man that great and true amphibium whose nature is disposed to live not only like other creatures in diverse elements but in divided and distinguished worlds" So wrote Sir Thomas Browne in *Religio Medici*. What are these "divided and distinguished worlds," and how is the tension between them experienced by characters in three works, including one from the early seventeenth century and one from the Restoration or eighteenth century?

12. In what ways is *Paradise Lost* also the story of Milton's life, and the Miltonic narrator a character who participates in the story as he tells it? Compare Milton's narrative self-portrait with those of two other writers we have studied. How does his or her fictive self—be it speaker, narrator, or character—correspond to what we know about the author from other sources.

13. Choose *three* of the following settings and discuss how, either directly or by implication, they reflect their authors' views about the social and political health of England: Faerielond (Spenser), Amalfi and Rome (Webster), Venice (Jonson), Jerusalem (Dryden), Vanity Fair (Bunyan), Surinam (Behn), Hyde Park (Congreve), Hampton Court (Pope), Lilliput (Swift), Aubrun (Goldsmith).

14. "The way of the world" stands for the principles that really drive society, not for high-minded ideals that nobody follows in practice. Compare those principles as they are acted out in Congreve's *The Way of the World* and Gay's *The Beggar's Opera*. What principles guide the characters' behavior? How might we understand "Honor" in these plays?

15. Describe the various notions of wit offered by Addison, Pope, and Johnson, and show how those notions shed light on some witty passages in Restoration and eighteenth-century texts of your choice.

16. How does Locke describe liberty? Using texts from the syllabus, describe how eighteenth-century writers drew attention to or accommodated the contradictions between the natural right to liberty and the institutions of marriage and slavery.

17. What differences are there between the experiences of childhood described by male and female writers in nineteenth- and twentieth-century poetry, fiction, and autobiography? Answer this question with reference to the work of one male and one female from the following list of authors: Barbauld, Baillie, Wordsworth, George Eliot, Lamb, Byron, Ruskin, Pater, Christina Rossetti (*Goblin Market*), Yeats, Woolf, Lawrence, Dylan Thomas.

18. It is sometimes said that the Romantic period was one in which writers "rediscovered" nature. It could hardly be said, however, that eighteenth-century writers like Swift, Pope, Johnson, or Gray ignored the natural world. Rather, it seems that writers from the earlier century looked on nature in somewhat different ways than the Romantics did. Compare the work of *two* writers from the earlier period with that of *two* of the Romantics in terms of the most important and revealing differences between their treatments of the natural world.

19. Compare and contrast the representation of ghosts, satanic dealings, or the supernatural in a work by a male writer and a work by a female writer from the Romantic period (e.g. Scott's "Wandering Willie's Tale" and Burn's "Tam O'Shanter," Coleridge's *Ancient Mariner*, Hemans's "A Spirit's Return," Mary Shelley's "Mortal Immortal").

20. Donna Julia writes to Don Juan, "Man's love is of man's life a thing apart, / 'Tis woman's whole existence." How does this summarize Byron's treatment of romantic love? Compare Byron's representation of women's social role with the writings of a Romantic era female author—for example, Wollstonecraft or Landon or Mary Shelley.

21. Compare Byron's Manfred and Mary Shelley's Frankenstein as Faustian overreachers (characters who attempt to go beyond human limitations to use supernatural power). Why do they suffer from remorse? Which character gets more sympathy from the reader (i.e., you)?

22. Discuss the Romantics' concern with communion (relatedness, connectedness, "togetherness," friendship, love, and so on). Name some writers and works treating the subject and explain (with selected examples) what they desire connection *with*.

23. "Man's love is of man's life a thing apart, / 'Tis woman's whole existence." Do you agree that this formulation (from Donna Julia's letter to Don Juan) sums up "the woman question" from Wollstonecraft to Woolf? Discuss with reference to the situations of several women authors and characters.

24. Why does Burns move in and out of Scots dialect in "To a Mouse"? In particular, trace the different effects of the language of the first stanza ("Thou need na start awa sae hasty, / Wi bickering brattle!") and the second ("I'm truly sorry man's dominion / Has broken nature's social union"). Think about the poet's choice of language (dialect vs. standard English) in the following paired works: Burns's "Auld Lang Syne" and "Afton Water"; Baillie's "Woo'd and married and a" and "Up! Quit thy bower"; Scott's "Jock of Hazeldean" and "Lochinvar."

25. Can we read Robinson's "The Poor Singing Dame" as allegorical of the plight of the woman poet in a culture hostile to female authorship? Who does the Lord of the castle represent, and why is there

such a pronounced class difference between this Lord and the old Dame in her poor little hovel? Explain why the Lord is haunted to death at the end of the ballad.

26. Dryden, Johnson, Wordsworth, Coleridge, Arnold, Pater, T. S. Eliot, and Woolf make up a distinguished line of critics, but they are critics working from different premises and preaching different aims and values. Compare and contrast the critical aims and methods of *three* critics, each from a different period.

27. A number of writers—Blake, Browning, Ruskin, Pater, Rossetti, and Yeats—were themselves either draftsmen and painters or were strongly interested in the relationship between literature and visual art. Their interest in this relationship took for each of them a variety of different preoccupations and forms. Compare and contrast the interests of three or four writers in visual art and its effect on their work.

28. It is often said that the greatest influence on Victorian poetry was the novel. Argue for or against this proposition, discussing the work of several poets, including Tennyson, Browning, and Barrett Browning.

29. Choose three women writers from *NAEL* and compare and contrast the ways in which you think gender shapes their work.

30. Such writers as Milton, Pope, Johnson, Byron, Shelley, Arnold, Swinburne, Housman, and Eliot, among others, were all strongly influenced by the classics. However, they looked back to the civilizations of ancient Greece and Rome with quite different attitudes and values in mind. Compare and contrast three writers from at least two different periods with respect to how they drew on the spirit of the classics.

31. Identify the use of non-Standard English in any one or more twentieth-century text(s), and discuss the effects of features of the language such as words or word order which you do not associate with Standard English.

32. Write a response to Achebe's "An Image of Africa: Racism in Conrad's *Heart of Darkness*," either defending *Heart of Darkness* on literary and/or historical grounds or considering the broader question of the political content of literary texts and their relation to the "task of the artist."

33. How have writers in different periods responded to advances in "natural philosophy" or science—e.g., as a contributor to human progress, evidence of God's universal plan, a meaningless and often filthy investigation of trivia, a threat to religion and the humanities, an instrument of patriarchy? Discuss with reference to three writers from at least two different periods. They might be drawn from the following list: Bacon, Newton, Swift, Pope, Keats, Tennyson, Browning, Arnold, Huxley, Raine ("A Martian Sends a Postcard Home"), Adcock ("The Ex-Queen among the Astronomers").

34. It has been said that ours is "the anti-heroic age," but if that is so, it has been in progress for a long time. When would you date its beginnings, and what do you think caused it? Discuss with reference to anti-heroes or anti-heroines from works by at least four writers. If you wish, you may argue that our age is as heroic as any, but our ideas of heroism have changed.

35. How do Heaney and Boland approach the concept of history? To what extent do gender and nationality enter into the work of each? What similarities and difference do you find in their poetry?

36. Although Mary Coleridge's "The Other Side of a Mirror" and Carol Ann Duffy's "Medusa" were composed more than a century apart, both have female narrators who describe themselves as monstrous and full of rage. Explore the concept of female identity in each poem. How do mirrors figure in each poem?

37. How does Michael Field (a pseudonym for poets Katherine Bradley and Edith Cooper) portray lesbian desire? How is this portrayal different from or similar to the frank sexuality in Swinburne's poetry?

38. In what way does the work of D. G. Rossetti, Swinburne, and Wilde reject the moral didacticism of such social critics as John Ruskin? Write an essay in which you develop an answer to this question.

39. Compare and contrast the portrayal of the working-class soldiers in Kipling's "Danny Deever" and "The Widow at Windsor." What are the thoughts and feelings of the men? What does the narrator think of them and their role in protecting the British Empire?

40. Explore the poetic techniques of any two of the following writers: Gerard Manley Hopkins, Louise Bennett, A. K. Ramanujan, or Les Murray. Consider their use of metaphor, diction, meter, rhyme, alliteration, and any other methods that significantly impact their poetry. What effects do these writers achieve by their craft?

PAPER TOPICS

The following topics are designed for short essays of approximately three to four typed pages (750 to 1,000 words). They cover a range of subjects in *NAEL*. A few are meant to develop techniques of analysis and close reading; most simply provide a chance to delve more deeply into works and issues that can be dealt with only generally in class. It is a good idea to accompany the first paper assignment with some instructions about format, citations, and organization. If the object is to talk about the text, students might be warned away from long general introductions.

1. Compare the *Beowulf* poet's treatment of Grendel and the dragon. Do these monsters contribute to our understanding of the ethical/ social values of Anglo-Saxon society? What purpose does the monster

serve in the poem? Do Grendel and the dragon represent different kinds of evil?

2. Discuss the use of humor and satire by Marie de France in *Lanval* and by Chaucer and the Wife of Bath in *The Wife's of Bath's Tale*. What is she/he making fun of—chivalry, romance, men, women? How can we differentiate Chaucer's comedy from Marie's and the Wife's?

3. How do clerks use scripture to attack the Wife of Bath and Margery Kempe? How does each woman use scripture in her defense?

4. In view of the striking differences between Old English and Middle English literature, is there any real justification in lumping these works together and referring to them as "medieval" literature? What, after all, do Chaucer and Langland have in common with the poets of *The Dream of the Rood*, *Beowulf*, and *The Wanderer* that sets them apart from later literature? Or, should the fourteenth and fifteenth centuries be considered part of the Renaissance?

5. Choose and analyze a portrait from *The General Prologue* not discussed in class. What is the effect of the choice of details? What is the pilgrim's "degree"—i.e., rank—and can you compare him with other pilgrims? Or discuss two portraits of pilgrims related in some way (e.g., Knight/Squire, Prioress/Monk, Sergeant of the Law/ Franklin, Parson/Plowman, Miller/Reeve, Summoner/Pardoner). In what ways do the members of the pair complement one another?

6. Look up the story of Noah and the Great Flood in the Bible. How has it been adapted for comic purposes by the author of *The Chester Play of Noah's Flood* and by Chaucer in *The Miller's Tale*?

7. The Green Knight says that he has only come to Arthur's court to ask "a Christmas game" (line 283). Much of the action in *Sir Gawain and the Green Knight* revolves around various kinds of games (including hunting games). How are all these games related? What are their purposes for the characters and for the reader?

8. Look up Ephesians 6.12–16 and apply St. Paul's symbolism in this passage to *Sir Gawain and the Green Knight* and to Passus 18 of *Piers Plowman* (the Crucifixion and Harrowing of Hell). What is the significance of armor and tournaments in these works?

9. Both *Everyman* and *The Second Shepherds' Play* attempt to deliver religious doctrine through a dramatic structure. Choose either the morality or the mystery play and discuss the strategies it employs to educate the audience. You might even want to discuss how the play might be staged to best convey its message to the audience.

10. Compare the treatment of the Crucifixion in *The Dream of the Rood* with that in either *Piers Plowman* or Julian of Norwich's *Showings*.

Can you develop any hypothesis about differences between Old and Middle English culture?

11. Write an analysis of a sixteenth-century sonnet. Consider such elements as structure, diction, imagery, figures of speech and symbols, tone, versification, and the sound of the language, though not all of these are equally important, and you should concentrate on only those aspects that are relevant and revealing. The object is to show the means by which the poem achieves its effects—whatever meaning and feeling it conveys. Consult the *NAEL* Glossary of Literary Terms. (Instructors may want to specify the sonnets the students may choose from.)

12. Discuss the character of Time (often personified) in Elizabethan sonnet sequences, especially Shakespeare's. Is the sense of time in Renaissance lyric different from that in medieval works you have read?

13. Explicate one of Shakespeare's sonnets both as a separate poem and as part of the sequence. You will want to read a few of the sonnets that precede and those that follow in *NAEL* or at the library. Do other poems in the sequence clarify the meaning? Instructors may want to specify the sonnet or provide a limited choice.

14. Write a comparative analysis of a pair of poems on a similar theme. Compare and contrast such aspects as (a) situation and point of view (what is stated or implied about the speaker, person(s) addressed, and circumstances), (b) figurative language, (c) tone, (d) diction, (e) versification, (f) rhyme scheme or stanza form. You don't need to talk about all of these elements, though. Focus on those that lend themselves to a significant comparison. In conclusion, in what respects does each poem exhibit the individual style of its author; in what respects does it belong to a "school"? Possible pairs: Marlowe, "The Passionate Shepherd to His Love" and Donne, "The Bait"; Herrick, "To the Virgins, to Make Much of Time" and Marvell, "To His Coy Mistress"; Donne, Sonnet 10 ("Death be not proud") and Herbert, "Death"; Waller, Song ("Go, lovely rose!") and Herbert, "Virtue"; Jonson, "Still to Be Neat" and Herrick, "Delight in Disorder."

15. Lady Mary Wroth, the poetic heir of her famous uncle Sir Philip Sidney and aunt Mary Sidney Herbert, exercised her own poetic strategies in her sonnet sequence *Pamphilia to Amphilanthus*. How does the language she uses about love and desire differ from that used by Donne? Are the differences comprehensible in terms of gender ideologies about proper male and female social roles? Is female desire represented differently from male desire? Look carefully at the imagery and discuss several poems in detail.

16. Dryden claimed Milton told him that Spenser was his "original"— presumably a primary poetic influence. Where do you see Spenserian influences in Milton's poetry, and how important is that influence in *Paradise Lost*? In what ways does Milton depart radically from that

"original"? Consider the allegorical characters but also topics such as verse form, subject matter, politics, conceptions of history, and so on.

17. How does Milton use imagery (both literal and figurative description) to manipulate the reader's response to Satan in *Paradise Lost*? Discuss examples from the first two books and some of the later books. Can you trace an emerging pattern?

18. How do the treatments of Cromwell by Milton, Lilburne, Winstanley, and Hyde display the attitudes of different factions during the Civil War? Does a close reading of Marvell's "Horatian Ode" reveal any partisanship? Discuss the usefulness and limitations of these documents as sources for a true portrait of Cromwell and how your own politics might guide your judgment of him.

19. In classical epic the gods play an active role in determining the fates of people. This is often referred to as "celestial machinery," defined as "the supernatural agents in epic action." How has Milton adapted celestial machinery in *Paradise Lost*? How has Pope, following Milton, used it in *The Rape of the Lock*?

20. Compare and contrast any two of the following as religious poets: Donne, Herbert, Vaughan, Crashaw. How do they represent themselves, their relationships to God, and the special responsibilities of the religious poet? Consider how their choices of subject, verse form, genre, and imagery bear on these issues.

21. What cultural differences emerge from a comparison of the treatments of madness in *King Lear* and "A Tale of a Tub"?

22. "Unhappy woman's but a slave at large," according to Mary Leapor. Discuss several Restoration and eighteenth-century works that look critically at the situation of woman and/or slaves. How well does Leapor's comparison hold? Where might it break down?

23. Many eighteenth-century poems, including Pope's "Epistle to Dr. Arbuthnot," Swift's "Verses on the Death of Dr. Swift," and Gray's "Elegy," conclude by drawing an idealized portrait of the poet's own character. Compare such portraits in three poems (at least one by a woman). What aspects of the self are singled out for praise?

24. Does the last book of *Gulliver's Travels* prove that Swift is both a misanthrope and a misogynist?

25. To what extent is "P" in Pope's "Epistle to Dr. Arbuthnot" a projection of the poet himself? To what extent is he a dramatic persona, a mask assumed to project several different and changing views of himself in what amounts to a brilliant self-defense?

26. Compare Dr. Johnson's "self-portraits" as "Sober" (*Idler* No. 31) and Imlac (*Rasselas*) with the depictions of him in Boswell's biography and Burney's journals. How well do they complement one another?

27. Compare and contrast the satiric mode of poetry that dominates until 1740 and the sentimental mode that emerges thereafter. Choose one or two poems from each period to demonstrate the characteristics of the mode.

28. Select one of the pairs of poems in *Songs of Innocence and of Experience* (e.g., Lamb/Tyger; the two Chimney Sweeper poems; the two Nurse's Song poems). How do they illustrate Blake's thesis that they show "Two Contrary States of the Human Soul"? Study the Blake illustrations in NAEL, and find in the library an edition of Blake's engravings; discuss the artwork in relation to the thesis mentioned above.

29. Discuss Coleridge's "conversation" poems as a genre. The two best are "This Lime-Tree Bower My Prison" and "Frost at Midnight." Analyze one of them, focusing on some but not all of the following:
   a. the structure—how the poem is organized, and whether or not it holds together
   b. nature description (and the relation of the description to the ideas of the poem)
   c. the philosophical/religious content
   (A variant of this topic would be to compare "Frost at Midnight" with Wordsworth's "Tintern Abbey" [the latter written a few months after the former].)

30. Consider causality in *The Rime of the Ancient Mariner*. Wordsworth criticized the plot as "having no necessary connection." Discuss connection and lack of connection in the poem. Where do we know why things happen, and where do we not know? Do you see it as a problem with the poem that we are not always told why things happen?

31. Dominant traits of Romanticism, while popular, were not without criticism in the literature of the era. Choose two works that criticize Romantic attitudes, such as Austen's *Love and Friendship* and Byron's *Don Juan*, and analyze the relationship each has to Romanticism.

32. Compare ideas of nature and natural process in Shelley's "Ode to the West Wind" and Keats's "To Autumn." Other poems for which such comparison would work are Barbauld's "A Summer Evening's Meditation," Smith's "Beachy Head," Baillie's "A Winter's Day," and Clare's "Nightingale's Nest."

33. Discuss causes of melancholy or dejection in poems by Smith (the sonnets), Wordsworth (e.g., "Tintern Abbey," "Resolution and Independence," "Ode: Intimations of Immortality"), Coleridge (e.g., introductory note and poetic text of "Kubla Khan," "Dejection: An Ode"), and Keats (e.g., "La Belle Dame Sans Merci," "Ode to a Nightingale," "Ode on Melancholy").

34. What arguments and rhetorical strategies do Wollstonecraft's *A Vindication of the Rights of Men* and *A Vindication of the Rights of*

Woman share? Given the concerns of the former text, is it surprising that two years later Wollstonecraft compared the situation of women to that of the poor, brought up in ignorance? What do you make of Wollstonecraft's assertion that women are like the rich of both sexes, trained in folly and vice, and like soldiers, instructed in gallantry, prejudice, and blind submission to authority? What is the effect of her making such a trio of comparisons?

35. Consider Robinson's two poems of the city, "London's Summer Morning" and "January, 1795," as seasonal poems. You might find it useful to contrast Blake's lyrics "To Spring" and "To Autumn," which use the conventions of apostrophe, personification of the season, and imagery drawn from the natural world. How does Robinson convey the essence of the season using only the cityscape and its human inhabitants? Given that Robinson's poems, written in the same year, share certain strategies—both proceed by itemization and addition, both use figurative language sparingly—how do they achieve such different effects?

36. Discuss the historical context of any one of Browning's dramatic monologues. What relationship does the poem have to problems and issues of the Victorian period? Why has Browning chosen to present them in a historical setting?

37. Both *In Memoriam* and *Thyrsis* are elegies for close college friends of the authors. What differences in form are there between these poems? Despite differences in form, do you find similarities in how they deal with grief and similarities in their resolutions?

38. A literary "source" is material a writer adapts and reworks for his own ends. Nearly all of Chaucer's tales and Shakespeare's plays are based on sources. Comparing a work with its source to see what has been added, changed, and left out can tell us a lot about an author's intentions and methods. Compare Tennyson's "Ulysses" with its source in Canto 26 of Dante's *Inferno* or compare *The Passing of Arthur* with its source in Malory's *Morte Darthur.*

39. Compare the representations of English civilization in Arnold's *Culture and Anarchy* and Kipling's *The Man Who Would Be King.*

40. Compare the use of the supernatural in Coleridge's *Christabel* and Gaskell's "The Old Nurse's Story."

41. Discuss the ways in which singing birds—Hardy's aged thrush and Yeats's creature of hammered gold—are figurations of the poet in "The Darkling Thrush" and "Sailing to Byzantium." In general, how is nature represented in these poems?

42. "Irish is not my language. . . . I'm sick of my own country, sick of it!" In Joyce's *The Dead*, the protagonist Gabriel reveals a great deal of ambivalence about Irish culture, Irish history, Irish nationalism, and

his own Irish identity. Compare Yeats's ambivalence about Ireland, particularly Irish nationalist politics, in "No Second Troy," "September 1913," and "To a Shade."

43. Most of the great modernist writers (e.g., Conrad, Joyce, Yeats, Eliot, Woolf) are closer in time to the Victorian age than they are to us. *The Waste Land* and *Ulysses* (1922) are chronologically closer to Tennyson's *Idylls of the King* than they are to the early twenty-first century. Choose a pair of nineteenth- and early-twentieth-century works and write an essay about the continuities and differences between them. In what respects, if any, is the twentieth-century work closer to our time than the nineteenth-century work? If you feel more attracted to the earlier work, explain why. Some possible pairings: Burns's "To a Mouse" and Lawrence's "Snake"; Keats's "Ode to a Nightingale" and Hardy's "Darkling Thrush"; Arnold's *Thyrsis* and Auden's "In Memory of W. B. Yeats"; Wordsworth's "Ode: Intimations of Immortality" and Yeats's "Among School Children"; Wollstonecraft's *Vindication of the Rights of Woman* and Woolf's *A Room of One's Own* and "Professions for Women"; a pair of your own choosing.

44. Compare the District Commissioner's scholarly treatise, The Pacification of the Primitive Tribes of the Lower Niger (Achebe, *Things Fall Apart*), with Kurtz's pamphlet for the International Society for the Suppression of Savage Customs (Conrad, *Heart of Darkness*). Why is each man writing his document, and how does his document elucidate his other work as a colonizer? How does each understand or classify the native peoples? Would Kurtz approve of the District Commissioner's methods, and vice versa?

45. Compare treatments of sexuality in one of the following pairs of works: *The Rape of the Lock/Visions of the Daughters of Albion*, *Christabel/Goblin Market*, *The Eve of St. Agnes/Don Juan*, *The Waste Land/*"The Horse-Dealer's Daughter."

46. Discuss the intersecting representations of sexuality and class in Lawrence's "Odour of Chrysanthemums" and Munro's "Walker Brothers Cowboy." How do class-based aspirations and class differences between marital partners cause or aggravate domestic tension in each of these stories?

47. Compare and contrast Gordimer's "The Moment Before the Gun Went Off" and Coetzee's *Waiting for the Barbarians* as explorations of the psychology of colonialism—that is, the ways in which one group explains, justifies, and perpetuates systematic dominance over another.

48. Irony is sometimes described as "the English disease." Analyze the different uses of irony in works by any of the following: Woolf, Lawrence, Smith, Larkin, MacNeice.

49. Discuss the parallels and differences between any of the following pairs of texts: Housman's *Epitaph on an Army of Mercenaries* and MacDiarmid's *Another Epitaph on an Army of Mercenaries*; Brooke's *The Soldier* and Owen's *Anthem for Doomed Youth*; Woolf's *Modern Fiction* and Lawrence's "Why the Novel Matters"; Joyce's *The Dead* and Mansfield's "The Garden Party." Your answer should refer to form, structure, and style, as well as to subject matter.

50. Pick out a work of some length (at least as long as one of Keats's odes) that you found strange or difficult but ultimately liked a lot. Explain why you found the work difficult, and devise a plan for teaching it either to high school students or to undergraduates (state who your audience is). What sort of information do the students need beyond what the introductions and notes provide? How would you get across the historical importance of the work? How would you explain to students what it means to you and help them to find personal meaning and significance in the work?

51. Explore the concept of marriage in the NAEL selections by George Meredith and Mona Caird. Contextualize your ideas with reference to work by John Ruskin, Coventry Patmore, or Sarah Stickney Ellis. How do Meredith and Caird counter conventional Victorian attitudes about women and marriage?

52. Explore the idea of religious faith in the poetry of Gerard Manley Hopkins and Les Murray. How does the natural world figure in the work of each?

53. Compare and contrast Ramanujan's "Elements of Composition" with Walcott's "A Far Cry from Africa." How do these authors develop the concept of identity?

54. Discuss the different ways in which the protagonists of Naipaul's "One Out of Many" and Rhys's "Let Them Call It Jazz" encounter their adopted countries. How does cultural dislocation affect the two characters?

55. Both Doris Lessing's "To Room Nineteen" and Katherine Mansfield's "The Daughters of the Late Colonel" describe women who have internalized the role of domestic angel with disastrous results. Discuss the correspondences and differences of the two stories.

CREATIVE ASSIGNMENTS

1. Write a sonnet in imitation of Elizabethan sonnets. Use the English form of three quatrains ending with a couplet, and be careful to observe the meter and rhyme scheme. It need not be a good poem, but it should be technically correct. If you want to try this but can't think

of anything to say, find a prose translation of Petrarch's or Ronsard's sonnets in the library and translate one of these as freely as you like into an English sonnet.

2. Write a satire in verse or prose, imitating either Pope's mock-heroic couplets or Swift's creation of a persona, as in "A Modest Proposal." For your subject, choose any aspect of contemporary life. For example, following Swift, you might come up with a satric argument about abolishing grades. If you choose Pope, use his technique of treating the trivial as though it were of immense importance, though you needn't employ all sorts of classical rhetoric. If you imitate Swift, make your persona consistent and convincing. Keep the target of your satire constantly in view.

3. It is often said that Pope mastered the heroic couplet in his translations of Homer. Imitating Pope's style, translate some earlier passage in *NAEL* into heroic couplets. Some possible subjects might be a portrait from Chaucer's *General Prologue*, a famous speech from one of Shakespeare's plays, a passage from *Paradise Lost*, Surrey's blank verse translation of Virgil, or Golding's translation of Ovid in "fourteeners." In the latter cases, look up the prose translations of the originals in the Loeb Classics at the library. Do at least twenty-five couplets; then write a two-page essay on the art of the heroic couplet and the problems you encountered in your imitation.

4. In the manner of Browning, write a dramatic monologue in blank verse, spoken by one of the authors or characters in *NAEL* (e.g., Hazlitt on an outing with Coleridge and Wordsworth, the Wedding Guest telling someone about his encounter with the Ancient Mariner).

STUDY QUESTIONS

Study questions can be a great help to students, especially at the beginning of the course. They can prepare students for discussion by focusing everyone's attention on a shared topic. Such questions, however, are no substitute for the texts, and, after a time, the texts should certainly begin to generate their own questions and incentives. Instructors will have to decide for themselves for how long such handouts are profitable and at what point to shift responsibility to individuals or the group. Similar decisions must be made about using questions to prompt the retention of facts or the development of interpretive skills.

Study questions can take many forms. There may be a whole battery of them to guide students through a text. Or there may be just one or two to start students thinking along the right track. We provide sample questions for the Middle Ages and the Romantic period introductions and a long (A) and short (B) form of study questions for three assignments.

Sample Study Questions

Historical Introductions

The Middle Ages

1. Into what three periods is medieval English literature divided?
2. To what family of tribes did the Angles and Saxons belong?
3. Why was most of the poetry of these tribes lost?
4. How was King Alfred indirectly responsible for the preservation of some of this poetry?
5. What is the form (i.e., the organizing principle of versification) in which Old English poetry was composed?
6. How did Old English poets represent biblical figures like Moses or Christ in terms of their own literary tradition?
7. What was the ancestry of the Norman conquerors of Britain? What language did they speak?
8. What language would have been used by a monk writing a theological treatise? During the period from 1066 to approximately 1200, what language would have been used by a poet writing a romance for the English court?
9. Point out one major difference between the subject matter of Old English and Middle English literature.
10. What pseudo-historical figure is Layamon's Brut named for, and what did he do?
11. In the Middle Ages, what distinction was there between the Britons and the English peoples? Which was King Arthur's nationality, and who were the invaders against whom he fought?
12. What is the name of the genre under which we classify adventure stories in the later Middle Ages? In what country was that genre chiefly developed?
13. What is the predominant subject matter of extant medieval literature?
14. Who were the three major authors of Middle English literature and during what quarter-century were they writing?
15. Name the first English printer and a major work he published.

The Romantic Period

1. Name two events of the French Revolution that alienated its English supporters.
2. What were the consequences of the Napoleonic wars for political life in England?
3. What did Disraeli mean by the "Two Nations"?
4. What was the Peterloo Massacre?
5. What reforms were instituted by the 1832 Reform Bill?

6. According to neoclassic poetic theory, art is "imitation." What key word would define the nature of art in Romantic theory?
7. According to neoclassic poetic theory, art should be produced according to rules. According to Romantic theory, how should art be produced?
8. Are Shelley's "Ode to the West Wind" and Keats's "Ode to a Nightingale" simply nature poems about the wind and a nightingale?
9. What quality in the experience of children was prized by the Romantic poets?
10. What qualities in medieval literature appealed to Romantic poets?
11. In what sense, according to Romantic theory, might an imperfect work of art be better than a perfect one?
12. What changes in journalism were instituted by the *Edinburgh Review*?
13. Name the three best-known essayists of the Romantic period.
14. Name the two major novelists of the Romantic period.

The General Prologue to The Canterbury Tales

A.

1. Focus on the first eighteen lines. What does the description of spring have to do with going on a pilgrimage? Why does Chaucer begin in this way? How does he define the motives for going on a pilgrimage? What do you know about pilgrimages? Who was Becket, and why did people seek him out?
2. Do you find your feelings about the Prioress (lines 118–62) changing as you read her portrait? In the end, do you like her or do you have some reservations?
3. Now look at the portrait of the Monk (lines 165–207). What was the idea of entering a monastery? What would you expect a monk to be like? Does this monk meet your expectations? Do you approve of him or not? Can you describe the tone of this passage?
4. Examine the Parson (lines 208–71) in the same way.
5. How and why does the poem enlist us in making judgments about these characters?
6. Are there pilgrims whose portraits are very favorable? Choose the most admiring and the most cutting portraits, and try to describe how the poem produces such "spin."
7. Chaucer tells us that he has tried to arrange the pilgrims in order of their "degree," i.e., their social rank, but he's not sure he has succeeded (lines 745–48). Are there other ways of ranking the pilgrims, and how might that change their order of presentation in the *General Prologue*? What kinds of persons are missing from this catalog of English society?
8. What is Chaucer apologizing for in lines 727–48? How does he present himself to his audience?

9. What agreement does the Host make with the pilgrims? What are his motives in proposing it?

10. Chaucer says he doesn't know whether it was "aventure, or sort, or cas" (luck, fate, or chance) that the Knight drew the short straw to determine that he would tell the first tale. What do you think it was?

B. What is the principle of order behind the arrangement of the portraits? Is there any argument in that order? Do you agree that the Prioress, Monk, and Parson are outstanding members of their religion?

The Rime of the Ancient Mariner

A.

1. Is the Mariner released from the curse at the end of the poem or not? Though he is allowed to return to port, why is he compelled to pass "from land to land" telling his story? Can this be understood as a punishment or a redemptive act? (His blessing of the water snakes is usually taken to be the act that redeems him.) Is the Hermit, a representative of orthodox religion, of any help to the Mariner?

2. Is the simple moral (lines 614–17) adequate to the poem as a whole, or does it merely characterize the Mariner, who is a simple man? Is the moral of any relevance or comfort to the Mariner or to the Wedding Guest? Coleridge once said of the poem that it should have next to no moral.

3. The American poet, novelist, and critic Robert Penn Warren interprets *The Rime of the Ancient Mariner* by noting which parts take place by moonlight and which by sunlight. In his reading, the moon symbolizes the imagination. Does this make sense to you? Does his scheme work out consistently?

4. Another critic, E. E. Bostetter, interprets the poem as symbolic of alienation, which is especially relevant to Coleridge's life but can also be applied more generally. He compares the Mariner's final situation to that of the poet at the end of "Kubla Khan." The poem inspires such interpretations because it seems so obviously symbolical. Many nineteenth-century critics, however, insisted that it was only an imitation of a medieval ballad. Which way of looking at this poem do you prefer, and why?

5. Why *did* the Mariner shoot the albatross? Is it a symbolic action, or is it completely inexplicable, the way things in ballads sometimes are?

B. The Ancient Mariner seems to be an archetypal figure forced to wander the earth in order to expiate a curse. Think about the symbolism of the story: Why does the Mariner's action have such enormous consequences not only for himself but also for the crew? Has he expiated the curse or does it continue? Why might the Wedding Guest be a "sadder" and a "wiser" man? What has he learned? Why might wisdom make one sad?

The Lady of Shalott

A.

1. Though one can read "The Lady of Shalott" literally, it also seems strongly allegorical. What is its subject? What is the poem about? Can you connect it in any way with the young Tennyson? Can you connect it in any way with yourself?
2. What do mirrors represent generally as symbols? What does this particular mirror represent?
3. What might the destruction of the mirror represent?
4. What are the basic differences between the Lady's island and the surrounding countryside?
5. Can you find color symbolism in the poem?
6. How does repetition, especially of the rhymes *Shalott, Lancelot, Camelot,* affect one's response to the poem? In medieval poetry such identical sounds were called "rich rhymes," but later poets avoided them. Why would Tennyson use them in this poem?

B. Try to develop an allegorical interpretation of the poem that accounts for the Lady of Shalott's confinement to her tower, her weaving, her mirror, the breaking of the mirror, and her death.

Special Problems
in Teaching Poetry and Drama

We want to address two general problems: teaching lyric poetry and teaching the staging of drama. The first involves strategies of reading; the second involves imagining plays in performance on the stages for which they were written. We provide general questions about poetry that have proved helpful to students in the past and a brief history of English stages that amplifies the discussions of pre-nineteenth-century staging in *NAEL* with information about the evolution of theaters, scenery, costuming, and acting styles.

TEACHING LYRICS

Lyrics are generally the hardest of all assignments to teach because students often come into a course in literary history with very little training in reading poems that contain no narrative thread. Most students have enjoyed reading fiction and watching drama on the stage, on television, or at the movies, and they feel comparatively at ease with those forms even when they happen to be written in verse. Faced with a lyric that doesn't obviously tell a story, however, students feel at a loss because they don't know what to look for.

Even though a historical approach is not the same as an introduction to poetry, the two are not incompatible. While one would want to avoid giving the impression that there is a "method" for anatomizing all poems, some instructors may wish to provide their students with a set of preliminary questions, with the caution that these are just a way to begin thinking about poems, especially difficult poems.

Exploratory Questions for the Analysis of Poetry

1. What is the meter, rhyme scheme, and stanza form, if the poem has these features? (Old-fashioned as this approach may be, it remains a useful way to classify and to identify poems, an inducement in a class where the exams will require the identification of passages. More important, this question may become part of a program to get students to listen to poems and to identify their characteristics by ear, not just by the way they look on the page.) Students may be referred to the literary terminology appendix in NAEL. See also Appendix B in this *Guide*, which contains a scansion exercise and suggestions for reading poetry aloud.

2. Does the poem have a relevant historical or generic context? Is it an occasional poem? Is it addressed to a private or to a public audience; or are we meant to be overhearing the poet's solitary meditation? Supposing yourself to be the poet's contemporary, would you already be familiar with similar poems; and, if so, does this poem resemble the others or is it in any respects different or original?

3. Does the poem contain any particular setting or circumstances: a place, a time of day, a season, a situation?

4. Does the poem advance an idea or a line of argument?

5. What is the poem's structure? Can you divide it into parts, based on stanzaic or other divisions; breaks in the syntax, the subject matter, the thought; changes of tone? Is there any progression of thought or feeling, or is the poem repetitive or circular, ending where it began?

6. Examine the images, including any figures of speech. Do they form any patterns? Does the poem contain any unusual metrical effects, contrasts, irony, understatement, hyperbole, and so forth?

7. Does the poem say anything to you personally? Can you relate it to your own thoughts, feelings, or experiences, or is its interest, as far as you are concerned, mainly historical?

A very useful aid in teaching lyric poetry is the section "Poems in Process" at the back of each volume. It is interesting in itself to see how poets go about their work. And, by comparing earlier drafts with the final versions as printed in the anthology, the students can themselves enter into the poetic process and come to see the reasons behind the revisions.

THE STAGING OF THE NAEL PLAYS

Most of our students have it some time been exposed to innovative staging that makes the audience rely on language and imagination instead of on scenery, lighting, and a curtain to locate them in dramatic space and time, and one may refer to such experience in explaining early English stages. Analogues might be drawn with the communal aspects of outdoor rock concerts, with performances at "Renaissance fairs," or with street theater. Some present-day street-theater companies perform on the backs of trucks—very much like the wagons used by the medieval guilds for the mystery plays.

A contemporary recount describes the wagon on which the mystery plays were presented as a "Theater . . . very large and high, placed upon wheels," while mother calls it "a high place made like a house with two rooms, being open at the top: [in] the lower room they apparelled and dressed themselves; and in the upper room they played." The spectators stood (or milled around) on all four sides of the wagon, which meant that actors were always aware of their audiences. The actors did not confine themselves to playing on the wagon: they acted scenes or entire plays in front of it. This playing space, the *platea*, was unlocalized. There was no realistic scenery of the sort we are used to; the wagons were, however, rather elaborately decorated, and some had machinery for God or angels to ascend or descend. A favorite wagon decoration was the "hell mouth," into which Satan and his fellow devils gleefully shoved lost souls. Costumes were rich, according to surviving financial records.

NAEL cannot include every kind of drama between the medieval plays and the plays of Marlowe and Shakespeare, so students may wonder how stages developed from the pageant wagons to the solid structure in the generalized illustration of a playhouse of Shakespeare's time in Volume I. In the years between the mysteries and the golden age of English theater, itinerant professional acting troupes performed brief dramas or interludes, often on and in front of a wagon which they set up in innyards or noble houses. Thus the upper stage and windows ("B" in the drawing) and the curtained recess ("C") were logical extensions of windows in the innyards. Another influence was that of the big Tudor halls, where dramatic entertainments might follow a dinner party. A screen traversed the lower end of the hall, flanked by two doors into the kitchen; compare the doors in the drawing. But note that whether in front of a wagon, in an innyard or on the floor of the hall, there is always a *platea* space.

When students look at the drawing and read the text, you may want to emphasize that James Burbage was not an architect but a carpenter: he did not invent the structure, but adapted elements from the innyards and halls. You may also want to stress that almost all the acting was done on the big thrust stage, projecting out into the audience, which (as we know from the contract, which has survived, to build the Fortune Theater) might measure as large as forty-three by twenty-seven feet. This thrust stage was the *platea*, which authors could turn into whatever locale they wanted: see, for example, *Twelfth Night* 4.2, where the clown Feste, disguised as Sir Topas the curate, visits Malvolio, who is in "prison" in Olivia's house. Malvolio speaks from "within" his offstage prison, where he will later be found "in a dark room and bound" (3.4).

Earlier twentieth-century reproductions of Elizabethan stages erred in emphasizing the recess and the upper gallery as playing areas. Indeed, modern scholarship questions whether earlier theaters even had the recess (the one surviving contemporary drawing of an Elizabethan theater shows none). In any case, the recess was, if employed, a "discovery space," in which Dr. Faustus or Volpone might be revealed. He would then immediately come out to the main acting area, where he would be surrounded by an audience standing on all three sides, wealthier spectators in boxes, and gallants actually sitting on the stage.

Very little is known about Elizabethan modes of acting, but we can infer from the plays themselves that physical agility was important. We can also infer, from a contemporary letter which states that performances averaged about two and a half hours, that speeches must have been delivered in a fast, bravura style. The Elizabethans were no doubt better listeners than we are.

The Elizabethans enjoyed spectacle as well as language. Philip Henslowe's inventory of his property room lists, for example, "i [*sic*] rock, i cage, i tomb, i Hell mouth . . . i tomb of Dido, i bedstead . . . i tree of golden apples"—that is, painted set pieces that could be moved onto the stage as needed; the hell mouth was a legacy from the mystery and morality plays. Essential also, for tragedies and histories, was the "state," or throne. Another aspect of spectacle was provided by bladders of pig's blood, which produced a gory realism in battle scenes. Finally, one must not forget the trapdoor ("D" in the drawing), which played its part in the last scene of Dr. Faustus, and, in some theaters, the flying throne that descended from the painted ceiling (under the roof). But as with every other aspect of Elizabethan staging, our knowledge is tantalizingly fragmentary and Henslowe's Admiral's Men may have been richer in props than other companies. Peter Thomson notes ("Playhouses and Players" in *The Cambridge Companion to Shakespeare Studies*, Cambridge, England, 1986, p. 81) that "we must assume that the platform on to which the Elizabethan actor walked was fairly empty. It was he who had to fill it."

Thomson also notes that costuming was "sumptuous." Leading actors were expected to provide their own costumes, and paid highly for them; for example, one actor, who perhaps had in annual income of £30, paid a tenth of that for "a man's gown of Peachcolour grain."

Dr. Faustus, Twelfth Night, King Lear, Volpone, and *The Duchess of Malfi* were all written to be performed on the public stage. It might be a useful exercise to ask students to direct a scene from one of these plays—either with other students as actors or in a short paper giving the "blocking moves"—so that they can experience for themselves the freedom of a big, unlocalized acting area.

Later in the period the public theaters were in competition with the more exclusive private theaters, such as the Blackfriars, which were indoors and artificially lighted. These were the prototypes of the Restoration theaters In this connection, students might read the description of masques in the Early Seventeenth Century section. These costly productions with innovations such as sliding wings, invented by Inigo Jones, also influenced staging during the Restoration During the Commonwealth the theaters were officially closed, but a few "underground" performances were also produced indoors. Some of the latter were quite elaborate, such as the operas staged by William D'Avenant, who subsequently received one of two royal licenses to operate a theater after the Restoration.

The new Restoration theaters were more intimate than the Elizabethan and Stuart private playhouses, though still larger than many college theaters today. Spectators now sat on benches in the pit (or, as we would say, the orchestra) instead of standing, or in the more expensive boxes, and they now faced a proscenium arch with its curtain. Prologues and epilogues were spoken on the forestage, and the curtain was drawn to reveal the "scenes." Most entrances and exits, however, were still made through the doors on either side of the proscenium arch. That, despite other changes in theater architecture, these doors remained as a holdover from the Tudor halls is a reminder that theater design is often conservative and ad hoc.

Restoration scenery was not three-dimensional but flat, facing the audience. The painted "flats" were set in grooves and were moved, for changes of scene, in full view of the audience; performances relied, as well, on stage machinery for impressive spectacles. Lighting was provided by the light in the auditorium, by footlights, and by hanging chandeliers.

The most important innovation was perhaps the substitution of actresses for the boy actors of the earlier theater. Many spectators in the new audiences had seen actresses in France during Charles's exile there, and, after the restrictions of the Puritan Commonwealth, the new sense of freedom seemed to apply to women as well. At first the recruitment of actresses was a problem because women had no tradition of acting; this is one reason why quick-witted women such as Nell Gwyn found early favor Together with young male actors, they were trained in the licensed theaters' acting schools, or "nurseries," to learn the manners and deportment of the gentry they were to play in the comedies.

With an indoor theater, a proscenium separating the audience from the stage, and scenery on that stage, we are within hailing distance of the "fourth-wall" theater familiar to students from their high schools. Indeed, the history of nineteenth-century staging might be very loosely summed up as the ongoing building-up of that fourth wall.

After the two licensed theaters—Covent Garden and Drury Lane—burned down in 1808, they were replaced by two "vast and ill-lighted" buildings, capable of housing the increasingly spectacular scenic effects demanded by growing audiences. Special effects obviously require distancing. By the 1820s most theaters were lit by gas, enabling the auditorium to be darkened, thereby, of course, separating the audience from the stage even more.

In 1848 licensing was repealed, and many new theaters were built to house the varied fare of the time. Many of the elaborate productions were done by actor-managers such as Henry Irving, who ran their own companies and also starred. Toward the end of the nineteenth century, however, some playwrights were making attempts at realistic drama and were served by companies working at a quieter and more natural style of acting. *The Importance of Being Earnest*, though lavishly produced, was performed in this more subdued and realistic style. In the productions of the Gilbert and Sullivan operettas, Gilbert and his producer, Richard D'Oyly Carte, also strove for realism in costuming and sets. Gilbert was one of the first directors: he worked out the blocking moves of his actors and actresses before rehearsals, and coached their readings of lines. Shaw reviewed many elaborate productions of bad plays before he began writing his own plays. Moreover, his earlier plays, too controversial for the commercial theater, had simple productions in lecture halls; hence he, too, was a force for theatrical realism.

The contemporary plays in *NAEL* could be, and have been, produced very satisfactorily on proscenium stages. But if the direction of the nineteenth-century theater was to build the fourth wall, one major direction of recent staging has been to demolish it. There is no space here to describe all the innovations of twentieth-century theater; suffice it to note the popularity of open stages or theaters in the round. The audience coming in to see *Endgame*, for example, might sit around the sheet-covered ashbins Clov examines in the opening tableau. From the epic theater of Bertolt Brecht and the music hall, among others, directors are now able to choose a variety of acting styles for their productions. To bring us full circle, in 1985 the poet Tony Harrison, in collaboration with the Cottesloe Company of the National Theatre, combined many of the medieval mystery plays into three evening-long productions, wherein all the action took place *among* the audience.

Scansion Exercise and Suggestions for Reading Poetry Aloud

SCANSION EXERCISE

Read about rhythm and meter in the *NAEL* Literary Terminology appendix. Following are two scansions for the first line of Shakespeare's Sonnet 116. The first is strictly according to meter. The second is according to a rhythmical reading of the line.

Lĕt mè nŏt tò thĕ màrriăge òf trŭe miǹds

Lèt mĕ nŏt tŏ thĕ màrriăge ŏf trùe miǹds

In metrical verse the rhythm is superimposed on the underlying regular meter, and there are often several ways of reading a line rhythmically, depending on where you place the stress. The formal meter, however, is quite regular. In this exercise, you are being asked to pick out the regular metrical beat. This means that an iambic pentameter should have five feet of two syllables, in each of which the second syllable receives the stress. Some lines end with an eleventh unstressed syllable (called a "feminine ending"). Never mind that some of these syllables may be very lightly stressed compared to others. For example, *to* and *of* are not important words in the first line of Sonnet 116, and *true*, in the last foot, is rhythmically more heavily stressed than *of*. However, within the foot, *of* is stressed relative to the last syllable of *marriage*, and *true* is slightly less stressed than the rhyming word *minds* (always stress the rhyming syllable). There is one metrical variation that you can indicate. In many feet, especially in the first foot of a line, the stress is inverted. Thus in the first foot of the sonnet, *Let* takes both metrical and rhythmical stress.

1. Identify the meter and number of feet in the following lines:

When I do count the clock that tells the time

Simple Simon met a Pieman

This is the forest primeval the murmuring pines and the hemlocks

'Tis the voice of the lobster I heard him declare

2. Scan the first stanza of Wyatt's *My Lute, Awake!*

3. In Volume I, The Sixteenth Century, there are two versions of the same poem by Wyatt (*They Flee from Me*). The first is from a manuscript. The second is from a famous edition of poetry by Richard Tottel (*Tottel's Miscellany*). Compare the scansion of lines 2, 3, 4, 5, and 16. What is the difference? Which do you prefer and why?

SUGGESTIONS FOR READING POETRY ALOUD

1. *Understand the meaning of the poem as best you can.*
If you know what the poet is saying and the poet's attitude to what is being said, you can then find an appropriate tone of voice and give the correct emphasis to each part of the poem.

2. *Read the poem silently to yourself before trying to read it aloud.*
Think of yourself as an actor with a script. Prepare your reading in advance (if you don't know how to pronounce a word, look it up in a dictionary). Mark the text for yourself, to indicate what to emphasize, where to pause (and how long), where to raise and lower your voice, etc.

3. *Read deliberately, as slowly as you can without exaggeration.*
You will almost invariably read faster in your audience's opinion than you imagine. You want the audience to appreciate your reading, not to be always conscious that you're in a hurry to get it over with.

4. *Don't recite in a mechanical way.*
The poem may have a definite and strong rhythm, but don't let your reading emphasize this at the expense of the sense. Watch the punctuation, making slight pauses for commas, a bit longer for semicolons and colons, and longer for full stops (periods, question marks, exclamation points). If your ear tells you the printed poem has a punctuation that is incorrect, change it.

5. *If the poem has rhymes, don't overemphasize them.*
A brief pause at the end of the line will be sufficient for the listener to get the point. This may cause some trouble with run-on lines, but it is more important for the listener to hear the rhymes.

Index